T0399089

Hitler's Personal Prisoner

Hitler's Personal Prisoner

The Life of Martin Niemöller

BENJAMIN ZIEMANN

Translated by

CHRISTINE BROCKS

OXFORD
UNIVERSITY PRESS

OXFORD
UNIVERSITY PRESS

Great Clarendon Street, Oxford, OX2 6DP,
United Kingdom

Oxford University Press is a department of the University of Oxford.
It furthers the University's objective of excellence in research, scholarship,
and education by publishing worldwide. Oxford is a registered trade mark of
Oxford University Press in the UK and in certain other countries

Published in the United States of America by Oxford University Press
198 Madison Avenue, New York, NY 10016, United States of America

British Library Cataloguing in Publication Data
Data available

Library of Congress Control Number: 2023937958

ISBN 978-0-19-286258-7

DOI: 10.1093/oso/9780192862587.001.0001

Printed and bound in the UK by
Clays Ltd, Elcograf S.p.A.

The translation of this book has been funded by

Geisteswissenschaften International—Translation Funding for Humanities
and Social Sciences from Germany. A joint initiative of the Fritz Thyssen
Foundation, the German Federal Foreign Office, the collecting society
VG WORT, and the German Publishers & Booksellers Association.

Acknowledgements

This book was first published in Germany with Deutsche Verlags-Anstalt. For the English translation, I have made considerable cuts and rewritten some passages. I am indebted to *Geisteswissenschaften International*, a joint initiative by the Fritz Thyssen Foundation, the German Federal Foreign Office, the German Collecting Society VG Wort and the Börsenverein des deutschen Buchhandels, which has recognized my book with one of its awards and funded the translation. At Oxford University Press, Stephanie Ireland commissioned my book. Stephanie, Matthew Cotton and Cathryn Steele offered expert advice and cheerful support all along the way. Thanks a lot!

During the research for this book I have accumulated a great debt of gratitude. I first want to thank institutions that provided crucial material support. The Gerda Henkel Foundation generously funded research leave via its MAN4HUMAN programme. Thomas Mergel was my host during the leave funded by the Gerda Henkel Foundation. His chair and the Faculty for History at Humboldt University Berlin offered further support. Thomas himself as well as staff at his chair, namely Claudia Gatzka, Felicia Kompio, Dagmar Lissat, Maria Neumann, and Dominique Rudin, made my stay in Berlin equally hospitable and memorable. Norbert Frei, Franka Maubach, and Kristina Meyer provided time to go to archives and reflect on my findings at a later stage via the Jena Centre for Twentieth Century History. My academic home, the Department of History at the University of Sheffield, offered both material and intellectual support. I am especially grateful to James Shaw and Adrian Bingham, my current and past Head of Department, respectively, my mentor Bob Moore, and my colleagues Miriam Dobson, Tom Leng, Saurabh Mishra, and Danica Summerlin. At various stages, Alrun Berger, Alessandra Exter, and Wenzel Seibold provided practical research support.

I am grateful to friends who took the time to comment on draft chapters, namely Joan Brüggemeier, Daniel Gerster, Benjamin Lahusen, Christoph Nübel, and Friedrich Veitl. Moritz Föllmer read and commented on a full draft. His trailblazing and highly innovative scholarship has continued to inspire me over many years. Mark Ruff generously offered advice on chapters in English translation. I am indebted to Christine Brocks for her meticulous translation of my German manuscript. This book is primarily based on research in altogether 28 archives in the Federal Republic, the UK, and Switzerland. I am grateful to the archivists who guided me through their collections, especially Jens Murken, Kerstin Stockhecke, and Peter Zocher. At the Evangelisches Zentralarchiv in Berlin, Henning Pahl not only provided friendly advice and good-humoured conversation, but also coffee and cookies—thank you! During my research, I uncovered the book-length manuscript with reflections on the history of the Christian Church that Niemöller wrote in Sachsenhausen concentration camp in 1939. I have greatly benefitted from collaborating with the theologian Alf Christophersen as we prepared the manuscript for publication.

Over the years, many other scholars provided ideas or copies of their own texts, pointed out primary sources, patiently answered my questions or shaped my thinking about twentieth-century Protestantism in other ways. I would like to thank Reiner Anselm, Nicolas Berg, Thomas Brodie, Simon Ditchfield, Manfred Gailus, Andreas Gestrich, Martin H. Geyer, Beatrice de Graaf, Carola Groppe, Thomas Großbölting, Christa Hämmerle, Wolfgang Hardtwig, Gerard den Hertog, Matthew Hockenos, Peter Jelavich, Peter Krumeich, Thomas Kühne, Claudia Lepp, Hugh McLeod, Arie L. Molendijk, Armin Nolzen, Andrew Oppenheimer, Detlef Pollack, Andrew Port, Till van Rahden, Michael Roper, Helmut W. Smith, Nick Stargardt, Sybille Steinbacher, Casey Strine, Todd Weir, Andreas Weiß, and Jonathan Wright. Kindly invited by Thomas Großbölting and Ulrich Pfister to speak at the University of Münster about Niemöller, I had an opportunity to chat with the late Martin Greschat, the doyen of Protestant church history in the Federal Republic. Greschat's many important books and articles have left a crucial mark on my thinking, and their traces can be found all over this book. I am grateful to Amanda Behm (University of York), Felix Schnell (University of Essex), Agnes Ohm (Museum und Gedenkstätte Sachsenhausen), Yoko Kitamura (Nagoya University), and Makiko Takemoto (Hiroshima Peace Institute), who gave me other opportunities to test my ideas in discussion with interested audiences. I would also like to thank five senior scholars whose own research, advice, and continuous support has been crucial for my career as a historian: Richard Bessel, Michael Geyer, Ian Kershaw, Dieter Langewiesche, and Josef Mooser.

Finally, I would like to express my gratitude to my family. My brother Alexander, his wife, Christiane Heiß, and their daughter Irina offered me a home during my extensive research stays in Berlin. Back at Sheffield, my wife Christine and our children Sophie and Jonathan were putting up with my extended absences. Ever since the draft of the introduction had been written, Sophie and Jonathan kept asking me why the book was still not completed. They call that 'happy banter', and I do love them not only for their very British sense of humour.

Benjamin Ziemann

Sheffield,
February 2023

Contents

List of Illustrations

Every effort has been made by the author to secure permissions for the images used in the book. If you believe that you hold copyright in any of these historical images, please apply in writing to Oxford University Press, and we will add your copyright information to any future printings of this book.

List of Abbreviations

ADE	Archiv für Demokratie und Entwicklung
AdsD	Archiv der sozialen Demokratie
AEM	Archiv des Erzbistums München und Freising
AK	Amtskalender (diary) Martin Niemöller (archived in ZEKHN, 62/6096 and 6097)
AKG	Archiv der Kirchengemeinde
ApU	Evangelische Kirche der altpreußischen Union (Protestant Church of the Old Prussian Union)
BArch	Bundesarchiv
BdD	Bund der Deutschen (Alliance of Germans)
BK	Bekennende Kirche (Confessing Church)
BMVtg	Bundesministerium der Verteidigung
BStU	Bundesbeauftragter für die Stasi-Unterlagen
CA	Central-Ausschuss der Inneren Mission (Central Committee for Inner Mission)
CDU	Christlich Demokratische Union (Christian Democratic Union)
CND	Campaign for Nuclear Disarmament
CSU	Christlich-Soziale Union (Christian-Social Union)
CSVD	Christlich-Sozialer Volksdienst (Christian-Social People's Service)
CVD	Christlicher Volksdienst (Christian People's Service)
DC	Deutsche Christen (German Christians)
DEK	Deutsche Evangelische Kirche (German Protestant Church)
DFG	Deutsche Friedensgesellschaft (German Peace Society)
DFG-VK	Deutsche Friedensgesellschaft-Vereinigte Kriegsdienstgegner (German Peace Society–United War Resisters)
DGB	Deutscher Gewerkschaftsbund (German Trade Union Confederation)
DKP	Deutsche Kommunistische Partei (German Communist Party)
DNVP	Deutschnationale Volkspartei (German National People's Party)
DVP	Deutsche Volkspartei (German People's Party)
DVSTB	*Deutschvölkischer Schutz- und Trutzbund* (German-Völkisch Protection and Defiance Federation)
ECPC	Ecumenical Council for Practical Christianity
EDC	European Defence Community
EKD	Evangelische Kirche in Deutschland (Protestant Church in Germany)
EKHN	Evangelische Kirche in Hessen und Nassau (Protestant Church in Hesse and Nassau)
ELAB	Evangelisches Landeskirchliches Archiv in Berlin
EN	Else Niemöller
EOK	Evangelischer Oberkirchenrat (Evangelical Supreme Church Council)

EZA	Evangelisches Zentralarchiv
FAZ	*Frankfurter Allgemeine Zeitung*
FCC	Federal Council of Churches
FoR	Fellowship of Reconciliation
GKR	Gemeindekirchenrat (parish council)
GSA	Gedenkstätte Sachsenhausen Archiv
GStA PK	Geheimes Staatsarchiv Preußischer Kulturbesitz Berlin
GVP	Gesamtdeutsche Volkspartei (All German People's Party)
HAB	Hauptarchiv der von Bodelschwinghschen Anstalten Bethel
HN	Heinrich Niemöller
IdK	Internationale der Kriegsdienstgegner (German section of the War Resisters' International)
IfZ	Institut für Zeitgeschichte München, Archiv
JK	*Junge Kirche*
KBA	Karl Barth Archiv
KOFAZ	Komitee für Frieden, Abrüstung und Zusammenarbeit (Committee for Peace, Disarmament, and Cooperation)
KPD	Kommunistische Partei Deutschlands (Communist Party of Germany)
LAB	Landesarchiv Berlin
LAV NRW W	Landesarchiv Nordrhein-Westfalen, Abt. Westfalen
LAV NRW R	Landesarchiv Nordrhein-Westfalen, Abt. Rheinland
LkA	Landeskirchliches Archiv
LKA	Landeskirchenausschuss (Regional Church Committee)
LkA EvKvW	Landeskirchliches Archiv der Evangelischen Kirche von Westfalen
LPL	Lambeth Palace Library
MfAA	Ministerium für Auswärtige Angelegenheiten der DDR
MN	Martin Niemöller
NDO	Nationalverband Deutscher Offiziere (National Federation of German Officers)
NKVD	People's Commissariat for Internal Affairs
OKW	Oberkommando der Wehrmacht (High Command of the Wehrmacht)
OSS	Office of Strategic Services
PA/AA	Politisches Archiv des Auswärtigen Amtes
PNB	Pfarrernotbund (Pastors' Emergency League)
PPU	Peace Pledge Union
RBR	Reichsbruderrat (Reich Council of Brethren)
RJM	Reichsministerium der Justiz (Reich Ministry of Justice)
RKA	Reichskirchenausschuss (Reich Church Committee)
SAPMO	Stiftung Archiv der Parteien und Massenorganisationen der DDR im Bundesarchiv
SD	Sicherheitsdienst (Security Service)
SE	Martin Niemöller, minutes of the *Sprecherlaubnis*, i.e. the visits of his wife to the Concentration Camps Sachsenhausen and Dachau on [date] (archived in: ZEKHN, 62/6179)
SDHA	SD-Hauptamt

SED	Sozialistische Einheitspartei Deutschlands (Socialist Unity Party of Germany)
SHAEF	Supreme Headquarters, Allied Expeditionary Force
SOVO	Seeoffizier-Vereinigung Ostsee (Naval Officers' Association, Baltic Sea)
SOZ	Soviet Occupation Zone
SPD	Sozialdemokratische Partei Deutschlands (Social Democratic Party of Germany)
StAM	Staatsarchiv München
UAMs	Universitätsarchiv Münster
USPD	Unabhängige Sozialdemokratische Partei Deutschlands (Independent Social Democratic Party of Germany)
USSR	Union of Soviet Socialist Republics
VELKD	Vereinigte Evangelisch-Lutherische Kirche Deutschlands (United Evangelical-Lutheran Church of Germany)
VK	Verband der Kriegsdienstgegner (Association of Conscientious Objectors)
VKL	Vorläufige Kirchenleitung (Temporary Church Leadership)
VVN	Vereinigung der Verfolgten des Naziregimes (Association of the Victims of the Nazi Regime)
WCC	World Council of Churches
WFFB	Westdeutsche Frauenfriedensbewegung (West German Women's Peace Movement)
WN	Wilhelm Niemöller
ZEKHN	Zentralarchiv der evangelischen Kirche in Hessen und Nassau

Note on Terminology and Translations

Confession: The German term *Konfession* has been translated throughout as confession. It refers to religious belief systems that were defined and shaped by the Christian confessions of faith during the Reformation and Counter-Reformation period, namely the 1530 Augsburg Confession of the Lutherans, the Reformed Heidelberg Catechism of 1563, and the Catholic 'Profession of the Tridentine Faith' of 1564. The notion of a divide between *Konfessionen* can refer to two different things. It refers firstly to the conflict between Catholics and Protestants, one of the major social cleavages in Germany from the 1860s to the 1950s. And, secondly, it refers to the confessional divide among Protestants, between Lutherans and Reformed Christians. All confessional churches, Protestant and Catholic, were incorporated as bodies under public law, and still are in the Federal Republic to the present day. Hence, it would be wrong to describe them as 'denominations'.

Jewry/Judaism: The German term *Judentum* can denote both the religion and the Jewish people who practise it, thus concealing the difference between Judaism and Jewry. In antisemitic discourse, the term *Judentum* is deliberately used to emphasize the ethnic or racial substance of the Jewish faith (i.e. the notion that the alleged 'problems' that Judaism creates relate back to the Jewish people). *Judentum* has been translated as Jewry, unless it was clear that Niemöller exclusively referred to the Jewish faith.

Old Prussian Union: The United Church in Prussia goes back to 1817, when King Frederick William III ordered a merger of the Lutheran and Reformed churches in Prussia, thus creating a united *Landeskirche*. However, the Union remained an administrative one, and never led to a joint order of worship. When Prussia annexed neighbouring states in 1866, among them the city of Frankfurt and the Kingdom of Hanover, their *Landeskirchen* (partly Lutheran, partly united, with some Reformed parish communities as well) remained independent. Hence, it was later called the Church of the Old Prussian Union, referring to the Prussian territory before 1866. The abolishment of the *summepiscopate* of the Prussian King in 1918 led to a name change. From 1922 to 1953, it was called the *Evangelische Kirche der altpreußischen Union* (Protestant Church of the Old Prussian Union), abbreviated ApU.

Protestant: The German term *evangelisch* has been translated as Protestant, unless occasionally when it was part of a name, or in those rare occasions when it refers to Evangelicalism (i.e. a strand of Protestantism that emphasizes the notion of being born again).

Regional churches: By 1933, 28 *Landeskirchen* (here translated as regional churches) existed in Germany. The division into *Landeskirchen* goes back to the Reformation era, when a ruler had control over the Protestant Church in his territory, a system that lasted with modifications until 1918, when the *summepiscopate* of the ruler was abolished in the wake of the revolution. For a list of the *Landeskirchen*, and for changes in their number due to mergers before and after 1945, see https://en.wikipedia.org/wiki/Landeskirche (accessed 4 Jan. 2023).

Introduction

The former Navy officer, parish pastor and church leader Martin Niemöller (1892–1984) ranks among the most prominent and influential German Protestants of the twentieth century. These days, he is often remembered for the so-called Niemöller 'quotation', four brief lines that were meant to encapsulate his inaction during the 'Third Reich'. While the core idea of the quotation goes back to speeches Niemöller delivered in the immediate post-war period, it was only canonized in the 1970s by his close associates. The most accurate rendition of the quotation, which Niemöller himself approved, goes as follows:

> First they came for the Communists, and I did not speak out—because I was not a socialist.
>
> Then they came for the trade unionists, and I did not speak out—because I was not a trade unionist.
>
> Then they came for the Jews, and I did not speak out—because I was not a Jew.
>
> Then they came for me—and there was no one left who could protest.[1]

This quotation puts Niemöller at the centre of post-war debates among Germans about their complicity with the murderous Nazi regime, and quite rightly so. But it would be wrong to reduce his life, which spanned nine decades from Imperial Germany to the final years of the 'old', pre-reunification Federal Republic, to the problem of German guilt. The biography of Martin Niemöller was marked by many dramatic moments and by periods of existential crisis. This book, however, is more than just an account of a turbulent life. I will combine a narrative of Niemöller's life with an analysis of three overarching themes that run through the book as a common thread. They all relate to core problems of twentieth-century German history.

The first theme is the transformation of Protestant nationalism. At its very heart, Germany was a Protestant nation. When the German nation state was established in 1871, Catholics were the minority. More importantly, the so-called 'lesser' German solution, founding a state that excluded German-speaking Austria, had severed the deep historical ties of the German-speaking lands to the Catholic Habsburg dynasty. To foster the internal cohesion of the newly founded state, Bismarck and the liberals cracked down on the Catholic Church in the so-called *Kulturkampf* (cultural struggle) from 1871 to 1886/7. Protestants interpreted the founding of the German nation state not only as a fulfilment of their political, but also of their religious and theological hopes. To them, the German appeared to be 'invented by God'.[2] The national Protestant blending of the German national idea and the Protestant faith led to a 'sacralization of the nation'.[3] A Protestant pastor, Friedrich von Bodelschwingh the elder—founder of the diaconal institution in Bethel near Bielefeld—inaugurated Sedan Day, the key national holiday in Imperial Germany. At crucial turning points in German history, in 1914 as well as in 1933, the national Protestant reading of German history was updated and interpreted as a specific mission for the German people. Thus, national Protestantism cultivated theological paradigms and political expectations that resulted in shared interests between Protestants and *völkisch* radical nationalists, both after 1918 and 1933.[4] The defeat of the 'Third Reich' in 1945 did not bring the national Protestant sacralization of the nation to an immediate halt. Protestants in the Federal Republic adopted key values of Western democracy, such as the acceptance of pluralism, albeit with a certain delay. Martin Niemöller is an important example for continuities of national Protestantism well into the post-war period.

The second theme of this book is the transformation of religious and confessional identities. Martin Niemöller's father was a Protestant pastor, and his son grew up within the rigid structures of a pious Lutheran milieu. A sense of confessional rivalry, if not outright hostility vis-à-vis the Catholic Church was an integral part of this environment. Yet the circumscribed world of Lutheranism had to adapt to changing circumstances after the end of the First World War. Socialist freethinker organizations were on the rise, and the fight against the secularism of the 'Godless' was part and parcel of the religious culture wars during the 1920s and early 1930s.[5] As functionary of the Inner Mission, an organization that was dedicated to a re-Christianization of the working class, Niemöller was at the forefront of this fight from 1924 to 1931. The struggle between the German Christians—the Nazi faction within the Protestant churches—and the Confessing Church during the 'Third Reich' was complicated by confessional irritations within Protestantism. Three of the 28 regional churches across Germany remained 'intact' as the German Christians could not seize control of them. Yet Niemöller was deeply disappointed about the actions of the leaders of these three churches—Lutheran bishops—and by those of the Lutherans more generally. He eagerly defended the 1934 'Barmen Declaration', the founding document of the Confessing Church, not least because it relativized the confessional difference between Lutheran and Reformed Protestants.

While he was detained as 'Hitler's Personal Prisoner' in the Sachsenhausen concentration camp from 1938 to 1941, the full extent of Niemöller's disillusionment with the parochial nature and questionable scriptural legitimacy of Lutheranism became apparent. Based on serious theological and church historical reflections, he was ready to convert to the Catholic Church. His wife Else resisted his plans, and so he did not make the leap. But his conversion plans were more than just a fleeting episode, concocted during a moment of deep personal distress. Niemöller's post-war activities in the Protestant Church bear this out. He retained a deep mistrust of the bureaucratic apparatus and limited spiritual commitment within the Protestant churches, issues that had been a key driver for his conversion plans. After he retired as church president of the Church of Hesse and Nassau in 1964, Niemöller's political engagement for pacifism and other progressive causes was more radical than ever before. In the 1960s and 1970s, the adoption of leftist ideas led to a 'politicization of Protestantism' in the Federal Republic.[6] Niemöller was an iconic representative of this trend.

During the last decade of his life, Niemöller publicly confirmed his deep disillusionment with the realities of organized Christianity, with churches that were protected and privileged as bodies under public law, yet seemed devoid of the fervour and effervescence that followers of Christ should display. Thus, he is a good example of the long-term destabilization of religious milieus, which were deeply fragmented, individualized, and insecure by the 1980s.[7] At the same time, Niemöller's biography is indicative of the ways Protestantism in the Federal Republic could gain new relevance whilst the number of church members dwindled dramatically. Niemöller's ethical and political statements showcased new ways in which the Protestant faith could have valency. Protestantism and protest are, after all, of the same ilk.

A third theme of this book is the long-term shifts of attitudes towards war and the military. Around 1900 in Imperial Germany, the military had a central place, and its norms and values deeply shaped civil society and attitudes especially among the middle classes. 'Militarism' was a contested concept, but also a lived reality.[8] Martin Niemöller shared a popular enthusiasm for the Imperial Navy, and his enlistment as an officer candidate was the logical consequence. During his wartime service as a navy officer from 1914 to 1918, he demonstrated an extreme belligerence and almost pathological hatred of the nation that was, in his view, Germany's main enemy: the United Kingdom. After Germany's defeat, his militarism was undiminished, as his active membership in various radical-nationalist combat leagues and officer associations confirms. In his part-autobiography, published in 1934, Niemöller claimed to have concluded the move *From U-Boat to Pulpit* by 1924. Yet upon publication of the book there was already mockery that he had moved 'With the U-Boat to the Pulpit'.[9] Niemöller volunteered for combat service in Hitler's Wehrmacht in September 1939, and contemplated this move again in the face of imminent German defeat in 1943. Even after years in concentration camp detention, Niemöller displayed the mindset of a navy officer.

Only in the years after 1945, Niemöller gradually changed his stance towards war and the military. He no longer saw war as a legitimate means of politics, not least because Germany would have been destroyed during the very first days of a nuclear conflict between the West and the East. Over the course of several years, he adopted pacifist positions. Henceforth, he became a figurehead of various campaigns against nuclear weapons, from the late 1950s to the early 1980s, and served as elected President of the German Peace Society (DFG), the traditional voice of German pacifism. When the people in West Germany turned away from the glorification of war and the military in the decades after 1945, this marked a major caesura in modern German history, a turn 'from a war culture to a peace culture'.[10] Martin Niemöller was both a symbol and a driving force behind this transformation. While he endorsed pacifist causes, Niemöller paradoxically also stayed true to his roots as a navy officer. In the late 1960s, he was readmitted into the Crew 1910, the group of navy cadets who had begun their training in April 1910, and enjoyed the company of his navy comrades.

I will summarize the key findings of this study in the conclusion, but should already address three key points here. First, we need to emphasize the xenophobic and antisemitic foundation of Niemöller's nationalism. During the First World War, he engaged in radical nationalist fantasies about the need to kill and annihilate as many British people as possible. This eliminatory nationalism transformed into *völkisch* nationalism in the wake of the trauma of defeat in 1918. At the centre of this world view was a racial antisemitism, which Niemöller actively engaged through membership of no less than eight radical-nationalist and racial-antisemitic organizations from 1919 to 1922. He first thought about Judaism in theological, rather than racial-antisemitic terms in 1932. Yet even then he continued to display a deep-seated social-cultural antisemitism, which not only shaped his actions during the 'Third Reich', but also his post-war engagement with the issue of German guilt.

His role in these post-war debates is the second point in which established views must be revised. Niemöller signed and supported the Stuttgart Declaration of Guilt by the Evangelische Kirche in Deutschland (EKD) in 1945, the new federation of churches set up after the war. Thus, he is often portrayed as a beacon of moral integrity, as someone who urged the Germans to acknowledge their guilt. On the contrary, I emphasize the highly instrumental nature of these reflections, which were designed to facilitate aid and relief work for the Germans. In his speeches on this issue, Niemöller portrayed the Germans as the real victims (namely of Allied occupation policy), often invoking antisemitic tropes in the process. And when invoking his own guilt, he described it as *silence* amidst the persecution of others, as in the now famous Niemöller-quotation. He never mentioned his own *actions* in support of fascism—such as membership of a fascist party in 1920/1, voting for the NSDAP in 1933, or volunteering for combat service in 1939. The persistence of his national Protestant world view casts a long shadow over his engagement with German guilt in the immediate post-war period.

Finally, his political activism in the post-war period needs to be reassessed. Niemöller claimed the capacity to act as prophetic guardian for the remnants of the Confessing Church, or more precisely for himself, both in church political conflicts and in 'secular' political debates. Anchoring his political positions in a specific interpretation of the Protestant faith, Niemöller immunized himself against critique. He denied a fundamental principle of democratic discourse, the need to listen to the arguments of others to reach a compromise. He also denounced the Federal Republic as a party dictatorship in disguise, thus downplaying the crucial differences between the Nazi dictatorship and the stable parliamentary democracy in West Germany.

A key element of the Niemöller legend is the notion of change. A landmark television interview with the journalist Günther Gaus in 1963 was entirely premised on the ways in which Niemöller had changed: the former Navy cadet who had become a pacifist; the staunch monarchist who learned to embrace democracy; the former anti-communist who now understood the imperative of Christ, to love one's political enemies; and, most importantly, someone who had displayed a 'certain reticence vis-à-vis Jewry [Judentum]', which he now 'deeply regretted'. Especially concerning the last point, Niemöller's assertions were highly misleading, if not an outright lie. He claimed this 'reticence' had been prevalent in the Navy, and he had simply failed to doubt the 'traditionally antisemitic sentiment' of the Westphalian peasants he grew up with.[11] No mention of his own racial antisemitism that became apparent in late 1918. No mention of the fact he had signed a declaration to be of 'Aryan' descent when he joined the German-Völkisch Protection and Defiance Federation (Deutschvölkischer Schutz- und Trutzbund, DVSTB), the first fascist mass party in Germany, in 1920. Equally interesting as these bogus claims is how Niemöller—not only on this occasion—explained why he had changed. He said this had happened during his long spell in concentration camp detention.[12] The benefit of such a claim is obvious: during his own lifetime, it was impossible to disprove. Since Niemöller's personal papers have become accessible, historians are able to reconstruct his political thinking during the years in concentration camp detention with precision. This is one of the reasons why this book offers a very detailed account of the period from 1938 to 1945, when Niemöller was 'Hitler's Personal Prisoner'.

Starting in the late 1960s, Protestant Church historians have published numerous biographies of the most important theologians and church leaders who were at the forefront of the conflicts within the Protestant churches and vis-à-vis the Nazi state from 1933 to 1945.[13] Yet a comprehensively researched biography of Martin Niemöller has so far not been published. The hagiographic book by the British historian James Bentley was mostly based on interviews the author conducted with Niemöller shortly before his death.[14] The recent book by Matthew Hockenos adopts a much more critical approach. Hockenos has also shed new light on Niemöller's turn towards pacifism and on his ecumenical work. Yet for the period prior up until 1945, his book is not based on substantial archival research, and he does not probe more deeply into the important issue of continuities in Niemöller's political positions beyond 1945.[15] All existing biographies of

Niemöller, as well as those of many other German Protestant Church leaders in the twentieth century, display an additional problem: an often single-minded focus on theological positions. Already Martin Luther was, however, not only a theologian, but a human being in flesh and blood, driven by anxieties and obsessions, involved in power struggles, schemes, and machinations. In her path-breaking biography of Luther, historian Lyndal Roper has demonstrated how an analysis of his often very 'worldly' ambitions can be used for a better understanding of the Reformer.[16] Inspired by Roper's book, I will highlight the extent to which Niemöller was often driven not by theological ideas, but by rather profane motives such as personal ambition, bossiness, and lust for power—both before and after his ordination as a priest.

Martin Niemöller's first biographer was his younger brother Wilhelm (1898–1983). He had commenced the study of Protestant theology a few months earlier than Martin in 1919. As a Protestant pastor, from 1930 in the city of Bielefeld, his career pattern was similar to that of his older brother. In 1923, Wilhelm Niemöller had joined the NSDAP. When he turned against the German Christians in 1933, the Nazi party tried in vain to exclude him from its ranks. Wilhelm Niemöller appealed against the decision, and continued to be an NSDAP member until May 1945.[17] During the years between 1933 and 1937, Wilhelm Niemöller joined his brother at all important Confessing synods both at Reich level, and in the Prussian Church. From 1945, Wilhelm turned from a pastor of the Confessing Church into its first historian. In 1946, Wilhelm Niemöller coined the term *Kirchenkampf* (Church Struggle), painting the image of a church 'fighting for its life' as it was persecuted by the Nazi regime.[18] Thus, he inaugurated the tradition to generally see the Confessing Church as part of the resistance against the Nazi regime, a view that has been since refuted by academic research.[19] Wilhelm Niemöller was instrumental in solidifying and expanding the Niemöller legend in post-war Germany, by portraying his older brother as a principled fighter against National Socialism in many booklets and brochures. He also worked behind the scenes, writing irate letters to people who had either painted the actions of his brother Martin during the 'Third Reich' in a less favourable light or who criticized his political interventions in the Federal Republic.

My portrayal of Martin Niemöller's life differs fundamentally from the rose-tinted accounts of his younger brother. It is based on a systematic and very extensive perusal of the personal papers of both Martin and Wilhelm Niemöller, and on the substantial collection of documents that the latter has gathered, which can now be found in the archive of the Westphalian Protestant Church in Bielefeld. These archival collections are invaluable due to the extended correspondence between different members of the Niemöller family, and other documents that relate to the church political activities of Martin Niemöller. In addition, I have conducted extensive research in many other state and church archives, partly with the aim to properly contextualize Niemöller's activities across nine decades, and partly to gauge how others viewed him, from the Imperial Navy to the West German peace movements of the early 1980s. One particular type of source material that is accessible in Niemöller's personal papers are his diaries, brief notes he jotted down on a daily basis from 1919 to 1983. From 1923, he used a specific type of diary that was produced for Protestant pastors. Hence, these diaries are called *Amtskalender* in German. Only the *Amtskalender* for 1937 is missing—it was confiscated by the Gestapo after his arrest. In 1943, Niemöller started to enter brief notes in a diary again. These calendar notes are indispensable for the years 1919 to 1936 and again from 1945 to 1968, as they allow us to reconstruct his personal network of friends and acquaintances that he met day in, day out. However, they are not diaries in a strict sense, as the *Amtskalender* had no space for extensive notes with observations and reflections, and Niemöller usually did not have time for this type of entry either. Nevertheless, the entries in the *Amtskalender* offer many deep insights into his political perceptions. The reader might ask, for instance, in which of the German political systems from 1918 Niemöller arrived at the following conclusion: 'We are "governed" by madmen.'[20] Was it in the Weimar Republic, during the Nazi dictatorship, or in the Federal Republic during the days of the first Grand Coalition, headed by Chancellor Kurt Georg Kiesinger from 1966 to 1969?

PART I
PROTESTANT NATIONALISM IN IMPERIAL GERMANY AND WEIMAR REPUBLIC

1
Childhood and Youth in a Parsonage

Looking back on his childhood and youth, Martin Niemöller occasionally stated that he was 'the offspring of a Westphalian peasant family' and had 'the nature of a Westphalian peasant'. Presumably, this was to emphasize his down-to-earth nature and toughness.[1] His earliest traceable ancestors made a living as hired hands and smallholders in Tecklenburg Land near Osnabrück in the north-west of Germany. His direct ancestors were millers, which is the origin of his name: Neumüller, that is, the new miller in the village. From the late seventeenth century, they were residents of the village Wersen. They came into some property as millers and thus achieved modest prosperity. The family's rapid social advancement during the nineteenth century, however, was owed to their acquisition of education. This process started with Martin's grandfather Gerhard Heinrich Niemöller (1819–1873), who worked as an elementary school teacher in Wersen. In 1850, Gerhard Heinrich married Christine Bäumer from Ibbenbüren, 10 miles away from Wersen. Heinrich Niemöller—Martin Niemöller's father—was born in 1859 as the sixth of eight siblings. The family spoke 'Platt' (Low German), a language variety close to Frisian and English, mostly spoken in north-western Germany. But the schoolteacher Gerhard Heinrich Niemöller also knew the classical languages Latin and Greek, which he used to prepare his children for secondary education.[2]

After her husband's death in April 1873, Christine Niemöller had to leave the parsonage. She initially found accommodation in some rooms at the Bringenburg, a hunting chateau near Wersen. The head of the district authority had promised Heinrich Niemöller a place at Schulpforta, a boarding school for boys in Naumburg upon Saale, founded in 1543 after the Reformation. He failed his first admission exam in autumn 1873. After some months of revising, he passed the test second-time and was admitted as a student at Schulpforta in April 1874.[3] Martin Niemöller's father Heinrich was not the only one of this generation of the family who passed the *Abitur*—final school exams and qualification for university entrance—, went to university, climbed the social ladder towards the middle class as an academic, and secured his social advancement. His education in Schulpforta, with its focus on humanist principles and classical languages, provided the necessary foundation. The dean offered the young Heinrich Niemöller, who had just passed the first theological exam at the consistory in October 1884, the post of an assistant pastor in Lippstadt. Two monks of the Augustinian abbey, founded in the Westphalian city in 1281, had brought the new doctrine of the Reformation to the city at the River Lippe in 1523. In 1890, Niemöller was elected second pastor of the town.[4]

Like his ancestors, Heinrich Niemöller had been baptized in a Reformed church parish. But receiving his school education and confirmation in Schulpforta—a Lutheran school that also trained candidates in theology and for Lutheran clergy—had a formative influence on him.[5] The parish in Lippstadt, where Heinrich Niemöller worked as a pastor from 1890 to 1900, had emerged from a lengthy and conflict-ridden process to unify Reformed and Lutheran parishes in the context of the Prussian Union of Churches. The Prussian King Friedrich Wilhelm III had endorsed the union of the two Protestant confessions. For this purpose, he drafted a new, unified order of worship, which was first celebrated on Reformation Day in 1817. However, Friedrich Wilhelm's order of worship was met with fierce resistance in Lutheran and Reformed regions alike, adding to the political opposition of Liberals against the king's imposition. Few parishes—not more than seven per cent in 1823—adopted the unified order of worship. Thus, the United Protestant Church in Prussia, created under the pressure of the sovereign in 1817, was mainly a legal and administrative union. It was headed by the Evangelischer Oberkirchenrat (EOK) in Berlin, the highest administrative body of the Prussian Protestant Church established in 1850. When Prussia annexed several of its neighbouring states in 1866—including the Lutheran Kingdom of Hanover and United Electoral Hesse—their regional churches remained independent and the Prussian Union was only applied to Old Prussian provinces. In 1922, it was officially renamed the Protestant Church of the Old Prussian Union. Ultimately, the foundation of the Union achieved the opposite of its intention: alongside Reformed and Lutheran churches, 'the Union de facto represented a third Protestant confession, furthering the fragmentation of the confessional landscape' among Protestants.[6]

Before taking up his post in Lippstadt, Heinrich Niemöller married Paula Müller in 1889. He had known the merchant's daughter, who lived in Westerkappeln close to Wersen and had a Huguenot background, since he was six years old. One year later, the first child was born, the son Gerhard Heinrich, who passed away in 1894 after a short illness. Thus, Martin Niemöller, born on 14 January 1892 and named after the reformer Martin Luther, became the oldest son. Four children followed: Magdalene (born in 1894), Pauline (born in 1896), Wilhelm (born in 1898), and Maria (born in 1901). Wilhelm attested that as the eldest, Martin played the undisputed 'leading role' among the siblings.[7] Wilhelm Niemöller 'admired' his elder brother.[8] After 1945, he contributed to creating the Niemöller legend and defended his brother against critics.

From 1898 to 1900, Martin Niemöller attended the Protestant elementary school in Lippstadt and, according to his surviving school reports, achieved good and outstanding grades.[9] During his solitary confinement in the Sachsenhausen concentration camp, he penned two brief notes about his childhood in 1939: 'in the Lippstadt garden: frock-coat, long pipe, meditating', he summarized 'what I remembered of my father'.[10] These sources paint the picture of a patriarchal paterfamilias who ruled over his wife and children with strictness and discipline, while occasionally showing generosity and tranquillity. In his *Pastorenspiegel*, a short booklet written for his sons Martin and Wilhelm published in 1927, Heinrich explained how he imagined the role of a Protestant pastor. The idea of the pastor as the 'paterfamilias' harked back to the emphatically idealized example of Martin Luther and his household in Wittenberg. Glorifying Luther as a model of national Protestantism, Heinrich Niemöller postulated that the thought of the 'cloister house' in Wittenberg would provide 'refreshment and 'edification', 'as long as there is a German history'. Referring to the relationship between Luther and Katharina von Bora, Heinrich claimed that 'the husband is the head of the wife'. And a father who had his children's best interests at heart had to keep in mind: 'spare the rod and spoil the child, but beside the rod, keep an apple to give'.[11] Growing up in a Protestant parsonage was shaped by strictness and rigour. In the Niemöller family, the mother was responsible for corporal punishment. As Martin Niemöller told a friend from elementary school, this was an advantage because 'it doesn't hurt that much when mothers hit'.[12] But occasionally Heinrich Niemöller himself, as 'sergeant on duty', carried out inspections of the children's rooms and monitored 'order and punctuality'. His son Martin would later adopt this practice (Fig. 1).[13]

Clearly the children of a Protestant pastor had to exercise Christian piety. For the Niemöller children this meant attending Sunday school, confirmation classes, and meetings for Bible studies alongside morning prayer and evensong within the family home. When Heinrich Niemöller took up a pastorate in Elberfeld in 1900, the children started attending normal church service held by their father.[14] During his imprisonment at the Sachsenhausen concentration camp, Niemöller often thought about his father's Sunday school and would have walked 'many many miles' only 'to finally attend Protestant church service'. In June 1943, he retrospectively wrote to his wife: 'how rich have we once been and only gently sensed it.'[15] However, just because Martin Niemöller participated in the religious life of his family and parish did not mean he was a pious child. 'We were not pious', Wilhelm Niemöller explained after 1945 to a journalist who was working on a piece about his brother.[16] It would have been more accurate to say that his brother Martin was no pious child, because the family and parish cherished Wilhelm as 'the pious lad', who was most likely to take up his father's profession.[17] That he grew up with Christian parents did not automatically turn Martin, the oldest and most independent of the five siblings, into a religious zealot.

Fig. 1 Heinrich Niemöller celebrates Christmas with his family on the eve of the First World War. Martin Niemöller sits to the right of his mother Paula, his brother Wilhelm to her left. Herbert Mochalski (ed.), *Der Mann in der Brandung. Ein Bildbuch um Martin Niemöller* (Frankfurt am Main, 1963), 17.

A Childhood Under the Banner of National Protestantism

His father's conservatism and national Protestantism shaped Martin's childhood and youth. The Lutheran pastor Heinrich Niemöller believed that the German nation, by word and deed, was based on Martin Luther's Reformation and the fight against Roman Catholicism. As a member of the Evangelischer Bund zur Wahrung der deutsch-protestantischen Interessen (Protestant League for the Safeguarding of German-Protestant Interests), founded in 1886–7, he was part of the anti-Catholic movement of the Protestant middle class, thus supporting the underlying prevalent *Kulturkampf* mood.[18] Being loyal to the Hohenzollern dynasty was a central element of the national Protestant mindset in Imperial Germany. Its head, the emperor, also was the *summus episcopus*, the supreme bishop of the Prussian Protestant Church, until the revolution in 1918–19. The most illustrious moments of Heinrich Niemöller's life were certainly when he could celebrate his loyalty to the emperor while also praising the Lutheran Reformation.

One of those moments was in October 1892 when Wilhelm II took part in the consecration of the converted All Saints' Church (commonly referred to as Schlosskirche) in Wittenberg, where Martin Luther is believed to have posted his—in Martin Niemöller's words 'world-shaking'—95 theses. With a fellow pastor, Martin's father watched the entry of the imperial couple in his preaching gown and threw his beret into the air just before the crowd was striking up the song *A Mighty Fortress is Our God*.[19] Shortly afterwards, Wilhelm II sent Friedrich Adler and Paul Groth, the two leading architects in Wittenberg, to Jerusalem. They were assigned to build the Protestant Church of the Redeemer in the Holy Land and, in doing so, defend the unity and radiant power of German Protestantism. Its consecration was celebrated on Reformation Day in 1898 as the most important event of the emperor's journey to Palestine, the first visit of a modern Western ruler and partly a personal pilgrimage, partly the official demonstration of imperial international standing of a Protestant nation. Heinrich Niemöller was part of the official church delegation to accompany Wilhelm II on his visit. Like the nationalist factory owner Diederich Heßling in Heinrich Mann's novel *Der Untertan* (*The Loyal Subject*), Heinrich Niemöller was very eager to be close to his emperor. Once again, the hymn *A Mighty Fortress is Our God* was sung, this time in the Jerusalem Church of the Redeemer on 31 October 1898. This moment was as unforgettable for the Lippstadt pastor as the entire visit. It was the 'highlight' of his life, particularly because he was accorded the honour of editing the official church remembrance book on the consecration of the Church of the Redeemer.[20] Father Heinrich's return from his visit to Jerusalem was deeply etched into little Martin's mind.[21] Not only his father but also school brought imperial nationalism of Wilhelmine Germany home to Martin. A lasting impression of his childhood in Lippstadt was the emperor's birthday on 27 January, which was celebrated by eating 'Korinthenbrötchen', sweet and spiced yeast buns with raisins. Schoolteachers gave speeches and Martin and his classmates sang songs to honour the emperor's day of glory, including the sentimental song *Der Kaiser ist ein lieber Mann* (*The Emperor is a Kind Man*).[22]

Around the turn of the century, Lippstadt was a placid, small town with about 10,000 inhabitants. Other than practising the rituals of imperial nationalism and Protestant faith as well as attending piano lessons, mandatory for children from families of the educated middle class, the *Bildungsbürgertum* in German parlance, Martin Niemöller had sufficient time to play 'in the streets' or 'go fishing in the River Lippe' behind the large garden of the parsonage. Potato bonfires, harvest, and marksmen festivals were fixed in Niemöller's memory of his time in Lippstadt. Despite all bourgeois conventions and regularities, it was a happy childhood.[23] Therefore, Martin and his siblings were not happy when the father took up the pastorate of the Lutheran parish of Elberfeld. In November 1900, the Niemöller family moved to the city at the River Wupper, which textile factories had made prosperous.[24] Particularly the sons rebelled against moving to the large city, which had more than 150,000 inhabitants. The eight-year-old Martin told his father bluntly: 'Father, how stupid have you been!'[25] Later, during his imprisonment at the concentration camp Sachsenhausen, Niemöller thought back to his childhood, writing he had never 'felt at home' in Elberfeld. Westphalia, in particular the Tecklenburg land with Westerkappeln and Wersen, where his grandparents lived, remained his home.[26]

Martin first attended the preparatory school of Elberfeld *Gymnasium* (secondary school in the German education system that prepared students for higher education) until Easter 1901. He continued at the *Gymnasium* and, in March 1910, took the *Abitur*, the school leaving exam that was needed for university entrance. His reports show he was a good, sometimes outstanding student in mathematics and classical languages, improving towards his final exams. But they also confirm Wilhelm's statement that his elder brother was not exemplary. Teachers repeatedly lamented that Martin was 'easily distracted' and was even 'prone to be disruptive'.[27] To be sure, the Wilhelmine *Gymnasium* was an authoritarian agent of socialization, yet the rather self-confident pastor's son was not easily impressed. According to his *Abitur* certificate, he finished school with an overall grade of 'outstanding' in March 1910.[28] During his navy officer training Martin occasionally remembered his schooldays at the Elberfeld *Gymnasium* in letters to his best friend and classmate Hermann Bremer, particularly the 'rather dull everyday school routine'.[29] According to the young naval cadet, everyday life at the humanist *Gymnasium* seemed to be relatively casual and offered a lot of freedom compared with the strictly organized military lifestyle of the imperial navy. After the first training months in Kiel, he wrote in 1910: 'I often think of the time at the *Gymnasium*. It was rather merry! Here, lessons are only for learning.'[30]

Heinrich and Paula Niemöller tried to give their eldest son a broad horizon. This included a stay in London, arranged with the help of a family acquaintance. Thus, the sixteen-year-old spent six weeks in the British capital in August and September 1908. He stayed in private accommodation and used his visit to go sightseeing in the metropolis. His first impression of the world power Great Britain was 'bleak' because 'the railways are useless'. But this negative verdict on the desolate British infrastructure soon faded. He frequently visited the Victoria and Albert Museum in South Kensington, attracted in particular by the galleries of model ships. During his stay with the Lumb family, where he was accommodated at the end of his time in London, he got a glimpse of Britain's religious life. On Sundays, the Lumb family attended church twice, first in the morning and then in the evening after supper. Martin preferred to read his copy of the New Testament, which he thought was lost and 'missed a lot', but eventually found in his luggage.[31]

Martin Niemöller's visit to London gave him many new impressions and improved his language skills, with which he boasted in letters to his friend Hermann Bremer.[32] During his journey, he also started to keep a diary to record his impressions and thoughts, but initially did not continue on his return to Elberfeld. Keeping a diary or journal to write down feelings and personal impressions was a popular practice among young people with a middle-class background around 1900. After a longer pause, Martin continued his diary. On 1 January 1909, two weeks before his seventeenth birthday, he penned the following, rather pathos-laden remark in his notebook, referred to as 'diary no. 1':

> A new year has started, a year that holds unusual importance for me. It is my final school year, it will bring the decision on my professional path and impact my character building and intellectual development. I'm taking many things from the old year into the new one, Christian faith, youthful patriotism, all kinds of knowledge, and an old, young, fervent love.[33]

This entry not only shows Martin Niemöller regarded faith and nationalism as self-evident core elements of his personality. It also shows how important he regarded his final school year for his life trajectory. As he stated more precisely the following day, the diary was supposed to help him grow up. Yet these earnest words were contradicted by the drinking song that Martin had composed the previous evening and written in his diary. He was aware of the gap between aspiration and practice. Part of growing up was the mentioned 'fervent love'. On 12 January, he confided to his diary a profession of love for a girl from a bourgeois Elberfeld family named Elisabeth Scheffner.[34] Despite lasting less than a year, this relationship probably had a profound impact on him.[35]

The Fascination of the Great Naval Game

When Martin Niemöller wrote in his diary on 1 January 1909, he also contemplated which career path he was going to take. Martin and his brother Wilhelm often said in retrospect that Martin had a 'life plan' and wanted to join the Navy at only four years old.[36] However, the German Navy only became popular with its expansion under Alfred von Tirpitz, who was appointed secretary of state of the German Imperial Naval Office in 1897. The first Naval Law of April 1898 stipulated building two squadrons with eight battleships each as well as cruisers and other escort ships over six years. The Naval Law of 1900 doubled the building programme to four squadrons. The expansion of the Navy was based on the assumption that a naval power was automatically a world power. The Imperial Navy thus represented Germany's imperialist aspiration of becoming a world power.[37] Therefore, the *Marineschauspiel* (Naval Displays) only unfolded their full impact on the bourgeois public of Imperial Germany after 1900. From then on, electric ship models, steered by an engineer hidden in the hull, demonstrated Germany's new power on artificial lakes. Thousands of enthusiastic spectators watched from galleries along the banks. In a wider sense, the 'Great Naval Game' became a metaphor of the naval enthusiasm from 1900 onwards, particularly among the Protestant bourgeoisie. This manifested itself in an increasing demand for postcards, popular brochures, and illustrated broadsheets. Carefully choreographed launches of Imperial Navy ships in Bremen, Hamburg, and Kiel were some of the most important rituals. The press department of the Imperial Naval Office, together with radical-national associations, influenced the press and public opinion, emphasizing the need for naval policy, that is, a series of laws to expand the Imperial Navy and start a naval arms race with Britain. But the enthusiasm was not only the result of manipulation from above. It also fed on the interplay between government, the military, and a broad public that embraced the technical, aesthetic, and imperial dimensions of the German Navy.[38]

The Great Naval Game also fascinated the young Martin Niemöller. The walls of his room in the Elberfeld parsonage were covered with pictures of Imperial Navy ships. His younger siblings had to learn the different types of war ships of the German navies. His sister Magdalene sewed signal flags. For Christmas, Martin asked for books about the navy; he even spent his own money on those books, which he earned from tutoring. He gradually acquired a small library. One of these books was the *Taschenbuch der Kriegsflotten*, edited annually by the former lieutenant at sea Bruno Weyer from 1900, which contained a broad overview on ship types and service regulations of European and non-European navies. It was this particular fascination for technical specifications and construction components of warships that led him to join the German Navy.[39]

Martin Niemöller's and his friends' youthful enthusiasm for the Imperial Navy found expression in setting up a 'Flottenkränzchen'; in Martin's eyes a 'very serious and well-organized matter'. This gathering of like-minded friends was an opportunity to talk shop about product series, engines, and armament of warships. Membership in this companionable circle was strictly formalized; Hermann Bremer, for example, could only join in July 1908 after receiving a formal invitation from Niemöller and three of his friends.[40] It is likely that members of the 'Flottenkränzchen' also talked about career choices immediately before their school leavers exams. The *Taschenbuch der Kriegsflotte* provided Niemöller with information about the admission requirements for a navy officer candidate, including an entrance examination in arithmetic, geometry, and trigonometry, as well as proof of good basic knowledge in natural sciences, usually in form of the *Abitur*. Only in English a minimum grade ('good') was required. This was no problem for Martin as he had been receiving 'outstanding' marks in English from 1909 onwards. Weyers *Taschenbuch* also informed about the career path and income levels of a naval officer.[41]

After the turn of the century it was not unusual for a pastor's son to aspire to a military career as an Imperial Navy officer. Out of the 96 naval cadets who started training in 1906, 24 were sons of academics or pastors, that is, members of the Protestant educated middle class.[42] Nonetheless, the question of Martin Niemöller's personal motives remains. Generally, young men chose the career path of a naval officer because the prospect of journeys across the seven seas appealed to their thirst for adventure or because naval officers were promoted more quickly than army officers. Karl Dönitz (1891–1980), who became Supreme Commander of the Navy in early 1943, joined the Imperial Navy thanks to his romantic ideas about travelling foreign countries.[43] Heinz Kraschutzki (1891–1982), son of a high-ranking army doctor, was told by his father from an early age that he was expected to become an officer. Kraschutzki chose the career of a naval officer; a trip to the Danish coast in 1907 with the radical nationalist Navy League contributed to this decision.[44] Dönitz, Kraschutzki, and Niemöller started their training as naval officers on 1 April 1910.

It remains unclear which factors—other than his fascination for the technology of ships and interest in seafaring—influenced Niemöller's decision. At any rate, his entry into the Imperial Navy was to a certain extent the result of a collective decision, as Karl Gerstberger, born in 1892 and one of the other members of the Elberfeld 'Flottenkränzchen', also started his officer training in April 1910. Hermann Bremer also joined on 1 April 1911.[45] Even in the dark hours during his training when the future naval officer regretted his decision, he always came to the conclusion that he lacked professional 'interest in anything else'.[46]

Biographical accounts should avoid speculation about childhood motives and experiences of their protagonists. We are only on firm ground with Niemöller's diary entry from 1 January 1909, where he described himself as a good Christian, a good German, and a good student eager to learn. His childhood and youth in a parsonage familiarized him with the core elements of a national Protestant mindset, including his admiration of the symbolic pillar of Wilhelmine Reich nationalism, Emperor Wilhelm II. What was still a juvenile enthusiasm for the emperor as a popular father figure in Lippstadt continued to shape Niemöller's adulthood. When he heard about Wilhelm II's death in June 1941 as an inmate of the Sachsenhausen concentration camp, he was 'rather moved'. Imprisonment provided ample opportunity for Niemöller to reminiscence about the 'idyll of my Lippstadt childhood'. This included memories of his enthusiasm for the Imperial Navy, which contributed to the young student's decision to be a naval officer.

2
Officer Candidate in the Imperial Navy

On 1 April 1910, Martin Niemöller, with 206 other naval cadets, reported for duty at the naval barracks of Kiel-Wik.[1] It had become common in the Imperial Navy to refer to the officer candidates of one year group as 'Crew'. Thus, Niemöller was a member of 'Crew 1910'. During his active service this affiliation had practical consequences, as promotions within officer ranks were carried out in accordance with length of service. Thus a member of Crew 1910 was generally unable to overtake a Crew 1909 officer in their promotion. Annual ranking lists were compiled separately for each year group. Even long after having left active service the affiliation to one's Crew still played a crucial role for officers. The Crew was not only a service community but also one of solidarity and remembrance. Shortly before his 90th birthday, after decades of peace movement activism, Niemöller attended the reunion of his Crew 1910 as if it was the most natural thing in the world. At that time, four decades after the end of the Second World War, most people in the Federal Republic considered comradeship a 'concept from another world'.[2] But not Niemöller. Obviously in a good mood, he met Karl Dönitz at the 1980 gathering of Crew 1910, the Grand Admiral of the Navy of the Third Reich, who succeeded Hitler as Reich President and Supreme Commander of the Armed Forces.[3] Another Crew comrade of Dönitz and Niemöller was Heinz Kraschutzki (1891–1982). In the early 1920s he had become a radical pacifist and emigrated to Spain in 1932. After being denunciated by the authorities of the Nazi state, he was incarcerated in the prisons of General Franco's military dictatorship from 1936 to 1943.[4] Thus, the members of Crew 1910 followed very different career paths and life plans, indicative of different developments within German twentieth-century history. And yet, despite all biographical differences they were bonded by overarching ties of comradeship.

More than the officers of the Prussian army, naval officers of the Imperial Navy were the 'emperor's elite corps'. This was due to Wilhelm II's direct influence on the appointment, promotion, and employment of naval officers that he exerted through the Naval Cabinet, founded by the emperor in 1889, as well as his unconditional approval for the programme of naval policy as world power politics, pursued by Admiral von Tirpitz, head of the Reich Naval Office. Naval officers were well aware that Wilhelm II was not only the Supreme Commander of the Imperial Navy but also one of its most influential advocates within the power political structures of Imperial Germany. He expressed his admiration for and paternalistic support of naval officers in a speech at the opening of the new naval school in Flensburg Mürwik in November 1910. Here, he declared that the naval officer corps, whose uniform he wore himself, had 'grown in my estimation', and addressed the cadets and officers present as 'my young comrades'.[5]

The elitist character of the naval officer corps aligned with the effort to recruit its members primarily from the socially 'desirable' circles. In addition to the sons of active officers, these included above all those of higher, academically trained civil servants, other members of the educated middle class that were, as professors or pastors, close to the state, and large landowners. Members of the economic middle class were less welcome, young men from lower social strata were de facto excluded, as were Jews and Social Democrats. The *Abitur* was not technically speaking an entry requirement for admission as a naval cadet. Due to the generally increasing level of education of the middle classes, but also to the growing technical and mathematical demands of a career as a naval officer, the number of high school graduates among naval cadets had risen rapidly from just 40 per cent in 1894 to 90 per cent in 1914.[6]

The naval officer corps was thus more bourgeois than the officer corps in the army. Of the naval cadets in the 1907 Crew, only 11 per cent were nobles and around 26 per cent were the sons of professional officers. Almost 46 per cent had—like Martin Niemöller—a father from the educated middle class with a university degree, and around 17 per cent came from families of the economic bourgeoisie.[7] The high costs paid by families for the military training of their sons already ensured the social exclusivity of the officer candidates. According to calculations of the Naval Command from 1910, around 4,800 marks for uniform, supplementary equipment, and allowances for living expenses were to be estimated for the four years up to the promotion to lieutenant at sea. A naval cadet's monthly wages of 40.50 marks did not even remotely cover this. However, studying at a university was particularly more expensive for parents due to accommodation costs.[8]

However, one should not overemphasize the educational demands placed on naval officers. Other factors were more important for the internal cohesion of the naval officer corps than the education formally proven by the *Abitur* and the technical knowledge acquired in the training process. This included the socially exclusive recruitment, specific ideas of honour, and a direct bond to the emperor, which was sworn as an oath at the beginning of the training. The group culture of naval officers was shaped by these factors. Regardless of the increased educational requirements, they therefore remained an 'estate', a specific social caste, and did not simply become a specialized 'profession'.[9] The activities of naval officers also supported this social orientation, as they were primarily responsible for command of the ships and their crew. Naval engineers, deck officers, and medical officers were involved in technical matters, navigation, and direct supervision of the crew. But before qualification and appointment as an officer came a three-and-a-half-year training period.[10] During this time they had to get used to the principles of military discipline and complete theoretical and practical training. The character formation of the officer candidates was also part of the curriculum, which included lessons in horse riding, fencing, and dancing.[11]

And yet, at the beginning of his time as a naval cadet in April 1910, other things were important to Martin Niemöller, about which he wrote in detailed letters to his friend Hermann Bremer, who remained in Elberfeld. Candidates had to pass an entrance exam in English to be admitted to the corps. After all, there were 372 applicants for the Crew 1910, with an assumed need for around 230 naval cadets. Niemöller noticed with concern that in the first few days some 'people were sent home'. Once his uniform measurements were taken, the sea cadets were distributed to the ships. Niemöller was assigned to SMS Hertha with 51 other men, one of the four training ships in use at the time. The group was divided into a starboard and port watch, and these in turn were divided into half-watches or sections of 14 men each. His Elberfeld friends Karl Gerstberger and Carl Pagenstecher also served in Niemöller's section.[12] After the six-week basic training programme, sniping and being fitted out with the naval cadets' dress-uniform were next on the agenda. The so-called 'monkey jackets' (Affenjäckchen) had been adopted from the Royal Navy in the UK. Niemöller felt homesick for the first time, but did not want to take part in the trivial everyday conversations in the barracks room or, like other sea cadets, seek diversion in cafes and shallow theatre plays. His firm hope was that he would never learn to 'enjoy himself' in such a mindless way.[13] This tension between the spiritual desolation of comradeship among the officer candidates and the striving for moral sublimation would become key to Niemöller's experiences in years to come.

Service on the Training Vessel SMS Hertha

Instruction on the training vessel began in May 1910. From 1908, SMS Hertha served for the training of officer candidates. The more than 110-metre-long ship had a crew of 300 men; 52 naval cadets slept in hammocks in the crowded naval cadet mess and the adjoining small mess. First Lieutenant Schaarschmidt gave instructions on the technical details of the boat, using a two-metre-long model. Of course, Martin was delighted. In addition, navigation lessons as well as fencing exercises and gymnastics were an important part of the naval cadet training programme.[14] In August 1910, the SMS Hertha embarked on her great trip overseas to the Mediterranean via San Sebastian, Barcelona, and Haifa, the Austrian Adriatic ports Cattaro and Pola, as well as Venice and Corfu, before returning to Kiel in March 1911. A highlight of the SMS Hertha's grand tour was when the ship cast anchor in the harbour of Port Said, Egypt in November. At very short notice, the Prussian Crown Prince Wilhelm (1882–1951) and his wife, Princess Cecilie, announced a visit onboard the ship. In great haste, the crew was gathered. Four naval cadets awaited the royal couple at the gangway; one of them was wearing the cockade of the uniform cap above the ear, another even had his trouser button open. But after this unsuccessful start, 'everything worked out fine'. When after her visit aboard the Crown Princess curtseyed on a motorboat casting off from the *Hertha* and shouted 'Thank you!' to the crew, the enthusiasm was great. 'It was splendid', Niemöller concluded. There was no greater joy for a future naval officer than a personal meeting with a member of the house Hohenzollern.[15]

In their free time the officer candidates enjoyed partying, usually with quite a lot of alcohol. On Christmas Day 1910, 20 naval cadets met in the small mess for an 'internal Christmas party', for which they had 'secretly' smuggled six bottles of Chianti, two bottles of liquor, one bottle of whiskey, and 50 litres of beer on board. This amount of alcohol explains why half of them had an 'immeasurable hang-over' the next day. However, at midnight First Officer of the *Hertha*, Corvette Captain Otto Hillebrand, put an end to the drinking bout. As he did not punish the young cadets for the unauthorized party, Niemöller fed on the remembrance of this joyful night 'for weeks on end'.[16]

Service in the Navy and even more so the everyday living together in the crowded quarters of a ship placed the young men at least temporarily in a forced community. Martin Niemöller had to get along with the other men, whether he wanted to or not. He acknowledged the necessity of military discipline, yet was in no way snobby towards his comrades. According to his observations, there was a great 'rivalry between port and starboard' among the 52 naval cadets of the *SMS Hertha*. He believed this was as regrettable as it was 'natural', since almost all aristocratic cadets served the starboard watch. This was why 'there was all cliquism. If someone is not part of the 3 cliques, he loses all credit. Then people are very reserved and perhaps even smug. At least that's what I call it when someone deems himself too good to shake hands with a German in the orient if he is only a vintner or something like that.'[17]

Niemöller, however, did not avoid any contact with aristocratic naval cadets. During basic training he already got acquainted with Otto Ferdinand Graf von Spee, the older son of Admiral Maximilian von Spee. Otto von Spee, alongside his father, his brother, and more than 2,000 other sailors of the Imperial Navy died on 8 December 1914 when British battleships sank a flotilla of the German East Asia Fleet near the Falkland Islands. In April 1910, Otto von Spee was enjoying himself at a sailing trip with Martin Niemöller on the Kiel Fjord. And at a stopover in Plymouth during the grand training trip he and Niemöller pooled their money to buy a copy of *Jane's All the World's Fighting Ships*, the British counterpart of Weyer's *Taschenbuch der Kriegsflotten*.[18] The fascination of the two young men for the technical features of the most modern warships transcended all social barriers.

At the beginning of basic training Niemöller already noted that 'there is a difference between friend and comrade'. With Karl Gerstberger and Carl Pagenstecher, he had two good friends from Elberfeld in the Crew 1910.

However, as Gerstberger served with a different watch than Niemöller, they seldom met. In September 1910, Niemöller already complained about loneliness, although there was ample opportunity to talk to his comrades. But his comrades were not his personal friends, like Hermann Bremer, whom he missed dearly.[19] After 1945, Karl Dönitz often mentioned he and Martin Niemöller had already been good friends and on a first name basis during their time as naval cadets.[20] At this point, Dönitz must have thought it beneficial to emphasize his friendship with a man who was globally well known as a critic of the National Socialist regime. However, in his letters and diaries from the time as naval cadet, Niemöller did not mention Dönitz once. At any rate, Dönitz served with the starboard watch of the SMS Hertha while Niemöller was part of the port watch. He did not have close personal friends here, but found this compensated by the harmonic atmosphere within the group: 'But comradeship is very good. We sometimes kick up a row and play tricks, drink sometimes one too many etc. According to those from starboard this a great crime and thus there is not much contact.'[21]

The inclination of Niemöller and his comrades from the port watch towards practical jokes and occasional drinking bouts did not mean the pastor's son was not committed to his training. On the contrary. In addition to their practical training, naval cadets had lessons in several subjects, including navigation and artillery, electrical engineering, and knowledge of service regulations. By the end of the trip on board the training vessel there was a three-day-long written exam, followed by a further inspection by the exam board upon return to Kiel. After passing this exam the cadets were promoted to Fähnrich zur See (with the British equivalent being navy petty officer) in April 1911.[22] Niemöller passed his final exam with outstanding results. A ranking list was compiled according to the exam results. Niemöller was in fifth place on the ranking list of Crew 1910, far above Otto Graf von Spee (15th) and Karl Dönitz (39th). In his memoirs from 1968, the later Grand Admiral tried hard to explain this rather mediocre result with a lack of ambition for learning the service regulations. At the same time, he pointed out that he was 'much higher in the list' of 1914—that is, after the promotion of Crew 1910 to lieutenant at sea in September 1913. This was true because Dönitz was in 29th place at the time. Niemöller, on the other hand, industrious and eager to learn as he was, had moved up to second place on the 1914 list.[23]

A Wasted Year at the Mürwik Naval School

After passing their petty officer's exam, the officer candidates moved to Flensburg-Mürwik for further theoretical training. On 21 November 1910, Wilhelm II had opened the new Naval School here, a large red brick building, located directly at the Flensburg Fjord. This new institution was the Naval Office's answer to the rapidly increased demand for naval officers in the wake of the Naval Laws of 1897.

During the 12-month training period in Mürwik, the cadets were constantly kept on their toes. There were more than 40 hours of lessons per week. In addition to navigation, which was taught most frequently, and technical subjects, the curriculum also included gymnastics, fencing, horse-riding, and ball dancing. Both the cadets' on-duty and off-duty behaviour were subject to strict rules (Fig. 2). A list of permitted Flensburg venues and premises regulated night entertainment.[24]

In hindsight, Mürwik Naval School was a wasted year for Niemöller. In early 1912, he told Hermann Bremer the time in Mürwik 'was not particularly rich in experiences' and he had 'the unsatisfying feeling' to 'not come much further'. He set all his hope on the time after Easter when several weapons training courses were scheduled. Then, Martin expected 'there will finally be proper work and one can rightly feel as a sailor again'.[25] Thus, the only highlight during the year at Mürwik was the long summer holiday, which Martin spent with his mother's family in Westerkappeln. He cycled to Wersen every morning, where he went

Fig. 2 The Crew 1910 in front of the Naval School in Flensburg-Mürwik. Niemöller is the third from the right in the front row, kneeling. The photo was taken around 15 April 1911, when the members of Crew 1910 were promoted to Fähnrich zur See (navy petty officer). The instructors, sitting or standing in the first row, wear the officer sabre. The petty officers of Crew 1910 were only granted permission to wear the sabre in December 1912—as so-called 'Säbelfähnriche' (sabre Fähnrich)–after they had successfully completed further training at the Ship Artillery School Sonderburg and on the SMS Württemberg. Marineschule Mürwik/WGAZ.

swimming with his siblings. In the evenings they sat outside, drank 'cold duck'—a punch with wine, sparkling wine, and lemon—and talked. Looking back from his solitary confinement in the concentration camp Sachsenhausen, the August of 1911, when he spent his time with his family, 'was the happiest and most carefree time of my whole life'.[26]

Life in Mürwik became increasingly boring, culminating in Niemöller beginning to have general doubts about the career as an officer at the end of the year.[27] Time and again he looked for opportunities for intellectual reflection and internalization and found them in educated middle-class culture. Apart from attending military church services, however, Protestant Christianity played almost no role at all in this respect. The first time Niemöller touched upon this topic was in April 1910 during his basic training. He had attended a religious service in Kiel with other naval cadets as it was common practice in the military.

> Shortly we will be led to Church, once again some intellectual work; the lessons are dull; though the sermon is still better, but I miss my father. [...] Church is over. Thank God, the sermon was much better than last time. I am starting to like the man. He preaches practical Christianity and I appreciate that.[28]

Niemöller did not expand on what he understood by 'practical Christianity'. Most likely he meant using the Ten Commandments and Luther's Small Catechism as a guideline of practical everyday morality.[29] In any case, referring to a church service as 'intellectual work' shows that Niemöller saw attending church above all as a welcome change from the dull training by the instructors of the Kiel naval battalion. During his training in Mürwik, sermons were not to his liking. When he attended church while at one of the weapons training courses in July 1912, he noted that he very much liked the sermon 'about the patriotism of Paul the Apostle'—a scriptural interpretation in the spirit of the national Protestant message of Germany's superiority—after everything he 'was used to from Mürwik'.[30]

Niemöller's interest in Protestant Christianity during his time in the Navy before 1914 did not go beyond mandatory church visits. Besides, if he could meet his friend Hermann Bremer on Sunday, he was happy to skip church.[31] That Niemöller's intellectual interest in the Protestant faith was very low at that time is shown by a diary entry of April 1913. He was, once again, contemplating his life plan—in particular the possibility of getting engaged:

> And yet I feel destined for some kind of special fate! Whether I can fulfil this destiny without a woman, whether it is only my imagination, whether I am strong enough to stand on my own feet? How come I no longer read the Sunday sermon; it would cost me more strength than I would gain from it. However, I do not want to be a heathen; I think I would have fit in well with the Greeks![32]

These remarks show Niemöller was looking for an intellectual guideline that would help him develop a life plan as a future naval officer, husband, and family father. But it was obvious that Protestant Christianity did not offer him suitable role models and values. Instead of looking to the Bible for inspiration, he preferred the idealized world of thought of Ancient Greece, which he had been taught at his humanist secondary school. Niemöller knew only a close relationship and the foundation of a family would give him the emotional stability and comfort that he longed for. He confided these ambivalent thoughts to his diary in July 1912:

> I increasingly come to the conclusion that as a naval officer—as wonderful as this profession might be and surely much more wonderful than any other—one has to do without a lot: family and a family life. And yet in my innermost being I very much depend on this kind of life and will always do so.[33]

At this time Niemöller had been in an emotionally deep relationship with Käthe Dilthey for some months. In May 1913 he recalled the year with her as the 'best one' since 'I'm alive and conscious'.[34] Katharina Dilthey—Käthe to her friends—was an old acquaintance of the Niemöller family. Her father Julius went to school with Heinrich Niemöller in Schulpforta. Both men had travelled to Jerusalem when the Lutheran Church of the Redeemer was dedicated by Wilhelm II in 1898. This event was the highlight of Heinrich Niemöller's life. After working as a teacher and deacon, Julius Dilthey was court chaplain in Weimar from 1889 until his untimely death in 1906.[35] Käthe had been a frequent and 'welcome' guest in the house of the Niemöller family in Lippstadt, particularly during the long summer holidays. Thus, Käthe, three years his senior, had been a good friend of Martin since his childhood and youth.[36]

Initially, Käthe's mother remained in Weimar after the early death of her husband. After the First World War she moved to Berlin, where Martin and Käthe again met regularly from 1931 onwards. Thus, between 1912 and 1914, Martin Niemöller and Käthe Dilthey had what today we would call a long-distance relationship. Aside from visits in Elberfeld or Weimar every once in a while, they used to write letters on a regular basis.[37] For Martin, this relationship was surely an emotional enrichment and a big hope, but at the same time the question arose in which direction it might go. Here, the navy service regulations came into play. In order to separate the naval officer corps according to their social status as an 'estate', marriage regulations played a prominent role. It was a constant worry of the Navy Command that an untimely marriage of the navy officers 'might lead to indebtedness, and hence to loss of social status on part of the junior executive in particular, and of the executive officer corps as a whole.'[38]

The Issue of Marital Consent

To avoid this, naval officers needed marital consent from the Naval Command. They not only had to provide detailed information about the familial and financial situation of the bride but also proof of assets. A lieutenant had to provide evidence of an annual income of at least 3,000 marks. Thus, Naval Command hoped to curb the number of marriage applications and ensure that naval officers got married in a way that benefitted their social status. In practice this meant that it was almost impossible for a naval officer to get married before being promoted to captain lieutenant, usually at the age of at least 30 years. Martin Niemöller was well aware of this.[39] The longer he thought about this, it was putting him off the relationship with Käthe Dilthey as well as a career as a naval officer in general. In January 1913 he confided to his diary:

> If I could get married, that is when I'm 32, she [Käthe] would be almost 35 years old and then the breath of life is over for the two of us, therefore I have no chance of being a happy family father; my life will become increasingly dull and empty, unless I do get absorbed in my career.[40]

This was a sober recognition of the facts related to marital consent and, at the same time, a gloomy assessment of the risks an unmarried naval officer faced in view of gradually increasing loneliness. While Niemöller reflected on the problem of loneliness, he also saw the danger of brutalization as the other side of a naval officer's life. Immediately following the diary entry cited above, he expressed his firm intention to continue his friendship with Käthe and thought about the alternative:

> I don't want to have superficial relations with women, as most of my comrades regrettably do, as long as I can endure it. That is beneath me. And the best cure against it is the friendship with a worthy woman, it makes one see what scum of the human race lives on God's beautiful earth [...]. Sometimes it is terrifying to see the joy and obsession with which they degrade this Holy [the family], make obscene and disgustingly unfunny jokes, screaming with laughter. I am sorry to speak of joy in this respect [...]. It is truly no small undertaking to remain an optimist under these circumstances as long as one takes it seriously. Often I find comfort in thinking that this is probably and hopefully only possible in our profession and in some other degenerated classes of society and that our German people has a healthy core, otherwise: woe betide such a people! In this case, a war with most terrible losses and extreme consequences, which will make the people aware of the last bits of its national honour, would be the last chance to create a resurrection for the better.[41]

This quote is interesting not because of Niemöller's decisiveness in condemning obscene jokes and short-lived dalliances with women, which were common among naval cadets. We would expect an attitude like that from the son of a Protestant pastor. Much more revealing is that he embedded his observations into a radical nationalist narrative about the declining moral core of the German people. It is ironic that Niemöller thereby deconstructed the ideological concept of the naval officer corps as the nation's elite. According to this view, the moral decay among naval officers corresponded to that of some 'degenerated classes of society'. Niemöller might have thought of those workers not reached by the social democratic labour movement. The narrative of decline, inscribed into the moral crisis of the German people, led him to a radical solution: the necessity of a war. According to this argument, only the efforts and sacrifices of war would improve the moral substance of the people. With these considerations Niemöller joined the ranks of a growing number of voices of the national Protestant and radical nationalist camp, which, just before 1914, spread the 'idea of the necessity of war' and claimed a war between the European great powers was inevitable.[42]

Niemöller's condemnation of superficial affairs made him feel morally superior. But it did not answer the question of whether he was to continue the relationship with Käthe. In May 1913, he wrote a letter to Käthe in which he broke up with her. But it was not that easy. Käthe assured Martin of her love, and thus they did not end the relationship. Shortly afterwards, however, Niemöller found himself in the exact same situation. In May 1914, he wrote another, this time final, letter.[43] After separating from Käthe Diltey, he again faced the inner loneliness that he deliberately preferred over the risk of brutalization related to the profession of an officer. Even more important, therefore, was his friendship with Hermann Bremer, who was a member of Crew 1911 and sometimes met Martin during the training in Kiel or Mürwik (Fig. 3). His school friend Hermann—whom he called Armin— gave Martin emotional stability and support during his time in the navy.[44] In November 1912, Martin confided to his diary how important the close contact with Bremer was for him and how much he needed his presence, not least to counterbalance the risk of brutalization in the navy.

If I could just see Armin for more than a few hours! He makes me feel calm when I am with him; I believe that is mainly the memory of the good old times back at home, this feeling of comfort and safety, to have people around who one knew and trusted. Life, reality is something completely different than this happy state of dreaming during the schoolyears. Until now it is only destructive and rough.[45]

These remarks reveal the soft side of the 20-year-old Niemöller, which did not quite fit in the harsh male world of the navy. During the First World War, Niemöller even complained about too many 'inherited female traits'.[46] But his

Fig. 3 Martin Niemöller (left) and his close friend Hermann Bremer, 1911–12. Bremer was a member of Crew 1911 and still naval cadet when the picture was taken. Unlike Niemöller, he did not yet have Oakleaves surrounding the Imperial Cockade on the service cap. Herbert Mochalski (ed.), *Der Mann in der Brandung. Ein Bildbuch um Martin Niemöller* (Frankfurt am Main, 1963), 18.

deeply rooted fear of moral brutalization did not result in the refusal to participate in all-male rituals common among officer candidates. One of these rituals was drinking together. To be sure, Emperor Wilhelm II had given clear instructions to the naval officer candidates at the inauguration of the Mürwik Naval School on

21 November 1910: 'The next war and the next naval battle will demand sound nerves from you. [...] There are destroyed by alcohol [...] and the nation which consumes the smallest amount of alcohol will win. And that is to be you, gentlemen!'[47] These remarks, framed and behind glass, hung on the wall of the officer mess of the Mürwik Naval School. Directly underneath it, cadets and naval officers often had merry drinking nights.[48]

Depending on their personal views on alcohol, the future naval officers developed different life plans, exemplified by Heinz Kraschutzki, Niemöller's Crew comrade. After the end of the first year in training and upon entering Mürwik Naval School in April 1911, Kraschutzki decided to completely abstain from alcohol. In doing so, Kraschutzki deliberately excluded himself from the male comradeship of the officer candidates, which manifested itself in regular drinking bouts. He even joined the Association of Teetotal Officers of the German Navy (Verein abstinenter Offiziere der deutschen Marine), which openly propagated the ideal of teetotalism. From 1915 onwards, Kraschutzki gradually turned into an opponent of war and a pacifist. His stand against alcohol already made him an outsider among the naval officer corps, a role that was cemented through his move towards pacifism.[49] But this was not the path Martin Niemöller chose before 1914. He participated in the drinking bouts and gambling games of his Crew comrades—albeit with a guilty conscience.[50]

Let us return to the chronological account of Niemöller's training course at Mürwik Naval School. At the end of the school year, in March 1912, the main naval officer exam was due, a written examination in several subjects. Niemöller achieved an 'outstanding' result with 117 points, the highest marks among all cadets of Crew 1910. Thus, he was first on the 1913 ranking list that determined seniority, before Otto Ciliax (1891–1964), the later admiral of the Navy of the Third Reich, who was the other of two cadets of Crew 1910 with an 'outstanding' performance.[51]

From April to September 1912, a number of different weapons training courses, each lasting several weeks, were scheduled. After the Ship Artillery School Sonderburg, the cadets attended Torpedo school and a special, several-week-long course in naval infantry. At the end of each training unit, the cadets had to take an exam.[52] Subsequently, the future officers were split into groups of six to ten and assigned to different battleships for further training. Niemöller and eight other cadets were allocated to the SMS Thüringen, based in Wilhelmshaven. The Helgoland class battleship, commissioned in 1911, had a crew of 1,000 men. After completing his special training courses, Niemöller was promoted to senior officer cadet and could wear an officer sabre. He qualified as a torpedo officer and in December 1912 already had the chance to become second torpedo officer on the Thüringen following the officer selection due in autumn 1913.[53] On the SMS Thüringen, Niemöller's life entered calmer waters. As he served with only a few Crew 1910 comrades on the ship, peer pressure was much lower than at Naval

School. Niemöller noted the 'relaxation' among the officer cadets in the mess. Because it was only a small group of people, 'it is possible to touch on subjects beyond amusement, shop talk, and rankings'.[54] On 27 September 1913, Niemöller was finally promoted to lieutenant at sea. While other officers of his Crew were assigned to other ships, Martin Niemöller remained on the SMS Thüringen.[55] At the age of only 21, he was already an officer of the Imperial Navy.

The account of Niemöller's time as an officer candidate would be incomplete without discussing his political views. Naval Command left no doubt that they expected their officers to be staunch anti-Social Democrats. The navy deemed Social Democracy as a party of revolution and upheaval.[56] During his training time, Niemöller rarely discussed political issues. But he could not ignore the political landslide of the Reichstag elections on 12 January 1912. The Social Democratic Party (SPD) could increase their share of the vote to 34.8 per cent of the votes cast. Now with 110 seats, it was the strongest parliamentary party by far. Niemöller described this result metaphorically as a 'red flood'. He mentioned the run-off election in Elberfeld between Friedrich Linz from the conservative German Reich Party (Deutsche Reichspartei), who had represented this constituency from 1907 on, and the Social Democrat Friedrich Ebert, who won. But even before the run-off elections Niemöller was convinced that the newly elected Reichstag was 'probably good for nothing'.[57]

These remarks not only reflected his political views but were also affected by professional circumstances. He reckoned the new Navy Bill would 'hardly have any chance for now' to get through a Reichstag with the SPD as the strongest party. Beginning in late summer 1911, the Naval Law was fiercely contested among Naval Command, the government under Reich Chancellor Bethmann Hollweg and the leaders of the bourgeois parties. As an insider, Niemöller was surprisingly well informed about the plans of the Navy Command around Alfred von Tirpitz although details were only published on 22 March 1912, after long conflicts and failed attempts of Lord Haldane, the British Secretary of State for War, to curb naval armament. In addition to a substantial 'increase in personnel', he wrote to Hermann Bremer, the 'commissioning of a third squadron' was intended. These plans directly affected Niemöller because they greatly increased his 'chances of promotion up to staff officer'—that is, up to the rank of a lieutenant commander (Korvettenkapitän).[58] While Niemöller's knowledge of the Navy's internal planning was indeed precise, his concerns that the SPD might block them altogether were rather exaggerated. When the bill passed the Reichstag in May 1912, only the Social Democrats and the representatives of national minorities voted against the law.[59]

On the issue of the Naval Law, growing pressure mounted on the government and Chancellor Bethmann Hollweg, as a 'nationalistic public demanded a massive armaments increase, which forced politicians to gradually give in'. A 'watershed' was the second Moroccan crisis in summer 1911. It triggered the formation of a radical right-wing camp against Bethmann Hollweg.[60] The German Foreign Secretary, Kiderlen-Wächter, wanted to use the French occupation of Fez and Rabat in April 1911 to impose a colonial compensation deal on France forcing the Paris government to give up the French Congo. The deployment of the German gunboat *Panther* to Agadir on 1 July and threats of war were intended to increase pressure on France. But when the British Chancellor of the Exchequer, Lloyd George, declared in a speech given in London that Britain was also ready for war, the German government backed down and agreed to a compromise. Germany recognized French interests in Morocco and was only granted a part of the French Congo.

Martin Niemöller commented on the Agadir incident in several letters. In late July he still hoped Britain would remain neutral and was optimistic that Germany would have to fight a war 'against the French alone'.[61] In early September, when the negotiations on an agreement between France and Germany were ongoing, his verdict was less hopeful and more aggressive. He wrote to Hermann Bremer:

> I wonder what will come out of the Moroccan question. It is almost funny how the newspapers write about war or not-war, seemingly with great calmness, but it is crazy that a 'German' colonial association issues a resolution that Morocco is not worth a war; as if this is only a matter of some lousy square miles of African sand. The German Michel [an allegorical figure representing the German national character, an equivalent to the English John Bull] has always been damn stupid!—By the way, Tirpitz reportedly said that we are not yet ready for war! (Please keep this to yourself!)—Well, we are not supposed to do politics and it is better anyway when other people make themselves immortal in doing so![62]

The last sentence of the quote echoes a deep disdain for the professional politicians of the government and the Reichstag. At the same time, Niemöller expressed his support for a war against France over Morocco, despite his internal knowledge of Germany's insufficient armament. Indeed, behind the scenes Alfred Tirpitz repeatedly criticized Kiderlen-Wächter's diplomatic approach during the Agadir incident and his threat of war because the German Navy was not yet ready.[63] The invective against the German 'Michel' reveals Niemöller's contempt for those circles who rejected an aggressive and imperialist policy determined to do anything for Germany's position as a world power. The letter can be read as an approval of the demands of the anti-governmental and radical right-wing camp, which was formed in the wake of the Agadir crisis. With their radical nationalism, these circles saw themselves in staunch opposition to Chancellor Bethmann Hollweg's politics, who was considered weak.[64]

After 1945, Wilhelm Niemöller tried to paint a positive picture of the years his brother Martin spent in the Imperial Navy. He claimed Martin Niemöller had been 'the prototype of a naval officer', which his comrades from Crew 1910 allegedly confirmed.[65] He also insisted Martin's time in the Navy had been 'happy years' with a lot of 'comradeship and friendship'.[66] Martin Niemöller himself emphasized in his 1934 memoirs that, before 1914, he 'was happy above measure in my calling as a naval officer'.[67] The sources used in this chapter have shown that this assessment is a retrospective whitewash of his biography. Niemöller's position in the ranking lists of the years from 1911 to 1914 demonstrates that he took his career very seriously.

Yet also clearly visible are Niemöller's deep emotional problems that resulted from his service. During the first year, he was still thrilled about service in the Navy, with the grand training tour and its manifold impressions playing a major role in this respect. But afterwards there was more than just one 'dull day' that passed in dreary monotony.[68] The fact that he was forced to postpone a potential engagement with Käthe Dilthey or break up with her, due to the Navy's policy of marital consent, massively impacted his emotional well-being. He longed for the comfort of family life, which he knew from his upbringing. For him the culture of the officer corps with its all-male rituals, its peer pressure, the superficial conversations, and the shop talk posed the dual threat of loneliness and brutalization. The harsh and all-male environment of the naval officers also prevented Niemöller from practising the faith he had adopted in his childhood. During the officer training, matters of Protestant faith were immaterial for him. After the beginning of the war in August 1914, Niemöller had to reacquire the Protestant tradition of his childhood and youth once again, this time based on the premises of wartime nationalism.

3

'May God Punish England'

Nationalism and the Great War 1914–1918

After four years of service in the Imperial Navy, Martin Niemöller increasingly felt that he was stuck in an inescapable rut. '[T]his never-ending everyday life makes one dull.'[1] These remarks, jotted down on 28 June 1914, provide several insights into his emotional state. He was unaware that on the very same day the heir to the Austrian throne was assassinated in Sarajevo, an incident that would subsequently trigger a war between the great European powers. A change of epoch was imminent. But what Martin Niemöller hoped for in June 1914 was a change in his personal life. The war that began shortly afterwards brought about both.

On 13 July, the *SMS Thüringen* embarked on its regular summer trip. On the high seas the crew was largely cut off from news about the events of the July crisis.[2] But on their return to Wilhelmshaven, a town shaped by the Imperial Navy, they found themselves in the thick of the events and the 'indescribable goings-on' directly preceding German mobilization. The shoreline of the Jade Bay was 'crowded with people' who waved farewell to the ships that left the harbour in rapid succession. As is well known today, the majority of German people reacted to the outbreak of the war partly with resigned scepticism, and partly with fear and anxiety. On 31 July, however, 'the enthusiasm' in Wilhelmshaven was 'boundless'. The crowd 'cheered on' every departing ship and 'sang the song *Wacht am Rhein* [a patriotic German anthem by Max Schneckenburger, lit. *The Watch at the Rhine*] and *Deutschland, Deutschland über alles*' (*Germany above all else*, which became the German national anthem in 1922). Niemöller took an active part in this awakening of the nation. He wrote to his parents that it was 'such a joy to experience this time', letting them know that should the war begin 'I will be a part of it with heart and soul!'[3] When German mobilization was announced on 1 August, the sailors on the *SMS Thüringen* sang 'all kinds of patriotic songs' until midnight. Martin was certain that the German Reich was acting 'in just cause', and not only to 'score off the Russians'.[4]

The beginning of the war in August 1914 was a moment when German national unity was symbolically invoked and substantiated. To be sure, the public display of war enthusiasm was mainly limited to situations such as the bidding of farewell to the troops in Wilhelmshaven. And yet, staging national unity in the name of the 'Burgfrieden'—a term referring to the political truce between the parties—had a deeper impact. It included and resonated even with the Social Democrats who had previously been considered 'unpatriotic fellows'. Not only every individual, but the nation as a whole, had to prove themselves in times of war. A widely held opinion which was particularly popular among the Protestant middle class claimed that the situation required 'national solidarity' in the sense of a 'harmonic social order born from the war'.[5] The belief in national unity based on the war seemed all the more self-evident since the Social Democrats approved the war credits on 4 August 1914. For the time being, the matter of how to flesh out the rather vague concept of a national community could be left open-ended. In the context of mobilization, the nation as an 'imagined order' facilitated the expression of intense emotions.[6]

These emotions were above all directed against the enemy. Only by 'creating boundaries' against external enemies could the nation consider itself a unity.[7] Thus, 'aggression' directed against nations that were seen as enemies complemented political 'participation' within one's own nation.[8] There was certainly no shortage of enemies of the German Reich in 1914. Alongside France, traditionally the 'archenemy' of the Germans since the Wars of Liberation against Napoleon from 1813 to 1815, was Tsarist Russia. Its authoritarian system of government was loathed by German liberals and social democrats alike. On 23 August 1914, a new enemy joined the ranks when Japan declared war on Germany. However, attention was primarily focused on England. During the July crisis, the government around Chancellor Bethmann Hollweg acted on the expectation of Great Britain remaining neutral. When London declared war on Germany on 4 August 1914, the disappointment of German nationalists quickly turned into rage. Within a few days, England became Germany's main enemy, at least in the eyes of Conservatives and radical nationalists. The 'Hymn of Hate against England' by the poet Ernst Lissauer, published shortly after the outbreak of the war, encapsulated this perception, in particular its chorus: 'We have one foe and one alone: England'.[9]

This radical national discourse focused on external enemies permeates Martin Niemöller's remarks from the first weeks and months of the war. Rather than drafting a conceptual framework of a new political order in Germany, he instead focused on pointedly expressing his feelings: which were primarily ones of resentment and open hostility against the war enemies, above all and from the very beginning against England. As early as 2 August, Martin penned the 'situation with the English is getting hairy', referring to England's looming entry into the war on the side of the Allies. His laconic comment used the stereotype of the British as a nation of shopkeepers: 'God willing, the customers will regret to have sided with the uncultured.' Either way, the war was, as he explained, 'a just cause for us'.[10] The malicious joke about the long legs of the English soldiers with which they would take to their heels and cowardly run away from the Germans flew easily from his pen. In his eyes, the Brits represented the 'worst type of soldier among our enemies'. He was amused by the thought that the sailors of the Royal Navy would 'have not much use' for their long legs.[11]

Remarks like these might be interpreted as part of a nationalist war folklore that tried to disparage Germany's enemies in a humorous fashion. However, only a few weeks after the beginning of the war it became obvious that Niemöller's humorous and radical anti-English invectives were part of a more comprehensive expectation of an imperialist reorganization of the world. According to this concept, the striving German nation had to eliminate the dominant British Empire as a rival. As early as 22 August, Niemöller wrote to his parents referring to the English people: 'We have to settle a score with this riffraff, the earth is too small for both peoples, one of them has to go and it won't be the German people!'[12] In Niemöller's view, all means possible should be used to eliminate the United Kingdom, even by stirring up anti-colonial resentments in the Middle East. He considered news on Turkey's imminent entry into the war as a welcome threat to the British position in Egypt. 'I firmly believe in the Holy War of Islam in Asia and Africa', was his comment, as then 'it will get hairy for our rivals.'[13] When it came to the imperialist competition with Great Britain, Niemöller did not shy away from any taboos—be they political, ethical, or religious.

As he developed his own version of anti-English war nationalism during the first weeks and months of the war, Martin Niemöller not only focused on top-level politics. The concept of the nation entailed that all individuals were supposed to find their place in it. Niemöller kept a diary to reflect on the meaning of life as a member of a belligerent nation. On 17 September, he resumed the series of sporadic entries in his 'log' that he had started in 1912. The following entry illustrates Niemöller expressed his radical anti-British nationalism towards his parents not simply to gain their approval. Moreover, it reveals to what extent the belligerent nation had become the substance of his own life:

Life has but one desire: to eradicate these alien dogs that have savaged our beautiful, wonderful, peaceful Reich. When this will have been achieved, I am a nobody without intent or purpose in the world.[14]

Germany would not be able to secure world power status, which Niemöller and other radical nationalists considered the legitimate goal of their ambitions, unless Great Britain was destroyed. However, Germans' willingness to make sacrifices was not the only precondition to achieving this goal. As a national Protestant, Niemöller saw the self-assertion of the German nation intrinsically linked to divine providence. In his eyes, God had chosen the Germans as a people that he would support unconditionally. This national Protestant idea became increasingly relevant during the First World War. Furthermore, the individual 'unconditional willingness to make sacrifices' gained full plausibility and validity by drawing on 'Christian semantics of sacrifice and love'. Thus, the concept of Christian charity lost its universal character and was instead reinterpreted as unconditional 'devotion' to one's own nation.[15]

For Martin Niemöller reflecting on the religious dimension of national Protestantism was a novelty. There is no evidence that the Lutheran belief, which he had encountered in his parents' home, gave him any cause for thought or triggered a continuously practised piety in the rather anti-religious atmosphere of the naval officer corps before 1914. This changed immediately following mobilization. One important aspect of his new interest in Protestant belief was the practice of military pastoral care which he carefully observed. On 2 August 1914, the chaplain of the Wilhelmshaven squadron held a service. Martin had wished for a text such as 'Be faithful, even to the point of death' as the core of the sermon. Instead, the chaplain read and preached about 'Do not fear, only believe!'. Niemöller was certain that 'talking about being scared' right at the beginning of the war would not 'enthral the soldier'.[16] Rather, the selfless willingness to sacrifice one's own life, the commitment 'till death', had to be emphasized as the main aspect of the soldiers' war service.

There is something else which indicates that Niemöller only began to embrace the religious dimension of national Protestantism in the war: his frequent references to God as almighty creator. Before 1914, as a high-school graduate and a naval cadet, there was not a single reference to God either in his letters or in his dairies—as far as the existing source material allows us to make such a judgment. This changed immediately after mobilization. From then on, he wrote about God in almost every letter and on every postcard, who would guarantee the German success against a multitude of enemy powers. For instance, on 18 August he wrote to his parents:

> Now Japan has joined in too!! All thanks to our dear cousin, the English. What a shame that the peace Bertha doesn't live to see this!—Life is getting interesting in the long run. When we finally start to let rip! […] God will not forsake the Germans. Hopefully the Brits, the scoundrels, will finally be swept away!'[17]

Niemöller's belief in God's providential work becomes apparent through these remarks. The German nation, chosen by God, could always rely on him. At the same time, the quote reveals the mechanisms of exclusion which the invocation of national unity necessarily entailed. All those who refused to 'dedicate' themselves to the nation had to be seen as 'sinners' from the perspective of national unity.[18] And yet, the internal enemy could indeed change. As we will see later, by the end of the war in 1918 Niemöller not only labelled defeatists and social democrats but also Jews as those who endangered national unity. In the above letter from 18 August 1914, he ridiculed the 'peace Bertha': Bertha von Suttner, pioneer and figurehead of European pacifism, the first women to be awarded the Nobel peace prize in 1905, had passed away shortly before on 21 June 1914. Niemöller's remarks on the war that had in fact become reality—despite her work and intentions—were a sarcastic obituary, at the same time illustrating the militaristic and anti-pacifist foundation of his nationalism.

Not every reference to God was a theologically elaborate statement. This is true also, and particularly, for the naval officer Niemöller. He most frequently used the plain phrase 'May God punish England' which gained currency shortly after the beginning of the war among nationalist circles and became a salutation in private conversation and correspondence. He usually closed his letters and postcards with the words: 'May God punish England! Yours Martin.'[19] The parents in Elberfeld might have added 'May he punish it' in their mind's eyes as the common salute in return. Besides, the moral dimension of Christianity was much more important for the everyday lives of German Protestants than any theological considerations. Protestant belief served as a moral compass in the daily contact with friends and strangers. It was a code of ethics for coexistence and appreciation, summarized in terms such as 'love of one's enemies', 'peaceableness', and 'compassion' that flagged up in the Sermon on the Mount as one of the key texts. It required, in particular, self-reflexion on what every individual Christian was able to do for their fellow human. However, the war propelled nationalist Protestants to abolish the inclusive dimension of their Christian ethics. Those who heaped abuse and hateful scorn on the enemies of Germany could no longer accept them as close fellow Christians with equal rights. Niemöller was fully aware of the consequences of this war ethics based on exclusion. As Christmas approached in 1914, he used clear words to express his fantasies on the extermination of the adversary and the consequences for him as a Christian:

> What I would most like to see is our troops on the English shore on Christmas Day helping these fellows celebrate. If the biblical term of the 'neighbour' includes people other than the Germans and their allies, I won't go to heaven: I hate all of them: the English, the French, the Americans and the Italians. The less of these scoundrels survive, the better for mankind.[20]

During the first weeks and months of the war, Niemöller gave considerable thought to the meaning of national enmity and the work of divine providence that would guarantee Germany's success. In letters to his parents and his brother he used a language derived from war nationalism which was charged with ravenous 'rage' about the enemies. He threatened—without any moral moderation—that 'no Englishman' should 'fall into my hands alive'.[21] These letters show Niemöller intellectually participated in the idea of the national awakening at the beginning of the war. However, on a practical level he felt increasingly disillusioned and frustrated when the war did nothing to change his daily routine as a naval officer. As early as 8 August, Martin wrote to his parents that he was 'pretty bored'. Four days later he expressed his displeasure about the disagreeable 'waiting'. On 22 August he regretted not to have joined the army where one could 'slog' the enemy. And in late October he wrote: 'If it wasn't in the newspapers, one would think that we were not at war at all.'[22]

Niemöller's discontent was grounded in the conduct of German naval warfare.[23] Before 1914, the German Navy's strategy was geared towards a confrontation with the British Royal Navy. Thus, Wilhelmshaven was the most important base of the High Seas Fleet from 1912 onwards, thanks to its vicinity to Great Britain. The Imperial Naval Office and the Admiralty Staff expected the Royal Navy to go on the offensive, in the event of war establishing a tight naval blockade off the German coast of the North Sea. According to Berlin, this would result in a possible 'decisive battle' near the island of Heligoland.[24] However, what exactly such a battle would decide remained unknown. Moreover, the German Admiralty failed to take into consideration the geostrategic situation of the German Reich. From 1911/12 onwards, the Royal Navy considered it sufficient to block access to the German North Sea coast by cordoning off the English Channel and the sea route between Scotland and Norway. This remote blockade minimized the risk to the Grand Fleet. In a war game in 1912, the German Admiralty explored possibilities to react to this strategic realignment of British operative planning. The answer was clear: a decisive battle could not be forced. And yet, the German Naval Command did not draw any conclusions from these insights and adhered to its previous planning.[25]

The consequences of this bad planning became apparent immediately after the beginning of the war. The Royal Navy established its remote blockade and, at the same time, launched a surprise attack near Heligoland on 28 August 1914, sinking three light cruisers and resulting in heavy casualties on the German side. Subsequently, the German Naval Command grew increasingly uncertain and restricted the already tight operational planning even further. Kaiser Wilhelm II's command stated that a potential 'decisive battle' was 'not to be jeopardized by premature casualties'. Chief of the Admiralty Staff, Hugo von Pohl, who became commander of the German High Seas Fleet in January 1915, was expected to follow this course.[26] Although some units of the German High Seas Fleet undertook minor forays into English east coast waters during autumn and winter of 1914/15, most ships lay idle in the harbour.

The Long Wait for a Mission

For Martin Niemöller, as for the vast majority of German naval officers, this was the beginning of 'the long wait' for a mission.[27] During 13 months from August 1914 to the end of August 1915, waiting was the defining experience of Niemöller's life. He had welcomed the beginning of the war as a way out of everyday routine, but now the service on the SMS Thüringen proved to be a dead end. He was on the verge of losing his professional honour and began to doubt the purposefulness of his service as an officer. There was no shortage of leisure activities, be it on board or in Wilhelmshaven when the ship was at the roadstead. However, as early as spring 1915, the 'universal stupor' reached a 'particular climax', and in summer 1915, military service on the *SMS Thüringen* had become a minor matter (Fig. 4).[28]

For Niemöller and many other young naval officers much more was at stake than just fighting boredom, for example by playing cards or drinking alcohol. Their professional honour was on the line, paramount to their collective rank consciousness and, at the core of the officer corps' honour, the oath of allegiance to the emperor as the supreme commander, which symbolized their attachment to the monarchy. The long wait for a mission was so unbearable for Martin Niemöller because his own professional honour as an officer was congruent with his willingness to serve the nation. Niemöller had become an officer because he wanted to serve the German cause. As a nationalist, he was prepared to die for Germany. In March 1915, he confided to his 'log' that not only could his nerves no longer take lying in the roads, but that, above all, his hopes associated with his career as an officer were profoundly disappointed by this idle waiting.

Fig. 4 Niemöller on board the *SMS Thüringen, c.*1913. Niemöller observes sailors setting up torpedo nets. Fixed on foldout beams and hanging several metres deep in the water, the steel nets were intended to prevent torpedoes from touching the hull. In response to torpedo nets, net scissors were developed. From 1916, the *SMS Thüringen* no longer used torpedo nets. United States Holocaust Memorial Museum.

My comrades: I believe they did not love their fatherland more than I did—they were allowed to fight, to bleed and to die. And I? I have to sit here, put a few drinks away and long for the end of this great time. [...] This war robs me of the chance to be a good officer. One becomes an officer to sacrifice one's blood, goods and life for the fatherland in the moment of truth and to train one's subordinates in the spirit of this offensive in times of peace. Now we are at war. Now they tell us: we don't want your life, just go on and do business as usual! [...] I have been cheated of my profession.[29]

But what was the alternative, given that the battle fleet lying in the harbours did not allow for the fulfilment of professional honour? Joining the Imperial German Flying Corps promised a participation in the romantically charged airborne fight. However, Niemöller's superiors failed to forward his request for transfer in August 1915.[30] In spring 1915, another opportunity emerged. The German Navy had an increasing need for submarine officers. For this reason, torpedo officers on large battleships such as the SMS Thüringen were declared dispensable as they could be replaced by petty officers. But Niemöller's immediate superior, Captain Lieutenant Wilhelm von Türcke, the first torpedo officer of the Thüringen, did not want to lose such an efficient officer. 'Everything will come to a standstill if I let N. go', he said to a fellow officer. Niemöller considered this a breach of trust as Türcke had promised him that he could train a petty officer who would 'fill in' in the case of Niemöller's reassignment. Niemöller's reaction was typical for a member of the officer corps: 'First of all, I got drunk, deliberately and with intent.'[31]

The nagging dissatisfaction with the work on board of the SMS Thüringen had both professional and personal reasons. Niemöller felt lonely, and he feared that the monotonous everyday life of an officer would dull his mind. The social life of the High Seas Fleet's officer corps was narrow. There were privileges such as communal parties and drinking in the mess, regular shore leave, and generous furlough.[32] However, Niemöller's social circle on board of the SMS Thüringen was small, not least due to the differences in ranks that formalized and ritualized contact with higher-ranking officers. In 1916, Martin wrote to his brother Wilhelm that 'spiritual values' withered away in the Navy. 'Friendship' among officers was rarely more than simply 'good comradeship'. Dealing with superiors was 'often difficult' and 'at the cost of honesty and inner peace'.[33]

With just a small number of comrades—in June 1913 Niemöller had counted five people—he had only one friend on board of the Thüringen: Hans Jochen Emsmann. Born in 1892, just like Niemöller, Emsmann had joined the Navy in 1910 as a naval cadet of the Crew 1910 and served on the SMS Hertha. Both men were assigned to the SMS Thüringen in autumn 1912. Niemöller became very close to this friend. Just how central a role he played for Niemöller's mental balance became apparent in the summer of 1915 when Emsmann took leave without prior notice.[34] Even playing the piano in the evenings did not console Niemöller in the absence of his friend. His only refuge was another ritual: 'May God punish England, also for my sake!'[35] Against this backdrop, it seems ironic that Niemöller left the SMS Thüringen at the very expense of Emsmann. Behind the back of his immediate superior, Türcke, some 'senior gentlemen' had suggested to reassign Niemöller. On 27 August, the commander of the ship, Hugo Langemak, told Niemöller that he—instead of Emsmann who was expecting the same—was to be reassigned to the U-boat fleet.[36] During the following weeks and months, the decision now and then fell into doubt before the reassignment finally took place as planned on 1 December 1915.[37]

Niemöller's 1915 qualification report described the lieutenant at sea as 'very well disposed', 'decisive', and 'vigorous', and explicitly emphasized that he was 'particularly suitable' for the service with the U-boat fleet. Thanks to this assessment, he was finally transferred.[38] When Niemöller reported for duty with the U-boat fleet in Kiel on 1 December 1916, his feelings were rather ambivalent since this branch of military service was 'not exactly my ideal', as he wrote to his parents.[39] Apparently, Niemöller considered it unethical to kill hundreds of people without warning with a U-boat. From his nationalist point of view, however, its terrible destructive power rendered it irreplaceable. A 'log' entry from September 1914 expressed this deep ambivalence: 'I hate the submarines. But this is good! The war will be very hard on Germany; on our enemies, however, it will be devastating if God wills!'[40] The nationalistic end of destroying England justified the means.

The rapid rise of the German U-boat force as a projection screen of imperialist power fantasies was not yet foreseeable at the beginning of the war. Alfred von Tirpitz, Secretary of State of the German Imperial Naval Office, did not include submarines in his design to win the war. Instead, he focused on the expansion of the battleship fleet for the final decisive battle against the British Royal Navy. For this reason, the first submarines were not built before 1904/5. Only 28 U-boats were completed by 1914.[41] The first submarine assignments during the war were exclusively against British battleships. The British remote blockade of German trade routes changed Naval Command's priorities. Admiralty and Imperial Naval Office realized the potential of a submarine war against merchant ships. On 4 February 1915, the area around the British Isles was publicly declared a war zone where enemy-flagged merchant vessels would be sunk without warning as required by the prize rules of the London Declaration of 1909 which codified maritime law. Furthermore, submarine commanders had to make sure that neutrally flagged merchant vessels were not in fact disguised enemy ships. In so doing, the German Reich did not introduce 'unrestricted' submarine warfare, as is often suggested. Contrary to this 'incorrect' interpretation, unrestricted submarine warfare did not start before February 1917.[42] At any rate, the use of submarines was a balancing act between the proper and the improper. Germany justified their attacks on enemy merchant vessels by ignoring prize rules as a means against the remote blockade by Great Britain that the Reich considered a breach of international law. Thus, in German eyes, extended submarine warfare was a 'necessary countermeasure' to force the United Kingdom to loosen the blockade.[43]

This was technically a plausible interpretation of maritime international law. And yet, by insisting on the legality of the German submarine war, government and Naval Command underestimated an important factor: the public opinion of neutral states. This became apparent in May 1915 when U-20 sunk the British passenger liner *Lusitania* off the shores of Ireland. Among the 1,200 killed were 128 American citizens, which propelled the government in Washington to intervene immediately and force the Germans to refrain from further attacks against passenger vessels.[44] The successful submarine war against enemy merchant vessels also challenged Britain. The still small German U-boat force—only 46 submarines were in service in September 1915—sank 500 merchant ships with 824,292 gross register tons during the first nine months of the year 1915. The government in London took countermeasures. British merchant ships started to sail armed and under neutral flags. So-called 'Q-ships', heavily armed auxiliary cruisers that were disguised as sailing or fishing boats with concealed weaponry, lured submarines into surfacing and opened fire with heavy-calibre artillery. This practice was a clear breach of international law.[45]

In late summer of 1915, the Q-ship *Baralong* sank two German submarines within four weeks. During the attack on U-27, British soldiers shot at 11 German crewmembers swimming in the sea. Other German sailors who had been rescued by the British freighter *Nicosian* were executed aboard.[46] When American crewmembers of the *Nicosian* made this incident public, it triggered widespread outrage. Martin Niemöller also reacted with anger and disgust to news of 'the murdered submarine crew'. He and his comrades on the SMS *Thüringen* were 'furious', as he wrote to his parents. His emotional reaction inevitably led to a call for revenge: 'I hope we will drop many more bombs on London, it is a great tool: what a pity that we made the decision to do so so late, but we are far from being the barbarians that we have to be in dealing with this riffraff!'[47]

Service in the U-Boat Force

His assignment to the U-boat force is the starting point of Niemöller's autobiographical book *From U-Boat to Pulpit*, written in 1934. Over 217 pages, he describes his path from leaving the SMS *Thüringen* in Wilhelmshaven on 30 November 1915 to his ordination as a Protestant pastor in June 1924. Urged by his friends of the Confessing Church, Niemöller quickly jotted the manuscript during his summer vacation in 1934. With this book, he wanted to emphasize that he and the Confessing Church were fully committed to the German nation.

Writing this manuscript was an easy task for Niemöller as between 1920 and 1932 he had frequently given speeches at several meetings of nationalist military associations about his experiences with the U-boat fleet from 1916 onwards. *From U-Boat to Pulpit* puts the fulfilment of duty towards the nation at the heart of the account. Niemöller does not elevate himself to heroic status; instead, he describes, in plain words, the routine of sinking gross tonnage as the core of the submarine warfare.[48] Previous biographers of Niemöller have taken his account at face value.[49] I will only draw on this text if no other source material is available.

Niemöller was first assigned to U-73, a minelayer not designed for attacking ships which could hardly keep up speed with freighters in surface cruising mode. Together with two officers and a crew of 28, Niemöller was second officer of the watch under Captain Lieutenant Gustav Sieß, with whom he got along well.[50] The operation order of the U-73 entailed the mission to lay mines in the Mediterranean. U-73 carried out the command before passing the Strait of Gibraltar and mined the entrance to the port of Lisbon, later areas at Malta and the Cyclades in the Aegean. However, the ship had many technical defects and, for this reason, lay in the roads in the Adriatic port of Pula for weeks on several occasions during the summer and autumn of 1916. Pula served as a base for the Austrian Navy. Niemöller had already been in Pula in 1910 as a cadet. Aside from German submarine officers, he met comrades from the Austrian fleet he knew from his first stay. Germans and Austrians were on friendly terms. They met regularly in the officers' mess or on board one of the ships. The summer of 1916 was a happy and easy-going time for Niemöller. On occasion, he took part in boat trips organized from Pula, and sometimes he and the other officers enjoyed sunbathing and a gush of cold sea water to cool down.[51] In March 1916, he had already been promoted to the rank of first lieutenant at sea.[52] However, this was only an interim goal for Niemöller, who remained restless and impatient through-out his entire life. Filled with envy, he wrote as early as in December that there were 'several commanders who have their own boat' among his age group of naval cadets, the Crew 1910.[53] He was only assigned his own command in 1918.

During the first months of 1917, Niemöller grew increasingly impatient with his position as officer of the watch on U73. He wanted nothing more than to get away from the 'old barge' and have his own command.[54] This was not unreason-able, given that younger officers, including from Crew 1910, increasingly served as commanders of small submarines without previously having been promoted to captain lieutenant. But Niemöller had to exercise patience. The Admiralty Staff had assigned him to cover for a sick officer working in the Mediterranean Department. He only stayed in Berlin from early May to late June 1917; however, during these few weeks he met the woman he would later marry and who would shape his life for the following 44 years and beyond.

Niemöller 'quite liked' the office work at the Admiralty. Berlin, where many urban amenities were still offered even at the end of the third year of war, made such an impression on him that he wanted to return to the capital 'in peace time'.[55] Besides, he was reunited with his old childhood friend from Elberfeld, Else Bremer. Else, born in 1890, was the one-year-older sister of Hermann Bremer, Martin's school friend and naval comrade. In 1940, Else recalled that she met Martin in November 1901, on Hermann's 10th birthday, for the first time. Martin, on the other hand, remembered meeting her around that time on an ice skating rink in Elberfeld. Be that as it may, the skinny boy failed to impress her, both back then and in the following years. For Martin, it seems to have been a different story. In July 1912, he wrote to his sister Magdalene that there had been 'a time' when he was 'interested' in Else, but that serious interests in a woman were 'futile' for a naval officer. However, since Martin was a frequent visitor of the Bremer family both as a school student and later as a naval cadet, he met Else on numerous occasions.[56]

Marie Elisabeth Bremer was the oldest of five children of the physician August Bremer and his wife Helene.[57] Because her mother suffered from impaired mobility at an early age, Else had to take up many responsibilities in the family at a very young age. This did not stop her from embarking on a career as a teacher. From the turn of the century onwards, an increasing number of young women with a bourgeois background chose this pathway of training in seeking to start a professional career and gain independence. The exam of a secondary school for girls qualified Else to study at the Municipal Educational Institute for Female Teachers in Elberfeld from 1907 to 1910. Then she worked as a teacher in German and singing at a public school in the county of Kent, England, illustrating her willingness to live an independent life. She also acquired an 'excellent command of English', which would prove useful on her extended journeys with Martin in the service of ecumenism some decades later.[58]

After her return from England, Else initially taught at an elementary school and at a secondary school for girls in Elberfeld (Mädchengymnasium) from 1912. Yet she still had not achieved her career goal. In May 1916, she enrolled for a degree in English, history, and German at the University of Bonn, seeking to qualify for a job as a graduate grammar school teacher. In October 1916, she moved to the Friedrich-Wilhelm University of Berlin, known today as Humboldt University. Until the summer semester of 1918, she attended, among others, lectures by the historian Otto Hintze, one of the pioneers of modern social history.[59] Apparently, Else very much enjoyed her time at university and her independent life in Berlin, which would have come to a rapid end once she had committed herself to a man. In Imperial Germany, female teachers were subjected to the so-called 'teachers' celibacy', meaning they were dismissed as civil servants as soon as they got married. This put Else in a quandary. Her work as a teacher was an important part of her life. At the same time, being in her mid-twenties she had reached the average age of a bourgeois woman to get married. Else was well aware of her dilemma. In September 1916 at her parents' house in Elberfeld, she confided these problems to her diary after she had met Martin again:

We had some lovely evenings meeting acquaintances such as Lewis, Buchfelds, Engels. By far the best was at Niemöllers (12 September). Martin was there. Herm.[ann], or rather Ms. Schmidt have told tales out of school about him and that puts me in a special relationship to him. I have rarely been so happy than on that night. I'm longing so much for love that brings the woman to the high level of development that she is able to achieve. It is so difficult to content oneself, even though if one believes that a different life is indeed possible.[60]

Thus, Else was torn between the desire for love and her awareness that a marriage would demand to 'content oneself'. In the end, desire prevailed. On 1 November she wrote: 'My heart is full of desire, but I must bury it.' But the next day it already seemed that everything 'will be fine'.[61] When Else and Martin met again in Berlin in May 1917, she was clearly expecting a potential relationship. Martin described these happy days in spring in letters to his parents. During the Whitsun holidays in late May, Martin, Else, her sister Käthe, and Käthe Dilthey went sailing twice on the Wannsee, a lake in Berlin, each time for three hours. Two weeks later, they again spent two days away from the bustling city sailing on the Wannsee. These days were certainly 'wonderful' not only for Martin. Thus he told his mother that he had a good reason to miss Whitsun Service, as he was going sailing.[62] In August, Martin again spent two days on official business in Berlin. In Else's company he 'thoroughly' stocked up on 'supplies of happiness'—using a mechanistic metaphor—for the upcoming long journey on board of U-151.[63] However, from this point onwards the development of the relationship ground to a halt. This was not due to the lack of mutual affection. Rather, three reasons were decisive.

Firstly, the war with all its uncertainties was not an ideal time for marriage, as shown by the radically decreasing number of weddings from 1915 onwards. Secondly, father Bremer harshly rebuked his daughter when she told him about the planned engagement and her decision to drop out of university.[64] The third and most crucial problem was the uncertainty of Martin's financial circumstances. In order to get married naval officers needed marital consent granted by the emperor for which proof of assets was required. This was supposed to prevent socially unacceptable marriages and to secure the financial basis of the officers' families. For a first lieutenant at sea such as Niemöller, this meant he had to provide proof of 'a guaranteed annual private income' of 3,000 marks in addition to his salary. When Martin revealed his 'marriage headaches' to his father in August 1918, he expected that he needed equity requirements of 60,000 marks, 'invested in 5 per cent war bonds'. He himself and Else only owned a tenth of this amount, which was already invested in war bonds. These assets were lost with Germany's military defeat in November 1918.[65]

Apparently, a complex process of coordination that lasted several months during autumn and winter 1917/18 was necessary to resolve these issues. It appears that Hermann Bremer, Else's brother, acted as an intermediary in this matter. 'Armin', as Martin always called him, established communication between Else and Martin, and possibly also between both families.[66] On 23 July 1918, Martin and Else celebrated their engagement.[67] At that time, Martin was on a three-week furlough. After returning to Pula he was optimistic that 'the sunshine of today' would 'stay in my future life forever'. 'Else is happy and me too, the worries about the war fundamentally cannot change that.'[68] The engagement with Else Bremer changed Niemöller's life significantly. Prospects of starting his own family promised independence from his parents, his own home, and thus a bourgeois life from which he as a bachelor had previously been shut out. In a letter to Wilhelm from June 1916 he expressed deep scepticism about the life of a naval officer, highlighting its monotony and intellectual narrowness that he knew only too well. He was 'afraid of the time when the first enthusiasm fades away. Then life gets lonely and empty for most of them.'[69] After his engagement, he no longer had to worry about this. The engagement had other consequences for Else, as she was certainly not the stereotypical young woman with a bourgeois background whose only aim in life was to get married within her social class. However, once engaged, she had to 'content herself' with this role, as she knew only too well.

Martin, on the other hand, was not at all prepared to content himself. In spring 1917, he still hoped that at any time soon he would be commanding his own submarine. Meanwhile, Waldemar Kophamel, who knew Niemöller from his time as commander of the Pula flotilla, became commander of U-151. Martin baulked, but could not evade Kophamel's request. Thus, from July until late December 1917, he served as 'first officer' on U-151, a 65m long Deutschland-class cruiser submarine. In 114 days, from late August to Christmas 1917, U-151 circumvented the British Isles and cruised through the Atlantic Sea to the Azores and the Canary Islands on the 'longest cruise of a German submarine'. It sunk about 50,000 gross register tons during this mission altogether.[70] In the meantime, the context of sinking gross tonnage had changed for German submarines. Taking office as chiefs of the Supreme Army Command in late August 1916, Erich Ludendorff and Paul von Hindenburg soon became the staunchest proponents of unrestricted submarine warfare. After Chancellor Bethmann Hollweg had tried to stall a decision for a long time, on 1 February 1917 Germany finally declared large areas around the British Isles, in the Atlantic, the North Sea, and the Mediterranean as prohibited zone in which any merchant vessel sailing under neutral flags would be sunk without warning as stipulated by prize rules. An anticipated sinking rate of 600,000 tons per month was supposed to stop Allies' supplies and bring Great Britain's economy to her knees.[71]

Disappointed Hopes for Victory

As most other radical nationalists, Niemöller shared the hope that the unrestricted submarine warfare would result in a swift German victory. In February 1917, he mouthed off about the prospect of submarine warfare, which became 'better by the month', believing that it would prevent the 'beefs'—that is, the beef-eating Brits—from putting out to sea 'at all'.[72] During the summer, he praised the third Army Supreme Command under Hindenburg and Ludendorff as a Godsend and saviour of the nation and made fun of the members of the Reichstag where the leader of the Centre Party, Matthias Erzberger, had demanded a negotiated peace without annexations on 6 July 1917: 'The submarine warfare must and will succeed [...]! Thank heavens that we have Hindenburg and Ludendorff.'[73] However, the strategy of radical nationalists and naval and army command did not pay off. On 3 February 1917, the USA broke off diplomatic relationships with Germany in response to the unrestricted submarine warfare. And yet Martin thought there was 'nothing to worry about' in this step of the 'wolves in sheep's clothing'.[74]

From summer 1917, another development attracted Niemöller's attention and changed his political thinking far beyond the end of the war. The mood among the civilian German population at the home front had deteriorated significantly from as early as 1916. Supply shortages and the perception of social inequality enraged broad sections of the population in urban and rural areas. From spring 1917, frustration and discontent became politically charged. In April, workers in Berlin, Leipzig, and other major cities went on strike against deficient food supplies. In 1917, the creation of the Reichstag Inter-party Committee consisting of Majority SPD, Centre Party, and Left Liberals showed that the majority parties of the Reichstag pressed for democratic reforms and the end of the war.[75]

It was no surprise that the Imperial naval officer Niemöller was strongly opposed to these strikes and reform attempts. Yet the emerging antagonism against the war among broad sections of the population raised a much more crucial concern. If the people turned against the emperor or even against the continuation of the war, were these people still at the very centre of the German nation? Protestant Reich nationalism considered the nation as a triad: the people embodied the substance of the nation, the state manifested it politically, and the emperor represented it as the symbolic capstone and head of the Reich. Niemöller had expressed his enormous adoration for the emperor when Wilhelm II gave his first war speech in front of units of the Navy in Wilhelmshaven on 4 February 1915. He quoted lengthy passages of this speech from memory, among other things Wilhelm's statement that from the beginning of the war he had been aware that 'we would have to fight against a superior number of enemies'. Niemöller was clearly deeply moved by this event, particularly because the emperor had personally greeted some selected officers before the speech:

Thus, I saw him at close range! The emperor has aged; but he looks unbelievably fresh and optimistic. This was a moment I will never forget. Afterwards, the emperor gave a speech from the upper deck of the 'Seydlitz'; magnificent—no: unsurpassed! Such a man comes only once every couple of centuries. He talked about the Navy, its spirit, its achievements, its tasks: without notes of course, very vividly and long![76]

However, the fact that the people protested against the state and objected to the war of the nation disrupted the harmony of the triad people–state–emperor and jeopardized the moral substance of the nation. Niemöller expressed this line of argument for the first time in August 1917, shortly before he embarked on the long war cruise with U–151:

> I am looking forward to the venture: thank God, at last we get to see something else than just long faces. There is nothing worse right now than to be stuck in the inner land among all those cretins who pretend to be the 'German people'![77]

Crucial in this passage are the inverted commas around the notion of the 'German people'. They indicate that for Niemöller the 'people' who were collectively protesting in summer 1917 were no longer qualified to represent the 'people' that was at the heart of the Reich nationalist world of ideas. This idealized *Volk* was supposed to pursue the war until German victory, since the nation was based on the enmity against other nations. In early October 1918, when German defeat was clearly looming, Niemöller came back to this thought, albeit differently worded:

> I'm happy with my achievements and would altogether be very happy if the domestic situation in the German Reich wasn't so terrible. But our people will only see reason when the enemy is in the country and clearly shows what they think of peace with us! But then it will be too late and the country will see a wave of emigration.[78]

It is interesting that Niemöller is addressing the idea of emigration from Germany in this letter. By October 1918, he considered it an option for himself, which he in fact pursued for a couple of months after armistice.[79] Emigration was here a cipher for Niemöller's feeling of being a stranger in his own country. However, the successes still outweighed the disappointments, albeit only at a personal level. In May 1918, Niemöller finally achieved his long-cherished goal: he was given his own submarine command. An internal qualification report regarding the time until late 1917 expressed confidence that Niemöller would 'perform well' as commander of a submarine.[80] After Martin received this message he wrote to Wilhelm: 'Now I have everything I need!'[81] His submarine was the UC-67, a mine-laying ship with a crew of 26 that was commissioned in late 1916. After some repairs Niemöller embarked on his first war cruise as captain on the last day in June. But after only a few days UC-67 was hit by an aeroplane and forced to return to Pula for repairs.[82]

After a furlough which he spent in Germany to get engaged, Niemöller came back to Pula in mid-August. On 28 August, UC-67 put out to sea again to lay mines off the coast of Marseilles according to its operation order. During the

1920s, Niemöller often found a grateful audience for his standard speech on the 'last war cruise' of UC-67 in front of radical nationalist associations, during which he would embellish his experiences.[83] However, the reality was more prosaic. During the deployment from 28 August to 26 September, Niemöller's UC-67 sank three steamboats with a combined tonnage of 14,500. On the first tour in early July, it had been one steamboat with 4,000 tons.[84] With altogether 18,500 tons, Niemöller's achievements as a submarine commander were rather modest, not only in comparison with the German tonnage kings. The most successful of them was Lothar von Arnauld de la Perière. With 485,000 gross register tons he was at the top of the list of the 'most successful submarine commanders' which was compiled in 1922. But at least Niemöller survived: 145 out of roughly 450 German submarine commanders died in the line of duty.[85] The reason for Niemöller's rather modest contribution to submarine warfare was not that the Mediterranean might have been a secondary theatre of war. In the third quarter of 1916, German submarines sunk 65 per cent of the overall tonnage, and in 1917 they were still significantly successful. But in 1918, German U-boats, which were susceptible to failure, lay in the roads in Pula for far too long. In addition, the Allies had introduced a new convoy system to protect their merchant vessels by escorting larger groups of them with Navy ships.[86] When Niemöller finally became U-boat commander in the Mediterranean, the submarine warfare was effectively already over.

In October 1918, while Niemöller was waiting for the repairs of UC-67 in Pula, his thoughts were already occupied with entirely different matters than his potential fame as a submarine commander. German defeat was looming, raising fundamental questions about honour and the continued existence of the nation, the moral failure and possible renewed ascent of the German people, and finally about a potential continuation of the fighting as an alternative to capitulation, which for Niemöller was 'the worst'.[87] The last issue in particular was under intense debate among nationalist circles that were discussing the possibility and form of a 'levée en masse', that is, total mobilization of all national reserves. Its proponents even accepted the—at least partial—self-destruction of Germany as a defence strategy by fighting French troops with guerrilla tactics on German territory. This 'catastrophic nationalism', as the historian Michael Geyer has called it, saw the demise of the nation as an opportunity for renewal.[88]

Martin Niemöller was among those who were concerned with such ideas. German defeat equated to the loss of honour of the nation. For this reason, Niemöller deemed it right to continue the fighting, particularly because the democratization of Imperial Germany—some hasty reforms to strengthen the Reichstag that were implemented in October 1918—had unravelled further the political balance of the nation:

> But what are the headaches about our little lives compared to the fact that everything is at stake now and that we will only get a peace which will force us

to get up again and defend our honour in a life-and-death war. Shouldn't we rather do this now? [...] As far as one can see, all privileges of the emperor are diminished or taken away. Where is it all leading? More than ever before, Germany needs a strong hand that can take the helm.[89]

However, the result of such a life-and-death fight seemed to promise death rather than life, and thus Niemöller remained indecisive in this matter. He wrote to his parents on 25 October in a last political statement before the revolution started:

Shall we fight this desperate war that will not save us, but might cost us the little energy and power our people still has? I'm glad that I don't have to decide on this matter. Maybe it will be better for the German people to go through all this hardship now and rise again after a few generations than to give up its national honour—albeit it is bruised and battered—and to capitulate.[90]

In late October 1918, when mutinies in the Austrian Navy started, some of the German submarines stationed in Pula were sunk while others embarked on their return voyage to Germany. UC-67 took to sea on 29 October, passing the Strait of Gibraltar and the Bay of Biscay, circumnavigating around the north of Great Britain past the Shetland Islands and briefly stopping over in a Norwegian harbour. The submarine was part of a small group of German ships, temporarily even a larger convoy. From newspaper reports Niemöller and his crew learned about the events in Germany, where the sailors' uprising in Kiel from 1 November ushered in the revolution, and the Social Democrat Philipp Scheidemann proclaimed the German republic from the balcony of the Reichstag on 9 November. Niemöller's account in his autobiographical book is quite believable when he writes that he had a 'faint hope' that a second revolution 'would efface the shame of the incidents of the 9 November'.[91] Yet these hopes—even if he had in fact cherished them—were disappointed when UC-67 entered Kiel submarine port on 29 November 1918.

Niemöller's actions and attitudes during the First World War characterize him as a typical member of the Wilhelmine naval officer corps. His hopes for victory, his fantasies of imperialistic omnipotence, his rejection of any democratic reform in Germany, his unwavering admiration of the emperor, and his disappointment about the political substance of the German people were similar to the mindset of other naval officers.[92] This applies particularly to the most significant aspect of his nationalistic world view: the almost pathological hatred of England. Before 1914, many members of the Protestant educated middle classes saw England as *the* Puritan nation par excellence, the shared Protestant religion being an important part of their perception, despite the imperialist rivalry between the two powers.[93] However, for Niemöller, this was of no relevance. He expressed his deeply rooted disapproval of the English by referring to them as 'beefs'.[94] He saw England as

Germany's main enemy, and the fact that the English people were also Protestants did not change that in any way. This corresponds to the fact that Niemöller attached little importance to the Protestant religion in his interpretation of the war. Other sons of pastors who served as officers at the front lines reflected intensely on the relevance of belief during the war, and practised their piety at every possible opportunity.[95] Yet, apart from his remarks on God's providential work, Niemöller did nothing of the sort. However, he cherished such hopes mainly in 1914. From mid-1915, he hardly ever mentioned religious topics. Niemöller's interpretation of the world war was the manifestation of Protestant nationalism rather than of a religiously inspired national Protestantism. It was not before 1919 that he fully adopted the religious tradition of his parental home.

4

Theological Studies and Counter-Revolution 1919–1923

In Kiel, the revolution was already over when Martin Niemöller and UC-67 entered the harbour on 29 November 1918. In Kiel, the revolutionary movement started on 1 November and the workers' and soldiers' council took over power as early as 6 November. It was content to control the administration and did not seek any other revolutionary change. On 7 November 1918, the revolution in Kiel was effectively finished.[1] For Niemöller, defeat and transition to the republic destroyed the foundations of his world view—the emperor and Germany's role as a world power—and would most likely end his professional career in the Navy. Niemöller's sense of honour was hurt in two ways: as a German and as an officer. It is not surprising he wrote in his autobiographical book that he felt like 'a stranger in my own country'.[2] That was not a retrospective embellishment but is corroborated in his first letters after returning to Germany. Here, Niemöller also addressed an issue that deeply concerned him from 1917 onwards in light of growing unrest on the home front. He believed the revolution, even more so than the mass strikes in 1917 and 1918, proved that the people's moral substance had disappeared. But on what basis should the nation be rebuilt? On 3 December Niemöller wrote to his parents:

> The question of what will come of Germany is futile; one can only abandon all hope of a better future when one sees how the people who actually yield the power today behave; and yet, the core of the people must be viable, but it must be taught the sense of responsibility. Who is going to do that? [...] If our government were only strong enough to uphold order and build the foundations of a new empire on the ruins! I'm no longer confident that this will happen.[3]

In addition to these political considerations, Niemöller was also concerned about his own future. Here he was still 'completely in the dark'. The Navy had been his home, not only professionally but also socially. However, now there was no longer any reason to stick to this career. Even before his return, Niemöller had learned that his childhood friend and brother-in-law Hermann Bremer—at that time Officer of the Watch on UB-104—had died in the North Sea off the Shetland Islands on 19 September.[4] Bremer had joined the Navy one year after Niemöller.

Since their schooldays they had shared their enthusiasm for the Imperial German fleet, which ultimately made them choose this career. In Kiel, Martin was told that Hans Jochen Emsmann had also been killed shortly before the end of the war. Thus all his personal ties with the Navy, which would have made him remain an officer, were severed. He wrote to his parents: 'I have become very lonely; thank God that I have Else and you!'[5] He was not the only one who faced loneliness. Out of 207 naval cadets of Crew 1910, 168 were active officers in May 1914. Out of these, 61—more than a third—had died in the war.[6] On 9 December, Niemöller bid farewell to the crew of UC-67. At that time, he thought it was 'almost impossible' for him to stay in Germany. He made 'contact with a group of naval officers' who wanted to 'establish a German colony in Argentina'. Emigration was planned for May 1919.[7] In mid-December Niemöller went on holiday. He initially met with Else at the home of his mother's relatives in Westerkappeln in the Tecklenburg Land. At Christmas both visited Martin's parents in Elberfeld. Other than what he thought to be a disastrous situation of the German nation, the planned emigration was the most important talking point during these days.[8]

On 10 January, Else and Martin travelled to Düsseldorf to meet an Argentinian consul. On their arrival they witnessed a 'shooting' between members of the KPD (Communist Party) and counter-demonstrators from the MSPD (Majority Social Democratic Party) and the left-liberal German Democratic Party. The communists opened fire against the demonstrators. Martin noted the 'shooting' and the fact that the 'railway station is in the hand of the Spartacists'.[9] He thus directly experienced the presence of communist politics in post-war Germany. Rejecting the KPD and its political stance would become an important aspect of his *völkisch* national world view. During the weeks and months after the war, Niemöller immersed himself in the mindscape of *völkisch* nationalism, drawing on the radical version of Reich nationalism and its enemy stereotypes, which he had already advocated during the war. The 'catastrophic nationalism' of the last months of the war, which considered the self-destruction of the nation the only chance of a possible resurgence, was still highly appealing to him even far beyond the end of the war. But the context of nationalist thinking had changed substantially: the emperor's forced flight into exile in the Netherlands had left an empty space within the symbolic landscape of Reich nationalism. Moreover, the German defeat demanded an explanation. How was it possible that despite its size and the power of its military machine the German Reich ultimately lost the war after four years of continuous fighting? Nationalists had to find answers to this question during the 1918 revolution.

Völkisch nationalism could help here. Instead of a common language, culture, and history, this concept considered the ethnic or racial substance of the Germans as the foundation of the national collective. Thinking in *völkisch* terms intensified the emphasis on a binary opposition between 'us' and 'them', which is inherent in every form of nationalism. Alleged enemies of 'the' Germans, apart from socialists and Bolshevists, were in particular the Jews. *Völkisch* nationalism did not see them as a religious community but a racial collective.[10] Only by considering this can we understand why Martin Niemöller could refer to Alice Salomon (1872–1948) as one of the 'damned Jews'. The well-known social reformist and pioneer of social work had been baptized a Protestant in 1914. In a *Berliner Tageblatt* article from early December, she discussed positive consequences of the introduction of female suffrage for the National Assembly elections in January 1919.[11] For Niemöller, who saw the revolution as a collapse of order, this only rubbed salt into the wound. Reflecting on the political situation shortly before Christmas 1918, he lashed out in rage and despair:

> The invasion by the Entente is probably the only rescue from this situation; I wouldn't bet a penny on the future of the German people. We will never be a great power again, and a people that celebrates a witches' sabbat on the ruins of its national honour and greatness does not deserve to rise again. German faithfulness! And our emperor has to leave the country because I'm dead sure that otherwise his people would have betrayed him. German women! And Alice Salomon signs in their name. These god damn Jews!—I can't make head and tails out of this mess. Never mind. It's getting crazier by the day in Berlin, the whole German Reich is a madhouse.[12]

Niemöller's national feelings were deeply hurt. He used the metaphor of a 'witches' sabbat', in which different levels of meaning, such as antisemitism, misogyny, and conspiracy theories, overlap. The binary logic and radical world view of *völkisch* nationalism are evident. It remained unclear, however, how the Germans would be able to find a way out of moral betrayal and political power decline.

In late January 1919, Niemöller returned to Kiel where on 31 January he received an order to report to the Submarine Inspector (Fig. 5). Niemöller was supposed to transfer a submarine to a British harbour. The Armistice agreement stipulated that the German High Seas Fleet was placed under Allied control within a certain time period. But Niemöller refused to execute the order. He asked for a meeting with the Inspector of Submarines, Commodore Paul Heinrich, and explained to him that he, Niemöller, had not sought for an armistice and would thus not carry out the transfer. 'Exempt through meeting with Commodore Heinrich', he wrote in a clearly agitated state, underlining the sentence in red.[13] Heinrich dismissed him and gave the transfer order to another officer. At this time, Niemöller must have known that the Commodore, a radical nationalist, sympathized with his refusal to fulfil the armistice conditions.[14] Either way, in January 1919 Niemöller was already well aware that for political reasons he could not serve the republic as an officer.

Fig. 5 Martin Niemöller—standing in the middle—with the crew of UC-67 in Kiel harbour, 29 November 1918. The U-boat had come into port this day. At this point in time, the revolution was already finished in Kiel. Immediately after docking, Niemöller had the Imperial War Flag taken down and stowed it into his suitcase. He included this photo in his 1934 memoirs *From U-Boat to Pulpit*. bpk no. 30017355.

Professional Alternatives

What other option did Niemöller have? In the revolutionary situation around the turn of the year 1918–19, he could have chosen paramilitary activities for the counter-revolution. There had in fact been opportunities. On 7 January 1919, the Provisional Government of the Council of People's Deputies called for the formation of military units to quell the uprisings of the radical Left. These free corps were initially formed out of units of the old imperial army, filling up the core of remaining officers and troops with recruited volunteers. The deployment of these free corps men, who were mostly anti-Socialist and anti-democratic, was a double-edged affair. In mid-November, naval officers in Kiel joined forces and founded the Naval Officers' Association, Baltic (Seeoffizier-Vereinigung Ostsee, SOVO). Its speaker was no other than the already-mentioned Commodore Heinrich. Because the counter-revolutionary naval officers of the SOVO expected the Kiel soldiers' council to resist, they did not appear in public but built a conspiratorial network among likeminded officers.[15]

Like most other naval officers in Kiel, Niemöller also attended secret meetings, including one in late January 1919 hosted by Wilhelm Canaris, later chief of the

German military intelligence service of the Wehrmacht.[16] Another senior member of the SOVO was Corvette Captain Wilfried von Loewenfeld, whom Niemöller knew from his time with *SMS Hertha*. He set up the anti-republican Marine Brigade Loewenfeld. In late January Niemöller had several conversations with Loewenfeld and Captain Lieutenant Arnauld de la Perière about joining this free corps, but finally decided against it.[17] In February and March 1919, when the Marinebrigade Loewenfeld was established, Niemöller was preoccupied with marriage plans. On 10 March, he wrote in his diary, double underlining the sentence: 'letter written to father Bremer'. And just a few days later: 'Parents agree, best regards Else.' Niemöller formally asked August Bremer for his daughter's hand in marriage. He had started a family.[18]

Moreover, that a government headed by Social Democrats used the free corps for their own ends made Niemöller suspicious. On 13 March, Reichswehr Minister Noske and Prussian Culture Minister Konrad Haenisch, both MSPD, encouraged students to join the temporary volunteer units for the 'border protection in the east' against the Bolsheviks.[19] Martin advised his brother Wilhelm, enrolled at Münster University where he studied theology, not to follow the government's call because the student free corps members would be nothing but a stopgap:

> Whether universities will be open in the next summer semester? We will hope so; but the Bolsheviks are at the doorstep, and the government considers intellectual circles just good enough to step into the breach and to bleed for them. I'm against joining the free corps as long as the government doesn't give a binding declaration.—To hell with the Jews and the comrades![20]

Deep-seated resentments against 'Jews' and 'comrades' were already a constant in Martin Niemöller's political world view. In mid-March it was still unclear in which professional direction he would go. Then he learned that the Navy granted three months of paid holiday for 'looking for a civilian position'. Shortly afterwards, father Bremer gave his permission to the marriage of his daughter Else with Martin. At that time, a brother of his mother from Westerkappeln got in touch with Martin. Instead of Argentina, he could also manage a farmstead in Germany. He, Martin's uncle, would be happy to help him find an apprenticeship in agriculture. His uncle thought Martin's savings, invested in war bonds, should be sufficient to purchase or share crop a farm.[21] In the meantime, Martin's plans to emigrate to Argentina were dashed. But in December he had already mentioned his wish to work 'on a farm'.[22] This plan gradually took form. Niemöller wanted to be a farm apprentice for two years and then have his own. One thing was clear: for this he needed 'loads of courage', particularly in these 'miserable times'.[23] After the decision was made, everything happened quickly. On 27 March, Niemöller handed in his letter of resignation. He was not the only one: out of 107 naval officers of Crew 1910 who had survived the war, only 22 still served in the Navy in 1924. Overall, Niemöller was glad that the 'suffering' in and from the Navy, which he believed acted spinelessly in the revolutionary transition phase, was finally over for him.[24]

On 20 April, Martin's and Else's church wedding took place in Elberfeld. On 30 April 1919, the newly-weds arrived in Westerkappeln, where they moved into a room that belonged to one of Martin's relatives (Fig. 6).[25] After only a few days Martin started his apprenticeship. Wieligmann's farm, approximately 40 hectares, was four kilometres away from the village of Westerkappeln. Niemöller was invited to join the house community of the Wieligmann family. There was enough

Fig. 6 Martin and Else Niemöller with some of their relatives in the Tecklenburg Land, 1919. When Else Bremer married Martin Niemöller in April 1919, she gave up her professional independence as a teacher and stood by her husband. Nevertheless, she remained an independent and self-confident woman, not only because of her husband's frequent absences during his years at the Inner Mission from 1924 to 1931. Especially during the long years when Martin was held in concentration camps, both felt how much they depended on each other—despite the conflicts of that time. When Martin told her during a visit to Sachsenhausen concentration camp in early 1940 that she 'had become very old', Else ironically replied to him in her next letter that she 'partly blamed this on a cold'. Quoting a song by Zarah Leander, she continued: 'But it is also said in the film "a woman only becomes beautiful through love" and since I had to do without love for 2½ years, this is no surprise.' Herbert Mochalski (ed.), *Der Mann in der Brandung. Ein Bildbuch um Martin Niemöller* (Frankfurt am Main, 1963), 22.

work, with the fields, pastures, and the barn with cows and horses requiring all the physical strength of a 27-year-old man. On some days Niemöller got up at 4.30 a.m.[26] He threw himself into the task with vigour. Later, Else proudly reported that her husband was known among the farmers of the area as 'the guy who works hard'.[27] Else initially stayed with her fiancé's relatives in Westerkappeln. In July, she also found a job on a farm where she could prepare for her future life as a farmer's wife. The farm Averwerser was located in Wersen, approximately five kilometres east of Westerkappeln. Else continued to live in Wersen on Schaberg's farm, with Aunt Johanna Schaberg, the eldest sister of Martin's father Heinrich Niemöller. Only the weekends offered a change from the strenuous work. On Saturday afternoons, Martin went to Westerkappeln to meet Else on foot. On Monday mornings, he walked back to work on Wieligmann's farm.[28] Opportunities to actively participate in politics were rare. In mid-June, Martin and Else took part in a meeting of the 'German Nationals'. This already shows their preference for the German National People's Party (Deutschnationale Volkspartei, DNVP), which had been founded in November 1918 as the successor of the two conservative parties and as a rallying point for other right-wing splinter groups.[29] Even if Martin did not note his party political preference, everything suggests that he voted for the DNVP in the elections to the National Assembly on 19 January 1919.[30]

Becoming a Pastor

The summer of 1919 passed without anything out of the ordinary happening. But even before the beginning of autumn, Niemöller decided to study theology. In his autobiographical book he put together a legend that was supposed to explain this decision and make the remarkable step 'from U-boat to pulpit' plausible. According to this legend, he and his wife during the summer of 1919 went to church on Sundays either in Kappeln or in Wersen. He states that reflecting on 'my people and my home' finally triggered his decision to become a pastor. While in light of the revolution he had initially alienated and distanced himself from the people, working on the farm had brought him closer to these foundations of national order. When in September it became clear that due to inflation the acquisition of his own farm was out of the question, he started to search for alternatives. He met with one of the two Kappeln pastors, Ernst Johann to Settel, on 17 September. On the same day he wrote in his diary: 'Am [I] going into the Church?'.[31]

Niemöller specifically stressed that it was 'not so much the theological aspect of it' that motivated him to study theology and become a pastor. This seems more than credible as the profession had a predominately pastoral rather than theological function. Yet the following paragraph of his autobiography is riddled with idealistic and sentimental remarks about Niemöller's career change as deeply anchored in his personality and family:

[...] I had, in my own life, seen cases when the hearing of the Word and the belief in Christ as our Lord and Saviour had made live anew and become free and strong. This teaching was one I took with me from the home of my childhood days and clung to it through all the vicissitudes of life. For that reason I felt I could serve my people with an honest and open heart, thereby helping them better in their present hopeless state than I could do by withdrawing myself to a farm.[32]

According to Niemöller in 1934, these thoughts had 'soon crystallized into a definite plan'. He finally asked farmer Wieligmann to release him from his work contract after the potato harvest.[33] That sounds noble and consistent with Niemöller's political views, given his turn to *völkisch* nationalism following the war and the revolution. But is it true? The surviving sources corroborate a rather different motive. First, regarding the chronology. It was not before a letter to his brother Wilhelm from 5 April 1919 that Martin first mentioned a possible career change. Here, he lamented his 'suffering' from the Navy, felt born to be a 'quiet husband', and finally remarked: 'When national bankruptcy comes, I will become a theologian.'[34]

This is the first mention that he might choose the profession of a pastor. It clearly reveals his economic motives. Niemöller was worried about the economic security of a farmstead, particularly because he wanted to start a family. In July, however, he still insisted that it was much better to attend an 'agricultural school' than 'university'. And yet he gradually realized that he lacked the financial resources to establish himself as a farmer. In late June he made a 'list of assets and incomes', followed by another summary of his financial situation on the last day of August. The result of these compilations must have been devastating. On 6 September, Else wrote in her diary that her husband had come to her in the evening: 'national bankruptcy, extradition [of German war criminals as demanded by the Allies], went to bed quite miserable'.[35] On 17 September, Martin met with Pastor Johann to Settel after finishing the potato harvest and penned in his diary: 'Am I becoming a theologian?'. But this was not the first time he talked to Johann to Settel during these weeks. On 1 September, both pastors of Westerkappeln, Wollschläger and Johann to Settel, and their wives had visited Niemöllers. This was 'a <u>very</u> nice evening' for Else, particularly when Martin joined them later. 'We are so happy together', she wrote expressing her joy about their young marriage. But when on 17 September Martin told her his plans to study theology she was at the end of her tether. 'I am very tired, weeping and whining in front of him.' The next day, Martin wrote letters to his father and a friend. Only after his father answered immediately—apparently in agreement—was the matter settled. On 24 September, Martin quit his job with farmer Wieligmann.[36]

So far, the chronology of the decision. But what about its motives? Was Martin Niemöller the pious Protestant Christian who attended church on a Sunday with his wife and could thus draw on a carefully nurtured tradition by choosing to become a pastor?[37] His diary paints a different picture. Specifically, that Martin attended church only four times during the four months from June to September: at Whitsun 'with the whole family'; once in August when his father held Sunday service in Wersen—which he could not miss; once with Else, an aunt and a friend; and finally on 21 September, the very day he decided to study theology. On some occasions he had good reasons to skip Sunday service—because of earaches that confined him to bed or on 20 July, Else's birthday. There were also profane and clearly understandable reasons after a week of strenuous physical labour: 'Fell asleep in the chair', while Else and a friend of hers went to church.[38] Else also attended church on other occasions with Martin staying at home. This corresponded with a trend towards feminization of religiosity that had emerged from the turn of the century: Protestant women received communion more often than Protestant men. During the last year of the war, the ratio—calculated per 100 communion service attendances—was 37 men to 63 women, and plateaued after the return of the frontline soldiers in 1919 at 40 to 60.[39]

And yet, Niemöller's merely sporadic practice of piety cannot be seen solely as a typical male reluctance towards going to church. Martin did attend Sunday service on a regular basis if he wanted to, for example in October, after he had decided to study theology. During this month, he was sitting on the pew every Sunday. On three Sundays he even noted the Bible passage that was preached on, and he praised Pastor Johann to Settel for his 'beautiful sermon'. Never before had he written down comments like this. Only after the decision of a career change did Else, Martin, and their friends discuss religious topics as well as political ones.[40] It was not his Christian upbringing that led Martin Niemöller to study theology; he only adopted this family tradition after deciding to become a pastor. The trigger for this change did not come from religion; it came from economics and politics.

In April, Niemöller mentioned the looming 'national bankruptcy' for the first time, which would make a change to theology necessary. In September, he revisited this topic and made his conclusions. The trigger for these concerns was inflation, which had already set in during the war, as the German Reich financed the costs of the war by printing banknotes. It continued and accelerated in 1919, although it was still far from the hyperinflation of 1923. Setting the exchange rate of the mark to the dollar for 1913 = 1, the index stood at 1.43 on average in 1918, but in September 1919 it was already at 5.73. At least during this time, the inflationary development was favourable for the German economy. The boom starting in spring enabled the smooth integration of demobilized soldiers and strengthened the export economy.[41]

However, nationalist circles, to whom Niemöller belonged, perceived the situation very differently. From the Prussian parliamentary elections in January, the DNVP had repeatedly stressed the imminent danger of national bankruptcy in its leaflets. Central to their agitation was the dual plundering of Germany by the victorious powers, on the one hand, and the revolutionary Left, on the other. They argued the workers' and soldiers' councils cost too much and moreover wasted money. 'National bankruptcy is inevitable', the DNVP warned with demagogic intent.[42] In July, DNVP politician Karl Helfferich sharpened his tone when he accused Reich Minister of Finance, Matthias Erzberger, of corruption and accepting undue advantage in a series of newspaper articles. Else and Martin Niemöller took careful notice of the 'Erzberger relevations'. Another important aspect was that both held a large part of their own savings in war bonds. In summer 1919, however, the market value of war bonds was about a quarter below that of mortgage bonds—although these earned lower interest rates. This showed a severe lack of confidence in the financial security of war bonds and growing 'fears of the audience of national bankruptcy'.[43]

Behind Niemöller's decision of a career change was therefore primarily the partly politically, partly economically motivated fear of a possible national bankruptcy and its consequences. Becoming a pastor promised a secure and regular income. Protestant theology had long been regarded as a degree that paid the bills and led to a 'civil servant-like career'. Economic reasons were often the decisive factor for the choice of this field of study.[44] It is fair to assume that Heinrich Niemöller explained these prospects to his son in letters. This is not to say that the motive Niemöller stressed in 1934—that is, the wish to contribute to the *völkisch* reconstruction of Germany—was pure fiction. After all, he emphasized this aspect as early as 1922 in his curriculum vitae, which he submitted when registering for his first ecclesiastical examination. It reads: 'In summer 1919 I decided to study theology to become a pastor because after the abolition of general conscription, this profession seemed to me a straightforward continuation of my old officer career.'[45] Niemöller had observed from his father that a Protestant pastor also served the nation. In September 1919, however, this motive was at best secondary.

The decision to become a pastor could 'not have been easy' for Niemöller. At least this was the opinion of his friend Käthe Dilthey, who knew him better than almost anyone else.[46] After making his decision, Niemöller set his hand to the task with typical determination. Pastor Johann to Settel agreed to give Niemöller Hebrew lessons, which was a prerequisite for studying theology. From early October, Niemöller spent every spare minute learning the language.[47] Although he had already enrolled for the autumn semester at the University of Münster, set up especially for returning soldiers, on 3 October 1919, he did not start attending lectures until after moving to Münster, which he and Else did shortly before Christmas 1919.[48] Heinrich Niemöller provided them with a place to stay. Walther Kähler, pastor and part-time consistorial councillor in Münster, had an attic apartment in his rectory to rent out. After viewing the flat, Martin was happy to accept the offer. Before that, there was good news: in late November, Niemöller received a letter from the Navy confirming his retirement from service, namely as a captain lieutenant, and with the right to wear uniform. This had the positive effect that Niemöller henceforth received a modest officer's pension, which did not cover the family's livelihood but nevertheless contributed to it.[49]

Radical Right-Wing Student Politician in Münster

Münster, episcopal see and, before 1803, centre of one of the Holy Roman Empire's ecclesiastical principalities, was essentially a Catholic city. But at the same time it was, from 1815 onwards, the capital of the Prussian province of Westphalia, had a university that was founded in 1902 after older predecessors, and hosted the General Command of the VII Army Corps, from which the Wehrkreiskommando VI emerged in late 1919 following the establishment of the Reichswehr. Münster was known as a city of civil servants, and many authorities located there employed Protestants. That was the most important reason why in 1910 at least 17 per cent of Münster's population was Protestant. The Catholic Centre Party was the Westphalian city's dominant political force. In the elections to the Prussian Constituent Assembly in January 1919, around 63 per cent voted for the Centre Party. The Majority SPD, the second strongest party, was far behind with about 14 per cent and the DNVP remained marginal with 5.8 per cent.[50]

Martin followed his brother in choosing Münster as his place of study. Wilhelm Niemöller had enrolled for Protestant theology at Münster University directly after his release from military service for the winter semester of 1918/19. From autumn 1919, he was active in the DNVP student group. In this, Martin also followed his younger brother. Immediately after arriving in Münster, he joined the DNVP student group and remained a member until the summer semester of 1922.[51] By joining this organization, Martin Niemöller entered the radical right-wing milieu that had started to flourish in 1920. This confusing network of competing parties, groups, and associations, most of them linked through multiple memberships, was a fluid form of sociability, with individual groups emerging and disappearing again, not least due to the pressure of legal prohibitions. In addition to divisive factors such as disputes about tactics, these groups had much common ground. Those active in this milieu championed a *völkisch* racist antisemitism, harboured deep bitterness about the consequences of the lost war to Germany, and strongly rejected the Weimar Republic. This 'commonality of the no'—as the DNVP politician Hans-Erdmann von Lindeiner-Wildau aptly put it—fed the cohesion of the radical right.[52]

The milieu of the radical national right in Münster primarily consisted of three groups of people. The first were members of the Protestant middle classes, including some university professors, who also served as intermediaries between the university and the wider radical right-wing milieu. The second group comprised Protestant students. Out of 4,400 students enrolled at the

University of Münster in 1919, almost a third were Protestants. In addition, there were—third—active officers based in Münster as well as decommissioned career officers of the old imperial army. Martin Niemöller represented all three groups. At the centre of Niemöller's political activity was the DNVP. Especially in 1919–20, before other *völkisch* groups emerged as a better radical alternative to the detested republic, the DNVP brought together nationalists and those angry about the defeat, rejected the peace dictated by the Allies, and resented Jews and communists. The DNVP student group, in which Niemöller was initially active, offered a rich and colourful variety of social events. There were sociable evenings and a vast range of lectures, either by student members or DNVP functionaries from the close vicinity of Münster. Several times, Niemöller spoke about his experiences in the U-boat fleet and thus developed a narrative that shaped his book *From U-Boat to Pulpit*, published in 1934.[53]

The DNVP student group coalesced around two political issues. The first was a deep longing for the restoration of the Hohenzollern monarchy, acknowledged above all at the annual birthday celebrations of Wilhelm II on 27 January.[54] The second one was antisemitic agitation. In March 1920, Leni, Else's sister, gave an insight into the everyday student life of the Niemöller couple:

Martin is just dictating a speech to Else that he will be giving at the local German National Student Group next Thursday. The topic is: his 4 months cruising the Atlantic Ocean in a U-boat. Hence, the First Secretary Else is already busy. Thus, let me endeavour to tell you all about us. [. . .] On Thursday [4 March 1920], I was at the German National Student Group with Martin and a student gave a talk about 'The Aim of Jewry' ['Das Ziel des Judentums']. Here, the issue of Jewry is very much a focal point. On Wednesday, a rabbi will give a speech, it is in some sense the response to a talk held by a Professor Werner from Gießen, a leader of the German Völkisch Federation. Everyone is quite excited about the evening.[55]

Said professor was Ferdinand Werner (1876–1961), a senior member of the German-Völkisch Protection and Defiance Federation (Deutschvölkischer Schutz- und Trutzbund, DVSTB), a fascist party that had a racially defined antisemitism at the core of its ideology.[56] The pronounced interest in Werner's speech among members of the DNVP student group, founded in 1919 and busy with antisemitic inflammatory propaganda from the moment of its establishment, shows that the boundaries between radical-nationalist and *völkisch* groups and their positions were blurred at this point. From spring 1920 to the end of the winter semester 1920–1, Niemöller was the chairman of the DNVP student group. However, this position was ultimately only a stepping stone for many other tasks that he tirelessly carried out for the DNVP from 1920 to 1922, and this beyond the scope of the student group for the local and regional party.[57]

An important turning point among the radical right-wing milieu in Münster was the Kapp putsch. Military men around the chief of the Reichswehr Group Command I, General Walther Freiherr von Lüttwitz, and Wolfgang Kapp, one of the founders of the radical nationalist Fatherland Party in 1917, joined forces to overthrow the republic. The coup began on 13 March, when the Marine Brigade of Hermann Ehrhardt marched into Berlin and occupied the government quarter. Subsequently, the Reich government under Chancellor Gustav Bauer (SPD) relocated to Stuttgart. Not only for nationalist students in Münster, the removal of a legitimate government was reason for jubilation. 'The old government is overthrown!', noted Martin enthusiastically in his diary. His brother Wilhelm was even more open: 'New Chancellor Kapp! Ebert-Bauer overthrown! Great enthusiasm! Black-white-red!'.[58] But jubilation soon turned into disillusionment when the Social Democratic Minister and leader of the SPD, Otto Wels, called for a general strike against the putschists the same day. The SPD-affiliated Free Trade Unions organized the strike, which was also supported by the KPD. After negotiations between the government and unions, the general strike was called off on 22 March. However, in the Ruhr area, where due to demilitarization regulations only few Reichswehr units were deployed and faced a large number of syndicalist or anarchist miners, it was continued. Immediately after the putsch began, left-wing workers in the Ruhr area armed themselves and organized the 'Red Ruhr Army' that mobilized up to 50,000 men. After news of the Kapp putsch spread, right-wing nationalist students demanded the call-up of the Akademische Wehr (Academic Defence), a unit of student volunteers. But Oskar von Watter, commander of the Wehrkreis VI in Münster, only mobilized the Akademische Wehr when the putschists surrendered on 17 March.[59] It comprised 750 students in three battalions. Niemöller took command of the third battalion with volunteers not affiliated with a student fraternity.

On 27 March, the Akademische Wehr advanced on the Red Ruhr Army. On 1 April, the third battalion under Niemöller charged the colliery Hermann II at Selm near Lünen. As early as 5 April, the remnants of the Red Ruhr Army dissolved. Thus, combat operations were practically over when on 4 April the Akademische Wehr crossed the River Lippe.[60] In his autobiographical account, Niemöller still glorified his unit as the 'liberator from the hell of Bolshevism'.[61] Yet only a small minority of Red Ruhr Army soldiers supported the KPD. But anti-Bolshevism—as political projection rather than as a description of political realities—was the most important political orientation of radical nationalist students. On 22 April, the Akademische Wehr returned to Münster. A few days later, Niemöller received an offer to join the Reichswehr as the adjutant of a major. But 'Else doesn't want me to', as Martin penned down, and with good reason: on 2 April, Brigitte was born, the couple's first child.[62]

After returning from the fight against the Red Ruhr Army, Niemöller's political activities radicalized further. In addition to work in the DNVP, he also became actively involved in the German-Völkisch Protection and Defiance Federation, which was founded in 1919 and should be considered the first fascist mass party in Germany. The DVSTB championed Germany's *völkisch* renewal, based on a racial antisemitism and firm anti-Bolshevism. With approximately 110,000 members nationwide at the end of 1920, the federation had a mass base for its *völkisch* politics. Many subsequent NSDAP functionaries started their political careers in the DVSTB.[63] Niemöller joined the German-*Völkisch* student group immediately after Reichstag elections of 6 June 1920. It had 158 members in summer 1920, and 24 of them were, like Niemöller, also members of the DNVP student group. According to the statutes of the DVSTB group, its members were obliged to fight against the 'corrupting influence' of the Jews on 'Germanness'. 'German'— that is, 'aryan' or rather non-Jewish—descent was a prerequisite for membership. Niemöller thus had to sign a declaration to be of German—that is 'Aryan'— descent when he joined the DVSTB, both for himself and his wife, a fact that he for obvious reasons failed to mention when debates over an Aryan certificate for pastors of the Prussian Church erupted in 1933.[64] The political impact of the DVSTB was far greater than on its original field of activity. It acted as a trans-mission belt in spreading racial antisemitism to other national associations that did not belong the core of the *völkisch* camp, but constituted a 'united antisemitic front against the republic' with *völkisch* organizations.[65]

Niemöller was active in all these associations: in the National Federation of German Officers (Nationalverband Deutscher Offiziere, NDO), which promoted antisemitic propaganda, the paramilitary group Organization Escherich and—after its ban in June 1921—its successor, the Westphalian League (Westfalenbund). In addition, he visited meetings of the Heimatbund Rote Erde, and of the Bund der Aufrechten, a radical nationalist association that worked towards the restoration of the Hohenzollern monarchy. Thus, between 1919 and 1923, the *völkisch* student politician Martin Niemöller was active in eight radical right-wing parties and associations that all promoted racial antisemitism one way or another.[66] All these organizations also cultivated the idea of a charismatic leader who was to save the nation. In November 1920, Niemöller went to a talk by Paul von Lettow-Vorbeck. He had become a heroic figure of mythical proportions in nationalist circles due to his guerrilla war against British troops in the German East Africa colony during the First World War. Niemöller had great expectations and remarked on Lettow-Vorbeck in his diary: 'The impression is overwhelming and makes the everyday mortal small and ugly.'[67]

Studying Theology with Practical Relevance

The fact that Niemöller still found time to study theology alongside his tireless activities in radical right-wing parties and associations owed to his specific circumstances. Martin was around 10 years older than his fellow students. Due to this age gap, he stayed away from the social life of fraternity students, who spent a lot of their time with excessive drinking sprees. The ancient languages did not 'burden' him, although his secondary school years had long since passed. As a career officer, he was used to systematic work and the quick, accurate intake of information. As a result, his lecture notes, made in neat handwriting, went 'from hand to hand' among theology students. Finally, the surviving transcripts provide another clue. The largest part is from summer 1921 and winter 1921–2, while there are only a few transcripts from 1920. This corresponds with Martin's political commitment which was tireless, especially in 1920. In the following two years, he focused more on his studies—although he was above all still active in the DNVP and the NDO.[68]

The Protestant theology department at the University of Münster had been formally opened in October 1914. It was equipped with six full professors, one honorary professor for Westphalian ecclesiastical history, and two associate professors. During the first years after the war, teaching had to be carried out under difficult material and spatial conditions. The department had only six rooms and lectures were held in the library. Lectures started early in the morning to reduce lighting costs. In winter, the students wore warm coats in lectures to save coal for heating. They sat close to each other, which facilitated close social contacts. In autumn 1920, slightly more than 100 students were enrolled in Protestant theology. By autumn 1922, that figure had dropped to 74. It was easy for a 30-year-old student like Niemöller to communicate with the lecturers on a more personal level in this small group and deepen his understanding of the subjects learned in these discussions. In particular, he soon established a friendly relationship with Georg Wehrung (1880–1959), who had been appointed as a professor at the University of Münster in spring 1920 and was only slightly older than Niemöller. Wehrung and Niemöller lived close to each other, and so both often walked home from university together. Their social contact also included their wives.[69]

Niemöller deliberately designed his studying in a very pragmatic and thus condensed way. It was not his aim to get to the bottom of and systematically reflect on theological theoretical questions, but to prepare himself for the profession of a 'pastor'. This is how he described his focus when, in August 1922, he submitted his curriculum vitae to register for his first ecclesiastical exam: 'My main focus is devoted to biblical exegesis, ecclesiastical history and systematics could only temporarily capture my attention while practical work became increasingly clear to me as a goal.' Focusing on exegesis and homiletic and catechetical work corresponded to his theological reading, above all the most important scriptural commentaries such as those by Theodor Zahn (1897–1899) and Hans Lietzmann (1906–10) as well as the Old Testament, translated and annotated by Emil Hautsch (1894).[70]

For Niemöller, the practical side of Christian preaching was more important than theological factional disputes. This is shown by his notes on Julius Smend's 'liturgy' lecture in autumn 1921. With 162 densely handwritten pages it is by far the most comprehensive of his notebooks.[71] However, the diligent study of how to prepare a Sunday service was one thing, another was putting it into practice. On 15 December 1921, a trial sermon was scheduled in Smend's homiletic seminar, with the professor and an audience of about 20 students. Niemöller had prepared his sermon on Mary's song of praise from the Gospel of Luke (Luke 1:46–55) and then 'memorized' and 'repeatedly practised' for eight full days. But he got stuck twice during the sermon and had to look at his notes. Even though his fellow students' criticism was friendly, this was anything but a hopeful beginning. Martin was depressed and asked his father for advice over the phone. Thus, only three days later, on the fourth advent, he had the opportunity to preach in his father's Elberfeld congregation and try and dispel the bad omen of the student trial sermon. This time, it went rather well.[72] But even in the following years, it was a permanent and much bigger problem for Niemöller to prepare a sermon in writing rather than to deliver it. On Easter Monday 1922, Martin already preached again in his father's Elberfeld congregation, and again he very much depended 'on his notes'.[73]

The successful completion of a university degree in theology was no requirement for the admission as a pastor. Rather, candidates had to submit proof of completing an at least three-year academic course and the successful completion of the first ecclesiastical examination. The next step was becoming a trainee vicar and the second ecclesiastical examination. Therefore, Niemöller registered with the consistory for the first examination in August 1922, after finishing his sixth semester. By mid-December, he had completed the two short academic essays that had to be submitted for the first exam. With a sermon and a catechetical essay, he handed in these papers to the consistory in January 1923. On 11 April, Martin and Wilhelm could celebrate the successful completion of the first ecclesiastical exam with Konsistorialrat Kähler.[74]

Meanwhile, from summer 1922 onwards, Martin and Else's financial situation increasingly deteriorated. In autumn 1921, inflation progressed and from early 1922 it developed into 'galloping inflation'. After the shock of the assassination attempt on Foreign Minister Walther Rathenau in June 1922, the confidence of foreign investors in the stability of the Weimar Republic had completely disappeared. From September 1922, the external value of the mark decreased dramatically, causing hyperinflation and an exponentially growing currency devaluation.[75] Recipients of nominally fixed incomes were particularly affected, and Martin Niemöller was one of them. Financially, he was retired and providing for his family on his modest Navy pension. When the real terms purchase power increasingly declined in 1922, he first searched for makeshift solutions. Martin and Wilhelm went to their peasant relatives in Wersen and Westerkappeln regularly on weekends to hoard food. Finally, in May 1922, Friedrich Bremer, Else's younger brother, who worked as a senior physician in Göttingen, stepped in. He helped his brother-in-law with a one-time cash payment. However, such emergency aid was no longer enough when Else's and Martin's second child, a boy, was born on 16 July 1922. He was christened Hans Jochen, after Martin's old naval comrade Hans Jochen Emsmann, who died shortly before the end of the war in 1918.[76] In August 1922, Niemöller finally found employment as a platelayer with the state railways, hard physical work that kept him busy all day. In September, this was followed by a short employment in the signal box. After that, he became an unskilled worker to the station cashier's office at the Reichsbahn, where the recalculation of wage bills that had to be adjusted weekly as a result of hyperinflation consumed an enormous amount of time.[77]

Niemöller's enormous tenacity and his ability to focus on his work allowed him to prepare for the successful completion of the first ecclesiastical examination in April 1923 under these conditions. Immediately afterwards he started as a trainee vicar on 1 May 1923. It usually took one year and was part of the practical preparation for service in the Church. Although a vicar could hold Sunday service and confirmation classes, he was not yet allowed to hold occasional services (baptism, confirmation, wedding, and funeral).

Martin was assigned to Konsistorialrat Walter Kähler as a vicar. As Kähler was appointed as a general superintendent in Stettin (nowadays the Polish city of Szczecin) shortly afterwards, only a few weeks remained to introduce the newly minted vicar Niemöller to the work of a pastor. In view of the family's economic situation, being a vicar soon fell completely behind. From August 1923, Martin again worked at the station cashier's office at the Reichsbahn. Only with the utmost discipline did he in late November successfully complete the thesis for his second ecclesiastical exam *Über die Berechtigung und die Schranken der religions-psychologischen Methode* (*On the Justification and the Limitations of the Method of Religious Psychology*). It was neatly hand-written and 23 pages long. When he registered with the consistory for the second theological examination on 12 November 1923, he needed the consent of the EOK. Together with the registration he submitted the admission that he was 'currently not in a position' to 'practically train for my profession'. The following day, Niemöller received the notice of termination from the station cashier's office of the Reichsbahn.[78] In November 1923, in the midst of the deep shock to state and society caused by hyperinflation and the Hitler putsch in Munich, his economic situation was more precarious than ever.

The collapse of Imperial Germany in November 1918 was a deep 'traumatization' for most German Protestants.[79] From a national Protestant perspective, the Great War had been much more than just an armed conflict. For Niemöller, too, the war had been about the acknowledgement of Germany's higher mission and moral superiority. This meant disappointment was all the greater in the face of defeat. Now key cornerstones of national Protestantism were unravelling. With the abdication of Wilhelm II, the guarantor and symbolic figurehead of Imperial

Germany was gone. Moreover, revolutionary upheaval created a sense of power-lessness as national Protestants watched helplessly when socialists gained political power. In Niemöller's and many other Protestants' eyes, the republic that emerged from the revolution had no legitimacy whatsoever. In a letter to Else's sister Leni from 1921, Niemöller openly showed his contempt for the new form of govern-ment when he congratulated the young women on her 20th birthday and thus on her right to vote. From now on, Niemöller advised, she had to follow politics because she could have a say in the 'future of the German Reich' to exactly the same extent as 'Reich President Ebert and other greats of the new regime'. The irony could not conceal Martin's deep shock about the revolution. There had been 'bad years' from early 1919, he wrote, and 'for our people' and the 'fatherland' 'maybe the worst' ever. If and when it would get better still remained open.[80]

The third trauma Protestants suffered was caused by the Versailles peace treaty. Even the newspaper *Die Hilfe*, published by the liberal Protestant Friedrich Naumann, in 1919 referred to the peace conditions of the Allies as a 'murder of a people'.[81] In an early 1920 letter to Samuel Jaeger, a pastor who worked at the Bethel diaconal institution in Bielefeld, Niemöller had made it clear how emo-tionally charged this topic was for him.[82] His tireless activities in several radical right-wing parties and associations primarily served the purpose to come to terms with and overcome the traumas caused by the German defeat. At the same time, however, he implicitly recognized the political realities in doing so. It is important to stress that in early 1919 Niemöller did not get actively involved in the para-military fight against the republic, as many other former officers did. Instead, he started a family and became active in the DNVP, a party that despite its aversion to the republic still followed its political rules. His service in the Akademische Wehr in the Ruhr area in 1920 was ultimately nothing more than a short episode that at best left nostalgic memories. In autumn 1940, Wilhelm wrote to his brother in the Sachsenhausen concentration camp that the battle of the Ruhr had been 'a very nice time' because 'one could fight for a good cause'.[83]

This 'cause' was the fight against socialism and Bolshevism, and it is symptom-atic of Wilhelm Niemöller's political mindset—with which his brother Martin might have agreed—that he, even seven years after Hitler's seizure of power, still continued to advocate such a view. When Martin Niemöller was a student, he devoted most of his time to fighting against the consequences of the 1918 revolution. On 8 June 1923, he took part in the commemoration ceremony in Elberfeld for Leo Schlageter, the *völkisch* activist who had been sentenced to death by a French court martial for his acts of sabotage against the occupation of the Ruhr area. The celebration was a parade of the radical nationalist right, with members of the Steel Helmet and other *völkisch* national associations appearing with the black–white–red flag of Imperial Germany.[84] But when Niemöller was about to complete his training as a pastor in late 1923, he had other priorities. He now had to think about how he would secure his family's livelihood in the future.

5

Inner Mission and People's Community 1924–1931

On 1 December 1923, Martin Niemöller was appointed full-time director of the Westphalian Provincial Federation of the Inner Mission in Münster. This had been initiated by Friedrich von Bodelschwingh the Younger (1877–1946), head of one of the most important centres of the Inner Mission in Germany, the Bodelschwingh Institution in Bethel, Bielefeld. Established by his father, Friedrich von Bodelschwingh the Elder (1831–1910), in 1872, the complex included numerous facilities for physically and mentally disabled people. At the height of hyperinflation, the institutions of the Inner Mission missed out on state funding because payment remittances were delayed. As the new director, Niemöller was tasked with changing this. Before he was appointed, Bodelschwingh had sought the advice of former consistorial councillor Walther Kähler, in whose house Else and Martin still lived. Kähler was full of praise. He characterized Niemöller as someone who combined 'the accuracy of a civil servant with the decisiveness of an officer <u>and</u> a particularly practical perspective and grip'. Kähler stated that Niemöller had 'learned something as a theologian, but not surrendered to criticism'. He had also 'developed fabulously' as a person during the time they were living together and had not, as initially feared, turned into 'a sleepy pastor'. Kähler concluded his recommendation by stating that Niemöller was an excellent choice for directing the Inner Mission: 'so industrious, so accurate, so clever and so practical'.[1]

What was the Inner Mission where Niemöller worked for more than seven years until the early summer of 1931?[2] Over the course of the nineteenth century, a broad network of Protestant associations had emerged, including those for occupational groups—for example for workers and artisans—and gender-specific associations. The foundation of the Evangelical League (Evangelischer Bund) in 1886 was, in turn, a reaction to the end of the *Kulturkampf* against the Catholic Church. With 470,000 members in 1911, it was the most powerful mass organization among all Protestant associations in Imperial Germany and mainly opposed Catholicism. Added to this were diaconal organizations heralded by Johann Hinrich Wichern (1808–1881), director of the Rauhe Haus Hamburg, at the first Protestant Church Congress in September 1848. Wichern outlined the programme of the Inner Mission in an impromptu speech as 'saving love'. For Wichern, who was influenced by the Neo-Pietist Awakening movement, Inner

Mission had a twofold focus: the annunciation of the Gospel, and personal care and diaconal support for those in need which were intended to curb secularization and, at the same time, solve the social question.[3] The Central Committee for Inner Mission of the Protestant Church (Central-Ausschuss für die Innere Mission der Deutschen Evangelischen Kirche, CA), based in Berlin, was founded in 1849 for this purpose. It coordinated all associations and institutions devoted to the Inner Mission. Benevolent societies at the regional and provincial level served as an organizational foundation. As Friedrich Bodelschwingh the Younger put it, gradually the CA developed into a 'general staff of the army of love'.[4]

During the Weimar Republic, the framework for the Inner Mission fundamentally changed. First, post-revolutionary Germany witnessed a massive secularization wave between 1919 and 1921, particularly among the socialist working class. In 1919 alone, almost 238,000 people—that is, 0.82 per cent of Protestant Christians—left the Church; 315,000 in 1920. From 1918 onwards, a completely secular milieu and a radically unchurched subculture emerged in big cities with a Protestant majority population. Brunswick had the highest number of confessionally unaffiliated people in Germany in 1925, with 11 per cent of people having no church affiliation. Anti-religious campaigns by socialist Freethinker associations, which gained hundreds of thousands of members from 1919, intensified this process. But it was in essence the war experience that propelled secularization. The navy officer Niemöller had glorified the war deployment of Germans as a fate controlled by God. Protestant factory workers, on the other hand, were disgusted by the inflammatory language of pastors who called for perseverance and were shaken in their belief by the futility of wartime death.[5]

The rapidly increasing milieu of unchurched socialist workers was the background of the Inner Mission's work after 1918. Wichern's nightmare scenario of an increasingly de-Christianized society had become reality. But the Weimar Republic also offered chances to spread Christian charitable activities. The expansion of the welfare state was enshrined in the new constitution. This did not only apply to social insurance schemes including health, accident and disability insurances, which had been established during Bismarck's time as chancellor. Included were social burdens caused by the war such as the care for war invalids, but also the systematic expansion of social welfare, for example through the 1922 Youth Welfare Law and the 1924 National Social Welfare Law. In 1919, the 'dual principle of social security' was born, which still underpins the German welfare state today, with both state actors at Reich, state, and municipal levels and independent welfare organizations as 'subsidiary' welfare providers. These were, above all, the Catholic Caritas Association and the Inner Mission. From the perspective of the state it was an advantage—and cost-effective—that these private agencies contributed their welfare expertise. At the same time, the associations could count on state funds, with the Caritas and the Inner Mission being the major beneficiaries.[6]

And this is where Martin Niemöller came into play. Incorporation of the Inner Mission into the dual system of social and welfare politics required its work to be professionalized, transitioning from a loosely connected 'club' to a systematically organized 'association'.[7] In Berlin, CA headquarters were established with several full-time employees, with a similar development following at the regional level.[8] In January 1922, the Westphalian Provincial Federation of the Inner Mission was founded. It included both local associations and institutions and was divided into departments for male and female diaconia, youth work, and other fields of social care.[9] This was the context in which Niemöller began work in December 1923. In early March 1924, the Westphalian Provincial Committee decided to permanently appoint him to the position of managing director. For Niemöller, this was an important decision, and so he double-underlined his diary entry: 'permanently employed'.[10]

Director of the Inner Mission in Westphalia

His relief was understandable. Only the permanent position of a managing director secured a bourgeois lifestyle for him and his family. On 6 January 1924, Heinz Hermann was born, Else and Martin Niemöller's third child. In the wake of deprivations from the inflation period, it was even more necessary to provide for the family and ensure their livelihood. After Niemöller passed the second ecclesiastical exam, he was ordained pastor by chief consistorial councillor Theodor Simon in the Münster Church of the Redeemer on 29 June 1924, with Niemöller's father Heinrich being the assistant pastor. In the afternoon of that day, Niemöller baptized his son Heinz Hermann in the small attic flat where the family still lived. He was named Heinz after his grandfather and Hermann in remembrance of Hermann Bremer, Martin's childhood friend and brother-in-law who had died on board UB-104 in 1918.[11] From early summer 1924, Niemöller's professional life became more and more structured. However, some concerns and tensions still remained, both in terms of his professional and family life. In the following years, it became increasingly clear that Martin's immense workload and frequent periods of absence from Münster were the reason for many marital conflicts with Else. In January 1924, for example, when Else went to Elberfeld with her three children, her husband wrote to her that he had been busy with paperwork for the Inner Mission 'until midnight'.[12]

Niemöller approached his new position in three steps. First, he took stock of the existing associations and institutions of the Inner Mission. Second, he improved networks at the municipal level, particularly through establishing local church welfare offices. Third, he organized a close cooperation between the Inner Mission and ecclesiastical authorities in Westphalia, especially the Provincial Federation bodies. A membership assembly with all institutions and individual associations took place once a year. A small working committee responsible for the practical work and convening every two months on a fixed date was at the core of the new organizational structure.[13] But it was the very organizational coordination of all people and interest groups involved in the Provincial Federation that initially proved extremely difficult and conflict-laden. The situation only improved in 1926, when Johannes Hymmen, Niemöller's main opponent in the bodies of the Inner Mission, was appointed consistorial councillor in Münster. From then on, Niemöller not only acted as managing director, but also as head of the Provincial Federation.[14]

Finally, he was able to draft a more detailed and programmatic outline of the diaconal work in Westphalia. In August 1925, he finished a 30-point blueprint in which he discussed the guiding principles of the Inner Mission. Completely in accordance with Wichern, Niemöller defined the aim of the Inner Mission as the 'saving' attention to those Christians 'who were alienated from the congregation'. In his eyes, mass secularization and renouncing God were at the bottom of the present social and political problems. Niemöller outlined three fields of action as equally important in his concept of diaconal work: first, 'spiritual help' through 'evangelization' and 'apologetics' that in practice manifested itself in the *Volksmission* (people's mission). Second, 'moral-educational help' that proved itself practically in the 'fight against alcohol' and the 'support of Christian schools'. 'External help' such as the 'fight against housing shortage', unemployment, or 'poor relief' only ranked third.[15] This was a broad definition of diaconal work, with its practical tasks to be seen as missionary activities, as evangelization.

Despite his personal problems, above all his permanent work overload, the years between 1924 and 1926 were an exciting time for Niemöller, who completely reorganized diaconal work in Westphalia. He made this very clear in the 1927 annual report that he drafted on behalf of the Provincial Federation. His 'largely strategic work for the Federation' during previous years, Niemöller concluded, 'has naturally been very exciting', offering numerous opportunities for 'free initiative'. But in 1927, 'no new aspects' had been added. Now, the 'new insights' had to be 'analysed and assessed and put into small scale practice'.[16] 'Small scale'— this phrase clearly indicates Niemöller was dissatisfied with the work at the Inner Mission, which had become routine over the previous three years. Despite his achievements, which in his own eyes not only included the *Volksmission* but also social care for vulnerable people and prisoner's aid, he considered the continuation of such routine-based operations as 'a grave danger for our association'. This disillusioning conclusion was probably mainly due to Niemöller's deep disappointment about the fact that redefining the Inner Mission's objectives was followed by the tedious process of putting these theoretical considerations into practice. However, Niemöller complaints about not having enough time for actual Inner Mission work were also the result of his exaggerated expectations of what the association could achieve. From Niemöller's perspective, there had not been a 'somewhat complete reorganization'.[17] His disappointment was ultimately the result of high expectations. The objective that diaconal work was to be a crucial part of the Church's work and, in addition to the moral 'salvation' of those estranged from the Church and the 'apologetics' of Protestant Christianity, was also supposed to enshrine the activities of private welfare agencies in the Weimar welfare state ultimately demanded too much of itself.

These excessive demands were also reflected in Niemöller's work schedule. Since it caused manifold quarrels with Else and a strain on their marriage, we will discuss this in more detail. The core task of the managing director, as Niemöller himself had formulated, was the networking of the many institutions of the Inner Mission in Westphalia. For this reason, he had to visit many homes and institutes as well as parishes that considered setting up a kindergarten or retirement home. Networking required personal presence and participating in parish conferences, church and foundation festivals, as well as regular meetings. Hence, the director had to go on one business trip after another, mostly day trips so that he usually came home late at night.[18]

And yet the high volume of travel for the Inner Mission was only part of the problem. On top of it was Niemöller's inability to say no when asked to perform other tasks. In March 1926, Else wrote in a letter to her sister Leni:

It's the 33rd time this year that I'm a grass widow. The director of the Bible school in Witten has fallen ill, and who has to step in? Your brother-in-law Martin! He had only one afternoon to catch his breath and was out for a walk with me, Kockelkes and Mrs Hymmen. I have expressed my disapproval, unfortunately under tears. As I learned later, the general [General Superintendent Zoellner] was on my side. Mind you, Martin longed for something other than files.[19]

It was only mid-March and Martin had spent more than a month travelling since the beginning of the year. His last minute assignment at the Witten Bible School kept him away from home for almost another two weeks. This example shows, at the same time, an important reason for his willingness to take on other tasks outside of his duties. 'Prying loose credits and poring over files', core tasks of his position as a managing director, had already lost their appeal after two years in the job. After a period of organizing and coordinating, Niemöller took on other activities in order to escape the tedious everyday routine. Physical overload was the immediate consequence. Thus, he was often 'irritable and nervous', and the 'marriage heaven was sometimes cloudy'.[20]

Else and Martin's relationship had its ups and downs. During the two years at the Inner Mission, Martin being unsatisfied with his routine work and his tendency of taking on additional tasks became a persistent pattern, which caused long periods of absence from home, and periodic anger about stress and conflicts at work, ultimately resulting in marriage tensions. Martin being away from home was an important factor that increasingly gained importance because of its frequency. He noted all his business trips away from Münster in his diary. He spent 137 days travelling in 1925, 174 days in 1926, and even 201 days in 1929.[21] If Else thought she was a grass widow in 1926 this feeling must have grown even stronger in the following years.

Life of a Pastor's Family

Else's attitude towards her husband's stressful work remained ambivalent. As early as August 1925, she assumed that Martin would not stay much longer in his position in Münster as it was 'so exhausting and back-breaking'.[22] Else noticed that Martin was overworked, as she wrote in a letter to her parents a few weeks later, not because he was 'complaining', but 'I unfortunately know the signs all too well.'[23] Martin was 'often distant' and 'even more silent than usual'. In these moments Else was not allowed to ask him about problems at work. If she wanted to know why he was anxious, she had to rummage through the files scattered in his study.[24] Else empathized with Martin, who was still having problems with his sermons. Niemöller preached several times a year in the Church of the Apostles, the main Protestant church in Münster, located in the Old Town. Preparation time was always scant, and thus he often had to work through one or two nights to complete his sermon. The stress that 'tormented and agonized' Martin, rubbed off on Else, who felt 'rather unhappy'. It was, however, only a seeming contradiction when she wrote in 1926 that Martin 'should work in the parish' because as a parish pastor the preparation of sermons would be one of his core pastoral duties and not an additional task to carry out under immense time pressure.[25]

Else became less and less understanding towards his permanent overload and frequent periods of absence. Conflicts were inevitable. As early as March 1926, she told Martin that she would no longer accept 'his constant travelling'. But this was rather an expression of her own exhaustion and she did not take action. 'What I have left in strength', she wrote one week later, 'is drunk up by little Jan, and he doesn't even get enough.'[26] Jan, the fourth child, had been born in December 1925. But there were also moments of relaxation and happiness between the two, for instance in February 1927:

> I'm sitting with Martin in the room. There is only a tiny corner left for me, everything else is covered with papers. Martin has been in Berlin for 2 days. Now he has to 'catch up'. One can hear the pen scratching over the paper. Today he is even faster than usual. I found the same when he played the piano earlier. [...] Today has been a day of sunshine. Martin and I were out for a walk for 1 ½ hours. [...] And I have sent the children outside. I would have liked to take them with *me*, but Martin had given the slogan: 'without children!'. If, like us, one is so often *not* together then one enjoys being together even more.[27]

But such a 'day of sunshine' was rare during the time in Münster. More common were frictions, sometimes even proper rows, like in February 1928, as Martin and Else both reported with equal wording, the latter in a letter to her father:

> In contrast, Martin doesn't like it when I'm mad at him, which I am right now, because when he works a lot it is too much. We had a proper row because of that. He has promised to think about not to overstraining himself when he takes on 'tasks'. Despite everything I'm happy if I have achieved this; because I fear a terrible end due to his lifestyle, which he doesn't want to be true.[28]

And yet it would be wrong to see the recurrent tensions between Martin and Else merely as a result of his tendency to take on new 'assignments'. We have to consider the wider context of the marriage: the Protestant parsonage with its gender-specific constrictions. To be sure, Martin was no parish pastor with immediate pastoral responsibilities. But the Niemöller household shared some typical structural features of a pastor's household. There was no separation between private and public sphere, which was typical of bourgeois families, in the Niemöller family, not least because the house in Erphostraße 60 was not only their family home but also hosted the offices of the Provincial Federation of the Inner Mission. A pastor's wife suffered multiple burdens: as the mother of the house she was responsible for bringing up the children, caring for all people living in the household, and assisting her husband with his professional tasks. This was so much not part of Else's duties during the years in Münster, apart from occasionally writing Martin's sermons and tidying up his file drawers. But children and household kept her busy, often until she was completely exhausted. Such 'selfless self-sacrifice' and 'total subordination under the husband's life' were, nevertheless, fully in accordance with contemporary expectations of a Protestant pastor's wife.[29]

The image of a pastor's wife, willing to make sacrifices and endure suffering, was not only an expectation of the church milieu. The gender-specific discourse around this role also shaped the self-image of those involved. One of Else's letters from 1926, where she complains to her sister about an aunt who had been visiting rather often lately, exemplifies this.

> You do know that I don't care much about her, despite all her good sides. But as a pastor's wife I'm probably not allow[ed] to say that but have to endure her with a loving heart. Until now no task has been too difficult for me.[30]

And there were plenty of tasks. Within eight years, Else gave birth to six children—Brigitte in 1920, Hans Joachim in 1922, Heinz Hermann in 1924, Jan in 1925, Hertha in 1927, and Jutta in 1928—and in 1921 a girl who died a few hours after birth.[31] After Hans Joachim's second birthday, Martin gave his wife a savings book so that she could buy birthday presents. Altogether, the father's contribution to parenting was scant, as Else ironically remarked in 1927: 'His achievements in parenting are substantial when he storms out of the room as Jupiter Tonans [Thundering Jove], calling his son to order and demanding silence from the daughter.'[32] Particularly during this year it became clear that 'domestic turmoil'—that is, noisy children—frayed his nerves more than his workload and caused further conflicts.[33] Bringing up children in a parsonage was based on strict obedience, with the father usually being responsible for enforcing this. Because Martin Niemöller was often away, this task fell to Else, who was not squeamish in her disciplinary measures. When Brigitte, the oldest, was seven, she was grounded because, as Else commented ironically: 'He that will not hear must feel. I need to be alert with her. In general, I am a proper policeman.'[34] But Else was much more than a 'policeman'. Because her husband was away most of the time, it was she who brought the children up as Protestant Christians. This included morning prayer, and she was thus delighted when the two-year-old Heinz Hermann tried to catch up with his brother Jochen, who was two years his senior, and said 'whole lines' of the morning prayer.[35]

And yet childcare was only one of Else Niemöller's responsibilities. In addition to this, there was the household. Even with the help of two maids this was a time-consuming and energy-sapping task. A parsonage was an open household, with not only relatives and friends but also colleague pastors and even their relatives visiting, who had to be cared for and accommodated. In March 1926, two pastors lived with the Niemöller family: Johannes Hymmen, about to move from Blankenstein upon Ruhr to Münster, and another one of Martin's colleagues. 'I have a big business', commented Else ironically.[36] In the next month, Hymmen's five-year-old daughter joined her father so that 'only'—another ironic comment—15 people spent the night at the Niemöller house.[37]

The periodic tensions and conflicts in the Niemöller family by no means resulted from Martin's potential character flaws. He did not have a violent temper towards the family and rather 'tormented himself', arousing Else's compassion.[38] Ultimately, both were suffering from intense pressure caused by the dual role of the parsonage as an open house, which impacted professional and family life. Despite all the tensions of everyday life, both were willing to bear this burden. There was hardly any personal freedom in this strict and, especially for Martin, tightly synchronized life style. His path 'from U-boat to pulpit' that he described in his 1934 autobiographical account was still not complete. Niemöller had not yet reached the pulpit because he was a 'theologian professional', as it was called in the Inner mission, instead of a parish pastor. At the same time, in his mind he had not completely left the U-boat and the Navy, shown in late 1930 when two old navy comrades from Essen came visiting. 'Martin was blissfully happy', wrote Else 'and suddenly transported into a different world'.[39]

His time in the Navy, and especially his experiences during the First World War, remained an important personal and political point of reference. During the war he had served the German nation and proved himself worthy of being an officer, a professional honour. At the same time, the German people and its defeatism had, in his view, directly contributed to the collapse in November 1918. From the very beginning, Niemöller's commitment at the Inner Mission aimed to rectify this moral emergency and create a foundation for the moral revival of the German nation. In publications written between 1927 and 1930, he discussed the link between Inner Mission, nation, and a much needed 'emerging sense of community', which was to manifest itself in the people's community, in more detail.[40] After beginning work at the Inner Mission in late autumn 1923, Niemöller's political activities in the radical right-wing milieu of Münster declined considerably. Reasons for this were mostly practical: he was no longer a student devoting limited time to his studies but had the strenuous position of a full-time managing director and did not have time to go to political meetings several times a week.

Between 1924 and 1930, Niemöller's political commitment rather took the form of commemorative politics. His continuing affiliation with the radical nationalist camp became predominantly visible in his speeches remembering the achievements of the Imperial Navy during the Great War. In May 1926, for example, he gave a talk in remembrance of the fallen of the Battle of Jutland in 1916—in his navy uniform. Between 1924 and 1930 he repeatedly held his standard speech on the 'last voyage' of UC-67.[41] But the highlight of Niemöller's political activities in the field of war commemoration during this Münster years occurred in 1930. On 8 June 1930, a memorial remembering the U-boat veterans of the First World War was inaugurated in Kiel Möltenort. On a 15-metre concrete pillar, tapering towards the top, stood an iron cast eagle of four metres that had spread its wings for take-off. This design symbolized the hope that Germany would be able to defend itself with a new submarine fleet.[42] Only a few days later, on 21 June, Crew 1910 met in Kiel to pay tribute to their fallen comrades. After the end of the war and the disbandment of the Imperial Navy, the character of Crew 1910 had changed. It was no longer a community of officers in service, but one of remembrance. The wives of the 1910 navy cadets were allowed to join in at the meetings. The crew meeting in 1930 lasted three days. On 20 June, Niemöller arrived in Kiel where he stayed at a comrade's house. A boozy 'beer evening' in the 'Skagerrak Club' was on the agenda.[43]

The next day, Niemöller picked up his wife from the station and went to a crew meeting at the Imperial Yacht Club. The whole group boarded two motor boats and visited the submarine memorial. From there they went to navy memorial in Laboe. Although it was only inaugurated in 1936, the 72-metre-high tower had been structurally completed in 1929. Niemöller gave a speech on behalf of his crew comrades, which according to Else was 'very touching in its sobriety and depth'. Afterwards, there were several minutes of silence before the organizers of the celebration shook Niemöller's hand in appreciation.[44] For the sake of simplicity Niemöller closely followed the text of the speech he already gave in 1926 to commemorate the Battle of Jutland. It contained the usual set pieces of nationalist commemorative rhetoric, ranging from 'proud morning' in remembrance of the fallen comrades to the line 'Germany must live, even if we have to die!', coined by Heinrich Lersch in 1914.[45] But more important than nationalist rhetoric was the social aspect of the crew meeting at the banquet in the evening. Else described the gathering as follows:

> Everyone was in high, but not exuberant, spirits. The gentlemen seemed as if they hadn't been separated for decades. Martin was jollier than he had been over the last years. One speech followed the next, some of them earnest, some more cheerful. In the end, they all told navy tales […]. Martin enjoyed the friendship of many. It was 3 am when we went home.[46]

The next morning they visited the *Königsberg*, a light cruiser of the Reich Navy.[47] The crew meeting shows there was nowhere Niemöller felt more comfortable than in the company of navy officers, even a dozen years after the end of the war. He still had not let go of the habits and political mindset of the professional officer.

The Inner Mission as a Service to the People's Community

It is difficult to precisely determine Niemöller's party political preferences between 1924 and 1930. In his statement before the Special Court Berlin in February 1938, he claimed he had always voted 'for the NSDAP from 1924 onwards'.[48] A handwritten note, the basis of his pleading, states more precisely that he voted NSDAP for the first time in Elberfeld on 7 December 1924, leaving it unclear if he referred to the Reichstag or the Prussian Diet elections that happened simultaneously. This claim, however, sounds extremely implausible, because there is no entry in his diary on that date, while he had recorded every other vote from 1919 to 1933.[49] In 1938 Niemöller pointed out that his brother Wilhelm had already joined the NSDAP in August 1923.[50] This is correct—Wilhelm Niemöller became a member of the Nazi party on 22 August 1923 and renewed his membership after the refoundation of the party in 1925, when he worked as a pastor in the Westphalian parish Schlüsselburg. Given that the—new—membership number was 26,850, he was one of the party's 'old fighters'.[51] In contrast, it seems rather unlikely that his brother Martin deviated from his existing preference for the German National People's Party in 1924. There is no reason why he should have taken such a step shortly after commencing work at the Inner Mission. As we will see in the following chapter, Niemöller's interest in National Socialism did not start before 1931–2.

We can only reconstruct Niemöller's political thinking and networks between 1924 and 1930 by drawing on some hints. There is, first of all, no evidence he was in contact with groups or individuals of the NSDAP in this time, which, in contrast, was the case for the DNVP, for example with its local branch in Elberfeld inviting him to give the keynote speech at a Hindenburg celebration. Niemöller was also in touch with the Steel Helmet, the radical nationalist League of Front-Line Soldiers, founded in late 1918. Due to a lack of time, he was unable to attend their meetings, for which he apologized with the 'German salute'.[52] In March 1929, however, Niemöller met with Franz Seldte, the founder and chairman of the Steel Helmet.[53] All this is indicative that Niemöller was still deeply embedded in the national Protestant milieu, his political home from 1919.

Existing sources that show Niemöller's political thinking confirm this finding. In September 1927, a retired major asked Niemöller to recommend publications for his talk on the 'Inner Renewal of the German People', considering the 'religious aspect'. Niemöller initially hesitated. Although he had concerned himself 'intensely' with such questions, he had not yet consulted 'specialized literature'. He ended up recommending publications by Hermann Jordan and Reinhold Seeberg.[54] The second recommendation in particular is relevant. Not only was Seeberg (1859–1935) a conservative Lutheran, advocating a positive theology in his fight against the liberal interpretation of Protestant Christianity, but he was also the chairman of the Central Committee of the Inner Mission in Berlin from 1923 to 1933, in addition to his professorship at Berlin University, and thus an important protagonist of conservative social Protestantism. Niemöller referred to one of Seeberg's brochures from 1915, where the latter elaborated his radical nationalist war theology.[55] All this shows that in the late 1920s Niemöller's mindset was still firmly entrenched in conservative national Lutheranism, a reaction to the crisis of the German nation caused by military defeat and revolution with a programme of moral-religious renewal.

Several articles written by Niemöller in the journal of the Inner Mission of Westphalia between 1927 and 1931 confirm this assumption. In these contributions he propagated the establishment of a 'true people's community'.[56] According to Niemöller, only the people's community made overcoming the functional differentiation of society viable, which made it impossible for private welfare agencies to see and address the 'entire human hardship' of people in need of help. Niemöller was well aware that the establishment of a community required personal commitment of every individual. How could the willingness to such commitment be created and fostered? Which possible motives for community formation could be thought of, given that—unlike in the Great War—one was no longer required to sacrifice one's life? Niemöller's answers remained vague. He referred to moral pleas and postulated the 'appreciation' that every 'people's comrade' was owed must be understood as the 'epitome of our *völkisch* honour'.[57]

Such remarks show the undecidedness of the discourse on the people's community during the Weimar Republic. The term itself only entered everyday political language during the First World War. In the 1920s, it was by no means just the Nazis who used it to signify their political core aim, namely the overcoming of class conflicts and deep cultural fragmentations of society. Especially among national Protestants, the 'people's community' was a widespread political watchword. The vagueness of this notion was one of its hallmarks. The people's community was not a programme or an actual plan of action. Rather, it was a political 'expectation structure', a conglomerate of vague hopes and longing for the revival of the nation.[58] There was only one aspect of clarity: both Niemöller and like-minded people rejected the 'demagogic poisoning' and the 'fanaticism' caused by political 'parties fighting each other'.[59]

Based on the criticism of parties, Niemöller developed the concept of a non-partisan gathering of all Protestant Christians, which shaped his political commitment from 1929. The starting point was his observation that anti-religious circles intended to drive back the 'confessional character'—in Niemöller's eyes: the Christian foundation—of voluntary welfare.[60] Shortly after taking on his position in 1924, he complained that the youth welfare office of Witten not only worked with representatives of the Inner Mission and the Catholic Caritas but also with 'Israelites' and 'free thinkers', a reference to social welfare workers of the socialist, SPD-affiliated Workers' Welfare Association (Arbeiterwohlfahrt).[61] More important than the antisemitic implication of his complaint is his hostile attitude towards the allegedly godless social democracy, which signified the general objective of the Inner Mission as contributing to the salvation of those estranged from God. When Niemöller returned to this topic in 1929 by using the example of youth welfare, he was convinced that the Workers' Welfare Association was launching a 'concentric assault' against diaconal work in this field, supported by the relevant municipal civil servant. Niemöller's conclusion was clear: it was necessary to actively intervene in local politics and let go of any 'aversion to all politics'.[62]

From these deliberations, the plan emerged to mobilize Protestant Christians for the local elections in Westphalia in November 1929 within the Provincial Federation of the Inner Mission. Prior to the polls, Niemöller published a leaflet on 'Aspects of Local Political Participation of the Protestant Population'. He discussed the advantages of mobilizing this group within the existing parties instead of establishing a separate 'Protestant Association' to canvass Protestant votes. Niemöller wanted to make the decision subject to the respective local constellation. It was, however, clear that a separate list was to be established in Münster devoted to the 'service to our people'.[63] This initiative came too late for the elections in November 1929. But when the vote was challenged due to a formal irregularity and repeated on 30 March 1930, a separate Protestant list, the 'Evangelical People's Service' (Evangelischer Volksdienst), was standing for election. It canvassed only once, on 28 March, proclaiming the enforcement of

Protestant interests against 'Bolshevism, free thought and secular school'. After critical remarks made by representatives of the NSDAP at this meeting, Niemöller stated that the Protestant list by no means intended a 'culture war'. On the contrary, the core objective, as he emphasized to applause, was to unify 'Protestants hitherto scattered across all parties'.[64] This minimal effort brought maximum results. The Protestant People's Service won 10.7 per cent of votes. In Münster, it overtook the national liberal DVP and the radical nationalist DNVP, which achieved 15.4 per cent with a joint bourgeois list in the November 1929 elections, but fell to 10.3 per cent in March 1930. The NSDAP was still insignificant in Münster with 3.4 per cent of the vote. Niemöller only joined the parliamentary party of the Protestant People's Service as a designated successor in late June 1930 and became its chairman. He did not leave much of a mark as a city councillor in Münster. He resigned his mandate as early as May 1931, as he was already on his way to Berlin Dahlem.[65]

The emergence of the Protestant People's Service is but one example of the profound political realignment that occurred among Protestant voters in Germany from 1929 onwards. The most important trigger for this development was a dramatic shift of the DNVP to the right after the media mogul Alfred Hugenberg became its chairman in late 1928. Hugenberg steered the party along a radical anti-republican course, which included an opportunistic cooperation with the NSDAP, for example promoting a referendum against the Young Plan in July 1929. This resulted in a splintering of the DNVP. From 1918, it had been the political home of most national Protestants, but in December 1929 the wing that represented working-class interests broke away from the party. Its members joined forces with Christian social groups represented from the mid-1920s in the Christian People's Service (Christlicher Volksdienst, CVD) and formed the Christian-Social People's Service (Christlich-Sozialer Volksdienst, CSVD). When Hermann Kling, one of the leading representatives of the CVD in Württemberg, visited North Germany in summer 1929 to maintain contact, he met with Niemöller several times. These meetings aimed to prevent a fragmentation of forces given the CVD was standing for election in competition with the existing Protestant lists, particularly in the elections for the Westphalian Provincial Diet.[66] In the run-up to the local elections on 30 March 1930, the Protestant People's Service emphasized it was 'independent from all sides', even from the CSVD and its parliamentary group in the Reichstag. However, in January 1931, the Münster voters' group did join the CSVD.[67]

In addition to this political involvement, Niemöller pursued various other activities during his time in Münster. In an autobiographical account from 1931, he mentioned 'sometimes very intensive teaching activities at the Bible school, welfare school, diaconal institution, also lecturing and sermons', as well as 'radio devotions'.[68] As early as 1925, Niemöller was also active in the Inner Mission beyond Westphalia, regularly attending meetings in Berlin. While these were initially consultations within the Prussian chapter, between 1930 and 1931 Niemöller also became involved in the national bodies of the Inner Mission. Their meetings usually took place in the Paulinum, a seminary for Protestant boys, located next to the building of the Central Committee in the Altensteinstraße in Dahlem, a Berlin suburb.[69] It is fair to assume that Niemöller's close contacts to the Central Committee and ecclesiastical bodies in Berlin were instrumental to his move to the parish of Dahlem. As we have seen, Else was already convinced that her husband had to become a parish pastor in 1926.

In 1929 it became clear that Niemöller would take up a pastorate. The only question was where? In previous years, he had already received invitations for trial sermons. In October 1929, Martin said to his wife that he felt 'like a hunted hound'.[70] This remark makes it abundantly clear that his permanent travelling soon had to come to an end. When Niemöller submitted his CV at the parish of Dahlem, he stated he had been considering a position as parish pastor 'for about two years' in order 'to end the restlessness of permanent travelling (200 to 250 days a year) and to finally become what I wanted to be when I started studying theology: a pastor'.[71] Trouble was added to this work overload. In early 1930, Niemöller had a conflict with General Superintendent Zoellner. In December 1930, he resigned his position in Münster as of 1 October 1931. His father was concerned about this step into the unknown.[72] But already on 6 January 1931, Niemöller received a letter from chief consistorial councillor Friedrich Jeremias, who worked with the Evangelical Supreme Church Council (EOK) in Berlin, offering him a pastorate in Berlin Dahlem. After a meeting with Jeremias, Niemöller initially hesitated because Dahlem was 'no Westphalia' and far from home. But Else mentioned in the same letter that the Dahlem pastorate was said to be 'one of the most sought after in Prussia'.[73]

As Martin Niemöller was well aware, he was not yet a 'pastor' in Münster between 1924 and 1931. Rather, he was a functionary who worked tirelessly, pooling the collective interests of the Inner Mission and representing them vis-à-vis the political authorities. As such, he was a well-known public figure when he left Münster, not only in Westphalia but far beyond. His job also had consequences for his political activities. In his student years, Niemöller had been involved in several völkisch-national groups with a radical anti-republican agenda. As a functionary, however, he had to accept the rules of the Weimar welfare state, which recognized private welfare agencies as independent actors. As managing director of the Westphalian Provincial Federation, Niemöller not only followed democratic principles within the association, for instance, by writing reports and minutes in preparation of votes. Working in the field of private welfare—in particular with such high professional standards as Niemöller's—tacitly implied acceptance of the republican state.

The political difficulty of Niemöller's diaconal work were his exaggerated expectations for the formation of a community. Following the founder of the

Inner Mission, Johann Hinrich Wichern, Niemöller determined the goal of the organization as the salvation of the de-Christianized masses through 'Christian love' and missionary activity. Welfare in the narrower sense was only one element of a more extensive concept that was intended to put a stop to de-Christianization—and thus the advance of allegedly 'godless' socialism and Bolshevism. The ultimate goal and the instrument for achieving this was the idea of a people's community, which would reach out across social classes and end the discord between the parties. The 'significance' of diaconal work culminated in its 'community forming effect'.[74]

The idea of the people's community resulted in a surplus of utopian expectations that could, given a certain constellation, turn against the Weimar Republic. This was not yet the case in 1931. On the contrary, Niemöller entered the stage of local politics in Münster with the aim of gathering all Protestants in a united list. Above all, this reflected the fact that many Protestants had turned away from the DNVP. Niemöller's commitment for the Protestant People's Service was only a small example of a profound change in party political preferences among Protestant voters across Germany during the late 1920s, which was a key precondition of the NSDAP's rise to a mass party.[75] In 1931, at least in Münster, these radical changes did not yet benefit the NSDAP.

6

As a Parish Priest in Berlin Dahlem
1931–1932

The rapidly growing Berlin suburb of Dahlem was mostly populated by members of the bourgeois elite. A tube line connecting it with the city centre was opened in October 1913, even before the suburb was incorporated into the metropolis Berlin in 1920. Three quarters of the residents in Dahlem were Protestants.[1] Referring to the fast increase in parishioners and extensive construction activities, the Dahlem parish requested approval of the consistory for a third parish priest in March 1930. From 1910, the parsonage in Cecilienallee 61 was available, directly next to the village Church St Annen. In 1926–7, a parish centre was built in Thielallee 1–3, and the new Jesus Christ Church in Hittorfstraße was consecrated in December 1931.[2] Doing these extensive construction works during a dramatic economic crisis would not have been possible without financial footing. Due to its upper middle-class residents, Dahlem was one of the richest parishes in Germany. After the establishment of a third pastorate, every Dahlem priest had to care for 3,500 souls, while the average ratio in 1933 Berlin, with 7,756 people per pastor, was more than twice as high.[3]

Pastorates in Dahlem were highly sought after. When Eberhard Röhricht (1888–1969) successfully applied for the recently established second pastorate in 1927, he outcompeted 50 other candidates in the parish election.[4] In Niemöller's case, the situation was different. He was appointed by the consistory as an ecclesiastical authority rather than elected by the parish. The reason was a pending lawsuit between the Prussian state and the Dahlem parish over whether St Annen Church was under state patronage, which would mean that the Prussian state had to pay for the Church's maintenance.[5] When Martin Niemöller arrived in Berlin on 13 January 1931 to discuss his move to Dahlem, he first reported to the EOK and met with chief consistorial councillor Jeremias, who had invited him to Berlin. The conversation was 'cool and unemotional', so that initially Niemöller had 'serious concerns' to expose his family to the 'Berlin atmosphere'. But then chief consistorial councillor Theodor Lang, who held the first Dahlem pastorate, sent him a 'warm letter', 'encouraging' Niemöller and promising that he would definitely get the post.[6] Lang emphasized the parish had large 'financial possibilities'. As a further advantage he pointed out that the three pastors alternated giving sermons, 'so that at least every third Sunday is free'. Thus, Lang skilfully used the wealth of the Dahlem parish as bait.[7] In late April, Niemöller received a message that the consistory's official confirmation was imminent.[8] Else and Niemöller were in agreement about the move to Berlin.[9]

On Sunday 17 May 1931, Martin Niemöller had to appear before the other Dahlem priests and Superintendent Max Diestel in the fully occupied St Annen Church. During this ritual, parishioners could voice their objections against the candidate chosen by the consistory. Needless to say, no objections were raised. In addition to a catechetical exercise, Niemöller delivered a trial sermon on John 15:26 ('But when the Comforter comes, whom I will send to you from the father'). In its report a local newspaper emphasized there was 'something ascetic and stern about' his appearance and his sermon had a 'vivid and energetic fighting spirit'. However, more important was what Niemöller vehemently rejected: rather than fussily lecturing his flock as was common, he preached the 'order to charge', the missionary mandate justified in the Gospel, spoke up against the 'advance of autonomy in all fields of life' and the 'battle cry of the Godless: away with this man!'[10]

What did he mean by this? Representatives of Cultural Protestantism such as the theologian Ernst Troeltsch used the term 'autonomy' (*Eigengesetzlichkeit*) to flag the observation that independent social fields emerge in modern society, including science, mass media, or the economy, which were marked by the autonomous regulation of their operations and thus no longer subject to religious normative framing. Sociologists refer to this process as the functional differentiation of society. Some supporters of liberal theology such as Otto Baumgarten not only noted this 'autonomy' but also emphasized that to posit religion as an overarching sphere that would have normative oversight over all cultural fields should be avoided.[11] Niemöller did not share this liberal understanding of Christian religion as a separate sphere, but rather advocated its claim to be a binding normative orientation across all cultural fields. He combined this with an aggressive stance against the advance of the 'Godless'. This term referred to the Bolshevist campaign that propagated atheism, promoted by the League of the Godless in the Soviet Union in 1925, but was also directed against the German Freethinker movement—divided into social democratic and communist wings. The movement became very successful after the revolution in 1918–19. A communist Freethinker magazine was titled *Der Gottlose* (*The Godless*). Niemöller fought against the secularism of the 'Godless' Freethinkers along lines that the Apologetic Centre of the Inner Mission had developed. Niemöller was very familiar with it from his work with the Berlin Central Committee (CA) of the Inner Mission. Challenging socialist secularism based on a coherent Christian world view could also help build a bridge between various radical nationalist groups in their fight against anti-Bolshevism.[12] In May 1931 it was not yet foreseeable whether Niemöller would cross this bridge. But he was interested in 'the movement of the Godless'. In December 1931, he gave a talk on this topic in Dahlem, and in a sermon from May 1932 he agitated against the 'offensive front of the Godless', who wanted to subvert a people as 'powerless, destitute, tormented' as the Germans from within and rob them of 'justice and morals and faith'.[13]

On 23 June 1931, the Niemöller family arrived in Berlin. The move to Dahlem was a profound turning point in Niemöller's life. At the age of 39, he started to work as a parish priest. Much depended on the personal constellation between Niemöller and the other two priests. Only a few weeks after Niemöller's start, Theodor Lang passed away in August 1931.[14] The parish elected Friedrich Müller (1889–1942) as his successor in November 1932. The biographical similarities between the three Dahlem pastors are striking. All three were born around 1890. All had served as active front soldiers in the rank of an officer or rather a reserve officer in the First World War and were awarded with the Iron Cross First Class. All three were national Protestants who rejected the Weimar Republic. Both Röhricht and Niemöller shared an affiliation with the Inner Mission and its programme of active re-Christianization. Müller had also proved himself in the fight against the 'Godless' as an assistant pastor in an industrial working-class parish in Lusatia (Lausitz), a region in the south of Brandenburg where he had worked from 1919.[15]

The three parish priests were forced to collaborate in their pastoral activities. However, there were implicit tensions between them. According to the number of years spent in Dahlem service and his temperament, Eberhard Röhricht was the senior of the three. This suggested that Niemöller would be keen to establish a good relationship with him. The families of Röhricht and Niemöller were on sociable terms, and in August 1931, after sitting together until almost midnight, Martin noted it had been a 'very pleasant evening'.[16] When, in a letter to father Bremer, Martin took stock of the first year in the Dahlem parish, he emphasized that he was 'grateful', not only for the 'unity in the parish' but also the 'good relationship to Röhrichts' and the parish council.[17] To form a 'closer relationship' with Fritz Müller took longer. When Niemöller wrote a eulogy to Müller in 1945, it was marked by great respect, even admiration, for Müller's 'general knowledge' and 'power of judgement' as a leader of the Confessing Church from 1933 to 1939. In Niemöller's eyes, Müller was 'the one church man of high calibre' that the Protestant Church had in its ranks during these critical years. But his description also suggests that patience was necessary to gain the trust of the sober-minded pastor colleague.[18]

Worries about Sermons and Number of Churchgoers

An important yardstick for the success of pastoral work and the popularity of a pastor in the parish was the number of churchgoers. At the end of his first sermon in Dahlem on 28 June 1931, Niemöller candidly touched on this topic. A pastor's 'effectiveness', he said, was 'measured by his success', just as the 'significance of the

Church' was 'expressed by the figures of the church statistic', namely those of churchgoers. Niemöller tried to put this observation into perspective by arguing that this was a rather 'pious self-deception', because ultimately the 'success or failure' of pastoral work did not lie in human hands.[19] But when not speaking from the pulpit, he was concerned how the number of visitors in his Sunday services would impact his standing in the parish. In September 1931, he wrote to his parents that the assembly hall of the Paulinum—where the Dahlem priests often held services before the opening of the Jesus Christus Church—had been 'packed to the roof' during his sermon on the Good Samaritan (Luke 10:25–37). Emphasizing this was clearly intended to combat his still nagging doubts about his capability to preach. In his view, his appearance in the pulpit had been 'less satisfying', while Else insisted 'all went well'. On this Sunday, Walter Hafa, one of the Central Committee directors from the Inner Mission, held a church service in the village church. But, as Niemöller insisted, St Annen Church was 'empty' that day. This comparison shows that for Niemöller the number of people who attended his services was a crucial yardstick of his position in the parish.[20]

Attendance of his services remained an important topic for Niemöller and his wife. In May 1932, Else wrote to her mother-in-law that Martin's services were 'very well attended' and that he received 'all kinds of recognition' in the parish. One parishioner had given him a book as a present. Martin attached great importance to such symbolic gestures of respect, as Else commented. 'This increases his confidence, which is rather necessary.'[21] One reason for Niemöller's lack of self-confidence as a parish priest was certainly the fact that—just like during the years in Münster—preparing his sermons was still 'agony' for him.[22] The solution to this problem was Else, who—like previously in Münster—helped him write his sermons, either by amending them or by choosing the topic. In November 1931, Else wrote to her father: 'I sense the sermons are getting better and better. On Sunday he speaks about revelation, 7. 9–17. I have chosen the passage. My contribution to the sermons is still considerable.'[23] As only four Dahlem sermons from 1931/2 have survived, it is impossible to ascertain whether Else's assessment was accurate. It is certain, though, that the sermons from before 1933 were the result of a cooperation between Else and Martin—with an almost equal contribution of the two.[24] It was only from 1933 that Martin Niemöller emerged as a self-confident and eloquent preacher.

Despite encouraging signs of growing acceptance among the parishioners, Niemöller experienced initial difficulties during his first two years in Dahlem. He still worried about the attendance of his services.[25] Churchgoer statistics show Eberhard Röhricht was initially the most popular pastor in Dahlem. On average, 344 people attended Niemöller's services in 1932, compared to 397 attending Röhricht's.[26] Apart from these concerns, Niemöller had enough time and opportunity to get settled into his new job. He swiftly established a daily routine. On weekdays, he gave confirmation classes between 8 and 9 a.m. After that he took care of paperwork in the parish office. In the afternoon he made house calls.

Accompanied by Else on these 'duty calls', he managed to visit almost all of the parish members until late 1931. There were also occasional services such as baptisms, weddings, and funerals. From Friday morning, sometimes already from Thursday afternoon, he focused on writing the sermon for the Sunday service, usually finishing the text by Saturday evening.[27] Other than Friday and Saturday night, his evenings were mostly free.

Unsurprisingly, Martin initially 'felt like a secret holidaymaker'. There was a big gap in his schedule over midday, which he used for reading and contemplating. We will discuss some of his reflections later. Martin and Else spent most of their free evenings at home with guests. Frequent visitors were Käthe Dilthey, Martin's early love, who worked in Berlin as a teacher, and Friedrich Bremer, Else's youngest brother, who worked as a senior consultant at a Berlin hospital, and his wife Gertrude.[28] Despite frequently entertaining guests, the Niemöllers spent most evenings at home alone. This was a radical change compared to the time in Münster when Martin's permanent travelling had been nerve-racking for all family members.[29] Like her husband, Else tried her best to settle down as a pastor's wife in the new surroundings of the parish, noticing every achievement on the way. In March 1932, she wrote to her father:

> Yesterday when I was at the market, a market women greeted me as her pastor's wife. Being this is great. Lately I have been worried about becoming a proper one. God grant that I have it in me. I'm more in favour of the saying: mulier tacet in ecclesia [based loosely on 1 Cor. 14: 34: 'Women should remain silent in the churches']. But one has to do it and try somehow. Don't be afraid. I will not say much about it. My children are my main focus.[30]

Else Niemöller was fully occupied by the children and household. Initially, the pattern of an overburdened housewife who argued with her husband over education issues that had dominated in Münster, continued in Dahlem. In September 1931, Martin had nothing else to say to the three younger children, Jan, Hertha, and Jutta, other than that they annoyed him 'with their racket'.[31] At the same time, the 'patriarch'—as Else sometimes called him—criticized Else that the household was 'not running properly' because she was too 'disorganized'.[32] Her workload was immense and sometimes she only found time to write letters around midnight.[33]

Thus, the move to Dahlem was much more positive for Martin than his wife, who was still overburdened with work. It is no surprise then that he declined other job offers. In December 1931, Admiral Erich Raeder, head of Naval Command, summoned Niemöller and offered him the position of first garrison chaplain in Kiel. Niemöller was flattered but 'of course' declined immediately.[34] Until 1933 Niemöller focused on his own parish, with one exception: his activities in pupils' Bible study groups. Emerging in 1883 in the context of the Awakening movement, this was a network of independent Bible study groups for young people. Niemöller had already been actively involved in pupils' Bible study groups in Münster. In Dahlem he was soon elected head of one of the three Berlin sections of pupils' Bible study groups with approximately 1,300 youths.[35] Through this engagement Niemöller developed a network of church contacts across Berlin and beyond, on which he could rely when the Pastors' Emergency League was founded in 1933. Even before 1933 he was already known to a wider public. In July 1932, a home story about 'the life story of a former U-boat commander' appeared in the popular family magazine *Beyers für Alle*. The article, illustrated with a photo of Niemöller smoking a cigar, anticipated many biographical clichés that Niemöller used in his autobiographical book *From U-Boat to Pulpit* two years later.[36]

While Niemöller gradually settled down in his new role as parish priest, the church elections of the Protestant Church of the Old Prussian Union (ApU) were due in November 1932. These regular elections chose the members of the self-governing bodies in the parishes. One of them was the parish council that, together with the parish priests, was responsible for all important decisions of the parish; another was the extended parish council that only seldom convened, for instance for the election of a pastor. The previous church elections had taken place in November 1928, with the 'Positives', the 'Liberals', and the 'Middle Party' standing for election. These three factions mirrored the tensions between different theological camps: the 'Liberals' on one side, the 'Positives', who insisted on the scriptural foundation of faith, on the other, and the third group in the middle. However, in approximately 80 per cent of Berlin parishes no elections took place in 1928 because the mandates were negotiated between the three groups in advance and presented to the parishes as a single election list.[37]

The German Christians

This fundamentally changed in 1932. At the beginning of the year, Wilhelm Kube, leader of the NSDAP Gau 'Ostmark' encouraged all 'Protestant National Socialists' to register in the parish election lists and conquer the ApU from within in the November elections. Shortly afterwards, all NSDAP-leaning pastors in Berlin, Brandenburg, and Saxony were urged to join a new working group. This circle met in Berlin in February 1932 to decide on the next steps. It made its first public appearance on 6 June as the 'Faith Movement German Christians'.[38] Its leader was Joachim Hossenfelder, pastor of the Berlin Christus parish from 1931, who had joined the NSDAP in 1929. As a national Protestant, Hossenfelder believed in the historical mission of the German people and need for a people's community. During the following one and a half years, he became a crucial figure of the German Protestant Church.[39]

On 6 June 1932, Hossenfelder presented the guidelines of the German Christians (Deutsche Christen, DC) in 10 points. Among other things, the DC demanded a merging of the 28 Protestant regional churches into one united national Church. This was a popular demand that even had the approval of many national Protestants who did not lean towards the Nazis. Furthermore, the DC referred to point 24 of the 1920 NSDAP party manifesto that propagated a 'positive Christianity' beyond the confessional divide. This wording was long considered to be a tactical concession to distract from the anti-religious character of the party's *völkisch* ideology. In contrast, historians today agree that the leading elite of the NSDAP in fact understood 'positive Christianity' as a means to overcome the confessional divide in Germany, which they considered an obstacle for the formation of a people's community. The precondition for this was an interpretation of Christian tradition purified from Jewish influences that, in its most radical version, understood Christ as an 'Aryan'. The guidelines of the DC were based on this *völkisch* reading of Christian faith, rejecting mission to the Jews as the 'gateway of foreign blood to our people's body' in point nine and demanding a ban on marriages between Jewish and non-Jewish Germans.[40] Overall, the guidelines were 'a *völkisch* appeal rather than an elaborated church political or theological programme'. They were simultaneously very close to positions of Protestant theology that emphasized the contribution of the Protestant faith to the nation.[41]

The election campaign of the DC corresponded with a general politicization of the German public in the context of the Reichstag elections in July and November 1932. It brought a large degree of polarization into the hitherto largely quiet everyday life of the parishes. The DC started their campaign in September 1932, displaying rather aggressive and rowdy behaviour in most Berlin parishes. Conflicts in parishes with a large share of workers were particularly pronounced because here support for the DC was greatest.[42]

In upper middle-class Dahlem, where a merchant named Karl von Elstermann represented the DC in 1932, manners were more civilized.[43] In view of the upcoming church elections, the pastors Röhricht and Niemöller—the post of Theodor Lang was still vacant—tried to prevent a polarization in their parish. Thus, the parish council and two pastors negotiated the possibility of a joint election list with the DC parish group, offering the DC 15 out of 40 seats in the extended parish council. One of the people involved stated 'we are in complete agreement on a personal level, but it [an agreement] failed due to "orders from higher up"', namely instructions of the DC leadership. Indeed, a quarter of Berlin parishes put up a joint election list in advance with distributing mandates between different groups.[44] The representatives of the majority in Dahlem, among them pastors Röhricht and Niemöller, named their election proposal 'Protestant non-political list'. In their appeals this group insisted the 'political fight' had to be kept away from 'parish life' at all costs. Due to its close connection with the NSDAP, the DC broke with this tradition.[45] Niemöller himself could draw on his activities for the Protestant People's Service in Münster in 1930, which he understood as the gathering of all Protestants irrespective of party-political affiliations.

And yet it is striking that representatives of the 'non-political list' never grew tired of emphasizing their substantive agreement with the DC. The draft of a flyer, written by Röhricht, insisted 'we do not oppose National Socialism as a political party in any way'. The author continued: 'And we have been "German Christians" long before this group called itself that.'[46] With this remark Röhricht tapped into the national Protestant associations that the cleverly chosen name of the DC evoked. Another flyer drafted by laymen of the election committee from the 'non-political list' went even further. On the one hand, they emphasized all parish work was bound by conscience, a swipe against the DC. On the other hand, they praised National Socialist 'Christian and German idealism', explicitly applauding their fight 'against the Godless movement, closely connected with Bolshevism' and against 'moral degeneration and decline' of the present as important fields of substantive agreement.[47] An election appeal signed by Niemöller refrained from pointing out substantive convergences, merely highlighting the 'burden' to church life that resulted from the DC's 'linking of political will and church will'.[48] Had Niemöller been a staunch National Socialist in autumn 1932—as he claimed in his statement to the special court in 1938—he would have followed the laymen in signalling a partial agreement with NSDAP politics.

The elections of 13 November 1932 had the following results: the DC list gained 352 or 23 per cent of the vote in Dahlem, the 'non-political list' supported by the pastors 1,170 votes. As a result, one representative of the DC joined five church elders in the parish council altogether. In the extended parish council, the DC gained nine out of 40 seats; considerably fewer than they would have if they had agreed on a single election list beforehand. Thus, even before the seizure of power, the Dahlem parish proved a difficult place for the National Socialists to win. The share of votes for the DC was only lower in the Berlin parish Grunewald, with 12.5 per cent, while on average it was 33 per cent in Berlin parishes where the DC stood as candidates. There is reason to assume the parish group of the DC gained even fewer votes than the NSDAP in Dahlem at the Reichstag elections on 6 November 1932.[49]

What was missing in Dahlem—in contrast to many other Berlin parishes—was a pastor who supported the goals of the DC and tried to influence his parishioners accordingly. Neither Röhricht nor Niemöller were willing to do so, even though Niemöller's relationship to National Socialism was deeply ambivalent, both before and after 1933. It is possible that Niemöller talked about the NSDAP with his brother in the years after 1923, when Wilhelm joined the party. From his time in the German Völkisch Protection and Defence League (Deutschvölkischer Schutz- und Trutzbund), one of the most important predecessors of the NSDAP, Martin Niemöller was very much familiar with the aims and purposes of *völkisch* parties. But it seems he only started to pay closer attention to the NSDAP after the Reichstag election on 14 September 1930. Surprised, he noted in his diary 'results of the Reichstag election (106 Nazis!)'. His interest was triggered, and shortly afterwards, in December 1930, he ordered and read Hitler's *Mein Kampf*.[50] The election success of the NSDAP in autumn 1930 motivated intensive reflections in both confessional camps, with pastors and laypeople trying to determine their view on the Nazi movement. In the process, a plethora of different positions emerged among Protestants. In 1931/2, 'Church and National Socialism' became one of the 'most debated and most contested topics' in Protestant magazines and at church conferences.[51]

One place where these debates took place was the Johannesstift in Berlin Spandau, a Protestant institution, founded by Johann Hinrich Wichern in 1858 for the support of the sick and poor. Here, the Apologetic Central Office of the Inner Mission offered courses for pastors. From 28 to 31 January 1931, one of them was concerned with 'The Position of the Church on National Problems of the Present'. Problems already surfaced during preparation stages. One member of 'a church office'—either consistory or EOK—phoned Gerhard Jacobi, pastor of the Kaiser Wilhelm Memorial Church who as the praeses of the Confessing Church in Berlin became a leading figure of the church struggle between 1933 and 1939. The cleric, whose name we do not know, complained to Jacobi that too many speakers in the Johannesstift such as Bruno Doehring and Wilhelm Stapel were 'from the political far right', which the church leadership 'does not like'.[52] Stapel (1882–1954) in particular was well known as the author and editor of several radical nationalist and antisemitic publications.[53] Martin Niemöller, who was in Berlin during these days, had registered to attend this highly sought-after course with 150 participants. He used the late morning of 30 January to speak with Theodor Lang in Dahlem about his potential new pastorate in the Berlin suburb. He was in the Johannesstift in Berlin Spandau during the early afternoon and listened to Stapel's lecture on 'The Worldview of National Socialism and Christianity'. 'Very interesting!' he penned in this diary.[54]

Given the extremely condensed phrasing Niemöller used in his diary, 'very interesting' was an expression of broad agreement, only topped by 'very nice'. In Spandau Niemöller also listened to the lecture by Otmar von Verschuer, a proponent of eugenics or, in German parlance, racial hygiene, on 'Heredity and Race in the German People'. Niemöller noted the topic—'biological race'—but did not deem Verschuer's deliberations worthy of praise.[55] Stapel expanded his Spandau lecture into a small brochure, which reached five editions by the end of 1931 and was therefore one of the more widely received comments on the relationship between the Protestant Church and National Socialism.[56] What was it Martin Niemöller considered 'very interesting'? What did Stapel talk about? His remarks demonstrated Stapel's deep fascination for the 'elementary move-ment' of National Socialism. After addressing three topics—'the race question', socialism, and nationalism—Stapel stated that there was no moral or religious reason for Christians to 'condemn' the National Socialists' nationalism. At the same time, he opposed syncretistic mingling of the religious and political spheres as advocated by many *völkisch* ideologists. Religious announcement had to emphasize the power of hell and 'eternity of damnation'. But, he continued, the nation needed Christianity so it could 'wield the sword with fear and trembling before the Almighty'.[57]

In essence, Stapel propagated a Lutheran political theology that separated nation and Christianity into two different realms but recognized the legitimacy of National Socialism and eliminated important points of criticism against it.[58] This sounded convincing in the ears of the national Protestant Lutheran Martin Niemöller, even though he went further in criticizing Judaism than the antisemite Stapel. We will discuss the controversy over the 'Aryan paragraph' in the Church in 1933 in Chapter 8. How Niemöller—in line with Stapel—differentiated between political demands on the nation and people's community and God's demands on man can be illustrated by the sermon-like address Niemöller gave on the National Day of Mourning in February 1932. He evoked the sacrifice of frontline soldiers and hope of 'a time of national greatness' that became even stronger in hindsight. He also emphasized the disillusionment that had emerged after 1918 with the end of the community of 'brotherly love', which had been so vibrant at the front. Neither the frequently invoked 'people's community' nor the attempt of keeping up the 'front spirit' could, as he stated, hide the fact that altruism, which had been a matter of course during the war, was lost. Only 'the word of the cross of our Lord Jesus Christ' could liberate the people from the spell of 'taking care just of myself'.[59] Thus the realm of the world and God's realm remained separate in Niemöller's neo-Lutheran reinterpretation of the doctrine of the two kingdoms. Despite his agreement with nationalist conviction and a readiness to make sacrifices, the latter had more dignity.

Rapid Shift to the Right in 1931–1932

By now it should be obvious there were many overlaps between Niemöller's national Protestant world view in 1931–2 and the National Socialist programme. Key examples are the fight against Bolshevism and other political forces that supported the advance of the 'Godless', praise for the heroism of German soldiers in the Great War, the demand for revitalizing the German nation domestically and externally, and the realization of a people's community. But what practical political demands did Niemöller support in 1931–2 and how did he comment on the hectic political events of this time? The limited source material from this time only allows for some insights. Niemöller was, for instance, in contact with people close to the Reichswehr and DNVP who were actively engaged in the Steel Helmet, the radical nationalist combat league. This is most likely why he was invited to a Steel Helmet rally in the Prussian House of Lords on 4 August 1931. This rally was held in the context of the Steel Helmet's ongoing campaign for the dissolution of the Prussian Diet. After the election success of the NSDAP in September 1930, when the cabinet of Chancellor Heinrich Brüning had to rely on emergency decrees according to article 48 of the constitution, the Prussian government under Social Democrat Otto Braun was one of the last strongholds of democracy in Germany. In March 1931, the Steel Helmet tried to bring down Braun with a referendum to dissolve the Prussian Diet, supported by DNVP, DVP, and NSDAP. When a sufficient number of voters approved holding a referendum—a constitutional requirement—the actual polling day was scheduled for 9 August 1931. During the rally in the Prussian House of Lords, Theodor Duesterberg, second leader of the Steel Helmet, attacked the democratically legitimized government of Otto Braun. Martin Niemöller's approval is documented in a letter written by Else: 'Düsterberg's speech was excellent, as the patriarch said.'[60]

Another testimony for Niemöller's political shift towards the right in 1931 is from October. On 7 October, Brüning and his cabinet resigned when the right-liberal DVP withdrew its support. At the same time, the radical right put even more pressure on Brüning. The establishment of the Harzburg Front on 11 October, an alliance between NSDAP, DNVP, and radical right-wing associations, was a powerful demonstration of their increased self-confidence. With his cabinet reshuffle Brüning shifted further right. And yet he barely survived a vote of no confidence in the Reichstag on 16 October 1931. The Centre Party, German State Party, and Christian-Social People's Service (CSVD) were the only bourgeois parties that still supported Brüning.[61] Else Niemöller described her husband's reaction to these events in a letter:

> It seems that Brüning gets a narrow majority after all. Martin was quite upset. That the Christian-Socials can vote like that! Well, it is not our party. Jochen prayed: 'Dear Lord, please do not let Brüning get a majority!'[62]

This passage sheds light on the prevailing political opinion of the Niemöller household in 1931. It is, first, striking how quickly Niemöller turned away from the Christian-Social People's Service he had represented only five months earlier as a city councillor in Münster. The CSVD was the only political group in the national Protestant camp that still firmly stood against the National Socialists. For Niemöller, the Catholic Centre Party politician Brüning was probably a red rag because in the Reichstag he depended on the toleration by the Social Democrats, which national Protestants like Niemöller associated with the assault of Godless secularists on the moral foundations of society. Striking also is that Else Niemöller approved of her just nine-year-old son's prayer. Here we gain a glimpse into a 'Steel Helmet pastor' family, as contemporaries dubbed those Protestant ministers who would do almost anything to achieve their nationalist goals.[63] Finally, there is the question of political goals. It is obvious that Niemöller not only opposed

Heinrich Brüning as a person but also his politics, as Brüning still operated within the framework of the Weimar constitution. What was the alternative? At the turn of the year 1931, this was the transition into an authoritarian regime with the complete elimination of the Reichstag—either supported by right-wing parties and under a chancellor appointed by them, or led by the NSDAP.[64] Whether Niemöller would have supported Hitler's appointment as chancellor must remain open because we do not have sources that answer this question.[65] It is, however, beyond doubt that he endorsed the destruction of the parliamentary democratic system.

During the trial at the Berlin Special Court in 1938, several witnesses for the defence from the Dahlem parish stated pastor Niemöller had been known as an 'age-old National Socialist' even before 1933.[66] However, these statements lack credibility because they aimed to exonerate the defendant. There are, moreover, no other sources from 1931–2 to corroborate them. Much closer to the truth was the statement by Ernst Brandenburg, at the time a head of department in the Reich Ministry of the Interior. According to his testimony, Niemöller was someone 'who brought up his children in the spirit of great patriotism', whose 'boys were all military-pious' and who 'himself was lovingly attached to his old soldierly memories'. Brandenburg referred to Niemöller as a 'passionate nationalist and believer' and a 'plain and devout Christian'—a characterization that corresponds with other available sources.[67]

While Niemöller's political opinion during the crisis years from 1931 to 1932 is difficult to pinpoint, we can reconstruct his deliberations on issues of Christian ethics rather accurately. As already mentioned, after settling down in his new job as parish priest in autumn 1931, Niemöller's daily schedule allowed for some free time that he used for in-depth reading and thinking.[68] His reading material was extensive, particularly on theological topics. It certainly encompassed books by Friedrich Naumann, Eduard Spranger, Marianne Weber, whose biographical book about her husband Max (*Ein Lebensbild*, 1926) he quoted, and Max Scheler (*On the Eternal in Man*, 1921). There were also articles written by theologians Karl Barth, Hermann Sasse, and Friedrich Gogarten.[69] Particularly the latter substantially influenced Niemöller. On 3 October 1932, he listened to a talk by Gogarten on '*Schöpfung und Volkstum* (Creation and Folkdom)' during the Berlin Mission Week and probably also read the written version in the magazine *Zwischen den Zeiten*.[70]

Niemöller appended almost 40 pages of excerpts and reflections on what he had read in his diary for 1932. These notes are undated, but as they start with a remark on Gogarten, and as excerpts of his speech and article take up much space, it is more than likely these diary entries were a reaction to Gogarten's presentation and were written in the last three months of 1932. Niemöller's notes revolved around two major issues other than pedagogical topics: he first discussed the position of the Old Testament—and thus also Judaism—within the Christian message of salvation under the title 'Old Testament and Gospel'. As this issue is closely connected with the emergence of German Christians in the Protestant Church we will address it in more detail in the following chapter.[71]

The other important topic in Niemöller's notes was the crisis of an individualistic understanding of Christianity as represented by liberal theology, and the associated crisis of individualism. An important symptom of this crisis, according to Niemöller, was the observation that 'there were no longer any generally recognized formulas and forms' because 'everything today is doubtful'. Here, Niemöller reacted on the relativization of all norms and values he saw as consequence of an individualistic understanding of freedom. Immanuel Kant's focus on the autonomy of the individual and its good will, Niemöller believed, had replaced heteronomy or the state of being ruled under the sway of another. He praised Gogarten for revealing 'the error of the present understanding of what is good', which was that people thought they could only defer to 'the norm when being free'. With this, man is believed to be as free as God, but, Niemöller continued, 'God is not the measure for man'.[72]

Like other Protestant theologians of the time, Niemöller understood the current crisis of ethics as the result of liberal society's corrosive tendencies, which stemmed from the autonomy or *Eigengesetzlichkeit* of societal fields. This applied to all aspects of life, mirrored by phrases such as 'politics as a vocation', 'economics as a vocation', or 'autonomy of pedagogy'. Thus, an overarching ethical framework had ceased to exist. However, Niemöller's answer to the crisis was not inner-worldly salvation, which was for example propagated by the totalitarian pseudo-religion of National Socialism with its belief in 'war, mass, leader'. Niemöller insisted it was 'impossible' to try and 'put the religious impulse into the cage of a [separate] practice'. Christian faith was not only the belief in salvation but also had to take God's 'demand' on man seriously, which covered all areas of society and of human life.[73]

In the face of this crisis of individualism, forces of cohesion that could counter the centrifugal tendencies of the liberal order were needed. Both in the political sphere and in theological debates many commentators believed that the German people and their *Volkstum* could create such cohesion. And this is precisely when, according to Niemöller, Friedrich Gogarten came into play. In his October 1932 speech, Gogarten addressed whether the '*volkhaft* cohesion' of man harked back to God's 'settings' or, rather, was 'arbitrary'. He recognized cohesion based on folkdom were 'similar' to God's demands, under which man was placed as part of creation. However, Gogarten opposed the metaphor of the people as 'a living organism', widespread among *völkisch* circles. He thought such ideas were 'dubious' and examples of 'gruesome thoughtlessness' typical of the time, and condemned the *völkisch* idea according to which the cohesion of folkdom was based on 'blood' or 'race'. Gogarten and Niemöller both believed this notion ignored the fundamental fact of man's 'bondage' under God's law.[74] Niemöller excerpted these passages with great approval. He also followed Gogarten in referring to God as the 'perfect Father' (Eph. 3:15), on whom—as Niemöller paraphrased in his own words—every 'fatherhood' was based.[75] There was hardly any firmer way of rebutting the National Socialist idea of a sacrally charged nation, in which the ethnic substance of the people, their *Volkstum*, was the source of inner-worldly salvation.

In the two final years of the Weimar Republic, Martin Niemöller reflected on the crisis of German society. He shared many ideas on the causes of this crisis with other conservative Protestants. According to this view, the crisis was caused by excessive individualism and by the consequences of functional differentiation, as functionally defined subsystems co-existed without an overarching ethical order. But Niemöller's critique of modern society's lack of cohesion and its ethical relativism did not make him join *völkisch* Protestants who sought to elevate the *Volkstum* of the Germans into an ethical substance. In 1932, there was a decisive difference between Niemöller and the National Socialist movement, not only in religious and theological, but also in church political terms. When the German Christians appeared on the scene in Dahlem in late 1932, Niemöller criticized that party politics had invaded the ecclesiastical space. He also refrained from highlighting similarities between him and the DC, although this would have been easy, as Niemöller shared their critique of liberalism and supported their fight against the political left and other parts of Nazi ideology. During 1931–2, he often emphasized the danger of the Freethinkers' anti-Christian secularism and the propaganda of the 'Godless', who aggressively attacked the nation's moral foundations. As for many other national Protestants, this marked an overlap with the anti-secularist propaganda of the NSDAP, and a potential bridge between Niemöller and the Nazis.[76] But Niemöller did not cross this bridge before Hitler's seizure of power in January 1933.

PART II
CHURCH QUARRELS AND CRISIS OF FAITH IN THE THIRD REICH

7

The Nazi Seizure of Power in 1933 as a 'Protestant Experience'

The National Socialist seizure of power in the months after 30 January 1933 was a gradual process. Step by step, Hitler used his powers as Reich Chancellor to get rid of the Weimar Republic's legal shackles and establish a totalitarian single-party state, among other means by violent terror against the socialist labour movement. After the Reichstag election on 5 March 1933—where the NSDAP could only gain an absolute majority in alliance with the Combat Front Black White Red (Kampffront Schwarz-Weiß-Rot), the former DNVP—the Reich government in Berlin pressed ahead with the 'coordination' of the *Länder* or federal states. With the passing of the Enabling Law on 22 March, the seizure of power was completed on a constitutional basis. Only one week later, on 1 April, the boycott of Jewish shops indicated that terror against the Jewish minority was a core element of the Nazi regime. The destruction of the socialist trade unions from 2 May onwards and the forced dissolution of the SPD and all other parties concluded this first phase of the violent consolidation of power.

However, explaining the 'coordination' of the German population through terror alone would fail to understand the historical significance of these months. There was another process alongside sheer terror, described by a contemporary observer as 'adjustment' (*Umstellung*). It encompassed numerous small steps and gestures, ranging from the re-reading of one's own war letters from the Great War to the flying of swastika flags, with which individuals willingly adapted to the new political realities.[1] The repercussions of this 'adjustment' reached deep into the middle classes. This is particularly true of the national Protestant milieu, to which Martin Niemöller belonged. Not only was this social group the 'main point where National Socialism penetrated German society', as can be shown by an analysis of NSDAP voters before 1933. But for many national Protestants, the Nazi seizure of power was also a moment 'of fulfilment of long-cherished expectations and hopes'. Many pastors agreed with the destruction of the hated Weimar system and the fight against Bolshevism, and shared the national Protestant hope for the creation of a *Volksgemeinschaft* or people's community. They thus considered the Nazi seizure of power as the 'beginning of a new era'. For middle-class Protestants, the sea change of 1933 was by no means a 'time of illusions' or 'self-deception' about the real nature of the regime. Rather, as historian Manfred Gailus has put it, it was a 'Protestant experience', a moment of religious and national self-discovery.[2] The church journal *Allgemeine evangelisch-lutherische Kirchenzeitung* summarized the situation in a nutshell, stating Hitler's appointment as Reich Chancellor was an 'obvious solution' for at least 80 per cent of German Protestants.[3]

Several of Niemöller's relatives, friends, and acquaintances participated in this moment of national awakening that followed the Nazi seizure of power. His mother Paula kept her children updated by letter from Elberfeld. On 3 February, she expressed her hopes that, with the new chancellor, 'things are finally looking up for our fatherland'. She lamented that another Reichstag election was still necessary. Ten days later she reported she had listened to speeches by Hitler, Alfred Hugenberg, and Franz von Papen on the radio with her husband. 'God help these people, so they achieve what they intend to do', she summarized her hopes.[4] In a typically national Protestant manner, Paula Niemöller expected God's plan of salvation for the renewal of the German nation. During the following months, she continued to report on symbolic gestures that made the active adjustment of the Niemöller family to the new political circumstances visible. In early June, her husband Heinrich Niemöller held a service in Elberfeld that concluded as follows: 'Today is a thanksgiving and rogation service. We thank God He has protected us from Bolshevism through the new government and we pray to Him that He rules the work in the Church through His Holy Spirit.' With his trust in the redemptive power of the Nazi regime, Heinrich Niemöller agreed with his parishioners, who presented him with a swastika flag as a gift. His wife wrote she had not yet flown it, but 'we will happily do so in the event of political successes'.[5] The moment to fly the flag came at a reminiscence of the German Empire, which fell in 1918. This occasion warranted a visit from Wilhelm II's fourth son, Prince August Wilhelm von Hohenzollern. Paula Niemöller reported from Elberfeld in September: 'Since yesterday our house flies the swastika flag, I put out our old black-white-red one [the colours of the German Empire] next to it.'[6]

The 'adjustment' of the Niemöller family in Bielefeld, where Wilhelm Niemöller had become pastor of the Jakobus parish in 1930, was even more emphatic. Martin's younger brother had already joined the NSDAP in 1923, and was thus very busy during spring 1933. As a celebrant preacher, he appeared at several flag consecrations of SA units and consecrated swastika flags. On 1 July, 'our old fighter pastor Niemöller'—as an article in a National Socialist newspaper read—carried out another consecration of the flag. 'Today is a great day', the pastor explained on this occasion. 'Our hearts are glowing and the realization that we need to live for Germany instead off Germany must take a firm hold in us.'[7] But Wilhelm Niemöller not only publicly called for support for the National Socialist people's community. He was also a member of the German Christians (DC). He did not disassociate himself from the Reich leadership of the DC before late June, which was promptly followed by proceedings to exclude him from the NSDAP that were pending from July 1933. However, Wilhelm Niemöller did not want to be ousted from the party. He—successfully—lodged his objection and remained a member of the NSDAP until 1945. During the proceedings in July 1933, he reaffirmed, if needs must, he would 'serve my Führer with my humble contribution even without a membership book'.[8]

Sermons in the Spirit of National Awakening

Martin Niemöller must have known how his closest relatives in Elberfeld and Bielefeld adapted to the 'Third Reich'. But what was his own reaction to the events following 30 January 1933? We do not have any letters written by him for the crucial months from February to April 1933, most likely because Wilhelm Niemöller removed them from his brother's personal papers and stored them elsewhere.[9] However, despite these missing documents one thing is very clear: Niemöller eloquently expressed his approval of the Nazi seizure of power as a moment of national unification and elevation.[10] Proof of this are his sermons in early 1933. During this time, Niemöller found his style as a preacher. His sermons were usually rather brief. 'No lengthy sermons ([not more than] 35 minutes)', was a piece of advice his father had given him as an important rule for a pastor.[11] Thus, Martin Niemöller's sermons were brief, concise, and antithetically structured with an exposition followed by a 'but'. In this second step, he put the topic at hand in the context of the Christian doctrine of salvation and its key demands: the necessary obedience to God and the adoption of the Christian message in word and sacrament. Unlike his brother Wilhelm, Martin Niemöller did not consecrate swastika flags or publicly call for obedience to Adolf Hitler. Nevertheless, he deemed it appropriate to put Hitler's birthday in his diary, next to his 14th wedding anniversary.[12] He spoke as a Lutheran pastor preaching the Christian message. However, this does not mean his political statements were inauthentic.

The sermon from 5 March 1933 makes this abundantly clear. The last Reichtag elections were held on this Sunday. In the afternoon Martin went 'to the polls with Else! List 1, and 5, respectively'. While Martin Niemöller voted for the NSDAP— most probably for the first time in his life—Else cast her vote for the Combat Front Black White Red, the electoral alliance between the DNVP and the paramilitary association Steel Helmet. Prior to this, at 10 a.m., Niemöller had preached in the Annen Church. In his diary, he described this service explicitly as a 'political sermon', which confirms the political statements in this sermon were based on his inner convictions.[13] These convictions were those of a national Protestant, who, on the same day, voted for the NSDAP. The meaning of his sermon only becomes clear when taking this vote into account. Niemöller preached about the Passion of Christ (Matthew 16:21–6), starting with the remark that focusing on this topic must be difficult for everyone given the 'abundance of impressions' during these days. The 'convenient phrase' that 'politics has no place in Church' would no longer suffice. The ongoing political events, Niemöller stated, decide 'on our and our people's fate'. Niemöller drove home that issues of national importance—including the establishment of a state based on a radical nationalistic ideology—did in fact have a place in the Church and demanded every individual Christian take a 'stance'.[14]

Thus, Niemöller tasked his parishioners with understanding the necessary 'adjustment' following Hitler's seizure of power as a personal challenge. He believed Christians played a key role in this process. Germans' 'becoming a people' (*Volkwerdung*) was 'spiritually based on Christianity', and 'without the positive Christianity of Lutherans and Reformed and Catholics' it would not be 'our people'. This was an approving reference to the NSDAP party programme, which, in article 24, referred to 'positive Christianity' without binding itself 'in the matter of creed to any particular confession'.[15] From this connection between the people and Christianity, Niemöller deduced 'there will never be a national rebirth of our German people [...] that is not spiritually based on an awakening of the Christian faith'. Suggesting religion was only 'a private matter'—Niemöller here referred to the Weimar Republic and its secularizing effects—would 'denationalize' the people.[16] Finally, Niemöller made a literal reference to the 'protection' Hitler had promised the Christian churches in his first speech on 1 February after his appointment as chancellor. Here, Hitler had committed his government to 'firmly protect' Christianity as the 'core of our people's and state body'.[17] The Dahlem priest explicitly cleared Hitler from the 'suspicion' of using 'God as a means to his goals and plans', in other words to have only referred to Christian faith for tactical reasons. Doing so, Niemöller argued, would be ignoring that a 'German statesman' always bore responsibility 'before God'.[18]

'However'—and here Niemöller applied one of his trademark rhetorical juxtapositions—a government that 'affirms the connection in fate between *Volkstum* and Christianity' alone was not enough to 'guarantee external rise and recovery to internal health'. Throughout the remainder of the sermon, Niemöller elaborated the simple but crucial reason for this qualification: it was, he explained, a precondition that the Christian faith became 'alive' and effective again in the nation. To achieve this, individual Christians had to follow 'the path of Christ' and commit themselves to obey God with this 'Christian service'. Only this was the actual and 'greatest service' of Christians to the German people: 'no rebirth of our people without Christian renewal!'[19] When on 5 March 1933, the NSDAP voter Martin Niemöller appeared in front of his parishioners, he reaffirmed the manifesto of the Nazi party, came to its leader's defence against potential criticism of his motives, and explicitly rejected the political system that had just been violently destroyed by the National Socialists. He also admonished his parishioners to be aware of the fateful nature of the radical change they were witnessing, and to update their faith to be able to contribute to the national 'rebirth' in a genuinely Christian fashion.

Niemöller's sermon on 5 March 1933 openly expressed his approval of the Nazi seizure of power and their project of national renewal. It is vivid evidence of the 'emphatic self-transformation' of Protestantism in early 1933 and its participation in the project of the National Socialist revolution.[20] Martin Niemöller differed only in one—but important—aspect from the euphoric celebration of the NSDAP and its leader that Wilhelm Niemöller and many other German Christian pastors preached from the pulpits: he avoided merging Christianity and *Volkstum* into a concept of *völkisch* religiosity. He commented rather sarcastically on the widespread 'watchword "*Volkstum* and Christianity"' and those 'optimistic voices' trying to exploit the 'favourable situation' to connect both.[21] Niemöller stuck to his criticism of identifying *Volkstum* with Christianity, which he had adopted from Friedrich Gogarten in late 1932. Gogarten himself, however, like many other Protestant theologians, had since revised his former position and supported the German Christians in 1933 briefly. As many others, he already left the DC after their scandalous *Sportpalast* rally in November 1933, which we will discuss in the next chapter.[22]

Niemöller's sermon on 5 March 1933 was no exception. On 30 April, he preached on the anniversary of the Berlin student bible groups. Again, there was a 'but'. It referred to the justification of the bible groups' work, which, given the great events of the time, seemed rather marginal. Yet Niemöller stated they proclaimed an extremely important 'message': God's demand to us was to accept 'His unconditional rule over us'. Before getting to the 'but', Niemöller expressed national passion, even more so than on 5 March. The German people were about to 'break the shackles of the enemies' hatred and thirst for revenge. The rallying cry of national rising is there and resonates in a way that exceeds the wildest expectations.' It was 'a miracle', Niemöller preached, that 'our entire people of 70 million' was 'marching', activated by one watchword. However, it was ultimately 'a few individual men' who determined the 'fate' of the people, as one could observe at the 'grave of the great Prussian king'. With this, Niemöller referred to the 'Day of Potsdam' on 21 March, when President Paul von Hindenburg swore in Hitler as chancellor at a ceremony in the Potsdam Garrison Church.[23] Niemöller's sermon combined military imagery with religious language, portraying the transformation of the German people into a community of 70 million ready to fight as a 'miracle'.

In an article published in May, Niemöller reflected on the consequences of the current 'revolution' for the individual. In this situation, when the individual might appear to be 'superfluous' given the importance of the community, many people started to 'look for God' again.[24] And, indeed, at first glance the 1933 figures evidenced a religious boom. While the number of people leaving the Protestant Church declined drastically—from almost 250,000 in 1931 to less than 50,000 in 1933—325,000 people joined the Protestant Church in 1933 alone. Of these, 95 per cent were unaffiliated with any Church, of which 50 per cent had left their

Church previously.[25] Which conclusion did Niemöller draw from this? In a time when the 'individual is completely overshadowed by the whole', it was 'Christianity's task to show the individual the place where he can be'.[26] In other words, every individual German could only experience their place in the people's community through Christian faith. In this respect, the sermon from 21 May displayed important nuances. Here, Niemöller demanded that the parish should defend the 'nuisance' of obedience to the Lord, particularly towards those 'who only wanted the Church for the sake of worldly hopes and national wishes'. This was an obvious dig at those National Socialists, like the German Christians, who wanted to use the Church as a vehicle of their worldly claims to power.[27]

From July 1933, Niemöller's sermons showed profound doubts as to whether the national awakening of the year 1933 indeed entailed a religious revival. On 23 July, he preached that 'our people' were 'by no means open-minded for Jesus' message about atonement and faith, about sin and mercy' and ultimately 'no religious movement' emerged 'from all the commotion and hustle and bustle'. In August he expressed his mistrust of the motives of those who had returned to the Church. And in October he voiced his frustration about the danger of the 'current revolution' creating nothing more than a 'natural religiosity' only knowing the self-centered claim 'God with us!'[28] By autumn 1933, Niemöller had become deeply sceptical of whether the national awakening following the Nazi seizure of power would benefit Protestant Christianity. However, there is no doubt about his initial national Protestant enthusiasm about the people's community of the 'Third Reich'. Looking back on 30 January 1933 in February 1935, when Niemöller had started to openly express criticism of the state's church policies, he emphasized the antagonism 'between the enthusiasm of our national feelings and the passion of our wishes for the Church', which had surfaced during the previous two years.[29]

Niemöller approved of the NSDAP's election victory on 5 March and the establishment of the dictatorship through the Enabling Law of 23 March. The German Christians also felt encouraged. They demanded the creation of a unified Reich Church that would encompass the 28 independent regional churches, the abolishment of parliamentary elements represented by the synods and the coord-ination of the Church with the Nazi state through the installation of state commissioners. On 25 April, Hitler officially appointed the former naval pastor Ludwig Müller as his plenipotentiary for the Protestant Church. Müller's task was to influence reform efforts within the Church. Meanwhile, the German Evangelical Church Confederation, a coordination body founded by the regional churches in 1922, had implemented a committee with three members named after its chair, Hermann Kapler. The Kapler committee was supposed to represent the Protestant Church to the outside world and advise the churches on reform matters and an intensified cooperation between them. In this capacity, the committee was also forced to work with Müller from May onwards.[30]

During these weeks, Martin Niemöller faced a dilemma. On the one hand, he was worried about the radical attitude of the German Christians in Berlin, which he knew well from the Dahlem parish election in November 1932. After the Reich meeting of the DC in Berlin from 3 to 5 April, he noted: 'The "German Christians" are becoming rebellious! Not a very pleasant prognosis.'[31] On the other hand, Niemöller's general approval of the Nazi seizure of power and its programme did not necessarily suggest a fundamental antagonism towards the DC. Hence it was, to a certain extent, a 'temptation', as Else Niemöller put it, when Horst Schirmacher, an old acquaintance from the Inner Mission in Westphalia, visited her husband in May 1933. Schirmacher was now one of the directors of the Berlin Inner Mission's Central Committee and adviser to Ludwig Müller, who was officially appointed patron of the DC on 16 May. The purpose of Schirmacher's visit was to persuade Niemöller to cooperate with the German Christians, but Niemöller let him leave empty-handed.[32]

The Young Reformation Movement

Schirmacher's visit may have also had the purpose of preventing Niemöller joining the Young Reformation movement, founded in Berlin on 9 May by, among others, Walter Künneth, head of the Apologetic Centre of the Inner Mission, and Hanns Lilje, general secretary of the German Student Christian Movement. Schirmacher visited Niemöller on 13 May for the first time. Four days later, first Künneth came to see the Dahlem pastor, noticing a signed photograph of Wilhelm II in uniform hanging over Niemöller's desk. Then, on the same evening, Schirmacher visited Cecilienallee 61 for several hours. Presumably, the two representatives of rival church groups courted the dynamic and well-known Dahlem parish priest. After many phone calls, his wife appears to have played a certain role in Niemöller's decision. When he was invited to a Young Reformation meeting, Else 'strongly' encouraged Martin.[33] As early as 19 May, Niemöller, with Künneth and Theodor Heckel, a chief consistorial councillor working for the Church Federation Office, participated in a press conference. They presented the guidelines of the movement, which had been co-drafted by Niemöller. On the same day, he, Künneth, and Lilje took on the leadership of the Young Reformation movement.[34] From the outset, the new movement drove home its positive attitude towards the Nazi state. One of its programmatic texts read: 'We demand that the Church acknowledges the state created by the German freedom movement with cheerful obedience.'[35] But such a docile acknowledgement was not enough to refute the accusations of the DC. They claimed the Young Reformers were part of 'reactionary' forces adversary to the revolution started by the NSDAP. Thus, in early June the Young Reformation movement established a 'National Socialist working group' that actively opposed the 'equalization of National Socialism and German Christians'.[36] Their 'organization plan', which was intended to give the top-heavy and Berlin-based Young Reformers a broader foundation through the incorporation of local brethren and associations, explicitly stated that all men appointed as 'parish leaders'—there were no women among the Young Reformers—should enjoy 'the trust of the national movement', that is, the local NSDAP.[37]

The still best partial biography of Martin Niemöller by Franz Hildebrandt (1909–1985) provides important information about the underlying reasons for such rhetoric. Hildebrandt, whose mother was from a Jewish family, was ordained in the Berlin Nicolai Church in June 1933. In September, when the Protestant Church of the Old Prussian Union introduced an 'Aryan paragraph' for pastors, he resigned from office. In February 1934 and again in July 1937, Hildebrandt took over for Niemöller in Dahlem after the latter was suspended or arrested, respectively. As a member of the Confessing Church and a friend of Dietrich Bonhoeffer from as early as 1927, Hildebrandt had independent and sound judgment of Niemöller. After his emigration to the UK, he wrote a biographical account of Niemöller that was anonymously published in 1938 under the title *Pastor Niemöller and his Creed*, printed and distributed by, among others, the Aid Organization of the Protestant Churches of Switzerland for the Confessing Church. Soon banned by censorship in Germany, a shorter version circulated with 60,000 copies.[38] Hildebrandt portrayed Niemöller as a man who joined the conflict within the Church in 1933 not only on the grounds of this national Protestant but also due to his National Socialist convictions. Specifically referring to the Young Reformers' statements, Hildebrandt claimed it had been Niemöller who 'insisted that the Church not only acknowledged the legitimacy of the new state but also its quality as a saviour and liberator. When others eliminated phrases like "upheaval" and "revolution", it was against Niemöller's express will.'[39]

The Young Reformers agreed with the German Christians in affirming the Nazi state. But there were more programmatic overlaps. Both groups welcomed the merger of the 28 regional churches into a national 'unity Church' with a Reich bishop at the top. This demand had been occasionally discussed in Protestant circles since the suspension of state rule over church governance in 1918. They also shared the same dislike for the, in their eyes, bureaucratic ossification of the administrative bodies of the regional churches. However, the Young Reformers staunchly opposed any attempt by the state to curb the Church's freedoms of taking care of its own affairs. They believed only the 'confession of the Reformation' could serve as the yardstick for all issues related to the reform of the Church, which emerged from discussions about topics including 'people, race, state'. This consequently resulted in opposing the DC's demand of excluding 'non-Aryans'—meaning Christians of Jewish descent—from the Church. In the eyes of the Young Reformers, 'Christians of all peoples and races' had 'to be uncondi-tionally recognized as equal children of the one Church before God'. However, the

Church should only appoint 'German people as its leaders', which ruled out the presence of 'Jewish Christians' in the leadership bodies of the churches.[40]

During May and June, debates within the Protestant churches revolved around the future Reich bishop. At the press reception on 19 May, Young Reformers had supported the proposed appointment of Friedrich von Bodelschwingh as Reich bishop. Niemöller, who was a good friend of Bodelschwingh from the time they worked together at the Inner Mission in Westphalia, was able to persuade the three-member Kapler committee, which decided on church constitutional issues, to support Bodelschwingh as a candidate.[41] Meanwhile, the German Christians were locked in a power struggle between supporters of Ludwig Müller, from mid-May the DC's patron who was supposed to strengthen the moderate wing, and the radical group around the Berlin pastor Joachim Hossenfelder. At a meeting of DC Gau leaders in Berlin, Hossenfelder prevailed. At the same time, German Christians promoted Ludwig Müller as their candidate for Reich bishop.[42] On 26 and 27 May, representatives of the regional churches met in the Berlin Church Confederation office to choose a Reich bishop. Niemöller accompanied Bodelschwingh to the meeting and clashed with the Bavarian Bishop Hans Meiser. The latter initially supported Müller because he expected more autonomy for the regional churches with him as Reich bishop, which an agitated Niemöller criticized as 'cowardice'. According to Bodelschwingh, 'for the first time' Niemöller showed a 'combative attitude that could only go forwards without consideration of others'. Precisely because Niemöller was close to the NSDAP, Bodelschwingh explained, 'he knew about the danger of this political force penetrating church life'. After several ballots, the majority of church representatives, except for three bishops, finally voted for Bodelschwingh as Reich bishop.[43]

However, Bodelschwingh's time in office as designated Reich bishop ended after four weeks. The reasons for this were threefold. The first was connected to procedures. The office of Reich bishop was filled before the future church constitution had been outlined in detail. Thus, it was an important task of the newly appointed bishop to participate in the shaping of the Reich Church constitution. However, uncertainty about the procedure weakened Bodelschwingh's position. This, secondly, enabled the German Christians to launch a campaign against him with the support of SA and Hitler Youth. The third, decisive factor, however, were developments in the Prussian regional church of the Old Prussian Union (ApU), by far the biggest in Germany. Not least as a result of the campaign against Bodelschwingh, Hermann Kapler, who was not only a member of the constitutional committee named after him, but also president of the Evangelical Supreme Church Council (Evangelischer Oberkirchenrat, EOK), the highest church authority of the ApU, resigned from his presidency on 8 June. Subsequently, the Church Senate of the ApU appointed Ernst Stoltenhoff, a general superintendent from the Rhineland, as acting president of the EOK. This, in turn, provided the perfect pretext for Prussian Minister of Education and Cultural Affairs, Bernhard

Rust, who deemed this course of action a violation of the church contract concluded in May between the Prussian state and the ApU, according to which the state had to scrutinize such an appointment. On 24 June, Rust appointed DC member and district court councillor August Jäger as state commissioner for all Prussian regional churches, including the ApU. Jäger dissolved all elected church bodies and appointed Friedrich Werner, a solicitor and Nazi careerist without any church affiliations, as president of the EOK, and Joachim Hossenfelder appointed Jäger as theological vice-president of the EOK. As a result, the leadership of the ApU was firmly under DC-control. When the representatives of the regional churches agreed with the view that Bodelschwingh could only be Reich bishop effectively after the conclusion of the constitutional deliberations, Bodelschwingh resigned on 24 June.[44]

On the day of his appointment as Reich bishop, Bodelschwingh had made Martin Niemöller and the Westphalian pastor Gerhard Stratenwerth his 'adjutants'. Both men immediately started to support the work of the designated Reich bishop behind the scenes and in public. Over Lent, Niemöller travelled to Bielefeld, where he met his brother Wilhelm and a group of pastors from the church province to discuss a public statement in favour of Bodelschwingh. Niemöller also supported Bodelschwingh within the Young Reformation movement. On 15 June, a delegation of Young Reformers paid Niemöller a visit. They expressly stated an 'agreement with Hossenfelder' was 'impossible', and one must not show the 'slightest weakness' towards the DC. They also suggested intensifying work on the constitutional draft for the future Reich Church to strengthen Bodelschwingh's position. Niemöller contributed to these parallel deliberations and helped draft several texts.[45] But some Lutheran regional churches weakened Bodelschwingh's position by expressing concerns regarding the legal validity of his appointment. Meanwhile, the German Christians continued their campaign against the Reich bishop. At a meeting in the Church Confederation Office on 17 June, Niemöller was running out of patience in view of this policy of obstruction. 'Exploded' and '[Ludwig] Müller stinks', he noted in his diary.[46]

On 23 and 24 June, church leaders met in Eisenach. At the end of this meeting, Bodelschwingh resigned as designated Reich bishop after the majority of the Lutheran bishops had withdrawn their confidence at a separate meeting, undermining his position vis-à-vis the German Christians.[47] Niemöller accompanied Bodelschwingh to Eisenach. Two days earlier, he had declared his 'demission' as his assistant. In this context, Niemöller explained to Bodelschwingh that many of his opponents would see it as a challenge if he, Niemöller, appeared in Eisenach. His role in the negotiations about changes in personnel matters had ended anyway. He insisted on immediately addressing the consequences of Bodelschwingh 'resigning or being forced to resign'. A decision had to be made about whether the future Protestant Church 'would be a salt for our people and our state or just a religious organization amidst a people decisively oriented towards this world!' An agreement with the opponents—the German Christians—would only be possible 'if the other side clearly shows the message of the Biblical Christ is at stake, particularly atonement and faith, sin and mercy, instead of a combative ideal of some sort.' The Church had 'to be based on the confession', rather than on the 'majority' of synods. If church leaders would not come together in supporting Bodelschwingh, one had to find the 'courage to accept a schism, should it be necessary'. And if in the process those would be forced into a schism who stood firmly with their confession, 'then the Church of the Reformation is destroyed'.[48]

It is striking how passionately Niemöller rejected the German Christians' 'heroic' concept of piety and instead focused on the dualism of sin and mercy as the core of a religion of salvation. Even more remarkable is that Niemöller already anticipated the separation of Confessing forces as a necessary 'schism' before the beginning of the church struggle and the formation of the Confessing Church. During Bodelschwingh's brief tenure as designated Reich bishop, Niemöller ultimately left the smaller stage of his Dahlem parish, entered the limelight of a wider church public, and played a crucial role at the centre of the 'Third Reich's' church conflicts.

As he stated in his letter to Bodelschwingh, Niemöller's readiness to gather and activate Confessing Christians had immediate consequences. As early as 26 June, representatives of the Young Reformers met in Niemöller's house in Dahlem. In a declaration they called on members of the movement to gather in their parishes and disseminate two declarations, authored by Bodelschwingh and by general superintendents in the ApU who had been threatened with removal from office, respectively. On 27 June, August Jäger deposed Otto Dibelius, general superintendent of Kurmark, who regularly participated in Niemöller's services in Dahlem. His Berlin colleague Emil Karow shared his fate the next day. A few days later, Niemöller and Kurt Scharf, pastor of the parish Sachsenhausen north of Berlin, wrote an appeal to the pastors of Mark Brandenburg, which was supported by more than 150 pastors of the church province Brandenburg. In Berlin, 106 pastors signed a similar declaration. Central to all these appeals and declarations was the effort to defend the freedom of the Church to promulgate the Gospel against state intervention. The declaration authored by Niemöller and Scharf emphasized the action of the Church had to 'exclusively' follow the Holy Scripture.[49] The superintendents' appeal, also drafted by Niemöller, vigorously protested against 'politically perverting' the Gospel.[50]

The conflict between the ApU church leadership, forcibly usurped by the German Christians, around Friedrich Werner and Joachim Hossenfelder, and the demoted Prussian general superintendents was building to an initial climax on 2 July 1933. On this Sunday, the general superintendents had appealed for a 'rogation and penitential service' that would express 'all our Church's hardship'. At the same time, the Supreme Church Council (EOK) controlled by German Christians called on parishes to hold thanksgiving services and deck the churches with swastika flags. In the Berlin Kaiser Wilhelm Memorial Church, SA flags were put up on both sides of the altar, and Joachim Hossenfelder preached in front of parishioners largely consisting of SA men in brownshirts.[51]

In Dahlem parish, Niemöller, Röhricht, and Fritz Müller held a joint penitential and rogation service in the Jesus Christ Church on 2 July. At the end, each pastor delivered a brief sermon. Niemöller focused on expressing that the state depended on the 'free proclamation' of Jesus' message and a 'free Church'. This was the core of his sermon, followed by a qualifying 'but', as was typical of his sermons, with which he came back to his introductory remarks on Christian proclamation. At the beginning of the sermon, Niemöller drove home that Christians always 'had to be good people's comrades and patriots, obedient citizens and subjects'.[52] This shows that, despite his fight for the inner independence of the Protestant Church, in July 1933 Niemöller was still not willing to abandon his emphatically nationalistic rhetoric. More interesting than the three pastors' speeches, however, was the structure of the service. It started with the reading of Hossenfelder's declaration and the superintendents' appeal. Subsequently, the three pastors alternated reading selected passages from Luther's works on the spiritual and worldly authorities. Pastors and parishioners spoke the Creed and the Lord's Prayer together. Many pastors had been reluctant to speak these prayers jointly with the parish. From the 1870s this had often caused controversy. In 1933, the Dahlem parish practised a liturgical form that many parishes of the Confessing Church later adopted, and which is still common in Lutheran churches in Germany today. Thus, the parish was able 'to express' its opposition 'in the form of the liturgy'.[53]

The conflict between German Christians and those circles around the Young Reformers who defended the confessional core of the Protestant Church had not yet escalated to the extent that reconciliation was completely off the table. Hindenburg responded to petitions submitted by the church opposition—one of them by Martin Niemöller—which called the Reich president to intervene. At a meeting on 29 June, Hindenburg urged Hitler to end the struggle in the Protestant Church.[54] As a result, a meeting between three representatives of Ludwig Müller and the Young Reformers' leadership, among them Walter Künneth and Martin Niemöller, was summoned on 3 July. In the summary minutes drawn up in advance, the Young Reformers agreed to cooperate with Ludwig Müller as Hitler's plenipotentiary for the 'new formation of the Church'. The prerequisite for this was the withdrawal of state commissioners in the ApU and the reversal of the suspensions they had announced as well as assurances that Young Reformers could freely publish their positions.[55]

However, against the backdrop of the hectic church political events during July 1933, the basis for such an agreement soon lapsed. At this point, Reich Minister of the Interior, Wilhelm Frick, interfered in order to calm the situation in the interest of the Nazi state—and against the Prussian government's policy of repression. At a meeting on 7 July with church representatives—among them Jäger and Müller as well as Lutheran bishops Hans Meiser and August Marahrens—Frick pushed for a swift conclusion of the deliberations on a new church constitution. To be sure, the negotiations had continued even after Kapler's resignation from the Kapler committee. However, it soon became apparent that establishing a unified Reich Church would fail due to opposition by the regional churches. They insisted on their independence and the distinctiveness of their confessions—be it Lutheran, Reformed, or a Union. Thus, the only possible compromise was a church confederation, albeit with a strong Reich bishop at the top, who appointed the members of a Spiritual Ministry. As early as 11 July, representatives of the regional churches gathered in Berlin and adopted the Church Constitution of the now-called German Protestant Church (Deutsche Evangelische Kirche, DEK). The Reich cabinet meeting on 14 July confirmed the new constitution, which came into legal effect through a law on the same day.[56] At the same time, August Jäger's role as state commissioner of the ApU came to an end and the commissioners of the church provinces that had been appointed by him were withdrawn.

The adoption of the new church constitution and the end of state interferences in the Prussian Church seemed to calm the church controversy that had flared up in May. On 14 July, Martin Niemöller, Walter Künneth, and Hanns Lilje drafted an appeal of the Young Reformation movement. They ceremoniously described the constitution as a 'turning point of church politics'. Some of their demands— they mainly referred to the position of the Reich bishop—were now 'fulfilled'. However, the Young Reformers would not give up their 'radical will' for renewal. The goal was a 'people's church as the true church of the Gospel'. This would require 'the work of a *Volksmission*', aiming to spread God's word to social strata 'alienated from the church'. The 'huge parishes' in many big cities with 30,000 or more souls had to be divided into 'small parish districts'. Members of church bodies and church officials should be chosen according to skills rather than in line with political considerations.[57] By emphasizing the idea of a *Volksmission*, the appeal drew on reflections Niemöller had developed in his practical work with the Inner Mission in Münster. Another declaration of the Young Reformers published in the journal *Junge Kirche* was much more passionate in tone. It rejected 'talking about schism', implicitly contradicting Niemöller, who had anticipated such a schism in his letter of 21 June to Bodelschwingh.[58]

The Church Elections on 23 July 1933

At a meeting with Wilhelm Frick and Ludwig Müller on 30 June, Hitler had decided to hold church elections throughout Germany immediately after the end of the church controversy in Prussia and the agreement on the church constitution. When Niemöller learned about these plans in advance, he vigorously opposed such elections because it was obvious that German Christians would be massively supported by NSDAP organizations to legally seize key roles in the Church. The Reich law on the DEK from 14 July determined elections were to be held on 23 July. It was hardly possible to organize elections at such a short notice, and the church opposition had great difficulties to prepare for them appropriately.[59] Therefore, the Young Reformers' leadership in Berlin started immediately. On 14 July, Niemöller, Lilje, and Künneth drafted 'guidelines' for the church elections under the watchword 'Gospel and Confession'. They contrasted the 'pure annunciation' with 'heresy and heretics' at the 'top and the centre' of the German Christians. With this, Niemöller and his fellow campaigners tried to win over moderate members of the DC. This revealed that the proposed establishment of a 'church unity front' was less unambiguous than suggested by the rhetoric.[60]

The Young Reformers' attitude towards the Nazi state was rather ambivalent. In the first 'word' on the elections addressed to the parishioners they firmly opposed the 'political methods' of the DC to 'ruthlessly seize power in the Church'. And yet, at the same time, they confessed to 'stand gratefully and decisively behind Hindenburg and Hitler as the leaders of our state'.[61] During the few days in the run-up to the 23 July elections, Niemöller was fully occupied with organizing the election campaign for the church opposition, whose list eventually ran under the name 'Gospel and Church'. He drafted flyers and appeals that the Young Reformers spread throughout the Reich. He was also involved in preparing the list and the elections in his own parish. The Dahlem office was, as Niemöller noted on 20 July, 'tremendously busy'.[62]

From the seizure of power on 30 January, Niemöller and his two colleagues had tried to establish a cooperative relationship with the DC parish group in Dahlem. The pastors allowed them to use the great hall in the community house for their events. On 19 March, a parish evening was organized with Niemöller and Georg Krahl, architect and chairman of the DC group, as speakers. Professor Iwan Alexandrowitsch Iljin, a Russian exile living in Berlin since 1923, spoke about Bolshevik anti-religious politics in the Soviet Union. Gerhard Klinge, priest of the Samariter parish, explained the impact of such politics in Germany by referring to the movement of the Godless. A song and 'closing words' by Niemöller concluded the evening with the motto: 'Put on the full armour of God, so you can take a stand against the devil's schemes' (Eph. 6:10–18).[63] Niemöller's participation in this event was a clear indication that, even after Hitler's seizure of power, the militant fight against 'evil'—atheism and Free Thinkers—formed a link between German Christians and the majority of the Dahlem parish, represented by the three pastors.

On Sunday 16 July, the three pastors opened a meeting in the Dahlem community hall to discuss the forthcoming elections. All three of them wore their Iron Crosses First Class and other medals from the Great War 'as testimony of their positive attitude towards the state'. Fritz Müller started the discussion, rejecting the accusation of the Church being 'alien to the people' by referring to its political stance during the Weimar Republic. Since 1918, Müller argued, the Church had fought against socialist anti-church politics, the 'shameful peace' of Versailles, and the 'war guilt lie'. Thus, the Church had helped pave the way, 'in its own fashion', 'for the present state, which it is wholeheartedly welcoming and willing to protect with heart and goods'.[64] To be fair, Fritz Müller's rhetoric, which glorified the Nazi regime and the Führer, could hardly be surpassed by his two colleagues. In January 1934, in a speech in Erfurt, he stated the 'loyalty to the Führer' was 'alive in all of us', and that one must thank God he had thwarted the dangers of Bolshevism 'through Adolf Hitler's action'.[65] In any case, Müller's remarks from 16 July 1933 were virtually undistinguishable from German Christian rhetoric.

Following Müller, Niemöller provided a brief overview of the church political events of recent weeks. He described the 'suspension of clerics' and other measures of repression employed by the state commissioners in the ApU, but also emphasized Hitler had helped abate the differences. Regarding the church elections, he stressed the two existing lists did not reflect 'party formation' but rather a 'boundary', which 'even crosses through the "German Christians" [...] The Church is based solely on God's word and the confession and cannot be the state in the guise of religion.' The subsequent discussion revealed 'a great will for agreement' between German Christians and the pastors and their list 'Gospel and Church'. The agreement over a Reich Concordat between the Nazi state and the Holy See, officially signed on 20 July, which was seen as a sign of lasting peace regarding church affairs, apparently contributed to the conciliatory atmosphere in Dahlem. The local newspaper summarized the mood of the meeting as follows: 'If during the last years all pastors in Germany had spoken like the three Dahlem pastors, the movement of German Christians would have been obsolete.'[66]

And yet, despite the pastors' insistence on their national reliability and on similarities of their list with German Christians, the Nazi state heavily interfered in the election campaign in favour of its party comrades. The Gestapo confiscated flyers and printing plates in the office of the list 'Gospel and Church', and the Nazi press declared it the duty of every Protestant Christian to vote for the DC. Finally, Hitler directly intervened in a speech broadcast on the radio on 22 July, the evening before the elections. He asked for the support of the forces 'based on the National Socialist state' such as the German Christians.[67] This made it abundantly clear that Niemöller's and the other Young Reformers' tactic to present themselves as loyal to the Nazi state through their speeches and appeals had come to nothing. Besides, many parishes and even entire regional churches, among them Baden, Hanover, and Saxony, had agreed on single lists granting the DC a great number of seats beforehand. In Berlin, 80 parishes voted, but the Dahlem parish was one of only three where the DC did not gain a majority. They received 1,046 votes while the list 'Gospel and Church' gained 1,447. 'Thank God', Niemöller commented on the results in his diary.[68]

The narrow defeat of the DC in the Dahlem parish could not hide the fact that the election result proved fundamental for setting a new course. From now on, the

German Christians could—via the election of representatives for provincial and general synods—legally seize power in the regional churches. At the same time, it became patently evident that a majority of German Protestants was willing to support the DC's reinterpretation of Christian tradition according to *völkisch* ideas.[69] On election day, Niemöller discussed the consequences of the election results for the Young Reformers with Walter Künneth. They decided the movement should withdraw from any church political activities. The next day, they and Hanns Lilje sent a corresponding telegram to the theology professor Karl Fezer on behalf of the Young Reformers' Reich leadership. Fezer, Ludwig Müller, the DC's patron, and others had been tasked with the acting leadership of the DEK on 23 July. In a public statement, the Young Reformers' leadership emphasized their willingness to 'contribute to the inner pacification and unity of the Church'. As a condition for this they requested 'free and unhindered activity' and a stop to any 'discrimination'.[70]

This statement could be seen as a sign that Niemöller and Künneth were willing to cooperate with DC moderates around Ludwig Müller. As a result, conflicts surfaced among Young Reformers, which until then had been concealed by the common goal to mobilize for the elections. They erupted at a meeting of the 'Gospel and Church'-list's Reich leadership, in which Fritz Müller represented the Dahlem pastors in Niemöller's absence. Gerhard Jacobi, whose circle of Berlin pastors formed one of the core groups of the Young Reformers, accused the leadership of 'washing their hands in innocence' like Pilate. But, Jacobi said, 'politics comes from *politeia*' (Greek for polity) and thus the task of restructuring the Church could 'not be abandoned'. Theodor Moldaenke had to defend Niemöller against the accusation that a compromise with the DC would benefit the Dahlem pastor in the form of a 'minor post' in the leading church bodies. But like Superintendent Max Diestel he also regarded the telegram as 'unfortunate'. Voices from other Berlin parishes expressed their disappointment with the Young Reformers' leaders: 'The fellows have surrendered.' Oskar Sohngen, who worked in the EOK, even assumed Niemöller and Künneth wanted to order 'a collective desertion' to the DC. Indeed, switches like this did occur after 23 July, albeit only in some individual cases.[71] It was, in fact, Künneth who considered putting the Young Reformers under Ludwig Müller's protection in early August. Rumours about the imminent realization of this idea circulated throughout the entire month.[72]

While these conflicts among Young Reformers continued, Niemöller went for a two-week holiday to the North Sea island Amrum, where his family would often go in the following years. He used the break to draft '16 theses' on the future course of action of the Young Reformers, which were published in the magazine *Junge Kirche*, the Young Reformers' newsletter, in August.[73] This was the first church political statement that was Niemöller's sole responsibility, and it is thus useful to take a closer look at it. He described the events of the last three months prosaically as a 'power struggle'. In his eyes, the inner church opposition lost this fight the moment that Hitler turned it into a 'state political struggle' in his speech of 22 July, stigmatizing the opponents of the German Christians as potential adversaries of the state. Continuing the struggle would mean expecting 'our own' church representatives to burden themselves 'with the flaw of lesser state political reliability'. But the 'status confessionis', that is, the violation of the Church's confessional position, had not yet been declared. Niemöller demanded 'clear-cut front lines' had to be established; however, he considered this a rather 'practical-congregational' and 'church-theological' task. Niemöller proposed 'to gather the believing members of the parishes' and advocate an 'inner course'. What this 'inner course' would be remained unclear. But Niemöller emphasized that 'there is a fundamental theological difference between the doctrine of the Reformation' and the theses of German Christians, even though the DC denied this. 'This ambiguity', he concluded, had 'to be clarified through a contemporary confession [zeitgemäßes Bekenntnis]'.[74]

This draft shows that Niemöller explicitly rejected the idea to fight for the rights of 'minorities' at the imminent synods of the Prussian Church of the ApU. Instead, he suggested to 'truly' help the DC take on their responsibility for the entire Church and not to wage a 'power struggle' at the synods.[75] Thus, his theses remained ambivalent. He demanded to strive for a 'contemporary confession', a demand that, during the conflict over Bodelschwingh's candidature, had already resulted in several declarations aiming to redirect the confessional basis of the Protestant churches. By adopting these demands, Niemöller attempted to restore the 'truth' and 'certainty' of Protestant faith. Thus, he placed the emphasis on a true confessional foundation of the church opposition.[76] His theses were marked by the illusion that an arrangement with the German Christians could be found. This hope was soon dashed. At the following synods of the Prussian Church, the German Christians enforced their goals ruthlessly and with brutal efficiency.

Like many other Protestant pastors, Martin Niemöller understood the beginning of the 'Third Reich' in 1933 and the promise of the people's community as a genuinely 'Protestant experience'.[77] In his sermons, he described the Nazi seizure of power as a moment of national 'rebirth'. He expected this transformation would also result in a renewal of Christian faith and a deepening of piety. Niemöller was actively engaged in the Young Reformation movement. His commitment was based on a hope to use the momentum and impetus of the Nazi seizure of power to reform the Church, particularly through the establishment of a unified Reich Church. His attitude in his Dahlem parish and during the conflict with Ludwig Müller showed he deemed it possible to cooperate with the moderate wing of the German Christians and maintain the state's neutrality in church political matters. However, both hopes were dashed by Hitler's speech on 22 July and the church elections on the following day. From now on it was clear that trouble was brewing. A power struggle flared up.

8

The Beginning of the Church Quarrel

After winning the church elections on 23 July, the German Christians began restructuring the Protestant Church according to the *Führer* principle and *völkisch* ideology. But the church opposition, with Niemöller as one of its leading figures by the end of 1933, did not simply surrender. A fight over hegemony within the Protestant Church began that contemporary observers named 'church quarrel' (*Kirchenstreit*).[1] This was not yet the *Kirchenkampf*, the church struggle of the Confessing Church, which only started in 1934. The term church quarrel referred to the church opposition in its defence of the confessional principles of the Reformation against the false doctrines of the German Christians. The Pastors' Emergency League represented the opposition in this conflict at an organizational level. Only in the church struggle the Emergency League pastors no longer saw themselves as one group among many others, but as representatives of the true Church.

At the Brandenburg provincial synod on 24 August 1933, all German Christians appeared in the brown uniforms of the NSDAP. Hastily and with a comfortable majority, they pushed several motions through to the general synod of the Protestant Church of the Old Prussian Union (ApU). Among them was a motion from Berlin DC leader Reinhold Krause urging the general synod to introduce a church law along the lines of the new civil service law. According to the Law for the Restoration of the Professional Civil Service from 7 April, civil servants of 'non-Aryan descent' were to be retired. For representatives of the church opposition—Niemöller among them—Gerhard Jacobi argued the adoption of state law for the appointment to church posts contradicted the 'nature of the Church'. DC delegates countered this with laughter and carried Krause's motion with a large majority.[2]

These events recurred at the general synod of the Old Prussian Church on 5 September. Again, several motions were hastily rubberstamped by the DC majority and objections drowned out by rowdy behaviour. Among them was Krause's motion to introduce an Aryan paragraph for church employees, which implied the mandatory retirement for ministers of 'non-Aryan descent'. Furthermore, Ludwig Müller was appointed regional bishop of the Old Prussian Church with dictator-like powers, and August Jäger became president of the EOK. This was the last step in the restructuring of the ApU at the will of the German Christians. Representing the minority was Karl Koch, who had just been elected as praeses of the Westphalian church province by its regional synod.

Koch's statement, which harshly denounced the German Christian's abuse of power, had been drafted by Niemöller and some other delegates the day before. When the synod delegates of the DC heckled Koch's speech, representatives of 'Gospel and Church' left the synod.[3]

The moment the church opposition left the Old Prussian synod set the course for the church political struggles in the 'Third Reich', paving the way for a church split ultimately resulting in the establishment of the Confessing Church. And yet on 5 September it was still open how this split would manifest itself. Members of the 'Jacobi circle'—young pastors from Berlin and Brandenburg around Gerhard Jacobi—met on 6 September. Dietrich Bonhoeffer and Franz Hildebrandt favoured the exit of the oppositional pastors and their parishes. Yet this would have established a Free Church that would have been defenceless against state reprisals. The majority of the pastors at the meeting therefore decided against this proposal. Instead, Bonhoeffer and Niemöller drafted a statement on behalf of the oppositional pastors that rejected the application of the 'Aryan paragraph' in the Church as contrary to the confessional principles—we will come back to this later.[4] Niemöller wanted to create a sort of oppositional pool. He suggested to Bodelschwingh to publicly invite the church opposition 'to form small parishes within the "parishes"' with 'the obligation of focusing on the Holy Scripture and confession of the Reformation'. This was intended to turn into a 'hidden Church' with an 'external organization' in the form of brethren councils, synods, and governing bodies.[5] The structure of this 'secret Church' was very similar to the Confessing Church that developed from 1934. Having said that, Niemöller did not yet suggest this 'secret Church' should consider itself to be the true Church. This was a position he only developed later under the influence of the Reformed theologian Karl Barth.

The Founding of the Pastors' Emergency League

From 7 September, several meetings of oppositional pastors took place in Berlin and the Rhineland to discuss the possibility of establishing an organizational structure. These plans were particularly urgent because a national synod of the DEK was scheduled in Wittenberg on 27 September. On 11 September, pastors Günter Jacob and Eugen Weschke proposed establishing a nationwide body of oppositional pastors to Niemöller. When Friedrich von Bodelschwingh hesitated to head such an organization, Niemöller decided to take over leadership of the Pastors' Emergency League (PEL)—the name already chosen some days earlier—himself.[6] This decision seems not to have been without controversy. Niemöller had to fend off the allegation that the 'Führer principle' was introduced in Berlin among oppositional pastors. Similar to when he had joined the Young Reformation Movement, Niemöller downplayed his role. He stated that 'without any contribution on my part' he had been 'drawn into this movement because colleagues from the countryside simply came into my house and asked for help'.[7] However, Niemöller's modesty was in stark contrast to his notorious zest for action and organizational skills.

In a circular letter from 21 September, Niemöller explained his reasons for founding the PEL. He argued there had been much 'confusion' and 'perplexity' among pastors after the general synod in Prussia. Responding to this 'emergency', an organization had been established. Even though recruitment relied on word of mouth, 1,300 pastors had already joined the Emergency League. The most important task of the League, Niemöller postulated, was regional Leagues 'supporting each other'. Otherwise one region after another would be 'purged'. He also suggested gathering laypeople in the parishes. Finally, Niemöller admitted 'this organization will not save the Church and move the world'. But one would owe it to the 'Lord of the Church' and the 'brethren' to do everything possible because 'today dithering and observing is denying'. The appeal 'Let Us Act!'[8] was in a sense the founding charter of the Confessing Church: the actions of the Emergency League were to bear witness and gather confessors, including laypeople.[9]

The first public proclamation of the PEL was published at the national synod of the DEK in Wittenberg on 27 September, drafted by Else and Martin Niemöller jointly with Friedrich Müller. It urged the synod delegates not to be 'fainthearted' and remain silent on 'contested questions'.[10] Since Hanover bishop Marahrens refused to read out the statement at the synod, Niemöller, Bonhoeffer, and the other Emergency League representatives from Berlin stuck posters with the text of the proclamation on house walls, trees, and telegraph posts. They then observed the brief negotiations of the synod from the spectator area of the Wittenberg Stadtkirche and witnessed Ludwig Müller being unanimously elected as Reich bishop of the DEK by the 60 delegates.[11]

Subsequently, Niemöller established the administrative apparatus of the PEL, based on technical support from the Dahlem parish office. On 20 October, a group of confidants from the Old Prussian Church and nine other regional Churches met in Dahlem to discuss organizational structures and next steps of the League. Those participating in the meeting formed a Council of Brethren with eight members as a governing body. Why Council of Brethren? In his partial biography of Niemöller published in 1938, Franz Hildebrandt explained the reasons. German Protestant pastors usually addressed one another with 'Herr Kollege' (colleague) or 'Herr Bruder' (brother). The name Council of Brethren, which later became common in the entire Confessing Church, semantically highlighted the equality and closeness between pastors in contrast to the National Socialist 'Führer principle'. This did not mean there were no conflicts or arguments between the brethren or that they were on first name terms with each other. It was not before summer 1937, when both men were imprisoned, that Niemöller offered Martin Albertz, pastor of the Reformed Church, Spandau Superintendent and one of

Niemöller's closest friends in the Confessing Church, to address him with the informal 'Du' via postcard.[12]

Apart from Niemöller, the Council of Brethren included Gerhard Jacobi and Karl Lücking, pastor and founder of a local circle of brothers in Westphalia. They discussed the next steps. Emergency League pastors should continue discussions with DC representatives, if possible, take on posts within the church leadership, and seek the advice of the PEL in case of an imminent coordination (Gleichschaltung) of church associations. All members of the Emergency League were to gather a group of laypeople in their parishes. Finally, participants of the Dahlem meeting decided that every pastor who wanted to join would be asked to sign a declaration of commitment drafted by Niemöller.[13] The four points of this pledge read as follows:

(1) I commit myself to conduct my office as a servant of the word, aligned only with the Holy Scripture and the confessions of the Reformation as the right interpretation of the Holy Scripture.
(2) I commit myself to unreservedly protest against all violations of this confessional state [Bekenntnisstand].
(3) I know I have, with my best abilities, a responsibility for those who are persecuted because of such confessional state.
(4) In such a commitment, I testify that the application of the Aryan Paragraph in the Church of Christ is a violation of this confessional state.[14]

Although the four articles of the Emergency League's pledge were to be seen as a unit, they emphasized different aspects. The first two points obliged the Emergency League pastors to preserve the confessional premises of the Church, the third and fourth to show solidarity with those who were persecuted due to violations of the confessional state. The last article clarified these were pastors of Jewish descent. The application of the Aryan paragraph, which the general synod decided to introduce in the Church, would remove them from the ministry. Thus, the PEL made active engagement for 'Jewish Christians'—the contemporary term for Christians of Jewish descent—among pastors the prime reason and touchstone for gathering oppositional forces in the Church. Only a small minority, 180 out of 18,000 Protestant parish priests in Germany, were affected by this measure.[15]

From spring 1933, despite their miniscule number, the issue of these 'Jewish Christians' developed into a focal point for the formation of the church opposition.[16] For a better understanding of Niemöller's resistance against the introduction of the Aryan paragraph in the Protestant Church and his activities in summer and autumn 1933, we must take the wider context of his attitudes towards the Jews into account. Niemöller had advocated a racial antisemitism as a member of the DNVP and the student group of the German Völkisch Protection and Defiance Federation in the early 1920s. He saw the Jews as a separate group, different from Germans in völkisch terms and disrupting the national community. These resentments still permeated one of his articles from 1928 where he railed against the 'leadership of elements alien to the German people and race' and their efforts to 'self-emasculate' the German people.[17] This indicates his racial antisemitism was still unwavering. There is no evidence that Niemöller used theological categories to interpret Judaism and Jewry through the lens of Christian anti-Judaist concepts during the 1920s. This changed in 1932.

Ambivalences in Niemöller's Perception of the Jews

As we have seen in Chapter 6, after having settled down in his new post as a pastor in Dahlem, Niemöller spent much time reading about theological and ethical issues, and making notes on what he had read. Among them were remarks on 'Old Testament and Gospel', written in late 1932. From 1930, the place of the Old Testament in Christian tradition attracted increasing attention. Several contributions by Protestant theologians that discussed the arguments of antisemitic authors are indicative of this.[18] For instance, Alfred Rosenberg, the leading race theorist of the NSDAP, suggested expunging the Old Testament from the Christian tradition in his 1930 book *The Myth of the Twentieth Century*. This was required to eradicate the Jewish influence from Christianity and to conceptualize Jesus as a representative of the Nordic race.[19]

Niemöller began his reflections on the Old Testament with the hypothesis: 'Protestant theology passes its judgement: religious charter [*Religionsurkunde*] of the people of Israel and of Judaism [*Judentum*]. From this perspective, the Old Testament is of no current value to us. Basic position!'[20] Presumably Niemöller had read the booklet by Johannes Hempel, professor for Old Testament at Göttingen University, titled *Away with the Old Testament?*. Hempel, who joined the German Christians in spring 1933, referred to the Old Testament as a 'Jewish religious charter' that was, nevertheless, 'an inwardly necessary preparation' to the New Testament. In this way, the Old Testament 'paved the way to Jesus' even though as a Christian one no longer wanted 'to go through all stages'. Only Protestant Christians who had strong reservations about the Old Testament should 'confidently leave it aside' in their practice of faith.[21] Although Niemöller adopted Hempel's term 'religious charter', he did not follow his further deliberations. He rather presumed the 'transience and relativity' of the biblical text. With this, he drew on the trend towards an empirical critique and historicization of the biblical texts, which had gained acceptance over the course of the nineteenth century. For Niemöller, the Old Testament was merely 'a part of literary history' with 'historical statements that are inaccurate' and others 'we do not like', as, for instance, the story of Joseph. For these reasons, he concluded, the Old Testament was only 'relative' and 'cannot be definitive'. Niemöller's conclusion from these reflections was unambiguous: 'The theologians cannot refute antisemitic objections.'[22]

It is obvious what Niemöller meant here: theologians such as Johannes Hempel, Emanuel Hirsch, and Friedrich Baumgärtel, who tried to challenge and riposte antisemitic attacks against the valency of the Old Testament in Christian tradition in 1931–2, had failed.[23] *Völkisch* authors who wanted to purge Christianity from in their view corruptive 'Jewish' influences of the Old Testament were right. But Niemöller's position raised further questions. What could be done when 'the Bible no longer is God's word'? 'We cannot prove, only confess!', Niemöller concluded, and reiterated even more explicitly: 'Is the Bible more than a religious charter? If so, then we can only confess to this!' [*können wir's nur bekennen*].[24] The terms 'confessing' and 'confession' do of course contain several layers of meaning. In the context of Niemöller's notes, confessing is to be understood as a demonstrative act of bearing witness.

But Niemöller also had a second answer that implicitly referred back to Hempel's notion of stages of development, according to which the part of the Christian tradition in the Old Testament must be understood as a 'preliminary to Jesus'.[25] Suppose the Old Testament was merely the 'preliminary stage' of the New Testament, Niemöller argued, then 'why do we need the elementary level?' Pointing to the difference between 'Prima' and 'Sexta'—the German terms for the first and the final year in secondary school—as an example, he suggested reversing the perspective on the two Testaments: 'Only from the perspective of the New Testament can we maintain the Old Testament is God's word. [...] We Christians are the chosen people. What they do in the synagogue—is basically an abuse of the Old Testament.'[26]

We can draw three conclusions from these fragmentary notes, clearly written only for himself. First, Niemöller reflected on Judaism from a Christian theological perspective rather than merely in categories of racial antisemitism for the first time in late 1932. To be sure, he still not only considered the Jews to be a religious community but also an ethnic group—a 'people', but not in an explicitly biological sense. Second, this did not stop him from claiming Judaism had no legitimacy as a religion of salvation. This claim, however, was very close to the assumptions of the German Christians. Like them, Niemöller assumed there was no place for the Old Testament in Christian tradition. By acknowledging anti-Jewish positions, which, as he claimed, Protestant theologians 'cannot refute', he at least implicitly accepted racial antisemitism as valid. Finally, excluding the Old Testament revealed an aporia of Christianity because it opened the doors for 'relativism', with relativism possibly 'having the final say', as Niemöller realized.[27] How was it possible to find a firm foundation for the Protestant faith under these circumstances? Niemöller's answer to this conundrum was 'confessing', that is the demonstrative performance of one's faith. Here, he established a position to which he returned during the hectic events of 1933.

With the German Christians demanding a Church with only 'Aryan' Christians, the question of how to deal with Christians of Jewish descent increasingly gained centre stage in church political debates during 1933. A parish evening on 28 May 1933 organized by the three Dahlem pastors offers a first insight into Niemöller's position. During the debate after his speech he admitted 'establishing a Church of merely Aryan Christians' was a possibility, but only if there was a 'simultaneous establishment of a Church of Jewish Christians that would be equally respected and equipped with equal rights'. Niemöller's following remark shows this position was still shaped by antisemitic thought patterns as, in his view, the 'equalization of the mission to the Gentiles with the mission to the Jews' must be rejected.[28] This did not fully correspond with the demands of the German Christians, who, in their June 1932 guidelines, completely rejected the missionary activities among Jews by referring to the danger of 'racial concealment and bastardization'.[29] But Niemöller's disregard for the mission to the Jews came close to the DC position, as well as his melodramatic remark at the end of the parish evening when he assured everybody of 'his unlimited trust in Reich Chancellor Hitler'.[30]

But immediately after the events of the Prussian general synod on 5 September, Niemöller reacted to the introduction of the Aryan paragraph in the Church of the Old Prussian Union. With Dietrich Bonhoeffer, who had already taken a firm stance regarding the Protestant position towards antisemitism in April 1933, Niemöller drafted a 'declaration' that all oppositional pastors were to sign. Bonhoeffer visited Niemöller in Dahlem with Franz Hildebrandt and some students on 6 September, and they discussed this declaration into the night. Else Niemöller described her husband's thoughts when she wrote to her sister on the same day: the 'implementation of the Aryan paragraph' touched 'on the nerve of the Church' and had to be seen as 'heresy'. At the same time, she explained the theological motivation of her husband's decision to act: the Aryan paragraph 'contradicts the 3rd article'. Here, she referred to the part of the Creed emphasizing faith in the Holy Spirit and the 'community of saints', that is, the equality of all baptized Christians. Else was delighted Martin was 'in great form' mentally. 'The more fighting the better', she aptly summarized his credo.[31]

Niemöller's and Bonhoeffer's declaration heralded the start of this fight. In three paragraphs, it condemned the Aryan paragraph as contradicting the confessional basis of the Protestant Church, because the 'office of parish priest' is only bound to 'his duly appointment' and not—as the declaration implicitly insinuated—his descent. Agreeing with such a 'violation of the confession' would result in 'exclusion from the community of the Church'. Thus, the Aryan paragraph was to be rescinded immediately.[32]

How could Niemöller take this position after firmly maintaining the lack of legitimacy of the Jewish synagogue practice in 1932? It seems he addressed the question of the 'baptism of Jews' during August for the first time. In any case, he noted a conversation about this topic on 21 August. The next day, the three Dahlem pastors held one of their open evenings, which they took in turns regularly from the summer onwards, to inform the parishioners about current church political developments. At this point, Niemöller still held the open evening in his own house in Cecilienallee, which was always overcrowded during these events. On 22 August 'questions regarding the confession' were discussed.[33] Thus, it was members of his parish that urged Niemöller to debate the position of Jews in Church and state. One of them was Elisabeth Schiemann (1881–1972), a renowned geneticist, one of the first female professors at German universities. From July 1933, she wrote several letters to Niemöller, urging him to publicly protest against the Nazi persecution of the Jews.[34]

Yet Niemöller rejected these proposals and argued the Church was not responsible. And he repeated typical antisemitic prejudices in the process. On 7 September, immediately after completing the declaration, Niemöller wrote to Schiemann 'the Church can only demand that the state does not impede the annunciation and leave the Church be the Church'. Only individual Christians 'who conceded to God's will' could then realize this will within the state. This view corresponded to Luther's doctrine of the two kingdoms that stipulated separate spheres of the rule of the state and the rule of the Church. To put it 'in dry words' this meant: 'The Church does not preach to the state, interfering in its powers (exercised justly or unjustly), which also applies to the Jewish question, rather, the Church speaks to the people in the parishes about God's will about man, also about Jews etc.' This would have been a consistent position within the framework of the doctrine of the two kingdoms, had Niemöller emphasized the dignity and rights of the unbaptized Jews—which he did not. In doing so, Niemöller essentially gave the Nazi state carte blanche for the persecution of the Jews. But he did not stop there. He asked for Schiemann's approval of his view that 'as a Christian I think like you when I also affirm the relative right of our people to firmly fend off the exaggerated [übergroßen] and damaging influence of Jewry that has existed in my view'.[35] This was a candid affirmation of antisemitic prejudices.

As we have seen, from 1932 Niemöller was no longer a racial antisemite. But he was still firmly convinced of the Jews' dominance and their negative influence on German society. This was what we can call a societal and cultural antisemitism. It offered sufficient congruence with Nazi racial policy so that Niemöller deemed solidarity with Jews a minor problem—if a problem at all.[36] The second important reason for Niemöller's silence towards the Nazi state's anti-Jewish policy in 1933 was the self-centred nature of his ecclesiastical thinking. This is particularly clear in the already mentioned letter to Elisabeth Schiemann, where he identified 'the fate of Luther's Church' and the question of 'how long this Church might be able to survive as an institutional entity' as 'the actual danger' of the time. In Niemöller's eyes, neither the Jews nor other victims of the Nazi state were in danger, but the Protestant Church, hard-pressed by 'Rome', the 'Free Churches', and 'völkisch-heathen groups'.[37]

Therefore, we must reject the comforting idea that Niemöller started to fundamentally criticize Nazi antisemitism in late summer 1933. He was exclusively focused on Christians of Jewish descent, for whom he, like other contemporaries, used the term 'Jewish Christians'. It was their removal from office that the pledge of the PEL opposed. However, Niemöller subsequently even watered down the position of the very pledge he himself had drafted in September. In October 1933, inquiries made by pastors and Emergency League members regarding the Aryan paragraph reached him on a daily basis.[38] In response, Niemöller wrote a brief article on 'Sentences on the Aryan Question in the Church' which he published in the journal *Junge Kirche* in early November.[39] In the following we will highlight only two aspects of his multi-layered and complex line of argument.

First, Niemöller repeated the basic position of the Emergency League that 'converted Jews' had to be recognized as 'fully entitled members of the Church through the Holy Spirit'. This applied to the conversion of individual Jews, which was the reason why Niemöller discarded the idea of a possible separate 'Jewish Christian Church'—which he had still advocated in May—explicitly as 'utopian'. On the other hand, he pointed out that in practice there were limits to the rights of baptized Jews. In yet another repetition of antisemitic resentment, he affirmed the assumption that 'we as a people have been heavily burdened with the influence of the Jewish people'. Therefore, recognizing equality among all who are baptized required 'considerable self-renunciation'. To be sure, the 'community of saints' was beyond any doubt. But one could at least expect 'due restraint' from pastors 'of Jewish descent'. In practice this meant pastors of 'non-Aryan descent' were not to hold an 'office in church leadership roles or a prominent post in the people's mission' and should thus not be part of the church leadership.[40]

This statement effectively blew up the unity of the pledge of the Pastors' Emergency League. By establishing conditions for the presence of baptized Jews in the Church, Niemöller abandoned the pledge's third and fourth article that promised a 'responsibility for those who are persecuted' and 'resistance of intro-ducing the Aryan paragraph in the Church'. Niemöller focused on the first two articles of the pledge.[41] We can explain why Niemöller watered down the promise of the pledge by pointing at his own ambivalent position towards Judaism and the Jews. His commitment to pastors of Jewish descent was limited, and these limitations were caused by his continuous societal and cultural hostility towards the Jews. Hence, Niemöller felt in no way responsible for the fate of members of the Jewish community who were subject to persecution and exclusion in 1933. Niemöller represented both: commitment to Christians of Jewish descent and disinterest in the fate of Jewish Germans who were persecuted by the Nazi regime.

Niemöller and the PEL drew a line when the Aryan paragraph was applied in the Church. But even active members of the League such as Gerhard Jacobi did not really understand why the struggle with the German Christians had sparked off in late October 'over the question of the Aryan paragraph, which was not as such crucial'.[42] Niemöller contributed to a sense of confusion and ambiguity within the Emergency League. In the first circular to its members from

2 November, he reprinted a telegram he had sent to the Reich Chancellor on 15 October 'on behalf of more than 2,500 pastors'. In this telegram he congratulated Hitler for Germany's exit from the League of Nations proclaimed the day before and thanked him 'for the manly deed and clear word that preserves Germany's honour'. At the same time, he promised that the Emergency League pastors were 'true followers' of the chancellor.[43] The idea to send the telegram was not Niemöller's, but originated from Wilhelm Harnisch, a pastor in Berlin. Even by 1957 Harnisch was still strongly convinced the League of Nations had no other purpose than to 'oppress Germany'. Harnisch and Niemöller had drafted the telegram, which reflected the view of both men.[44] Elsewhere Niemöller emphasized that the difference between German Christians and PEL members did not spring from being 'old or young, conservative or progressive, dogmatic-orthodox or dogmatic-liberal, nor from being National Socialist or politically reactionary, because many old National Socialist fighters are members of the Pastors' Emergency League'. Rather, the difference accrued from 'the assessment of what the Church might be and must be. It must not be a place where religious questions are pushed forward forcefully. It is Christ, not current affairs, that must be its centre.'[45]

Critique of Niemöller's Views

These remarks can be seen as currying favours with the Nazi regime, and that is exactly how they were understood in the Emergency League. On 24 October, Franz Hildebrandt wrote a letter to Niemöller expressing his deep discomfort with this course of action. For 'a long time' he had no longer been in agreement with the line of the Young Reformation Movement and the Emergency League:

> It is in my eyes completely incomprehensible that one can joyfully welcome the political step in Geneva [exit from the League of Nations] without firmly saying No to a Church that time and time again denies us 'equality', a Church with which we must not even show false solidarity on the surface if one is convinced that Christ's Church is with us and not with the other Church. It seems [...] as if again the watchword of 'cooperation' has been victorious at all costs.[46]

Hildebrandt not only criticized Niemöller's course of 'cooperation at all costs', but also drew personal consequences. In early November he followed Bonhoeffer to London. However, at Niemöller's urgent request, Hildebrandt returned to Dahlem as early as January 1934, became treasurer of the Emergency League and deputized for Niemöller, who by that time was suspended from office.[47]

Criticism also came from elsewhere. On 30 October 1933, the Reformed theologian Karl Barth gave a talk in Berlin. The following day he had three meetings with Berlin Emergency League pastors. The first gathering took place in the private home of Gerhard Jacobi. Barth urged the pastors not to meet with Bishop Ludwig Müller. Doing so would 'recognize' his leadership of the Church.[48] Niemöller rejected this allegation indignantly and referred to the exit of oppositional pastors from the Old Prussian synod on 5 September as an example of fundamental opposition. The only purpose of recent meetings with moderate German Christians had been to resolve theological issues. He also explained that as a pastor he did in fact differentiate in his pastoral practice. He would walk past a theologian of the DC who came to him for Communion. Yet to a layman he would offer the Communion cup.[49] It is particularly striking that none of the League pastors at this meeting understood Barth's thesis 'We are the true Protestant Church'. Barth's remark, which anticipated the constitution of the opposition as the Confessing Church, fell on deaf ears. Moreover, his pressing concern whether the Church would be willing to react to the terror in concentration camps, and to 'what has been done to the Jews', remained unanswered.[50]

In the afternoon, a meeting took place with Barth and 150 pastors. Barth repeated his suggestion that the oppositional pastors should gather a 'free synod' and constitute themselves the 'legitimate representatives of the true German Church'. But a conversation about this option—which in May 1934 eventually was pursued at the synod of Barmen—did not happen. The American church representative Charles Macfarland, who met Hitler on that day, informed Jacobi via telephone that the chancellor was willing to meet him, Jacobi, as the representative of the church opposition. When Jacobi announced this to the gathered pastors, everyone 'was cheering'.[51] This reaction shows how complicated church politics had become. Of all people, the Emergency League pastors put their hope in a Catholic politician to recognize their demands. Jacobi suggested Barth accompany him. But apart from Jacobi, the Council of Brethren of the PEL unanimously rejected this idea at a meeting on 9 November. The brethren considered it unthinkable that Barth, a Swiss national and former SPD member, would meet with Hitler. Instead, the opportunistic proposal that Wilhelm Niemöller, a staunch Nazi supporter, should accompany Jacobi was accepted.[52]

The meeting between Hitler and the church representatives took place in a different constellation and not before 25 January 1934. It achieved the opposite of what the Emergency League pastors had hoped for at their gathering on Reformation Day 1933. The discussions on 31 October 1933 had revealed Niemöller and the majority of the other participants were not willing to follow Barth's fundamental criticism of German Christians and his insistence to establish a Church true to the confession. Especially Niemöller still hoped Ludwig Müller and the church leadership would recognize the wishes of the Emergency League and curb the radical wing of the DC.[53] And yet there was evidence this radical wing had already pushed forward within the DC. At the same time, the German Christians pushed back against oppositional pastors. On 6 November, the Dahlem

DC group requested from the EOK to appoint a DC pastor to one of the three pastorates in their parish. If Niemöller were the one to be removed, one would get rid of the 'most active adversary' in the parish. At that point in time, Niemöller was deemed—probably not only in the view of the DC—as 'the most important Dahlem pastor'. By the end of 1933, Niemöller had surpassed Eberhard Röhricht as the most popular Dahlem pastor. The average number of parish members attending their services was 438 for Niemöller, compared to 407 for Röhricht. In 1934, Niemöller attracted an average of 1,112 parishioners to his services. The fact that even the DC recognized Niemöller's 'significant qualities as a pastor' caused a dilemma: on the one hand, the Dahlem DC group advocated for Niemöller to remain in his post 'in the interest of the parish'; on the other hand, it suggested to remove him due to 'his attitude against our movement'.[54]

Meanwhile the Reich leadership of the DC prepared for a missionary offensive to be inaugurated at a mass rally in the Berlin Sportpalast on 13 November. Two days earlier, the consistory suspended Niemöller, Kurt Scharf, and Eitel-Friedrich von Rabenau, three prominent Emergency League pastors, from office. Protests by the Dahlem parish and the intervention of President von Hindenburg made sure the suspension was lifted on 16 November.[55] The Sportpalast rally on 13 November with 20,000 participants was a typical National Socialist mass event. Alongside the Bishop of Brandenburg, Joachim Hossenfelder, almost all members of the EOK under its president, Nazi lawyer Friedrich Werner, took part. The main speaker was the Gau leader of the Berlin DC, Reinhold Krause. Krause's speech caused a scandal when he demanded to purge the Church from the Old Testament and its 'Jewish stories of cattle traders and pimps', directly referring to Alfred Rosenberg's *Myth of the Twentieth Century*. He also suggested removing the 'inferior theology of the Rabbi Paul' from the New Testament. Instead, Krause wanted to place a *völkisch*-Germanic religiosity at the heart of the Protestant Church. The participants enthusiastically adopted a resolution along these lines.[56] These developments confirmed Martin Niemöller's observation that a large number of German Christians had got increasingly tied up with a *völkisch* and neo-pagan current and completely abandoned Christian tradition. At the heart of these efforts was the German Faith Movement (Deutsche Glaubensbewegung), established by Indologist Jakob Hauer in 1933, which combined Indo-Germanic and mystic clichés.[57]

Niemöller reacted immediately. In the afternoon of 14 November, he, Gerhard Jacobi, and his brother Wilhelm met Ludwig Müller and the Reformed theologian Otto Weber, a member of the Spiritual Ministry of the DEK, the German Protestant Church. The Emergency League pastors gave Müller an ultimatum to step down as patron of the DC and dismiss all church office holders that were present in the Sportpalast. The reason behind this, as Jacobi explained, was to increase divisions among the DC and significantly damage their radical wing. Martin Niemöller's main goal was Hossenfelder's dismissal. This might have appeared as a personal vendetta—which it was. Over the course of the meeting it became increasingly obvious that Niemöller's actions were guided by disappointed hopes. To Müller's surprise, Niemöller stated that in May 1933, when the moderate guidelines of the East Prussian DC were published, 'the whole Young Reformation Movement was ready to follow you'. But Hossenfelder's dominance over the DC had dashed Niemöller's hopes for a broad national church agreement.[58] When put under such pressure, Müller was evasive and played for time. At the end of this dramatic meeting, the conversation between the two old navy comrades Niemöller and Müller took a turn to the sentimental. Niemöller made it clear he would not comply with the pending suspension from his pastorate. 'I respectfully report my second insubordination.' He had committed the first one in 1919 when he refused to surrender a submarine to the British at Scapa Flow. In response, as the minutes read, Müller 'tenderly touched Niemöller's lapels and amicably shook his hand'.[59]

Müller stalled. Immediately after the meeting he dismissed Krause and publicly dissociated himself from his speech. But he refused to accept any further demands of the Emergency League pastors, again in a second conversation on 16 November.[60] On the evening of 14 November, the Emergency League pastors again met with Karl Barth and Friedrich Bodelschwingh, who both swiftly travelled to Berlin. Again, Niemöller clashed with Barth, just like on Reformation Day. Barth wanted a 'comprehensive opposition' in response to the attacks against the Church, explicitly also directed against the Nazi state that had given the German Christians a position of power by appointing the state commissioner for the Old Prussian Church in late June. Niemöller, however, was unwilling to reject Ludwig Müller's authority as Reich bishop, as long as he was also the Bishop of the Old Prussian Church. He lectured Barth arrogantly: 'After all, we are Lutherans!', pointing out the Lutheran bishops had elected Müller. Niemöller insisted to continue negotiations with Müller and, in doing so, precipitate the DC's split. Particularly with an eye to his Dahlem parish, Niemöller hoped Müller would 'survive for the time being' for the benefit of the Emergency League, as the parishes could only develop under this 'pressure'.[61]

This argument revealed a fundamental weakness of the church opposition in Berlin. So far it had only involved pastors without including laypeople in the parishes. Niemöller's admission prompted Georg Schulz, pastor in Bremen and head of the Sydow brethren, to make the ironic remark—directed against Niemöller—that his parish 'understood very well' when he explained the 'confusion of word and violence' as the essence of the DC 'heresy'.[62] But Niemöller prevailed. How he did this was described by Barth in a letter to Günter Jacob a few weeks later. According to Barth, the Council of Brethren of the Emergency League and a larger group of PEL pastors met in Jacobi's flat on 15 November. The Council drafted a petition to the Reich bishop containing seven points, by and large repeating the demands verbally made at the meeting with Müller on

14 November. In a 'decisive moment', Barth stated, Niemöller 'formally' sent Bodelschwingh and himself 'out of the room' and subsequently 'amended and concluded' the draft with his followers.[63] Present at the meeting was Christa Müller, a young doctoral student of theology, who started her internship at Dahlem shortly afterwards and worked closely with Niemöller. At one point during the tumultuous meeting Karl Barth whispered despairingly in her ear: 'Your Niemöller is terrible!'. Müller herself, who despite their close work relationship still had a critical view of Niemöller, stated a few weeks later that he 'is a committed Nazi'.[64] Only after prolonged pressure, Niemöller met Barth's wish to draft a 'fundamental word' that Barth subsequently published as six theses under the title *Church Opposition*.[65]

The renewed encounter with Niemöller and his insistence on further negotiations annoyed Barth. He vented his anger a few days later in a letter to his former student Richard Karwehl, describing Berlin members of the Emergency League as an 'anthill of nervous pastors' who were 'under the dictatorship of the U-boat commander Niemöller', who would 'not tolerate' any 'theological hesitation in the name of the "parish"'.[66] When Barth repeated his concerns—this time in more obliging words—in a new instalment of his series *Theologische Existenz heute* (Theological Existence Today), Gerhard Jacobi complained about this, in his eyes, deplorable criticism. But Barth remained adamant, claiming Niemöller still did not understand 'what kind of antagonism was at stake'. The Emergency League only pursued 'church politics' in 'a bad sense of the word', because it 'constantly had its eye on the benevolence of the Nazis'. The Council of Brethren only wanted to 'get a fig leaf with a swastika painted on', rather than 'not giving a damn about compromising itself in the view of the state!' Given his view that Niemöller was currying favours with the NSDAP and the church leadership it had put in power, it must come as a surprise that Barth 'really liked' Niemöller 'as a person'.[67]

Even so, Niemöller knew how to use the Sportpalast scandal to activate the church opposition. On 16 November, he sent a circular to all Emergency League pastors where he summarized the events in the wake of 13 November and demanded to read out a pulpit declaration in the parishes. This declaration informed parishes about the course of the conflicts in the Church for the first time since 2 July.[68] The PEL took the step to go public, and this unequivocal position was reflected in growing membership. It increased from 3,000 in mid-November to 5,500 in mid-December. In mid-January 1934 membership reached a peak with approximately 7,000, more than a third of all German pastors. Predominantly in Westphalia and the Rhineland 'passive resistance against the representatives of this church leadership' started, with many pastors and parishes submitting petitions 'rejecting the bishops imposed onto them'.[69] Niemöller simultaneously expanded the oppositional forces. On 24 November, he and Gerhard Stratenwerth met with the three bishops of the regional churches Hanover, Bavaria, and Württemberg, which were still 'intact' and not yet destroyed by the DC—August Marahrens, Hans Meiser, and Theophil Wurm—as well as with Karl Koch, praeses of the only 'intact' Prussian church province in Westphalia. With this meeting, a 'Confessing Front' of all oppositional forces against the German Christians was established. All participants again demanded the dismissal of Hossenfelder.[70]

However, the church opposition was not able to translate its newly found strength into direct success. Müller's backing of Hossenfelder proved a tactical mistake when a growing number of parish priests and parishes broke with the German Christians because they did not want to support Hossenfelder's neo-pagan assault on Christianity. This heralded in the downfall of this religious movement, which had shaped the course of German church history in such a fatal manner during 1932–3. On 6 December, Ludwig Müller stood down as patron of the DC, and Hossenfelder resigned from all his church offices and as Reich leader of the DC on 21 December. The remaining DC members split into several competing groups.[71] After Niemöller had focused his oppositional activities on Hossenfelder for several months, this should have been the hour of his triumph. But he had miscalculated the situation. Shortly after the Sportpalast scandal Niemöller learned in a meeting with the Berlin theologian Erich Seeberg, who was close to the German Christians, that Hossenfelder's downfall did not necessarily imply the same fate for Müller, which dashed Niemöller's hopes. The 'opposite' was the case, Seeberg predicted. Thanks to the elimination of the radical DC leader, he argued, the Reich bishop would become the 'saviour of the Church' and be stronger than before.[72]

Seeberg's prognosis was generally accurate. Until the end of the year, Ludwig Müller was able to frustrate all attempts of the Confessing Front to establish a new church leadership of its liking through delaying tactics. After many meetings and conversations behind closed doors Niemöller was completely exhausted in early December. At an open evening in the church hall on 5 December he admitted he felt 'like a hollowed out crater and would love to visit my parishioners instead of driving across the city via taxi six times a day'.[73] But Müller did not only manoeuvre, he also acted. He used open repression to silence the church opposition. On 4 January he issued the so-called 'muzzle decree' that prohibited any church political statements, flyers, and circulars and threatened parish priests with disciplinary proceedings in case of any violation.[74] Niemöller strongly condemned the decree as a 'terrorist regime based on violence', and the Emergency League responded with a further pulpit declaration and a protest rally in Berlin. Müller subsequently suspended about 50 parish priests who had read out the pulpit declaration. He also successfully persuaded the church leaders summoned to a meeting in Berlin on 13 January 1934—namely also those who like Meiser and Wurm were members of the Confessing Front—to agree to a 'fortress truce' until a meeting between Müller and Hitler scheduled for 17 January would bring clarity.[75]

On 11 January, Niemöller noted the church political situation 'was foggy'. On this day, President von Hindenburg met Ludwig Müller and expressed his concerns about Müller's course of action. A few days later, Hindenburg informed Hitler about these concerns. The chancellor was tired of the continuous struggle within the Protestant Church and, in a meeting with Minister of the Interior Frick on 18 January, agreed the situation should be clarified at a Chancellery meeting with the leaders of both church political camps.[76] In his preparations for this meeting Frick followed Hitler's view, who favoured state neutrality towards the quarrelling camps in the Protestant Church. Apart from Müller, seven representatives each from the German Christians and the Confessing Front were invited, including the Bishops Marahrens, Meiser, and Wurm, the Westphalian praeses Karl Koch—and Niemöller. Although theologian Karl Fezer and two former members of the Reich Church Ministry, Hermann Wolfgang Beyer and Otto Weber, represented the DC in the meeting, these three now actually belonged to the church opposition.[77]

Thus, with a ratio of 10:4 the opposition against Müller's supporters was in the majority. During the run-up to the meeting, this fuelled the hopes among the Confessing Front to succeed in removing Ludwig Müller as Reich bishop and fend off efforts to establish a national Church. The invitees—church leaders, Emergency League pastors, and professors from throughout Germany—who met a few days before the 25 January to prepare for the meeting, all agreed on this point. They were also on the same page that only Hitler was able to find a solution out of this stalemate, an assessment Niemöller wholeheartedly shared: 'The only point with which one might be able to fight against this [DC policy] is the Führer.' For Niemöller, the moment to decide on the basic ideological and spiritual position of the German people had arrived. He pointed out to the participants of the preliminary meeting that 'the coexistence of Protestant Christianity and a disguised *völkisch* ideology' was 'in the long-term' hard to imagine.[78]

The Chancellor's Reception on 25 January 1934

In the hagiographic literature on Niemöller, his encounter with Hitler takes centre stage of the one-hour chancellor's reception.[79] This, however, does not correspond with the actual facts, but results from Niemöller's efforts to retrospectively whitewash his role in this debacle of the church opposition. And yet the day had started well for Niemöller. He was well rested and put on all his First World War medals and badges of honour before heading for the Chancellery to present himself appropriately to the war veteran Hitler. There was a preliminary meeting with the invited church representatives at 12 p.m. At 1 p.m. the reception started in the rooms of the Reich Chancellery with the introduction of the participants through

Interior Minister, Wilhelm Frick, who stood next to Hitler with Hermann Göring and Hans Heinrich Lammers, Chief of the Reich Chancellery. But soon came 'Göring's ricochet shot', as Niemöller noted in his diary later that evening.[80]

Without the church opposition noticing, Ludwig Müller had gained the support of the Prussian minister president for his church politics. In a conversation with Hitler on 20 January, Göring solely blamed the church opposition for the church quarrel and insinuated political motives. Hitler thus authorized him to gather material. Among other things, Göring ordered the wiretapping of Niemöller's phone. Hence, he could read out the minutes of a phone call between Niemöller and Walter Künneth shortly before the former had left for the Reich Chancellery that morning. Niemöller referred to a meeting between Hitler and Hindenburg scheduled for 12 noon, where, as the church opposition hoped, the president would convince Hitler of the necessary dismissal of the Reich bishop. 'The Last Rites before the meeting!', as Niemöller formulated according to the minutes. And yet, it was not him who said these words, but Ernst Eisenhardt, speaking on a second receiver. Eisenhardt had started working as Niemöller's voluntary 'adjutant' in May 1933. In the phone call Niemöller also praised himself that 'we have orchestrated everything so well via Meißner'. He meant Otto Meißner, head of the president's office, who had conveyed the proposals of the church opposition to Hindenburg.[81]

In autumn 1938, Else Niemöller still had to answer Gestapo officer's questions in Sachsenhausen concentration camp about the now famous expression of the 'Last Rites'.[82] Revelations about the phone call immediately put the representatives of the church opposition on the defensive. Now it seemed as if Niemöller had used the president to manipulate Hitler. Niemöller, who stepped forward when his name was called, had to confirm the phone call had happened. When he tried to implore Hitler that he had acted in the best interest of the Church, but also of the people and the state, Hitler snubbed: 'You leave the Third Reich to me and care for the Church!'. The conversation between Niemöller and Hitler was not the central event of the reception. After this short exchange Niemöller repeatedly tried to be given the floor, but was 'deliberately overlooked'.[83] Then Hitler pointed out that the Church itself had elected Müller as Reich bishop and he neither wanted to back nor dismiss him. The completely baffled bishops Wurm and Meiser were unable to concisely express their objections to Müller and, in reply to a question from Hitler, had to admit a Reich bishop from the Confessing Front could not ensure peace within the Church. Hitler ended the reception with an appeal for unity and—failing this—threatened with the withdrawal of state funding for the Church. The reception was a 'complete victory' for Hitler. Bishop Theophil Wurm bitterly commented the events a few days later: 'This time the U-boat commander has torpedoed himself instead of the enemy!'[84]

This comment reflected how the church leaders viewed the meeting, solely blaming Niemöller for the debacle. On the following day the Bavarian bishop

Hans Meiser phoned Niemöller and urged him to resign as chairman of the Emergency League.[85] On the same day, the church leaders started negotiations with the Reich bishop without inviting representatives of the Emergency League. On 27 January, these negotiations resulted in a joint declaration. The church leaders backed Müller and his decrees, including the muzzle decree.[86] This, as Niemöller put it, amounted to a 'capitulation of the church leaders' before the Reich bishop.

Niemöller was aware of the debacle he had caused. In the afternoon of 25 January, he and other Emergency League pastors met with Ulrich von Sell (1884–1945), a member of the Dahlem parish. The mood at this gathering was 'first class consternation', as Niemöller noted.[87] Two weeks after the church leaders' capitulation, Niemöller tried to put a positive spin on the chancellor's reception. On balance, he concluded, it was 'neither a victory of one side nor a disaster of the other one', but an 'appeal for unity'. The fact that a 'disaster' followed, was only decided later.[88]

Ultimately Niemöller passed the blame for the chancellor's reception 'solely' to the Reich bishop, even though the pugnacious pastor had every reason for self-criticism.[89] But this was not one of his strong suits. First, he himself, longer than other members of the Confessing Front, had advocated negotiations with Müller and thus strengthened his position. Second, it was doubtful whether Niemöller's harsh negotiation style was in fact purposeful. Indeed, in the decisive moment he had nothing but hollow nationalist phrases as a counter to Hitler. In late 1933, Georg Schulz, a member of the Sydow brethren, already pointed to Niemöller's rhetoric weakness. To be sure, he did so out of wounded vanity after the Emergency League pastors who gathered at Jacobi's house on 12 November decided on Martin and Wilhelm Niemöller instead on him as possible representatives for the chancellor's reception. Schulz admitted probing into a subject during negotiations was not his strong suit. Niemöller himself argued this very skill was a crucial precondition to achieve a success at the meeting with Hitler. However, Schulz correctly stated that Niemöller had not achieved anything in his former negotiations with the Reich bishop either. 'Like chain smokers, there are also chain speakers', he said about the Dahlem pastor.[90] This was an apt criticism, as the events of 25 January 1934 had shown.

In the second half of 1933, Martin Niemöller took centre stage in the church political conflicts of the 'Third Reich'. With the PEL, he had a power basis that he could put in the balance independently from the bishops of the 'intact' regional churches of Bavaria, Hanover, and Württemberg, even after the debacle of the chancellor's reception on 25 January 1934. Despite his often radical rhetoric, Niemöller's church political course was still leaning towards compromise. He hoped for a split of the German Christians longer than other members of the church opposition and counted on negotiations with the unpopular Reich bishop. Compromises and ambivalences also shaped the way he dealt with the central trigger of the conflict—the 'Aryan paragraph' in the Church. By 1932 Niemöller had already abandoned racial antisemitism and started to interpret Judaism according to theological categories. But he had also concluded theologians could not refute the key elements of antisemitic critique of Judaism. The pledge of the Emergency League drafted by Niemöller, with its unconditional recognition of baptized Jews in the ministry, clearly distinguished the League from the German Christians. However, Niemöller was still shaped by a cultural and social antisemitism and, as a result, was willing to compromise in realizing the pledge. In addition, he did not show any solidarity with members of the Jewish faith. This judgment is not a historian's fault-finding based on hindsight. There was already sharp criticism of Niemöller's course coming from within his own ranks of the church opposition, both from pastors and theologians such as Karl Barth, Franz Hildebrandt, Gerhard Jacobi, and Georg Schulz as well as from laypeople like Elisabeth Schiemann. Niemöller's ambivalences were the result of his unwavering national Protestant position rather than manifestations of character weaknesses.

9

Building the Confessing Church, 1934

After the chancellor's reception, with its disastrous outcome for the church opposition, Niemöller and the PEL had to rethink their strategy. They realized that they were unable to oust Ludwig Müller from his dual position as Reich bishop and bishop of the Old Prussian Church. Emanating from regional initiatives, in 1934 the church opposition became increasingly aware that it could constitute itself as the true Protestant Church. The Barmen Confessing Synod in late May 1934 was the first culmination of this process. At the same time, Martin Niemöller was increasingly exposed to defamation and repression in the wake of the chancellor's reception, by the state, church authorities, and by the DC.

This already started two days after the chancellor's reception. On 27 January, the Gestapo conducted a house search in Niemöller's parsonage in Cecilienallee 61. The officers confiscated documents belonging to the Emergency League. On the next day, a Sunday afternoon, Niemöller was picked up by Gestapo officers and taken to the Gestapo headquarters in Prinz-Albrecht Straße 8, where he was interrogated about the Emergency League's 'foreign relations'. At the chancellor's reception, Göring had already referred to the League's alleged relations with the foreign press as evidence of its subversive activities. On 30 January, Niemöller was interrogated again, from midday to early evening, this time with Ernst Eisenhardt, his 'adjutant' and tireless aid in practical issues.[1] On 29 January, the London *Times* reported on the result of the chancellor's reception and Niemöller's Gestapo detention under the headline 'Collapse of Opposition'. In an internal memo, the Gestapo clarified that, in contrast to the article in the *Times*, Niemöller had only been interviewed and released without charge.[2]

However, these police interrogations were not the end. On 22 January, the Gestapo had already classified the PEL as a 'melting pot of reactionary groups'. No less than 8,000 copies of the circular to Emergency League pastors mentioned in the previous chapter, in which Niemöller gave his version of the events at the chancellor's reception, were confiscated in a Berlin printing house.[3] There were also personal attacks on Niemöller. On the morning of 10 February, unknown persons threw a can filled with explosives into the hallway of the Dahlem parsonage. The explosion caused only minor damage. The search for the perpetrators was unsuccessful.[4] Niemöller also experienced very disturbing verbal abuses as 'liar' and 'agitator' by German Christian rioters at events of the Saxon Emergency League in April.[5]

Niemöller, who understood his work with the Young Reformers and the PEL as a contribution to the national awakening of 30 January 1933, was shocked by these experiences. His Dahlem sermons can serve as a seismograph for the extent of his shock. On 4 March, he held his easterly Passion sermon on Luke 22, 31–4, where Jesus predicts Peter's threefold denial before the crowing of the cock. Niemöller used this passage for a pessimistic retrospect of the church political developments from January 1933 onwards by comparing them with the persecution of the Christians in the Roman Empire. In view of this persecution, the general question arose in imitation of Christ: 'confessing or denying?'. Niemöller admitted the previous year had also brought some positives, namely 'some honest confession in word and deed'. But, he insisted, 'heroic Christianity'—a phrase frequently used by German Christians—was neither required nor called for, as Christ 'did not fall on the battlefield' but was 'crucified'. He did not die as a 'martyr' but 'a criminal against the state' (*Staatsverbrecher*). This was a gloomy metaphor in stark contrast to invoking 'the love of Christ', as Niemöller had concluded his Passion sermon in 1933.[6] The change in language mirrors the change in Niemöller's attitude towards the Nazi state.

Not only German Christian rioters and the Gestapo took drastic measures against Niemöller and the PEL after the church leaders' capitulation to the Reich bishop on 27 January 1934. The church leadership with Ludwig Müller at the top also applied repression. On 26 January, one day after the chancellor's reception, Müller, in his capacity as Old Prussian bishop, ordered the consistory to temporarily suspend Niemöller 'due to his untenable church political and state political attitude'.[7] A decree issued by Müller on the same day served as legal basis for this step. As Reich bishop, Müller granted himself—in his other capacity as bishop of the Old Prussian Church—the authority to issue orders to the EOK and all subordinate church authorities of the ApU. This would not be the last time that church authorities used circular decrees against Niemöller. To expand the legal basis for measures against the Dahlem pastor and his recalcitrant colleagues, Müller published two further decrees a few days later which allowed him to temporarily retire parish priests. This gave him a strong enough legal lever to put Niemöller into temporary retirement with effect from 1 March.[8]

The Dahlem parish council and 600 parishioners protested against these measures in separate resolutions, as did the PEL. Niemöller himself accused Müller in a letter that this step was a 'personal act of revenge' because the decree only applied to him. Niemöller strongly repudiated the suggestion that he did not 'guarantee to fully support the national state at any time', as a section of the decree claimed.[9] This is evidence that Niemöller continued to emphasize his national stance in the face of repression, claiming his church political opposition only referred to unpolitical, purely ecclesiastical issues. The means to do so were not uncontested. At a meeting of Emergency League pastors in March, Niemöller suggested joining the NSDAP collectively to thwart further measures by the state police.[10] These tactical manoeuvres prompted Dietrich Bonhoeffer to harshly criticize Niemöller in a letter to a Swiss friend in late April:

> Fantasists and naïves such as Niemöller still think they are true National Socialists—it might be a benevolent Providence that keeps them in their state of self-deception and it also might be in the interest of the church struggle—if there is anyone who is still interested in this church struggle anyway.[11]

However, Niemöller was not quite as naïve as Bonhoeffer suggested. He used uncompromising language when communicating with like-minded people rather than state or church authorities. This is demonstrated by his attitude at an open evening in his Dahlem parish on 27 March 1934. Here Niemöller explained that putting him in compulsory retirement was directed against him as 'Führer of the Pastors' Emergency League'—this choice of words shows the extent to which the language of the 'Führer' state had even penetrated the Church. Furthermore, he openly described the 'continuous acts of violence' against the Church, particularly the suspension and forced redeployment of several pastors. Regarding his own suspension, Niemöller—with his usual bluntness—took the view that he could 'simply keep on preaching' because no disciplinary proceedings had removed him from the clergy.[12] And thus, after a short break, Niemöller continued to preach and confirm, supported by the two other parish priests in Dahlem, as if nothing had happened.

The Dahlem parish responded with the same mixture of decisiveness and defiance when in late March the Berlin Consistory, backed by Ludwig Müller, started attempts to appoint Pastor Alexander Schaerffenberg as acting priest to replace Niemöller. During a telephone conversation Eberhard Röhricht unambiguously told Schaerffenberg that he was unwanted in the parish and did not need to come to Dahlem in the first place. The consistory regarded this 'open rebellion' with suspicion, particularly because the London *Times* had reported on Niemöller's suspension. But chief consistorial councillor Otto Gruhl could persuade neither Röhricht nor Superintendent Max Diestel to give in. Frustrated, he wrote in a marginal note: 'It will be fine.'[13] It was, however, not fine. Niemöller went on the offensive and filed a law suit against his own parish to enforce the continuation of his salary. On 5 July, the district court Berlin decided these civil proceedings in his favour and found the Reich bishop's decree from 26 January, which was the legal basis of all following decrees in this case, to be unconstitutional.[14] Niemöller skilfully used the opportunities offered by the judicial system of the National Socialist 'dual state' (Ernst Fraenkel). While the terrorist 'prerogative state' bypassed the rule of law, the 'normative state' remained largely intact.[15] As a result, measures of church leadership bodies could be successfully challenged in civil courts. The Dahlem parish must have seemed like an impregnable 'fortress' to Ludwig Müller and his subordinate church authorities.[16]

The controversies over Niemöller's temporary suspension attracted the attention of the international press. Apart from British newspapers, press outlets in Austria and Switzerland covered the Dahlem parish and its charismatic priest in detail. Even the American weekly *Literary Digest* reported on Niemöller.[17] For the Basel *National-Zeitung*, he embodied the 'free, composed, platitude-free, self-responsible German man'. He was, the newspaper wrote, 'famous' throughout the whole of Germany as 'the soul of the resistance of the free Church against state despotism'.[18] The liberal Viennese daily *Neue Freie Presse* tried to convey Niemöller's ambivalences to its readers. He 'unconditionally and unreservedly' recognized 'Adolf Hitler's worldly leadership'. Ultimately, Niemöller belonged to those Germans who had already 'paved the way' for the 'National Socialist revolution' before 1933. It was, therefore, 'particularly tragic' that he had 'fallen victim' himself. The newspaper correspondent noted many 'high-ranking officials' of the Nazi regime belonged to the Dahlem parish and many people in uniform participated in Niemöller's services. 'Needless to say that the parishioners welcome their shepherd with the Hitler salute, which he returns by putting his right arm high up.'[19] It cannot be stressed enough that the Dahlem parish was not a bastion of political resistance against the Nazi regime, but the centre of the opposition against state interference into church affairs.

The international press was not so much interested in Niemöller's well-known political ambivalences, but rather in his qualities as a preacher. 'Absolute propriety' was how a Viennese journalist summarized his impressions: 'properly parted dark hair, stand-up collar worn to the proper standards, proper posture, gesture, proper creases. Is the fire in his eyes also proper?' Niemöller was 'no Savonarola, no passionate monk, no angle with a flaming sword, but a Prussian confessor'.[20] The *Neue Zürcher Zeitung* reported how visitors of the Jesus Christ Church 'were crowded in the central aisle and on the stairs to the altar': 'The atmosphere of a strong sense of community and religious revival, which fills the light and unadorned church room on such days, can hardly be put into words.'[21]

In his sermon from 8 April 1934 to which the article referred, Niemöller defended Christian faith against the demand 'to adopt to the methods and laws of the world'. Many thought Christianity was 'the expression of a religion alienated from people and race, which had to be discarded' or which was only bearable if it 'corresponds with our German nature'. For these critics, Jesus 'must not have been a Jew'. That was a courageous and clear criticism of '*völkisch* religiosity', a German Christian current within the NSDAP that propagated the wholesale departure from Christian tradition in the name of a Germanic religiosity.[22] Since the Sportpalast scandal in November 1933, this movement increasingly took centre stage in Niemöller's apologetic efforts to defend Christianity. Even though it never had more than 30,000 organized members, it seemed clear to Niemöller that not only state interference, but the existence of Christianity itself was at stake.[23]

The reprisals in the wake of the chancellor's reception offered a taste of what was to come. With the capitulation of the church leaders on 27 January 1934, the contact between the PEL and the bishops of the intact regional churches was broken. The Württemberg section of the League was suspended. Several pastors, also from other parts of Germany, left the PEL and its membership swiftly declined to 5,500.[24] What was the church opposition supposed to do? Niemöller discussed this question in the journal *Junge Kirche*. He took it as evidence of the confusing situation that many urged the PEL to call for a 'church-leaving movement'.[25] Niemöller was aware that the 'struggle over church governance' he had started fighting for in June 1933 was over. But what was the alternative? Drifting off and becoming a 'sect' was not an option. Thus, Niemöller again voiced the idea of the gathering of true Christians 'from within the parishes', which he had first contemplated in 1933. This time, however, he connected this idea with blunt criticism of the unquestioned 'equalization of people and Church', which was traditionally at the core of the concept of a people's church (*Volkskirche*). Niemöller was convinced the time of this 'formation' was 'drawing to an end'.[26]

This was a deep rift in Niemöller's ecclesiological ideas, his thinking about the shape and substance of the Church. At the Inner Mission in Münster, the missionary activation of social strata alienated from the Church had been at the centre of his work. At that time, Niemöller was convinced that the Protestant Church could only provide moral orientation and stabilize the nation when it was a people's church that encompassed all social groups. In retrospect, he had to admit that this idea was dashed in 1933 precisely because the establishment of a national church was intended to place church life exclusively 'in the service of the people's formation [*Volksaufbau*]'. The *völkisch* utilization of the people's church had reduced this concept to absurdity.[27] Only few of those pastors and theologians who set up the Confessing Church in 1934, such as Franz Hildebrandt, promoted the establishment of a Free Church, equivalent to an association. The majority of the Confessing Church understood its structure, consisting of synods and councils of brethren which was implemented over the course of 1934, as a church with the status of a statuary body under public law, like the existing Protestant churches and the Catholic Church in Germany. However, this served the purpose of giving the Confessing Church legal legitimacy without claiming to represent all Protestant Christians. In Niemöller's eyes, a people's church without true confession was a 'hollow thing'.[28]

The 'gathering of Christians among Christians'—The Confessing Church

In February 1934, Niemöller spoke about the task of 'gathering Christians among Christians, the community within the community, the church within the church'.[29] This very much sounded like the separation of religious virtuosos from the masses of ordinary Christians who practised their faith only superficially. In a speech delivered in Barmen in March, Niemöller clarified his ideas about the reconstruction of the church from below. The outer appearance and leadership of the Church were 'not decisive', as long as it was not 'filled with life'. 'No church without community', this was his credo. The community did not live off the confession, but lived 'solely off the word'. A community that 'subordinates itself to the word' was a 'confessing community'. Niemöller pointed out that by now parishes in the west of Germany were starting to 'bestir' in this way and 'to act as a church'.[30]

Niemöller referred to developments that had started in parishes of the Rhineland in January and ultimately paved the way for the establishment of the Confessing Church. A Free Reformed synod in Barmen on 4 January with representatives of 167 Reformed parishes from the Rhineland broke the ground. This initiative corresponded with the Reformed tradition of building church from below, through presbyters and synodal structures. The synod adopted a declaration drafted by Karl Barth. The first article rejected the idea that 'alongside God's revelation, God's mercy, and God's honour' the 'high-handedness of man' was to determine 'the form of the Church'. In other words, Church was wherever God's revelation and His word were expressed in sermon and service. At the same time, the Reformed synodal members called on all Protestant Christians, whether Lutheran, Reformed, or United Protestants, to realize and emphasize the 'essential unity of their faith'. On 18 and 19 February another Free synod with pastors and laymen of 30 out of the 33 district synods of the Rhineland followed. It now included Lutheran, Reformed, and United Protestants. They adopted a resolution that called believers to resist DC-led church authorities and support parish priests who defended the confessional basis of the church. This made it obvious that the Confessing Church would remain within existing church structures, re-establishing them based on the confession.[31] This gave the confession a new function: no longer expression of 'a merely personal religious conviction', it was considered the 'sign of the Church' as in the sixteenth century.[32]

Martin Niemöller was one of the first to grasp the implications of these developments. At his proposal, on 20 February the Council of Brethren of the PEL decided to collectively join the new Rhenish synod. In a circular, it informed the Emergency League pastors this was 'the only still possible way of "church" action beyond individual parishes'. The League's pastors in other German regions were urged to join the Free synod. The hope was that groups throughout Germany would gather in a 'Free Evangelical National Synod'.[33] This was particularly urgent in the Old Prussian Church because the leadership of the DEK under Reich bishop Ludwig Müller was threatening the independence of the regional churches. The driving force was the Nazi lawyer August Jäger, who had briefly headed the ApU as state commissioner in summer 1933. With Müller's approval, he pursued a policy of coordination of the regional churches from early February 1934, using a simple trick: first Müller transferred the regional churches' powers to the Reich Church, subsequently appointing a new regional church leadership according to his will. In Prussia, this incorporation took place on 2 March. In the same vein, Jäger 'incorporated' 14 further regional churches into the centralized structure of the Reich Church during the following months.[34]

Again, the Emergency League was the first to respond to the incorporation of the Old Prussian Church. At Niemöller's initiative, the League planned the 'reconstruction' of the Church in Prussia through Free Synods as in the Rhineland. The DEK could 'no longer be considered a Church' in its 'visible form'. It was still unclear which legal form a reconstruction of church structures would take and what its position in relation to existing institutions would be. These problems were never completely solved during the further establishment of the Confessing Church. The Westphalian provincial synod resisted its dissolution through the DEK and constituted itself as Westphalian Confessing Synod on 16 March. As a result, two church leaderships, one German Christian, the other Confessing, existed in Westphalia. To support the latter, Praeses Karl Koch asked Confessing parishes and Councils of Brethren to transfer their church tax income to the escrow account of the Confessing Westphalian Church.[35] This was the first step towards parallel church structures, for Niemöller 'the most important church event since many months'.[36]

What was missing was the connection of Confessing forces in the north and west of Germany with the intact southern regional churches in Württemberg and Bavaria. After the debacle of the chancellor's reception, this connection was severed from both sides, by Bishops Wurm and Meiser and the Emergency League around Niemöller. On 13 March, Wurm and Meiser met with Hitler again, where they voiced their concerns about Jäger's incorporation policy. Hitler made it clear he would continue to support Ludwig Müller. On 12 April, Jäger was appointed to the Spiritual Ministry of the DEK as 'Rechtswalter' (authorized administrator) and could continue his policy of compulsory incorporation of all regional churches. First, he took action against the Württemberg church and its Bishop Wurm. But Jäger failed, as his actions triggered a broad wave of solidarity with the bishop in the parishes of Württemberg. One day before Jäger's inauguration on 11 April, representatives of Confessing groups from north and south Germany met in Nuremberg and established a 'Nuremberg Committee'. Immediately after Jäger's attack on Wurm, Meiser convened the Nuremberg Committee, this time in Munich. Niemöller was also invited to this meeting. He and Meiser reconciled in Meiser's apartment on the evening of 17 April.[37]

Hugo Hahn, a Dresden pastor who was also invited to Munich, suggested holding a large-scale joint rally of the newly constituted Confessing community in Ulm Minster on 22 April, where Wurm was already scheduled to preach. On 22 April, Meiser read out the 'Ulm declaration' in front of an audience of 5,000 people. Niemöller was not present because he had left Munich to go on holiday. In this first foundational document of the Confessing Church, Confessing groups and regional churches throughout Germany declared to be 'the legitimate Protestant Church of Germany'. A young Lutheran pastor, Hans Asmussen from Hamburg-Altona, had contributed this phrase. The Nuremberg Committee then decided to meet this high expectation by convening a German Confessing synod, scheduled in Barmen from 29 to 31 May.

Niemöller arrived in Wuppertal-Barmen on 28 May. The other two Dahlem priests, Müller and Röhricht, were also among the 138 synod delegates eligible to vote—83 pastors or theologians and 55 laymen—who represented 18 regional churches. Franz Hildebrandt and other representatives of the Emergency League were among the 200 guests in Barmen. On 29 May, Niemöller started his day at 10 a.m. Before the start of the Confessing synod of the DEK, a Confessing synod of the Old Prussian Church convened. For Niemöller this meant 'work through the whole day'. But the result was satisfying: 'very good! [...] 2 resolutions!' was his conclusion.[38] As we will see below, the two resolutions of the Old Prussian synod even exceeded what the Confessing synod of the DEK in Barmen decided. The latter was opened with a service on the evening of 29 May. A 'Lutheran convent' convened by the Munich Bishop Hans Meiser followed, whose deliberations Niemöller found extremely 'difficult'.[39] The details of these discussions were not recorded, but the participants apparently engaged in heated debates. This separate convent was necessary because Meiser and other Lutherans still had reservations against the draft of a theological declaration that Karl Barth, Hans Asmussen, and the Lutheran member of the Bavarian High Consistory Thomas Breit had prepared.[40]

The concerns of the Lutherans were important because they marked a potential rift in the Confessing Church that opened not long after the synod. At the Kassel meeting on 7 May, Meiser had already voiced his concerns against the plan to adopt a joint confession in Barmen. Like other Lutherans, he feared their confessional identity, traditionally based on Lutheran confessional sixteenth-century texts, would be watered down, particularly under the influence of the Reformed theologian Barth. Niemöller respected the reservations of the Lutherans from southern Germany against a 'single confession' (*Einheitsbekenntnis*) in the run-up to Barmen. But it seems that this line of argument, repeated on the evening of 29 May, no longer convinced him.[41] Thus, it was decided to appoint a small committee of Lutherans that would discuss the draft until the early morning. The next day, Asmussen would explain the declaration at the plenary meeting of the delegates, and it would only be adopted in conjunction with his explanations. Subsequently, separate meetings of the Lutheran and Reformed convents took place. Pastor Friedrich Graeber from Essen criticized this procedure, arguing that theological 'truths' could not be decided 'like in a joint stock company'.[42] Niemöller was right when he commented on the deliberations of the first day in

Fig. 7 The three Dahlem pastors Martin Niemöller, Friedrich Müller, and Franz Hildebrandt at the Confessing synod of the DEK in Barmen, May 1934. ekir.de/ Archiv/Susanne Pfannschmidt.

his diary: 'far reaching consensus'.[43] Only the Lutheran theologian Hermann Sasse refused to join this consensus. He left Barmen even before the final plenary sessions started, 'solemnly' voicing his protest 'against the violation of the Protestant Lutheran Church' in writing to the president of the synod, Praeses Karl Koch (Fig. 7).[44]

Niemöller intervened only briefly in the plenary sessions of the synod. He was clearly more interested in the practical consequences of the resolution for the pastors of the Emergency League. 'Who decides on the principles of how to exercise pastorhood? Who initiates the selection of pastors?'[45] In Barmen, Niemöller waited in vain for answers to his questions. But this did not matter. The 'real highlight of the entire conference' was the moment when five representatives of the different confessional groups—from Lutheran, Reformed, and United Churches—voiced their approval of the final version of the Theological Declaration. Karl Koch subsequently called for a vote: 'Adoption of the

Declaration.—Unanimously!', Niemöller recorded in his diary.[46] In a newspaper article published a few weeks later, he explained that the Theological Declaration did not aim to 'blur the boundaries between the different confessions' or even create a 'new version'. Rather, its purpose was to 'give coherent answers' to the pressing problems of the Church.[47] Niemöller referred to the preamble of the Declaration that explicitly stated 'we want to be and remain true to our different confessions' while it remained open 'what this might mean for the relationship between the Confessing churches among themselves'.[48]

The Theological Declaration of the Barmen Synod

Niemöller referred to the Theological Declaration, consisting of a preamble and six articles, as a confession in an emphatic manner and as the foundation of a new church community only some time after the Barmen synod. In an article written in 1936, he described confessing as the actualization of the Christian message, which 'inevitably entails an either-or: mercy or God's judgment!' In Barmen, he stated, the synod had vehemently rejected the opinion that alongside God's revelation 'other sanctuaries such as race, blood, and soil' existed, which had started to permeate the Church in 1933. And precisely in this context the Barmen Declaration was a 'confession': it caused 'the separation' between confessors and their opponents as well as between 'doctrine' and 'false doctrine'. The 'new community of believing and confessing' founded in Barmen was the 'Confessing Church'.[49] With this, Niemöller referred to the first thesis of the Theological Declaration:

> Jesus Christ, as he is attested for us in Holy Scripture, is the one word of God which we have to hear and which we have to trust and obey in life and in death. We reject the false doctrine that the Church could and would have to acknowledge as a source of its proclamation, beyond and besides this one Word of God, yet other events and powers, figures and truths, as God's revelation.[50]

Hans Asmussen emphasized this thesis at the Barmen synod: as rejection of the German Christians' claim to consider 'the events of 1933 as binding for the proclamation and interpretation of the Gospel', thus placing *Volkstum* as a further source of revelation alongside God's word. Asmussen clarified that the synod members by no means protested 'against the new state as citizens', but against 'the development which has gradually paved the way for the devastation of the Church for more than 200 years'. Thus, he also criticized theological liberalism, historicism, and Cultural Protestantism, which in his eyes had placed 'reason, culture, aesthetic sensibility' as sources of faith alongside the Holy Scripture.[51]

This justification of the first Barmen thesis was and is controversial. Niemöller most likely agreed with the critique of liberal theology.[52] But it is fair to assume he primarily understood the thesis as a powerful restating of the three principles of the Reformation—solus Christus, sola scriptura, and sola fide (solely through Christ, Scripture, and faith).[53] The second Barmen thesis, according to which Jesus Christ was 'God's mighty claim upon our entire life', was essentially the confirmation of a position that Niemöller himself had often advocated: men could 'never and nowhere' escape from God's 'claim', and this constituted the limits of all other claims, both political and ethical.[54] Clearly, Barmen remained a profoundly formative experience for Niemöller. His commitment to the Confessing Church was always a fight for the Theological Declaration and its first article. In a letter to Karl Barth from 1966, Niemöller emphasized the significance of the Barmen synod:

> [In 1933,] theology ceased to be a thinking theory and theoretical thinking. What happened in Barmen was life and a true event; and from then on, the first Barmen thesis has not only been hanging on the wall, framed and under glass, in my study, reminding me of a church political event that I witnessed. It has, from then on, determined my thoughts and my life and filled my work.—Since then I know that I, albeit late but still irrevocably, have become and still am your student. Thank you and thank God, our Lord, that it turned out this way.[55]

Barmen constituted the Confessing forces as the rightful Church. At the same time, the Confessing synod had no intention of replacing the National Synod and set up a new church authority that competed with the Reich bishop and Reich church leadership bodies. It settled for constituting the Nuremberg Committee, which had prepared the synod, as a Reich Council of Brethren (Reichsbruderrat) with the task of continuing deliberations on the Barmen resolution. In addition, a permanent representation of the Confessing Church was based in Bad Oeynhausen, Westphalia, with Praeses Karl Koch, as well as Hans Asmussen and Eberhard Fiedler as advisors, dealing with day-to-day administrative tasks.[56]

How the claim to gather the members of the Confessing Church should be put into practice remained unclear on 30 and 31 May. The delegates of the synod of the DEK were not willing to 'deviate from positive law' as the Reich church governance under Ludwig Müller was still formally head of the Church. In contrast, the Confessing synod of the Old Prussian Church, which was in session in Barmen on 29 May immediately before that of the DEK, took a different course of action. With recourse to an 'interim law', which was later specified as an 'emergency law', the Prussian synod claimed to represent the rightful Church even in places where Confessing parishes were a minority. On this basis, they started setting up synod structures, ranging from the parish level, to the district and provincial level, to a Confessing synod of the ApU, a regional Council of

Brethren and a permanent committee for administrative matters. At the same time, parishes were called on to pay 10 per cent of church taxes as levy to the Confessing Church. In a separate resolution, the synod stated all decrees and laws issued by German Christian church leadership bodies from the 23 July 1933 church elections onwards were rendered invalid.[57]

Niemöller flagged these two resolutions as 'very good' in his diary on 29 May. He had authored the drafts for the Old Prussian Confessing synod. In the weeks after the Barmen synod, Niemöller repeatedly urged the Old Prussian Council of Brethren to put the resolutions into practice. He met some resistance in the process, causing 'great disappointment'. It was not before 5 July that the Council of Brethren decided to establish two theological seminaries, issued regulations for the ordinations of pastors of the Confessing Church and set up offices in Bad Oeynhausen and in Berlin. The Council also adopted the wording of a pledge for ordinary parishioners. Soon afterwards, the Dahlem parish, like other parishes throughout Germany, started to give out so-called 'red cards' to members of the Confessing Church.[58]

Niemöller had been at the vanguard of the church struggle while normal business in the Dahlem parish continued. He had to preach and give confirmation classes, tasks he carried out with great care. The parsonage in Cecilienallee 61 was much more than a family home. Even after Praeses Karl Koch's office in Bad Oeynhausen had taken over the administrative leadership of the Confessing Church in spring 1934, Dahlem remained the real nerve centre of the church struggle. Franz Hildebrandt has vividly described what this meant for Niemöller and his family:

> Everyone who is visiting this house for the first time immediately senses the tension and restlessness: in all rooms are people waiting, doorbell and telephone are ringing constantly, office and children's noise pervades the walls, and 'he' is only ever visible between two or three things that have to be done at the same time, and then for only a few moments. [...] At 9 am the secretary arrives to take dictation of the letters, this goes on for half of the morning and is interrupted by telephone calls and consultation visitors; around midday he hurries into the city to attend the next meeting of pastors or the Council of Brethren, which has usually already started in the morning and where Niemöller is eagerly awaited. [...] If he can stay at home for once, he never goes to bed before midnight as there are meetings, night gatherings or friends visiting scheduled. [...] He never has the chance to sit still, and indeed he is not cut out for it. [... An] important part of the church struggle happens in the hundreds of local and long-distance calls that Niemöller holds and whose tone is well-known by friend and foe just as that of his letters.[59]

Despite the hustle and bustle, Niemöller was not inclined to delegate his tasks. From summer 1933 onwards, only his 'adjutant' Ernst Eisenhardt assisted him.

An old navy comrade from the Crew 1902 who lived in Dahlem, retired Frigate Captain Martin Schulze, initially helped with administrative tasks of the Pastors' Emergency League. When he stopped in this job in early 1934, Franz Hildebrandt stepped in. From his own, probably sometimes painful, experience he concluded 'a calm assistant' was 'the best one', given Niemöller's 'explosive temper'.[60] Martin and Else Niemöller had only very few moments of rest together. There were occasional visits to the cinema, at the Ufa Palace or the Titania Palace in Steglitz, with its programme following the Nazi party line. Both Martin and Else preferred the light—and shallow—entertainment of Nazi mass culture. They watched, for example, the operetta movie *I liked Kissing Women* (*Gern hab ich die Frau'n geküßt*) with Theo Lingen as one of the main characters or the comedy *Love and the First Railway* (*Die Liebe und die erste Eisenbahn*).[61]

On 21 July 1934, the Niemöller family went to the Baltic Sea spa Zinnowitz on the island Usedom for their summer vacation. But even here, Niemöller could not get away from the church struggle. He immediately started drafting his partial biography *From U-Boat to Pulpit*. On 16 August, he completed the manuscript. Three days later, the family returned to Dahlem. Niemöller could finish the book in such a short time because he had developed the narrative since his student days in Münster. Niemöller's publisher, Martin Warneck, and members of his family had urged him to write down his U-boat experiences. This should demonstrate that the Confessing Church was as committed to the nation as the Nazis—despite allegations to the contrary on the part of the German Christians and the Nazi press.[62]

Niemöller's account is marked by a narrative of duty and is deeply entrenched in the Reich nationalism of Wilhelmine Germany. Only the last sentence of the book refers to the situation in the 'Third Reich'. Here, Niemöller emphasized the necessary service of the Church to the Word of God so 'that the great work of unifying and elevating' our people, 'which we have begun, should receive a sure foundation and a lasting stability'.[63] By the end of 1934, 60,000 copies had been sold. The reception in Germany, focusing on the central motif of fighting for the nation, was positive. Reviewers highlighted that Niemöller had selflessly placed himself at the service of the nation as a navy officer in 1914, of which he gave a true account in his book (Fig. 8). Even the Gestapo appreciated the nationalist attitude of the author: 'The content of the book itself cannot be found fault with.' With these lapidary words, the Gestapo censorship office still acknowledged Niemöller's life story in September 1938—after he was sent to Sachsenhausen concentration camp. Initially, the authorities abstained from prohibiting the book. It was not before 5 September 1940 that the Reich Ministry of Public Enlightenment and Propaganda banned the dissemination of Niemöller's book, most likely on direct order of Joseph Goebbels.[64]

While Niemöller explicitly emphasized his national allegiance in the book, the Confessing Church did not protest against the terrorism and brutality of the Nazi

Fig. 8 Martin Niemöller, here in 1917 in the officer uniform of the Imperial Navy with the Iron Cross and other badges of honour on his chest, boldly and proudly looking into the camera. Niemöller used this photo as the frontispiece of his 1934 memoirs *From U-Boat to Pulpit*. The note in Niemöller's own handwriting states that the photo shows him as a 'First Lieutenant at sea'. The use of the photo intends to emphasize his commitment to the German nation as the core of his life's work by focusing on his military service in the First World War. Martin Niemöller, *Vom U-Boot zur Kanzel* (Berlin, 1934), frontispiece.

regime. There would have been an opportunity to do so on 2 July 1934, when the 15 members of the Reich Council of Brethren, inaugurated at the Barmen synod, met in Würzburg for the second time. Members of the Westphalian church had urged to send Hitler a telegram congratulating him on the killing of the SA leader Ernst Röhm and other politicians, including the former Chancellor Kurt von Schleicher. At least, Hans Asmussen rejected this request, referring to the basic principle stated in Romans 13 that Christians owe obedience to the authorities and stating that the Confessing Church would abstain from domestic political statements. It goes without saying that, on this basis, it was futile to expect criticism of the brutal killing of the SA leadership. Apparently, Niemöller was shocked by the 'alarming news' that reached him on 30 June.[65] But when he suggested that the Church should 'say a grave word of atonement as response to the situation' at the meeting of the Brethren Council on 2 July, he only referred to the church political situation.[66]

When he criticized state intervention in church matters, Niemöller usually found clear words. In early 1934, he voiced sharp protest to the official in the Interior Ministry responsible for church matters, Rudolf Buttmann, against a decree that prohibited all public deliberations of the church struggle except for declarations of the Reich bishop. His tone became increasingly critical when he was interrogated by two Gestapo officers on 14 August during his holidays in Zinnowitz. The reason for this interview was a pulpit declaration of the Reich Council of Brethren from 12 August, directed against Ludwig Müller's and August Jäger's integration politics at the national synod of the DEK on 9 August. Only a few delegates of the Confessing Church were present at this synod.[67] In his letter to Buttmann, Niemöller harshly criticized the 'persecutions of Christians' by Müller and the Reich church leadership and the 'false account' on the church political situation by August Jäger. The Confessing Church would continue to 'loyally obey' orders of the worldly 'authorities', 'even by sacrifice of life. And these are not empty words.' From today's perspective, this might sound like hollow pathos. But we must bear in mind that Niemöller decided to volunteer for military service in the Wehrmacht in September 1939. Niemöller urged Buttmann, and the state in general, to deal with 'the dynamics of church matters' and intervene. The Confessing forces would certainly not be able to 'be silent' if the Church 'was ruled by Satan and this Satan calls himself Christ'.[68]

Niemöller had good reasons to employ such dramatic rhetoric. In late summer 1934, the Confessing Church's fate was 'on a knife's edge'.[69] After the coordination of the national synod on 9 August, Bavaria and Württemberg were the only Protestant regional churches that August Jäger as *Rechtswalter* of the DEK had not yet robbed of their independence. On 3 September, he issued a decree that also placed these two churches under the leadership of Reich bishop Müller. Theophil Wurm protested and called on the pastors in Württemberg to support him. Jäger and his entourage visited the Stuttgart church office on 8 and 14 September, declaring Wurm to be disposed. On 6 October, Wurm was placed under house arrest to break the resistance. The campaign against the Bavarian Bishop Meiser started with a rally on 17 September and articles in the Franconian dailies. On 11 October, Jäger arrived in Munich to depose the Bavarian bishop, who was placed under house arrest the next day. A wave of public protests in solidarity with the pressurized bishops swept through Württemberg and Bavaria. On 20 October, the Bavarian Minister President had to inform Berlin that a delegation of 15 NSDAP members on behalf of 60,000 Franconian farmers had reported 'a rebellion' which would only be stopped by releasing and reinstating Meiser immediately.[70]

The Confessing Church did not hesitate to support the two southern German bishops in their struggle against these unlawful dismissals. At a meeting of the

Reich Council of Brethren on 18 September, Niemöller and two other members drafted a declaration that was read out from the pulpits on 23 September. Here, the Council of Brethren postulated that through their actions the members of the Reich church leadership around Ludwig Müller had excluded themselves from the church community.[71] For Niemöller, the events in Bavaria and Württemberg were further proof that the Confessing Church had to organizationally dissociate itself from the existing church leadership structures, not only in Prussia, where this process had already started in the wake of the Barmen synod, but throughout the whole of Germany. On 17 July at a meeting of the Reich Council of Brethren, he had demanded that 'we have no longer anything to do with this Reich Church [...] We must accuse the Reich church leadership of deliberate dishonesty in front of the church community. We must abandon the church-bourgeois attitude. In this respect, one should also confront the state authorities.'[72]

At this point—that is, before the campaigns against Meiser and Wurm—Niemöller's main concern was that a 'formation of a middle group from the circle of non-combatants' would be on the cards.[73] Niemöller was thinking of those Lutherans who, soon after the Barmen synod, expressed criticism of its Theological Declaration and emphasized their separate confessional identity. The initial step was the so-called *Ansbacher Ratschlag* (Ansbacher Counsel) from 11 June, a declaration of eight theologians, among them Paul Althaus, who was known for his recent antisemitic statements. It argued against the revelation theology of the Barmen theses, instead highlighting natural orders of creation such as people, family, and state. Erlangen-based theologian Werner Elert, the driving force behind the '*Ansbacher Anschlag* (attack)'—as the Confessing Church mocked—expressed confessional objections. Lutheran theologians and church leaders were concerned that, in the wake of Barmen, confessional differences between Lutherans and Reformed were levelled and replaced by a union theology designed by the Reformed theologian Karl Barth. Many influential Lutherans shared this concern: from Marahrens, Meiser, and Niemöller's former superior, the Westphalian General Superintendent Wilhelm Zoellner, to Friedrich Bodelschwingh.[74]

The theological differences amplified diverging interests. Prior to August Jäger's intervention, the intact south German regional churches in Württemberg and Bavaria were not interested in setting up separate Confessing Church structures as they would weaken their functioning church leadership. Furthermore, some destroyed regional churches were discontent with Niemöller and the PEL. A statement by the Saxon Superintendent Arno Spranger, who was initially an active DC member and switched to the church political centre in 1934, is indicative of this discontent. He accused the Emergency League of fighting a mere 'negative' battle against the Reich bishop and his church leadership. In Saxony, he explained, the 'Lutheran character' of the Church was to be preserved and deepened, establishing a 'joint labour front' beyond 'all church political camps'.[75]

Spranger—and with him many Lutherans outside the Old Prussian Union—hoped to end the internal church conflict along those lines. To voice their concerns, senior Lutherans gathered for a meeting in Hanover on 24 and 25 August, chaired by the Hanoverian Bishop Marahrens. To consolidate their joint interests, they established a Lutheran Council, with the bishops of the three still intact Lutheran regional churches and representatives of theological departments and associations as members. The meeting culminated in complaints about the Barmen synod and the levelling of confessional differences that had been allegedly concluded there.[76] This gathering of Lutherans and centrist groups not directly involved in the church struggle opened up a fissure that would ultimately result in the split of the Confessing Church.

The Dahlem Synod and the Implementation of Church Emergency Law

All these problems—the quarrels over the Barmen synod as well as August Jäger's attacks on the Bishops Wurm and Meiser—convinced the Reich Council of Brethren to prepare a new Confessing synod. After the plan had initially been postponed in September, the Council decided on 10 October to convene a synod at the end of the month. When a cry for help from Munich, where Jäger disposed Bishop Meiser on 11 October, reached the Council of Brethren, they moved the synod forward by 10 days. Only very little time remained for preparation. The second Confessing synod of the DEK took place in the community hall of the Dahlem parish on 19 and 20 October 1934. Niemöller's parish was yet again a central site of the church struggle. Unlike at Barmen, Niemöller had a strong presence during the debates of the Dahlem synod. He often took the floor and made detailed contributions; he was emotionally deeply involved and pulled out all the stops rhetorically. When he urged the delegates to find clarifying words on the 'emergency of the Church' and the need of an 'emergency law' because anything else would be a 'denial of Christ our Lord', the minutes recorded 'continuous applause'.[77] The theological 'message' of the Dahlem synod was influenced by the destruction of the hitherto intact regional churches of Bavaria and Württemberg that had just happened. Against this backdrop, Niemöller urged for a 'complete break' with German Christian church leadership bodies and thus for the consequent separation from existing ecclesiastical structures.[78]

The third part of the declaration adopted in Dahlem executed this break. The synod declared the DEK leadership had been passed over from Ludwig Müller to the Confessing synod. In doing so, the synod implemented the same church emergency law for the whole of Germany that the Old Prussian synod had adopted in Barmen for Prussia only. This part of the declaration was highly controversial. Some of the delegates voiced the same concerns as the Lutherans.

They demanded the newly established leadership bodies of the Confessing Church—the Reich Council of Brethren, now expanded to 22 members, and a six-member council responsible for dealing with ongoing questions—should be structured along confessional lines, with a proportional presence of Lutherans, Reformed and United representatives. Others rejected the termination of all contacts with the church leadership under Müller as practically impossible. Niemöller confronted them head-on. 'They cannot circumvent to say the word, to show disobedience towards a regiment which is that of the devil, to take it seriously, up to their fingertips and to the construction of community houses and the submitting of statistical forms.' Even the joint reading of the Gospel with German Christians was, he formulated sharply, 'spiritual adultery'.[79] Not least owing to Niemöller's emotional intervention, the delegates approved the more decisive statement of the Reich Council of Brethren.

Church historian Klaus Scholder has identified a 'weakness' of the Dahlem synod. This weakness, he argued, became apparent when only 52 members of the synod voted in favour of the third sentence in the third paragraph of the message's final draft. This meant only one third of the delegates supported the radical separation from the existing church leadership. Furthermore, Scholder explains, adopting the majority resolution violated the 'fundamental principle of a church order based on councils of brethren and synods' that decisions had to be unanimously. As a result, Dahlem had become a 'heavy burden' for the unity of the Confessing Church.[80] In this perspective, Niemöller was the driving force behind a development that ultimately led to the self-destruction of the Confessing Church. Contrary to this I argue practical reasons caused problems during this election. It took place on Saturday, the second day of the synod, when only 72 of the altogether 143 synod delegates were still present. Many delegates from the south of Germany had already left. This allows their priorities to be queried, particularly because it had been the Bavarian cry for help that led to the synod being hastily moved forward.[81] And even though it is true that the Dahlem resolutions weighed on some Lutherans' conscience—their confessional separation had become apparent much earlier. It was the Lutherans' criticism of the decisions made in Barmen that ultimately resulted in the split of the Confessing Church in 1936.

However, another important factor in this process was the Nazi state—namely Adolf Hitler. As early as summer 1934, the bodies of the emerging ecumenical movement intervened in favour of the Confessing Church. In late August, the meeting of the ecumenical World Council for Practical Christianity in Fanö, Denmark, adopted a resolution that condemned the restriction of church freedom in Germany. From late June onwards, Foreign Minister Konstantin von Neurath repeatedly pointed out to Hitler that August Jäger's ruthless regime in the DEK put a strain on foreign relations, particularly with the United Kingdom. However, concerns over a legal humiliation, rather than foreign policy considerations, ultimately tipped the scales of Hitler's decision. On 24 October, Reich Minister of Justice Franz Gürtner, informed the chancellor about an appeal that the Dahlem parish had initiated against the decision of the Berlin District Court from 5 July 1934. As mentioned above, the District Court had rescinded Niemöller's dismissal from late January and declared Müller's decree from 26 January on the 'unified leadership' of the ApU unconstitutional. The Dahlem parish had subsequently lodged an appeal at the Reich Court to obtain a confirmation by the Supreme Court of this legal criticism of Ludwig Müller.[82]

On 24 October, Gürtner informed Hitler that the Reich Court would declare the Reich bishop's decree unlawful. Hitler decided to perform a U-turn in church policy. He cancelled his appearance at Müller's official inauguration as Reich bishop scheduled for the next day. And he urged the Munich authorities to repeal Bishop Meiser's house arrest. Pressured by state authorities and some German Christian church leaders, August Jäger resigned as *Rechtswalter* of the DEK on 26 October, and from his state and party offices three days later.[83] His policy of forcibly integrating the regional churches into the DEK had failed. This, however, did not mean Hitler would drop Ludwig Müller as Reich bishop or dissociate himself from the German Christians. He conveyed this to Meiser and Wurm, who had just been released from house arrest, at a reception of the two bishops and Bishop Marahrens in the Reich Chancellery on 30 October. After the meeting with Hitler, the three bishops of the intact churches advocated a temporary solution to the church leadership problem. With August Marahrens in mind, they proposed a *Reichskirchenverweser*, an administrator who should restructure the Church in consultation with the state authorities. Niemöller remained sceptical that the state would recognize the Confessing Church. He insisted on the validity of the Dahlem synod resolutions. If someone was to be temporarily appointed as *Reichskirchenverweser*, it could, in Niemöller's view, only be Praeses Koch, who, unlike Marahrens, enjoyed Niemöller's trust.[84]

Thomas Breit, Meiser's deputy, drafted a proposal for an emergency church governance structure with Hermann Beyer, Julius Schniewind, and Friedrich Schumann—all professors of theology. He followed ideas of the Justice and Interior Ministries that Praeses Koch had discussed with Gürtner. At a meeting of the Reich Council of Brethren in Dahlem on 9 November, the debate on this proposal ended in a confrontation between the Lutheran bishops, represented by Meiser, and the Prussian supporters of the course decided at the Dahlem synod, among them Niemöller as well as the young Reformed theologian Karl Immer, Paul Humburg, and Karl Lücking from Westphalia. Niemöller was angry and agitated. He flatly refused 'to listen to some professors who were German Christians half a year ago'. With this he referred to Schumann, who had only left the German Christians after the Sportpalast rally in November 1933, and Beyer, who at that time was a United minister in Müller's second Reich church cabinet. In Niemöller's eyes the situation was crystal clear: 'There is a legitimate system of church governance: it has been introduced at the Dahlem synod.' In the gloomy tone that, from 1934, would become characteristic for him he added: 'If we deviate from Dahlem, we are heading for the abyss.' Hans Meiser vehemently contradicted him. If Niemöller defined the Church as identical with the Confessing synod, Meiser argued, 'there is a danger of turning it into a sect'. He furthermore refused to accept that 'whoever wants to belong with us must sign the Theological Declaration [of Barmen] and that his assurance he is true to the confession is not enough'. Heinrich Kloppenburg, senior member of the Pastors' Emergency League and the Confessing Church in Oldenburg, had nothing but scorn and derision for Meiser. What qualified as confession in Bavaria—only the 'sola fide' and 'sola gratia', he mocked—'the German Christians in the North offer with pleasure'.[85]

At this meeting, various conflicts surfaced, including differences about the right tactic to restore 'constitutional conditions' (Meiser) in Bavaria and Württemberg. From his point of view, the resolutions of the Dahlem synod were already outdated three weeks after they had been adopted. Meiser also voiced his objections to the Barmen Declaration. In addition, the Lutherans were eager to find a broad basis for the new structure of the Church. A 'people's Church', Wilhelm Pressel explained, was to encompass 'everyone', even those who were not openly committed to Barmen. A vast gulf separated south German Lutherans from the Dahlemite wing of the Confessing Church around Niemöller. Asmussen's attempt at compromise failed, even though Niemöller was willing to meet the other side half-way. He would have agreed on the establishment of a temporary church leadership body, as long as it was in Koch's hands. Eventually, the members of the Council of Brethren left the meeting after 10 hours in the early evening of 9 November, without understanding the other side, let alone having reached a tangible result.[86]

After the meeting failed to reach an agreement, the members parted ways.[87] The same evening, Niemöller, Praeses Koch, and Gerhard Jacobi spoke in front of an audience of 15,000 in the exhibition halls at the Radio Tower Berlin. Niemöller denied a 'split of the Confessing Church', although the writing had been on the wall earlier the same day. He polemicized against the attempt to strike a 'cheap compromise' between the conflicting parties. 'No compromise, no half measures. All for the Confessing community', was his credo.[88]

This event was only one of several mass rallies in major German cities where Niemöller propagated the Confessing Church.[89] Through his appearances, he defied a decree of Minister of the Interior Frick, who had banned all publications and public statements about the situation of the Protestant Church on 6 November. Ludwig Müller, on the other hand, could still spread his 'lies among the people', as Niemöller protested in strong terms, implying Frick.[90] Meanwhile, the bishops of the three intact regional churches met with the regional bishop of Baden, Kühlewein, and some theologians to prepare a temporary church leadership body. On 20 November, Ludwig Müller rescinded the decree on the incorporation of the ApU. The majority of the Council of Brethren consented to these plans, and the way was clear for the reorganization. On 22 November, Praeses Koch signed the agreement on the establishment of a Temporary Church Leadership (Vorläufige Kirchenleitung, VKL) with five members headed by August Marahrens. This agreement was the result of a deal between the Reich Council of Brethren and the three intact regional churches. The VKL was meant to follow the spirit of the Barmen and Dahlem synods in its task of reorganizing church matters, while simultaneously abiding by the provisions of the Reich Church constitution of 11 July 1933. Until the convening of a new national synod—which ultimately never happened—the Reich Council of Brethren represented the synodal element within the DEK.[91]

From the perspective of the proponents—among them Praeses Koch, who joined the VKL—this was a necessary compromise. It had become inevitable, they argued, after the two south German churches returned into the hands of their legitimate bishops. Given the concerns about the Dahlem declaration, it did not seem right to put churches that were intact under the control of the Council of Brethren, which was only legitimized by emergency law. There were also confessional worries, formulated by the Lutheran theologian Walther Künneth in a memorandum from early November. In his view, the Reich Council of Brethren was dominated by a majority of Reformed and United representatives. The VKL, on the other hand, consisted of one Reformed, one United, and one Lutheran theologian under the leadership of the Lutheran Marahrens, which much better represented the confessional interests of Lutheranism.[92]

Niemöller was not convinced by this line of argument. Jointly with the Reformed theologians Karl Barth, Karl Immer, and Hermann Albert Hesse, he left the Reich Council of Brethren after it had agreed to the establishment of the VKL. As he explained to his former university teacher, Georg Wehrung—who was professor in Tübingen at the time—he by no means started a 'fight' against the VKL. He was willing to 'give it [the VKL] a chance', but did not want to take 'responsibility' for its course. He had learned 'the bitter lesson' from the chancellor's reception in January that first one must devise an 'unerring course' and then establish a 'broad church front'. In his view, it looked 'like restoration' that Mahrarens chaired the VKL.[93] Niemöller and his Reformed friends considered the Hanover bishop untenable because he neither supported the Confessing community nor had joined the Confessing synods—apart from a matins in Barmen that concluded with a profession of faith to the 'Führer'. It was even worse that Marahrens was nominated as head of the VKL due to pressure by the state authorities. This was diametrically opposed to the resolution adopted in Dahlem, according to which only the Church was to decide about its own internal affairs.[94]

By the end of the year, Niemöller and Barth, who both rejected the VKL and Marahrens as a person, came into closer contact. Only now their close cooperation began, which would shape the work of the Dahlemite wing of the Confessing Church. Barth made the first move by writing to Niemöller. He assured Niemöller that he had 'always liked him', despite their previous conflicts. Now he was delighted to 'be on the same side' as Niemöller. The Swiss theologian regarded the 'system of Marahrens' as 'representative of a secret secularism'. Particularly 'unedifying' in Barth's eyes was that his and Niemöller's position in the Council of Brethren 'was always referred to as the "Reformed" view'. Criticizing the efforts of the Lutherans for proportional representation, Barth was convinced 'that we are not making any headway with this confessionalism today, just as we did not with unionism during the time of the pre-revolutionary Church'.[95] Niemöller emphatically agreed and voiced his 'delight' that he would stand 'closely' together with Barth and Asmussen in future church political struggles, and promised to coordinate with them on a regular basis.[96]

Over the course of 1933, Niemöller's church political actions were marked by ambivalences, because he approved of the Nazi project of the people's community, but also because he believed he could convince Reich bishop Ludwig Müller to recognize the church opposition. Following the debacle of the chancellor's reception, Niemöller entered church politics in 1934 rather disillusioned and more decisive. He now adopted the view, already previously held by Karl Barth, that the church opposition had to be considered the true Protestant Church. And he defended this position tooth and nail against all those in the Confessing front who expected it would benefit from the integration of previously neutral Protestants and former German Christians. When the Barmen synod established a programmatic basis for the Confessing Church, Niemöller immediately seized the opportunity. Not only did he use the Barmen theses to establish the Confessing Church in the Old Prussian Union, but he also defended the declaration against its Lutheran critics. In his opposition to the Lutherans, he made a fault line visible that ultimately resulted in the split of the Confessing Church. From our current viewpoint, the events of 1934 mark the enduring historical significance of Niemöller's work in the Confessing Church. He resolutely advocated the Barmen theses against his own Lutheran instincts. Nowadays, the Barmen Declaration is an important confessional capstone of Protestantism in the Federal Republic.

10

The Split of the Confessing Church
1935–1936

The conflicts that led to the split of the Confessing Church had already become visible at the lengthy meeting of the Reich Council of Brethren on 9 November 1934. The representatives of the intact regional churches around the Bishops Wurm and Meiser distanced themselves from the resolutions of the Dahlem synod and were not willing to adopt the structure of the Confessing Church in their bishoprics. They were, however, interested in a separate gathering of the Lutherans. For Niemöller and his mostly Reformed fellow campaigners from the Church of the Old Prussian Union, the brethren-based structure of the Confessing Church was the only way of protecting the confessional foundation of the Protestant Church. Furthermore, Niemöller was sceptical about broadening the opposition if this would include not only conservative Lutherans but also former German Christians. A further conflict arose in November 1934, when the Temporary Church Leadership (Vorläufige Kirchenleitung, VKL) voiced their willingness to cooperate with state authorities in reorganizing church affairs. When Hanns Kerrl was appointed Reich Minister for Church Affairs in July 1935, Niemöller's criticism of state interference in church matters and of those parts of the Confessing Front who were willing to cooperate with the state intensified. At the synod in Bad Oeynhausen in February 1936, the Confessing Church finally split. A second VKL was established, dominated by a group of pastors from the Church of the Old Prussian Union who were associated with Niemöller.

Under the leadership of Hanover bishop August Marahrens, the VKL tested the waters for a reorganization of the Reich Church Leadership in accordance with the state, initially negotiating with East Prussian NSDAP Gauleiter Erich Koch. Yet these attempts came to nothing because Hitler still did not want to drop Ludwig Müller as Reich bishop. Simultaneously, the VKL strived to reach an understanding with DC church leaders. VKL members met with Baden regional bishop Julius Kühlewein and Otto Zänker, bishop of the Prussian church province of Silesia.[1] These attempts to integrate former or current German Christians sparked Niemöller's criticism of the VKL under Marahrens. In mid-January, he explained his position to his former superior, Wilhelm Zoellner: 'Am I really a Unionist', he replied to Zoellner's allegations, 'if I answer to the DC heresy in the same way as the Reformed brethren?' The 'Dahlem front', Niemöller insisted in retrospect, had been 'smashed solely by "Lutheran" special requests'. He was still angry that, in a letter to the Marburg theological department, Marahrens supported the decision to accept the German Christian bishop Heinrich Oberheid, who had been one of the main supporters of the forced coordination of the regional churches in 1934, as a university teacher. By his own account, Niemöller parted with the Reich Council of Brethren because of this letter, which he had asked Marahrens to retract. He summarized the current situation by using a military metaphor: when the 'Confessing community' found itself 'fighting the final battle against Rosenberg's paganism and the Romanism of the DC', this 'combat front' collapsed because 'a new field commander [Marahrens] was elected, who did not even belong to this front'.[2]

In February 1935, Niemöller publicly criticized the course of the VKL in a circular to the members of the Pastors' Emergency League. The actions of the VKL, he wrote, created the impression that 'the days of peace were in immediate reach'. From the perspective of the destroyed regional churches, particularly the ApU, this was clearly an illusion as news about the dismissal of pastors arrived on a daily basis. Niemöller stated the 'rescue of the Protestant Church' would ultimately be decided 'in the parishes' rather than 'by the church leadership'.[3]

Nevertheless, in the first half of 1935, Niemöller was open to talks and still ready to compromise with the VKL. Besides, he could rightly point out that he refrained from personal attacks on Marahrens in public. This was the basis for a meeting of Marahrens and Niemöller in Berlin on 27 February 1935, in which the Hanover bishop advocated the case of the Confessing Front clearer than ever and rejected any involvement of German Christians in the Church leadership. For Niemöller this was reason enough to endorse a fresh rapprochement between VKL and the Reich Council of Brethren, which resulted in a joint meeting of both bodies on 7 March. A committee was established for the preparation of a new Confessing synod of the DEK—the third after Barmen and Dahlem. Eventually, it took place in Augsburg from 4 to 6 June 1935, after it had been postponed several times.[4]

At the national level, the conflict within the Confessing Front was slightly defused. The situation in the Old Prussian Church was still dire. Starting in January 1935, Niemöller urged his fellow campaigners to convene a Confessing synod, which, he thought, could launch 'an attack on Rosenberg' and the *völkisch* neo-paganism of the Nazi ideologist in-chief.[5] Heinrich Vogel's statement *To the Parishes* was the most important result of this second Confessing synod of the Church of the Old Prussian Union, held in Dahlem from 4 to 5 March 1935. 'Disobedience' of the first commandment, it read, was 'the new religion', and the 'racial-*völkisch* ideology' made 'myth, blood and race, folkdom, honour, and freedom an idol'. This 'delusional belief' had nothing to do with 'positive Christianity'—as quoted in the NSDAP manifesto—but was 'anti-Christianity'. The Church recognized the authority of the state, but would not bow to the 'claim to totality' that 'the new religion ascribed to the state'.[6] This was a clear rejection of the totalitarian National Socialist concept of the state.[7]

A Wave of Repression from the Nazi State

At the Dahlem synod, the delegates decided this message should be read from the pulpit in the parishes. On the following Sunday, 10 March, Niemöller read it out in his Dahlem parish. His temporary detention by the Gestapo, followed by an interrogation in the Ministry of the Interior on 13 March, prevented a second reading. This was only the beginning of a wave of repression orchestrated by the Reich Minister of the Interior, Wilhelm Frick. He instructed the police to halt the reading of the word that the Emergency League planned for 17 March. Overall, 715 pastors of the Old Prussian Church were temporarily arrested. Indeed, a reading of the word on this specific day was not uncontested among pastors of the PEL as a state ceremony was planned on 17 March to mark the reintroduction of compulsory military service. However, at a meeting on 13 March, Niemöller had pushed for the reading because there were 'people at the top' of the state 'who had broken their word'.[8] Thanks to negotiations between Wilhelm Frick and Praeses Koch, the arrested pastors were soon released. A compromise had been agreed. The reading of the word would be prefaced by an opening paragraph, emphasizing that the message of the Confessing Church was directed against neo-paganism— not against the state.[9] But the temporary restraint of the Prussian state was only due to tactical considerations. With the approval of the German Christian bishops of Nassau-Hesse and Saxony, the police deported approximately 40 pastors to concentration camps. In late April, several Prussian PEL pastors were also taken to Sachsenhausen concentration camp.[10]

Martin Niemöller was outraged about this new wave of repression. He wrote to the Minister of Finance, Lutz Count Schwerin von Krosigk, who was not an NSDAP member and close to the Confessing Church. Krosigk had acted as an intermediary between church groups and President von Hindenburg in 1933–4. In this letter, Niemöller used drastic words, referring to a 'persecution of Christians', as 'arrests, house searches, confiscations' had ultimately made the pastors 'fair game'. But he was still not ready to abandon the national Protestant premises of his political thinking: he emphasized the pastors of the Emergency League had not only been 'best friends, but trailblazers [Vorkämpfer] of the Third Reich'.[11] In Niemöller's eyes, the continuous readiness of the VKL to compromise a greater problem than the inflexibility of state authorities. Marahrens negotiated with Minister of the Interior Frick on 2 May about the potential release of arrested pastors from Saxony and Hesse. The Saxonian bishop Friedrich Coch, who had ordered the transfer of these pastors to the concentration camp in the first place, was present. For Niemöller, this was a clear breach of a key decision of the Dahlem synod from October 1934, not to engage in negotiations with a DC Church leadership body. Moreover, the VKL had ordered the parishes to hold intercessions on 20 April, Hitler's birthday, that should express the joy of the entire church about this 'Führer'. This was simply 'unbearable' for Niemöller. In a letter to Koch, he voiced the accusation against the Temporary Church Leadership that it scatters Frankincense for the Führer, that it completely misrepresents and influences the feelings of the Protestant church members, while a great number of Protestant pastors are held in concentration camps, in prison stripes and with shaved head. [...] I prefer the bones of an honest Protestant pastor over the entire so-called bishop clergy that still stands exactly where it has been standing on 27 January 1934: the state orders and we are silent and obey![12]

Two things stand out in this letter. First, there was the trauma that the chancellor's reception had left, and second, Niemöller's increasing resentment against the Lutheran bishops of the intact regional churches, which quickly widened to a polemic against Lutheranism altogether and would shape his actions far beyond 1945. In the context of the conflicts in spring 1935, the harsh letter did serve its purpose, as Niemöller temporarily left all his offices in the Confessing Church vacant. Thus, he finally persuaded Marahrens to make further negotiations with the state conditional on the release of the arrested pastors. Hence, Niemöller and his Reformed friends could rejoin the Reich Council of Brethren that they had left in November 1934. Immediately before the beginning of the Augsburg Confessing synod of the DEK on 4 June 1935, the detained pastors were released.[13]

The most important result of the deliberations in Augsburg was the regulation of competencies of the VKL, the Reich Council of Brethren, and the Confessing synod. It quickly became clear that the expansion of synodal structures in all regional churches, as envisaged by the emergency law of the Dahlem synod in October 1934, was off the table. Hans Ehlers, member of the Council of Brethren of the ApU, clarified a significant change of the Reich church constitution of 11 July 1933 was not intended and that all resolutions of the Dahlem synod were merely meant as 'temporary solutions' until new structures approved by all sides were established.[14]

Other than clarifying procedural issues, Augsburg brought no substantial results to speak of. A 'Word to the Authorities' repudiated the insinuation the Confessing Church supported or backed 'political resistance'. The government was urged not to 'create a rift between Christianity and people's community [Volksgemeinschaft]'.[15] This was empty talk to pacify the authorities. It immediately drew criticism from Karl Barth and Dietrich Bonhoeffer that the synod had remained silent on pressing issues such as the persecution of the Jews and political opponents of the regime.[16] Hans Asmussen repeated this criticism at a joint meeting of the Reich Council of Brethren and VKL on 20 August. 'We cannot remain silent about the actions of the state', he urged his fellow brethren. 'This silence will be the end of the Confessing Church.'[17] Thus, the Augsburg synod was little more than a formulaic compromise that obscured rather than resolved the conflicts between the Dahlemite wing of the Confessing Church and the intact Lutheran regional churches. From 2 to 5 July, Lutherans from all over Germany gathered in Hanover under the leadership of Marahrens and Hans Meiser, celebrating a so-called 'German Lutheran Day'. Blatant criticism of the new cross-confessional creed that Barmen and Dahlem had allegedly created, and demands to dissolve the Church of the Old Prussian Union—because it stood in the way of gathering all Lutherans on the basis of a purely Lutheran confession—were frequently voiced during this event.[18]

At the Augsburg synod, Niemöller defended the Church of the Old Prussian Union. In his eyes, it was not only a 'union in a legal sense' but also a church community with 'Lutherans and United and Reformed Protestants sharing the burden of fighting and confessing against several different heresies and enemies'.[19] To prevent further compromises and a fragmentation of the Confessing Church into confessional groups, Niemöller and his closest allies—among them Hans Asmussen and Karl Immer—decided to activate the Pastors' Emergency League. He invited 50 Emergence League pastors to a meeting in Dahlem on 30 July 1935. The participants adopted a circular titled *To Our Brethren in Office*, drafted by Asmussen and revised by Niemöller and others. It emphasized the 'disappointment' following the 'wait for a resounding success of our church leadership' during the last months. This was a blatant criticism of the VKL under Marahrens. The circular also committed the pastors to 'take a tough stance against all attempts to resolve church matters contrary to the resolutions of Barmen and Dahlem'.[20]

Reactions were mixed. Dietrich Bonhoeffer sent congratulations from Finkenwalde, where he worked as head of a Confessing Church seminary from April 1935. He suggested to Niemöller the establishment of 'an Emergency League within the Emergency League', based on a fundamentally different interpretation of Matthew 22:21 ('Render therefore to Caesar the things that are Caesar's; and to God the things that are God's').[21] Friedrich Bodelschwingh, however, openly criticized his former protégé Niemöller in a letter to Karl Immer. Niemöller's exit from the Reich Council of Brethren and his criticism of Marahrens, Bodelschwingh wrote, had damaged the authority of the VKL and impeded the recognition of the Confessing Church by the state. Bodelschwingh criticized the 'canonization of the resolutions of Barmen and Dahlem'. As already during the Dahlem synod, the bone of contention was the resolution on article III, 3—the demand of a radical separation from any DC church leadership. To get 'beyond Dahlem' was Bodelschwingh's 'watchword'.[22] The fierce debate about Niemöller's criticism of the VKL and of the circular initiated by him were the dominant talking points of two joint meetings of VKL and Reich Council of Brethren on 31 July and 20 August 1935. With good reason, Niemöller could refute the claim that he intended to canonize the decisions of the Dahlem synod: 'I don't cling to Dahlem. It might have been fallible.' But in his eyes, the VKL's course of action towards the state was merely tactical. And in the process, the actual concern of the Confessing Church—the commitment to the confession and God's word as the only source of revelation—had 'increasingly disappeared'.[23]

The 'Pacification' Policy of Reich Minister
for Church Affairs Kerrl

These controversies within the Confessing Church in the weeks after the Augsburg synod did not have any profound repercussions as the relationship between the Nazi state and the churches fundamentally changed in July 1935. Until then, the regime's church policy had fluctuated: periods of benevolent neutrality followed the initial staunch support for the DC. After August, Jäger's policy of forced integration had failed in October 1934—a decision had to be made: either the complete withdrawal of the state or its direct control of the churches. Hitler settled for the latter and tasked Hanns Kerrl to take care of church affairs with a decree on 16 July 1935. Kerrl (1887–1941) was an 'old fighter' who had become minister without portfolio in 1934. Based on the decree, Kerrl made himself Reich and Prussian Minister for Church Affairs—with Hitler's subsequent approval. The relevant departments of the Ministries of Education and the Interior provided the organizational structure for the new ministry. However, Kerrl did not have the authority to appoint chairs of theology, and his ministry had a weak position within the polycratic maze of institutions of the Nazi state.[24]

During these hectic days, little Martin Niemöller was born on 11 August, the seventh child of Else and Martin and much younger than the others. The parents always called him Tini. But the church struggle still had priority for his father. Thus it was Else who bore the brunt of raising Tini and her other children.

Initially, Kerrl took a moderate course of action and understood his endeavours as a 'pacification work' (*Befriedungswerk*) aiming for a cautious domestication of the Confessing Church. In this vein, he ordered the authorities to desist from repressive measures such as arresting pastors without his explicit approval in early September.[25] Several meetings between Kerrl and representatives of the churches were intended to build trust. On 23 August, Kerrl met with representatives of the Confessing Church. The Minister for Church Affairs presented himself as a devout Protestant Christian. Kerrl assured his interlocutors that he wanted to 'protect Christianity', namely against 'neo-paganism'. But at the same time, he was convinced 'Luther would have stood enthusiastically by the Führer's side if he were alive today.' On behalf of the church representatives, Marahrens expressed his delight about Kerrl's appointment as minister, emphasizing their opposition to the DC was 'solely ecclesiastic' and did not affect the relationship to the state.[26] Kerrl, in return, affirmed he did not want to establish a 'state church'. The other church representatives also tried to accommodate Kerrl as much as possible, above all Bodelschwingh. According to his own notes, Bodelschwingh put on record: 'We are the linchpin of the state.'[27] Niemöller's notes, however, show he went even further, expressing his joy about the Protestant Church being 'more alive' than ever since the Reformation and glorifying the 'Führer' as someone who had 'done more for the Church' than anyone else during the 'last centuries'. In light of such euphoria, Kerrl felt compelled to insist on the need to proceed 'with caution'.[28]

The relaxed atmosphere encouraged Niemöller to provide insights into the core of his religious thoughts, including—unsurprisingly—polemics against theological liberalism. Niemöller insisted the promulgation of Christ was the 'life centre' of the Church. 'In the confession of the Church, liberalism has not been acknowledged on an equal footing. We do not want to make the Church even more liberal today.' This was a clear rejection of a pluralization of religious belief that Cultural Protestantism propagated. The idea of obligation (*Bindung*) was at the core of Niemöller's theological thinking and in direct contradiction to the liberal postulate of freedom. 'We are bound by God's word.'[29] He implicitly accepted this might be seen as an approval of the anti-liberal policies of the Nazi regime, particularly at the meeting with a Reich minister. However, Niemöller's theological preferences by no means increased his willingness to compromise. When Bodelschwingh tried to persuade him to cooperate with Kerrl, Niemöller responded with a 'hard no'.[30]

Three days later, on 26 August, Niemöller had the chance to suggest a way out of the messy situation in a personal encounter with Kerrl. He essentially suggested a Simultaneum, a parallel structure with two spiritual church leadership bodies in every regional church or church province, respectively: one led by the DC, one by the Confessing Church. '*Treuhandstellen*'—or 'trust offices'—like those established by the Confessing Church in autumn 1934 to distribute church tax funds, were to take care of financial matters under state supervision. Otherwise, the state had to 'wait and see'.[31] Niemöller's plan was illusionary for two reasons: first, with the law of 11 March 1935 the state had introduced financial departments, initially for the ApU, that were already in charge of financial matters. This had already indicated a change of course in regard to church politics. In a decree from 22 August, Kerrl prohibited the fiduciary collection of church tax money by the Confessing Church and confiscated the existing funds. Niemöller tried to shield the Dahlem parish from this policy, but had to watch helplessly when the Prussian state took financial authority away from the parish.[32] Second, Niemöller's ideas met staunch opposition from Marahrens and Bodelschwingh, who hoped that moderate German Christians might defect to the Confessing Front. They accused Niemöller of forgetting the neutral centre, which would never bow to the 'governance methods of the brethren councils'. In a letter to Marahrens, Bodelschwingh accused Niemöller of 'building walls of separation' between the moderate centre and the Dahlemite radicals 'with his recurring public explosions'.[33]

At several meetings with Julius Stahn, a high-ranking official of the Church Ministry, Niemöller and Otto Dibelius learned in late August about Kerrl's plans to introduce a state-controlled body that was to manage the affairs of the Protestant Church and pacify the conflicts between the different factions. Niemöller immediately voiced protest against these plans and warned every direct 'state intervention' would end in a 'catastrophe', because the Confessing Church was no longer 'a "church group"', but *the* Protestant Church. It would be better if the state just accepted the 'fact that the Church has already split'. But interventions like this via letter—even when signed with 'Heil Hitler'—were futile.[34] On 24 September 1935, the 'Law for the Safeguarding of the German Protestant Church' was introduced, on the premise that the state had to take over church affairs as a 'custodian'. For this reason, the law authorized the church minister to issue binding decrees for the entire DEK and the regional churches.[35]

This 'safeguarding law' was passed when another Confessing synod of the Old Prussian Church was held in Berlin Steglitz from 23 to 26 September. For the first time in the history of the Confessing synods from 1933, a state representative, Julius Stahn, made the introduction. He explained why Kerrl considered the synod of the ApU an undesired disturbance of his pacification efforts. When he urged the synod members to 'take heed, and be quiet' (Isa. 7:4), he was met with scornful laughter.[36]

The Steglitz synod had two focal points. First, the Confessing Church in Prussia looked at how to respond to increased state intervention into church matters. These efforts had already begun prior to the appointment of Kerrl, when financial departments were established to manage the financial affairs of the Prussian regional churches, and a decision-making body was set up at the Ministry of the Interior to deal with church legal issues. The resolutions of the Steglitz synod outright refused cooperation of bodies of the Confessing Church with these offices.[37]

Persisting Anti-Jewish Stereotypes in the Confessing Church

Much more controversial was the second focal point of the synod: how to deal with Christians of Jewish descent in the Church. Niemöller had initiated this discussion. On 12 August, he sent a resolution of the Council of Brethren of the PEL to Praeses Koch. The Emergency League pastors emphasized the fourth point of their commitment—opposition to the 'Aryan paragraph' in the Church—and asked for a 'clarifying word' on this matter. Niemöller pointed out that statements as those by the director of the Berlin city mission would damage 'the reputation of the Confessing Church'.[38] He referred to an article by Siegfried Knak, director of the Berlin city mission since 1921. In 1933, Knak sympathized with the DC, but had switched to the Confessing Church afterwards. Yet he did not abandon his *völkisch* world view. In his brief text, Knak not only repeated antisemitic allegations such as the 'ruin' that the Jewish people brought to the nations, among which 'it is scattered'. He also ascribed the Nazi state the sole authority to regulate mixed marriages between Germans and Jews—that is, between non-Jewish and Jewish Germans—as, according to his credo, a 'Jew does not become a German through baptism and faith'.[39]

In light of these remarks, Knak's general support of the Christian mission among Jews was easily overlooked. But exactly this point was controversial in the Confessing Church. Praeses Koch, for instance, questioned whether the 'Jewish Question' should be discussed at the synod at all. One day before the synod began, the Old Prussian Council of Brehren agreed that the mission among the Jews had 'no promise'. Bavarian Bishop Meiser even predicted a 'self-inflicted martyrdom' in case the synod would discuss this topic.[40] Pastor Günter Jacob told Niemöller he was worried a statement would be politically misinterpreted in the current 'struggle for existence of our people'. Jacob pointed out that the 1933 Bethel Confession—in its final version that was no longer authorized by Dietrich Bonhoeffer—essentially confirmed the 'truth of modern racial doctrine [Rassenlehre]'.[41] Parallel to these and other interventions, a theological commission of the Old Prussian Council of Bethren convened from 5 to 23 September. It tasked Niemöller, Franz Hildebrandt, and Heinrich Vogel to draft a text for the message of the synod.[42]

This draft, which was given out to synod members, defended the mission among Jews by referring to Galatians 3:28: 'There is neither Jew nor Greek, there is neither bond nor free, there is neither male nor female: for ye are all one in Christ Jesus.' The draft also contained a paragraph—deleted at the synod— which reminded the Church that it was not 'absolved from Jesus Christ's commandment of love' even towards unbaptized Jews. However, this decisive statement was immediately qualified: 'Baptism, however, does not justify anybody's worldly claims and rights.'[43] The draft presented in Steglitz went even further, explaining baptism did not 'confer worldly civil rights'.[44] On 15 September, the Reichstag had passed the so-called Nuremberg Race Laws, which removed the citizenship of German Jews according to racial criteria—this definition included Christians of Jewish descent. Thus, this passage of the theological draft resolution can be interpreted as an approval of the political criteria of the Nuremberg Laws.

At the synod, Berlin pastor and superintendent Martin Albertz, supported by Franz Hildebrandt and Dietrich Bonhoeffer, pushed through the deletion of this paragraph. But this simultaneously resulted in the omission of the commandment of love towards the members of the Jewish faith—on the insistence of Praeses Karl Koch.[45] There were still several contentious points left to debate, which reflect the ambivalence of Niemöller and the entire Confessing Church towards the fate of the Jews persecuted by the Nazi state. In an intervention explicitly motivated with an eye on the 'minutes of the synod'—and thus on his legacy—Niemöller called the adopted resolution 'less than a provisional minimum'. He referred to the work of the Pastors' Emergency League after 1933 and claimed that, beyond granting baptism, Christians of Jewish descent had to be offered an equal place in the Church. This was a practical necessity 'in these times of persecution of the Church'. This choice of words shows Niemöller was not willing to seriously consider Nazi persecution of other groups than the Protestant Church.[46]

The only female delegate, Stephanie von Mackensen, who had come from the DC to the Confessing Church in 1933, staunchly opposed Niemöller. The rejection of the 'Aryan Paragraph' in the Church, she explained, had been uncontroversial among the members of the theological commission, just like the fact that 'baptized Jewish fellow Christians [...] are equal members of the community'. The only contested issue was whether 'baptism makes someone a German'. Siegfried Knak, who had answered this question in the negative in his article, supported von Mackensen. Dahlem Pastor Eberhard Röhricht voiced the openly antisemitic opinion that 'non-Aryans' desired to be baptized 'because they seek economic community' with Germans for their own benefit. Ernst Hornig from Breslau rejected the baptism of Jews in general on 'racial grounds'. Niemöller affirmed his conviction of the equalizing effect of baptism and insisted the expression 'we Germans' had to include Christians of Jewish descent. In light of the focus on this rather small group, only Gerhard Jacobi, who had initiated the church opposition with his conversation group for Berlin pastors in 1933, asked the crucial question: 'How does the Church stand towards the non-baptized Jews?'[47] Yet none of the delegates was willing to answer him, including Martin Niemöller. While the Nazi regime drastically increased the persecution of the Jews, the Confessing Church remained fixated on its own internal problems. A Gestapo report compiled prior to the Steglitz synod correctly stated that 'leading men of the Confessing Front [...] generally support the position of the state towards the Jewish Question'.[48]

These findings about the Steglitz synod are disillusioning. Precisely the topic that had led to the gathering of the church opposition in 1933—the rejection of anti-Jewish measures in the Church—now became the cause of a dispute within the Confessing Church of the Old Prussian Union. Its deeply ambivalent position also harked back to Niemöller's own ambivalences. At a meeting of the Old Prussian Council of Brethren on the first day of the synod, Reformed theologian Karl Immer courageously demanded to oppose 'the shameless pornography of the Stürmer', the fiercely antisemitic newspaper edited by Julius Streicher. Niemöller, whose word as a leading member of the Council would surely have had considerable impact, hid behind technical questions.[49] In the statement he gave at the synod, he talked about 'baptized Christian brethren who, in terms of their flesh [nach dem Fleische], are Jews or half-Jews'. With this ambiguous phraseology, he not only adopted the racial terminology of the Nazi regime but perhaps also the notion of a biological core of the Jews.[50]

Niemöller's sermons from this time also show that he continued to use traditional anti-Jewish stereotypes. On 25 August 1935 he talked about the 'impossible existence' of the Jewish people and the 'curse' of the 'Eternal Jew' as a 'restless wanderer who has no home and finds no peace', reproducing the legend of Ahasver, the Eternal Jew.[51] Only very few of his Dahlem sermons between 1933 and 1937 contain such anti-Jewish stereotypes. A speech on the relevance of the

Old Testament from 1936, which he published shortly afterwards, gives some indication of his thinking about Judaism. Niemöller argued the Old Testament had 'changed hands'. Since its beginnings, he explained, the Christian community had denied 'the Jews the right to claim the book for themselves'. Following God's revelation in Jesus Christ, Christians had become 'God's people'. Only the process of salvation described in the Gospels provided the key to understanding the Old Testament, and 'Jewry does not have this key'.[52] With this line of argument, Niemöller turned against those National Socialists and German Christians who intended to purge Christian tradition from all Jewish traits. At the same time, he affirmed what he had already noted in his diary in 1932, that Judaism lacked any legitimacy as a religion of salvation.

As the Nazi regime brutally cracked down against the Jewish community in Germany, these remarks were highly problematic. Niemöller's national Protestantism was also undiminished in political terms, as he deliberately emphasized his agreement with the regime's policies. A prominent example is his speech on 'God's peace as the strength of the combative [wehrhaft] man', delivered at the Evangelical Week in Hanover in late August 1935 and published shortly afterwards.[53] In June 1943, months after the German defeat at Stalingrad, Niemöller touched upon this text in a conversation with his wife during one of her regular visits at Dachau concentration camp. With great satisfaction he recalled how his brother Wilhelm once told him it was 'the best I have ever written'.[54] The talk in Hanover was delivered a few months after the reintroduction of military service in March 1935, a deliberate breach of the Treaty of Versailles and a crucial step in the Nazi regime's policy of rearmament.

Against this backdrop, Niemöller declared it an 'irresponsible utopian dream' to suggest one would live 'in a world of peace', and portrayed the Germans as a 'defenceless people'. It was 'imperative and necessary that a state with the task to defend a great people from injustice' would do so by establishing a strong 'Wehrmacht'. The looming 'struggle for existence' that the Germans would have to wage 'to the bitter end' required the nurturing of 'truly soldierly virtues'. Thus, Protestant Christians had to see the 'Christian brother' in the 'combative man'. It was paramount to reject the wrong view that Christian faith would have to lead to 'unmanly' behaviour.[55] Twenty years earlier, Niemöller had struggled to adapt to the norms of hegemonic masculinity within the officer corps. That was now forgotten. In August 1936, he retrospectively claimed he 'deliberately' stood against 'all declarations of political loyalty' from mid-1935 onwards.[56] And yet his speech in Hanover was a declaration of political loyalty to the Nazi regime. The unreserved recognition of state authorities ordained by God was still a fixed constant in Niemöller's political world view in 1935. It found expression in a sermon he delivered in February. With reference to Romans 13, he preached from the pulpit of the Jesus Christ Church that 'a Protestant Church hostile to the state is a contradiction in terms'.[57]

The Law for the Safeguarding of the German Protestant Church, enacted on 24 September 1935, provided Hanns Kerl with the authority to issue legally binding decrees for the DEK and regional churches. With the first decree that implemented this law, published on 3 October, the Minister for Church Affairs created a Reich Church Committee (Reichskirchenausschuss, RKA), a Regional Church Committee (Landeskirchenausschuss, LKA) for the Church of the Old Prussian Union, and committees for individual church provinces. These committees were intended—initially for a limited period of time—to take over leadership of the Church, including decisions about the appointment of church officials. When he selected committee members, Kerrl took advice from Bishop Marahrens. As chairman of the RKA Kerrl chose Wilhelm Zoellner, the former Westphalian General Superintendent who had retired in 1931. As a moderate Lutheran with both sympathies for the Confessing Church and an understanding of the aims of the German Christians, Zoellner represented those in the middle of the Protestant Church that Kerrl wanted his pacification policies to be based upon. As chairman of the Prussian LKA he appointed Johannes Eger, the former Saxon General Superintendent. Prior to these personnel decisions, Kerrl also coordinated with national representatives of the German Christians, which seemed to secure broad agreement with his course of action. A programmatic statement by RKA and LKA from 17 October emphasized the orientation towards Scripture and confession, but also affirmed the 'National Socialist becoming of a people (*Volkwerdung*)' in 'race, blood, and soil'.[58]

This wording allowed critical inquiries into whether the new bodies would uphold the confessional basis of the church. But it was not clear if any critics would make an appearance in the first place. On 12 October, Paul Winckler, one of Zoellner's confidants, stressed the new committees were only facing potential opposition from Niemöller and his friends. This opposition, however, could become a huge burden for the whole Confessing Church.[59] And this was exactly what happened between October 1935 and February 1936. The VKL under Marahrens immediately advocated the nomination of members for the committees created by Kerrl. Yet the Old Prussian Council of Brethren warned against such a course of action and declared participation in these committees incompatible with membership of the bodies of the Confessing Church. Niemöller argued that by recognizing the committees, the Confessing Church would give up its claim to represent the true Protestant Church. The Reich Council of Brethren supported Niemöller's view in a crucial vote on 15 November. At two meetings with the VKL and the Old Prussian Council of Brethren on 27 November, Kerrl tried to solicit approval for his course of action. Apart from the Reformed member Paul Humburg, the VKL indicated its support. Fritz Müller, however, as representative of the Council of Brethren, abandoned negotiations, when Kerrl discarded the ideas of the Confessing Church as 'worthless'. Kerrl responded immediately with another—by then the fifth—decree for the implementation of the safeguarding law, dated 2 December. It barred all church groups—yet was solely directed against the Confessing Church—from exercising functions that were reserved for church leadership bodies, including examining and ordaining pastors or conducting Confessing synods.[60]

After the establishment of church committees, Niemöller demanded a clear 'dissociation' from all members of the Confessing Church who were ready to cooperate with the new bodies and, in his eyes, entered into a 'union with the German Christians'. A practical example was the East Prussian church province of the ApU. The chairman of the East Prussian Provincial Council of Brethren, Theodor Kueßner, was persuaded by Marahrens to join the RKA. Lay members of the Confessing Church from the province contacted Niemöller, who immediately arranged for Kueßner's removal from the Council of Brethren of the ApU.[61] Thus, the claim of the church committees set up by Kerrl to speak for the entire Protestant Church became the catalyst for the ultimate split of the Confessing Church. Its internal lines of conflict had become apparent in late 1934, when representatives of the intact regional churches refused to implement the resolutions of the Dahlem synod and the Lutherans gathered separately. This conflict escalated in late 1935. When Kerrl tried to stop the Confessing Church from exercising church leadership functions with the decree of 2 December, Niemöller increased the pressure on the VKL members to dissociate themselves from this course of action. The ultimate split occurred at a meeting of the Reich Council of Brethren on 3 January 1936. During the meeting, Marahrens insisted the VKL had tried to hold the diverging forces together. Friedrich Müller put forward a motion aiming to replace the VKL because its members had violated the resolutions of the Confessing synod by cooperating with the RKA. Niemöller and Asmussen seconded Müller in advocating the Dahlem position. As at many previous meetings—from the Barmen synod in 1934 to earlier meetings of the Reich Council of Brethren—it was Hans Asmussen, who put his finger on the key problem with great clarity. Niemöller, who on this occasion only spoke briefly, was the tireless driving force of the Confessing Church—and its public face. At important turning points, however, he often only addressed technical or organizational issues. Asmussen was another leading figure of the Confessing Church, at least on a par with Niemöller in intellectual and theological terms, and able to clarify crucial points in decisive interventions. On 3 January 1936 he explained:

The Church thrives on bearing witness to the Gospel, which also includes to discard heresy. Some members of the Temporary Leadership think this bearing witness could be done by writing to the state committees—while we believe that it must be preached from the roof tops. The Temporary Leadership can only gain authority by publicly witnessing the Gospel and discarding heresy—and it has not done so for 1 ¼ years.[62]

The vote resulted in a majority of 17 to 11 in favour of the position of the Dahlemite wing around Müller and Niemöller. Both groups immediately continued negotiations separately.[63] During the following weeks, the conflict within the Confessing Church played out at the legal level with expert opinions and counter expert opinions. Both sides denied the legitimacy of the course of action the other had taken, and the minority contested the legitimacy of the vote that had been conducted on 3 January.[64]

At the heart of the split of the Confessing Church was a different understanding of ecclesiology held by Niemöller and his followers, on the one hand, and by moderate Lutherans, on the other. The establishment of church committees was 'the final push for the separation' because it indicated a possible reorganization of the relationship between the Church and the Nazi state, based on Lutheran ecclesiology.[65] And Niemöller was not willing to take such a step—which in his eyes equalled surrendering the resolutions of Barmen, Dahlem, and Augsburg.[66] Yet he had also lost confidence in Lutherans' bona fides. As early as October 1935, Niemöller had told his Dahlem parish that, according to his information, it was the 'intent' of the church committees 'to split the Confessing Church'. However, he did not realize that he himself had an active role in aggravating the conflicts. Rather, he regretted to 'have let himself be persuaded to show false restraint' from November 1934, when conflicts in the Reich Council of Brethren erupted.[67]

The Formal Split of the Confessing Church in Bad Oeynhausen

After the conflict within the Reich Council of Brethren had erupted on 3 January 1936, it was still necessary to finalize the split of the Confessing Church on a formal level. Both sides agreed that a new Confessing synod of the DEK was needed. From the perspective of the intact Lutheran churches, this synod had only one 'task, to liquidate' the Confessing Church, as Bishop Meiser put it.[68] From 3 January until the start of the synod—which finally took place in Bad Oeynhausen from 18 to 22 February 1936—both sides were busy pulling strings behind the scenes to create an optimal starting position for themselves.[69]

At the synod, Marahrens and Niemöller outlined the position of their respective camps in two lengthy introductory speeches. Niemöller emphasized the 'de-Christianization of our people', which had become apparent with the appointment of Reich bishop Müller in 1933. For him and his fellow campaigners from the destroyed church provinces of the ApU, the forces that aimed for such de-Christianization were 'not anonymous', but had 'a face': he referred to the radical, neo-pagan wing of the German Christians, and called for a 'final missionary full attack' to halt the advance of 'heathendom'.[70] This choice of words shows that from 1935, the church struggle increasingly developed into a fight for the re-Christianization of German society for Niemöller. In an article titled

'Missionary Church', he even agreed with DC criticism of a Church that had become 'self-sufficient' and 'complacent'. Insistence on the proper confessional basis of the Church was a precondition to reach those who had been so far 'unreachable'.[71] Niemöller's understanding of ecclesiology was clearly shaped by his long work at the Inner Mission.

In its final resolution 'On Church Leadership', the Bad Oeynhausen synod condemned the state-imposed church committees and their claim to lead the Church. The remaining members of the first VKL—Paul Humburg had already resigned—stepped down. Simultaneously, a new Reich Council of Brethren was established. The synod then petered out in debates on bylaws and procedural motions.[72] An acting leadership committee was appointed, consisting of Fritz Müller, Hans Böhm, and Martin Albertz, until a new VKL would be elected. On 12 March, the Reich Council of Brethren voted in this Second VKL with Müller as its chairman. Otto Fricke and Bernhard Heinrich Forck complemented the committee. At the same time, the Council appointed a seven-member council of the DEK, headed by Niemöller, which was intended to advise the VKL.[73]

These resolutions formally implemented the split at the top of the Confessing Church. The new, second VKL continued the work of the Confessing Church in the spirit of the synods of Barmen, Dahlem, and Augsburg. However, the intact regional churches of Hanover, Württemberg, and Bavaria did not recognize the Second VKL as a legitimate church leadership. Hence, the influence of the Second VKL hardly extended beyond the territory of the Old Prussian Union. The split also affected the grassroots level. Nowhere was this more obvious than in Niemöller's Dahlem parish. After their joint service on 2 July 1933, the three Dahlem pastors had worked together peacefully to establish a Confessing community and later the Confessing Church. Alongside Niemöller, Friedrich Müller and Eberhard Röhricht participated in the Barmen synod in May 1934. The mood had already changed by late 1935. Röhricht signalled his approval of the church committees. In 1936, he joined the Berlin consistory, which was subordinate to the church committees, and stopped paying fees to the Pastors' Emergency League.[74]

Soon after the official split of the Confessing Church, the bridges in Dahlem were burnt. In April 1936, only a few weeks after the establishment of the Second VKL, Niemöller and Röhricht concluded there was 'no longer a common foundation for cooperation'.[75] Increasing quips and allegations led to a 'terrible conflict'. By September, Niemöller thought the strife would 'break up the parish'. Thus, in November 1936, Niemöller, Hildebrandt, and Müller asked Röhricht to allocate their pastoral work according to districts to minimize further friction.[76] Even before Niemöller's arrest in July 1937, the split of the Dahlem parish spread to the active laity. In June 1937, a member of the group that helped with Sunday school complained to Niemöller that Sunday school had started with a 20-minute delay because the Jesus Christ Church emptied only slowly after his Communion service. Apparently, Röhricht, who held Sunday school, had threatened to mobilize the parents against Niemöller.[77]

In the wake of Bad Oeynhausen and with the establishment of the Second VKL, the Dahlemite wing around Niemöller prevailed in the Confessing Church of the ApU. At the same time, the intact regional churches started a close cooperation focused on their Lutheran confession. In February 1935, the bishops of Hanover, Württemberg, and Bavaria had already formed the 'Lutheran Pact' to initiate cooperation in liturgical terms. The 'Lutheran Day' in July 1935 was a more broadly conceived consultation of Lutheran organizations. Finally, on 18 March 1936, the 'Lutheran Council' was established in Leipzig. Bishops of the three intact regional churches as well as representatives of the Regional Councils of Brethren of Saxony, Mecklenburg, and Thuringia joined. Formally, the Lutheran churches acknowledged the synod resolutions of Barmen, Dahlem, and Augsburg. In practice, however, the Lutheran Council cooperated with church leadership bodies that had formerly belonged to the German Christians. At the same time, it claimed to represent Lutherans of the Eastern Prussian church provinces, which ultimately put up the very existence of the ApU 'for negotiation'.[78] In the following months, Niemöller took every opportunity to rail against the establishment of the Lutheran Council and its politics. At a meeting of the Reich Council of Brethren on 12 March, he lashed out at the intact regional churches as being 'indecent' and 'dishonest'.[79] In a letter to Bodelschwingh from April, he complained that Lutherans 'not only demanded love and understanding for the representatives of heresy [of the German Christians], but also for the heresy itself'. Marahrens, Meiser, and Wurm, he claimed, had 'smashed' the Confessing Church 'in order to survive'. This was nothing other than 'betrayal'.[80] These were strong words, indicating how agitated Niemöller was about the split of the Confessing Church. They also clearly pointed the finger at the three Lutheran bishops. The conflicts within the EKD during the early 1950s showed that, even 15 years later, Niemöller's anger about their 'betrayal' was still strong.

After the split of the Confessing Church, Niemöller fought even harder against the de-Christianization of society, which the Nazi state facilitated under the misleading watchword of 'de-confessionalization'.[81] In a speech held on 1 May 1936, Robert Ley, head of the German Labour Front, blamed Christianity for creating an 'inferiority complex' that would be 'alien' to the German race. Niemöller responded with a postcard to Wilhelm Zoellner, mocking him that it remained to be seen 'whether the Reich Church Committee has a mouth through which the Church of Jesus Christ speaks'.[82] In a letter, probably from early summer 1936, he emphasized the fulfilment of ordination vows required 'a confessing and daring commitment due to the blatant hostility against the Christian faith'. Initially, this had only been present 'in a concealed fashion' through the German Christian faith. 'Today', however, 'the German Christian myth has started an open and down-the-line attack on Christian doctrine'.

Niemöller still trusted that his fight against de-Christianization was in line with the law and would not put him 'in opposition to the people's community', but rather 'as a serving member in its middle'. Otherwise, the self-deification of man would end 'in Bolshevism' for the German people.[83]

The Memorandum of the Second VKL to Hitler

The fight against Christianity's marginalization in important functional fields of society, including education and mass media, was not only a personal matter for Niemöller, but a concern for all Christians. The Fulda Catholic Bishops' Conference, for example, lamented the various attacks on Christianity in a memorandum to Hitler from 20 August 1935. In the run-up to the Reichstag election on 29 March 1936—which the Nazi regime used to prove public support for the deployment of German troops in the demilitarized Rhineland—the VKL discussed a 'word to the parishes and the state' for the first time. Yet the timing seemed bad, so the VKL abandoned the plan for the time being. But when they placed it back on their agenda in 1936, the VKL stuck to its initial intention: the memorandum should combine information and advice for the faithful, and a plea to the state leadership.[84] Niemöller was neither one of the authors of the memorandum—as is sometimes wrongly suggested—nor was he involved in its compilation from the outset. Rather, it was Pastor Wilhelm Jannasch from Lübeck, whom the DC had expelled from office in 1934, who played a significant role in writing and editing several drafts. Niemöller was first involved at a joint meeting of the Second VKL and the Council of the DEK on 30 April 1936. At this point, the fourth version of the memorandum was under review.[85]

Niemöller was only directly involved in the sixth and final version. On 22 May, he, Asmussen, and Jannasch edited this draft, deleted potentially offensive expressions and changed the overall tone: now, no 'expectation' was voiced, only a 'plea' to the state. The 'realization that the state was the adversary of the Church and Christianity', which had been 'clearly expressed in previous versions', was 'significantly mitigated', as historian Martin Greschat has argued.[86] The introduction of the final draft acknowledged the 'activists of the National Socialist revolution', as their 'victory over Bolshevism' had also defeated 'the enemy' of Christianity. Hence, the authors of the memorandum defined the opposition between Bolshevism and Christianity as the core of the confrontation—exactly what Niemöller had already expressed publicly in 1932–3.[87] Thus, Niemöller mainly watered down the critical core of the message and even reversed it through the reference to the dangers of Bolshevism. Yet after 1945, Niemöller and his supporters never missed an opportunity to praise his contribution to the memorandum as the highlight of his resistance against the Nazi regime.

It is no contradiction to simultaneously stress the historical significance of the memorandum. Neither before nor after during the 'Third Reich' did a group of Protestants stand up so firmly for 'justice and decency' and called the 'existing injustice' by name.[88] Apart from condemning anti-church measures, the memorandum pointed to election fraud. It explicitly mentioned the 'measures of the Secret State Police [Gestapo]', which were beyond 'judicial control', and the 'concentration camps'. It countered antisemitism, which 'compels to hate Jews', with 'the Christian command to love'. These were brave words, addressed to the 'Führer and Reich Chancellor'.[89] On 4 June, Wilhelm Jannasch delivered one of only three copies in person to the Presidential Chancellery for onward transmission to Hitler. On 24 June at a joint meeting of the Second VKL and Council of the DEK—whose members had jointly signed the memorandum—disillusionment set in when Jannasch reported that the Presidential Chancellery had forwarded the memorandum to the Ministry for Church Affairs. Hitler was not willing to engage in discussions with the Confessing Church, this much was clear.

The memorandum was strictly confidential and only intended for Hitler's eyes. Its authors therefore got into considerable trouble when the *New York Herald Tribune* reported on its content on 16 July and the *Basler Nachrichten* printed the text in full on 23 July. The VKL soon suspected Friedrich Weißler (1891–1937) as the source of the leak. Weißler came from a Jewish family, but his father had him baptized. After 1918, he made a stellar career in the Prussian judicial service, which came to an abrupt end in the 'Third Reich'. In April 1933, Weißler was dismissed as a civil servant. In late 1934, he started working as a clerk, later as an office supervisor and legal counsel for both the First and the Second VKL. In this capacity, he was involved in drafting the memorandum as secretary and counsel. The revelations in the press forced the top bodies of the Confessing Church onto the defensive. In August, Praeses Karl Koch asked the Ministry of Justice for an inquiry into the events that had led to the publications. In mid-September, the VKL suspended Weißler from office. On 7 October 1936, he was arrested by the Gestapo and after long interrogation transferred to Sachsenhausen concentration camp. He died there from severe physical abuse by the security guards on 19 February 1937.[90]

It is impossible to establish with certainty whether Weißler was in fact responsible for leaking the document to the *Basler Nachrichten*, but there are good reasons to doubt it.[91] To be sure, he had leaked information on church political issues to the foreign press on previous occasions with Werner Koch, a vicar working with Dietrich Bonhoeffer, and his friend Ernst Tillich. He justified this by pointing out that Christians abroad had the right to learn more about church affairs in Germany. With these leaks, Weißler crossed 'a line' the 'Confessing Church did not want to cross: from the church struggle on one's own account to political action, ultimately embarking on a path to Christian resistance.'[92] This was a path Niemöller by no means wanted to go down, as he emphasized several times in the context of the affair about the leak in the VKL, which was surrounded by many rumours, second-guessing, and finger-pointing. In a letter from early September to a pastor of the Confessing Church, he dismissed the insinuation, apparently made by the Erlangen theologian Hermann Sasse, that the memorandum had been intended for direct political impact. 'None of us', Niemöller insisted, 'has tried to force the state to intervene "before the Olympic Games", as we generally do not care whether the state does this or that and only care about our own office and our own duty.'[93] Niemöller also denied that he and Karl Barth, whom he had last met in April for a 'nice and brief get-together with Else', had initiated the memorandum.[94] One week after Weißler's arrest, Niemöller explained it was 'simply impossible' to keep the already suspended office supervisor further employed. And in the Reich Council of Brethren, he firmly demanded on 29 October: 'We must immediately draw a clear line against Weißler.'[95] A few days later, Weißler was dismissed. Only a small number of theologians of the Confessing Church—above all Martin Albertz—showed solidarity with Weißler and took care of him and his family.[96] Like the majority of the VKL members, Niemöller dropped the hard-pressed jurist like a hot potato.

From the outset, the VKL memorandum had been intended as both a plea to the state and a word to the parish communities. When it became clear Hitler had no inclination to respond to the petition, the VKL began to prepare a pulpit declaration. In mid-July, Wilhelm Jannasch completed a draft that culminated in the demand to the parishes to make 'a written declaration of your belonging' to the Confessing Church, which 'will give you strength and support and will be an admonition to our state and its leaders'. This was a call for a written 'no', a protestation of faithfulness in opposition to the regime.[97] But after the memorandum was published by the international press, such a call for action was no longer advisable. When the Reich Council of Brethren met on 30 July, Martin Niemöller and three other members came together to edit a text drafted by Otto Dibelius, which was passed the same day. The new pulpit declaration refrained from any political references such as the condemnation of concentration camps that the memorandum had contained. The Confessing Church only called on believers to 'witness' their faith, without mentioning a written declaration to the state leadership. However, even this final version was still a courageous proclamation against the Nazi policy of the 'de-confessionalization of public life' and 'spying on church work'.[98]

On 23 August, the pulpit declaration was read out in the parishes. About three quarters of the pastors of the ApU and other 'destroyed' churches read the word, while in Bavaria and Württemberg declarations of their church leaderships were read out. The Ministry for Church Affairs explicitly decreed that pastors who read out the word were not to be disciplined. The Security Service of the Reich Leader SS, tasked with the surveillance of political opponents of the regime, tried to prevent the spread of a flyer with the text of the declaration without success.[99] On

23 August, Niemöller gave a very brief sermon in the Dahlem Jesus Christ Church on the letter of Paul to the Philippians (Phil. 1:27b). He compared the Confessing Church with the situation of Paul, who was imprisoned when he wrote the letter. Subsequently, Niemöller left the pulpit and read out the declaration at the floor level. As the London *Times* correspondent assumed with good reason, Niemöller did so to avoid violating the pulpit law. Section 130a of the Penal Code, which originated from Bismarck's 'culture war' against the Catholics, penalized disturbing public peace by clerics. When Niemöller had finished, 'many women were in tears', as the newspaper reported. The 'fervour' with which the parishioners finally sang 'A Mighty Fortress is our God' left 'no doubt about the deep feelings the religious conflict [in Germany] has caused'.[100] But one person did not participate. 'Röhricht does not read the pulpit declaration', Niemöller noted in disgust in his diary.[101]

In 1935–6, Niemöller firmly, and increasingly stubbornly, adhered to the resolutions of the synods of Barmen and Dahlem. He realized that Hanns Kerrl's church policies and the church committees appointed by him ultimately aimed to marginalize the Confessing Church and to establish state control of the Protestant Church. In January 1936 he published a brochure, written by Otto Dibelius, but edited and accounted for by Niemöller, titled *The State Church is there!*.[102] Dibelius and Niemöller argued that the state, via the church committees, not only interfered in the Church's financial and administrative, but also in its spiritual matters and that this course of action was safeguarded by the 'cooperation with the Secret Security Police'. There was only one command against the 'state imprisonment of the Church': 'One must obey God more than man.'[103] From Niemöller's perspective, the split of the Confessing Church in early 1936 was not necessarily only a defeat. On the one hand, he saw it as a 'betrayal' of the cause of the Confessing Church on the part of the Lutherans—and particularly the bishops of the three intact Lutheran regional churches. He denied any personal responsibility for the split—and rightly so. This perception would shape Niemöller's assessment of the Lutheran regional churches and the office of the regional bishop not only during his concentration camp imprisonment but far beyond 1945. The split of the Confessing Church enabled Niemöller to further pursue his decisive course without the need to make compromises, and to gather the remaining members of the Dahlemite wing of the Confessing Church in the Old Prussian Union. The first direct consequence of this course was that Niemöller used increasingly clear and strong words in criticizing the Nazi state and its church political measures from summer 1936 onwards. Already before he did that, his role in 'preserving the liberty of the Christian Gospel' was recognized internationally. In June 1936, Eden Theological Seminary in St Louis, Missouri, a Protestant seminary founded by German pastors in 1850, awarded Niemöller the honorary degree of Doctor Divinitatis. Only more than 10 years later, in January 1947, during his extended trip to the USA, was Niemöller able to express his gratitude to students and faculty at Eden Theological Seminary in person.[104]

11
Arrest and Trial 1937–1938

After the Confessing Church had informed the parishes about the content of its memorandum to Hitler in a pulpit declaration, Niemöller's public rhetoric noticeably changed. Speaking about church politics from summer 1933, he had used clear and strong words, more than once irritating both his church-internal opponents and his friends. Up till then, however, he had saved personal attacks against representatives of the state and the NSDAP for his letters to friends in the Confessing Church. Henceforth, this changed. A process of verbal radicalization started, in which increasingly pessimistic remarks about the situation of the Church, persecuted by the Nazi regime, were thrown into the mix. A little over 10 months after the pulpit declaration, on 1 July 1937, Niemöller was arrested in his Dahlem parsonage by the Gestapo.

It is hardly a coincidence that his increasingly sharp rhetoric started in the wake of the pulpit declaration about the VKL memorandum to Hitler. This statement seemed to have spurred on Niemöller's combative spirit.[1] He talked about this subject at his open evening in the overcrowded Dahlem parish hall on 21 September 1936, only a few weeks after the pulpit declaration. Thanks to the report compiled by a Gestapo officer, we are well-informed about what happened. Participation in the meetings on Monday evenings, when Niemöller talked about church political issues, was only open for those with a 'Red Card', the membership card of the Confessing Church. This was not a problem for the Gestapo officer, although entrance checks were 'particularly thorough' this evening. But the 'cold shower' followed when Niemöller started his talk by asking the Gestapo officer to leave the room. When his request for 'decency' fell on deaf ears, he got started. He described how his house was searched on 18 September. To the amusement of his audience, he ridiculed that it took—according to his diary—five officers hours to search for documents that had been lying openly on his desk.[2] Niemöller confessed he always acknowledged Gestapo orders to 'just continue doing the same thing' as soon as the officers had turned their backs on him. But he not only mocked the Gestapo. He also denounced the moral poisoning of the youth through the propaganda of Julius Streicher's *Stürmer* and the gagging of Protestant newspapers. This was reason enough for the Gestapo officer to lament Niemöller's 'malice', suggesting the pastor's 'constant agitation' should no longer be tolerated.[3]

Popular support for the Nazi regime peaked in 1936. Niemöller's open evenings in the Dahlem parish were one of the few spaces where a critical discussion of church affairs and political issues was still possible in a—limited—public environment. The impact of these evenings should not be underestimated, as they attracted large crowds. Soon after 1933, Niemöller had moved them from his parsonage to the parish hall, which held up to 800 people. In early 1937, he moved them to the Jesus Christ Church. With up to 1,500 participants, entrance checks alone took one hour.[4] Niemöller also created an uncensored public through the several talks he gave throughout the country between autumn 1936 and spring 1937, which the public prosecutor's indictment later listed meticulously.[5] On all these occasions he mostly talked about church political issues. He criticized that the church committees implemented by Kerrl arbitrarily interfered in the work of regional churches and parishes. He did not hold back in his scorn for the Minister for Church Affairs and Ludwig Müller, who still received the exuberant salary of a Reich minister although he no longer played a role in church politics after the establishment of the Ministry for Church Affairs.[6] Niemöller described the situation of Christianity and the Church in increasingly gloomy terms. In October 1936, in front of theology students in Westphalia, he explained the Confessing Church had 'lost every right'. All church doors, as he put it metaphorically, were now guarded by two posts, from the inside by the church committees and from the outside by the Gestapo. To the amusement of his audience, he made jokes about the Secret State Police, whose officers had failed to find the addressing machine he used to dispatch printed materials despite several house searches. These sarcastic attacks were followed by the complaint that Christians lived 'the life of a Church in catacombs'.[7]

At this point, Niemöller did not even shy away from blatant attacks on the leadership of the Nazi state. During an open evening in Dahlem in September 1936, he referred to the church committees as 'special departments of the Propaganda Ministry' that really had to operate 'under the company name "Joseph Goebbels"'.[8] He sprinkled his talks with satirical jibes against Heinrich Himmler and Baldur von Schirach and mocked: 'there might come the time that we are again good enough to control the people with Romans 13.'[9] This was a self-criticism of the tradition of Lutheran social ethics, which, with reference to Romans 13:1 ('Let every soul be subject under the higher powers'), demanded unconditional obedience towards the state. Only Hitler was mostly spared from such verbal attacks. In front of students in Dortmund he insisted one had to obey God more than man, and 'even Adolf Hitler is only flesh'.[10] Otherwise, despite all criticism of the Nazi regime's church policies, Niemöller still shared the Führer myth. The Dahlem parishioner August Kopff, as a witness in the trial, recalled that, at the open evening on 20 April 1936, Niemöller used Hitler's birthday as an opportunity 'to pray for the Führer in a very emphatic and relatively long prayer'.[11] His family still did so even after the Second World War had started. Their daughter Hertha, born in 1927, prayed for her detained father, but also for the Führer and the soldiers of the Wehrmacht.[12]

During public talks such as in Gütersloh in November 1936, Niemöller insisted that the Confessing Church members were 'anything but the enemies of the state'. Yet the Gestapo, whose officers carefully penned down this remark, begged to differ. In June 1936, detectives began to record Niemöller's speeches and ser-mons.[13] In January 1937, nine Confessing Church pastors from the Lübeck regional church, who had been suspended by the DC church leadership, were placed under house arrest. Wilhelm Zoellner, who wanted to hold a service on behalf of the suspended pastors in February, was hindered in doing so by Gestapo officers on orders from the Church Ministry. In response, the Reich Church Committee that he headed unanimously resigned on 12 February. However, the leaders of the regional churches—bishops and leaders of the regional church committees—who had previously signalled their support for Zoellner, let him down. Kerrl reacted promptly. In a speech on 13 February, he outlined plans for a DEK church leadership body subordinate to his ministry. When he referred to the dogma of Jesus as God's son as 'ridiculous', Niemöller and his fellow campaigners felt vindicated in their objections to Kerrl, who in their view echoed DC ideas.[14] Kerrl's plans, however, never materialized because Hitler did not support them. The anticipated foreign policy ramifications made a state leadership of the Church problematic. Instead, Hitler changed his church policy again. On 15 February, he signed a decree tasking Kerrl to prepare church elections for a general synod of the DEK. These elections never happened. But they dominated the agenda of the Protestant Church until November 1937, when Kerrl officially abandoned them.[15]

The Second VKL immediately imposed conditions for participation in the elections, and denied Kerrl the right to hold them.[16] The pressure resulting from the declaration of church elections led to a temporary rapprochement of the Confessing Church's different wings. After a long break, the Reich Council of Brethren reconvened and suggested a working group with members of the Second VKL and the Lutheran Council, which was established on 11 March 1937. This was a mere 'alliance of convenience' to strengthen joint positions in the run-up to the elections. Niemöller, whose motion to boycott the election had been outvoted in the Reich Council of Brethren, soon criticized the watering down of core positions of the Confessing Church due to this cooperation.[17] He still distrusted the Lutheran bishops of the intact regional churches who oscillated between VKL and regional church committees—which Niemöller considered non-confessional—'without deciding for one or the other side'.[18]

Niemöller closely followed the situation of the Catholic Church in light of the growing pressure from the Minister for Church Affairs. In late 1936, the Catholic population of the Oldenburg Münsterland had successfully resisted a decree to remove crucifixes and other religious symbols from confessional schools. At a tumultuous meeting in Cloppenburg, the Gau leader of the NSDAP had been forced to revoke the decree. In January 1937, Niemöller expressed his admiration for these 'powerful' protests. 'It could make one envious if', he qualified, 'we were not Protestant Christians'.[19] The confessional animosity towards Catholics no longer prevented Niemöller from contemplating a joint course of action against Nazi church politics with leading representatives of the Catholic Church. In March 1937, the Catholic Bishop of Berlin, Konrad von Preysing, visited the Dahlem parsonage. Niemöller suggested forming a 'unity front' of Confessing Church and Catholic Church. Yet Preysing thought such an 'alliance' would be a burden for the work of the Confessing Church.[20] In April 1937, Niemöller had a similar conversation with Clemens August von Galen, the Catholic Bishop of Münster.[21] In his last open evenings in Dahlem in June Niemöller pointed out state repression of the Catholic Church and Galen's resistance against interference with confessional schools.[22]

While the representatives of the Confessing Church struggled to agree on a joint position against the election decree, Hans Kerrl created a fait accompli. With another implementing regulation—now the thirteenth—of the 1935 Safeguarding Law from 20 March he appointed Friedrich Werner, the DC president of the Supreme Church Council (EOK) of the Old Prussian Church, as head of the DEK administration. Now both functions were in the hands of a National Socialist jurist, who in Niemöller's eyes had 'no relationship to the Protestant Church and its message'.[23] Further repression against the Confessing Church in the north and west of Germany followed immediately. In April and May 1937, the Second VKL and leaders of the regional churches sought to negotiate a solution for the leadership of the Old Prussian Church.[24] Niemöller, who was hardly involved in these debates, preferred to comment on the plight of the Confessing Church in several speeches. One that stood out in particular was a talk about the besieged city of God, which he held several times between March and May. It became a subject of the lawsuit against Niemöller because he referred to the Church Minister as a 'minister against church matters'.[25]

The speech was based on the biblical story of the Assyrian King Sennacherib, whose troops besieged Jerusalem. Sennacherib sent envoys to the city walls who ridiculed the God of the Israelites because he was unable to protect the citizens (2 Chr.:32). Niemöller clearly expressed the analogy:

> Just as it happened in the city of Jerusalem, which was besieged, it has been happening today with the Church for the last four years. Enemies encircle and besiege the city of God, and the enemy army, today's state, has encircled the Church with the force of its political power. But one day the besiegers will start to advance and will try to destroy Christianity by force. And we have to prepare for this day.[26]

While Erich Ludendorff, Niemöller continued, could spread his *völkisch*-pagan religious ideas unhindered, the Confessing Church was subjected to 'arrests and house searches' as well as gag orders. The Gestapo—in Niemöller's analogy the 'enemy troops'—had 'never had as much to do with the Church' than since the election decree from 15 February. In light of the looming final battle, Niemöller called on Christians to read the Bible in 'the streets and on the tube' and provoke 'opposition' in doing so.[27]

And Niemöller's strong remarks did provoke opposition, namely that of the Secret State Police—or the 'enemy troops'.[28] From late March onwards, he was repeatedly summoned to the Gestapo office at Berlin Alexanderplatz for interrogations. The judicial authorities also showed an interest in Niemöller's criminal prosecution. Starting in May at the latest, the attorney general at the Berlin regional court took the lead. In May 1937, Ludwig Chantré, at the Berlin Gestapo headquarters responsible for church affairs, had gathered enough evidence to press charges against Niemöller. All that was still needed was the delinquent's arrest.

The Decision to Arrest Niemöller

The assumption that Hitler himself was the driving force behind Niemöller's prosecution is false. Hitler had quickly lost interest in church political matters after the election decree and, with an eye on international reactions, shied away from a direct confrontation with the Confessing Church. Rather, the initiative to try Niemöller in court came from Church Minister Kerrl. However, all authorities involved agreed that Niemöller's arrest required Hitler's approval. On 2 June 1937, Theo Gahrmann, the SD Main Office official responsible for the surveillance of the Protestant churches, noted that, according to the Gestapo, 'the decision about Niemöller's arrest has been submitted to the Führer'. In his view, 'every day Niemöller is not yet arrested means a tremendous loss of prestige for the Third Reich due to the increasingly growing rabble-rousing activities of pastor Niemöller [...].'[29]

The decision to arrest Niemöller was finally made in late June 1937. Notes about the three open evenings in June that he held in the fully occupied Jesus Christ Church illuminate the run-up to the arrest. They describe a hectic sequence of events, in which Niemöller was brave, showed no fear, and indicated he knew about his looming arrest. On Monday 7 June, Niemöller listed 16 gag orders, 22 expulsions, and 11 arrests recently imposed on pastors of the Confessing Church. He reported hours-long interrogations through the public prosecutor's office without any charge. Because the 'Führer' had publicly stated that the 'living space' of the Protestant Church would not be narrowed, Niemöller argued that no one could accuse him of acting against the state when he 'fought for the German people remaining a Christian people'. He openly criticized the 'intimidation methods' of the Gestapo.[30]

On 21 June, Niemöller told his audience about the events after the previous open evening. Assessor Chantré and other Gestapo men had been sitting in a café close to the parish hall. 'Red card holders'—members of the Confessing Church—had told them what Niemöller had said an hour earlier. The participants of the open evening, who left the event at 10 p.m. 'in an agitated state', had seen SA and Hitler Youth members in the streets, trying to 'provoke'. Niemöller assumed they wanted to stage an incident and create the pretext that he was 'no longer safe' in his parish, making it possible to take him into protective custody. He talked about other pastors who had been arrested, and about Hans Asmussen, who—on Niemöller's suggestion—was in hiding. Finally, he denounced a decree issued by Kerrl in February 1937 that penalized public announcement of the numbers of church-leavers. This was exactly what Niemöller—in accordance with a resolution of the Old Prussian Council of Brethren—had done repeatedly during his services.[31]

In the following week, events came thick and fast. On 23 June, the members of the Old Prussian Council of Brethren gathered in the Friedrichswerder Church rather than in Dahlem, where the parish hall was surrounded by Gestapo men. Soon after the meeting had started, Gestapo officers entered the Church, arrested eight members of the Council and the VKL and confiscated documents. Alongside praeses Koch and Hans Asmussen, who had gone underground, Niemöller was the last member of the Council of Brethren of the Old Prussian Church who was not yet arrested. At the open evening on 28 June, the Monday after his last Dahlem service, Niemöller told his audience about the arrests and about an interrogation by Berlin Chief Public Prosecutor Ernst Lautz after the previous Monday evening. 'Will the Confessing Church be banned?', Niemöller asked. He did not think so but if it happened 'it will not destroy the Church of Jesus Christ'. Niemöller compared the situation with that of front line soldiers during the Great War, whose hearts thumped wildly before the attack started. But when 'one was in the thick of the fighting, one was completely calm'. That evening, with a joint intercessory prayer for the prisoners of the Confessing Church, he said goodbye to his parish.[32] On 29 June, he travelled to Wiesbaden and gave several talks. On 30 June, he spontaneously met with his brother Wilhelm, Friedrich Bodelschwingh, and the bishops Meiser and Wurm in Bielefeld. Back in Dahlem, he was arrested by the Gestapo in his parsonage in the morning of 1 July and brought to Moabit remand prison.[33] On 2 July, the Nazi-newspaper *Völkischer Beobachter* offered a brief article reporting that Niemöller had been arrested for 'permanent agitation from the pulpit' and had been brought before a judge.[34]

Being in Moabit remand prison marked a deep caesura in Niemöller's life. Not so much because of the restriction of his personal freedom, which he got used to surprisingly quickly, at least during the first weeks. Rather, he struggled with the sudden cessation of the relentless succession of meetings, discussions, and talks that had characterized the past four years. When he flicked through his diary of the previous year in February 1938, he was startled: 'How did I ever endure that'. The church struggle had left no time for a private life. The couple's last visit to the cinema—the only leisurely pleasure they had left—was on 24 January 1937. Therefore, 'taken out of service' through detention was, at least initially, 'certainly no loss'.[35]

In social terms, however, his imprisonment was a drastic change. In his parish and across Germany, Niemöller had met hundreds, even thousands of fellow citizens during the years after 1933. Niemöller was a sociable individual, who loved to engage in conversations even beyond church political discussions. Now his social circle was rapidly reduced to a handful of people, including—apart from his prison guards and the Protestant prison chaplain—Else and his three solicitors headed by Dr Horst Holstein (1894–1945). Holstein was a well-versed lawyer and church elder in the Dreifaltigkeit Church in Berlin. Upon Niemöller's wish, he had represented the Confessing Church in many trials from 1934. He was also a delegate at important Confessing synods, such as in Steglitz and Augsburg in 1935.[36] During the long months of remand, Niemöller and Holstein got closer on a personal level; they became friends. During his solitary confinement at Sachsenhausen concentration camp and especially during the so-called *Wartestandsaffäre* in 1939–40, Holstein, as Niemöller's personal advisor, was a central figure in his life. His letters and legal papers give insight into the work of a jurist with great legal expertise and a lot of common sense, who often saved his impatient client from rash and ill-advised actions. He was drafted into the Wehrmacht in July 1940. After the end of the war, Niemöller hoped Holstein would contribute to the re-establishment of the Church, but he passed away in November 1945.[37]

Niemöller's second lawyer was Dr Hans Koch (1893–1945). In 1937, he had represented Gerhard Jacobi, praeses of the Berlin Confessing Church. Koch also remained Niemöller's lawyer after the trial. In 1940, he joined the resistance group around Hans von Dohnanyi and Hans Oster, was arrested in the wake of the 20 July 1944 plot and murdered by the SS on 24 April 1945.[38] The third solicitor was Judicial Councillor Dr Willy Hahn, one of the most adept criminal lawyers in Berlin. Politically conservative and leaning towards the DNVP before 1933, Hahn was associated with the Confessing Church as a lay member of the Provincial Council of Brethren in Brandenburg. Hahn died in 1942.[39]

By far the most important contact person during Niemöller's remand was his wife. Else Niemöller could see her husband in Moabit prison every 10 days for 15 minutes. She often brought one of the children.[40] Perhaps even more important than the visits was their correspondence. Niemöller wrote a letter to his wife almost every day, and every letter shows his quest for emotional closeness and his worries about the well-being of the children. In September, he was in a depressed state, probably caused by the 'permanent wrangling' during the last months before the arrest. But overall, Niemöller was holding up alright. He explained this with his 'Westphalian peasant nature'.[41]

Global Solidarity with the Imprisoned Pastor

While he was confined to his cell in Moabit prison, Niemöller and his family experienced a huge wave of sympathy and solidarity. Already by the evening of 1 July, just a few hours after Niemöller's arrest, a small crowd gathered in the Dahlem Cecilienallee in front of the parsonage. The group—among them Bible school students of the Burkhardthaus, an institution for girls' welfare close by— finally walked to St Annen Church where Helmut Gollwitzer (1908–1993), a student of Karl Barth, held a short devotion. On 4 July, Gollwitzer held another evening service. This was the start of a series of intercessory services that were held in Dahlem on a daily basis until 1945. The Confessing Church had held interces- sory prayers for persecuted members before; Niemöller himself had led some of them in 1935. The novelty was that this daily practice resulted in the formation of a community based on intercession. It separated from the official Dahlem parish and became the core of the Confessing Church in Dahlem.[42] When Niemöller received a letter signed by about 250 members of this 'intercession community' in January 1938, he was overjoyed. It gave him reason to hope that his arrest would help gather the 'alienated brethren' around the 'flag' of the Barmen synod. If this was the case, he commented, then 'I'm happy to 'do time' (Fig. 9).[43]

Intercessions, pulpit declarations, and other acts of support and solidarity not only came from Dahlem and the bodies of the Confessing Church in Berlin and the Old Prussian Union.[44] There were also international protests against Niemöller's arrest. George Bell (1883–1958), Bishop of Chichester, was the first who voiced his criticism. Bell was one of the most respected Anglican bishops. 'This bell never rings for nothing', as an observer in 1925 described Bell's ability to bring his reputation to bear in the British public. And Bell's voice did not only count in Britain, but far beyond. As president of the Ecumenical Council for Practical Christianity he led the core organization of the ecumenical movement that emerged in the 1930s.[45] Bell had followed the church political development in Germany closely—always reliably informed by Dietrich Bonhoeffer—and supported the Confessing Church after 1933. On one of his tours through Germany he finally met Niemöller on 29 January 1937. Niemöller's charisma and energy distinguished him from the amicable but detached church leaders Marahrens and Zoellner—the latter 'was obviously much too old for his job', as Bell observed. Bell sensed that Niemöller's devotion and loyalty to the basic principles of the Christian faith and his missionary impulse were authentic and real. The Anglican bishop was, as his notes show, spellbound:

> He was like a man on fire, but smiling and friendly all the time; and a man of great faith. He was not just a fighter, although he was that too. He said faith was greater than organization and that there had been too much interest in organization everywhere. [...] Now the Church was being persecuted, but he emphasized the fact that the life of the Christian was a life with an obligation. [...] We could not have had a happier or more illuminating talk.[46]

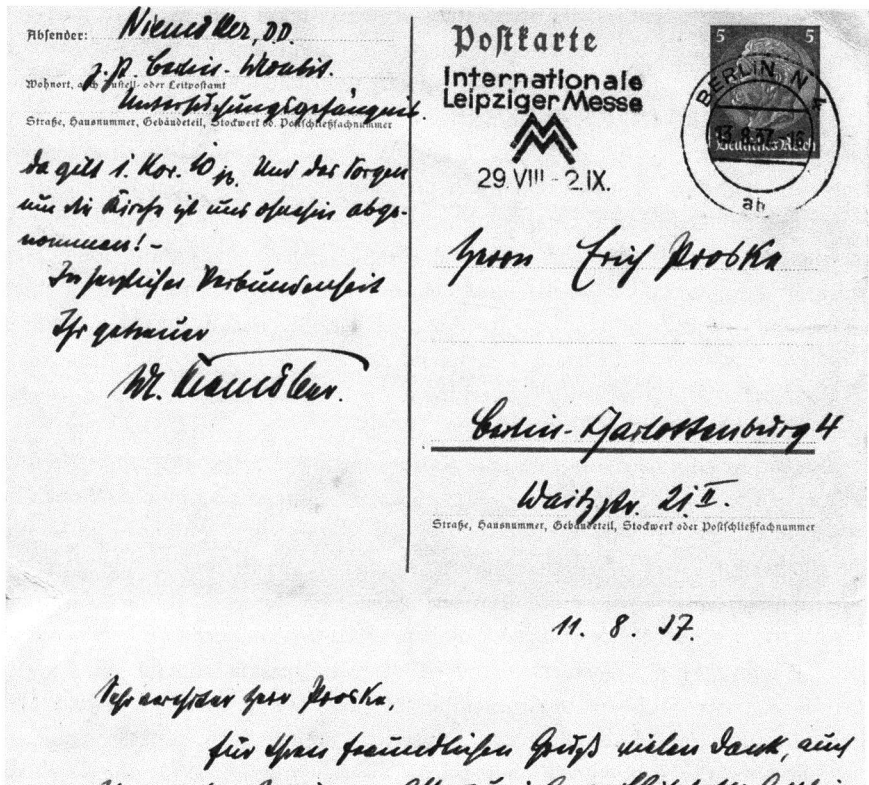

Fig. 9 Martin Niemöller wrote this card to Erich Proske, a good acquaintance from his Dahlem parish, on 11 August 1937. Optimistically, he states 'Thank God, I am well and I see the matter [his imprisonment], above all, as a well-deserved rest, but also as an opportunity to draw from God's word and thereby to refresh spiritually. And finally, such a forced training in patience is also good for my impatient soul. So I am better off after these 6 weeks than before, and rejoice every day when it comes and when it goes.' Private possession, Dr Alejandro Zorzin, Göttingen.

After Niemöller's arrest, Bell immediately wrote to Rudolf Heß, whom he had met in Munich in 1935. The detention of the pastor, famous in Germany and abroad, he reasoned, must appear as an 'attack on Christian religion as a whole'. With an eye on the ecumenical world conference in Oxford on 12 July 1937, he skilfully argued that such an act of aggression would 'inevitably unite all churches on the side of the suffering Christians in Germany'.[47] Bell hinted at the fact that pressure from ecumenical organizations had influenced the Nazi regime's church political decisions before, namely when August Jäger's integration policy was abruptly terminated in November 1934. But the hoped-for response did not come. Heß replied politely but firmly that Niemöller had exploited the pulpit for agitation against the state. Bell would certainly not agree with a German national criticizing the British government for the treatment of Catholic clerics in Ireland, or would he?[48]

Bell did not stop at an appeal to the Nazi leadership. He also wrote a letter to the editor of the London *Times*, an effective means of influencing public opinion in Great Britain at that time. He referred to Niemöller as being 'famous in the whole of Christianity' and posed the rhetorical question of whether a 'high-ranking German statesman', whose children Niemöller had baptized, would now speak up for the 'teacher' of his children.[49] This referred to a conversation between Bell and Joachim von Ribbentrop—from 1938 Minister of Foreign Affairs—in November 1934. Ribbentrop, a member of the Dahlem parish, had told Bell that, in July 1933, Niemöller had refused to baptize his youngest daughter Ursula after the Ribbentrop couple had shown sympathies for the German Christians.[50] Bell's letter to the *Times* was indicative of the rapidly growing interest of the British public in Niemöller. While in 1935 and 1936 only ten and eight articles in the London *Times*, respectively, mentioned Niemöller, this figure rose to 33 in 1937, and in 1938 even to 53.[51] In a similar vein, this also applied to the *Manchester Guardian*.[52] British laypeople also supported Niemöller. A Methodist community in Poplar in the London East End put up a banner on the wall of their parish hall asking to 'Pray for Pastor Niemöller'.[53] But bishops like George Bell and actively engaged laypeople like the Quaker Dorothy Buxton, who unreservedly supported the Confessing Church, also met with opposition. Arthur Headlam, for example, the Anglican Bishop of Gloucester, voiced the same opinion as Rudolf Heß: Niemöller was a fanatic who stood trial quite rightly if he had violated the laws of the land.[54]

In remand custody, the Dahlem pastor Martin Niemöller gradually became the international figurehead of the Confessing Church and of resistance against Hitler. This was not to be expected as Niemöller's career had already begun to falter at the time of his arrest, also because Hans Asmussen—and not Niemöller—was the foremost intellectual of the Confessing Church. Niemöller's position was primarily based on the power of the Pastors' Emergency League, which peaked in 1933 with 7,036 members. This figure already dropped significantly through the collective exit of 1,200 Bavarian pastors in 1934. In 1938, the Emergency League only counted 3,933 pastors, approximately 20 per cent of all ministers in active employment.[55]

In detention, Niemöller became *the* public symbol of church persecution in the 'Third Reich'. In this role, he even appealed to those who were initially critical of him. One of them was Hermann Klugkist Hesse, pastor of the Reformed parish of Elberfeld, who, as a member of the Confessing Church, had already been removed from office in 1934. His diary illuminates how much admiration Niemöller enjoyed from members of the Confessing Church. In November 1936, Hesse heard a speech Niemöller held in Elberfeld and found it 'excellent' as Niemöller was 'outspoken' as usual, describing the situation of the Church with catchy metaphors.[56] Hesse followed Niemöller's arrest and detention with great sympathies. Yet when the trial began in February 1938 and the Lutheran parish of Elberfeld held a rogation service for Niemöller, Hesse had had enough: as he noted in his diary, he believed 'we do too much and might give the impression as if Niemöller was the Confessing Church. This obsession with Niemöller [*Niemöllerei*], in my view, is an excessive reverence of man. Every Sunday, every Bible study session, every Confessing Church gathering commemorates Niemöller.'[57] But when Niemöller was deported to Sachsenhausen concentration camp, criticism gave way to unbounded adoration. When Hesse learned about the news, he even 'felt ill', wondering whether the Confessing Church might have been 'damned' by the Lord. Subsequently, the Reformed pastor pleaded 'God might hear our prayers' for Niemöller.[58]

Niemöller himself did not really know how to deal with his new international fame. When he received a letter from the USA asking for autographs of 'world famous people', Niemöller thought about making a stuffed 'duplicate' of himself who would carry out those tasks. When Else told him that Otto Dibelius had predicted Niemöller would feature 'in all text books of Church history', Niemöller answered—quite rightly, it can be argued—they were 'boring anyway'.[59]

Indictment and Niemöller's Defence Strategy

On 13 July, the public prosecutor presented the indictment. It contained three charges: violations of the Pulpit Law, section 130a of the Penal Code, which penalized public utterances by clerics that disturbed public peace. For remarks against the Ministers Kerrl and Goebbels, Niemöller was also charged with an offence under the Treachery Act issued on 20 December 1934, which penalized critical remarks against the NSDAP and the government. Third, Niemöller faced a charge of violating the ban on public announcements of the numbers of people leaving the church, issued by Kerrl on 28 February 1938.[60]

The defence presented several character witnesses who testified on the former Navy officer's nationalist attitude and loyalty to the state, among others the physician Ferdinand Sauerbruch, Ulrich von Hassell, and General Oskar von Watter, under whose command Niemöller had fought against the Red Ruhr Army in 1920. The prosecution had filed for a trial before the Special Court at the Regional Court of Berlin. In 1933, Special Courts had been established in the wake of the so-called Reichstag Fire Decree, which nullified many civil liberties. They were intended to accelerate criminal trials. In Niemöller's case, the opposite was true. The start of the trial, scheduled for August, was postponed, evidently following pressure from the SD (Security Service). On 17 January 1938, the prosecution added a supplementary charge to bolster its position. Simultaneously, the court sent out the summons for the main trial, scheduled for eight days starting on 7 February.[61]

Thus, Niemöller waited seven months for his trial to start. But he saw no reason to 'become bitter'. The many letters from pastors and entire parishes, even from the intact regional churches of Hanover, Württemberg, and Bavaria, indicated that the 'ship of the Church was afloat again'. 'The paint is faded, the masts are broken, the whole sight is an eyesore; but the Lord Jesus Christ is still at the helm and the ship is floating!'[62] The nautical imagery was no coincidence. Remanded in custody, Niemöller's love of the navy became 'vividly alive' again. First, he read a book by the British Admiral John Jellicoe with great enthusiasm. Then he asked his wife to bring him some volumes of Weyer's *Taschenbuch der Kriegsflotten* (*Pocketbook of War Fleets*), which had once fuelled his youthful enthusiasm for the Imperial Navy. Niemöller, as Else stressed, 'was and remained' a soldier.[63]

Meanwhile, different party and state offices vied to influence the trial behind the scenes. On 21 January, Joseph Goebbels phoned Reinhard Heydrich. Goebbels hoped to reduce the duration of the trial 'to 2 days'. For this purpose, he wanted Heydrich's SD to provide him with information about the judges.[64] On 30 January, Hitler, Gürtner, and Goebbels met to set out the 'framework of the trial'. They decided the trial should be kept 'low key', and not be exploited for propaganda purposes.[65] Finally, on 5 February, Goebbels met with one of the prosecutors and Wilhelm Crohne from the Justice Ministry to draft a road map for the trial. The guiding principles were clear: 'as short as possible, hard punishment, no public. [...] And it goes without saying that Niemöller doesn't walk free.'[66] Evidently, Goebbels had tried to persuade Hitler early on that Niemöller had to be taken into protective custody immediately after the verdict, come what may. He could count on Hitler's approval. As early as December 1937, it was known in the Church Ministry that Hitler would prevent Niemöller's release from remand custody in case the court would rescind the arrest warrant.[67]

But not everything went according to plan for Goebbels. The first day of the proceedings began with a scandal before the trial even properly started. After the defendant's personal details had been read out, the chief prosecutor moved to close the trial to the public—just as had been discussed with Goebbels before. In response, representatives of the Confessing Church as well as those of Nazi and state organizations tried to secure access for their observers. Alongside Superintendent Max Diestel—Niemöller's direct superior—the court allowed four further church representatives. On the second day of the trial, however, the court granted a motion by the prosecution to exclude all church representatives apart from Diestel.[68]

The list of regime representatives was much longer and included observers from the Ministries for Propaganda, Church Affairs, Justice and Interior Affairs, the staff of Rudolf Heß and Ribbentrop's offices as well as representatives of Hitler Youth and Gestapo. Theo Gahrmann observed the proceedings for the SD. The ordained pastor Wilhelm Brachmann, who was deemed a 'miscreant theologian' in the Confessing Church, did so for the Rosenberg Office. Brachmann's presence prompted Niemöller's dramatic response: he contradicted the prosecutor, who had asked the court to exclude the representatives of the Confessing Church, by pointing out 'ideological anti-Christian groups' were still present. He was thus prepared to withdraw his lawyers' mandate. But the court did not back down, appointed another defence counsel, and postponed the proceedings to 19 February.[69]

At least Niemöller was questioned on the first day of the trial. The court allowed the defendant to talk about his life in detail. Niemöller seized the opportunity and gave a speech that contained many elements of the narrative in *From U-Boat to Pulpit*. He presented himself as a navy officer and U-boat commander, who had risked his life for the fatherland and wanted to serve the 'uprooted German people' as a 'free corps fighter' in 1920, as a student of theology and as a pastor. He claimed to have 'always voted for the NSDAP from 1924 onwards'.[70] That was evidently untrue, as all accessible information shows that Niemöller voted for the NSDAP for the first time on 5 March 1933. Other parts of his deliberations, however, were not purely self-protecting assertions. For example, the fact that Niemöller congratulated Hitler in 1933 on Germany's exit from the League of Nations. And his remark that Jews were 'alien' to him and he 'disliked' them downplayed his attitude towards the Jews in light of his former membership in the racial-antisemitic German *Völkisch* Protection and Defiance Federation.[71]

Niemöller's strategy to emphasize his nationalist stance and his successes as an officer and anti-Bolshevik free corps fighter not only made an impression on the judges. After only two days, Brachmann was sure the defendant would end up as a 'great martyr'. No one, he opined, should treat the 'freedom of a German man' like the court had treated Niemöller. After the second day of the trial, one of the prosecutors asked him to procure 'solid material' against Niemöller for the prosecution.[72] The following day, Joseph Goebbels invited two representatives of the SD to a meeting about the trial. He phoned Roland Freisler in their presence and asked him why the Justice Ministry had failed to comply with his orders. After the call, he stated it was high time to abolish 'the independence of judges'.[73]

As he confided to his diary, Goebbels was furious.[74] But that did not change the still existing independence of judges. The trial continued with Niemöller's statement on 18 February. When questioned about the charges, Niemöller countered allegations of his outright criticism of the Gestapo and proved a 'very skilful defender' of himself.[75] The interrogation of the witnesses also did not get anywhere. The defence presented several well-known witnesses, while the prosecution could only put forward 'minor and, to some extent, inept detectives', as the SD complained.[76] On 24 February, the prosecutors held the final pleading. They demanded 25 months detention, summed up to an overall penalty of 1 year and 10 months. The defence pleaded for acquittal. Niemöller made his closing remarks. He emphasized his obligation to two oaths, his soldier's oath and the ordination vow, and his loyalty to the state 'as the Führer wants it'. He insisted that he had always only defended Christianity and asked his parish to do the same. 'Lieutenant Commander Niemöller' of yore was standing here before the court as Pastor Niemöller 'in his entire earthly existence, deeply rooted in a national sense of honour'.[77] This was no self-protective assertion. Only on 26 January 1938, one day before the birthday of the 'old gentlemen in Doorn', Emperor Wilhelm II—for whom he had strong sentimental feelings—Niemöller had expressed his political leanings in a letter to his wife: he still felt 'the same faithful and patriotic German man I used to be when I was promoted to imperial lieutenant 25 years ago'.[78]

Emphasizing his nationalist stance had clearly impressed the court. On the fifth day of the trial, the chief judge, Robert Hoepke, noted that everyone in the court hall had gained the impression of Niemöller as a 'fighter'.[79] On 2 March, the court pronounced the sentence. It considered several of Niemöller's speeches as a continuous violation of the pulpit law, section 130a of the Penal Code. With regard to the public naming of church-leavers, it confirmed the violation of the so-called Reichstag Fire Decree of 28 February 1933. In its sentencing, the court explicitly took the person and character of the defendant into account, citing parts of his own narrative in his book *From U-Boat to Pulpit*. As the judges stated, Niemöller was an 'outstanding officer' with 'firm patriotic convictions'. He had presented himself as a 'man of unreserved love of the truth'. The court concluded Niemöller had acted 'with honourable motives'. The sentence was seven months of fortress confinement, a privileged form of detention for the violation of the Pulpit Law, and a fine of 2,000 marks for the other offences. The prison sentence and a part of the fine were served by time spent in remand. The arrest warrant was repealed.[80]

The opinion of the court was delivered behind closed doors. The public was only allowed access for the pronouncement of the sentence. Meanwhile, a crowd had gathered in front of the Moabit courthouse to welcome Niemöller, albeit in vein. Niemöller was initially brought back to the nearby remand prison. At midnight he was picked up by a Gestapo car and brought to Sachsenhausen concentration camp, north of Berlin. Hitler had already ordered Niemöller's deportation to Sachsenhausen one day before the pronouncement of the sentence, on 1 March 1938. In light of Security Service reports on the trial, Hitler anticipated that the judges would not issue a long prison sentence.[81] With the deportation to Sachsenhausen, Niemöller's active involvement in the church political debates of the 'Third Reich' was finished.

As the following chapters will show, Niemöller gained the reputation of a particularly tenacious adversary of the Nazi regime thanks to his status as 'Hitler's personal prisoner', his long imprisonment and growing sympathy of international Christian churches and groups. But were Martin Niemöller and the Confessing Church really part of the resistance movement against National Socialism? This question was often asked after 1945. One crucial aspect of any answer is whether the work of the Confessing Church had a political quality and, if so, whether it was only geared towards church politics or towards the criminal policies of the Nazi regime more generally. Niemöller himself was well aware of the significance this question posed. In September 1945, he contacted Hans Ehrenberg, the Bochum pastor who as one of the first members of the Confessing Church championed the firm rejection of antisemitic positions. Ehrenberg had emigrated to England after his release from Sachsenhausen concentration camp in 1939. In 1945, Niemöller asked Ehrenberg to send him a copy of the memorandum of the Second VKL to Hitler from May 1936, which had been published in the British press. He wrote that the memorandum 'would be quite valuable to me as a proof that the struggle of the Confessing Church was obliged to draw political consequences and in fact did so', and as 'important evidence that we did not wait for the Roman Catholic Church before protesting against concentration camps and similar evils'.[82]

Any answer by historians very much depends on the definition of resistance they apply. A narrow concept of resistance is focused on a general political rejection of the Nazi regime. Viewed from this vantage point, the answer is negative. Neither Martin Niemöller himself nor the Dahlemite wing of the Confessing Church rejected the criminal policies of the Nazi regime more generally, nor did they support attempts to topple the regime. Such a form of resistance was only practised by small groups within the Confessing Church and by individuals such as Dietrich Bonhoeffer and Friedrich Justus Perels. Mediated by Hans von Dohnanyi, Bonhoeffer's brother-in-law, both men got into contact with individuals of the military resistance around Ludwig Beck. Due to their conspiratorial work with the resistance, they were targeted by the Gestapo, later arrested and ultimately murdered by the SS in April 1945.[83] It is no coincidence that, in 1945, Niemöller referred to the memorandum of the Second VKL to evidence the political stance of his church work: it was this document more than any other that was testament to the Confessing Church's potential for resistance in the sense of a more general critique of the regime.[84] Just to bear in mind, apart from softening the wording of an earlier, much more strident draft, Niemöller had no involvement in drawing up this memorandum. And the pulpit declaration for the public omitted precisely those statements about concentration camps and other aspects of the injustice of the regime that Niemöller emphasized after 1945.

These remarks might prompt the objection that Niemöller bravely bore witness to the assaults on the Christian faith in the 'Third Reich'. This is undoubtedly right. However, his protests against the German Christians' usurpation of church functions, against the implementation of the 'Aryan paragraph' in the Church or against Hanns Kerrl's church policies were all focused on fending off interventions by the state and the Nazi party in church matters, and to secure the Church's autonomy. What mattered to Niemöller was the bond of Protestant Christians with God's word and their obedience towards God. His church political activities between 1933 and 1937 emerged from his missionary understanding of pastoral work that he developed during his time in Münster. In a speech to students in Göttingen in February 1937, Niemöller denounced recent restrictions of the Church's preaching in word and script, pointing out the alternative:

> It means the state today can decide where the Gospel may be preached and where it must not be preached. This is a situation where the Church is faced with the question whether it will obey God or man. If it obeys man, it stops being Church.[85]

Niemöller did not call upon the students to disobey the Nazi state. But by publicly criticizing its interferences in church matters, he himself practised disobedience— or church disobedience, to use a term derived from Niemöller's own remarks and that is hence not analytical, but reflects the semantics of the time.

During recent decades, a consensus has been reached among historians to the effect that the term 'resistance' should not be inflated and reserved for those groups and individuals who opposed the Nazi regime as a matter of principle. This was never Niemöller's position. To use a category coined by historians, we can speak of a social 'refusal' or a 'withdrawal of loyalty' to describe Niemöller's attitude towards the 'Third Reich'. This means he effectively limited the 'claim to total rule' of the Nazi state in one particular field of society—the Protestant Church.[86] For Niemöller, it is important to stress that his 'refusal' or 'withdrawal of loyalty' was primarily directed towards the regime's church policy rather than its ideological foundations. As his behaviour during the 1938 trial shows, there was broad agreement between Niemöller's national Protestant stance and the Nazi ideology of the *Volksgemeinschaft*. Especially Niemöller's antisemitism makes it very clear that he did not oppose the 'Third Reich' as a matter of principle. The same applies to his support of the foreign policy of the Nazi regime, and in fact its conduct of war against Poland and the Soviet Union, as we will see in the next chapter.

The comparison with Dietrich Bonhoeffer is illuminating. As early as 1933, in his famous article 'The Church and the Jewish Question', Bonhoeffer had discussed the need for the Church to intervene in case 'any such group of state subjects' were made 'lawless'. Then, Bonhoeffer argued, clearly implying the members of the Jewish community, it might be necessary 'not merely to bandage those under the wheel, but to attack the spokes of the wheel itself'.[87] Following historian Michael Geyer, resistance can, in the broadest sense, be understood as solidarity with strangers.[88] But showing solidarity for people who did not belong to the Protestant Church was far from Niemöller's mind. The fact that he did not stand up for the Jews who were persecuted by the Nazi regime demonstrates this.

12

'Hitler's Personal Prisoner'

Imprisoned in Concentration Camps

When he was deported to Sachsenhausen concentration camp, Niemöller did not expect to remain imprisoned for the following seven years. Solitary confinement soon became a physical and mental strain. Detached from conflicts over church policy and with time for reading and contemplation, he developed profound doubts about the legitimacy and promise of the Protestant Church. When the Church of the ApU planned to force him into temporary retirement (*Wartestand*) in 1939, his criticism intensified, resulting in the decision to convert to the Catholic faith. It was ultimately his wife, Else Niemöller, who prevented him from taking this step. The attempts to force him into temporary retirement, the so-called *Wartestandsaffäre*, marked the rock bottom of Niemöller's life. Almost completely cut off from the outside world first in Sachsenhausen and then in Dachau concentration camps, he became a symbol of the resistance against Hitler far beyond Germany. The tension between the glorification of the prisoner Niemöller and his unabated national Protestant beliefs would cause irritation after 1945.

After he was sentenced by the special court on 2 March 1938, Niemöller was initially transferred back to remand prison. Shortly before midnight he was brought to a Gestapo car in the prison yard, where Ludwig Chantré told him he would be 'transferred to a concentration camp at the Führer's command'. Niemöller described the arrival at the gate of Sachsenhausen concentration camp north of Berlin in 1946 as follows:

> A young officer steps out of the guard house and starts shouting: 'Finally, there is the rare bird!', and soon he is surrounded by the entire guard detail. I don't know what the people are shouting and screaming; like in a dream I let everything happen to me. They are dragging me through the guard house and out through another door. For a moment I realize that I am now within the camp and behind barbed wire; but soon I am standing in front of a gate again; a bell is ringing, and after a while the gate opens. I'm in an inner courtyard in front of a long, low-rise building with a big door and many barred windows; a prison within a prison.[1]

Niemöller was brought to cell 1 of the so-called 'Kommandaturarrest' or cell block where an SS guard removed his pair of braces. The following morning the camp commander, Hans Helwig, came into his cell:

I'm the commander of the camp. You have been brought here tonight as the Führer's personal prisoner. I have not yet received instructions in regards to you. The board on the wall says how you have to behave.

Helwig then asked the prisoner about his wishes. Niemöller requested his Bible, which had been removed on his admission.

I sense the camp commander is unsure about what to do; he has no instructions and doesn't want to do anything wrong; for a moment he hesitates. Then he addresses an SS man: "Go to my office and bring the Bible that is on my desk!".[2]

Niemöller's status as 'the Führer's personal prisoner' was not clearly defined. The term was not used in official correspondence about Niemöller. We only know about it through Niemöller's recollection. However, immediately after Niemöller's internment, the SD found out that he would enjoy 'privileged treatment' in the concentration camp.[3] Niemöller belonged to the broader category of 'special and honourable prisoners' (Sonder- und Ehrenhäftlinge) who were interned by the SS in concentration camps. Most of them were high-ranking politicians and dignitaries of states that had been occupied in the wake of the expansion policy of the 'Third Reich'. An early example was the Austrian Chancellor Kurt Schuschnigg, who was transferred to Sachsenhausen directly after Austria's 'Anschluss' in March 1938. Georg Elser, who carried out the assassination attempt on Hitler in the Munich Bürgerbräukeller in November 1939, was another of Hitler's personal prisoners.[4]

Indicative of Niemöller's privileged position among these special prisoners was the fact that Hans Lammers, Chief of the Reich Chancellery, repeatedly informed Hitler about the pastor's requests for his release. This also applies to a petition by Dahlem parish council from 31 March. Lammers subsequently invited some members of the parish council for a meeting to the Reich Chancellery. Subject of the discussion was again Niemöller's phone call from 25 January 1934, with which Göring had made such an impact at the chancellor's reception. The next day, Lammers informed Hitler about the outcome of the meeting. But the Führer still refused to release Niemöller—just as on all other following occasions.[5]

What were Hitler's reasons for this decision? The response to Else Niemöller's handwritten request for her husband's release on their 20th wedding anniversary and Hitler's 50th birthday in 1939 sheds some light on this question. As Lammers explained in his—negative—response, Hitler was of the opinion that, soon after his release, Niemöller would 'again be the centre of a group of individuals that are hostile towards National Socialism' and jeopardize 'the unity of the German people'.[6] Niemöller remained imprisoned because the activities of the Dahlemite wing of the Confessing Church ran contrary to the pacification of church politics and the completion of the people's community in religious terms. These were important aims of the Nazi regime's leadership. To achieve them, the regime accepted that parts of the Protestant population and the international public showed solidarity with Niemöller.

This became clear when Else, Wilhelm, and Heinrich Niemöller applied through solicitor Hans Koch, to grant Niemöller furlough on occasion of the golden wedding anniversary of his parents on 23 July 1939. Himmler flatly rejected this request. Even a short-term furlough would 'impede' the 'pacification' of the conflicts around the Protestant Church. Moreover, the international press— particularly that of German emigrants—would interpret it as a 'hesitancy of the state leadership' that could be exploited for anti-regime propaganda. An official of the Reich Chancellery, however, pointed out that such a gesture would create gratitude not only in church circles and was therefore useful domestically.[7] Hitler again rejected the request, a decision which Lammers had already anticipated.[8] Hitler also prohibited any review of his decision to arrest Niemöller by other authorities of the 'Third Reich'.[9] Himmler's conversation with the Norwegian Bishop Eivind Berggrav—who became a symbol of the resistance after the German occupation—in February 1941 sheds further light on the reasons why Niemöller remained imprisoned until the end of the war: 'Because it was his doing that England used his preaching against us. [...] This is treason. We do not tolerate that.'[10]

Release through a Declaration to Cease and Desist?

Would Niemöller have been released after signing a declaration to cease and desist, by refraining from further church political interventions? Niemöller himself contemplated this question shortly before Christmas 1937. Was his remand only 'a kind of imprisonment for contempt' and an attempt of the Nazi regime to coerce him into signing a 'declaration of loyalty'? Niemöller asked his wife to arrange a meeting with Minister of Justice Gürtner to clarify the conditions. If the government indeed demanded a signature from him then 'we will need a great deal of patience', he wrote to Else—a sign that, at this point in time, Niemöller was not prepared to sign such a declaration.[11] Directly after the sentence and his transfer to Sachsenhausen, this question resurfaced. On 3 March 1938, the *Manchester Guardian* reported that Niemöller would only be released when he signed a 'declaration of obligation', promising to give up 'his principles'. According to the article, the rumour that Niemöller could have achieved his release by complying already circulated among supporters of the Confessing Church during the time of his trial. However, Niemöller, the report read, refused to do so.[12]

If this rumour is true then Niemöller changed his mind after only two months of imprisonment in Sachsenhausen. On 6 May, he received a visit by Admiral

Wilhelm von Lans, the former commander of the 1st squadron of the High Seas Fleet until 1915 and in this capacity Niemöller's superior. Lans suggested Niemöller should put out a statement 'which, in his view, would enable the Gestapo to rescind my detention'. This was a surprising change of events for the imprisoned pastor. In early April, replying to his query how long he would be detained, Gestapo officers in the Berlin headquarters had assured him that this depended on 'how the pastors and parishes outside responded to his arrest'. He himself could do no more than 'calming his friends down'. After von Lans' visit, Niemöller was prepared to accommodate the regime. Regarding the pulpit law, he referred to his interrogation at Gestapo headquarters on 4 March 1938. In the future, he had stated then, he would always 'inform the state police' in case his duties as a cleric and as a citizen clashed. He had 'no other wish and no other goal' than to serve 'my people' by preaching the Gospel. And in court he had already stated 'in detail' that 'I am and will be aware of my love for the people and the Reich'.[13]

Niemöller explained all this in a letter to the commander of the Sachsenhausen concentration camp that was passed on to the Gestapo with certainty.[14] Well after 1945, Wilhelm Niemöller claimed his brother had rejected Admiral Lans' suggestion to sign a declaration to cease and desist.[15] On this occasion, this misinformation did probably not result from Wilhelm's eagerness to create a heroic narrative about his older brother but from the fact that Martin did not tell him the whole truth. Wilhelm had suddenly been given permission to see his brother in Sachsenhausen and met him on 29 August 1938. According to his notes, Martin smiled 'almost bashfully' when he told him that family and friends would not have to worry about him signing such a declaration.[16] The news that Niemöller, a man with principles, was willing to sign a declaration would have sent shock waves through the Confessing Church.

But this letter was not the only attempt to achieve Niemöller's release through signing a declaration to cease and desist. Behind the scenes, his navy comrades worked on his behalf. Lans cooperated with Admiral Erich Raeder, who, as the commander-in-chief of the German Navy, was one of the leading members of the military elite in the Third Reich. A letter written by Else makes it clear that Raeder had beseeched Niemöller in 1936 to support the church committees and contribute to pacifying church politics. Apparently, Raeder's dedication to help Niemöller was not without inconsistencies. Else Niemöller complained that Lans had made defamatory remarks about her husband towards the national leaders of the German pastors' associations.[17] Nevertheless, Raeder tried to explore the conditions for Niemöller's release behind the scenes. He did not reveal any details to Else Niemöller, but assured her that he was acting for the benefit of the Protestant Church.[18] Raeder probably talked to Hitler or other high-ranking Nazi leaders in private.[19] In January 1939, however, he told Heinrich Niemöller that his and Lans' activities to help his son Martin had remained unsuccessful.[20] At the same time, in

Führer's headquarters, Hitler remarked that Raeder could try to support Niemöller 'out of old navy loyalty' as much as he liked, but he would 'remain as tough as iron' and would not 'release him into freedom'.[21]

The question of a potential declaration to cease and desist caused a considerable stir among members of the Confessing Church, particularly when the international press also raised this issue. In July 1938, the London *Times* published a letter to the editors by Arthur Headlam, the Anglican Bishop of Gloucester. Headlam repeated his well-known opinion that Niemöller had been rightly arrested for violating state laws. He also claimed it had been indicated to him that Niemöller could be released if he refrained from using the pulpit for political purposes.[22] As Headlam had contacts to government circles in Berlin, his suggestion caused a sensation within the Confessing Church. Hans Böhm, member of the Second VKL and in this capacity responsible for ecumenical issues, immediately tried to get information about Headlam's sources, albeit to no avail.[23] Preaching from the pulpit of the Jesus Christ Church in Dahlem—where he repeatedly held church service on behalf of his brother—Wilhelm Niemöller repudiated Headlam's suggestion in an improvised pulpit declaration. When rumours about Niemöller's imminent release were spreading, the Propaganda Ministry in 1939 repeatedly banned all press coverage of the Niemöller case so that foreign countries would not be provided 'with ammunition'.[24] Niemöller himself remained unaffected by all these speculations. In March 1939, he noted after a conversation with his wife that, regarding the question of a declaration, he 'could only answer: I don't know anything.'[25]

In late 1940, both Hitler and Goebbels agreed that Niemöller had to be treated well to not appear as a 'martyr'. But his release was 'out of the question'.[26] However, Else Niemöller continued to fight tirelessly for her husband's release in the following years. She was supported by the Württemberg bishop Theophil Wurm, who took a deep personal interest in Niemöller's situation. In June 1943, Wurm made another attempt to explore the conditions for Niemöller's release in a letter to Heinrich Himmler. The reply, signed by Ernst Kaltenbrunner, head of the Reich Security Main Office, made it a precondition that Niemöller would no longer disturb 'the establishment of the National Socialist people's community under the pretext of religious matters'. But this was, as Wurm soon realized, only an excuse. When the bishop offered to persuade Niemöller to sign such a declaration, he received a negative reply, stating his release was out of the question.[27]

In Sachsenhausen, Niemöller lived in solitary confinement in the so-called 'cell block'. The t-shaped compound, surrounded by a wall, consisted of 80 cells and served as prison within the camp. Other special prisoners held here alongside Niemöller were, for example, Georg Elser and, from 1940, the Polish bishop Władysław Goral. Niemöller was strictly isolated from other inmates. Unlike regular detainees in the camp, he did not have to work and did not experience torture, abuse, and humiliation from the hands of the SS.[28] His encounters with SS men in the cell block were kept to a minimum. Niemöller only met other prisoners when he was treated by nurses or dentists in the infirmary.[29] On the way back from the so-called *Kommandantur*, the building of the camp command where the meetings with his wife took place, Niemöller saw Heinrich Grüber twice and once Heinrich Bokeloh, a pastor from East Frisia, 'standing in line' at roll call.[30] Otherwise, he was only informed about the events in the camp as an earwitness: in the courtyard of the cell block prisoners were physically punished. Niemöller could hear the screaming of the tortured fellow inmates.[31] His cell was located on the right-hand side, next to the entrance to the cell block. As Niemöller recalled, it measured 3.5m by 2.2m and was equipped with a bunk, a small table with footstool and a small shelf for crockery. The loo was in a corner to the right of the door.[32] Once a day in the afternoon, the prisoner was brought to the 'arrest court' of the camp for a stroll.[33]

Only few visitors were allowed. One of them was Kurt Scharf, pastor of the Sachsenhausen parish and active member of the Confessing Church since its beginnings. He was able to get a visitor's permit for Good Friday 1938. On this occasion he could—in the presence of the camp commander and two SS officers—celebrate Holy Communion with Niemöller in an empty cell opposite Niemöller's.[34] A permit for regular visits was only given to Else. They took place once a month, initially at the Berlin Gestapo headquarters on Alexanderplatz, with an assessor or police constable always being present, occasionally two or even three officials.[35] In spring 1939, these visits were moved to the Sachsenhausen concentration camp.

On 26 May 1939, his oldest daughter Brigitte visited Niemöller for the first time with her mother. The previous day, Else Niemöller had learned at Heinrich Himmler's adjutancy, where she was treated in a 'very accommodating way', that her children above the age of 17 were allowed to accompany her. But when Brigitte 'saw her father in prison stripes, tears gushed from her eyes'.[36] This was also a new sight for Else as Niemöller had always worn civilian clothes during visits at Gestapo headquarters. However, she found it 'more informal' to have visits in the concentration camp and got used to the prison uniform after just a few minutes.[37] From August 1939, the Gestapo granted her a visitor's permit every fortnight—probably in response to one of her petitions.[38] One of the young theologians who covered for Niemöller in the Dahlem parish—including Hans Peter Jessen, Wolfgang Saß, who worked as an assistant preacher in Dahlem from summer 1937, and Helmut Gollwitzer, who was assigned to substitute for Niemöller from April 1938— used to accompany Else on her way from Dahlem to the camp gate. Else Niemöller and her companion occasionally took a horse or motorcar cab for the approximately two-kilometre journey from the S-Bahn station Oranienburg to the concentration camp. But most of the time she walked.[39]

In March 1939, Niemöller started to compile detailed, three- or four-page-long handwritten minutes of every meeting with Else. He started writing as soon as he was back in his cell—Else's visits were mostly around lunchtime—and sometimes spent one or two more days to complete his notes. These minutes show that Martin and Else's conversations followed a constant pattern and both acted according to a certain 'routine'.[40] First, they exchanged news about their mutual well-being and the things Niemöller cared most about in 1939 and 1940: his forced temporary retirement and the planned conversion—both of which we will discuss in detail further below. Then Else reported on the seven children, starting with the eldest. The next talking point was Dora and Anni, the two house maids, without whose support Else could not have managed to keep house in the parsonage. This was followed by 'death notices'—which increased especially from the beginning of the Second World War—and news about 'sick people'. Finally, Martin asked Else to pass on his best wishes to close friends and many members of the Dahlem parish.[41]

For Niemöller's first year in the concentration camp—that is, before he started to draft these notes—we must rely on his letters to Else as a source for his state of mind. They show that solitary confinement in Sachsenhausen affected him much worse than the time in remand custody, which practically flew by. Health problems were one reason for this. Over the course of several months, Niemöller suffered from recurrent neuralgic headaches. When her husband told Else about visual impairment caused by the neuralgia in February 1939, she turned to Heinrich Himmler. Immediately, the camp commander, Hermann Baranowski, was brought in, who requested the camp doctor to submit a report. Himmler's adjutant showed Else this report in addition to the minutes of an interrogation with Niemöller about his health, which was supposed to reassure her.[42] These efforts demonstrate the Nazi regime was very keen to avoid negative news about Hitler's personal prisoner.[43]

But health issues were only some of Niemöller's problems. More important was that his transfer to the concentration camp had crashed any hope of being released soon. And this clearly got to him. As he wrote to Else in July 1938, he lacked 'the mental capability, I can't stand it any longer'. These emotional problems also put a strain on the few hours Niemöller had with his wife. It reached the point that he only 'felt secure in his cell', and thus some of Else's visits went by without a proper conversation.[44] The 'present is not life', Niemöller penned in August 1938, and he was 'really only living in the past'. He wrote notes about his childhood and delved into books on battle fleets that he had last read as a young man.[45] In February 1939, Else heard alarm bells ringing when Martin told her that his life was really 'nothing more than a very prolonged dying'.[46] She immediately assured him how 'affectionate' he had been during her last visit, urging him 'not to think about death all the time', even though she could imagine this was understandable in his situation. Else obviously feared Martin was thinking of taking his own life. She suggested having 'happy and grateful thoughts' about herself and the seven children every day for 15 minutes each. This would fill two hours of the 'endless, long day'.[47] For Martin, however, this well-intended advice was 'mere theory', and it might have made him even more acutely aware of his dire situation.[48] After only a few months of imprisonment, he painfully realized that he was 'increasingly ousted as a family father'. It was of small comfort that this happened to the benefit of 'good friends' and 'loyal neighbours' who stepped up to fulfil this role.[49]

This remark referred to a circle of close friends that played an increasingly important role for Else. They were by her side on a daily basis and assisted her in the upbringing of the children. For example, in their letters the couple mentioned a friend of Else named 'Gisela'. This was code for Hans Bernd Gisevius (1904–1974), who had helped establish the Gestapo in 1933–4 but was active in the military resistance from 1938 onwards. Using a code name was a wise precaution: after the 20 July 1944 plot, Gisevius had to go into hiding. Thus, the Gestapo never discovered his relationship to Niemöller.[50] Hans Asmussen, who visited the parsonage frequently, became Else's 'loyal adviser'.[51] Even more important was Helmut Gollwitzer, who, for example, spent Christmas Eve 1938 with Else and the children. After the German invasion of Poland in September 1939, the wine cellar of Cecilienallee 61 became a provisional air-raid shelter, where Gollwitzer spent several nights to reassure the family. In April 1940, Else wrote about the pastor always ready to help: 'above all he is very good with the boys, and can even handle Brigitte'.[52] Of all pastors and supporters of the Confessing Church who visited her house every day—17 people on average, as she wrote in June 1940—it was Gollwitzer she got along with 'the best', even though his punctuality left 'a lot to be desired'.[53]

It was no problem for Niemöller that close family friends helped Else with everyday life. It did, however, bother him that—with increasing duration of his imprisonment—his wife not only demonstrated her willingness but also the ability to manage family and parsonage on her own, take responsibility, and even deny her husband's wishes. This did not correspond with Niemöller's paternalistic image of himself in particular and of a husband in general. In a letter written in remand custody, he had denounced two men who were not mentioned by name as 'Lau-Männer' ('pussies'), whose weakness he, as a 'German man', very much disliked. 'How', he asked rhetorically, did those men present themselves 'in front of their wives', whose '"masters" they should really be!'.[54] During his imprisonment in Sachsenhausen, Niemöller gradually realized he could not act up as such a 'master' towards his wife. Else Niemöller was well aware that her newly found autonomy, which resulted from her husband's imprisonment, could strain their relationship. In August 1939, she wrote to Martin:

> I have gradually learned to make my own decisions. I know it is very hard for you to accept that and only knowing this makes me somewhat bear your wrong impression of me.[55]

The knowledge of Niemöller's problems to accept his wife's new autonomy did not stop her standing her ground in all important crises and conflicts between

1938 and 1941, even against her husband's will, and blocking decisions that would have had drastic consequences, not only for the Niemöller couple. One example was her refusal to emigrate to England with the children. Martin Niemöller had first voiced this idea while remanded in custody to spare his children the embarrassment of having a father in prison. In Sachsenhausen, he soon came back to this topic. Anna Riethmüller—the widow of Otto Riethmüller, director of the Dahlem Burckhardthaus who had passed away in 1938—had calculated how much money Else would get from her widow's pension in case Martin died. In his eyes, the amount was so small that moving to England with the help of friends of the Confessing Church seemed the best option. But when, during a visit in March 1939, he tried to urge Else to make a decision, she simply answered: 'I can't.'[56] And that was the end of that.

Wartestandsaffäre and Voluntary Application for Military Service

The so-called Wartestandsaffäre turned out to be even more fraught with conflict. On 2 June 1939, the Consistory of the Protestant Church of Mark Brandenburg informed Niemöller that he had been placed into temporary retirement.[57] Immediately after his deportation to Sachsenhausen concentration camp, the Evangelical Supreme Church Council (EOK) had considered opening disciplinary proceedings against Niemöller and removing him from his Dahlem pastorate. The Consistory had opposed such a step. It was not before March 1939 that the president of the EOK, Nazi jurist Friedrich Werner, issued a decree which had long been in preparation: the decree on transferring clergy for official reasons. It enabled church authorities to place a pastor into temporary retirement without a public hearing and burden of proof that applied to disciplinary proceedings. Under this decree, it was justification enough to point out Niemöller could no longer fulfil his pastoral duties because he had been imprisoned for two years. This procedure was obviously a farce, even more so because Friedrich Werner, the spiritus rector of the decree, was also the only and final arbiter on any complaints.[58]

Niemöller was beside himself. He immediately told his lawyers to file a complaint. But on 25 November 1939, the Consistory confirmed the decision and announced his temporary retirement beginning 1 January 1940. This ultimately never happened because the church authorities soon decided to suspend these and other measures against undesirable pastors to pacify the Church during the war. But Niemöller had no knowledge of this. Horst Holstein only informed him the decision was suspended in May 1940. Thus, for almost one year, Niemöller was convinced the Wartestand was a done deal. He was sure to lose his pastoral office on 1 January 1940 and his family to be removed from the parsonage. Hence, the Wartestandsaffäre marked the absolute low point of his entire life.

Niemöller could not refrain from expressing his bitterness, anger, and frustration. He wrote two letters to this effect. In a lengthy document he not only lectured Friedrich Werner that the measures he had implemented made a mockery of orderly procedures. Niemöller also added a verbal insult in form of a 'classical quote'—referring to Goethe's play *Götz von Berlichingen* and its protagonist saying: 'He can lick my a . . .'. But even more important was the conclusion Niemöller drew from the actions of the EOK and the Consistory. For him, the regional church of the ApU—he always put *Landeskirche* in inverted commas to ironize the notion it was a church at all—was a merely 'worldly organization, completely separated from the Church', only concerned with three tasks: administering funds that were extracted from parishes that were the real owners of these assets; redistributing these levies in favour of the German Christians; and 'the removal of undesirable personalities of the Church who stand in the way of the silent liquidation of the Protestant Church'. Consequently, this meant:

> In this organization, the ecclesial confession and the constitution of the Protestant Church of the Old Prussian Union are practically, and largely also substantially, suspended. Thus, for a Christian, it is irrelevant and superfluous.[59]

At the end of his letter to Friedrich Werner, Niemöller again emphasized what he had already told the president of the consistory, Johannes Heinrich, 10 days earlier, on 12 December 1939:

> Until your principal [referring to the EOK] has made a final decision in this matter, I have, by way of precaution, arranged for me and my family to leave the "Protestant regional church".[60]

In doing so, Niemöller severed ties with the Protestant Church. This decision came in the context of his long-lasting deliberations to convert to Catholicism, which we will look at in more detail in the next section. However, being placed into temporary retirement was the final trigger of his decision to leave the Protestant Church. On 13 December, following their previous letters and conversations, Niemöller instructed his wife to do the same for herself and the children who had not yet reached the age of religious maturity. We do not know what exactly Else discussed with her husband at her following visit to Sachsenhausen on 21 December, as no notes about this conversation exist. According to Martin Niemöller's notes about Else's next visit on 4 January, the one in December had been 'unfortunate'.[61] It is fair to assume Else was not prepared to leave the Church and told him so. It appears she did not want to follow him in this for him profoundly existential question.

However, Martin could count on Else's support in another matter, which stirred up more global interest and bewilderment than any other episode in his life as it did not correspond in the slightest with the legend of Niemöller as a principled resistance fighter: his volunteering for military service in the Wehrmacht. We need to discuss this step in connection with his temporary retirement—the *Wartestandsaffäre*—as it can only be fully understood in this context. On 7 September 1939, one week after the German attack on Poland, Niemöller sent a handwritten letter to the High Command of the Navy in Berlin:

> As I have waited in vain to be drafted for military service, despite having submitted in time all required reports and information about my time as a former active naval officer since the time of the "Black Reichswehr", I hereby apply explicitly as a volunteer for military service.[62]

This application, Niemöller clarified, applied to 'any deployment in military service'. He referred to his active service in the '1914–18 war' and again in the 1920 'Spartacist uprising in the Ruhr area'. His 'crew comrades', he wrote, were surely willing to provide information about him—meaning about his suitability and attitude. Niemöller concluded this military-style letter with the closing 'Heil Hitler!'—a phrase he did not use for the first time.[63]

The letter provides some clues about the expectations that led to the application for military service. In August 1935, in a speech delivered in Hanover, Niemöller had explicitly tasked the Nazi state with building a strong 'Wehrmacht' for the looming 'struggle for existence' of the German people. Undoubtedly, Niemöller supported the rearmament policy of the Nazi regime. When his brother Wilhelm visited him in August 1938, he had just read in the newspaper—his daily reading in Sachsenhausen included the *Völkischer Beobachter*—that all former officers had to report for military service until the end of September. Martin asked Wilhelm to arrange this for him, still wondering whether the Wehrmacht was even interested in his contribution after his one-and-a-half-year detention in a concentration camp.[64] It was thus only logical that he instructed Else on 24 August 1939 to look for the mobilization order in the event of war that he kept in an 'iron box' in the parsonage. Like Martin, Else was convinced a war was 'to be expected soon'.[65] On 4 September, she wrote to her husband her inquiries at the recruitment district office (*Wehrbezirk*) had established that everything was 'alright' with the mobilization order. In this letter she used phrases typical of the national Protestant discourse—now in the context of the war against Poland—claiming that the German people, chosen by God, was under His protection:

> Let us hope that God will put our beloved German fatherland under his specific protection! Many words from the Bible acquire a new ring in this new situation! Our lives as well, and yours, are in His hand, and God will guide us as He sees fit. More than at any other times, we must stop ruminating.[66]

What she meant was that Martin should start acting rather than brooding. The decision to act was made at the meeting on 7 September. Martin learned that his brother Wilhelm was already drafted as first lieutenant of the reserve and did military service in Osnabrück. He talked about his own situation with Else and asked for her thoughts on his plan to apply for voluntary service, explaining all the 'problems' this involved—probably referring to a potential refusal. Among his closest friends from the Confessing Church, Jacobi had 'already gone' to Poland, while Fritz Müller still waited to be drafted. Else reported that their closest friends were 'divided' on the matter. Captain Martin Schulze, a close colleague since the beginnings of the PEL, and Niemöller's solicitor recommended reporting for voluntary service. As her husband noted, Else 'was a bit more cautious but still said she thought it the right thing to do'. With this, Niemöller had all necessary information to make a decision. He asked Else to talk to Walter Lohmann (1891–1955), an old comrade of Crew 1910, who was head of the navy budget department at the High Command of the Navy. It is likely this conversation was intended to sound out whether or not a concentration camp inmate's application for voluntary service was likely to be accepted by the Navy Command, and, if possible, to increase its chances. Niemöller concluded, as he wrote after his conversation with Else, to make a decision 'within 24 hours'. But he submitted his application the same day.[67]

Never shy of misrepresenting historical facts when it served his brother's reputation, after 1945 Wilhelm Niemöller claimed he was 'sure' the 'encouragement' to report for voluntary service came from the Dahlem parish and that Else conveyed this to Martin on 7 September. It was 'absurd' to suggest Martin Niemöller had acted on account of 'nationalist and militarist' motives. Rather, he demanded 'freedom' to 'speak as a Christian'.[68] However, the notes about the conversation with Else on 7 September contain no mention of encouragement from the parish.[69] The news about his brother and Jacobi having been drafted put certainly moral pressure on Martin Niemöller to apply for military service himself. But the decision was his, and his alone, 'cautiously' supported by his wife, who probably—and rightly so—feared for his life. This decision was, first and foremost, that of a career soldier who would not shy away from risking his life for his nation in the event of a war. A note to the Secret State Police Office (*Gestapa*) in Berlin, written on the same sheet of paper as the application for voluntary military service to the High Command of the Navy, reveals that Niemöller's motive was by no means his liberation from concentration camp detention:

I would like to remark explicitly that I would have preferred to be drafted immediately, which would made my application for voluntary service unnecessary, because now it could give rise to the impression I would seek for an escape from the concentration camp. Hence, I declare on my own account that I will, as a matter of course, make myself available to continue my protective custody immediately after my release from military service.[70]

When Else returned to Sachsenhausen on 19 October, the Gestapo assessor present let her know in passing that the High Command of the Armed Forces—rather than that of the Navy that Niemöller had sent his application to—had refused to accept his voluntary military service. Niemöller 'was dumbfounded' and 'Else had tears streaming from her eyes'. The terse letter, signed by Wilhelm Keitel, was given to Niemöller on the same day.[71] On 2 November, Martin explained to his wife the exact wording of the letter and the probable reasons for it. He asked her to instruct his lawyers to submit the sentence of the 1938 trial 'to the relevant authorities', probably hoping to stress his honourable motives for his church political actions. Then he said to Else he was 'standing exactly where we started in 1919', that is, before he started studying theology.[72] This must be seen as a reference to the *Wartestandsaffäre*. After all, in autumn 1939 Niemöller expected to be removed from his Dahlem pastorate at the end of the year. What would be more obvious in this situation than returning to his old job instead of hoping for a new position as a pastor?

The most important reason for this decision, however, was Niemöller's intention to defend the German nation in the event of war, which had already become visible in 1938. The fact that he understood this as a service for the nation rather than for the Nazi regime—although a definite dividing line could, for all practical purposes, not be drawn between the two—is illustrated by one of Niemöller's earlier decisions. On 25 February 1939, he read an article by Joseph Goebbels in the *Völkischer Beobachter*. The Propaganda Minister denounced 'enemies of the German people abroad', who were in cahoots with a 'small clique of intellectuals and professional nay-sayers' in Germany. For these reasons, Goebbels opined, 'the anti-German newspapers in Paris, London, and New York adore Niemöller and the Confessing front'.[73] This went against Niemöller's grain. He did not see himself as an enemy of the German people, but as a Protestant nationalist. Goebbels had attacked his honour, and Niemöller responded according to the code of honour of a German officer. The same day he wrote to Admiral of the Fleet Raeder, letting him know that he henceforth waived the right to wear uniform that he had retained with his discharge from the Navy in 1919. When Raeder failed to answer, he repeated this waiver in August, adding this was a 'necessary requirement due to my respect for the robe of honour', which he had worn, and served his 'personal cleanliness'.[74]

Niemöller's reaction demonstrates that, even two decades after his release from active service, he still adhered to and acted in line with the officer corps' code of honour. This self-evidently included his willingness to serve his country in arms in the event of war. Analysing the expectations that caused Niemöller's decision to report for voluntary service in 1939 clarifies this motive. Niemöller was convinced that the war against Poland was inevitable. Otherwise he would not have said that the 'news about how the Poles are conducting this war' weighed 'certainly heavily' on his daughter Brigitte's 'heart', who just got engaged with a staff surgeon of the Wehrmacht.[75] Undoubtedly, Niemöller's isolation in the concentration camp contributed to him believing in the Nazi news coverage on atrocities committed by the Polish army. But first and foremost, he acted in accordance with the habits of a career officer who was inclined to ascribe inferior motives to the enemy. Else confirmed this view when she told Martin about Captain Carl Schako in October 1939, an old friend from the work with the Bible study groups. She thought her husband 'will be pleased to hear' that Schako had been awarded the Clasp to the Iron Cross First Class for his 'daring enterprises' against the Polish. This military decoration was given to those soldiers who had already been awarded with the Iron Cross in the First World War.[76]

The campaign against Poland was soon over and ended in a clear victory of the German troops, which commenced their policy of ethnic cleansing in occupied countries. 'Operation Barbarossa'—the German attack on the Soviet Union in June 1941—brought success and enormous territorial gains. However, after the lost battle of Stalingrad in 1943, it could no longer be overlooked that, in the east, the German army had been forced onto the defensive. Niemöller, at this time detained in Dachau concentration camp, started brooding again. In late April 1943, he wrote to Else:

> Sometimes I am tormented by the thought that the whole bloody fighting might end for us in Bolshevism; but we—you and me—can't do anything about it except pray that we and our country and people will be spared such a terrible fate; and sometimes I think of the devotion I held in Bielefeld 15 years ago at the Inner Mission Week, before Professor Auhagen spoke about his impressions in Russia, about Ephesian 6:11–12. I am still—and more than ever—convinced the Apostle guides us the only possible way.[77]

The defensive war situation in 1943 refreshed Niemöller's anti-Bolshevism, which he had already cultivated during his time in Münster at the Inner Mission, whose work he understood as a fight against the secularism of the 'godless' communists. At the 1929 Inner Mission Week in Bielefeld, Otto Auhagen had delivered a speech. Auhagen was a political science professor and Protestant Christian, who, as an agricultural expert at the German embassy in Moscow, reported on the devastating consequences of Stalin's collectivization.[78] Consistent with his anti-Bolshevism, Niemöller again drew on the national Protestant interpretation of history: in the sense of Apostle Paul (Eph. 6:11: 'Put on the whole armour of God, that ye may be able to stand against the wiles of the devil!') the success of the German people and its victory in the fight against the wiles of the enemy was at

stake and had to be prayed for. In June 1943, Niemöller summarized his deliberations in a letter to Else:

> During the last weeks and months I have often thought about the question
> whether I should try again and apply for voluntary service; but Keitel's letter in
> response to my first attempt does not leave me with the possibility to take the
> initiative again, although it makes me sick to watch. As long as everything
> seemed to go well, it was not even half as difficult—but let's drop that![79]

When Niemöller considered signing up for military service again in 1943, it
seemed to him that his contribution was even more urgent than in 1939, when a
swift victory of the Wehrmacht in Poland was foreseeable. In both cases, the
driving force behind his wish to join the German troops was the willingness of a
nationalist former career officer to fight for his fatherland.

The news about his volunteering for military service spread rapidly in
September 1939; first among members of the Confessing Church, then among
the international public. In a circular published during the Advent season, Helmut
Gollwitzer reminded his friends that 'no one' could 'really put himself in his
shoes'. Even though Niemöller's action 'was a mistake', 'no one should be swayed
about him'. This statement would have been more convincing had Gollwitzer not
proudly reported on Fritz Müller's conscription in the following, who was 'now
wearing the honourable uniform of a lieutenant'.[80] It remains an open question
whether, like Niemöller, Müller had volunteered for military service in the
Wehrmacht after he had been removed as a pastor in March 1939.[81] Karl Barth,
who was informed about Niemöller through family friends, initially denied the
rumour of his volunteering, and the *Daily Telegraph* published this disclaimer.
After he had been informed of the facts, he entered into a correspondence with
Bishop George Bell. Parts of this correspondence were printed in the French
media in December. In a letter to Adolf Keller, an ecumenist based in Geneva,
Barth showed surprisingly good insight into Niemöller's state of mind. He was,
Barth wrote, an 'old German-National' and 'fighter for order against the com-
munists', who 'had not moved on from the malign tradition of the majority of
German Protestantism as much as one would have hoped for' (Fig. 10).[82]

A Dutch newspaper already covered Niemöller's voluntary application on 17
October 1939, claiming that, according to their information, his motivation had
been the 'love of the fatherland' rather than the 'wish to be released'.[83] The London
Times also published the story, confirming Niemöller's intention 'to serve his
fatherland'.[84] In November, the *Observer* quoted a report in the *Neue Zürcher
Zeitung*, which shows how quickly the story travelled internationally.[85] But all
these reports were nothing compared to the wave of indignation that Niemöller
experienced after the liberation in 1945 because of the decision he made on
7 September 1939.

Fig. 10 George Bell (left) and Franz Hildebrandt (centre) in front of St Martin-in-the-Fields in London on 1 July 1941 after an intercession service for the imprisoned Niemöller. George Bell was the most important advocate of the Confessing Church in English-speaking countries. After Niemöller's arrest, he kept in touch with Else Niemöller and visited her in Berlin in 1938. On 1 July 1938, the anniversary of Niemöller's arrest, Bell organized the first service of intercession for the imprisoned pastor at St Martin-in-the-Fields. He repeated this every year until 1944, always delivering the sermon himself. bpk no. 00103118.

The Planned Conversion to the Catholic Church

The application for voluntary service is an important episode of Niemöller's time in Sachsenhausen, particularly because it had considerable impact on his public image after 1945. The prevailing topic of the time between 1938 and 1941, however, was Niemöller's planned conversion to the Catholic Church. The thought that he might have become a Catholic is apparently such a disturbing one that previous biographers of Niemöller decided to only mention this in passing, as a brief, fleeting episode.[86] And yet, his planned conversion was an extremely multi-layered matter that defies simplistic attributions.[87] Before we discuss some of its many dimensions in detail, let us have a look at the chronology. As his letters to Else show, Niemöller started to intensively engage with Catholicism in August 1938, after someone had sent him a Catholic Mass book. Niemöller was 'surprised about the richness of prayers and biblical lections' that it contained. In Easter 1939, he received a copy of the *Breviarum Romanum* with the liturgy of the hours. The Catholic practice of piety helped him enrich the meagre 'spiritual self-catering' he faced in solitary confinement without the chance of receiving Holy Communion. In the *Breviarum* and the early church hymns, he discovered 'quite a few things that have died away due to the sterility of our Protestant, often mistakenly so-called theology'.[88]

In spring 1939, this voyage of discovery into a world of piety that had hitherto been unknown to Niemöller, gradually turned into critical reflections about inconsistencies of the Reformation principle of sola scriptura, according to which the Holy Scripture is the only source of the message of salvation. He entered into a dialogue with his wife—both by letter and in conversation—and with Hans Asmussen, arranged and mediated by Else. From July 1939, these reflections deepened into the plan to convert. The immediate reason was the *Wartestandsaffäre*. His placement into temporary retirement had convinced him that the Protestant regional churches—that of the Old Prussian Union and all others—were nothing more than bureaucratic entities, programmed to secure their continued existence, but devoid of any authority to talk about salvation. The Protestant Church, he wrote in July 1939, had 'never been a Christian Church', not even in the sense of the sixteenth-century confessional documents.[89] A few days earlier, he had—as mentioned above—already declared his exit from this Church in a letter to the president of the consistory. This was the first step of his path towards the Catholic Church.

This decision, made in July 1939, was the beginning of an intense battle between Martin and Else, who was supported by her closest advisers. It lasted the following 18 months and became a heavy burden on the relationship between Else and Martin Niemöller. And yet, during all these months, a resolution of the conflict was never on the horizon. On 9 February 1941, Niemöller wrote to Else he had 'apparently missed the right time for a decision'.[90] But his plan was not yet off the table. Else's visit on 22 February 1941 turned into a decisive confrontation:

> Else became really dramatic when she beseeched me not to become Catholic, but to my surprise she came up with economic reasons for this! "Then you can become a street sweeper; and how are we then going to survive with the children? We can't feed more than 3 then!"—I promised her that I would not take any step in this direction without her knowledge, and that I was reading Newman at the time.[91]

The Anglican priest John Henry Newman (1801–1890) had himself converted to the Catholic Church in 1845, where he later became a cardinal. It is not surprising that Niemöller would turn to his writings as he himself thought of emulating Newman's example. Three days later, Else again implored him in a letter not to make a decision yet, particularly because there was no 'right moment' anyway. She also pointed out the consequences of such a step for Niemöller's friends and acquaintances, and for the Protestant Church as a whole. For some of them, his conversion would be a 'beacon' and an instigation to follow him immediately.[92] On 6 March, Niemöller noted after the meeting with Else that he was 'rather shaken': 'quousque tandem?!'—'How much longer?' On 17 April, Else wanted to know whether he did a lot of reading, which Niemöller answered in the negative. When she asked him cockily if he was sucking his thumb instead, he broke off the meeting 'because I am very much on the edge'.[93] On 23 March, his father had died, which left him completely devastated.[94] At this point in time, Niemöller weighed less than 133 pounds and had lost any physical and mental energy.

Immediately after this meeting, Else abruptly stopped asking about Martin's conversion plans both in her letters and during the visits to Sachsenhausen. Instead she recommended light novels in English language.[95] In light of Niemöller's poor physical and mental health, this strategy of distraction and de-thematization proved successful. In a letter from 4 May, he still insisted he had no reason to 'revise his objective opinion' in this matter. But he confirmed 'a concession', namely his promise to Else from 22 February not to decide on the conversion without informing her in advance. Letters from the following months hardly ever touch upon this topic. Niemöller had to admit that reading theological books had 'not saved' him 'from slowly descending into idiocy'. Instead he played solitaire 'from morning to night'.[96] On 11 July 1941, he was transferred to Dachau concentration camp. This move came as a complete surprise. On 18 July, he met Else there for the first time. When Martin told her that he was accommodated with two Catholic priests, Else said: 'Just don't become a Catholic now!'[97] At this point, this remark was not much more than a little joke. Clearly, the plan to convert to the Catholic Church was already off the table for Niemöller even before he was transferred to Dachau.

What was theological and spiritual context of the conversion? The first dimension was—as already mentioned—the Catholic practice of piety that Niemöller gradually adopted in the face of his forced 'spiritual self-catering'. The legal dimension of *Wartestandsaffäre* came second. Indeed, Niemöller was willing to 'seek and re-establish contact to the Church'. But he waited for a 'clear sign that will clear the path for me'. As he wrote to his wife in July 1939, this sign came when he was notified about his temporary retirement.[98] When he initiated leaving the ApU, several legal problems arose, which Niemöller discussed with his lawyers.[99] A third dimension was related to the weakening of the confessional dichotomy between Protestants and Catholics, which was deeply embedded in the religious history of the territories of the Holy Roman Empire since the Reformation. This divide, however, had started to soften from 1933, due to a number of reasons. Growing numbers of staunch Nazis left the Christian churches and referred to themselves as '*gottgläubig*', 'believing in God', a Nazi term for belief beyond and outside the Christian confessions. In addition, Protestants who had previously left their churches now started to re-enter. An increasing number of people converted to the Catholic Church. Between 1933 and 1945, 70,000 Germans converted to the Catholic Church, most of them Protestants. This figure is the absolute minimum, as there are no data for a period of four years. From 1933, conflicts over church politics led to a pluralization of the entire sphere of religion.[100] At the same time, the opposition between the confessions softened.

In this situation, Niemöller realized that Protestant identity was to a great extent based on opposition to the Catholics. As we have already seen, in 1936 he was prepared to join forces with the Catholics in the fight against Nazi neo-paganism. But now it was about something else: Niemöller had become convinced that Protestants only had a 'confessional consciousness'—rather than an awareness of the specific qualities of their Church—which he understood as being solely based on the 'defence against Rome'. He considered the work of the Protestant League, in which his father had been active for years, a symptom of this problem. He also believed the name of this association was misleading: 'Only the name "anti-Rome" or "anti-Catholic League"', he wrote, would have reflected its true nature 'so that even the uninitiated can recognize what it is about!'[101] The 'attitude' that found expression in the Protestant League was therefore 'basically neither religious nor church-related, but political and at best ideological'.[102]

Not only the predominantly political nature of the Protestants' confessional identity proved dubious and hollow on second thought, as Niemöller now realized. Protestants also had an inadequate understanding of their own faith:

> One should try and ask some average Lutheran Christians who go to Church every Sunday about the separating difference between us and the Catholics and one will get the strangest answers, as I know from experience: everything but not the one which was crucial for Luther. But everything else is deemed to be strictly rejected because it is Catholic: the saints, the priest garb, making the sign of the cross, kneeling in Church, the confession, celibacy, monasticism! Even regular church visits are valued as Catholic and thus as superstition.—But how is it possible to recognize, address and effectively perform the task of the Church under such a confusion of concepts?!!![103]

This quote indicates the fourth aspect of Niemöller's theological reflections, his focus on the 'task of the Church'. It needed to embody and proclaim Jesus Christ's message of salvation both adequately and authoritatively. Niemöller paid great attention to ecclesiology, writing a manuscript titled *Thoughts on the Path of the Christian Church* from late August to early November 1939. It was a remarkable feat that he could produce 215 handwritten pages in less than three months. Ever since the Reformation, that was the key argument of his book, the Christian Church had been on the wrong path. The introduction of regional churches with the territorial ruler as *summus episcopus* (highest bishop) had led to a bureaucratic ossification. Decisions were solely based on 'political and fiscal considerations, while the assignment [*Auftrag*] given by Jesus Christ only applies when it is granted permission by the authorities on a case-to-case basis. As a result, the Lutheran Church became sterile.'[104] Even the cessation of the summe-piscopate in 1918 could not free the Church from this 'deadly grip' of the state.[105] Seen from this angle, the church policies of the Nazi state and the adaptation of many regional churches to its *völkisch* guidelines seemed to be a late consequence of a development that had already started in the sixteenth century. Niemöller also criticized that the incorporation of the Protestant churches in the territory of a ruler had resulted in the loss of Christianity's universal and missionary impetus. Hence, Niemöller had words of praise for eighteenth-century pietism and the work of the Inner Mission, which he understood as a 'church reform movement'. For him, the deaconesses—whose lifestyle he greatly idealized—were one of the few groups which could be seen as 'evidence' that 'a Christian life can grow and mature even on the basis of Lutheran faith'.[106]

For Niemöller, the ties to secular rulers had led to an emptiness at the very heart of the Reformation churches. He identified the loss of the teaching office of the Church as the second dramatic aberration since the Reformation. Lutheranism, he wrote, had 'replaced it with the Holy Bible and a sixteenth-century confession drawn from Scripture'. Focusing on the principle of sola scriptura 'ended in absurdity right in front our eyes, and we call on the apostolic ministry for help, without which there is no unity of the Church'.[107] Long passages of the manuscript are trying to prove that only the organic adaptation of a canon based on an authoritative tradition of teaching could ensure the liveliness of the Church. Niemöller followed a naïve Biblicism. He deduced an immediately valid truth from his reading of the New Testament, without taking any contemporary theological debates into account. In addition, he displayed an idealized view of the Roman Catholic Church and especially the office of the Pope, which he considered indispensable for maintaining tradition.[108]

In his conversations with Else, Niemöller referred to his *Thoughts on the Path of the Christian Church* as his 'book', which demonstrates that his reflections were intended to lend substance to his planned conversion. He also told Else he wanted to account for his motives and reasons towards his 'travelling companions'.[109] Above all, he referred to Hans Asmussen, who also queried a self-assured Protestant identity at that time. His reflections were met with great reservation among the members of the Confessing Church in Berlin, who suspected a drift towards Catholicism. Niemöller developed his church historical and theological arguments in the seclusion of solitary confinement. But he was not the only member of the Confessing Church who substantially criticized the ecclesiological legitimacy of the Protestant churches. A letter by Heinz Kloppenburg, written in 1941, is illuminating in this respect. Kloppenburg, a Lutheran pastor and theologian, was a leading member of the Confessing Church in the Oldenburg regional church. He was one of Niemöller's closest political allies in his pacifist activism in the decades after 1945. In March 1941, he responded to the rumour that Niemöller had already converted, stating

> [t]he beginning and the end of Niemöller's thoughts on this issue are without doubt the question of the church as a community in the Body of Christ in its shape here on earth. [...] The experiences of recent years inevitably lead to the question whether the evangelical church with its consistories, its German-Christian bishops and with its administrations that act entirely in accordance with the law of the secular world rather than in accordance with the Gospel, whether it is possible to belief in this church as the church of Jesus Christ in the sense of the third article of faith. For many earnest Christians, the answer to this question is today: no![110]

Kloppenburg also agreed with Niemöller's assessment that the 'introduction of the summepiscopate' was the key reason for these deformations, as it had turned the Protestant churches into a 'pawn of the worldly rulers'. Whether or not Niemöller would finally make the leap and convert to the Catholic Church: for Kloppenburg, this was ultimately a 'very secondary question'. Observing his friend from a distance, his conclusions were very clear:

> Personally, I can only rate it positively and can see a true question of the faith in the rumours about Martin Niemöller, as they put to us once again the question of the reality of the church in such an unmistakeable fashion.[111]

Kloppenburg's statement shows Niemöller's critique of the Reformation should not only be seen in the context of his planned conversion. Niemöller expressed ideas that several of his close companions could relate to, while they opposed the solution proposed by Niemöller.

Kloppenburg's letter also clarifies the fifth dimension of Niemöller's potential conversion, their consequences for German Protestants more generally. His brother Wilhelm was one of the first to address them:

> It pains me a lot when I hear from Else that you are considering conversion. I agree it is inappropriate to point out that you are 'no private person'. I am convinced such a step would have a bad impact on Christianity in our country, particularly on the Confessing Church, but one has to do what one's conscience tells him to do.[112]

The calmness Wilhelm Niemöller showed here in regard to his brother's conversion, which he treated as a matter of personal conscience, was only rhetorical. Behind the scenes, he provided Else with good arguments against such a step. At the time the letter was written, in November 1940, only family members and

Martin Niemöller's closest friends knew about his interest in converting to the Catholic Church. It was not before early 1941 that the news spread among Dahlem parish laypeople who continued to support the Confessing Church. Upheaval was the immediate consequence. In several controversial conversations and speeches, parishioners debated the question whether one should be 'Protestant' or 'Catholic'.[113] Ludwig Bartning, church master of the Dahlem parish and close friend of the Niemöller family, admitted to Else that he had already considered a 'conversion' at the end of the First World War, namely 'out of fear losing the salvation of his soul'.[114]

The Dahlem parish had hardly started to discuss Niemöller's potential conversion, when stories about it surfaced in the international press. This suggests that the news was leaked to a broader public by members of the Confessing Church. The London *Times* covered the story like many other newspapers in the United Kingdom, Switzerland, France, and the USA, erroneously reporting that Niemöller had already gone through with the conversion.[115] Finally, even the pope was involved. Berlin Bishop Konrad von Preysing was informed by Georg von Sachsen SJ, the last Saxon crown prince, a convert who had joined the Jesuit order, and perhaps also via Hans Asmusen, of Niemöller's plans. Preysing asked Pius XII how he should react and whether he should intervene in the process of conversion. But the pope felt reassured to hear that 'he who has searched for the truth has gone his way without interference from outside'.[116]

Nonetheless, there was indeed interference from outside. It came from the only person who had direct access to Niemöller: his wife. Only Else Niemöller had the power to prevent her husband's plans. Thus the conversion was—and this is the sixth and ultimately most important dimension—part of a marital power struggle between Else and Martin Niemöller. This conflict is best described as a war of attrition, in which Else demonstrated that she was a strong woman. She knew about her husband's weaknesses and how to exploit her advantages: she had almost complete control over the information flowing into the Sachsenhausen concentration camp and had been the most important person in Niemöller's life for more than two decades. In the seclusion of his solitary cell, Martin needed her encouragement and affection more than ever, and Else was well aware of this. In February 1940, Martin wrote to her that he did not read her letters 'to turn to some other nice entertainment afterwards, but that they fill and hold sway over my life until the next letter arrives or it is time for the next visit'.[117]

From the outset, Else was determined to prevent her husband's planned conversion and used all means within her reach to do so. On some occasions, she bluntly provoked a scene during her visit and drove him into a corner. This happened, for example, on 2 November 1939. At this point in time, the *Wartestandsaffäre* was pending and Niemöller once again assumed his wife did not inform him about everything; at least, her information did not match that provided by Horst Holstein. The following dialogue took place:

> I want to know whether they can come after me based on existing state law if
> I leave the regional church, likewise if I join the Catholic Church.—Else protested
> passionately: rubbish, crazy, etc. and she started crying. I told her that I was
> pretty clear about this, and it would be neither rubbish nor crazy.[118]

When they said good-bye, Else started crying again and Niemöller was 'on the
brink of joining her'.[119] But such direct confrontation was the exception. However,
threats were another part of Else's repertoire. At a visit in August 1940, she
initially assured him she had highlighted whole passages on theological questions
in his letters and learned them 'by heart'. Then she told him, rather unexpectedly:
'Father [Heinrich Niemöller] is going to kill himself.' This threat was followed by
the request 'to give her time' until 1 July 1941, which he 'reluctantly agreed on'.[120]
Else stalled, and repeatedly used this tactic, trying to convince her husband 'not to
make any decisions as long as I am not free'.[121] In her letters she used a broad
range of arguments and rhetorical figures. She reminded Martin that he was 'no
longer a private person' and could only convert 'if you take those who are listening
to you with you'.[122] Finally, she also urged him to think about the significance of a
conversion not only for Church and parish but also for 'your family'. This
conversation ended in the already-mentioned eruption in February 1941 when
she suggested Niemöller would become a 'street sweeper'.[123]

Else Niemöller's core motive is clear: she did not share his thoughts at all.
Supported by Hans Asmussen, who contributed key formulations in the background, Else addressed her husband's theological arguments and made some
tactical concessions. But she was still confident that she was on the right path as
a Protestant Christian. In December 1939, she wrote: 'My faith and my confidence
[. . .] are even stronger than before.'[124] Furthermore, Else defended the integrity
and unity of her family, just like she had done during the two decades when her
husband, the 'Jupiter tonans', was there for the family only every now and then.
We can only speculate about what her husband's conversion would have really
meant for Else. Martin Niemöller could have become a lay Catholic—or he could
have intended to enter priesthood in the short- or medium-term, which, as Else
must have assumed, would entail celibacy and the end of their marriage.[125]

Apparently, Martin Niemöller never raised the spectre of this option. But there
were quite a few hints. In Moabit prison, he reminded Else that she knew his
'(theoretical) penchant for church celibacy'.[126] In February 1941, he returned to
this topic. The eldest daughter Brigitte had broken off her engagement with a
Wehrmacht doctor, when he did not obtain the marital consent necessary for this
marriage. But this was not the end of the matter. Immediately afterwards, other
men proposed to Brigitte, and her parents discussed how they could control this
process. Niemöller finally came to believe that Erich Klapproth, a young priest
who worked for the Confessing Church in Berlin and who had proposed to
Brigitte, was 'too good' for the disappointment his daughter would certainly

bring. Instead of marrying Brigitte, Niemöller recommended, Klapproth should 'really wait until Hertha [their second daughter, born in 1927] is ready, if he doesn't rather go with 1 Corinthian 7:7–8 (Luther's old translation) anyway, which I think is the better way for a theologian of today'.[127] Paul, who in this passage taught the Corinthians about issues of marriage, said here: 'I say therefore to the unmarried and widows, it is good for them if they abide even as I', which is celibate. Although he did not express it explicitly, Else could assume her husband considered celibacy the best way of life for himself after conversion.[128]

But it did not come to that. Else Niemöller's tactic of attrition, her varied approach of using threats, listening and stalling was successful. After almost two years of reflection—from July 1939 to spring 1941—Martin Niemöller refrained from converting. But Else's success came at a price. It was not so much the permanent conflict about the pros and cons of a conversion that strained the marriage. The relationship between Else and Martin was marked by deep affection and tenderness, and it could bear the strain.[129] More importantly, Niemöller once again realized that he had not only lost his freedom but also his agency. His volunteering for military service was perhaps already an attempt to regain agency and become 'a German man' once again. After the long debates about conversion, it was clear that Else Niemöller had decisively used her newly won autonomy, and had limited that of her husband in the process. Losing his autonomy in the field of religion was very difficult for Niemöller, but in the end he had to concede. Losing his autonomy in the family, however, was a serious affront for him, to which he reacted with anger.

In order to understand the way he felt insulted, we need to look closer at the story of Brigitte Niemöller's engagement that we have already alluded to. We do not do this to peep through the keyhole and observe intimate details of the Niemöllers' personal lives. This episode reveals important aspects of Martin Niemöller's relationship to his family and, at the same time, lays bare a crisis that, in some respects, was even more profound than the *Wartestandsaffäre*.

According to her parents, Brigitte (born 1920), the oldest daughter, had many admirers. In August 1939, Niemöller learned that Brigitte wanted to get engaged to a Wehrmacht doctor. He was a member of the NSDAP, but did not consider 'the worldview' a hindrance, as Else told Martin. Niemöller, who was not happy that he not been consulted in this matter, recommended to 'delay' until his daughter finished her training.[130] Finally he yielded to the pressure of his daughter and wife. But the wedding, planned for March 1940, had to be postponed because the marital consent of the Wehrmacht had not arrived in time. In May, Else hinted that the decision might go 'up higher and higher'.[131] In September 1940, Niemöller learned that the consent had been rejected. But it was even worse that Else had only told him eight weeks later. More importantly, the doctor suggested a 'morganatic marriage'—a marriage that would limit the rights of the bride. As this type of marriage was legally abolished since 1919, the doctor's suggestion could only mean an informal legitimation of the relation with no legal guarantees for Brigitte. On top of this, the bridegroom had already left the Church. Niemöller was completely distraught. He suspected Brigitte already had an intimate relation with the doctor, which, in his view, would have been put right with her marrying the man, even though he was not exactly to Niemöller's liking. 'Now everything is over!' And he continued: 'I blamed Else to have deliberately deceived me, and told her that her letters are completely worthless to me!' And while he was at it, he also complained that 'there had been no theological discussion' about the conversion 'that I wanted for ages', but which Else had successfully delayed. Niemöller's reaction is striking: during the same visit when he learned about the rejected marital consent, he ordered Else to ask his lawyer Hans Koch whether he should 'submit a request for retirement or for court of honour proceedings'.[132] His daughter's cancelled marriage had shaken up Niemöller's honour as a family father, pastor, and officer to such an extent that the only appropriate solution was to immediately resign from his second and third roles.

A letter to Hans Koch shows Niemöller initially considered solving the matter through an 'affair of honour', that is, a duel.[133] This again illustrates that for Niemöller the code of honour of an imperial naval officer was still valid. As conducting a duel was impossible, Niemöller, in a second letter—which he never sent—asked Koch to inform the Dahlem parish that he would retire from his pastoral office. This was the consequence of a 'mental breakdown' he experienced in the wake of the cancelled engagement. But it was also a consequence of the understanding that the Church of the ApU 'was no part of the Christian Church'.[134] As was the case during the *Wartestandsaffäre*, Koch was able to talk his impatient client out of this impulsive decision, with legal advice and a lot of common sense. This, however, only applied to Niemöller's role as an officer and pastor. In carefully chosen words, Koch clarified that none of the involved could be the judge of Brigitte, only 'an educator'.[135] But the plea to Martin Niemöller, the family father, not to condemn his daughter, was in vain.

Niemöller felt so insulted in his honour as a father that he decided to disown his eldest daughter. Two weeks after Else had told him the news of the broken-off engagement, he informed her about his decision: 'I told her she [Brigitte] must leave the house and I no longer want to know anything about her.' Else had expected such a reaction. Her attempt to defend Brigitte was thus rather half-hearted. The meeting ended in tears: 'Else cried, me too—terrible!'[136]

Niemöller knew full well that this situation could not last. But the consequences for his daughter followed instantly: on 3 October, Hans Asmussen and Hans Koch told the bewildered Brigitte she had to move into the Protestant orphanage in Lippstadt as an au pair. When she refused, Asmussen, who acted in her father's place, sharply rebuffed her. She finally resigned herself to her fate. Brigitte returned to the Dahlem parsonage after a few months, but the matter remained unresolved. As Niemöller considered taking legal steps against the doctor and the worries about Brigitte did not go away, Else and Martin had to deal with the matter well into 1941. It was another aspect of Niemöller's deep existential crisis during the period between 1939 and 1941, which at the same time highlighted his profoundly paternalistic and authoritative attitude as a family father and the strains that his limited agency in this role brought. He could, as he complained in May 1941, 'not accept that she lives at home again'.[137]

Interned in Dachau Concentration Camp
with Three Catholic Priests

Niemöller's transfer to Dachau concentration camp on 11 July 1941 brought some relief from these problems. Two Catholic priests were transferred to Bavaria with him: Johannes Neuhäusler (1888–1973), who became auxiliary bishop of the archdiocese of Munich and Freising after the war. Neuhäusler had been arrested by the Gestapo in February 1941 due to his reports on anti-church policies of the Nazi regime, which he had started to compile in 1933 on behalf of Munich Cardinal Faulhaber.[138] The second one was Michael Höck (1903–1996). He had been arrested by the Gestapo in May 1941, right after he had been acquitted at a trial in his capacity as editor of the *Münchener Katholische Kirchenzeitung*.[139] It has often been assumed the Gestapo transferred Niemöller to Dachau and interned him with two Catholic priests so that he would go through with his conversion plan.[140] There is, however, no evidence to back this up. Furthermore, this assumption is implausible for two reasons: first, the SS could just as well have put him together with Höck and Neuhäusler in Sachsenhausen. Second, the Gestapo knew from Niemöller's letters and the surveillance of his conversations with Else that he had already given up the plan to convert in spring 1941.[141]

Niemöller was transferred because from late 1940 clerics of both confessions and all nationalities were brought together in Dachau.[142] However, Niemöller, Höck, and Neuhäusler were not placed in one of the camp's priest blocks but in the *Zellenbau* or 'bunker', a prison within the concentration camp. The SS used it to isolate certain prisoners, but also to torture or kill them. Over the course of reconstruction work at Dachau concentration camp, a new cell building had been erected in spring 1938, which ran for 196 metres parallel to the service building in a west–east direction. All cells were the same size (2.20 x 2.90 metres) and had the same equipment, consisting of a cot, washbasin, and toilet.[143] Shortly before the end of 1941, another Catholic priest, Aachen Cathedral Chaplain Nikolaus Jansen (1880–1965), who had been arrested in August 1941, joined the group. The four clerics were initially placed in solitary cells located in the middle of the building next to a bathroom. Presumably in late 1942, at the latest in early 1943, they were moved to four cells at the western part of the *Zellenbau*. There were four more cells which the group could use jointly for having meals, for prayers, and celebrating mass with a suitcase altar. A door separated the end of the corridor occupied by the four clerics from the other cells in the western half of the bunker.[144]

In his first letter to Else from Dachau Niemöller emphasized he got on 'very well with the two brothers'.[145] A daily routine quickly emerged. In the morning, the three devoted one or two hours to reading the Holy Scripture together in Greek. They began with the Revelation of John and continued with other books of the New Testament. For Niemöller, this was the 'best, admittedly also the most exhausting hour of the day'.[146] After lunch and a short break they moved on to some light reading, with Niemöller usually doing the reading aloud. First on the programme were volumes from the 16-part *Jalna* novel series by Canadian author Mazo de la Roche.[147] Initially, they spent the evening separately in their cells. However, the options expanded with Nikolaus Jansen's arrival, as Niemöller reported in January 1942:

> We four live in good harmony and the evening Skat game is good for us; in any case I am glad that the long period of loneliness is over and that I have not yet become completely useless for social life.[148]

Both Niemöller and Höck seemed to have a good, but slightly distanced relationship with Neuhäusler. After all, one of them—or both?—taught him card games such as skat and rummy.[149] Höck leaned closely on Niemöller, who was more than 10 years his senior. The world-famous Protestant pastor's recognition and willingness to talk helped him see a deeper meaning in his imprisonment.[150] The affection was mutual. Niemöller saw an important interlocutor in the younger Catholic priest, 'despite all the differences in our theological views'.[151] And he gave Höck great credit for making every effort not to give Niemöller the feeling that he was a 'class apart' in the group. After a good six months, however, routine set in. Niemöller now spent more time alone in his cell than in the months before, either reading or sleeping. And he came to the conclusion that one had to 'take the involuntary community as it is'. In this context, 'silence', according to his maxim, was 'sometimes golden'.[152] For this reason, the actual theological conversation between Niemöller and the priests was soon limited to 'occasional details'.[153]

There were various reasons for this development. For one thing, Niemöller's view of the 'confessional problem' slowly began 'to shift', as he now saw 'Protestant Christianity' as a 'correction of Catholicism'.[154] During the first months of his Dachau imprisonment, Niemöller, right after his conversion crisis, met his Catholic brothers in the spirit of openness and deep respect for their faith. But this window of open dialogue gradually closed. The theological discussions remained 'unfruitful'.[155] Furthermore, Niemöller increasingly focused on details of the Catholic faith that irritated him, such as the veneration of saints, and accused Catholics of distorting Christian faith with a 'semi-Pelagian view of the path of salvation'.[156] In late antiquity, the monk Pelagius had taught that man was without original sin. For Niemöller, however, it was precisely man's sinfulness that necessitated redemption through Christ's death on the cross. Moreover, group dynamics changed with the arrival of Nikolaus Jansen.[157] For Niemöller, 'living together as a foursome was considerably more strenuous then living together as a threesome like before', and there is reason to believe this was mainly due to Jansen's personality.[158] Full of empathy, Martin told Else that Neuhäusler's character was borderline 'melancholic'. The label 'sanguine person', who caused 'problems' in living together, could only refer to Jansen.[159]

From spring 1942, routine dominated the daily lives of the four prisoners in Dachau. After reading the New Testament together, Niemöller read from the Psalms for a while every day. In the morning, they held hourly prayers together from the Catholic breviary book. After lunch, everyone dozed off. In the evening, they played cards.[160] In early 1943, the daily routine started to show a welcome change (Fig. 11). This was because a new SS man was put in charge for the special prisoners. His name was Wilhelm Beyer. He had worked as an employee in the judicial service until the war and had then been called up for the Wehrmacht. According to his personnel records, he had joined the SS in early 1936. In November 1942, he was transferred to Dachau concentration camp.[161] Niemöller seems to have established rapport with the Untersturmführer very quickly. They had a lot in common: Beyer was only two years younger than Niemöller and a Protestant family man. In addition, Beyer had served as a front-line soldier in the First World War.[162] Niemöller often had long conversations with Beyer, who on some days visited him twice in his cell and sometimes supervised Else's visits. Niemöller found this 'very nice', presumably because Beyer did not listen that closely. When the SS man was transferred to Lublin in November 1943, he said goodbye to Niemöller in person.[163]

Not only Niemöller but also his three Catholic fellow prisoners benefited from the good relation to Beyer. On 20 March, Beyer took all four of them on an excursion to the game park for the first time. The park was situated north of the site used for the detainees, the *Schutzhaftlager*. It had been laid out for the then commander Hans Loritz. Concentration camp prisoners had provided hard manual labour from 1937 to spring 1938. With trees, ornamental shrubs, lawns, and an artificial pond, it was used for the SS men's recreation. Loritz himself celebrated parties there in a log cabin.[164] The 'extended run' in the game park gave Niemöller 'a new vital impulse'. It was, he wrote, 'a piece of German home soil on which one stands and that the eyes absorb with love'. All four clerics were 'buzzing with exhilaration' the whole day. He asked Else to send him swimming trunks because there were rowing boats on the lake.[165] Such excursions to the game park soon became normality. Beyer took Niemöller and the other clerics there a dozen times until October 1943. The longest trip lasted four hours.[166]

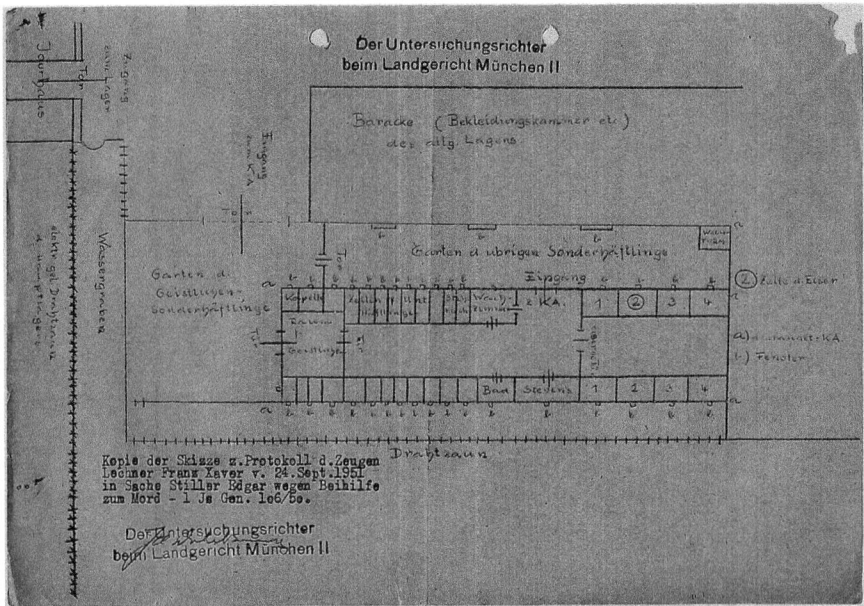

Fig. 11 SS Obersturmführer Edgar Stiller was in charge of the special prisoners in the *Zellenbau* or bunker of Dachau concentration camp. Due to his possible involvement in the murder of Georg Elser in April 1945, the public prosecutor's office at the Munich II Regional Court conducted an investigation against him in 1951, in which Franz Xaver Lechner, an SS Rottenführer who had been working in the bunker from 1944, also testified. Lechner made the template for this sketch of the prison situation there. Niemöller and the three Catholic priests were housed in a separate area on the west side of the bunker, which was separated from the corridor by a door. Another door opened onto what Lechner called a 'garden' area, which only the four clerics used. There, they could sunbathe in good weather. Staatsarchiv München, Staatsanwaltschaften 34475/5.

Sunbathing in the game park was not the only perk for the four special prisoners. Beyer also took them to the bowling alley a few times, which was otherwise only available to the SS men. 'A lot of wine was drunk' during a round of bowling in July 1943. When Else visited the following day, she asked her husband whether he was hungover.[167] Niemöller was also allowed to visit the cinema that was set up for the SS men. He watched films such as *Kleiner Mann ganz groß* (1938) and *Nacht ohne Abschied*.[168] But the two greatest privileges were granted to the prisoners in July 1943. On 1 July, Niemöller 'went to the tailor with Mr Beyer: dressing in civilian clothes'.[169] On her next visit, Else was able to admire her husband wearing 'an elegant suit'. But soon afterwards she voiced criticism because he was wearing what she thought was an 'unfitting nightgown tie'.[170] During those days, Niemöller and the three priests were allocated sprung beds.

After six years on a hard cot, Niemöller had to get used to a proper mattress.[171] From now on, the meetings with Else were full of harmony, particularly because conditions became more relaxed (Fig. 12). Sometimes the supervising officer turned his back to them and immersed himself in his files. On another occasion, Else and Martin were 'alone in the room several times'. Then, according to Niemöller, 'we used the time to kiss heartily'.[172] Even if Beyer did not take the four clerics to the game park or the cinema, they enjoyed other freedoms. A door at the western end of the 'bunker' led outside, and they could go into the courtyard, which was separated from the *Schutzhaft* camp by a wall, to stretch their legs or sunbathe. It is no surprise that Niemöller described his situation to his wife as follows in August 1943: 'I told her about myself, that I had lain in the sun a lot, and that my imprisonment was now rather to be called "internment"'.[173]

While Martin Niemöller was relaxing in the sun, his wife's living conditions became extremely problematic. She was still responsible for running the parish household in Dahlem and had to make the long train journey to Munich every fortnight, often accompanied by one of her children. She did not lack support: one or two times, the Munich bishop Hans Meiser and his wife invited Else Niemöller for dinner and offered her accommodation for the night. On other occasions, she stayed in a hotel run by the Caritas Association, or a hospice in Schliersee served as accommodation.[174] Meanwhile, the war had reached Germany and Allied bomber units flew air raids against German major cities. When Hamburg became the target of a devastating wave of Royal Air Force bombers on 24 July 1943, Goebbels, as Nazi Gau leader of Berlin, called on all women and children to leave the capital by 1 August. During these days, Else was in Bavaria with her children Martin and Jutta as well as the housekeeper Dora Schulz, and constantly had to change accommodation. The way back to Berlin seemed blocked to her, so she telegraphed to the Gestapo that she would stay in southern Germany for the time being. But where?[175]

As always, the ever so helpful Hans Asmussen had a recommendation for her. Initially only for a fortnight, Else found accommodation at the holiday home of Maria Lempp—Albert Lempp's widow—in Leoni at Lake Starnberg. Lempp had managed the Christian Kaiser publishing house until his sudden death in June 1943. Martin Niemöller had met him in 1936 when the publisher took *Stimme der Gemeinde*, a journal of the Confessing Church, under his wing.[176] The provisional situation in Leoni soon became permanent, lasting until November 1945. On 'instructions from above'—probably from the Gestapo in Berlin—the mayor of Leoni had convinced Maria Lempp to take in Else Niemöller, the children Martin, Jutta, and Hertha, and Dora Schulz. In view of the cramped living conditions, this soon led to a dispute. Eventually Maria Lempp moved out temporarily and only dropped in sporadically as a 'control commission'—Else's ironic choice of words—to check the house for cleanliness and order.[177]

Fig. 12 On 18 September 1941, Helmut Gollwitzer—here in Wehrmacht uniform—, his fiancée, the actress Eva Bildt, and Elsie von Stryk accompanied Else Niemöller (centre) to Dachau concentration camp to visit her husband. The photo was taken by Elsie von Stryk, who had been employed as a parish helper in the Dahlem parish from January 1938. On that day, Else Niemöller wore, as her husband noted afterwards, 'her blue dress and grey autumn coat'. Niemöller helped her with her coat and the two sat down on two armchairs in the camp commander's office, where the visit took place. Niemöller wrote: 'We adhered to our old order in our conversation': after practical matters and Else's health, they spoke about the children, then about relatives and acquaintances. Niemöller specifically inquired about the last air raid by British bombers on Berlin on the night of 7–8 September. Else replied: 'It was ghastly, we haven't experienced anything like this before.' The conversation that day, however, once again centred on the ongoing conflict over their eldest daughter Brigitte and her recent engagement. EZA 500/17936.

The Looming German Defeat as 'the Decline of the West'

Which perceptions preoccupied Martin Niemöller during the last two years of the war, when the military defeat of the 'Third Reich' was looming? The climate in Dachau had noticeably changed, and not just thanks to Wilhelm Beyer and his courteous attitude. Time and again there were moments when Martin and Else were alone for a short time during her visits. This would have been an opportunity to speak freely about the criminal policies of the Nazi regime. Else could have reported from Dahlem, where the Confessing Church, initiated by Helmut Gollwitzer, had taken practical measures of solidarity with 'non-Aryan' Christians, from the November pogrom in 1938 to the introduction of the Yellow Star in September 1941.[178] But there is no trace in Niemöller's notes—which the SS never checked during Niemöller's entire imprisonment, just as they did not read any other of his papers—that such conversations happened at all. From summer 1943 there was only one topic: the threat to the German nation posed by the events of the war, which seemed to become increasingly gloomy. The conversation first revolved around the accounts of several family members. In December 1943, Dora Schulz reported on the destruction in Berlin caused by the last air raids and on unexploded bombs that lay around in Dahlem. Niemöller's mother and his sister Magdalene, who stayed in Leoni for a while in April 1944, reported on air raids on Elberfeld in June of the previous year: 'The escape from the burning sea of houses (in wet bathrobes!)', Martin noted what Else had told him, 'must have been terrible. There is almost nothing left of Elberfeld.'[179]

In autumn 1943, the 18-year-old son Jan Niemöller was drafted into the Wehrmacht. His father was worried when the news came in January 1944 that Jan would be deployed to the Eastern Front. In a letter, he assured Else they need not worry about his 'attitude as a soldier': 'The boy is "right" and will fill his place—wherever this may be. But what will happen when the Bolshevik wave will come over Europe and over our fatherland cannot be thought of calmly and in acquiescence, one can only pray: "Lord, have mercy!" Daniel 9:15–19.'[180] Niemöller's anti-Bolshevik reflexes were still intact, and he continued to adhere to the national Protestant stance which demanded that each German put his individual interests behind those of the people. In this vein, Niemöller did not see himself but the German national collective as the real victim. In July 1943, while he enjoyed bowling and swimming in the lake at the game park, he thought about his 'drone existence'. It struck him as 'strange' and questionable that he himself was 'having enough to eat and a good night's sleep while millions at home don't know whether they will still have a roof over their heads the next night and millions outside are facing the enemy'. This contradiction was only bearable for him as long as he could 'believe that God had his fatherly hand at work here'—which was very much in line with national Protestant thought.[181]

During 1944, the Allied troops moved ever closer to the pre-1938 German borders. Every day Niemöller waited 'with excitement for the Wehrmacht reports', 'which, for all their restraint and brevity, do reveal something of the seriousness of the situation. If only the war would come to an end that would open a way into the future for our people!'[182] In early 1944, Niemöller began to summarize the Wehrmacht reports with diligent regularity in a calendar: 'Army report not very satisfactory' was a typical entry.[183] It was 'hardly satisfactory' not because the day of liberation was delayed again, but because the Allies' grip on Germany tightened. In November 1944, when the army report was once again 'rather gloomy', Niemöller noted: 'but V2!', expressing his hope that the attacks of the 'wonder weapon' on London might yet bring a turnaround.[184]

In view of the destruction of large parts of Germany and the annihilation of many 'irreplaceable assets', Niemöller thought the 'word of the Decline of the West is truly no longer a figure of speech', especially because 'one must admit that today's generation is simply lacking all mental and cultural prerequisites for the creation of something equivalent.'[185] When Niemöller thought of the down-fall of the Christian West, he initially had the destructive dynamics of commun-ism in mind, an idea deeply ingrained in his political mindset from 1919 onwards. In November 1944, he wrote to Else: 'Bolshevism hangs over all of us like a terrible threat, even if one believes that we do not have much left to lose; it is still quite a lot!'[186] But the enemies of the German people and its Christian civilization were not only to be found in the East. In March 1945, Niemöller was shocked to read in the Wehrmacht report: 'In the West, the enemy is on the Rhine and in Trier!'[187]

On 28 February 1945, Jochen, his eldest son, died as a Wehrmacht soldier in Pomerania. One month earlier, he had visited his father in the concentration camp. At the end of 1944, Jutta, his younger sister, born in 1928, had died unexpectedly of an illness, and Jochen, like his father, was still under the shock of this loss during the visit. Jochen was a machine gunner and felt at home with his unit. His comrades knew who his father was, and could not understand why Jochen had not yet been promoted to officer candidate. Following his instinct as a professional officer, the father responded to this news as follows: 'I openly expressed my bitterness and told him to do his duty but no more, to which he replied: "That is difficult, the name does oblige!"'[188]

From the son's perspective, the name Niemöller stood, above all, for the ethos of the officer. Shortly before his death, Jochen had written a letter to his father, asking a question that had been on his mind during these weeks: 'Was Spengler right after all?' Was *The Decline of the West* imminent, as the philosopher Oswald Spengler had suggested in his successful book, first published in two volumes in 1918 and 1922, whose title has since become a proverb. His father's answer, sent to Else by letter, was unequivocal:

I don't see how this question could be answered in the negative; because I cannot imagine that the Anglo-Americans care in the slightest about the fate of the European culture; besides, what is left of it anyway? Ruins and a pile of shards.[189]

For Niemöller, the military defeat of the 'Third Reich' was first and foremost a defeat of the German nation. Occupied and defeated by Bolsheviks and Anglo-Americans, it was threatened with an uncertain future. Nevertheless, he observed the end of National Socialism with satisfaction. On 1 February 1945, he told Else about his 'joy that now the district leaders' [*Kreisleiter* of the NSDAP] number was up'. But even this was, at least to a certain extent, a self-centred attitude because Niemöller was 'up to his neck in rage' at that moment as his renewed application for leave had been rejected in Berlin.[190] In terms of his ambivalent stance on the conquest of Germany, Niemöller was no exception. For many Germans it was a 'must to hold the front line' in order to delay the advance of Bolshevism. Even a victim of Nazi racial policy like the professor of Romance literature Victor Klemperer, who was forced to live with his wife in a 'Jewish house' for years due to his Jewish descent, perceived the end of the war as both liberation and defeat.[191]

There were some changes during the last period of Niemöller's imprisonment in Dachau. In April 1944, Nikolaus Jansen was transferred to the so-called Priest Barracks. The SS put Corbinian Hofmeister, the abbot of the Benedictine Abbey of Metten, in his cell.[192] From late 1944, more and more special prisoners arrived in the bunker as the SS drew them together in Dachau from other camps. When a group of nine Italian officers joined them in March, Niemöller felt isolated.[193] At the same time, the imminent end of the Nazi regime brought new freedoms. On 13 January, Niemöller and Corbinian Hofmeister, accompanied by an SS Storm Squad leader named Bossenigk, took a walk to the town of Dachau, where they stopped at Café Fuchs.[194] A week later, Niemöller and Johannes Neuhäusler went on a tour to the Schlossberg for three hours, followed by a leisurely coffee break at Café Brüller. Further excursions of this kind followed every few days well into March, each time accompanied by an SS man. On 1 March 1945, they met the Catholic priest of Dachau, Friedrich Pfanzelt. On the morning of that day, Niemöller had seen his wife for an hour, which was followed by an air raid alarm shortly afterwards. Niemöller, Michael Höck, and the SS man went by the station to inquire whether Else's train had managed to leave before the alarm.[195] But this privilege of carefree excursions to the city centre suddenly stopped, and Niemöller was not able to name the reason.[196]

Tensions and uncertainty grew in the hectic atmosphere of the last weeks of the war. On 3 April 1945, Niemöller noted the ominous statement of an SS man called Bruno Lenzkowski: 'Lenzkowski said he wanted to shoot all special prisoners before the end!'.[197] To be sure, Lenzkowski was not to decide on this, but his statement did cause some unease. Only two days later, on 4 April, Michael Höck and Corbinian Hofmeister were released unexpectedly. Niemöller gave Höck his personal papers—copies of letters and manuscripts—to take with him, which thus ended up in the hands of the Dachau priest Friedrich Pfanzelt on the same day.[198] A guard told Johannes Neuhäusler he had originally also been on the release list, but had to stay on 'so that Niemöller would not be alone'.[199] On 16 April, SS Obersturmführer Edgar Stiller, who was in charge of the special prisoners from late 1943, informed them that they had to move into the former brothel barracks. But during those days, the power of the SS in the camp disintegrated, and Niemöller had a mind of his own anyway. 'I refuse', he noted, 'with success'.[200] The same thing happened a day later when the departure of the special prisoners was unexpectedly announced. Niemöller refused, saying he would not let himself be 'dragged to Katyn'—where the NKVD had murdered thousands of Polish officers in spring 1940.[201]

On 20 April, Else visited her husband in Dachau for the last time. Their conversation lasted 90 minutes and was dominated by Martin's report on the hectic events in the camp. Then there was an air raid alarm, and Else 'shouldered her backpack; our good-bye was heartily and joyful if I may say so.' Else, as he summarized after seven years of concentration camp detention, was 'a woman like few others'.[202] On this day, both parted in high spirits. Three days later, the marching order for the special prisoners arrived. Some asked Niemöller whether he would join them. He agreed but successfully insisted that two 'nasty' SS men from Buchenwald concentration camp did not accompany the transport. On 24 April, about 160 special prisoners boarded lorries and buses.[203] In the following days, they drove to Niederndorf in South Tyrol via Innsbruck and the Brenner pass. Whether the SS really intended to liquidate the special prisoners in case its plan to use them as bargaining chips in negotiations with the Allies failed, cannot be stated with certainty. It is, however, certain the prisoners feared for their lives until, on 30 April, a Wehrmacht unit under Wichard von Alvensleben took them into custody and under its protection. On 4 May, troops of the US Army finally liberated the high-profile prisoners.[204]

After 1945, Niemöller often told the public that his political views had fundamentally changed during the years of concentration camp imprisonment, particularly in Dachau. Above all, he stated, he had developed a growing empathy with communists and other victims of the Nazi terror. All previous biographers have followed Niemöller's testimony without hesitation and suggested his political thinking and his attitude towards nationalism 'radically changed' during his time in Dachau.[205] A close examination of the evidence demonstrates nothing could be further from the truth. Niemöller's anti-Bolshevik attitude remained as consistent as his nationalism. Filled with shock and horror, he noted that Wehrmacht troops had to retreat before the Red Army. According to Niemöller's nationalist mindset, the German people was, above all, the victim of the Allies' bombing war. Shortly before the concentration camp was liberated, he interpreted the defeat of the

German nation as the decline of the West. If anything changed during the long years of concentration camp imprisonment, it was Niemöller's attitude towards the Protestant Church. Largely thanks to the stubborn resistance of his wife, he did not convert to the Catholic Church after all. Nevertheless, this was more than just a fleeting episode in Niemöller's life. In the years after 1945 it often seemed as if he wanted to compensate for his conversion plans with a decidedly anti-Catholic stance. However, the distance to the Protestant Church he scorned as a mere bureaucratic apparatus, a perception which had emboldened his conversion plans, remained in place even after he had abandoned these plans.

PART III

CHURCH POLITICS, PEACE ACTIVISM, AND ECUMENICAL WORK FROM 1945

13
New Beginnings—Delayed

After his liberation by a US army unit on 4 May 1945, a period of transition began for Martin Niemöller. The return to his family in Leoni was delayed. Finding a suitable position in the Church—and thus a permanent place of residence—took until late 1947. After eight years of imprisonment, the general public saw Niemöller as a martyr of resistance against the 'Third Reich'. Thus, the surprise was all the greater when his first public remarks after liberation revealed that his nationalist mindset was largely intact. Until 1947, controversies about his actions during the Nazi period kept flaring up. As a result, Niemöller was often at the centre of conflicts that negotiated how to come to terms with the legacy of the 'Third Reich'.

The Wehrmacht unit under Wichard von Alvensleben brought the special prisoners from the concentration camp Dachau to the Hotel Pragser Wildsee in the South Tyrolean Dolomite Alps. Upon their arrival on 4 May, the US army first registered the prisoners' personal data. The next day they experienced an 'invasion by journalists and photographers of the seventh Army'.[1] Thus, it was possible that an extensive interview with Niemöller, presented as the 'anti-Nazi pastor', appeared in the *New York Times* as early as 8 May. Niemöller stated that Germany would only be able to survive the following months with the help of the Protestant Church.[2] On 8 May the former special prisoners were brought to Verona, and three days later by plane to Naples. The headquarters of the Mediterranean Allied troops under the command of British Field Marshall Harold Alexander, responsible for the prisoners from then on, were in Caserta, close to Naples. Niemöller was still very worried. 'Where is Else, where are the children?' It was not before 18 May that Niemöller learned about his family's whereabouts when he read an interview with Else in the army newspaper *Stars and Stripes*.[3]

During the following days, Field Marshall Alexander and several American ministers from different Protestant denominations met with Niemöller.[4] On 5 June, he held a press conference with Johannes Neuhäusler, Hermann Pünder, Josef Müller, and Reinhard Goerdeler, the son of Carl Friedrich Goerdeler, who had been taken prisoner by the SS for his father's involvement in the assassination attempt on Hitler on 20 July 1944.[5] The reports of the New York newspapers focused on Niemöller, who, they claimed, had become famous for his 'courageous opposition to the Nazis'. But what the famous pastor conveyed from the podium did not match the image of a fearless resistance fighter. He admitted that in

September 1939, imprisoned in Sachsenhausen, he had offered his service as a navy officer 'in every capacity', including combat missions.[6] He also emphasized that he did not claim to be part of the opposition to the Nazi regime. He truthfully stated that as a man of the Church he had not been interested in politics, but only in fending off state interference with the autonomy of the Church.[7]

Consequently, the New York Times commented Niemöller was a 'hero with limitations'.[8] Among the American officers in Naples alarm bells started to ring after the interview. On 13 June, Niemöller, Hjalmar Schacht, Pünder, and some other Dachau special prisoners were flown to Paris and three days later, on 16 June, to Frankfurt. But Niemöller was not yet released. The American military authorities detained him in an interview centre in Wiesbaden. [9] On 18 June, an all-day interview followed, including a long conversation with Major Marshall C. Knappen, who headed the Religious Affairs Section of the Supreme Headquearters, Allied Expeditionary Force (SHAEF). In this capacity Knappen, a former pastor, was in charge of drafting the church policy of the Western Allies. Niemöller experienced the conversation with the Major as 'very intense'.[10] In the afternoon, two officers of the US intelligence service Office of Strategic Services (OSS) interrogated the German pastor.[11]

Both interviews could not disperse American concerns about Niemöller's political views. In regard to his volunteering in 1939, he told the two OSS officers he had seen 'no alternative' to the decision to fight for his nation. He claimed that reports on 'Polish terror'—which were the pretext for the Nazi invasion of Poland—had been accurate; he himself knew German pastors who had been 'slaughtered' by the Poles. Given that Niemöller still believed in National Socialist atrocity propaganda, it is no surprise he considered a 'contagious disease' to be the reason for the systematic terror in the concentration camps to which not only the Germans, but also other peoples might have succumbed.[12] In the report of his conversation with Niemöller, Knappen emphasized that the Western press had incorrectly amplified and distorted his image as an 'anti-Nazi martyr'. He, in contrast, saw in him a rather 'provincially minded pastor'. Knappen cautiously distinguished between the popular 'religious leader' and the politically minded former navy officer. The former deserved respect, while the latter, especially if he discredited the politics of the US military authorities, should be 'watched carefully'.[13] Knappen suggested releasing Niemöller soon, who in the meantime had gone on hunger strike. The two advisers of the British and American military administration ordered his release the next day.[14] But this was not an uncontested step within the military administration. The army was worried that Niemöller could publicly criticize his treatment after being released, which would result in a 'dog fight'.[15]

Niemöller's first contacts with the American occupation authorities had consequences far beyond his brief detention. They confirmed the Americans' intention to choose Bishop Theophil Wurm rather than the impulsive Dahlem pastor as the leading figure to re-establish the Protestant Church in Germany.[16] The stumbling block was again Niemöller's declared willingness to fight for his nation as an officer during the war. Niemöller was aware of this. In the following months, he attempted to defuse this dangerous subject and presented a whitewashed version of his motives in September 1939. The first occasion to do so was a letter to George Bell, Bishop of Chichester, who had spoken up for him during the entirety of his imprisonment. Niemöller explained the dilemma he allegedly experienced in 1939. Hitler's defeat would have resulted in Germany's destruction. Thus he, just like many other Germans, hoped the war, which had already started, would lead to the downfall of the regime, 'which could be performed naturally not without the help of the armed forces'.[17] Niemöller implied that he had only volunteered to join the 20 July 1944 conspirators.[18] This was of course mere fiction, because the resistance movement around officers such as Wilhelm Canaris only shaped up after Niemöller's arrest in summer 1937.

After his release from American internment on 21 June, Niemöller first met his sister Pauline and friends from the Confessing Church in Frankfurt. The next day, Theophil Wurm and Hans Asmussen joined them for long conversations. Only then did Niemöller drive to Leoni, where he woke up his wife and little Martin and Hertha. Hans Asmussen concluded the long day full of many joyful conversations with a brief devotion.[19] However, the American military authorities remained Niemöller's primary contacts. Niemöller planned journeys abroad, for which he needed permission. He intended to organize fundraisers in Switzerland and Great Britain for the suffering German population. But his relationship with the US authorities was strained. Major Knappen reported Niemöller told a US officer in Munich that he had been treated better in Dachau than by the Americans. Whenever he requested to speak with an SS officer in the concentration camp, his wish had been answered. When interned in Wiesbaden, the guards just told him: 'Forget it'. Unsurprisingly, Knappen agreed with Hugh Davis, the press secretary of the American military government in Frankfurt, to decline Niemöller's travel applications.[20] Niemöller remained, as Knappen wrote in a memo, 'potentially dangerous as a political leader'.[21] General Clarence L. Adcock, head of SHAEF's G-5 department responsible for contacts with the civilian population, concluded matter-of-factly that Niemöller was 'just another German' and therefore should stay in Germany.[22] But some of the ministers working for the US military supported Niemöller. One of them was Frank P. Hladky, who also worked at the Allied headquarters. He put in a good word for Niemöller with Knappen to allow the German pastor a speech in front of American militaries, scheduled in Frankfurt for 31 July. An audience of approximately 1,000 people had already gathered when the chief-of-staff cancelled the event at the last minute.[23]

The text of Niemöller's speech, however, has survived, and it is worth taking a closer look at what he would have said in his first public talk after liberation. Niemöller presented the Confessing Church as the 'only hope' for Germany's spiritual 'rebirth'. Discussing topics such as education, schools, and the economy, he pointed out how only the Church could fulfil these hopes. At the centre of his deliberations was the demand that 'no area' of social life should develop 'according to its own rules'; rather, 'they must always answer the law of God'.[24] This was essentially a rejection of the autonomy of modern society's functional sub-systems.[25] His position can be described as religious fundamentalism in the sense that he understood faith as the overall yardstick of any type of social action. The continuity of Niemöller's thoughts is remarkable in this respect. He had already rejected the concept of an 'autonomy' of modern society's functional sub-systems in his Dahlem trial sermon on 17 May 1931. The second thesis of the Barmen Theological Declaration of 1934, which emphasizes God's claim to 'our entire life', also rejected such an autonomy.[26]

In early August, the American journalist Percy Knauth, who worked for *Time Magazine*, met Niemöller in Frankfurt. He encountered an 'extremely bitter, extremely negative' man, who wore American army trousers and lit American cigarettes with an American Zippo lighter. His appearance contrasted with his strong resentment against Americans. He honestly believed that American newspapers followed a 'directive' to report nothing positive about him. Knauth tried in vain to explain the concept of press freedom to him. Niemöller still complained about his treatment by the Americans. He was certain the Allies wanted to see Germany's 'total ruin' and make Germany the battlefield of a new war that would end the German nation.[27]

The 'Historical' Niemöller and the Myth of the Resistance Fighter

Niemöller's allegations about American objectives are indicative of his anti-Americanism, which did not stop him from appreciating affluence and mass culture in the USA. Recently liberated from the concentration camp, Niemöller was surprised to learn that the world public had celebrated him as a hero of the resistance and now condemned him due to his voluntary application for military service.[28] To understand his fall from hero to villain, we have to consider the public image of Niemöller in the USA. A good bellwether of American interest in him is the *New York Times*: the newspaper reported on Niemöller and his fate no less than 167 times from the time of his arrest until Germany's capitulation.[29]

US Protestant churches in particular went head over heels in their admiration for him as a Christian martyr.[30] All Protestants in the USA were called to commemorate him at the anniversary of his arrest on 1 July. The driving force behind this initiative was Henry Smith Leiper, a Congregationalist and well-connected leading member of the Federal Council of Churches—the umbrella organization for Protestant Churches in the USA—and the World Council of

Churches (WCC). During the run-up to the commemorations on 1 July he referred to Niemöller as a 'symbol of undying human thirst for freedom of conscience', whose 'martyrdom' begun with his arrest. Hitler, Leiper claimed, had justified this measure against the brave pastor by saying: 'Niemöller or I'. Because this—fictional—remark was repeated time and time again, Niemöller appeared to have been the most important adversary of the brutal dictator.[31] In 1939, a pastor in Brooklyn went so far as to re-enact Niemöller's arrest during his Sunday service. The moment he went up to the pulpit, two men in brown Nazi uniforms dragged him away. Subsequently, the American pastor delivered the sermon behind a staged cell door with bars and the inscription 'Sachsenhausen'.[32]

And yet, not only Protestants considered Niemöller a symbol of resistance against Hitler. American rabbis praised the imprisoned cleric and likened him to the Old Testament prophet Jeremiah. New York rabbi William Rosenblum stated the prisoner would go down in history as the 'martyr Niemöller' because he preferred to wear a prisoner's gown instead of 'neo-pagan vestments'.[33] The media amplified this perception. In 1942, the book *I was in Hell with Niemöller* was published. Its author, Leo Stein, described how as one of Niemöller's fellow inmates in Sachsenhausen he witnessed how the SS subjected Niemöller to brutal treatment.[34] The real identity of the author, whose book is a piece of fiction, has not been established until today. To be sure, soon after publication doubts arose in the US media about the authenticity of the story, but if anything this increased interest in the fate of the imprisoned pastor.[35] Niemöller even appeared on cinema screens. The anarchist and playwright Ernst Toller, in US exile from 1937, wrote the play *Pastor Hall*, unmistakably following Niemöller's biography in narrating the church struggle. Based on this play, in 1939 two English directors made a film that was released in British and American cinemas after a short delay in autumn 1940. The *New York Times* reported that Eleanor Roosevelt, the president's wife, watched the film several times—her son, who worked for a Hollywood studio, was involved in its release.[36]

Nobody prepared Niemöller for the fact that a global public expected a resistance hero and martyr. In his first letter to Niemöller after his liberation from Dachau, dated 9 July 1945, Karl Barth, whose ironical remarks often hit the nail on the head, put the problem as follows:

> I'm not exaggerating when I tell you that there has been hardly anyone during our time who was so much loved and admired, for whom so many Christians prayed and so many children of the world showed so much respect than you. [...] [T]he newspapers never grew tired to occasionally mention you, and in America you have been an official hero on the cinema screen. You have been the symbol of the resistance against Hitler. I have sometimes tried to humbly remind of the "historical" Niemöller, whom I remembered not only in large format but also at least in his relationship to Hitler and particularly to pre-Hitler German nationalism having

less easy contours. But there was no stopping. [...] Afterwards you have—surely without suspecting it—done powerful things to thwart this myth: I mean the interview in Naples between you and one or several American journalists. Good grief, the declaration that a proper German does not ask whether his fatherland is in the right or in the wrong when there is a war! Oh, at this point I recognized the old, the "historical" Martin Niemöller![37]

Barth's remarks aptly describe the extent of the hero's fall. Behind the symbolic image of Niemöller as resistance fighter and hero of the church struggle, Barth unmasked the 'historical' figure, the militarist, nationalist, and supporter of National Socialism. Niemöller instinctively reacted to the negative press coverage by blaming the media for creating distorted stories. In November 1945, he expressed his surprise that many people 'are still gullible to the newspapers, even after our experiences with Goebbels'.[38] It did not occur to him that mass media in a pluralistic society had an important purpose. In this vein, scolding the press remained his first reaction to negative reports during the years that followed.[39]

While Niemöller tried to settle in post-war German society, he faced many practical problems. In Leoni, he, his wife, little Martin, Hertha, Brigitte, and the maid Dora Schulz lived in three rooms in Mrs Lempp's holiday home. Only one of them could be properly heated in winter. This situation caused many arguments, which Niemöller found 'intolerable'.[40] First he clashed with Brigitte and Dora Schulz. When the latter returned to Dahlem to take care of the parsonage, he kept arguing with his oldest daughter; the conflict harking back to her engagement which was broken off in 1940.[41] At least Niemöller, after some efforts, was able to get instalments of his salary from the Dahlem pastorate transferred to Bavaria. But he was never involved in the Bavarian regional church, and the trips to Frankfurt were as exhausting as the living conditions in Leoni. So what was more natural than returning to Dahlem?

Whether the Niemöller family would return to Berlin or not was a charade that lasted two years, and had a protagonist who, in the end, had almost forgotten what he had actually wanted. It was not before autumn 1945 that Martin and Else Niemöller travelled to Dahlem. Their first visit was to their old friend and church master of the parish, Ludwig Bartning. They then went to the house in Cecilienallee 61 where they met their son Heinz-Hermann, who had reached Berlin via some detours from the eastern front.[42] On 23 October, Niemöller and his wife visited the Brandenburg Confessing Synod convened in Spandau. The delegates welcomed him with the song *Now Thank We All Our God*. They then asked him to move back to Berlin, which gave the impression that a leading position in the Church was in the offing.[43] Niemöller later vehemently denied such an offer had been made. He perceived church politics in Berlin as toxic because Otto Dibelius had himself made Bishop of Berlin on his own authority in May 1945 and gave Niemöller, who had after all been in a concentration camp, the cold shoulder. In a letter to Franz Hildebrandt from 1945, Niemöller maliciously suggested Dibelius ruled 'according to the Führer principle'.[44] In another letter directly to Dibelius from July 1946, Niemöller complained his Dahlem fellow pastors did not even feel the need 'to say hello' to him and the Berlin Church 'has not made one word of contact with me'.[45] But both claims were inaccurate. In a long personal letter from August 1946, Kurt Scharf reminded Niemöller of the real events at the Brandenburg synod.[46]

Testimony from the initial days in Dahlem corroborate Niemöller was indeed looking forward to returning to Berlin. On 29 October 1945, the Dahlem parish council convened and Niemöller expressed his intent to return to his old parish.[47] In the following months, however, he sent out conflicting signals. In a letter to a Berlin pastor from July 1946 Niemöller stated he would 'love nothing more than' to return to Dahlem. Yet at that time he was already involved with the Confessing Church in Hesse-Nassau and wanted to support his fellow brethren there in their 'fight against the restoration of the Church'.[48] Niemöller was indecisive. He assured Martin Albertz, his old comrade from the Confessing Church in Berlin, that he would move to Berlin in 1947.[49] At first it seemed that precisely this would happen. On 28 June 1947, the parish council convened for another meeting. Eberhard Röhricht welcomed Niemöller's 'return home to Dahlem' in a 'lengthy speech' and conferred the chairmanship of the parish council and management of the parish upon him.[50] But while the parishioners were largely happy about this decision, their joy was short-lived. Four months later, in November 1947, Niemöller informed the parish council he would terminate his position as pastor in Dahlem and accept a leading post in the Protestant Church in Hesse and Nassau (EKHN).[51] Later he told his brother Wilhelm that Walter Dreß had tipped the scales of this decision. Despite extended negotiations, the consistory was not willing to remove Dreß, whom Niemöller deemed a declared opponent of the Confessing Church, from the Dahlem parish.[52] However, the real reason for his farewell to Berlin was most likely that the Berlin Church had become too small a stage for Niemöller. The position in the EKHN, located in Darmstadt close to Frankfurt airport, seemed to be a stepping stone into the wide world of ecumenism and was also in close vicinity to the US military authorities. As Otto Dibelius' rise in the EKD and the ecumenical movement shows, this calculation proved to be wrong. But perhaps Niemöller simply did not want to work and live in the same place as Dibelius. Niemöller's commitment to the EKHN was also a result of his move to Hesse in mid-November 1945. He and his family lived in a spacious flat in Büdingen Castle, an old Staufian water castle 60 kilometres east of Frankfurt. This was again temporary accommodation, but much more spacious than the tiny rooms in Leoni—and heated. Niemöller also had an office and a secretary for his extensive correspondence.[53]

While the move to Büdingen brought some calm into Niemöller's life—at least on the surface—the controversies over his attitude during and towards the 'Third

Reich' did not end. Several months after the interview in Naples, the Americans still did not know what to make of him. Major General Morrison C. Stayer, responsible for public health, concluded in September 1945 that it was 'too early to predict' whether the former U-boat officer 'will wholeheartedly reject militaristic, nationalistic concepts of the German state' which had been connected with the Protestant Church for such a long time. Stayer was convinced that Niemöller's remarks in Naples were not an 'isolated utterance', but corresponded with 'good Lutheran theology'.[54]

Public controversies over Niemöller between 1945 and 1946 mostly revolved around his remarks on the issue of guilt, which we will discuss throughout the following chapter in greater detail. In 1947, public attention again focused on Niemöller. The first occasion was a press conference on 28 March 1947, held by Robert W. Kempner, deputy chief prosecutor of the Nuremberg trials. Kempner read out excerpts of a report compiled by Wilhelm Brachmann for the Office Rosenberg about Niemöller's appearance during the first day of his trial in 1938. The press coverage in 1947 focused mainly on Niemöller's remarks—falsely—claiming he had voted NSDAP from 1924 onwards, and that he had 'disliked' the Jews—a massive understatement. The newspapers concluded he had been a 'sympathizer of the NSDAP'.[55] In the mass media, the 'Niemöller case' emerged—not for the last time.[56] Old friends from the Confessing Church, including Hans Böhm, who had joined the Second VKL in 1936 and became Provost of Berlin in 1945, responded swiftly. He praised Niemöller as the 'soul of the resistance' of the Church and highlighted the 1936 memorandum.[57] However, as Niemöller was still in the USA at the time and unable to respond to the press allegations, media coverage remained critical. The Jewish German-language weekly *Aufbau*, published in New York, strongly criticized Niemöller, claiming his statements from 1938 'unmasked' him.[58]

The Germans as Victims and Niemöller's Antisemitism

The next controversy loomed even before Niemöller returned from the USA. At the end of his long journey, Niemöller wrote an open letter to Frederik J. Forell, a Silesian pastor who had fled the Nazis in 1933 and finally arrived in the USA in 1940. As head of the Emergency Committee for German Protestantism, Forell was committed to organizing cash and care packets for the suffering German population and was thus an important contact for Niemöller.[59] Intended as a moving moral appeal, the rhetoric of Niemöller's letter missed the mark completely when he portrayed the Germans as victims. Niemöller claimed Germans in the British occupation zone had received 'only 700 calories' recently, less than the lowest ration that had ever been reportedly given out in a National Socialist concentration camp. The result was, he wrote, 'starving to death in the proper sense'.[60] To be sure, Germany suffered a hunger crisis in winter 1946–7. But only in some isolated places did the average ratio of calories per person sink to the levels suggested by Niemöller. On average, Germans in the British zone received a minimum of 1,100 calories per day in spring 1947.[61] The comparison with concentration camp food rations insinuated that the treatment of Germans under Allied occupation was worse than that of the victims of Nazi terror. And this was not all. Niemöller also indulged in wild number games, suggesting since the capitulation of the 'Third Reich' in May 1945 'at least 6 million Germans have disappeared'. This was nothing less than 'putting the Morgenthau plan into practice, intending to exterminate an entire people to the roots'. Allied rule over Germany was in essence nothing but the 'continuation' of the 'rule of terror by the Gestapo'.[62]

Such frenzied rhetoric was not only problematic due to the harsh allegations against the Allies—who had liberated Germany from the Nazi rule of terror with great sacrifice after all. The accusation that Henry Morgenthau, a Jewish American from New York, wanted to exterminate the Germans had clear antisemitic connotations, as a staff member of the US military government critically remarked.[63] But at the core of the letter was the claim of German victimization, specifically the assumption that Germans were victims whose suffering exceeded that of the concentration camp inmates. 'Less than concentration camp rations', read the headline in a German newspaper.[64] As the letter targeted the American public, the German media response to Niemöller's abysmal deliberations remained subdued. And yet another controversy erupted which cast an even darker shadow on Niemöller's public image.

In June 1947, his housekeeper approached Wilhelm Beez, district chairman of the Association of the Persecutees of the Nazi Regime (Vereinigung der Verfolgten des Naziregimes, VVN). In this capacity Beez was in charge of distributing additional food rations to victims of the Nazi regime, which Niemöller and his family had been receiving since their move to Büdingen. Beez must have seen a note by the local SPD group in Büdingen on the distribution of care packets that Niemöller had organized in the USA. According to the note, Prince Hubertus von Preußen, the grandson of Kaiser Wilhelm II who also lived at Büdingen Castle since the end of the war, received care packets. The same applied to the Prince's family and former National Socialists. In contrast, local Social Democrats and Communists, who were genuine victims of the Nazi regime, were left in the cold. Beez used this as an opportunity to deny Niemöller's housekeeper additional ration cards.[65] In response, Niemöller went to see Beez himself on 14 June. 'Made a row', reads the brief entry in his diary.[66] A few weeks later, the *Spiegel* reported how this row had panned out: Niemöller had complained, accusing the distribution office: 'So you only support friends of the Jews [*Judenfreunde*]?'. Niemöller never denied having made this allegation.[67]

The executive board of the VVN in Hesse used these events to exclude Niemöller. The Jewish emigrant and journalist Hans Mayer, founding member and chairman of the Hessian VVN, explained this decision in late July. He made it clear that the events at the district administration office were only the final nail in the coffin. For a long time there had been discussions about Niemöller's political views. Those VVN members who had been victims of religious persecution were convinced 'a religious struggle had to be simultaneously in full ideological and political opposition against the Third Reich'. In this context, it seemed highly disconcerting that Niemöller stated he had rejected the Nazi regime solely on religious grounds. The publication of Niemöller's statements before the 1938 Special Court again proved crucial in this respect. Mayer admitted that, when interviewed by the Gestapo, many VVN members had made statements to protect themselves. But Niemöller's remarks from 1938 on antisemitism and National Socialism, Mayer concluded, were of a different quality.[68]

The decision of the VVN garnered broad media attention, not only in Germany but also in Switzerland, Great Britain, and the USA. Niemöller, the *Manchester Guardian* titled, was 'Not a Nazi Victim', while an American army newspaper reported that Niemöller was 'Ousted by Nazi Victims Unit, Termed Anti-Semite'.[69] Only a few German newspapers explicitly defended Niemöller, among them *Die Zeit*, which dismissed the story as 'foolish' and insisted that Niemöller could not be denied his status as a victim of Nazi persecution.[70] Uncertainty spread in the VVN about how to deal with the press frenzy. In an internal memo, Hans Mayer pointed out that representatives of all parties on the regional executive board of the VVN in Hesse supported the decision, including those from the CDU such as Eugen Kogon.[71] Niemöller's response was clumsy. He was about to leave for Oslo when the controversy began in late July. German newspapers quoted him saying that those behind the decision were 'full of hatred and worshipped the principle "an eye for an eye, a tooth for a tooth"'.[72] The antisemitic implications of this remark, referring to the Old Testament (Exod. 21:24), were obvious.

Upon returning from Oslo, Niemöller added injury to insult by declaring he would prove the 'validity' of his claim that only 'friends of the Jews' benefited from care packages.[73] On 10 August he delivered a speech in the Büdingen Church to 'comment on the attacks'.[74] This was in essence an attempt to portray himself as the innocent victim of a campaign. He claimed the attacks on him had followed a pattern that 'has been common during the last fifteen years'. To put it plainly, he accused the VVN of using Nazi methods. With more than a touch of self-righteousness he insisted he did not need to prove to anyone that 'he had been anti-Nazi'.[75] He might have convinced the Büdingen parish, and hence it was a 'good evening' for him.[76] But he did not convince the mass media. A KPD-leaning newspaper published excerpts of Franz Hildebrandt's book *Martin Niemöller and his Creed*, published anonymously in 1938, which highlighted Niemöller's proximity to National Socialism. The history of the fight against Hitler, the newspaper concluded, should not concentrate on those who had 'fondly welcomed' 30 January 1933 'as the fulfilment of long cherished hopes'.[77]

As the scandal was initiated by an antisemitic remark, it was deeply ironic that Niemöller tried to end the controversy by persuading a Jew to publicly exonerate him. On 18 August he met with Philipp Auerbach in Munich. Auerbach, who came from a Hamburg Jewish family, had been a prisoner in Auschwitz and became Bavarian State Commissioner for 'racial, religious, and political persecution' in 1946, an office established on the request of the US military government in the interests of Nazi victims.[78] The main purpose of Niemöller's meeting with Auerbach was to publish a joint press release. It stated that Niemöller considered the allegation of antisemitism to be 'a personal offence'. After all, he had been the 'spearhead of justice and truth'. After initial sympathy, he had turned away from the NSDAP when Hitler glorified the Potempa murders.[79] This was blatantly false. The brutal murder of a Communist worker in the Upper Silesian parish of Potempa happened in August 1932, months before Niemöller declared his approval of the Nazi regime from the pulpit and voted for the NSDAP in March 1933. But in 1947 these facts were unknown. As a further result of the meeting, Auerbach, a founding member of the VVN, promised to mediate with the Hessian regional office and resolve the conflict.[80]

The controversies around Niemöller show he had great difficulties dealing with a broad international public. The world expected a martyr of the fight against Hitler, but were instead faced with Niemöller's highly contradictory statements regarding the Nazi regime. Another point in question was his statement to the 1938 Special Court, where his anti-Jewish remarks attracted public attention. All this begs the question of Niemöller's attitude towards antiemitism after 1945. In this context attention is commonly drawn to his public statements about the question of guilt, which we will discuss in greater detail throughout the next chapter. On 22 January 1946, for instance, Niemöller gave a speech in the Erlangen Neustädter Church in front of approximately 1,200 students. He pointed out he did not dare 'to open my mouth' when he witnessed 'that the Jews were abused' in the concentration camp. And, he continued, the '5.6 million dead Jews' were 'the debt of our people'.[81] The gist of these remarks was that Niemöller blamed Protestant Christians for the murder of the Jews not in an abstract sense, as the collective responsibility of the German people, but in the sense of a personal responsibility. He also spoke of an encounter with a 'Jew who had lost everything' and was the 'only survivor in his family'. So he 'could not help' saying to him:

Dear brother, man, and Jew, before you say something let me tell you: I plead guilty and beg you: forgive me and my people our guilt. Only this will open the path again, only then the message can work again and new live start.[82]

It is striking that in these remarks Niemöller not only begged for forgiveness for himself, but for the German people collectively. Something else is eye-catching: the instrumental meaning of the desired forgiveness. It was not an end in itself, but ultimately served to facilitate and strengthen the announcement of the Christian message. But who was the Jew that Niemöller addressed so personally and inclusively as 'brother' and 'man'? Another of Niemöller's many speeches from 1945–6, titled *Der Weg ins Freie* (The Road into the Open), can shed a light on this question. Here, Niemöller elaborated on the encounter with this 'brother'. He described an incident in his Dahlem parsonage in October 1945. A man visited him whose parents had 'starved to death in Theresienstadt' and whose sister had been 'gassed'. Niemöller told him, in a similar vein: 'Dear brother, I know that my people and I have sinned against you and your people.'[83] The brother, as Niemöller pointed out, was 'a Jewish Christian from my parish I had last seen in 1936–37'.[84] In other words, the gesture of personal forgiveness did not refer to a member of the Jewish faith, but to a Christian of Jewish descent, a 'brother' who like himself had found his way to the true religion of Christianity. For Niemöller, the actual 'Jew' remained a chimera, an abstract imagination.

This is not to deny that Niemöller made great efforts to address the Church's guilt for the persecution of the Jews. In his speeches from 1945 and 1946 he drove home that the guilt for the Holocaust was not only a heavy burden on 'the German people and the German name' but also 'on Christianity'.[85] He also became active in church circles. At a conference on 'The Church and Judaism' in Darmstadt in 1948, he gave the welcome address, emphasizing that 'during the years of persecution' he had realized 'Christianity's guilt'. The topic of the conference, he claimed, had become 'a problem of paramount importance'. Thus he supported the aim to make the 'Jewish question' a concern of the entire German Church.[86] It is no semantic sophistry to point out that the term 'Jewish question' only makes sense in the context of an antisemitic discourse. From their own perspective, Jews pose neither a 'problem' nor a 'question' that needs to be resolved. This is but one example illustrating the lack of historical depth and reflexivity in Niemöller's deliberations on the theological dimension of Christian antisemitism during the immediate post-war years.

Furthermore, a blanket distancing from antisemitism in Sunday speeches and synod decisions is not necessarily proof of a fundamental change of heart, particularly as Niemöller at the same time repeatedly insinuated that 'the Jews' were the masterminds behind negative developments. We have already discussed some examples for this. It is striking that Niemöller used antisemitic tropes especially whenever he wanted to rhetorically disassociate himself from Nazi racial thinking about the Jews.[87] At a press conference in New York in January 1947 he declared there was no longer any antisemitism in Germany. Some rabbis, who were in contact with Jewish Displaced Persons in Germany and knew that they were victims of antisemitic resentment almost on a daily basis, vehemently protested. A US journalist commented on Niemöller's remark ironically: 'Pastor Niemöller has come to America to tell us antisemitism in Germany is dead. If the pastor were to look a bit more closely he would see it is the Jews that are dead.'[88] In an interview with the German-Jewish weekly *Aufbau* Niemöller was asked whether the emigrated Jews would return to Germany. First he expressed his dismay that 'six million people' had been 'slaughtered in such a horrendous way'. But his verbal empathy swiftly turned into resentment when he asked what the returning Jews should do in a 'crowded and impoverished Germany'—'provided they don't want to become farmers'.[89] This rhetorical question relied on the anti-semitic stereotype that Jews were neither willing nor able to do hard physical work.

After his return to Germany from the USA, Niemöller continued his rhetorical low blows. In late 1947, he held a press conference in Berlin where he addressed his journey to America and political issues in great detail. When asked how prevalent antisemitism was in Germany and the USA, he again drew on anti-semitic stereotypes. Racial antisemitism in Germany had been 'beaten to death'—his unfortunate choice of words according to the stenographic minutes—when the synagogues burned in 1938. But, Niemöller continued, during recent months antisemitism in Germany had resurfaced as a 'general feeling', in the form it had been around before 1933. The reason? 'Everywhere in American institutions [...] Jews are placed. Let's be honest and call a spade a spade.' What's more, Niemöller also gave an explanation as to why the Jews in US military government did 'not want reconciliation' with the Germans: 'If I were a Jew coming from America to Germany after having escaped slaughtering under Hitler, I would also deal in politics of hatred and revenge, provided that I am not a Christian.'[90] With this line of argument, Niemöller reversed the roles of victim and perpetrator, a core element of antisemitic discourse, by turning the victims of the Holocaust into perpetrators, who had themselves to blame for anti-Jewish resentment.[91]

Niemöller's reference to the revengeful and hateful Jew, who can only be freed of his ills by baptism, was another established anti-Jewish stereotype. The assumption that this was an isolated faux pas does not hold water, as Niemöller made similar remarks on other occasions. On 7 March 1946, for instance, representatives of the Swiss Protestant Church Aid for the Confessing Church in Zurich welcomed Niemöller for a speech and subsequent discussion. The pastor Paul Vogt had founded the organization in 1937.[92] The meeting started with a friendly gesture. Vogt presented Else and Martin Niemöller with a bouquet of carnations, a 'practical greeting in the form of a Swiss banknote', and, to highlight the ecumenical character of the meeting, a 'German banknote'. Both Vogt and Karl Barth, who was also present, insisted the subsequent discussions should not be leaked to the press.[93] During the debate a female participant inquired about the 'Jewish question in Germany'. Barth added that this question would put 'the grave problem of antisemitism on the agenda'.[94] Niemöller answered the question as follows:

There is a new antisemitism in Germany, but it has nothing to do with the returning Jews. It is caused by the Americans letting Jews carry out the denazi-fication.[95]

Again, Niemöller employed the antisemitic trope of reversing victims and perpetrators, in which Jews are guilty of the resentment against them. At the end of the almost four-hour debate, a final remark by Niemöller gave insight into his personality when he stressed that 'despite everything he does not want to be anything other than a German'.[96] Even after 1945, nationalism was still at the core of his political thinking. And because nationalism always has a dark side, tending to aggression, exclusion, and xenophobia, antisemitism was still part of Niemöller's world view.[97] After 1945 he took the first steps to break away from Christian anti-Judaism, yet at the same time still reaffirmed key elements of a socio-cultural antisemitism.

The only novelty after 1945 was that Niemöller expressed his antisemitic resentment in the context of an anti-American discourse. He blamed the Jews—that is, the Jews in America—for all the problems that emerged in Germany. In autumn 1947 he wrote to the Methodist Ewart Turner, a close personal friend of Martin and Else Niemöller who had been a pastor of the American Church in Berlin between 1930 and 1934.[98] Niemöller complained that food rations were cut to 100 grams of meat per week. Ordinary people, he predicted, would starve to death during the following winter. Therefore 'the Jew [in the US military government] would be proved right, who answered my question of what would happen with the too many people in the Western zones with: "Don't worry, we will take care of that, this problem will be resolved in a natural way!"'[99] For Niemöller it was the Jews who starved Germans to death, not the other way round. At the same time, he repeatedly used a juxtaposition, which revealed the hypocrisy of the Protestant discourse of guilt after 1945: only Christians were ready for remorse and reconciliation. When Jews did not accept the offered declaration of guilt, they only affirmed what Niemöller kept on emphasizing: Jews were driven by hatred and revenge.

For Niemöller, new beginnings upon liberation were delayed. That was partly due to his personal situation. Initially, he lived in isolated and cramped conditions in Leoni, later with more freedom and space, but still a 'lodger', in Büdingen. Only in May 1948—after he was already in the post of church president in Hesse-Nassau for several months—did he and his family move into a house in Brentanostraße in Wiesbaden, where he would live until his death. A crucial reason for this delay was his own indecisiveness about his career path. His vociferous criticism of Otto Dibelius—part of the conflicts over church politics that erupted in 1945—should not obscure the fact that it took Niemöller quite a while until he definitively ruled out a return to the Dahlem parish. In the wake of liberation from the concentration camp Dachau, the international public expected to find a martyr and hero of the resistance against Hitler in Niemöller. The astonishment was therefore all the greater when it turned out that the 'historical' Niemöller—as Karl Barth put it—still existed and expressed his unwavering nationalist stance in interviews. His attitude towards the Jews was another continuity that went beyond 1945. To be sure, he was involved in initial attempts of the Protestant Church to come to terms with the legacy of Christian anti-Judaism. But his personal antisemitic resentment, his habitual, deeply entrenched socio-cultural hostility towards the Jews, became visible on several occasions both in private and public settings.

14

Rebuilding the Protestant Church

The collapse of the 'Third Reich' and the end of the war in 1945 gave rise to hope for both Protestants and Catholics. The Christian churches were the only institutions that survived the end of the Nazi regime intact, even though this was only true in a very limited sense for many Protestant regional churches due to the fierce conflicts of the church struggle. An administrative apparatus survived which remained operational in the moment of German defeat. More importantly, the caesura of 1945 provided a chance to discuss ideas for a renewal of morality and society after the catastrophe of National Socialism. Leading representatives of the Protestant churches—including Martin Niemöller—felt they had great responsibility in this respect and, at the same time, hoped the churches would have an excellent opportunity to spread the message of the Gospel. In this sense, Bavarian bishop Hans Meiser stated as early as January 1945 that the 'hour of the Church' was now 'newly on the rise'.[1]

These expectations were informed by often contradicting interpretations, which can be subsumed under the opposition between secularization and re-Christianization.[2] Even before 1945, this had been a widespread notion among clerics of both confessions, which was now brought up to date. According to this idea, National Socialism had been the result of a renunciation of Christianity, and the attack on Christian faith been the core of its ideology. Martin Niemöller adopted this interpretation after the Sportpalast scandal in November 1933, and modified it from 1935 as a *völkisch*-pagan religiosity made considerable advances among National Socialists. His interpretation of National Socialism as an anti-religious force led him to the conclusion that there was more at stake in 1945 than just to hope for a rising number of churchgoers and the return to the Church's fold of those who had left it after 1933. For Niemöller, re-Christianization meant that Germans—far beyond nominal church members—had to find their way back to God. The destructive legacy of the 'Third Reich' could only be overcome when all areas of society oriented themselves towards Christian norms. In his speech to representatives of the US occupation troops, scheduled for 31 July 1945, Niemöller advocated that Christian imperatives should guide all fields of society.[3] From the outset, the idea of re-Christianizing German society was wishful thinking, lacking any basis in social reality. But the concept of re-Christianization was relevant even as a chimera-like illusion, as it interpreted and structured social reality. This was particularly true for Martin Niemöller, who, during the first months after his long imprisonment, had no reliable information about the situation of the Protestant Church after the end of the war. In letters to fellow campaigners from the Confessing Church in July 1945, he time and again emphasized that he was 'completely in the dark' about the events from 1937 onwards.[4]

However, being uninformed did not stop him from expressing concrete ideas about the situation of the Church and steps that should be taken. From his point of view, four measures were necessary to eliminate the legacy of National Socialism and get the renewal of the Church off the ground. First, all offices established after 1933—and this included in his view the DEK, the church chancery, and the newly appointed bishops—had to 'vanish', as well as, second, those office holders who had 'supported or condoned the Nazi regime in the Church'; here Niemöller specifically referred to Hanover bishop Marahrens. The Confessing Church, third, should 'take the lead' in the parishes. Niemöller adhered to the idea he had developed during the church struggle, that missionary work of Confessing Christians had to be based on the parish. The fourth step, building new church leadership bodies, could only be taken 'slowly'. Based on universal church elections, Confessing synods were to take the relevant decisions.[5]

In late July 1945, Niemöller drafted a memorandum about the 'Situation and Prospects of the Protestant Church'. Its primary purpose was to obtain permission from the US military authorities to hold a meeting of the Reich Council of Brethren. According to Niemöller's account, the Confessing Church was—in essence—little more than the Pastors' Emergency League (PEL) led by himself. At the same time, he went as far as to say that, in this understanding, the Confessing Church 'has been home to the vast majority of Protestant Christians in Germany for many years' insofar 'they actively participate in church life'.[6] This was far from the reality. By 1938, only a fifth of all pastors in active service were members of the PEL, and this ratio is likely to be similar for lay members of the Confessing Church.[7] But Niemöller was not bothered by such details. Thus, it was no surprise that he not only predicted a large majority for the Confessing Church (as he saw it) in the church elections but also spoke of himself as someone who was 'doubtlessly seen as the leader of the German Church by the entire Protestant Christianity in Germany and beyond'.[8]

The strategic purpose of these remarks is obvious. Niemöller wanted to drive home to the occupation authorities that only the Confessing Church, led by him, 'could lead the right way based on the Gospel' and thus 'help the German people achieve a spiritual rebirth'.[9] Seen from this angle, he himself embodied the promise of Germany's re-Christianization. While Niemöller still praised the Confessing Church, understood from the perspective of the 1934 Dahlem synod, as the only force for the moral renewal of the German people, others had created a fait accompli. As we have already seen, the American occupation authorities had considerable reservations about Niemöller and decided to rely on Württemberg bishop Theophil Wurm for the rebuilding of the Protestant Church. Beginning in

1941, Wurm had made great efforts to reconcile the quarrelling factions within the Protestant Church. By Easter 1943, he had summarized his ideas on the 'Mission and Nature of the Church' in 13 points, an initiative which was met with support from representatives of all relevant church groups except for the DC.[10]

Wurm's conciliatory approach was firmly committed to the ideals of the Confessing Front, and had not only gained him respect from church circles. Representatives of the World Council of Churches (WCC) in Geneva, which was in the process of being established, also favoured Wurm. Willem Visser 't Hooft, driving force of the ecumenical movement as WCC secretary general from 1948, was explicitly against Niemöller. He should rather not become the leader of the Protestant Church, 't Hooft suggested, because he was 'no states-man'.[11] When travelling through the American and British occupation zones in June 1945, Wurm was able to win the support of regional church representatives, the Allies, and the ecumenical movement for his plan to establish a *Kirchenbund* (federation of churches) to reorganize the Church. On 21 July, the US government gave Wurm the go-ahead for a conference where 'church leaders'—referring to leading representatives of the regional churches—should discuss the 'reorganization' of the Protestant Church in Germany. Four days later, Wurm sent out invitations to this meeting, which was to be held in the Hessian town of Treysa from 27 to 31 August 1945.[12]

The Treysa Conference

Before the start of the actual conference, the representatives of the Lutheran Council met in Treysa on 25 August. Bavarian bishop Meiser wanted to use the opportunity to declare the establishment of a united Lutheran Church. When Wurm tried to persuade him and the other participants to await the results of the negotiations with the representatives of the Council of Brethren at the upcoming conference, the mood turned against him. When the Lutherans learned that Karl Barth, whom they despised, would also come to Treysa, it triggered a massive outrage. Niemöller was also targeted. Eugen Gerstenmaier, who had worked in the Church Office for Foreign Affairs (*Kirchliches Außenamt*) until his arrest as a member of the resistance group Kreisauer Kreis on 20 July 1944, reprimanded the pastor for his 'unbelievable' statements about the German people in his interviews in Naples.[13]

Thus, when church representatives from all across Germany, including the Soviet Occupation Zone, arrived in Treysa on 27 August 1945, the atmosphere was already sour. Originally, Wurm had invited 40 delegates, but this number increased, not least thanks to the inclusion of the Council of Brethren, to 88. Including others who were not official delegates, there were 120 to 150 people present at the plenary meetings.[14] The conference was opened on 28 August with addresses by Wurm and Niemöller. Three sets of written notes on the conversations held between 28 and 31 August are available. None of it gives a true indication of the atmosphere at the church conference.[15] To get an idea of the prevailing mood in Treysa, we need to consult the notes of neutral observers. One of them was Colonel Russell L. Sedgwick, the leader of the 'Religious Affairs Branch' of the British military government. Sedgwick had converted from the Anglican Church to Catholicism and thus had a healthy distance to German Protestantism. He was not enthused about the deliberations in the plenary meetings of the conference. 'Some of these talks', he wrote in his report, 'were interminably long, academic and sometimes abstruse. Not just a few were frankly dull.'[16] In addition, Sedgwick had many conversations with individual participants, which gave him disillusioning insights into the general mood:

> One could not help remarking that many of the delegates were tired, dispirited and anxious. Many of those who had put up any fight against National Socialism were now spiritually and physically exhausted. Some expressed their shame that they had not spoken up against the regime early enough—or had not spoken at all. Many feared for the future.[17]

'But for a handful of real, fighting men'—apart from Wurm and Niemöller, he also referred to Asmussen and Lilje—'the conference would have been a valley of dry bones', as Sedgwick wrote, in allusion to Hesekiel 37:1–14.[18] The British officer was particularly impressed by Niemöller. He had four long conversations with him and his wife Else. During the Second World War, Sedgwick had harboured 'suspicion' against the German pastor, not least after his perusal of *From U-Boat to Pulpit*, which was 'not easy to forget'. Yet this changed in Treysa:

> In spite of these misgivings I found myself "converted" by Niemöller's quite strong and intensely spiritual personality. He is, of course, a patriotic German like Bishop Graf von Galen of Münster, and we should not expect him to be anything else. He never referred to his imprisonment, nor sought to pose as a martyr. He is all-out to get on with the job of re-christianizing Germany [...].[19]

What Sedgwick failed to realize in his enthusiasm for the energetic pastor was the intense dislike the Lutherans had for Niemöller and the other representatives of the Council of Brethren. Niemöller had to accept he was seen 'as a dictator'.[20] On the evening of the first conference day, a harsh confrontation erupted when Hans Meiser claimed the representatives of the Reich Council of Brethren had no right to participate in the conference. Theologian Helmuth Schreiner went even further, suggesting 'threats' had been made by the Brethren. He said the Brethren were giving orders just like 'the party' had previously, which blatantly alluded to 'Nazi methods'. In response, Hans Asmussen protested against this 'infamous perfidiousness'.[21] Nerves were raw on both sides, and only Theophil Wurm's negotiation skills ensured the conference could continue successfully. The conflicts got to Niemöller, even though he was rather thick-skinned. At midday during the second conference day, he suffered a 'fainting episode', had to consult a doctor and lie down for a few hours. According to Colonel Sedgwick, it had been a heart attack.[22]

Overall, Karl Barth was quite right when he wrote in a report for the American military government that he could not recall a single moment that the people involved had 'engaged in an open and generally objective conversation'.[23] Instead, a tug of war over the responsibilities of the new church leadership bodies prevailed, which immediately turned into haggling about posts. Ultimately, a compromise was made. The conference adopted a Provisional Constitution of the Protestant Church in Germany (Evangelische Kirche in Deutschland, EKD), which repealed the DEK's church governance established in 1933 but maintained the independence of regional churches. A Council consisting of twelve members—six Lutherans, four United and two Reformed Protestants—was to represent the EKD internally and externally. Seven of them acted as speakers of the Council. It was expressly stated that the Council of Brethren of the Confessing Church would transfer its function as church leadership body—which was in any case only exercised on paper—to the Council of the EKD, at least temporarily until a permanent regulation was agreed on. What the relationship between the EKD and regional churches would look like remained open. It was quite obvious that, in the long run, the EKD would be nothing more than a church federation rather than a church in its own right. However, at this point in time it was more about people than structures, specifically about whether Hans Meiser would be a member of the Council. This was unavoidable to prevent a split with the Lutherans. Ultimately, the Bavarian bishop became a member of the EKD Council and one of its seven speakers. But Wurm was the chairman and Niemöller vice chairman.[24] The EKD Council convened in Treysa for a brief first meeting. Hans Asmussen was in charge of the church chancery and Niemöller headed the Church Office for Foreign Affairs, which was responsible for 'ecumenical relations and German parishes abroad'.[25] There was a clear reason for this decision. The church leaders thought, as the figurehead of the church opposition against National Socialism, only Niemöller was capable of representing the Church of Germany in view of critical, if not hostile, attitudes abroad.[26]

It is the nature of compromise that all sides involved can see themselves as losers.[27] And this was precisely the case here. Meiser loudly lamented the 'methods' used in Treysa and the opening address given by Niemöller, which Meiser considered 'tactless'. He primarily saw the conferences as an incentive to press ahead with the cooperation of Lutherans. However, it was not before July 1948 that he could realize his plans with the foundation of the United Evangelical Lutheran Church of Germany (Vereinigte Evangelisch-Lutherische Kirche

Deutschlands, VELKD), which encompassed 10 of the 13 Lutheran regional churches.[28] Niemöller, on the other hand, complained to Wurm only two days after the conclusion of the negotiations that the 'Bavarian obstruction' continued in the EKD Council without interruption. He also put on record that he had not agreed to the compromise 'voluntarily'.[29] However, as he told his brother Wilhelm, he was also deeply disappointed and 'depressed' about the development of the Confessing Church during his imprisonment. Too many brethren had drifted away to the 'Berneuchen line'. This was a reference to the Berneuchen Movement, a group that originated from the youth movement and, from the 1920s, practised a renewal of the faith through the sacrament of the Eucharist and the ritual of penitence.[30] It is fair to assume such emphasis on ritualized piety irritated Niemöller, not least because it was an embarrassing reminder of his own conversion plans. Yet he was focused on the future. He had to explain to the Councils of Brethren what their further tasks were after they had handed over their church leadership authority in Treysa. He stressed the Council of Brethren would still have a purpose as guardians until church elections would take place. The Confessing Church should see itself as the 'mouth of the Church', organizing a 'core of the church' in the parishes.[31]

But this was easier said than done, all the more in the seclusion of Leoni, where Niemöller initially returned to. Niemöller felt weighed down after the conclusion of the Treysa conference and was in a 'mood of despair'. He lamented there was no 'visible way' forward in church matters.[32] And yet, he could have been content. Not only was he vice president of the EKD Council and thus prominent 'to the whole world' as a representative of German Protestants, as Martin Albertz phrased it.[33] He also headed the Church Office for Foreign Affairs, one of the two offices of the EKD, while the EKD at this point—without any administrative apparatus— only existed during the meetings of the Council. Reich Bishop Ludwig Müller had established the Church Office for Foreign Affairs in February 1934 over the course of the DEK's transition into a Reich Church. It was responsible for Protestant parishes abroad, established and run by German Protestants in many European countries, America, and Asia. Its second task was to maintain relations with the ecumenical movement that had emerged during the 1930s.[34]

It is ironic that none other than Niemöller headed the Church Office for Foreign Affairs and vehemently defended its work against critics during the following decade. In Treysa, he had emphatically expressed the view that the church chancery and the Office for Foreign Affairs as institutions of the DEK had to be 'liquidated'.[35] The reasons for his swift change of mind are obvious: after the Council of Brethren had given up any immediate claim to a church leadership function, a church office in the EKD was an ideal platform for representing the interests of the Confessing Church. The problem, however, was that this office only existed on paper, or rather as a pile of papers in Niemöller's tiny study in Leoni. The situation only improved when the Niemöller family moved to

Büdingen. From the outset, Niemöller's work at the Office for Foreign Affairs was fraught with controversy. He moaned he was being side-lined. At the same time, there were many complaints that he neglected the work of the Office for Foreign Affairs. Niemöller was well aware he spread himself thin by dashing from one talk to the other. To cope with his personal correspondence, he employed a secretary in Büdingen who also worked for the Office for Foreign Affairs. She ultimately resigned in 1948 due to permanent disputes about the allocation of tasks. In December 1947, Niemöller complained to his secretary: 'The work is eating me up.' As to the Office for Foreign Affairs, he knew very well that he 'needed to be there much more often'. But this 'constant travelling is hellish'.[36]

Between 1945 and 1947, Niemöller's 'constant travelling' took him to many German cities where he gave talks on the Germans' guilt of National Socialism. Like no other representative of the Protestant Church, Niemöller made the issue of guilt his own topic. His interventions on this theme are his most important contribution to the rebuilding of the Protestant Church after 1945. In his many speeches and articles on the guilt of the Germans, Niemöller often talked about his personal guilt. However, it is important in what context he did this and how he expressed his and the Germans' guilt. We also need to explore why Niemöller addressed this topic. To be sure, the answer to this question can only be deduced indirectly, by mapping out the chronology of his engagement with this topic.

Leading representatives of the Confessing Church had already commented on the guilt of the Church during the Second World War. In autumn 1940, in his *Ethik*, a major treatise on Christian ethics, Dietrich Bonhoeffer wrote that the 'Church has become guilty of the lives of the weakest and most vulnerable brothers of Jesus Christ'. This was a direct reference to the persecution of the Jews by the Nazi regime, details of which he documented a year later in a report for the circles of the military resistance.[37] In a letter to Visser 't Hooft from December 1942, Hans Asmussen also addressed the issue of guilt, for which Christians had to answer to God. For the members of the ecumenical movement in Switzerland, addressing guilt was the first sign for the willingness of the German Church to pave the way for a re-encounter after the end of the war.[38] While some members of the Confessing Church started a discussion about the time after Hitler, Niemöller had different priorities at this point. Deeply alarmed by the offensive of the Red Army that he learned about in his Dachau cell, he thought about submitting a second application for voluntary military service, eager to contribute to turning the fortunes of war in Germany's favour.[39]

Even during the first weeks after his delayed return to Germany, Niemöller did not concern himself with German guilt. On the contrary, during July 1945 he was busy arguing with the American military authorities about the permission for a meeting of the Reich Council of Brethren, which in the end took place in August.

In this context, he wrote a letter to Colonel Hugh O. Davis, the officer of the US military government in Frankfurt in charge of public relations. At the beginning of his letter, Niemöller referred to information conveyed by Otto Dibelius about suicides among Protestant pastors in Greater Berlin. He continued by describing the post-war situation of the Germans as victims, marked by impoverishment, despair, and mass deaths:

> In addition to all this I got direct news from Berlin yesterday, announcing that in the last few weeks about twenty Protestant pastors in that area had committed suicide in full despair, an event not heard of in the whole history of the Christian Church. I think you will try to understand what that may mean to me, but I doubt you can, even if you wish. And when I read two women of my own household [in the Dahlem parish, BZ] had been ravished, when the rectory was robbed, that millions of people are dying from starvation without help and hope, and that in this way the guiltless are put to death with the guilty without mercy, I only had to pray to God, He might free my heart of hatred and lead me the right way. I know very well that you might say: Your people has done the same things, but I doubt God will hear this excuse, and I doubt that wrong will be right on the day of judgment in any case. For me the question is not that of guilt, but as a Christian I have to look upon the misery and try to help as well as I can. [...] Now I see it is too late for helping, that winter is coming in a few weeks, that my people must pay with its life and lives what has been done by its criminal government and its followers [...].[40]

This letter is vivid evidence for the continuity of Niemöller's national Protestant mindset. He was certain God would only hear the Germans rather than the excuses of the Americans. At the same time, it is a shocking example of self-righteousness and bigotry dressed up as Christian ethics. The hatred Niemöller wanted to free himself from by praying was not directed against the Nazi dictatorship and its legacy, but against the Allies who had just liberated the German people from Nazi oppression. Yet in Niemöller's eyes, the Nazi dictatorship had only been the work of the government and its core supporters. The majority of Germans, on the other hand, were passive victims, and thus the question of guilt did not even arise in Niemöller's view.[41] In any case, he lacked any feeling that the solidarity with the German people he demanded from the Americans in the form of relief goods required empathy with their fate, an attitude which he denied Colonel Davis lock, stock, and barrel. He went even further, underpinning the groundlessness of the guilt question by accusations against the Allies. He himself had hated 'Hitlerism' from the moment 'I saw what Hitlerism was, and that was a good deal earlier than the statesmen of Great Britain and France admitted Hitler was not to be trusted.'[42]

The Question of Guilt and the Discourse of Victimization

In his first statement on the question of guilt, Niemöller focused on the victimization of the Germans. They were victims of the Allies' failure to render assistance, which made them perpetrators. However, it soon became apparent Niemöller was a quick learner. At the Frankfurt meeting of the Reich Council of Brethren in August, he addressed the question of guilt in his opening address. The Church, he said, was partially responsible for the developments after 1933. But, just like in his letter to Davis, he understood this responsibility not as the burden of guilt towards the victims of National Socialism, but towards the 'hardship' and 'horrors' of war that Germans had had to endure. References to the suicides of the Berlin pastors and the 'white shroud' that would cover starving Germans in the following winter framed his rhetoric of victimization.[43] A day later, the participants of the meeting discussed a word to the pastors drafted by Asmussen, in which the Lutheran theologian addressed the 'guilt with which our people has burdened itself'. In the same breath, however, he devalued this admission by speculating about the demonic nature of power as cause of the Nazi atrocities. He also insinuated the 'temptation' of the Allies to retaliate by committing new atrocities.[44]

In the following discussion, Niemöller opposed qualifying the German guilt. Accusations against the occupation powers should be omitted for the time being because 'the Americans don't hear it yet'. First of all, pastors and parishes were 'obliged to confess their own guilt', particularly the Confessing Church, which had let itself be 'silenced by fear'.[45] The instrumental character of this understanding of guilt is striking. In contrast to July, Niemöller now described the task of the Confessing Church to speak of its own guilt. This could be offset with that of the Allies, although the time to do this had not 'yet' come, as he had learned when Colonel Davis did not reply to his aggressive letter.

In his Treysa opening address, Niemöller again shifted the emphasis of the discourse of victimization. In his first sentences, he rejected referring to the Germans' hardship, which had previously always been the opening part of his deliberations about this topic. This hardship, he explained, was a manifestation of the fact that Germany had lost the war, rather than 'primarily the responsibility of our people and that of the Nazis', who had not seen any alternative. The true guilt for the current misery was with the Confessing Church, which was 'the only one that knew the chosen path would lead into disaster' and still did not call out the 'injustice'.[46] What consequences were to be drawn? Niemöller rejected the idea of bringing charges against former Nazis, because they would find 'their prosecutors and judges'. This was extremely naïve, indicating Niemöller's complete lack of interest in legally punishing criminal guilt. But the Church's guilt discourse was never about issues that were crucial for coming to terms with the legacy of National Socialism. The only important thing was occupying the moral high ground. The consequence Niemöller drew was that 'we'—that is, the Church—'must accuse ourselves'.[47] In his speech, he explained what this meant in practice: in a departure from 'a misconceived Lutheranism', the Church had to be renewed from below in the spirit of a 'true and earnest Reformation'.[48] In plain language this meant: the Councils of Brethren had gained moral legitimacy to lead the renewal of the Church because they recognized their guilt. This was the instrumental purpose when Niemöller acknowledged German guilt.

Niemöller would have had an opportunity to convey his take on the question of German guilt—as explained in Treysa—to an international audience. The representatives of ecumenism waited for a statement by the German church in summer 1945, their view an essential precondition for re-establishing church contacts and organizing relief supplies. But Niemöller was still occupied with the victimization of Germans. Two weeks after the Treysa conference, he repeated the stories about atrocities and his view of Germans as victims in a letter to Karl Barth. The 'decent people' in the country had 'stopped railing against the Nazis'. Instead, the most-discussed topics were news that allegedly 80 per cent of all women in Berlin had been raped and 'a mortality rate that practically meant biological extinction'. And yet, Niemöller had failed to mention the 'biological extinction' of the European Jews in his many letters or talks up to then. Instead he clarified who, in his view, was responsible for Germans' hardship: The 'Americans drive lorry after lorry with coke and coal briquettes over thousands of kilometres so that they won't freeze in winter', while nothing was done for the German population.[49]

Hence, it was only external pressure that made Niemöller stop referring to the Germans as victims and motivated him to prioritize German guilt. The second meeting of the EKD Council was scheduled in Stuttgart on 18 October. On 27 September, Visser 't Hooft asked Niemöller to invite a delegation of ecumenical representatives to Stuttgart as head of the Church Office for Foreign Affairs. A day later, Karl Barth wrote in a letter to Niemöller what the ecumenical circles and the 'Christian countries abroad' expected from the EKD Council: an unambiguous statement of the Protestant Church of Germany that it was 'co-responsible' for the 'wrong track' from 1933 onwards. Barth hoped Niemöller could 'embrace this matter'.[50] Niemöller immediately responded that he had already done so with his Treysa address.[51] But Barth, who had heard the speech, was not convinced. While the EKD Council's declaration of guilt was without doubt not the result of extortion by international church representatives—as national Protestant apologists suggested until far into the 1970s[52]—it was also not a free choice of conscience made by EKD Council members including Niemöller. At any rate, there was not only an implicit connection between the re-establishment of church relations and the admission of German guilt, and pressure on the EKD Council played an important role (Fig. 13).[53]

The six-member ecumenical delegation headed by Visser 't Hooft arrived in Stuttgart on the evening of 16 October. Bishop Georg Bell joined them on

Fig. 13 Martin Niemöller and Otto Dibelius, 1945. Despite their different theological positions, Niemöller and Dibelius worked closely together during the church struggle. After Niemöller's arrest on 1 July 1937, Dibelius took over Niemöller's confirmation classes and covered for him holding church services in Dahlem, which Niemöller very much appreciated. From 1945, their relationship was burdened by dramatic conflicts. When the conflict over the Church Foreign Office escalated in 1954–5 and Niemöller once again roared and raved, Dibelius compared him to the figure Michael Kohlhaas from Heinrich von Kleist's novella, whose relentless insistence on justice led him to excessive actions. EZA 500/4221.

18 October. Bishop Wurm met the group on 17 October, but only for a brief conversation in the afternoon, since there were two public events scheduled for the evening with Dibelius and Niemöller as speakers.[54] Niemöller started his

address as usual, emphasizing the current 'hardship' the Germans faced. But on this occasion he used this rhetorical figure to draw attention to the Germans' own responsibility for their fate. The Christians were 'to blame for the path our people has chosen because we have kept quiet when we should have spoken up'. The far-reaching implications of this silence were crystal clear to him: 'We are responsible for millions and millions of people being murdered, slaughtered, destroyed, thrown into hardship and chased out to foreign lands, poor human beings, brothers and sisters in all countries of Europe.' While this invocation of German crimes was indeed powerful, Niemöller's description of the consequences remained vague and abstract. Christians had to act 'as usual' by proclaiming the Gospel so that it would be 'heard and understood'. Niemöller's recognition of German guilt had no practical consequences whatsoever, as he urged to 'practise forgiveness' and 'preach love'.[55]

Essentially, Niemöller addressed the genocide committed by the Germans in the style of a harmless, edifying Sunday sermon. But because the ecumenical delegates, above all Visser 't Hooft, were operating within the limits of this Protestant moral discourse, they were impressed by Niemöller's speech. The following day, on 18 October, the delegation and the Council of the EKD first conferred separately and met later in the afternoon for a joint meeting. In the late evening, the Council adopted the Stuttgart Declaration of Guilt, based on drafts by Asmussen and Dibelius. The text, which consists of three brief paragraphs, is contradictory. In rather conventional Christian rhetoric, the Declaration expressed the 'guilt' of the 'whole Church' for 'not standing to our beliefs more courageously, for not praying more faithfully, for not believing more joyously, and for not loving more ardently'. At the same time, the authors claimed they 'did fight for long years in the name of Jesus Christ against the mentality that found its awful expression in the National Socialist regime of violence'. Secularism was the root cause of the 'Third Reich', re-Christianization hence the core mission of the Church. Finally, the Declaration expressed the hope that all churches would counter the 'spirit of violence and revenge'. In coded language, the EKD flagged that it perceived the Germans as victims of the occupation powers.[56]

The Stuttgart Declaration of Guilt was an important moment in German church history after 1945. It was supported by all strands within the EKD, which had been fiercely fighting each other at the Treysa conference. Thus, it marked the actual foundation of the EKD and its Council, which took collective responsibility for the first time. Despite its weaknesses and internal contradictions, the Declaration became the central point of reference for anyone in the Protestant Church who wanted to address the legacy of National Socialism.[57] It was received, discussed, and interpreted immediately after its publication, with critical voices dominating from the outset. Only four of the 27 regional churches and some provincial synods adopted the Stuttgart Declaration until 1946. A great number of pastors, parishes, and individual laypeople rejected both the gist and the intention of the Declaration.[58]

In an influential commentary to the Stuttgart Declaration, Hans Asmussen concluded that it could only be understood in its religious dimension. If repentant Christians turned towards God, they could talk of God's law to others and thus 'speak up for their right'.[59] In consequence, this meant, after unreservedly recognizing German guilt, the moment had come to address the guilt of the occupation powers. The members of the EKD Council saw themselves as advocates of the German people, who had to address negative consequences of denazification as well as material hardship of the population.[60] At a meeting in December 1945, the EKD Council discussed the draft of an open letter entitled 'To the Christians in England', which applied the same logic and was also adopted with Niemöller's consent. On the surface, the letter opposed the idea of an 'offset' of moral claims and counter-claims. But what else did the Council members mean, when they criticized that German 'injustice' was surpassed by 'even greater injustice'? Just like Niemöller in his previous statements on the question of guilt, the letter denounced the Allies for starving 'millions of innocent people'.[61]

The topic of German guilt kept the EKD Council busy far into 1946. Hans Asmussen took the next step. He not only wanted to talk about the 'guilt of others', but adopt a public act of grace granted by the Church for all of those who would admit their guilt. Yet this proposal was unanimously rejected by the EKD Council in November 1946. Even those Council members who emphasized the victimhood of the German people vis-à-vis the Allies after 1945 believed it impossible that Germans could 'grant themselves general absolution'.[62] At this point, Niemöller could no longer follow his old friend and companion. He pointed out to Asmussen that he, Niemöller, had indeed taken every opportunity to publicly talk 'about the guilt of the others' during the last months, but that he had done so in a way '[...] that we are not the others' judges'. The real reason for Niemöller's opposition, however, was that he did not trust that the German Church 'really wanted to do penance' in Stuttgart. In London, his talk about the 'culpable failure' of the British occupiers had always fallen on sympathetic ears, Niemöller wrote to Asmussen. An official 'proclamation' of the EKD, however, would not be heard there.[63] In plain language this meant only Niemöller himself, as a former concentration camp inmate, had the moral authority to read Christians in other countries the riot act. He strove for forgiveness as the result of recognition of guilt, which had already been the core of his speech in Stuttgart.

Niemöller's approach to the question of guilt was based on his authority as a concentration camp inmate who nevertheless bore part of the responsibility for the Nazi regime. In countless speeches, he told an anecdote to illustrate his deep dismay. In autumn 1945, the story went, on his way back to Leoni with Else, he took a detour to Dachau to show her his cell in the camp prison. They passed the crematorium of the former concentration camp where a sign—erroneously—gave the number of inmates who had been burnt here as 238,756.[64] Niemöller described that Else was distraught about the high figure. He himself, however, was rather troubled by the fact that inmates had already been burnt in Dachau from 1933 onwards. While he had an 'alibi' before God as a 'concentration camp inmate' for the time following 1937, he did not have one for the first four years of the Nazi regime. He should have known from newspaper coverage that communists had been deported to concentration camps as early as 1933. Because he had not been 'bothered' about their fate, he took a share of the guilt of the German people.[65] Niemöller told this story often and in different variations. It must remain open how much of it was real dismay, and how much rhetorical embellishment. Yet he did indeed visit the former concentration camp with Else on 8 November 1945. The entry in his diary—'after dinner in the camp (crematorium!)'—indicates that the site of mass murder touched him emotionally.[66]

With the constant repetition of this story, Niemöller took a personal approach to the question of guilt, injecting a sense of urgency in his appeal to all Germans to address their guilt and do penance. If he as a former concentration camp inmate did so, all others had to do it as well. Niemöller developed a rhetorical figure that illustrates which groups of victims he felt guilty towards. If the Lord Christ called him on Judgement Day, Niemöller explained, he could ask him (following Matt. 25:42–3):

For I was imprisoned (and he [Christ] points to the Communists in the 1933 concentration camp) and ye visited me not; for I was hungered (and he points to the mass graves of starved Greeks) and ye gave me no meat; for I was murdered (and he points to millions of urns of my Jewish fellow men) and ye said 'I do not know the man'.[67]

The paratactic stringing together of three groups of victims clearly brings to mind the structure of the Niemöller 'quotation' which became world-famous in its 1970s version. This quote has its roots in Niemöller's numerous speeches and sermons between 1945 and 1947, when he confessed his guilt.[68] Yet for all his emphatic insistence on his personal guilt, he never said what this actually meant. In every speech he emphasized that he had not spoken up for the victims. But was he also guilty due to his actions and speeches? Occasionally, Niemöller said he was 'guilty because I voted for Hitler in 1933'.[69] And yet, millions of Germans had done the same, and none of them was considered guilty of severe wrongdoing in public post-war debates. If Niemöller had really wanted to emphasize his personal responsibility, he could have mentioned that he joined a party that excluded Jews via an 'Aryan paragraph' as early as 1920. Or that, in autumn 1933, he confirmed the 'right of our people' to 'firmly defend itself against the ultra-large and harmful influence of Jewry'—with which he gave carte blanche to the Nazi regime and the persecution of the Jews that started immediately after their seizure of power.[70]

The crucial problem of Niemöller's public expressions of German guilt was that the genocide of the European Jews only featured marginally at best. In a speech delivered in Zurich in March 1946, for example, Niemöller mentioned the persecution of the Jews under the Nazi regime with a single sentence, in the same breath and on a par with the fate of persecuted communists. 'We should have recognized Lord Jesus Christ in the brother who suffered and was persecuted, regardless of whether he was a communist or a Jew.' He was much more elaborate in describing the hardship of the German population in the post-war period, referencing the 'millions of people who have lost their homes, commodities, property and belongings' as they had fled from the Soviets to West Germany. In sympathetic words, he described meeting a 'bombed-out young girl' on a visit to his old Dahlem parish, who put aside the first slice of a loaf of bread for the starving 'refugee masses'. The lack of food in Germany was generally at the core of his speeches and addresses in 1946–7. In Zurich he talked about those who were 'in the process of starving' because their ration cards—which he called 'perishing cards' (*Sterbekarten*)—only provided for 1,000 calories a day and were thus insufficient to survive. He painted a drastic picture of the hardships of Germans 'in despair' and 'distress', which culminated in the dramatic—and clearly grotesquely exaggerated—lament of several suicides, which happened in the wake of the 'invasion of the Russians' in the east of Germany and Berlin in 1945. He suggested '200 people' had taken their lives in one day in his Dahlem parish alone.[71]

All this shows that Niemöller could speak vividly and with empathy about suffering in the wake of the Second World War. But this empathy was always reserved for the Germans as victims of the bombing war, expulsion, and the Allied occupation regime. The German guilt towards the Jews was briefly mentioned, but its roots in Christian anti-Judaism and antisemitism were not explained. Niemöller always referenced 'the' Jew, an abstraction, a chimaera. He even expected this 'Jew' to take 'this guilt' away 'from between' the two, 'so that we can come together'.[72] It was not the Germans that had to recompense for their guilt, but the Jews! Niemöller painted a vivid picture of the hardships and misery of the German people in the post-war period. This was in stark contrast to the few words that he found to describe the suffering and death of Jews in the reach of power of the Nazi regime. Effectively, Niemöller played down German guilt for the mass murder of the European Jews by emphasizing the hardship and victim-hood of the Germans after 1945.

It soon became evident that, in regard to the question of guilt, most members of the EKD Council adhered to their national Protestant stance beyond the end of the war. They primarily saw themselves as advocates of the German people and therefore started to denounce the hardship of Germans immediately after the adoption of the Stuttgart Declaration of Guilt. Niemöller was more than willing to speak of the 'others' guilt'. Like other Protestant church leaders he considered Germans to be victims. But in contrast to the majority of the EKD Council, he acknowledged two things: first, that injustice did not become 'justice by pointing out the injustice of others'. Second, Niemöller knew that the 'songs of mockery and derision' about Germans would not be over until they had provided a sufficient sign that they understood their guilt. A confession of guilt which 'at the same time stresses the guilt of others' was in fact none.[73] Niemöller shared the national Protestant mindset of his fellow EKD Council members, but he saw emphasizing one's own guilt as the more effective tactic for steering Christians abroad towards a more positive view of Germany.[74]

Thus, he set out to discuss the guilt question and the significance of the Stuttgart Declaration of Guilt across the three Western occupation zones. In doing so, Niemöller alienated a lot of people. He dismissed the notion of collective guilt and instead talked about 'collective liability'.[75] But this did not stop angry letter writers from insulting him as a 'rascal' and 'traitor' who dragged his fatherland through the dirt. In the end, a broad public considered Niemöller to have created the notion of German 'collective guilt', which fuelled the controversy about his political statements even further.[76] Students reacted with particular sensitivity to the debate about German guilt. At some universities, a third of all students were former Wehrmacht officers. Niemöller gave a talk at Göttingen University on 17 January 1946, and the resentment of the students was palpable.[77]

Five days later, he delivered the same speech in Erlangen in front of 1,200 students. Many of them were shuffling their feet and stomped when Niemöller spoke of the guilt towards Poland. He noted a 'ruckus' in his diary, but played down this incident later in a letter to the vice-chancellor. A broad press coverage already scandalized the students' reaction so that even the Bavarian Council of Ministers had to address the affair.[78] On 3 February, Niemöller held a sermon in Marburg on the significance of German guilt for the Church. A speech on 'The Political Responsibility of Christians in Academia', organized by the Protestant student community, was scheduled for the following day. A female Marburg student recorded the events of this evening:

Everyone knew about the events in Erlangen. From Göttingen the rumour spread that he had been beaten up. I don't know what really caused these outrages [*Ausschreitungen*]. Apparently, Niemöller has put such drastic emphasis on every single German person being guilty for the war so that the students who had sacrificed their lives, freedom, and health at the front lines for six years were unable to listen to this without voicing their opinion on it. Niemöller's reputation, which preceded him, resulted in the students here in Marburg bringing themselves into position in front of the hall two hours before the start, some of them armed with sticks, pokers, whistles etc., and literally storming the venue when it opened and getting increasingly worked up by shouting [...] A broken chair with the label 'victims of fascism' was passed from one row to the next. And suddenly a tall and lean and squatting American appeared in the first row from these waves of turmoil. He turned and looked with horrified children's eyes at the

> masses storming the hall. [...] Vice President Ebbinghaus appeared. The
> evangelical maidens were on stage, ready to sing, the students held their sticks
> ready and heckled. Suddenly His Magnificence vanished looking very dismayed,
> and soon afterwards a man, invisible in the crowd, declared with a resolute voice
> that the speech was cancelled.[79]

The furious students performed a rough music, a ritual of cleansing, which
declared Niemöller's declaration of guilt a breach of the norms of their community. The broken chair signified their contempt for prioritizing the suffering of the
Nazi victims. It remained unclear whether Niemöller's speech was cancelled due
to 'overcrowding and noise', as he noted in his diary, or whether he himself
refused to give a talk in such an agitated atmosphere, as the Marburg theologian
Rudolf Bultmann and the local press reported.[80] This may very well have been a
self-serving declaration on the part of the university, which did not want to
become involved in a 'press polemic' like the one that ensued after the Erlangen
talk. Niemöller only returned to Marburg on 4 May to deliver his speech after all.[81]
In the following months, he restlessly travelled around to speak about the
Declaration of Guilt and explain its content.

   Yet in summer 1947, his zeal in this matter waned rather abruptly. Presumably
he realized the rhetorical cliché he always used in these cases—namely the claim
that a concentration camp prisoner and Nazi victim was confessing his own
guilt—was no longer plausible after the revelations about his antisemitic statements in the 1938 trial and his conflict with the VVN in Hesse.[82]

   Niemöller's position in the debate about German guilt was therefore much
more complex than often portrayed. Only when ecumenical circles and his friend
Karl Barth put pressure on him did he stop to focus primarily on the victimhood
of the Germans. In line with the majority of the EKD Council, he held the view
that the guilt of others had also to be discussed. But in contrast to this majority he
believed this could only be done with some chance of success and in a credible
fashion if German Protestants would adopt the Stuttgart Declaration of Guilt. This
was the main reason why he promoted it tirelessly. When his reputation as a
victim of National Socialism, which he always used as an entry point to discussing
German guilt, came under attack, he stopped this promotion.

   Niemöller's unwavering national Protestantism was even clearer with respect to
his attitude towards denazification. On this topic, the EKD Council showed unity
in opposing the policies of the Western Allies. The US occupation authorities were
committed to pursuing this policy, while their French and British counterparts
were rather pragmatic. The American authorities removed compromised persons
from the civil service and dismissed around 140,000 public administration officials
up until March 1946. Then the 'Law for Liberation from National Socialism and
Militarism' came into effect, turning over responsibility for the process of denazification to German civil courts, the *Spruchkammern*. They classified suspects into

five categories: from main perpetrators to harmless followers (*Mitläufer*) to exonerated people. This procedure was soon taken up in the French and British zones. With the help of many Protestant pastors who gave out masses of denazification certificates without proper checks, this policy soon became akin to a 'factory-scale production of followers', which turned the goal of denazification on its head.[83] And yet the Council of the EKD, above all Theophil Wurm, considered the approach of the Allies outrageous. On 2 May 1946, the Council unanimously adopted a resolution that rejected the Liberation Law. It eloquently lamented the dismissal of people who had carried out their tasks 'impeccably'. Using a disproportionate rhetoric, the resolution stated that denazification would go even further than measures of the Nazi regime, referring to the dismissal of Jewish civil servants in 1933. Only criminal offences—that is, Nazi crimes— should be punished.[84]

When Karl Barth read this intervention, he was outraged. In a long letter to Niemöller, he refuted the logic of the EKD resolution point by point and lectured his friend that denazification was primarily a 'matter of political morality'. Full of bitterness, he lamented that Niemöller and his colleagues in the Council had apparently 'already forgotten' the fate of the persecuted Jews.[85] Niemöller's reply throws light on the persistence of his national Protestant mindset and, corresponding with this, his ignorance of the relevance of denazification. He rejected Barth's criticism of the unfortunate comparison with Nazi anti-Jewish policy because 'no reasonable person' would assume Jews fell under the category of 'apolitical officials'. Niemöller quite obviously lacked empathy with the thousands of Jewish civil servants who were dismissed in 1933. Instead, he again invoked the victimhood of Germans. He claimed the true objective of denazification was to eliminate the 'intelligentsia in Germany'. And the 'remaining remnants of our people'—here he again referred to the ominous legend of millions of Germans who were allegedly starved to death from 1945—were too weak to protest. Finally, Niemöller insisted one could not put a sheet of paper between him and the other Council members regarding this question.[86]

The resolution of May 1946 was not the end of Niemöller's fight against denazification. In early 1948, rumours spread that the US military authorities were to mitigate the practice of the *Spruchkammern* and thus terminate denazification effectively. Information about the imminent end of denazification and internal criticism of members of the Protestant Church in Hesse and Nassau (EKHN) church leadership did not stop Niemöller—who had become church president of the EKHN on 1 October 1947—from bulldozing through a resolution to issue a pulpit declaration against the Liberation Law to the parishes on 1 February. It was based on a draft by Niemöller, in which he deplored the spirit of 'revenge'—which allegedly characterized the law—made the allegation of 'collective punishment' (*Sippenstrafe*) and finally repeated the comparison between denazification and the situation during the 'years of horror that lie behind us'. The pulpit declaration culminated in a blatant call to the pastors and parishioners to boycott the *Spruchkammer* procedures.[87] Niemöller came up with flimsy excuses to rebuff internal criticism of this course of action.[88] Representatives of the US authorities could only make sense of this extraordinary plea, which could easily be refuted by the facts, by assuming Niemöller was a 'pseudo Nazi' and nationalist who fought against denazification because it targeted the radical nationalism that was still widespread among Germans. The workers who renovated the Frankfurt Paulskirche threatened to go on strike if Niemöller was not disinvited as a speaker at the re-inauguration of this symbol of German democracy on 18 May 1948. The Frankfurt Social Democratic mayor, who was also a member of the EKHN synod, ultimately gave in to this demand.[89] The Darmstadt-based district president, Ludwig Bergsträsser, also an SPD member, welcomed this step, noting in his diary that a better title for Niemöller's autobiographical book would have been *With the U-Boat to the Pulpit.*[90]

Niemöller's advocacy for those accused by the Allies of being Nazi war criminals was an integral part of his fight against denazification. He did not only stand up for individuals who, in his view, had been wrongly accused or severely punished. Like other members of the EKD Council, he criticized the legal sanctioning of war crimes in a fundamental fashion, putting forward the alleged arbitrariness of proceedings as well as humanitarian aspects, and rejecting the death penalty against convicted war criminals. In this spirit, he participated in the deliberations of a commission established by the EKD Council in February 1949. It compiled a memorandum of 160 pages that was handed over to John McCloy, the US High Commissioner for Germany, in February 1950.[91] Niemöller even took advantage of his contacts to ecumenism to support heavily incriminated Nazi criminals. For instance, he contacted George Bell on behalf of the release of Erich Koch, the chief of civil administration in the Reichskommissariat Ukraine from 1941, who was directly responsible for the murder of hundreds of thousands of Ukrainian Jews.[92] This example shows how Niemöller's national Protestant position hampered critical engagement with the crimes of the Third Reich after 1945.

Church Politics in Hesse-Nassau and in the EKD

In the previous chapter we have seen that until summer 1947, Niemöller intended to return to his old Dahlem pastorate. At the same time, there had been efforts from autumn 1945 to appoint him as church leader of the Protestant Church in Hesse and Nassau, which finally happened in autumn 1947. At the Church Congress in Friedberg on 30 September 1947, the founding of the EKHN was confirmed. A day later, on 1 October, Niemöller was elected church president of the EKHN with a large majority. The term 'church president' emphasized the collegial understanding of church governance. Niemöller did not want to be a bishop.[93] It was important for him that the leadership of the EKHN operated in the style of a Council of Brethren because, in his view, this was the only way to maintain the legacy of the Confessing Church.[94] Another central motivation of Niemöller's work in the EKHN was to overcome the confessional fragmentation of Protestantism. In the EKHN, Lutheran, Reformed, and United parishes had been merged into one whole. As Niemöller wrote to an American Lutheran: 'We have drawn a crucial consequence from the past of the Confessing Church, namely that our confessional differences have no bearing on the Church as an institution.'[95] Accordingly, the EKHN admitted all members of the regional churches of the EKD to Holy Communion regardless of their confession.[96]

Niemöller was church president of the EKHN until 1964. In the regional church in Hesse and Nassau, he was able to rely on a relatively stable power base for 17 years. At the national level, however, his influence on church politics waned. The reorganization of the Protestant Church was not complete with the establishment of the EKD Council in August 1945. Until a constitution was adopted and complementary bodies such as the synod were formed, the compromise of Treysa was only provisional. Negotiations on the basic constitution of the EKD dragged on for three long years. They were largely concerned with the question of whether the EKD was just a federation of churches or a proper church. With the possibility of a full eucharistic fellowship, the latter would allow Protestant Christians to receive Communion in all regional churches, regardless of their confession. Lutherans, however, defended the Lutheran Communion as a 'treasure' from the sixteenth century that they did not want to abandon.[97] When the delegates of the regional churches met in Eisenach between 11 and 13 July 1948 to adopt the constitution of the EKD, signs were pointing to the imminent partition of Germany. The EKD, which included the regional churches in the GDR, took a stand against. After lengthy debates, Niemöller finally opened the way for the adoption of the constitution by abandoning the idea of a full intercommunion between churches of the EKD. It was only realized in 1973 with the adoption of the Leuenberg Concord. Today, the EKD still is a church confederation in which the regional churches enjoy a high degree of autonomy.[98]

In January 1949, at the first synod of the EKD in Bethel, a new Council and Council chairperson had to be elected as, due to his age, Theophil Wurm was no longer available. Especially the delegates from the Soviet Occupation Zone backed Dibelius. They appreciated him as a supporter of their interests, all the more against the backdrop of the still ongoing Berlin blockade imposed by the USSR. The Bethel synod elected a Council with 12 members, among them Niemöller. Dibelius was made chairman of the Council and Hanns Lilje his deputy, over Niemöller, who got only two votes in the second ballot. As Visser 't Hooft, who was present at the meeting, reported to George Bell, the whole synod was characterized by a 'strong anti-Niemöller tendency'. It primarily resulted from his relentless criticism of Lutheranism and the constantly polemic way of voicing his views.[99]

The Bethel synod indicated that, four years after the end of the war, Niemöller had lost much of his influence in German church politics. But he still headed the Church Office for Foreign Affairs, which he mainly used to establish contacts with the ecumenical movement. Ever since taking over this office, Niemöller had sensed his church political opponents wanted to remove him from it. When the 1954 Berlin EKD synod decided the Office for Foreign Affairs should take the 'confessional structure' of the parishes abroad into account—that is, the relations between Reformed and Lutheran Protestants—smouldering tensions erupted into gloves-off conflict. Ultimately, the EKD appointed someone else as head of the Church Foreign Office in 1956.[100] This conflict created deep personal tensions between the members of the EKD Council. It was not the first time that they were triggered by Niemöller's harsh tone, which was equally well-known and infamous. In April 1952, Niemöller told Martin Haug, Wurm's successor as bishop of Württemberg, that he had to 'cut him short because of his arrogant manner'. A leading church official in Stuttgart commented in a memorandum as follows: 'Unfortunately, completing the 60th year of age does not guarantee that one has outgrown one's loutish years [Niemöller had just celebrated his 60th birthday in January].'[101] In the conflict over the Church Foreign Office, Niemöller's verbal attacks predominantly targeted Otto Dibelius, who even had to interrupt a phone call because of his own 'state of agitation'.[102] Niemöller tried Dibelius' patience to the very limit. Dibelius expressed his anger in July 1955: 'Niemöller is raging. I've had enough of this. But I can't help it.'[103]

Even Niemöller's closest friends were frustrated by his erratic behaviour. Helmut Gollwitzer, for example, complained to Gustav Heinemann in February 1956, who had participated in the Confessing synod of Barmen in 1934 and was praeses of the EKD synod from 1949 to 1955: 'As has happened before, the problematic aspect of his actions is not the justification of the individual action itself, but that he prefers to play a lone hand and does not communicate his actions.'[104] In June 1956, the EKD Council appointed his successor as head of the Church Foreign Office, whereupon Niemöller resigned from the Council. This was the end of his role in the rebuilding of the German Protestant Church after 1945.

In June 1946, Niemöller wrote a long letter to Hans Asmussen with a litany of complaints. It started with a description of having a flat tyre on the motorway just before Mannheim: not a small problem for Niemöller, who was always on the move. Next on the list was his 'disappointment' about Dibelius' alleged 'self-declaration' as bishop of Berlin. Finally he complained about being side-lined as deputy chairman of the EKD Council and that his work as director of the Church Foreign Office had been 'sabotaged at every possible occasion and to a considerable extent'. In addition, there was his frustration about the 'policy of restoration and reaction' in the regional churches, the 'confessionalistic eccentricity' of the

Lutherans and the neglect of German guilt.[105] This was the beginning of another disappointment for Niemöller: first gradual alienation, then open conflict and finally permanently breaking off all relations with Hans Asmussen, his friend, indispensable advisor of his wife, and Lutheran theologian who had fought at Niemöller's side during the church struggle like no one else.[106] Niemöller's letter is an early acknowledgement of the fact that he failed to achieve his goals regarding a post-1945 church renewal. There was no re-Christianization, the brethren wing of the Confessing Church only played a marginal and further diminishing role in the rebuilding of the Church, and Niemöller's work in the EKD Council did not give him substantial influence. He was also largely alone in insisting on the relevance of German guilt before he stopped his commitment for this cause due to controversies around himself. In his considerate reply to Niemöller's list of complaints, Asmussen offered yet another insight into the reasons for his limited impact on church policy after 1945:

> You are not unhappy because you are suffering from several technical difficulties. And you are not suffering because Wurm or I have allegedly sabotaged your work, which, by the way, is certainly not the case. You are suffering because you are lonely. You are lonely because you assume an independence in word and advice from the brethren, which the brethren have not given you.[107]

15

The Political Pastor

Niemöller as a Critic of the Federal Republic

Upon his return to Germany in June 1945, Niemöller replied to a question from an American military chaplain about whether he would possibly accept an office in government that he was 'a cleric and no politician'.[1] He repeated this statement on numerous occasions over the following three decades. Nevertheless, like hardly any other Protestant church representative, Niemöller was repeatedly at the centre of public controversies over politics in post-war Germany. In the following we take a closer look at Niemöller's political statements between 1945 and the mid-1950s.

Back in Germany, Niemöller elaborated on his criticism of democratic governance that he had already alluded to in Naples in June 1945. He told the US military authorities that Germans had never been better off than under the constitutional monarchy of Imperial Germany. Since a restoration of the monarchy was impossible, a democratic system had to provide 'strong authority' for the chief of the executive. Niemöller imagined Germany's political reconstruction similar to his ideas for the renewal of the Church: local self-governing bodies should be established, instead of centralized political institutions. The number of political parties should be limited and parties without sufficient voters were to be banned.[2] On another occasion, he expressed the hope that the political parties which had existed prior to 1933 would not be re-established.[3] And yet, in autumn 1945 the Western Allies permitted parties initially at district and state level, and as a result a four-party system, which included the KPD and the CDU as the only genuinely new party, was quickly re-established. For Niemöller, this was a restoration, akin to that in the Protestant Church. At a press conference in Berlin in June 1947, he fulminated the re-establishment of the parties with 'the old apparatus and the old men with old beards' had put the wrong people in the driving seat.[4]

Nevertheless, influenced by Karl Barth, Niemöller quickly and unreservedly recognized the democratic form of government. In his opening address at Treysa on 28 August 1945, Niemöller declared that all people as God's children had a 'claim to justice and freedom'. Thus, democracy was closer to Christianity than any 'authoritarian form of government'. This was a decisive, bold and deliberate break with the long tradition of obedience towards the authorities according to the Lutheran understanding of the state. Niemöller reminded his audience of the fatal consequences of this tradition that had forced Christians to accept 'obedience'.[5]

Niemöller was not alone in this view. Other speakers at Treysa such as Otto Dibelius and Theophil Wurm expressed their willingness to contribute to democratic reconstruction, even though their statements still indicated their adherence to a conservative Lutheran understanding of the state. For Dibelius and Wurm, the task of the Church was solely to define general moral guidelines. Their implementation was left to the state. How democratic institutions should function in practice was of secondary relevance. Like the majority of the EKD Council members, Dibelius supported the CDU.[6]

The Lutheran understanding of the state was marked by a dualism between state and Church. Its core problem was to determine the relationship between the two spheres. In practice, this primarily referred to the specific form of church presence in politics. Niemöller's understanding of the role that Church and Gospel should play in politics was fundamentally different to positions of moderate Lutherans such as Dibelius. In line with his friend and mentor Karl Barth, Niemöller drew on the Second Thesis of the Barmen Declaration, which rejected the 'false doctrine' according to which 'there were areas of our lives in which we did not belong to Jesus Christ but to other lords, areas in which we did not need justification and sanctification through him'. 'God's powerful claim on our whole life'—as the thesis formulated in the positive—thus also applied to the political sphere, and it was the task of every Protestant Christian to bring the 'kingship' of Jesus Christ to fruition in this area.[7]

The Prophetic Guardianship of the Church

As Niemöller had already declared in Treysa, Christians' responsibility for shaping the political sphere bore an important consequence: the Church had to be 'a guardian' and to offer 'admonition!'.[8] Another transcript of Niemöller's speech reads: 'We have to say something to the people that only we have to say.'[9] Both remarks implied that the Church could make absolute claims in the political sphere, based on its 'duty to be a guardian' (*Wächteramt*). With these remarks, Niemöller tapped into the Reformed tradition of a third office of Christ besides Kingship and Priesthood, the office of the prophetic guardian. Jean Calvin had turned this *munus proheticum* into a cornerstone of his Christology.[10] After the crimes of the Nazi regime, this notion of the prophetic guardian could be seen as an important ethical corrective against any abuse of power. But this position also raised a significant problem. If Niemöller based his political interventions on assuming the office of a prophetic guardian, it was doubtful whether he was open to critique. Democratic governance thrives on the ability of all parties involved to revise their own opinions. Whether Niemöller's political interventions were compatible with this requirement remained to be seen.

The first test was a publication of the EKD Council of Brethren on the 'political path of our people', the so-called Darmstadt Word (*Darmstädter Wort*). It harked back to a discussion held in Darmstadt in July 1947 in response to a speech by Karl Barth. The theologian Hans Joachim Iwand made a passionate plea that the Confessing Church, represented by the Council of Brethren, should inaugurate a new style of politics. The most important point was the 'termination of the alliance between Christian and conservative' which had determined the political actions of the Protestant Church ever since 1871.[11] During the heated discussion about the draft of the *Darmstädter Wort*, Niemöller was interested in the authority that enabled political speech in the first place. 'Does God want us to speak something new?', was his rhetorical question. It mattered most to him that the Church, through speaking 'prophetically', left behind the guilt of the past and thus created space for a political reorganization based on the Gospel.[12] There were certainly concrete questions that the Council of Brethren could have discussed. Ulrich Bunzel, for example, pointed to the 'satanism of Bolshevism'. He was dean in the Protestant Church of Silesian Upper Lusatia located in the Soviet Occupation Zone (SOZ), where he witnessed state repression against the Church on a daily basis. In Darmstadt, he gave a 'harrowing report' about his experiences. But the majority of the Council of Brethren had no time for this. Removing the traditional opposition between Christianity and Marxism was more important to them.[13]

This was another major objective of the *Darmstädter Wort*, which was adopted in August 1947. In seven theses it repudiated four fallacies, including the 'dream of a special German mission' and the concept of the power state, the 'alliance of the Church' with conservative forces as well as the blanket rejection of Marxism and thus the failure to advocate the 'cause of the poor and the disenfranchised'.[14] The *Darmstädter Wort* already lacked unanimous support among its authors. Only 12 of the 43 members of the Council of Brethren participated in the vote, and thus it reflected their private opinion rather than the decision of the whole body.[15] Outside of the Council, the *Darmstädter Wort* faced a massive backlash among a wider Protestant public. The critics—among them prominently Hans Asmussen—found fault with the general recognition of socialism as a political option. However, the real 'touchstone' of the *Darmstädter Wort* was the question of how its authors reconciled their commitment to social justice with the conditions in the SOZ, where SED and Soviet occupation forces promised the implementation of socialism.[16]

This issue came to the fore in October 1947 when the Council of Brethren convened again, with a larger number of members from the areas east of the Elbe attending. The Berlin Provost Kurt Scharf summed up their opinion with the claim that the *Darmstädter Wort* 'tramples all over the disenfranchized' in the SOZ. To him it seemed obvious that the Protestant Church in West and East spoke 'completely different languages'.[17] Niemöller showed contrition, regretting that 'no one from the East' had been present at the discussion about the

Darmstädter Wort.[18] He had probably not paid attention when Dean Bunzel reported from Upper Lusatia in July. But the Hessian church president was concerned with something more important anyway, namely the political 'guardianship of the Church'. It needed sufficient 'legitimacy', which, according to the second article of the Barmen Declaration, could only come from God. For Niemöller this meant he did not want to say anything about the 'suffering of our brethren in the East' rather than 'seeing ourselves as subject to the same judgement'. He justified this by saying:

> They want to hear us denouncing the Russian methods, but do they want to hear this as a word of Christian consolation? Where has God called me to reproach a foreign government or responsible authorities, to whom He has given executive powers, for their sins—in the name of the Church? I did not appoint the Russians as my rulers, God did. Where is my legitimacy from God to approach these people? [...] The question is: Lord, what do You want me to do and say?[19]

Niemöller had no sympathies for state socialism, which was installed in the SOZ with the help of the Soviet Secret Police. Hence, he could in good conscience reject an allegation to this effect, which was raised by Asmussen at the meeting.[20] There is ample evidence that Niemöller voiced fundamental criticism of communism during the 1950s, particularly during his visits to the GDR. In a speech to 800 students in the Halle city mission in October 1952, he asked how Bolshevism 'can advocate peace on the one hand', and 'propagate hatred against the Americans' on the other. In December 1953, only a few months after the 17 June Uprising in the GDR, Niemöller was even more explicit in his talk at the Prediger Church to an audience of 1,200. 'Marxism is doomed, both in the East and in the West', he stated. 'Even people who propagate and support it, would not believe in it.'[21]

Niemöller did not keep quiet about repression in the SOZ at the 1947 meeting of the Council of Brethren because he supported communism. Rather, it was his interpretation of the prophetic guardianship, which he claimed for himself and the Council of Brethren of the Confessing Church, following the second thesis of the Barmen Declaration. In plain English, this meant a statement derived from his prophetic capacity simply failed to materialize when Niemöller did not deem it legitimized by God. 'Lord, what do You want me to do and say?' Niemöller often repeated this rhetorical question in the following decades when he wanted to address political problems. But in autumn 1947, when his main concern was to break with the Protestant tradition of anti-socialism, the Lord's call failed to materialize when the hardship of Christians in the SOZ came up for discussion. Even Hermann Diem, who always supported Niemöller's peace politics throughout the following decades and shared his belief in the prophetic mission of the Church, was appalled. He felt it was 'not enough to say we exercise guardianship' and then keep quiet about the injustice in the SOZ.[22]

A problematic aspect of the political guardianship that Niemöller and his friends in the Council of Brethren claimed becomes apparent: it was based on an 'ethical claim to absoluteness'.[23] Claiming to act as a prophetic guardian, Niemöller did not see the need for critical discussion of his own views and for compromise, and did not recognize the pluralistic diversity of political positions. As a prophetic guardian, Niemöller claimed to be guided by God and His authority, thus insulating himself against any criticism. While he formally endorsed democracy, there were clear limits to his recognition of democratic procedures in practice.[24]

In 1947, another political problem provoked Niemöller to take a stand: the prospect of German partition. In March 1947, US president Truman inaugurated the policy of 'containment' of the communist zone of influence. Tensions between the Western powers and the Soviet Union came to the fore, and a separate state in the three Western occupation zones was on the horizon. Niemöller observed this development with great unease, particularly because he did not consider Western integration as the superior option. A letter to his friend Hans Bernd Gisevius, written a few days after the London Foreign Minister Conference in December 1947, which marked the final break between the USA and the USSR on the German question, illustrates his position:

> Either we must finally become Russian to enable a new beginning (maybe, maybe), or we need to go to war again with the blind and deluded West, a fight where justice is by no means on our side. It looks very, very dark if one tries to picture the future development.[25]

Niemöller's deeply critical view of Western integration was, on the one hand, a result of his negative perception of the USA, which we will discuss in greater detail in the context of his ecumenical work. On the other hand, his view of the confessional conflict between Catholics and Protestants—in which he considered the USA to be an advocate of Roman Catholicism—played a role. His anti-Catholic rhetoric intensified after the founding of the Federal Republic on 23 May 1949 and the first Bundestag elections on 14 August in the same year. Niemöller had ostentatiously not voted—he was travelling in Australia with Else. He told his friend Gustav Heinemann, who was Minister of the Interior in Adenauer's first cabinet, that the foundation of the West German state was a 'mistake'. It would only benefit the Western powers and the 'Roman Church', which had set its sight on 'the permanent separation of the German people'.[26]

Anti-Catholic resentment surfaced again in the famous Higgins interview, published under the headline 'Niemoeller for United Reich, Even if It's Red' in the *New York Herald Tribune* in December 1949.[27] The American journalist Marguerite Higgins quoted Niemöller saying that Germans would 'take the risk of Communism' if it offered 'the prospect of reuniting the country under a foreign dictatorship'. He doubted the West German state could survive. As a reason for his critical stance he cited his 'bitterness' over 'the preponderance of Catholics in the present West German government', which in fact did not exist. In this context he stated the West German government 'was conceived in the Vatican and born in Washington. Continuing the West German state means the death of Continental Protestantism.'[28] The interview was soon reprinted everywhere, sparking a storm of outrage, not only in the West German press. Adenauer himself wrote to Niemöller several times, asking him for the exact wording of the conversation. The French High Commissioner André François-Poncet reported to Paris about the interview, albeit with the reassuring conclusion that the majority of the German population rejected Niemöller's ideas. The pastor, on the other hand, brusquely rebuffed Adenauer's criticism.[29]

The Higgins interview was further proof of Niemöller's inexperience in dealing with the media. But it was more than this. Whenever he did not like a published opinion, he outright denounced reports in the mass media as 'propaganda', which still operated 'like under Joseph Goebbels'.[30] Remarks like these not only reveal that Niemöller did not understand how the mass media work, but also a deep distrust in their contribution to a pluralistic public sphere. After the Higgins interview, Niemöller did what he would often do: he immediately submitted a statement and claimed to have been misrepresented. He repeated a proposal, which he had already mentioned in the interview, to transfer the control of partitioned Germany from the occupation powers to the UN, which would let the 'Iron Curtain [...] collapse' immediately.[31]

When criticism of the Higgins interview did not wane, Niemöller once again attempted to explain himself with a publicized letter to Gustav Heinemann. He felt compelled to 'speak out' as long as there was 'still time'. With this remark he identified the Higgins interview as part of his task as prophetic guardian. Niemöller also remained true to himself in the matter of the imbalance of the confessions. Since the Reformation, he claimed, Protestantism had not suffered a loss 'of its external existence' as great as the 'amputation of East Germany', with millions of Protestants remaining behind the Iron Curtain.[32] This was correct in one respect: the founding of the two German states had made the Federal Republic more Catholic. While one third of the population of the pre-1938 German Reich was Catholic, this proportion rose to about 44 per cent in the Federal Republic, as core Protestant regions now belonged to the GDR.[33]

But since Protestants in the GDR did not simply disappear, only someone who still thought within the categories of a nation state shaped by the hegemony of Protestantism would try to scandalize this fact. The Higgins interview must be seen, above all, as evidence for the continuing relevance of Niemöller's national Protestantism. Confessional reservations against the Catholic Church added to this, and by no means solely in Niemöller's case. Well into the mid-1950s, mutual animosities and tensions marked the relationship between the two churches. In 1953, the *Süddeutsche Zeitung* even spoke of a 'confessional war' between Protestants and Catholics, while other observers detected a new 'culture war'.[34] Niemöller viewed Protestants as the victims. He was convinced 'confessionalization' was 'pushed forward by the Catholic Church with power [...] because Rome has never operated in a different fashion and always used other "confessions" and ideologies as a stepping stone until it sits firmly in the saddle'.[35] During the 1950s, Niemöller's anti-Catholic resentments became as acrimonious as they had been prior to 1936. However, we cannot directly prove whether a guilty conscience about his own conversion plans played a part in this.

The founding of the Federal Republic was the first milestone on the path to Western integration that Adenauer pursued. A policy of concessions was intended to gradually restore the sovereignty of the West German partial state. With the beginning of the Korean War in June 1950, Adenauer saw an opportunity to accelerate the establishment of the Federal Republic's full sovereignty by providing a German troop contingent. France, concerned about these intentions, immediately reacted with the Pleven Plan presented on 24 October 1950. Under this proposal, the German troop contingent was to be integrated into the European Army of a European Defence Community (EDC).[36] Niemöller still staunchly rejected Adenauer's policy of Western integration after the foundation of the Federal Republic. He suggested to his friend Gustav Heinemann, as Minister of the Interior, to ask the cabinet what steps would be taken for a peace settlement for the entire German people. 'One gets the impression', he added, 'as if the establishment of the West German state has only been given permission by the authorities of the occupation powers under the condition that this very question is not raised'.[37]

Critic of German Rearmament

A few days after the start of the Korean War, Niemöller already sensed the chancellor would use the war as an opportunity to establish a German army.[38] Niemöller was willing to use every possible leverage to publicly denounce Adenauer's policies. Franz Beyer, a former general in the Wehrmacht, came to his aid. After his release from captivity in 1947, Beyer worked as a private secretary for Niemöller, whom he knew as a member of Crew 1911. Niemöller demonstrated once again that he was always happy to help old naval comrades. In late September, Paul Mahlmann approached Beyer, who had served under his command towards the end of the Second World War. He informed him the 'outrage against Heinemann among Protestant career soldiers' was so great 'because Heinemann, after all, holds a top position in the Church, which proves that men with un-Christian spirit are in the church leadership'. But it was the following line that immediately attracted Beyer's attention: 'It will be of interest for you',

Mahlmann wrote, 'that, from 1 October this year, I will be taking over the leadership of an organizational staff that is setting up German units for the European Wehrmacht.'[39]

This appeared to be evidence that Niemöller could use against Adenauer. In an open letter to the chancellor from 4 October 1950, he decried that, despite statements to the contrary, 're-militarization' was already under way 'by all available means'. 'Organizational staff units' for German troops in a 'European army' had already started operating this month—in direct reference to the information conveyed by Mahlmann. Niemöller combined the accusation with an attack against the Basic Law: 'After all, this constitution is so cleverly crafted that the German people can be plunged into war again without even being asked first.' Niemöller criticized the Basic Law for not providing plebiscites. The daunting experiences of the Weimar Republic had led the fathers and mothers of the constitution in the Parliamentary Council in 1948 to not allow referenda at federal level. If a plebiscite was impossible, Niemöller demanded, at least snap elections should be held.[40]

In October 1950, Adenauer was under domestic pressure. In August, he had passed a proposal on a West German troop contingent to US High Commissioner McCloy. As a result, Minister of the Interior Heinemann resigned, having only learned of this memorandum from the newspapers on the day of the cabinet meeting on 31 August. To underline his position, Heinemann handed Adenauer a letter that emphasized the responsibility of the Western powers for the protection of the Federal Republic. He also drove home that his decision was by no means based on general pacifism.[41]

Niemöller had hoped to help his friend Heinemann by writing his open letter to Adenauer, yet the opposite happened. The chancellor used it to push for Heinemann's dismissal after the latter refused to distance himself from Niemöller. At the same time, the reason for Niemöller's accusation quickly collapsed. First, Mahlmann complained that Niemöller had publicly exploited his private letter. Then it turned out he was not in charge of German troops at all, but of labour commandos in the service of the US army that belonged to the so-called service groups.[42] Niemöller, however, did not want to acknowledge this until November and became embroiled in an ongoing—and ultimately unsuccessful—dispute with the news agency *Deutsche Presse-Agentur* over the question whether Mahlmann had denied the statement he had used.[43]

All this was embarrassing enough. But even more important than the lacking factual basis of Niemöller's open letter to Adenauer was its impact in the GDR. In East Germany, a new 'church struggle' was raging in the run-up to the first *Volkskammer* elections on 15 October 1950. The SED state took aggressive action against the Protestant Church.[44] In this context, Niemöller's letter to Adenauer was literally a Godsend. It was printed in all daily newspapers of the GDR and distributed as hundreds of thousands of leaflets. In contrast to the conservative bishops and warmongering chancellor, the GDR media celebrated Niemöller as a progressive Christian. Dibelius told Niemöller about the many Protestant Christians in the GDR who complained the letter was 'stabbing them in the back' in their fight against the communists. Niemöller had nothing better to say than to rehash his already refuted accusations about Major Mahlmann's 'police force' and insinuate the Federal government had 'undoubtedly worked to influence the press so that all my anti-communist statements were suppressed'.[45] Niemöller lacked any sensitivity for the negative effects of this statement on the position of the Protestant Church in the GDR. However, this did not prevent him from presenting himself as an advocate for the people in the East at the same time. At a church event in Frankfurt, he declared the Church was the 'only power that can still raise its voice for the freedom of the whole people'. In November 1950, he even claimed that no one cared about the people in the GDR, especially not the Americans and the British.[46]

Adenauer himself was deeply outraged about the open letter and its impact. In the cabinet meeting on 17 October 1950, he burst out that Niemöller was 'insane' and his letter 'naked treason and nothing else'. Ultimately, Adenauer suggested, the Hessian church president 'belongs behind bars'.[47] Leaving aside the personal invectives, this episode shows how close Niemöller and Adenauer were in their reservations about democratic procedures. The former portrayed the democratically legitimized institutions of the West German state as a puppet of the Allies and implied the press was controlled by the government. The latter understood public dissent as a kind of lèse majesté, punishable by immediate imprisonment. Both shared a deep mistrust of the democratic legitimacy of political action based on formal procedures and legally controlled institutions.

And yet, Adenauer had no need to fear Niemöller's interventions. This was indicated by the result of an opinion poll commissioned by the Press and Information Office of the Federal government in December 1950. According to the survey, 76 per cent of the West German people knew who Niemöller was. But only 11 per cent agreed with his 'statements' on German rearmament. Five per cent believed he was indeed right, but his assumptions were 'harmful'. Just as many respondents rejected him personally because he 'constantly changes his point of view'. Even larger than the group of his critics were those who knew Niemöller himself, but had not yet heard of his security policy theses.[48]

While Niemöller's political interventions were a mere nuisance for the CDU-led government, they proved to be a stress test for the Council of the EKD.[49] In a letter to the Council members, Hans Asmussen bitterly complained that the controversies unleashed by Niemöller and Heinemann had completely lost sight of the question of 'existence in light of the Last Judgement', which was to be at the heart of the Church. Asmussen did not doubt Niemöller's intention to help East Germany. In reality, however, most Protestant Christians were extremely poorly informed about the 'suffering' in the GDR, which was also due to the fact that, under Niemöller's leadership, the brethren in Hesse-Nassau dismissed reports in the mass media as 'American propaganda'. It was, Asmussen stated, a 'monstrosity' that Niemöller only raised his voice 'so quietly' against the rearmament of East Germany, particularly given that his personal life was shaped by the fight against dictatorship.[50] But Otto Dibelius knew only too well that, as Council chairman, it was impossible for him to give in to the numerous critics of Niemöller in this body and try to push him out the EKD Council. This would result in the GDR mass media declaring 'the progressive prophet of peace' was brought down by the 'warmongering bishops', which would have 'devastating consequences' on church politics.[51] There were voices from Lutheran circles that, in reaction to the open letter, demanded Niemöller's removal as head of the Church Foreign Office. It was only with difficulty that Dibelius managed to keep the quarrelling parties together at an EKD Council meeting on 17 November 1950. The result was a declaration that criticized the sharp tone of Niemöller's and Adenauer's statements, but, at the same time, stated there could be no 'uniformity of political judgements' in the community of faith.[52]

Niemöller's attacks on Adenauer's policy of rearmament were not motivated by pacifism, but by a nationalist stance. The combative church president explained this position in a pamphlet from early 1951, in which he described the 'plight of the Germans', whose country would either be a 'theatre of war or a bridge'.[53] According to the premise of his argument, the Cold War had made Germans 'mere objects' of the plans of other powers. In terms of the bipolar logic of the Cold War, Germans were called upon to choose between the East and the West. To be sure, the West was 'more tempting', but only because, as Niemöller wrote, there was 'plenty' of 'money'. 'Living in freedom' as promised by the West was only a 'bonus', which in reality did not exist, just like 'social justice' promised in the East did not exist. If Germans followed the logic of the Cold War and chose one of the two sides, they would only achieve the 'perpetuation of our misery' and 'unfreedom'.[54] These phrases show that, for Niemöller, freedom was not defined as the protection of the individual, but as the ability of national self-determination. On this precise point, Niemöller agreed with a sizeable part of the West German public which rejected German rearmament. This rejection was based on 'national, if not even decidedly nationalist' motives. Adenauer's plans were also rejected because he proposed a German contribution to a European army rather than a national German army.[55]

After Niemöller's attack on Adenauer, it was obvious the SED would try to use his political stance for its own purposes. The chosen vehicle was the Peace Council of the GDR, an organization controlled by the SED, which on the surface advocated disarmament and international rapprochement, but in practice firmly toed the pro-Soviet line. The Peace Council was the East German section of the World Peace Council, founded in Warsaw by communist intellectuals from East and West Europe in November 1950.[56] In September 1951, Niemöller met

Heinz Willmann, the secretary-general of the German Peace Council, in Wiesbaden. Willmann alluded that Moscow was interested in Niemöller getting first-hand knowledge of the Soviet Union. Niemöller immediately signalled he was very much willing to do that. Both agreed the patriarch of the Russian Orthodox Church would send him an invitation for a visit in January 1952. At a further meeting on 23 December, it was agreed to inform the press about the trip to Moscow only after Christmas and to spin its purpose as 'ecumenical information', based on contacts with the Orthodox Church, which had been under way for a long time.[57] This was deliberate misinformation.[58] But it was not in Niemöller's interest to let the true reason for his journey become known at the very moment when the Protestant churches in the GDR had to defend themselves against massive pressure from the SED state to join the Peace Council.[59]

On 29 December, Niemöller met close friends, including Heinrich Held and Ernst Wilm, to prepare his journey. Gollwitzer, who was unable to attend, sent a detailed letter in which he welcomed the opportunity to show the Soviets that the churches in the West were not all 'war mongers'. But he also urged Niemöller that the patriarch and the Orthodox Church had 'no freedom of action at all' and were ultimately nothing else but mouthpieces of the Communist Party of the Soviet Union (CPSU). Discussing peace politics was completely 'pointless' as long as Niemöller did not voice what the holders of power did not want to hear. For Gollwitzer, this meant: to convey the message that the Soviet Union's 'imperialist will to power' also had to be curbed to facilitate peace. Otherwise, the whole visit would be 'useless'.[60]

Measured against Gollwitzer's recommendations, Niemöller's visit was indeed useless. For his stay in Moscow from 2 to 8 January 1952, his hosts had put together a varied and tightly scheduled programme. Alongside conversations with political representatives about the possible repatriation of German contract workers, and with Patriarch Alexeij, the primate of the Russian Orthodox Church, Niemöller visited churches and abbeys, museums and theatre performances and met representatives of Russian Baptist parishes. His daughter Hertha, who studied Slavonic studies, and a Russian interpreter provided by the Soviets, accompanied him.[61] After his return, Niemöller emphasized in a detailed report in the *Spiegel* magazine that his visit had served solely to initiate ecumenical relations, in addition to his effort for German contract workers and prisoners or war.[62]

His report demonstrates that Niemöller had completely disregarded Gollwitzer's warnings. He stressed in all seriousness that he and his daughter had 'never been under police surveillance'. He also indulged in ethnic psychological generalizations, claiming 'the Russian' had particularly deep religious feelings. And he answered the question of whether the Church was 'under Bolshevik pressure' in the negative. Full churches, the intense liturgy of the Orthodox service, and the impressive spirituality of his church interlocutors were proof enough for him. He simply omitted the fact that the Russian Orthodox Church itself cooperated with the communist regime—which Gollwitzer had pointed out.[63]

Niemöller's report was characterized by an almost boundless naivety.[64] But his uncritical observation of religious life in the Soviet Union was the least of the problems. Added to this was his grave hubris in ascribing himself a political role that he did not possess and which was not beneficial to the political interests of the Federal Republic. A crucial case in point are the minutes of a conversation that Niemöller was able to fit into his densely packed schedule on 4 January, but for good reasons did not mention to anyone after his return from Moscow. It was a meeting with the ambassador of the GDR in Moscow, Rudolf Appelt, arranged at Niemöller's own request which the patriarch had conveyed. The one-hour conversation initially revolved around details of the visit and the humanitarian situation of German contract workers. But then Appelt skilfully steered the conversation towards the question of German–Soviet relations. What followed was grist to the mill of the SED regime:

> Pastor Niemöller declared he was a firm supporter of the German-Soviet friendship and that the German people could not exist without a good relationship with the Soviet Union. He referred to Bismarck, among others. [...] When asked about his impressions in Moscow, he literally stated: "I have already seen so much in one day on the streets that I can refute a thousand assertions of the West." During the discussion about the question of establishing a German army he said much depended on postponing it until the 1953 Bundestag elections. Any party that advocates the establishment of an army in West Germany will suffer a crushing defeat in the coming Bundestag elections.[65]

Niemöller's deliberations were nothing other than propaganda support for the CPSU. No surprise then that the head of department responsible for German affairs in the Soviet Foreign Office was delighted when Appelt promptly told him what Niemöller had said.[66] Niemöller enjoyed the esteem in which he was held. At the end of his visit, a reception organized by the department for church matters of the Council of Ministers took place, at which Niemöller was 'celebrated as a peace fighter'. As a token of appreciation, the patriarch presented him with a large wooden cross set with precious stones, while his daughter Hertha received a smaller version set with brilliants.[67]

The reaction of the West German public to Niemöller's Moscow visit was extremely critical. Some press commentators at least gave Niemöller credit for the fact that his trip had stimulated 'some reflections' on the East–West conflict.[68] On his return to Wiesbaden, Niemöller was greeted by a banner saying 'Go Back to Moscow!'. Church representatives complained that Niemöller had painted the situation of the churches in the Soviet Union in a much too rosy light. Adenauer expressed regret over the fact Niemöller had stabbed the Federal government in the back with his journey.[69] The combative pastor justified himself by pointing out Protestants had 'a prophetic task' in politics.[70] And yet, his friend Gollwitzer had explicitly warned him to separate prophetic talk from political assessments. His self-declared prophetic guardianship had a highly problematic effect on Niemöller and those around him.[71] For example, a lecture Niemöller gave in Darmstadt shortly after his return from Moscow was widely distributed as a brochure. Its first paragraphs made it clear that Niemöller understood his political commitment as a form of resistance and, in doing so, fatally levelled the difference between the Third Reich and the Federal Republic. He saw the trip to Moscow and his other peace political activities as part of a task to which the Church 'had also had to devote itself in the Third Reich'.[72] Niemöller still adhered to the national Protestant idea that 'God let arise a German people'. This was also the reason for his preference for securing German unity over Western integration because the 'separation of our people' meant deep 'suffering' for Germans. As a means to this end, Niemöller propagated the 'neutralization' of the two German states, which was to be achieved through a Four Power Agreement or a UN statute.[73]

Niemöller and the Neutralists

It was only logical that Niemöller banded together with bourgeois-conservative critics of Western integration who advocated a neutral Germany. One of them was, for example, historian Ulrich Noack, member of the CSU (Christian Social Union), and Günter Gereke, who had been expelled from the CDU (Christian Democratic Union) because of his contacts to the SED. In December 1950, Niemöller organized a gathering in his Wiesbaden house with Heinemann, Noack, and Gereke to explore a possible organizational framework for a pro-neutralist policy. The initial result was a *Call for Peace* that, in addition to renouncing rearmament of the Federal Republic and the GDR, demanded a plebiscite on these matters. Heinemann soon dissociated himself from this initiative because he was suspicious of the wide spectrum of supporters, ranging from right-wing conservatives to some left-wing radicals. Niemöller, on the other hand, had no problems with this. 'Our people and the whole world are staring into the abyss', he wrote to Heinemann. And in this situation, he was not willing to 'check the firefighters, who are supposed to extinguish and save, for their social qualifications'.[74] He wrote to Noack that the broad spectrum of supporters indicated it was not about an issue of a 'party manifesto', but about 'the vital question of our people'. At the same time, he expressed his joy that despite the 'gagging of the German press', resistance to remilitarization was growing.[75] Again he showed no appreciation for the fact that there was no press censorship in the Federal Republic.

Despite distancing himself from the *Call for Peace*, Gustav Heinemann was not deterred from his search for an organizational platform against Adenauer's policy of rearmament and for neutralism. Soon he found new allies, among them Helene Wessel from the Catholic Centre Party. With them, he founded the Emergency Association for Peace (Notgemeinschaft für den Frieden) in November 1951. Up until autumn 1952, they collected 150,000 signatures for a petition to the Bundestag. Niemöller supported the Emergency Association as a platform against the policy of Western integration from behind the scenes. But, as he told Heinemann, he was sceptical whether 'you and your friends can stand up with us against this windfall of dollars, or rather curse of dollars' with which 'Adenauer takes his last chance'.[76] This metaphor demonstrates Niemöller not only saw the chancellor as a puppet of a modernity dominated by the USA, whose superficial materialism the Protestant pastor deeply disliked. On another occasion, Niemöller talked about the 'Dance around the Golden Calf' shaping the West German public. 'Money trumps and money today means dollar.'[77] In contrast, the 'people in Russia' were characterized by 'moral and spiritually ethical cleanliness', as Niemöller idealized the Soviet Union after his return from Moscow.[78]

The Emergency Association's push for a non-partisan gathering of all opponents of Western integration and rearmament was largely unsuccessful. Moreover, the foreign policy constellation had changed in 1952. The so-called Stalin Note of 10 March 1951, which proposed the unification of a neutralized Germany, made negotiations about the establishment of an EDC more urgent. Adenauer rejected the Stalin Note immediately. On 26 and 27 May 1952, the treaty establishing the EDC was signed in Paris, together with the General Treaty that revised the Occupation Statute for Germany. The GDR reacted by implementing a prohibited zone along the border of the Federal Republic. The German partition had all at once become 'unmistakable'.[79]

The Treaty of Paris intensified deliberations among Emergency Association members to establish a political party. Niemöller had already urged Heinemann to do so in 1950. 'Our people here in the West need a rallying bourgeois party', he wrote to Heinemann, 'that is neither confessional nor "Christian", but that knows to some extent what it wants.'[80] But Heinemann hesitated. Finally, in November 1952, Emergency Association members launched the All-German People's Party (Gesamtdeutsche Volkspartei, GVP) with Heinemann among its leaders. In terms of foreign policy, the GVP advocated a neutralist position, referred to as 'Germany's exclusion' from the two military blocs.[81]

The founding of the GVP came in the run-up to the second Bundestag elections on 6 September 1953, when the Protestant camp was involved in fierce disputes about rearmament and Western integration. Niemöller started the debate with an open statement on 15 July 1953, which could only be understood as an endorsement for the GVP. Niemöller asked for a party that advocated a 'peaceful unification'. He accused the Federal government of 'carelessly disregarding the

288 HITLER'S PERSONAL PRISONER

opinion of the people', preventing the 'education of the people' and vilifying 'its opponents as communists in disguise'. Only the 'power of propaganda and money' had been effective, while 'millions' of Federal citizens rejected to be drawn into 'the deadly opposition between East and West'.[82] Niemöller also urged all opponents of rearmament to join forces. Such an alliance came into being with an electoral coalition between the GVP and the Alliance of Germans (Bund der Deutschen, BdD) with its leader Joseph Wirth, a former Centre Party politician. Heinemann initially opposed this coalition because he, like other observers, assumed the BdD was infiltrated by communists. But Niemöller and his close associate Herbert Mochalski, who ran as a candidate for the GVP, endorsed it. The disillusionment was all the greater when it became known in August 1953 that the SED supported the BdD financially. In the meantime, Hermann Ehlers, president of the Bundestag, was at the forefront of Niemöller's critics in the CDU. He accused the pastor of having disparaged the Basic Law with his appeal.[83]

Niemöller hoped his friends would for once 'shoot' at Ehlers and Eugen Gerstenmaier, another of his critics in the CDU, and release him from the 'burden of fighting'.[84] But this hope was futile. He remained the public face of Protestant resistance to rearmament and Western integration. Ehlers even supported the idea of preventing Niemöller from giving a speech at the Protestant Church Congress (*Kirchentag*) in Hamburg in August.[85] The result of the Bundestag elections was devastating. The CDU/CSU gained a majority with 45.2 per cent of the vote, while the SPD stagnated at 28.8 per cent. The GVP only reached 1.16 per cent. Otto Dibelius was right when he wrote the election result was 'also a defeat of the Niemöller circle' that 'has been 100 per cent wrong about its political influence'.[86]

The disappointing result of the 1953 Bundestag election was certainly an important reason that Niemöller cut back his general political interventions and focused on peace politics, which we will discuss in the next chapter. But 1953 was also a watershed in another respect. Hermann Ehlers did not prevail with his demand of preventing Niemöller from speaking at the Hamburg Church Congress. So he did give a speech there on 14 August on the topic 'Our People among Other Peoples' in front of an audience of 20,000 people. In it, he criticized the concept of the nation as solely based on descent or a common language. To be a 'people', he explained, was also about the 'will' to be together, implicating a voluntaristic concept of nationhood. At the same time, Niemöller abandoned the idea of a 'people privileged by God'. Located at the interface between East and West, he ascribed the German people the task of serving as a 'bridge' between peoples and nations, calling the idea that one must act 'only in the interest of one's own people' questionable. One also had to acknowledge that the partition of Germany was a result of the Second World War and that the Germans themselves were therefore to some extent to blame.[87] With this seminal speech, Niemöller clearly and permanently abandoned the national Protestant idea of the German nation's God-given superiority.[88] Thus, he renounced an important tradition that had shaped his political thinking from 1914 up to this point.

In 1979, Niemöller wrote an article that looked back on the 30 years since the founding of the Federal Republic. He criticized the illusion—which he himself had cherished in 1945—that the 'forces of the past' had vanished at the end of the war, while they 'secretly' worked towards a restoration and also found 'allies' among the Western occupation powers. With this view of history, which was tinged with a touch of conspiracy theory, he interpreted the policy of Western integration as a process largely controlled by West German industry. 'No one' wanted rearmament, he claimed. But why then did the CDU/CSU, which promoted this policy, win convincing election victories in 1953 and 1957? Niemöller had an explanation at hand. The big parties simply exercised a 'dictatorial regime' and the people were 'not being allowed to vote for anything other than *their* opinion'. Since he saw the Federal Republic as a dictatorship in disguise, it was obvious to Niemöller that an 'inner resistance' was necessary, similar to that against the 'Third Reich'. Otherwise the 'prophetic word' applied: 'Ye cannot serve God and mammon' (Matt. 6:24).[89]

This article demonstrates the profound reservations Niemöller still harboured about parliamentary democracy, even 30 years after the foundation of the West German state. In August 1945, at the conference of Treysa, he had emphatically declared his support for the democratic form of government. But, in practice, this commitment was thwarted by a series of reservations. Niemöller, firstly, struggled to adapt to the reality of a pluralistic media landscape. Since he was constantly embroiled in public controversies and contradictions—not least due to his own shortcomings in dealing with the press—he repeatedly sensed a propaganda reminiscent of Joseph Goebbels at work. Niemöller's opposition to Adenauer's policy of Western integration drove him, secondly, into a resentment against the mechanism of parliamentary representation. In order to stop rearmament, he called for a referendum and thus a plebiscitary element. In 1949, Niemöller was not the only German Protestant who had reservations about the foundation of the West German partial state and the constitutional order based on the Basic Law. The Protestant churches did not constructively influence the drafting of the constitution. Viewing Germany's partition as a result of the founding of the West German state, many Protestants showed traces of a 'considerable emotional distance towards the emerging Federal Republic'.[90]

This sceptical attitude soon disappeared through the practical commitment of renowned Protestants such as Asmussen or Ehlers in the CDU. But this did not apply to Niemöller. The idea of the Church's prophetic guardianship often gave him licence to harshly criticize concrete political decisions. This was Niemöller's third and most profound reservation about representative democracy, which he maintained until the end of his life. Prophetic criticism of political conditions, as theologian Friedrich Wilhelm Graf aptly put it, 'makes itself immune to criticism'.[91] Niemöller always took an absolute point of view. He was not prepared to seriously appreciate the arguments of his companions presented in the spirit of brotherhood or to recognize their honest motives for dissenting opinions.

16
Pacifism

Niemöller and the Fight against
Nuclear Armament

Niemöller's political commitment after 1945 is best known today for his involvement in the peace movement. And for good reasons: even in old age after he had
resigned all church political functions, he relentlessly championed peace and
supported pacifist organizations. As one of the first signatories of the 1980
Krefeld Appeal, the almost 90-year old Niemöller, alongside Petra Kelly, became
the public face of the protest against the NATO Dual Track decision which made
millions in the Federal Republic take to the streets. Without pathos he put the
moral authority of a person in the balance who, after being involved in the Great
War as an officer of the Imperial Navy, came to the right conclusions, though with
a lengthy delay. Niemöller never denied that, in 1945, he was by no means a
staunch pacifist. Similar to his turn away from national Protestantism, his shift
towards pacifist ideas took several years.

One of the US military questionnaires Niemöller had to answer in 1945 asked
questions relating to German militarism and measures that would prevent its
rekindling. Niemöller had no difficulties providing an answer. Germany, he wrote,
was 'cured' of the evils of militarism 'for the following decades'. Christian education in family and school would prevent a return of militarist attitudes.[1] Given the
destruction of the Second World War in Germany, particularly during its final
stage, Niemöller found it unimaginable that Germans would ever be enthusiastic
again about the military. But the shock about the terrors of war did not make
Niemöller a pacifist. When tensions between the world powers aggravated in the
wake of the Cold War from 1948 onwards, the EKD also addressed the threat to
peace. On Easter Monday 1949, it organized a rally on this topic in the Frankfurt
Paulskirche, with speeches by Dibelius, Lilje, and Niemöller, who emphasized
impulses emanating from the 1948 plenary assembly of the WCC in Amsterdam.
A resolution adopted at the meeting stated: 'War is not God's will.' Niemöller
thought growing ecumenical contacts were testament of the peoples' wish for a
'brotherly encounter' despite all hostilities. Thus German Christians had to turn to
Christianity around the world, begging 'Give us Peace!'.[2] With this Niemöller
made it clear that he considered the commitment to peace a Christian duty. But
despite the hopes he placed in ecumenism, he did not quite trust this peace

rhetoric. After the Frankfurt rally he noted in his diary: 'Give us peace! (Oh well)'. This 'Oh well' can only be read as an ironic comment to this well-intended wish.[3]

And yet, Niemöller's scepticism towards a Christian justification of peace did not prevent him from continuing to talk about the Church's responsibility for peace. However, he caveated that this would not easily translate into a programme or principle. Hence, he did not believe a specifically 'Christian pacifism' existed. Despite this qualification, his statements from 1950 did indicate some practical steps the Church could undertake. First and foremost, the logic of *se vis pacem, para bellum* (if you want peace, prepare for war) had to be rejected, which presented deterrence as a contribution to peacekeeping.[4]

As we have already seen, Niemöller's opposition to German rearmament was a contribution to the first major debate on defence politics in the Federal Republic. It came in the context of a broad mass mobilization against the deployment of German troops, which, throughout 1950, became well-known as the 'Without Me' movement because young men wanted to avoid a future draft. Several local action groups supported this campaign. Traditional pacifist organizations such as the German Peace Society (Deutsche Friedensgesellschaft, DFG) cooperated with other anti-militarist groups and, on a local level, even with members of the KPD. But not all supporters of the peace movement agreed with this. The SPD wanted to disassociate it from the Communists. An informal referendum conducted in 1951 at the behest of the KPD on rearmament was persecuted by police and legal authorities.[5] The Committee for a Referendum against Remilitarization, founded in spring 1951 and dominated by Communists, explicitly referred to Niemöller's open letter to Adenauer to justify their endeavour.[6] Despite this, Niemöller was not in direct contact with the protagonists of the 'Without Me' movement.

Not even his opposition to a German military contribution made Niemöller a pacifist. This became apparent in January 1951 when he gave a speech to an audience of 1,200 in Potsdam after a meeting of the EKD Council. With an eye to the Korean War, he spoke about all Germans' fear of a new war and the 'millions and millions' of victims it would entail. It would 'start again with nights of bombing', with people running through the streets 'until they fall down'.[7] As a prisoner in the Dachau concentration camp Niemöller only experienced the air raids on Munich from a distance. But during her visits Else had told him about them in great detail, as well as about the devastation in Berlin she had heard from. Thus, in Niemöller's perception the bombing war was very real. The war in Korea refreshed these fears, and Niemöller explained to his audience in Potsdam that 'weapons' could 'only be a bad thing' on both sides of the Iron Curtain. Hence, he said, he politically intervened against a rearmament of the Federal Republic. However, after careful consideration Niemöller was still certain: 'I am no pacifist in general.'[8] This was precisely what he established two years later, in November 1952, in front of an audience in Switzerland.[9]

Niemöller's Path to Pacifism

Five years after his appearance in Switzerland, Niemöller was elected president of the DFG. How did this happen? His wife's influence certainly contributed to the development. After 1945, Else Niemöller became a speaker in her own right. In April 1950, she gave a talk in Wiesbaden on what 'Christian women can do for peace'. She reminded her audience of the last war's horror, invoking man's desire for peace. Her justification of women's special calling for peace was quite conventional: women were the family's natural arbitrators and carers. Furthermore, she called on women to pray to Jesus Christ, the 'prince of peace', for 'rapprochement between people and peoples'.[10] In a speech, probably delivered in 1952, Else Niemöller used the motive of women as 'protectors of life' as a reason for their commitment towards peace. Other than prayers, she referred to the West German Women's Peace Movement (Westdeutsche Frauenfriedensbewegung, WFFB), founded in 1952, which advocated against German rearmament and whose chairwoman, Klara Marie Faßbinder, ran as a candidate for the Gesamtdeutsche Volkspartei (All-German People's Party, GVP).[11] Soon after its foundation, Else Niemöller joined the WFFB and was actively involved in the movement as a speaker and participant in events. On Faßbinder's initiative, she was eventually appointed honorary president of the WFFB.[12]

Else Niemöller's commitment to peace certainly had only limited effect on her husband, who—except for the extreme situation of concentration camp imprisonment—always followed his own ideas. But impulses also came from elsewhere, particularly from Christian pacifists in Germany and the USA. In July 1950, Niemöller took part in a WCC meeting in Toronto and drafted a statement with the theologian Reinhold Niebuhr on the American intervention in Korea. Because it was authorized by the UN, Niemöller and Niebuhr approved it as a 'police measure'. The WCC adopted their resolution draft. This was reason enough for Abraham J. Muste to arrange a meeting with Niemöller in New York in late July 1950. Muste (1885–1967), born in the Netherlands and raised in the tradition of the Reformed Church, had emigrated to the USA with his family as a child. He intermittently supported the Fellowship of Reconciliation, a Protestant pacifist organization active in many countries, including the USA, with Martin Luther King as one of its members.[13] Muste pressed Niemöller to state under which circumstances he still considered war justified and expressed his rejection of the Toronto resolution because it associated churches with the war of the West in Korea. Niemöller admitted that he himself had meanwhile developed reservations against the resolution.[14]

But Muste was not satisfied. He followed up their conversation by letter, trying to weaken Niemöller's aversion to the term 'pacifism'. Niemöller understood pacifism as an idealistic and abstract 'principle'. He preferred to apply it to a specific situation, following Christ. This, Muste answered, was precisely how he understood pacifism, as a way of life in 'the spirit of love'. Political problems were secondary. However, the Christian spirit of reconciliation had to inform decision over the use of violence. Muste hoped for a resolution explicitly condemning the Korean War signed by church representatives.[15] Eventually, Friedrich Siegmund-Schultze (1885–1969), who was in close contact with Muste, joined the discussion with Niemöller. Siegmund-Schultze, Wilhelm II's former court pastor, and an English Quaker had jointly founded the first national section of the International Fellowship of Reconciliation in 1914 as a reaction to the Great War. Siegmund-Schultze did not want to waste time with terminological quibbles and insisted that, unlike his American friends—including Muste—he 'never used' the term pacifist for himself. Instead, he emphasized the similarities of the aim, particularly the fight 'against Germany's rearmament', and invited Niemöller to cooperate.[16]

This approach was successful. On Easter Monday 1952, Niemöller and Heinrich Grüber travelled to Heidelberg to deliver a speech on Germany's reunification at the annual meeting of the International Fellowship of Reconciliation. This was very much after Niemöller's own heart as he could present himself as an advocate of a neutral and demilitarized united Germany without describing himself as a pacifist. At the end of the speech, Niemöller briefly mentioned people's fear as a problem of peace politics, defining it vaguely as 'a fear of the unfaithful' in the context of his hopes for re-Christianization.[17] With this he had touched upon a topic that he would pay great attention to as part of his subsequent commitment against nuclear weapons.[18]

His 1952 journey to Heidelberg indicated that Niemöller was keen to meet representatives of organized pacifism and that he saw his political work in this context. He only joined the International Fellowship in 1954 when its executive board invited him to do so, but he was already 'in very close contact' with the organization during the years before.[19] Yet Niemöller also had no reservations towards liaising with the World Peace Council, orchestrated and funded by the CPSU. On 15 June 1953, he spontaneously flew to Budapest, where representatives of the World Peace Council held a conference. Until then Niemöller had rejected official contacts to the organization by referring to the 'anti-Christian stance of the GDR government'. But in early June 1953, when the economic and political crisis in the GDR took a dramatic turn with the popular uprising on 17 June, the SED leadership abruptly changed course. At a meeting with EKD representatives on 10 June, Minister President Otto Grotewohl carefully listened to their grievances, holding out the prospect of ending anti-church politics. When the EKD Council convened the day after, Dibelius warned against meeting Grotewohl's wish to send a bishop to Budapest.[20] But Niemöller was always inclined to do the opposite of what Dibelius suggested.

In Budapest, Niemöller talked about 'reconciliation with the adversary' and 'coexistence' as necessary preconditions of peace as well as about people in East and West living in 'fear' of each other, based on an 'artificially' enhanced 'mistrust'. These were constructive thoughts on the reduction of enemy images. He then discussed the situation in Germany and a further 'shift', which would enable the Church to make the case for 'peaceful reconciliation' between East and West, hinting at the communiqué issued by the EKD and SED leadership on 10 June. When the delegates in Budapest accordingly adopted a resolution directed against Adenauer's alleged war policy, Niemöller had already left the Hungarian capital.[21] He naively assured his friends in the American Fellowship, who strictly rejected cooperating with the World Peace Council as a Soviet propaganda machine, that he supported every commitment to peace, regardless of its motives.[22]

Thus, Niemöller had started moving towards the groups and organizations of organized pacifism from 1950, establishing important contacts in the process. His turn towards pacifist positions—namely the unconditional rejection of every war—was not the result of a sudden spur of the moment, as he occasionally stated.[23] However, the events in the wake of Castle Bravo played a crucial role. Detonated on 1 March 1954, Castle Bravo was the first in a series of seven above-ground H-bomb test explosions conducted by the US military. This H-bomb was more than 1,000 times as powerful as the nuclear bombs that destroyed Hiroshima and Nagasaki in 1945. The test made global headlines when the crew of the Japanese fishing boat *Daigo Fukuryu Maru* (*Happy Dragon*) returned to its home port Yaizu on 14 March. On the day of the explosion the boat had been miles away from what the US military had flagged as a danger zone. Despite this, the crew members showed severe symptoms of acute radiation sickness. The incident brought home the new dangers caused by the H-bomb to a global public and provoked pacifist groups to rethink their strategies against the nuclear threat.[24]

The EKD council responded immediately. At a meeting on 21 May, it adopted an 'appeal to all Christian church leaderships', addressing the dangers caused by the new weapon in drastic words. They 'exceed everything what has hitherto been considered conceivable' so that 'every human heart recoils'. As emphatic as these words were, the suggestions to remedy the problem were vague, no more than a wake-up call for the individual conscience.[25] Niemöller was not satisfied with the declaration; therefore, he did something very sensible: he invited three leading German experts for nuclear fission and nuclear technology, who explained the current capabilities of nuclear weapons and their future potential to Otto Dibelius and him. On 9 June 1954, Otto Hahn, a former member of the Dahlem parish, Werner Heisenberg, and Carl Friedrich Weizsäcker gathered in a Wiesbaden hotel restaurant and met with Dibelius, Niemöller himself, and his confidant Helmut Gollwitzer.[26] Afterwards, Gollwitzer compiled an extensive report about the most important results of the two-hour conversation. According to this document, the three experts disagreed with the physicist Pascual Jordan, who informed the EKD Council about the current state of technology by playing down the fate of the

Daigo Fukuryu Maru as a sort of workplace accident. Jordan's assessment, they concluded, only applied to the 'current H-bomb which will be outdated shortly'. The largest part of the conversation was on possibilities to confine the new technology by measures of international law.[27]

Niemöller did not agree with his friend's summary of the meeting. He had experienced the evening differently, as he clarified immediately. In his view Hahn claimed that in the near future it would be possible to 'make the surface of the planet uninhabitable for human beings'. This remark was crucial for him, he explained, also in respect to what Weizsäcker formulated as the alternative. According to the physicist, only two attitudes towards nuclear weapons technology were possible: either strongly endorsing further research on the H-bomb, like the American physicist Edward Teller, who was significantly involved in its development in the first place, or promoting a 'resolute pacifism'. Given a potential nuclear war that would 'make the planet inhabitable', Weizsäcker was leaning towards the latter.[28] Thus, Niemöller did not become a pacifist on theological grounds, but because the H-bomb threatened the self-destruction of the human race.[29] Only later did he justify his decision theologically.

'Fight Atomic Death'

Niemöller immediately used the new insight to cause trouble in the EKD Council. At a meeting on 24 June 1954, members discussed a letter written by Niemöller to Pascual Jordan, the physicist Dibelius had asked for his expertise. In this letter Niemöller lashed out at Jordan so hard that the Württemberg bishop Martin Haug banged his fist on the table, exclaiming the Council had 'enough and will no longer put up with this'.[30] Niemöller was well aware he could not hope the EKD would support his peace policy goals. Thus he searched for other allies, for instance among the nuclear physicists who had already advised him on the consequences of nuclear weapons. They came into play when the Federal government under Adenauer planned to equip the Bundeswehr with tactical nuclear weapons in 1956–7. This included Honest John rockets with nuclear warheads of one to four kilotons of explosive power. They could be fired from a mobile launcher with a range of up to 28 kilometres. Bundeswehr units were equipped with these weapons from 1959.[31]

Adenauer made a grave faux pas at a press conference on 4 April 1957, when he referred to these tactical nuclear weapons as a 'mere further development of artillery', carelessly repeating the official version he had picked up from US diplomats and militaries.[32] Members of the CDU national executive board, who held several serious discussions on the topic, became increasingly sceptical of the terminology on and functionality of nuclear weapons. Furthermore, since the NATO exercise *Carte Blanche* in summer 1955 the German public knew that tactical nuclear weapons would be deployed on the battlefield. In case of a Soviet attack, this battlefield would be the Federal Republic with estimated hundreds of thousands, if not millions, of deaths in only a few days.[33] The response followed promptly. On 12 April 1957, eighteen acclaimed German nuclear physicists published the so-called Göttingen Manifesto. The declaration stated that even tactical nuclear weapons had a destruction power similar to that of the Hiroshima bomb. The signatories, among them Otto Hahn and Carl Friedrich von Weizsäcker, supported Western freedom in no uncertain terms and recognized the logic of nuclear deterrence. For a sustainable policy of preserving peace, however, they deemed nuclear weapons unsuitable. The Federal Republic, they wrote to Adenauer and Minister of Defence Strauß, should explicitly abstain from the possession of nuclear weapons.[34]

Adenauer was able to defuse the Manifesto's impact. A few days after its publication, he invited five of the signatories, including Weizsäcker, to the Chancellery and issued a joint communiqué emphasizing the shared interest in nuclear disarmament, which eased tensions.[35] Nevertheless, the Göttingen Manifesto made waves in the West German public, not least because only a few days later, on 23 April 1957, Albert Schweitzer made an appeal via radio that was broadcast in many countries, warning of the danger of radioactivity and nuclear weapons. Schweitzer, a good friend of Niemöller, had huge moral authority, which gave the nuclear physicists' concerns even more weight. According to 1958 opinion polls, more than 80 per cent of West German citizens were against the nuclear armament of the Bundeswehr.[36] On 15 April 1957, Niemöller and other prominent Protestants, including Heinemann and Gollwitzer, thanked the authors of the Göttingen Manifesto for their 'warning of the nuclear threat'. In summer 1957, Helmut Gollwitzer published a book titled *Die Christen und die Atomwaffen* (*Christians and Nuclear Weapons*), igniting an extensive and controversial theological debate on nuclear deterrence.[37]

Niemöller was only marginally involved in these discussions. He was more interested in political mobilization against the nuclear armament of the Bundeswehr, particularly because the CDU/CSU gained an absolute majority in the Bundestag elections on 15 September 1957, which gave Adenauer even more leverage. The SPD felt encouraged to act when Gustav Heinemann, the former CDU Minister of the Interior who joined the SPD in 1957, attacked Adenauer and his policy towards the division into two German states in the Bundestag on 23 January 1958, asking him to resign. Simultaneously, several protest demonstrations against the Federal government's armament politics were launched in German cities. SPD leader Erich Ollenhauer propagated a broad campaign against nuclear armament and Adenauer's rearmament policy, trying to encourage his demoralized party after the election defeat and open up to new allies and supporters. Given the broad public aversion to nuclear weapons, this was a realistic goal.[38]

For this purpose, the SPD held a meeting in Bad Godesberg on 22 February 1958. Participants included Ollenhauer and Walther Menzel, both SPD, Helene Wessel and Heinemann as former representatives of the GVP which had been dissolved in 1957, representatives of the liberal FDP and the DGB, the German Trade Union Confederation, Max Born for the Göttingen 18 as well as several Protestant representatives such as Niemöller and his confidant Heinz Kloppenburg. The meeting agreed to the SPD proposal of launching a broad movement with a public appeal, posters, and rallies. The campaign 'Fight Atomic Death' (*Kampf dem Atomtod*) was inaugurated. The appeal urged the government to support the establishment of a nuclear weapons-free zone in Europe, in accordance with the so-called Rapacki Plan, proposed by the Polish Foreign Minister Adam Rapacki.[39] During the discussion it quickly became apparent that, more than anyone else, Niemöller championed a mass mobilization wave. The campaign only had 'real sense', he declared, 'if a considerable public movement emerges'. The Paulskirche movement of SPD and GVP representatives in early 1955 against German rearmament had 'come to nothing because it failed to create the impression that the people wanted something'. Niemöller drove home the need for a strategy of dramatization. Nobel Prize winner Max Born pointed out American tactical nuclear weapons already deployed in Europe had more firepower than the Hiroshima bomb. Niemöller found this line of argument too weak. To be sure, the 'first salvo' of nuclear weapons would be directed against US rockets deployed in the Federal Republic, he explained. But this was not all. He predicted that 'the cobalt bomb will be fired in the first hour of the third war'.[40]

This referred to a thought experiment developed in 1950 by the nuclear physicist Leo Szilard, who worked in the USA. An H-bomb covered by cobalt could release even more radioactive radiation, making the Earth permanently uninhabitable—a 'doomsday device'.[41] But Niemöller not only wanted to paint a picture of the threat caused by nuclear armament that was as drastic as possible. He also aimed to present the Germans as the real victims through a rhetoric of victimization. The 'German people' faced 'certain death', was his message.[42] The appeal's declaration, published on 10 March 1958 and not only signed by the participants of the Godesberg meeting but also by several politicians from SPD and FDP, theologians, and intellectuals, harked back to a remark made by Niemöller at the meeting on 22 February: 'We will keep going on and on, as long as nuclear death threatens our people.'[43]

The campaign 'Fight Atomic Death' evolved into a mass movement in spring 1958 with public rallies and events in many German cities. A Quaker group around the couple Hans-Konrad and Helga Tempel held a two-week vigil on the Hamburg Rathausplatz, introducing a new form of protest to the German peace movement. In spring 1958, an Augsburg-based group around Walter Oehmichen and artist Carlo Schellemann organized a touring exhibition with prominent painters and graphic artists, which showcased paintings, woodcuts, and copper engravings visualizing the unimaginable—nuclear destruction. The exhibition was on show in 40 cities of the Federal Republic until 1963. Between early April and late June 1958, approximately 325,000 people took part in demonstrations of the campaign 'Fight Atomic Death', not including participants of May Day marches organized by the DGB, which were also held under the banner of the fight against nuclear weapons.[44] It goes without saying that Niemöller took part in several of these rallies, with the most appearances occurring in June 1958.[45]

On 7 April, when the campaign was about to start, Niemöller travelled to London and from there to Aldermaston, in the county of Berkshire. The final rally of the first Easter march, organized by the pacifist Direct Action Committee and supported by the Campaign for Nuclear Disarmament (CND), finished there in front of a military research facility. CND, founded in November 1957 and represented by the philosopher Bertrand Russell and the Anglican priest John Collins, was the British counterpart to the campaign 'Fight Atomic Death'. CND advocated unilateral nuclear disarmament by the United Kingdom. As in Germany, it comprised a broad coalition of socialist politicians from the Labour Party's left wing, Protestant Christians, and artists and writers.[46] On 7 April 1958, instead of meeting representatives of CND, Niemöller was picked up from the airport by Stuart Morris, an Anglican cleric and leading member of the Peace Pledge Union. This movement, founded in 1934, was controversial in the UK— and rightly so. In the struggle over the policy of appeasement, some of its members had considered the 'Third Reich' as a partner in peace-keeping. At Aldermaston, Niemöller delivered one of many speeches, praised the 'good organization' of the rally, but did not meet 'any acquaintances'.[47] It was a first step: the German campaign against the Bundeswehr's nuclear armament became part of a transnational peace movement, aiming to abolish nuclear weapons.[48]

In March 1958, the SPD decided to support the campaign 'Fight Atomic Death' at the parliamentary level by introducing draft bills for a referendum on nuclear armament in state and Federal parliaments. However, the government submitted a complaint to the Federal Constitutional Court. When the judges in Karlsruhe decided to prohibit these referenda on 30 March, 'Fight Atomic Death' was effectively finished as a broad movement.[49] While Niemöller had predominantly understood his contribution to the campaign as an attempt to garner a broad political alliance, soon controversies over the theological position towards nuclear weapons erupted within the Church. But theological reflection on the legitimacy of atomic war did not lead to the core of the problem, as Niemöller admitted, as it did not address the new threat caused by nuclear weapons. Niemöller asked whether nuclear warheads could still be referred to as 'weapons'. Was there not need for a 'complete rethink' because 'the terms we usually use are no longer sufficient' to understand the new technology? H-bombs were more than just weapons, means of destruction that could be deployed for a certain purpose, the defeat of the opponent. For Niemöller they were a means of self-destruction, as the conventional distinction between combatants and civilians could no longer be applied. They not only threatened those who were targeted and those who deployed them, but the existence of 'all living creatures' on Earth. Did human beings have the right, he asked, to 'seize control from God the Creator' and destroy what he had created, 'namely life itself'?[50] In another speech, Niemöller elaborated on these reflections. Again he pointed at the confusion and semantic inversion of the terminology, which had taken place in the shadow of the bomb. Peace and war could no longer be separated because the threat of the bomb impacted everyone, even in times of peace, and nuclear radiation already caused the death of human beings in the wake of nuclear weapons tests. As nuclear war would make all human beings victims and render the distinction between friend and foe obsolete, it could no longer be referred to as war. The most important point for Niemöller was the new power of destruction, which no longer only threatened groups of people but could destroy 'mankind' and 'life' per se.[51]

Niemöller's justification of nuclear pacifism, rejecting the 'production, storage, usage of' as well as 'threatening with nuclear weapons' as a 'sin', was clearly based on the theology of creation.[52] In terminological terms, Niemöller's line of argument is strikingly close to that of the philosopher Günther Anders (1902–1992) and his radical criticism of the atom bomb, for instance in the first volume of his book *The Obsolescence of Man*. Anders also focused on the fundamental reversal, or rather dissolution, of the juxtaposition of war and peace as well as ends and means which resulted from the novel destructive power of nuclear weapons. And just like Niemöller—albeit with a more precise terminology—Anders emphasized that this destructive capacity pointed towards a new level of destruction, no longer aiming for the extermination of entire nations or groups of people, as with genocides, but the extermination of mankind in its entirety, the omnicide or 'globocide'.[53]

His contribution to the movement 'Fight Atomic Death' made Niemöller one of the leading figures of a social mass movement that went public targeting one particular point: the nuclear armament of the Bundeswehr (Fig. 14). This was in line with a trend that emerged after 1945, which saw peace movements based on a broad alliance of supporters and selective mobilization campaigns superseding traditional pacifism with its general opposition to war supported by small circles and associations.[54] However, established pacifist organizations, banned by the National Socialists immediately after the seizure of power in 1933, were re-founded after 1945. Other than the German branch of the International Fellowship for Reconciliation, which Niemöller joined in 1954, there was the German section of the War Resisters' International, the Internationale der Kriegsdienstgegner (IdK), a radical pacifist organization founded in the wake of the First World War that propagated conscientious objection to military service in war and mobilized against conscription. The mother of all pacifist associations, however, was the German Peace Society (Deutsche Friedensgesellschaft, DFG),

Fig. 14 Martin Niemöller at an anti-nuclear vigil in Cologne on 6 August 1958. The Cologne group of the *Verband der Kriegsdienstverweigerer* (VK), a section of War Resisters' International, had organized this event. Once the Bundeswehr had been established in 1955, the issue of conscientious objection mobilized many younger men who were eligible for the draft. In addition, the Cologne VK local group experimented with new forms of protest, such as a motorcade against the conscription of the year group of 1922, or the depicted vigil with a dummy missile. During the six-day anti-nuclear vigil, the VK group collected 15,000 signatures for a petition to the Bundestag against nuclear rearmament of the Bundeswehr. © AKG Images, AKG75258.

founded by Bertha von Suttner and Alfred Hermann Fried in 1892 and re-founded in 1946. Its president was retired Major General Paul Freiherr von Schoenaich (1866–1954), who had already held this post between 1929 and 1933. Like other prominent pacifists in the Weimar Republic, he had made a career in the Prussian military before the experiences of the First World War and the Reichswehr's reactionary policy drove him into the pacifist camp.[55]

President of the German Peace Society

From 1948 the DFG got caught in the crossfire of the Cold War. Like all pacifist organizations in the Federal Republic, it came under general suspicion of serving the cause of communism or being infiltrated by the SED due to its reference to peace. Its membership shrank to 4,435 paying members in 1949, largely from the older generation.[56] In late October 1957, the DFG *Bundestag* meeting took place in Mühlheim. The meeting agreed to suggest Niemöller as the new DFG president. The only question was whether the busy church president would accept. Niemöller, who had become a member of the DFG curatorium in 1956, was not present. He was informed about the meeting's proposal over the phone and immediately accepted. The relief was great. With this president, 'who was well known and respected like no other German in Washington, Moscow, and Sydney likewise', the DFG Federal chairman, Max Stierwaldt, explained, the DFG could look forward.[57]

This accolade was no mean feat. For a start, the DFG was not 'founded by Christians', and thus its choice of 'a Protestant priest' as president was surprising, according to Erica Küppers (1881–1968), one of the first female theologians in Germany and a close friend of Niemöller, who ordained her in the EKHN in 1950. In early 1960, Küppers visited a meeting of the Berlin DFG local group and told the participants about her friend's eventful life. This was met with great interest, but 'the committed atheists', Küppers observed, 'retreated into the sulking corner'.[58] Niemöller's military past was another problem. It was none other than Stierwaldt himself who had expressed his reservations when, in 1950, Niemöller made head-lines with his criticism of Germany's rearmament. Someone who 'is a militarist once', Stierwaldt wrote, 'who volunteers again for service in the U-boat force and then develops a passion for pacifism cannot expect interest from us'.[59] Some years later, the DFG had no choice as its personnel thinned out. It was common knowledge that Niemöller attracted the masses; his events filled the halls.[60] But the revival that followed Niemöller's election as president came at a price. The honoured elderly veterans of traditional German pacifism had to give up their organizational egoism as the world famous pastor did not want to work within their narrow-minded environment. Heinz Kraschutzki, a leading member of the IdK, interceded with the IdK in 1957 to elect Niemöller as its president, which indeed happened in 1958. Kraschutzki praised his old Crew 1910 comrade's qualities, explaining he was 'not associated with any political party' and, more importantly, was 'not afraid of anything'. Niemöller as president would also facilitate a 'merger' between DFG and IdK, which was, however, not put into practice before 1968.[61]

Niemöller made the peace movement and its positions visible in public debates and caused controversies. A prime example is the reactions to his Kassel speech on 25 January 1959 at an event titled *Christians against Nuclear Threats*.[62] First, seven vigil candles were lit, one of them as an appeal to the soldiers of all countries to free themselves from the 'error' that hardship could be remedied by 'bloody violence'.[63] In his speech, Niemöller repeated rhetorical elements he had used in the campaign against atomic death, for instance the assumption that 10 cobalt bombs could self-destruct all life on Earth. Niemöller concluded that the enhanced effects of nuclear weaponry, which eliminated the difference between victors and losers, had made the traditional church doctrine of a just war obsolete.[64]

Niemöller only deviated from his standard speech against the risks of nuclear armament in one aspect: on 27 January, newspapers quoted him as saying 'the training of soldiers and high-ranking officers in superior headquarter posts must today be called the higher education of career criminals'.[65] Niemöller immediately requested rectification, and rightly so. In his speech he had talked about 'commandos' rather than military headquarters, that is, special units of the Wehrmacht High Command which trained civilians for operations behind enemy lines.[66] But the Bundeswehr machine was no longer stoppable. Alarm bells started ringing in the Federal Ministry of Defence on the morning of 27 January. The relevant Military District Command Mainz had informed the Ministry's press department about the incriminated remarks already on Monday 26 January.[67] Minister of Defence Franz Josef Strauß instructed the legal department of his ministry to 'report an offence' on the same day. The legal department, however, concluded there was no legal basis for such an approach. It was an offence to defame the Bundeswehr in its entirety (sec. 186 Criminal Code), but Niemöller had not even mentioned the Bundeswehr. Malicious gossip (sec. 185 Criminal Code) was applicable when defamatory facts were disseminated. But the legal department argued that Niemöller's remarks had to be seen as a 'value judgment', so that even sec. 109d Criminal Code—which provided that 'disruptive propaganda against the Bundeswehr' was an offence punishable with imprisonment—was not applicable.[68] Despite these objections, Strauß—known for being impulsive—did not shy away from further steps, signed the criminal charge against Niemöller, and sent it to the Kassel chief prosecutor.[69] Critique from within the Bundeswehr may have contributed to this hasty action. Officers exerted pressure on representatives of the Protestant Church to take a stand against Niemöller. Former Wehrmacht Lieutenant-General Bodo Zimmermann decried Niemöller's remarks as an 'egregious insult' against an 'entire profession'. He did not, however, consider whether it rather was the German soldiers' actions between 1939 and 1945 that had discredited them in the first place.[70]

Eugen Gerstenmaier, president of the Bundestag, rejected Strauß's imposition on the Protestant Church to officially dissociate itself from Niemöller.[71] As in previous controversies around Niemöller, the public was split. His supporters saw another campaign at work against him, while the weekly *Die Zeit* identified a pattern of behaviour: repeated denials to fend off the 'evil press'.[72] Niemöller's claim of having changed his view as declared in his Kassel speech was also brought into the public eye. A reader's letter argued that Niemöller could not be blamed for offering his service to Hitler in 1939, but indeed for not professing in hindsight that he did—in contrast to his still unwavering commitment to his service in the Imperial Navy. Niemöller, the letter read, always thought 'to be in the right'.[73] DEFA, a GDR film company, had recorded Niemöller's Kassel speech and published the entire text. The Frankfurt chief prosecutor closed the proceedings against Niemöller as early as March.[74]

After the prohibition of the referendum against nuclear rearmament of the Bundeswehr, the campaign 'Fight Atomic Death' swiftly tailed off and the anti-nuclear peace movement lacked momentum during the entire 1960s. This was mainly due to the lack of support from SPD and DGB, which had used the campaign for their own political purposes. Public perception of the nuclear threat also waned. In early 1958, the USSR declared a unilateral moratorium of nuclear tests. In August 1963, after lengthy negotiations, a treaty that banned all tests of nuclear weapons over ground was signed by all nuclear powers except China and France. Several small activists' groups did not give up, for instance the Association of Conscientious Objectors (Verband der Kriegsdienstgegner, VK), founded in 1958 by former GVP and trade union members. Among them was Hamburg Quaker Hans-Konrad Tempel and members of the anti-militarist IdK where Hans Kraschutzki was active. When the public learned about the first deployment of British Honest John tactical nuclear weapons at Bergen-Hohne in late 1959, these groups organized the first Easter March, with some hundreds of activists participating on Good Friday 1960. From 1961, Easter Marches became a common annual event in many cities of the Federal Republic, with already more than 100,000 people taking part in 1964.[75]

Niemöller was a constant participant from 1961 onwards—in this particular year as a contributor to the closing rally. Meanwhile in his seventies, he was a strong driver of the Easter March movement as a speaker and supporter, putting his weight in the balance with public appeals and calls to participate in the Easter Marches.[76] From the outset, an important goal of the movement was to extend political discourse beyond the parliamentary sphere and create a counter-public. In this sense, the Easter Marches are part of the prehistory of extra-parliamentary opposition that started in 1967. In this vein Adolf Freudenberg, a close friend of Niemöller, declared in his speech at the closing rally at the Frankfurt Römerberg in 1962 that it was imperative to make 'the voice of the truth' heard against the mass media's 'conspiracy of silence'. Simultaneously, Freudenberg repudiated the accusation of communist infiltration, which had been made against every pacifist activity in the Federal Republic from 1949. The answer, he said, lay in the counter-question: 'Who actually dominates the formation of political will in our country?'. It was paramount to do the 'sensible and decent thing' against the 'petty fear of infiltration' in the fight for peace.[77] Niemöller shared his friend's line of argument, when, at the 1964 Easter March, he said that communism again 'serves as a spectre'; thus, it was the movement's task to create a real public opinion against the 'printed propaganda'.[78]

Pacifism for the 'Family of Humans'

Niemöller not only drove the Easter March movement forward through his presence. Over the course of the 1960s he developed a new understanding of pacifism, in line with other peace movement activists.[79] Like the DFG, Niemöller took the nation as a starting point in his fight against German rearmament. In his view, pacifist politics defended the Germans' physical and political existence as well as their moral integrity as a nation and understood 'peace' as the peaceful coexistence of nation states. During the campaign 'Fight Atomic Death', Niemöller was convinced that Germans were the main victims of a future nuclear war. He changed his view in this respect. The 'atomic cloud with its deadly cargo', he argued now, would cross the border between East and West, poor and rich, and threaten people everywhere.[80] Soon afterwards, Niemöller extended this line of argument into the general insight that pacifist politics had to bear in mind the 'vital necessities of the entire human kind and all peoples'. It was not just about failed armament policies of the super powers and other countries of the global North but about grave hardship of 'people less privileged, starving and dying of hunger' in the global South.[81] Thus, Niemöller significantly contributed to overcoming the Eurocentrism of the West German peace movement and seeing peace as a goal that could only adequately be understood in the context of the 'human family'.[82]

When Niemöller and other members of the DFG recognized global 'people's solidarity' as a necessary element of peace policy, attention for conflicts at the periphery of the Cold War increased.[83] An important trigger was the escalation of the Vietnam War from the mid-1960s. Niemöller initiated the 'Relief Action Vietnam' in early 1966 with other members of the DFG and the International Fellowship of Reconciliation, collecting donations for humanitarian actions such as a hospital ship for Vietnamese civilians. On a journey to Hanoi in 1967 with Georg Hüssler, secretary general of the Catholic Caritas Association who was also active in Vietnam, Niemöller sounded out the possibility of humanitarian help for North Vietnamese civilians.[84] Representatives of the communist World Peace

Council welcomed the small delegation at the airport and socialized with them over a 'festive dinner' the following evening. There were several bomb alarms during the inspections, and the North Vietnamese hosts introduced Niemöller to a 'Napalm victim' to demonstrate the suffering of the civilian population. Finally, Niemöller accepted an invitation from Ho Chi Minh, who, according to Niemöller, 'staunchly' insisted: 'The Amis have to get out of here, then we'll invite them for tea!'[85]

Immediately after his return from Hanoi, Niemöller published his key conclusion from the journey in the *Spiegel* magazine: North Vietnamese people, according to their view, were not even at war and the US bombardments had to stop immediately.[86] A detailed report for his old Dahlem parish from June 1967 made the ambivalence of Niemöller's pacifist solidarity with the North Vietnamese struggle even more apparent. Just like during his journey to Moscow in 1952, he claimed that in Hanoi he was allowed to move freely, while on his visit to Saigon in 1965 there was an American chaperon with him all the time. Remarks like these reveal boundless naivety. However, in contrast to his many references to the 'Gospel of peace', Niemöller's report was quite clear that he did not expect the North Vietnamese to make any efforts to end the war. He had not met any North Vietnamese person 'who is tired of war' and thus the military conflict would continue until US troops withdrew.[87] The attentive observer could not help but notice that Niemöller sympathized with the armed resistance of the Vietcong against the US military. Such remarks were not isolated utterances. In the late 1960s, a conflict emerged within the DFG between pacifists who insisted on the principle of non-violence and those who endorsed the anti-imperialist fight of peoples from the 'Third World' as a necessary exception. Both positions clashed at the DFG federal congress in October 1972. Niemöller went on record saying: 'When slaves defend themselves then this is a just war. We will not join in, but our sympathies are with the Vietnamese people.'[88]

Contacts with Christian pacifists including Abraham J. Muste and Friedrich Siegmund-Schultze had led Niemöller to his commitment to peace. Shortly after he had developed the key elements of his anti-nuclear pacifism, he focused on cooperating with 'secular peace movements', including the DFG and the campaign 'Fight Atomic Death'. This had a practical reason: Niemöller knew he would not be able to win a majority for his positions in the Protestant Church.[89] But there was also a programmatic reason for Niemöller to cooperate with any person who was willing to serve peace. He would not ask if someone who wanted to help him 'save people in need' was a Christian or an atheist, Niemöller stated in 1967. If he failed to save people because of such objections, 'then I am no Christian'.[90] The aim of re-Christianizing society, which had guided Niemöller's church political activities since he started working for the Inner Mission in 1924, lost its significance in the context of the peace movement.

The peace movement's problem of working with groups and individuals who were detached from Christian values became particularly apparent in regard to cooperation with communists. Pacifists in the Federal Republic constantly faced allegations of being close to the KPD—which was banned in 1956—and the East German state party SED. When Niemöller delivered a pacifist speech in June 1959, he was asked about his relationship to communism. He explained that he rejected the communist state order because the people behind the Iron Curtain were degraded to 'function-driven creatures' (*Funktionswesen*).[91] However, during the 1960s he strongly supported DFG cooperation with communists, namely the World Peace Council controlled by Moscow and its affiliate, the Peace Council of the GDR. While the DFG had long maintained the concept of 'living together' and 'talking together' with the GDR Peace Council, in 1963 Niemöller endorsed the policy of 'working together' for the first time.[92] His position was met with broad approval. Some DFG members saw the necessity of officially recognizing the existence of the GDR. The motives of Niemöller and his friends in the DFG for aligning with communists were multi-layered. The disproportionate number of older people among DFG activists—there was not one member in the local group Hamburg-Bergedorf younger than 50—made it urgent to search for allies. Niemöller in particular took the view that 'ousting allegedly unpopular people' who supported communist positions did not improve the DFG's 'reputation'. Other DFG members, on the other hand, were concerned that 'criticism of the East German system' would be stifled in the process.[93]

In addition, Niemöller had deep-seated reservations about the parliamentary system of the Federal Republic. The long-winded debate on the emergency laws, with the Ministry of the Interior presenting one draft bill after the other from 1956, strengthened this view. The DFG organized a protest rally against the emergency laws in 1963. Explaining his rejection of the bill, Niemöller argued left-wing positions were again persecuted in Germany, with the new law being 'another step on this fatal path'.[94] Thus, Niemöller saw the Federal Republic as being on a path to a new 1933. Fogged by his moral relativism, he was no longer able to distinguish between the political systems. In the run-up to the 1965 Bundestag elections, he therefore called on the public to submit spoilt ballot papers. He justified his position that, as a 'friend of peace', it was 'impossible' for him to 'agree with this alleged two-party system, which it isn't, with a simultaneously strong independent and influential "Wehrmacht"'.[95] The result was howls of protest by representatives of all political parties that he had just denounced as accessories of a dictatorship dressed up as a democracy. Gustav Heinemann, Niemöller's old friend, also vented his anger about Niemöller in a letter to a pastor in the Ruhr area:

> If Niemöller for example characterizes political work as the only form of activity that does not require education, training or a certificate of competence, then it can hardly be a surprise for him that a man with a biography such as [Herbert] Wehner reacts with anger [...] I object that men of the Church always measure

politics using the yardstick of loyalty to one's faith [...]. Politics is different to religion; it has to deal with political views and power relations instead of questions of truth.[96]

In the late 1960s this course, supported and endorsed by Niemöller ensured that the DKP (German Communist Party), a party founded in 1968, increasingly gained influence over the DFG. In this spirit, the associations DFG-IdK and VK merged into DFG-VK, with Niemöller as honorary president. Many members of the new organization considered anti-communism to be the most important cause of war. As a result, pacifists advocating a staunch anti-militarism, such as Heinz Kraschutzki, withdrew from the association.[97] In the same year, individuals close to the DKP founded the Committee for Peace, Disarmament, and Cooperation (Komitee für Frieden, Abrüstung und Zusammenarbeit, KOFAZ) and won Martin Niemöller as a supporter. Its communist agenda, which soon became apparent, proved a problem for this organization so that it failed to resonate with the public.[98]

The anti-nuclear peace movement only started to mobilize the masses after the NATO Dual Track decision in December 1979, when it had a clear objective that brought together a broad coalition of Social Democrats, Greens, Protestant and Catholic Christians, and left radicals. The November 1980 Krefeld Appeal, which Niemöller supported as one of its first signatories, expressed the minimum consensus of this mass movement demanding 'Nuclear Death is a threat to us all—no new nuclear weapons in Europe!'. The small group of DKP-leaning cadres was not able to considerably influence its dynamics.[99] Focusing on 'Nuclear Death' as a key notion, the new mobilization wave drew on the campaign 'Fight Atomic Death' that Niemöller had co-initiated in 1958. In the 1980s peace movement, Niemöller, by now very advanced in his years, only had a symbolic presence. Due to health reasons he was unable to attend the movement's first major rally on 10 October 1981 in the Bonn Hofgarten, which had 300,000 participants. But his speech, in which he remembered the 1958 Easter March to Aldermaston and passed the baton of his commitment for peace to the youth, was read out in Bonn.[100]

Martin Niemöller was not the first former career officer who had a leading position in the German peace movement. Two generals of the imperial army, Paul von Schoenaich and Berthold von Deimling, were among the most popular speakers of the German Peace Society during the Weimar Republic. In the Federal Republic, there was no longer room for this type of symbolic representation of pacifism. August Bangel, long-time national chairman of the DFG, aptly summarized the change in 1964. He reminisced that during the Weimar period Schoenaich 'could say at every meeting that he as a Prussian general had done the right thing and that he was proud of this time; today every meeting' of a pacifist organization 'would laugh at him'.[101] Like Schoenaich, Niemöller tapped into his biographical background as a career officer in his work for the peace movement. But he did not do so while boasting about his former heroic deeds. Self-critically he regretted not having learned and drawn the consequences immediately after the First World War as his friend Heinz Kraschutzki had done.[102] His turn to anti-nuclear pacifism was not a sudden conversion but the result of a long-time learning curve. Niemöller took as a starting point the assumption that Germans would be the first victims of a nuclear war and gradually moved to reject war as a political means as a matter of principle, influenced by his wife and contacts with Christians pacifists. However, only the knowledge of the potentially global destructive power of the H-bomb made this a permanent change of mind. The historical significance of Niemöller's commitment to pacifism was that his departure from pacifist politics that were grounded in theological arguments made him a pioneer of a peace movement based on a broad coalition of different political groups, both Christian and secular.

17

'The World Is My Parish'

Ecumenical Work

Martin Niemöller grew up in the national Protestant culture of late Imperial Germany, which deemed the German nation to have God's special calling. The Nazi seizure of power in 1933 even strengthened this nationalist framework. The conflict between the Confessing Church and the German Christians put relations with Protestant churches outside Germany on the agenda. Who was to represent German Protestants on the international stage: the DEK, headed by Reich Bishop Ludwig Müller, or the Confessing Church, claiming to be the true Protestant Church at the 1934 Barmen Confession Synod? This question became relevant when the emerging ecumenical movement became embroiled in the German church struggle. Niemöller first encountered ecumenism in this context, although his arrest in 1937 prevented him from getting into direct contact.

The ecumenical movement shaped up in the wake of the 1910 World Missionary Conference in Edinburgh. Its name was indicative of its cause in two respects: the conference predominantly gathered representatives of Anglo-American missionary societies rather than those of national churches. 'Ecumenism' referred to its ancient Greek meaning: *oikumene*, the whole inhabited world. The main topic was the coordination and global networking of missionary activities, according to the motto 'The Evangelization of the World in this Generation', coined by the American Methodist John Mott in 1901. Mott headed the discussions in Edinburgh. Only 17 of the more than 1,200 delegates in Edinburgh came from the so-called young churches in Africa and Asia. Representatives of the Orthodox churches of the East and the Roman Catholic Church were not even invited. Prior to the Second Vatican Council (1962–5), the term ecumenism did not have the same meaning it has today, reconciliation between Protestant and Catholic Christians. Ecumenism was first a Protestant endeavour to network Christian—which meant Protestant—religious communities across the globe. Only over the course of ecumenical work did the focus shift from missionary goals to emphasizing the unity of all Christians.[1]

After the starting gun had been fired in Edinburgh in 1910, the ecumenical movement split into three wings: first the International Missionary Council, which predominantly understood ecumenism as mission; second the Ecumenical Council for Practical Christianity (ECPC), which was strongly influenced by the US American 'social gospel' in which liberal progressive Protestants tackled social problems; third the Faith and Order Commission, which emerged from the

Edinburgh conference. The second and third groups only came together at a meeting in Utrecht in 1938 and decided to establish a World Council of Churches (WCC) with headquarters in Geneva.[2] The ECPC was the first ecumenical organization and as such confronted with the German church struggle. In autumn 1933, it decided to accept the membership of the DEK, headed by Reich Bishop Ludwig Müller, but not to acknowledge its Nazi-dominated leadership. In doing so, it was willing to keep the door open for Germany. Initially, Niemöller's Pastors' Emergency League was highly sceptical towards influence from abroad. Only Dietrich Bonhoeffer recognized the strategic advantage for the Confessing Church by establishing contacts with ecumenism.[3]

In the following years, the ECPC still did not acknowledge the Confessing Church as the only German Church. The conflict over the German representative came to a head in the run-up to the great conference organized by the ECPC in Oxford in July 1937. After the Reich Church Committee's failure in February 1937, the German Church's foreign relations fell into the hands of Theodor Heckel, director of the Church Office for Foreign Affairs. As an internal memo of the German Foreign Office stated, this matter was of grave foreign political importance for the 'Third Reich'. Particularly in Anglo-Saxon countries, 'more is written and talked about the alleged persecution of Christians than about that of the Jews'. It would do 'considerable harm to Germany's cultural political reputation' if no German delegation was sent to Oxford.[4] Against this backdrop, Heckel enforced the sending of a united German delegation. The Confessing Church appointed Niemöller, among others. In response, Heckel changed his mind and decided against German participation. Probably upon his instigation, the Gestapo seized Niemöller's and other designated Confessing Church representatives' passports in mid-May 1937.[5] A few weeks later, Niemöller was arrested. He thus had no opportunity to play an active role in the ecumenical movement before 1945.[6]

His manuscript *Gedanken über den Weg der christlichen Kirche* (*Thoughts on the Path of the Christian Church*), written in solitary confinement in Sachsenhausen in 1939, shows he was well-informed about the activities of the ecumenical movement. For Niemöller, the ecumenical movement was indicative of the fragmentation of the many non-legitimate churches that had broken away from Rome. The path to 'true ecumenical work' would only open when Protestant Christians proved why they were unable to 'integrate into the Roman Church'. All current ecumenical work only served the 'pious interests' of a culture that believed its 'future to be threatened' and thus invested into the global spread of Christianity.[7]

Niemöller came to this conclusion as he was convinced only the Roman Catholic Church represented the Imitation of Christ in an authentic fashion. Niemöller changed his mind about the conversion before he was transferred to Dachau concentration camp. In open discussions with his three Catholic fellow prisoners, he initially tried to clear up basic theological problems. Only when these conversations waned, Niemöller's longing for the community with Protestant Christians grew. On 31 October 1942, he wrote to his wife:

> I feel lonelier, particularly on a day like today when the Protestant Church commemorates Reformation! Catholic piety—this has become quite clear to me now—does not practically place Lord Christ and his work centre-stage.[8]

After lent 1944, he declared he 'very much' missed 'Protestant service'. The Catholic priests in the concentration camp block 26, the so-called Priest Barracks, were allowed to celebrate mass in the camp's chapel. When Niemöller heard a prayer from the chapel on Whit Sunday 1944, his mood, as he wrote to Else,

> changed, and I remembered the happy and free Whit Sunday services that we could once celebrate and celebrated [...]. And then I feel I belong to the Protestant community and the thought of leaving it seems to be completely absurd.[9]

However, Niemöller was unable to participate in Protestant services in Dachau, while his two, later three, Catholic fellow prisoners could use an empty cell to celebrate Holy Mass daily from late autumn 1941. From December 1941 they used a mass suitcase with a folding altar, a present from Michael von Faulhaber, archbishop of Munich and Freising.[10] Niemöller, who became increasingly aware of confessional differences with the three Catholics during his lengthy detention, did not participate in these services.[11]

Ecumenical Encounters in the Face of Death: Dachau Sermons

The situation did not change before late 1944. One of the prominent special prisoners in the cell block, the former Dutch defence minister, Johannes C. van Dijk, asked for the permission to celebrate a Protestant service. His request was approved and, as Niemöller was the only pastor among the Protestants in the cell block, he held the service on Christmas Eve 1944.[12] Van Dijk, two Norwegians, a Brit, a Yugoslav, and a Macedonian formed the small group around Niemöller. He preached on the good news of the Christmas story (Luke 2:10–12), but the joy over Jesus' birth in his exegesis was mixed with 'deadly fear', which all who were gathered around the foldout altar knew and shared.[13] After 1945 the American Methodist Ewart Turner said the 'ecumenical Niemöller' was born this evening.[14] Among the participants of the mass service were one Anglican as well as Lutherans, Reformed, and Orthodox Christians. And yet, Turner missed the point here, Niemöller's view of the communion service on 24 December 1944 was rather different.[15]

For Niemöller, the service on Christmas Eve 1944, as well as five more until his removal from Dachau concentration camp, were marked by the fear of death and his anxiety about losing his faith in God in view of the destruction of human life. However, he was not thinking of Jews, communists, and Soviet prisoners of war who wasted away in the barracks of Dachau concentration camp, but of his family and the German people. On 17 December, his brother-in-law, Fritz Bremer, died at only 50 years old. Niemöller wrote to Else: 'So this Christmas threw a shadow of death for you as it did for all of us and the majority of our people.' For this reason he did not put up a small Christmas tree in his cell, as he had done the year before, and admitted to his wife he was 'rather disheartened'. In this desperate situation he remembered a remark by Pastor Wolfgang Saß, who was his substitute in Dahlem:

> I understand now what dear Sass meant when he said he was looking forward to eternity; no man is able to dry the many tears flowing right now, so that we have good reason to wait with the sighing creature for the hour and hope that 'God shall wipe away all tears from our eyes' [Rev. 21:4].[16]

His mood darkened further when he learned about the death of his daughter Jutta the day before New Year's Eve 1944. Thus, he did not devote his Dachau sermons to ecumenism. They were, in contrast, marked by the experience of mass death and a fundamental problem: how could God allow such an imperfect world to be created in his plenitude of power? In his Dachau sermons, Niemöller addressed the problem of theodicy—without finding an answer.[17]

The ecumenical movement's 'first task after the war', as the longstanding secretary general of the WCC, Willem Visser 't Hooft, explained, was the 'reconciliation of the churches whose countries had fought each other'.[18] One condition for this was that German Protestants acknowledged their guilt. The Stuttgart Declaration of Guilt from October 1945 paved the way for this. While the public in the three Western occupation zones harshly criticized the declaration, it was 'met with great joy' in France and the Netherlands, as Visser 't Hooft assured Niemöller.[19] Niemöller had been appointed director of the EKD's Church Office for Foreign Affairs in Treysa in August 1945 and was thus responsible for ecumenical relations of the Protestant churches of Germany. In practice, this involved regular communication with Visser 't Hooft and other staff members of the secretariat general of the WCC in Geneva. However, it proved exceedingly difficult for him to travel to Switzerland. While Swiss authorities granted Niemöller an entry visa without further ado, the US military authorities in Frankfurt delayed a travel permit.

American Protestants had considerable influence in the ecumenical movement after 1945. Their critique of establishing ecumenical contacts with German Protestants was not only rooted in objections to Niemöller, but also sparked off by church political questions. Lutherans among them raised the question of whether an organization such as the EKD could become a member of the WCC in the first place. Particularly Franklin Clark Fry, president of the United Lutheran Church, a merger of Lutheran churches, took this view. It was based on the concern that German Lutherans were not available for the expansion of the Lutheran World Federation, founded in 1947. Fry also feared the EKD had 'strong tendencies towards Unionism' as in the ApU, for which he blamed Niemöller. Visser 't Hooft, who was obliged to remain neutral, indicated to Niemöller that he rejected the 'isolation of confessions' in ecumenism.[20]

When Niemöller finally travelled to Switzerland for the first time in February 1946, his 10-day stay was not only an ecumenical endeavour, but also a 'recreational' trip for him and Else. During his second visit in March, he met Karl Barth and other representatives of the Swiss Protestant Aid Organization for the Confessing Church (Schweizerisches Evangelisches Hilfswerk für die Bekennende Kirche) in Basel. Niemöller admitted to these friends, who had supported him and his family financially from 1937, that 'he felt like being taken out of the world since he has crossed the Swiss border'.[21] In Switzerland he experienced the comfortable bourgeois lifestyle that he was deprived of during his years in concentration camp imprisonment and in post-war Germany, where life was shaped by malnutrition, unheated rooms, and other material hardships. During the first post-war years, ecumenism was an encounter with the world of plenty for Niemöller.

On his visit to Geneva in February 1946, Niemöller participated in meetings organized by the WCC. First, a smaller group of the committee gathered. Niemöller was not sure how the other participants would react to him. But when Bishop Eivind Berggrav from Oslo, who had spent part of the years of German occupation in prison, entered, he went straight to Niemöller, kissed him on both cheeks, and said: 'Dear brother Niemöller, how many, many months have I waited for this moment.'[22] Next on the itinerary was a meeting of the Preliminary Committee of the WCC. It was the first plenary meeting since the beginning of the Second World War in 1939. Expectations among the around 50 participants were running high. Niemöller was again 'afraid' of how representatives of the countries recently occupied by the Wehrmacht would react to him. The Danish representative broke the ice, briefly describing the persecution of the Protestant Church in Denmark and emphasizing that it would not have been possible to survive this time of deprivation of rights without the example of the Confessing Church.[23] The symbolic meaning of Niemöller's involvement with the Confessing Church and his concentration camp imprisonment considerably facilitated the return of the German Protestant Church to the ecumenical movement after the war.

Niemöller's ecumenical work started with fleeting visits to Switzerland and to England, where he met George Bell and Franz Hildebrandt in early November 1946.[24] Niemöller understood ecumenism as the encounter with Christians all over the world, and thus his numerous travels were at the centre of his ecumenical efforts. Contacts within Europe were only the beginning. Since his liberation through the US army, he planned a trip to the USA. On 15 May 1945 he met Garfield Bromley Oxnam (1891–1963) in Naples, a Methodist bishop who was also chairman of the Federal Council of Churches (FCC). Founded in 1908, this organization was the ecumenical umbrella body of several dozens of Protestant denominations in the USA, ranging from Baptists and Methodists to Presbyterians and Lutherans to Quakers. During their conversation, Oxnam invited Niemöller to visit the USA as soon as possible. These plans came to nothing, owing to the controversies over Niemöller's press conference in Naples. But Oxnam was adamant and renewed his invitation when he met Niemöller again in Geneva in March 1946, this time in his official capacity on behalf of the FCC. Other Reformed and Lutheran US representatives in Geneva joined in and affirmed this invitation on behalf of their churches.[25]

Considerable obstacles had to be overcome until Else and Martin could finally embark on their journey to the USA. Dean Acheson, the US Vice-Secretary of State and responsible for visa issues, wanted an 'indisputable' representative of the democratic forces in Germany as the first official German visitor after the war. In his eyes, Niemöller was not such a person due to his nationalist and militarist views, and his initial support for the Nazi regime. Jewish representatives, for example Rabbi Stephen Wise, president of the American Jewish Congress, opposed a visit by Niemöller because of his questionable statements on antisemitism. In spring and summer 1946, Samuel Cavert, secretary general of the FCC, tried to overcome the resistance of Acheson, Wise, and other critics in lengthy negotiations. He finally succeeded: on 21 November 1946, Martin and Else Niemöller were the first prominent German civilians who were granted visas for the USA in November 1946.[26] After the bad experiences with Niemöller's interviews in Naples, his American supporters sought to make provisions. They provided a chaperone who was supposed to prevent Niemöller from making inconsiderate remarks. Ewart E. Turner took on this role, a Methodist who had been appointed pastor of the American Church in Berlin in 1930 and subsequently became Niemöller's friend and confidant. After his liberation, Turner met Niemöller and his wife in Leoni. They spent Christmas 1945 together in Büdingen.[27]

Evangelization in the Superlative: Niemöller's Trip to the USA, 1946–1947

Turner welcomed Martin and Else Niemöller at the airport in New York on the morning of 3 December 1946. With only one layover, they continued their trip in his company to Seattle, where Niemöller was to give a talk at a meeting of the FCC. But Turner soon realized that Niemöller's spontaneous remarks were by no means the only practical problem. Originally, a round trip of about three months through the most important US states had been planned. But the demand for Niemöller's lectures and sermons exceeded all expectations, and thus it was not before 19 May 1947, almost half a year later, when Else and Martin Niemöller finally returned to Germany.[28]

Visits to no less than 52 cities were planned for Niemöller. This ecumenical trip was a marathon. In Portland, Martin developed heart problems, but still spoke in front of an audience of 12,000 after brief treatment. From then on, Turner made sure to have a doctor available at every stop. Wherever the Niemöller couple appeared, they were surrounded by 'journalists, congratulators, and autograph hunters'. Turner tried to control the influx of visitors through a local welcome team. He also made sure there were stenotypists available in every hotel to help Niemöller with his correspondence with numerous Americans who wrote to him. In Los Angeles he looked for a secretary who would accompany the Niemöllers during their long railway journeys. The pastor of the First Congregational Church of Los Angeles helped him, while Else and Martin Niemöller met the actor Bing Crosby in one of the Hollywood studios, whose film *Going My Way* they very much liked. When they arrived at the railway station of Los Angeles a few hours later to continue their journey, Miss Gladys Boggess, one of the resourceful pastor's secretaries, waited for them on the platform with her suitcase packed. During the following months she accompanied Else and Martin all the way to New York, the last stop of their journey, and became a family friend.[29]

Niemöller's first trip to the USA was a huge endeavour. His report for the EKD about the journey reflected this: it was a seemingly endless list of superlatives, mentioning 200 talks in 22 US states and two Canadian cities, in front of huge audiences and 40 gatherings of pastors—including a meeting in Columbus with an audience of 2,000, almost all Protestant ministers in the state of Ohio—and 17 universities and theological seminars. All his lectures were played back via loudspeakers in the surrounding churches. According to his own estimation, Niemöller reached 'at least' half a million people directly and a much larger audience through his radio broadcasts. He agreed with the Americans who, as he put it, loved 'superlatives', that such an 'evangelization across all of the states' of the USA had never happened before.[30] Niemöller had made it a condition to speak only at 'interconfessional' events that were supported by all local Protestant churches. The practical implementation was mostly the responsibility of the local Council of Churches, which represented the relevant denominations.[31] In form and performative setting Niemöller's appearances—mass events with an audience multiplied by mass media and a dynamic orator, who gave interviews the minute he arrived at the airport or railway station—resembled the 'crusades' practised by the young evangelical Baptist pastor Billy Graham throughout the USA from autumn 1947.[32]

When Niemöller embarked on his trip to the USA, he faced harsh criticism from the German public because of his remarks on the question of guilt. In America, he only addressed the topic of German guilt once when he spoke to a largely German audience in Manhattan in January 1947.[33] Otherwise Niemöller was keen to present the good Germany to his American audiences, to raise understanding for the Germans' material hardship, and thus to appeal to the Americans' sympathy. He started all his talks with a thank you for the intercession he had particularly received in the USA during his long imprisonment in the concentration camp. He explained he was a 'victim' of the Nazi regime, but simultaneously a member of the German nation. The invitation to the USA was building a bridge and his trip illustrated the 'ecumenical liveliness of the universal Church'. When Niemöller talked about the Church Struggle, he described it—incorrectly—as a 'political battle' and painted an idealized picture of 'Christian resistance'. And he stated that the Confessing Church had been a new form of Christian community with Lutherans, Reformed, and United Protestants coming together. Only in retrospect did the members of the Confessing Church realize they had created an 'ecumenical Church' by unifying different confessions in one 'fellowship of brethren'.[34] With this overly smooth interpretation, he omitted that the very tensions between Lutherans and those in United Churches had contributed considerably to the split of the Confessing Church. In the USA, he highlighted the opposition of the Confessing Church against Hitler's crimes and its persecution through the Nazi state by describing the fate of some selected 'martyrs', including Friedrich Weißler and Paul Schneider.[35]

Wherever Niemöller appeared, the interest and affection of the audience went out to him. From Seattle, the start of the trip, Else and Martin travelled to Chicago at a gallop in only 18 days, where they spent some quiet days over Christmas with a local pastor. On New Year's Eve 1946 they headed to the Southern states of Georgia, Virginia, and Kentucky, afterwards to the Midwest and Washington DC. After a detour to Toronto, their itinerary finally included the New England states in March 1947. In many cities, Else Niemöller also gave talks organized by Ewart Turner. She often spoke in front of Protestant women, describing the events of the Church Struggle in the Dahlem parish. Her moving stories, recited in perfect English, captured the audience. In January 1947, Else Niemöller went on a three-week lecture trip to Florida without her husband. 'In flight', she wrote in English to Martin, using the headed stationary of Eastern Airlines. She very much liked West Palm Beach ('gorgeous'), clearly enjoying her trip to a world of plenty and full of friendly encounters.[36] Martin also often noted pleasant impressions in his diary. Be it Hartford, Charlotte, Richmond, or St. Louis, he got a huge reception everywhere, sometimes even at the railway station, where the mayor or local dignitaries welcomed him. An audience of 5,000 people expected him in St. Louis, in addition to masses of people in three other halls. In Columbus, the capital of Ohio, he was very moved by a local pastor's farewell wishes: 'You have become a pastor of us all.'[37] Theologians were also impressed. Don E. Smucker, a Mennonite preacher and theologian, declared the two sermons Niemöller held there as 'two of the most magnificent messages I have ever heard'.[38]

While Protestant Christians gathered in many places throughout the USA to see and hear the world-famous German pastor, the American media response was rather critical. Eleanor Roosevelt, widow of the former US president and author of a regular column in the *New York Times*, set the tone. She warned that in over-glorifying Niemöller it might be forgotten that the German people had enabled the dictator Hitler. When Cavert immediately wrote a letter in protest against such a statement, Eleanor Roosevelt advised him that one should not look too favourably upon the Germans. The touchstone of Niemöller's public reception in the USA were his remarks on German antisemitism, particularly his assertion that anti-semitism had been waning after the war in favour of sympathy for the Jews' suffering. Several rabbis publicly protested against this insinuation. The Jewish magazine *B'nai B'rith Messenger* called Niemöller's assumption a deliberate lie intended to invoke a new German Reich. It was not helpful when the influential Protestant theologian Reinhold Niebuhr insisted that the Jewish community in the USA should not interfere in Protestants' internal affairs. In this respect, Niemöller's trip worsened relations between Jews and Protestants in the USA.[39]

Protests against Niemöller's appearances in 1946–7 did not occur. This changed during a second trip to the USA in spring 1952. After a speech at Southern College in Lakeland (Florida), around a hundred students approached the dean, calling 'Niemöller's anti-American deliberations' an imposition.[40] They criticized that he denied the danger of a Soviet attack and conveyed his positive impressions from his visit to Moscow. However, Niemöller had already been irritated by critical media coverage during his first journey in 1946–7. He com-plained about 'bad press' in his diary, but also in his report for the bodies of the EKD where he attributed 'attacks of the press' solely to the proponents of the Morgenthau plan and 'certain Jewish and political circles'. In America, he declared, 'one is afraid of the press', explaining Samuel Cavert's restrictive media relations.[41] In a letter to Ludwig Bartning with clear antisemitic undertones, Niemöller blamed those for public criticism who 'once and for all have made it their mission to relentlessly hate all German people'.[42] Niemöller's strained view of the US media was part of his deeply ambivalent, partly condescending, partly explicitly hostile perception of American society as a whole. Reflecting this perception, he wrote a manuscript on his return about 'The "Good" Americans'. Right at the start he made it clear that the title was meant to counter the 'American watchword' that there were 'no good Germans'. To rebut the 'fairy tale of the collective guilt' of Germans—something the Allies had never spoken of—Niemöller pushed all buttons: many Germans, he claimed, accused Americans of 'deliberate hypocrisy' and the 'intended mass murder of a people' [i.e. the Germans] that had 'unconditionally surrendered to the victors'. Both accusations, he continued, were 'difficult to refute'. The Americans had not brought democracy to Germany. Since the end of the war, 'more German people were missing and had died' than during 12 years of 'murdering under Hitler's terror regime, including the allegedly 6 million missing Jews'.[43]

With these completely baseless accusations, Niemöller drove home that he considered the German people—rather than the people persecuted by the Nazi regime or the countries occupied by the Wehrmacht—as the true victims of the 'Third Reich'. In passing he also indicated that, although not denying the genocide of the European Jews, he did indeed doubt its extent. To corroborate these accusations, Niemöller insisted he had not met one single politically well-informed person with an interest in Europe and Germany on his trip across the USA. Even Americans working with humanitarian organizations considered aid for Germany morally dubious. In Niemöller's eyes this revealed an extent of 'moral self-righteousness' that was hard to beat.[44] This assessment retrospectively falls back on Niemöller, who often became outraged quickly. After making all these accusations he admitted there also were 'good Americans', but they were in the minority. Here, he only referred to Christians—with which he primarily meant Protestants. And yet he even criticized those. He had travelled the USA contemplating whether the Western concept of democracy could become a man-made and thus 'intolerant' religion. After five months he had to answer this question in the affirmative. In the USA, the constitution was the highest value. Hence there were 'countless "American Christians" for which the American is more than Christ'.[45]

With these remarks, he referred to what sociologist Robert N. Bellah described as 'civil religion' in a landmark article published in 1967. This notion considers the American people and the US constitution sacred, creating a religious belief system in its own right.[46] Yet Niemöller stated that Protestant church life in the USA also had its good points. He pinpointed the much higher number of churchgoers and the stronger presence of faith in public life. But, according to Niemöller, 'forgiveness of sins' through Christ's crucifixion—for him the heart of Christianity—was 'empty words' in the USA because people here believed in shaping a human being through education.[47] As a symptom of this problem, Niemöller pointed to the possibility of Christian pastors and rabbis filling in for each other in celebrating services. The vapid 'ethos sermon' that underpinned these practices and represented the lowest common denominator lost sight of the meaning of Christ's death on the cross. This is why he had told the US military chaplains in Naples in 1945 that they required 'Christian missionaries'.[48] He found drastic words to express his perception of a divide in terms of civilization to his friend Gisevius: one had to speak 'at a very primitive level' with the 'very primitive people' in the USA 'so that they can understand'.[49]

Niemöller summarized his negative assessment of the USA in a letter to his mother, written during his trip, referring to the United States as a 'country of this-worldliness', in which a sense of the netherworld was lacking. He would 'rather starve to death in Germany than to emigrate here'.[50] Americans lived in material affluence that was 'dauntingly huge'.[51] Yet the price was the moral shallowness and theological emptiness of Protestant Christianity in the USA. He did not advocate principled anti-Americanism, in the sense of understanding America as the most important 'metaphor for a modernity that is threatening one's own community'.[52] He fully approved of some aspects of US mass culture, shown by his enthusiasm for Bing Crosby and entertaining Hollywood films, which Martin and Else watched 'with a lot of laughter'.[53] It is, however, deeply ironic that, in said report to the bodies of the EKD, Niemöller highlighted his journey as a great success for ecumenical relations and simultaneously expressed fundamental objections to the culture of Protestant Christianity in the USA and its flattening of the Gospel's message, when he condemned American 'pragmatic utilitarianism'.[54]

Yet the trip to the USA also made a lasting impression on Niemöller because it opened his eyes to a lively Christianity created by local community life, which he thought was much more vibrant than that in Germany. In a letter to Elsa Freudenberg, written in the USA, he emphasized his 'tendency towards Congregationalism has increased considerably, that is I again doubt whether the major church organizations mean anything at all for the truly spiritual life and whether it might be better to put every focus on individual parishes'.[55] Especially in regard to ecumenical work, Niemöller's trip to the USA remained ambivalent. It clearly showed that Niemöller could reach a great number of people with his personal testimony as a preacher, leaving the often pedantic conflicts between the Protestant churches in Germany far behind. However, after his return from the USA at an EKD meeting in Treysa in June 1947 he realized immediately that the actual strength of his ecumenical work lay in direct encounters with Christians of other countries. Niemöller initially talked about his trip using the superlatives mentioned earlier and emphasized that he had given talks only at interdenominational meetings. Oldenburg pastor Wilhelm Wilkens then asked him whether he attached more importance to all this than to the 'confessional conversation'.[56] This 'confessional conversation', referring to the Lutherans' narrow-minded struggle for hegemony within the EKD, dominated the rest of the meeting in Treysa.

Meanwhile, the institutional structures of ecumenism expanded, and Niemöller played a leading role. In late August 1948, the WCC was officially founded in Amsterdam; 351 delegates from 44 countries who represented 147 different churches were present. Fixed structures were implemented: a plenary assembly was to be convened every five years—the next one in Evanston near Chicago in 1954—headed by six presidents and a central committee with 90 members, including Niemöller. The plenary assembly in Amsterdam adopted a message to all Christians of the world. Under the lead of the busy Secretary General Visser 't Hooft, despite emphasizing personal freedom as a precondition of faith and thus criticizing communist totalitarianism, the WCC steered clear of a one-sided statement in favour of the capitalist model of society. However, the resonance of these ecumenical activities among German Protestants remained limited well into the 1950s.[57]

Niemöller himself was not always impressed by the legwork of the WCC committees. After a meeting in Amsterdam in 1948 on missionary questions he noted that he was 'very unhappy', because all this 'is just so much talk!'. A public event in the Concertgebouw, where he gave a talk alongside Sarah Chakko, an Indian-born representative of the Syrian Orthodox Church, and John Baillie, a Scottish theologian, was more to his liking and therefore 'a great and good thing'.[58] Niemöller championed the idea of the necessarily prophetic function of Protestant Christianity also in the context of ecumenism, which provoked considerable irritations. After the meeting in Amsterdam, the American theologian Reinhold Niebuhr noted that, emphasizing eschatological ideas, Niemöller had spoken 'so contemptuously' about a theology based on reasonable reflection that some participants felt 'uneasy'.[59]

Soon, Niemöller started travelling again for the cause of ecumenism. In autumn 1949, Else and Martin spent several weeks in New Zealand and Australia. Niemöller wrote about his cooperation with the Open Air Campaigners in Australia with pride and joy. This organization, founded in the late nineteenth century and still operating today in many countries of the world, was in his eyes an 'interdenominational group doing missionary work outside the churches', trying to reach out to the people via street stalls and open air events. 'They are', Niemöller reported, 'quite young and active people who are doing this work, some of them Anglicans, some Free Churchers. Our experiences with them are the very best and I have become very fond of them.' After extensive trips across New South Wales, Else and Martin returned to Sydney, where Martin gave talks during a 'tent mission' to 4,000 to 5,000 mostly young people every night for a whole week: 'I really enjoyed that!' At the same time, George Bell was travelling in Australia, giving speeches about the work of the WCC. Niemöller met him several times, but was clearly more interested in ecumenical missionary work that operated through public mass events. For this purpose, he cooperated with evangelical Awakening movements such as the Open Air Campaigners, who, like all Evangelicals, placed the spiritual rebirth of those they approached centre stage.[60]

Already in the 1950s, Niemöller's ecumenical horizon had broadened, reaching beyond the countries of Europe and North America to the regions of the world referred to at the time as the 'Third World'.[61] In December 1952, he took part in the Third World Conference of the Christian Youth during an extensive journey through India. M.M. Thomas, the leading Indian ecumenist at the time, chaired this meeting of delegates from 54 nations in the south Indian city of Kottayam. For the first time, this event took place in a non-Western state, indicating a gradual shift within ecumenism and the end of Anglo-American Protestants' hegemony.

One of the young participants in Kottayam was Hans de Boer, a merchant's son from Hamburg, who worked with his father's company in Namibia. De Boer gave a vibrant account of his journey, describing how Niemöller impressed the mostly young delegates of the ecumenical meeting with his 'open and casual attitude' by queuing for food like everyone else and sitting on the floor during discussions—unlike the participating bishops. In the wake of Niemöller's trip to Moscow, the American delegates came to Kottayam with an 'anti-Niemöller attitude'. But Niemöller could dispel their objections in an open conversation and win the respect of the young Indian communists with whom he discussed the problems of capitalism. After Kottayam, Niemöller travelled to northern India for a meeting of the WCC central committee in Lucknow, which was also attended by the Hanover regional bishop Hanns Lilje. De Boer, who also was in Lucknow, observed that, in spite of the tropical heat, Lilje did not take off his black bishop's gown for status reasons, while Niemöller wore light trousers and a light-coloured shirt.[62]

Niemöller adopted manners that differed substantially from those in the hierarchical German Protestant Church. It was more difficult for him to order his manifold impressions from this trip to India. In his written reflections about this topic, the situation of Christianity in India or the question of missionary work in this country was of secondary importance. Niemöller instinctively understood that the demographic and social problems of 'Third World' countries shifted the Cold War coordinates, as they put both the relevance of the East–West conflict and the partition of Germany into perspective.[63] In a lecture from 1956 he addressed the situation of the young churches, that is, the Christian communities in regions colonized by European imperialist powers. From his experiences gained at ecumenical meetings over previous years, he concluded that 'white Christianity' no longer mattered for bringing the Good News of Jesus into the world. Niemöller observed a global shift from the traditional churches of Europe towards the dynamic Christian communities in Africa and Asia. In his view, the reason for this radical change was not only the demographic development, namely Europe's rapidly shrinking share of the global population. Crucial for him was the greater strength of the Christian announcement in 'real life' that shaped these communities. Therefore, as he ironically put it, it was high time to send Christian missionaries from India and Africa to Europe. The ecumenist Niemöller also observed that the so-called young churches set to overcome the fragmentation of Protestant denominations—Anglicans, Lutherans, Methodists, and Baptists—were a legacy of imperialism's colonial mission.[64]

Thus, Niemöller championed a 'de-Westernization' of the ecumenical movement, and actively contributed to it. An important milestone on this path was the third plenary assembly of the WCC in New Delhi in late 1961, not only indicated by the place of the event but also by the representation of churches in Asia, Africa, and Latin America, who accounted for 40 per cent of conference attendees.

The Indian prime minister urged the WCC delegates to stand back from the animosities of the Cold War, and the Indian Marxist M.M. Thomas emphasized Christians' political responsibility for creating decent living conditions in Asia and Africa. In this sense the assembly in New Delhi was indeed a milestone on the path to global ecumenism and a globalization of its programmatic self-conception.[65] During the run-up to the conference, Niemöller had defined the conference's task exactly along these lines, and afterwards he commented and propagated it in the same vein—as a long overdue shift of ecumenism away from the countries of the West.[66] At New Delhi, his contribution to the ecumenical movement was recognized by election as one of the six presidents of the WCC. The nomination recognized his stance from 1933 to 1945, but also acknowledged his contribution to ecumenical dialogue with the Russian Orthodox Church, which became a member of the WCC in 1961.[67] Niemöller held this office until the next WCC assembly in Uppsala in 1968. Over the course of the 1960s, he increasingly focused his ecumenical work on the fight against racism in the USA and other countries, including South Africa during a journey in 1966. In 1964, he publicly supported the campaign for awarding the Nobel Peace Prize to Martin Luther King and wrote him a letter thanking him for his work in the civil rights movement.[68]

In January 1938, when Niemöller was detained in Moabit, he wrote to Else that—in the words of John Wesley, the English theologian who around 1740 had founded Methodism—'The world is my parish.'[69] He knew not only Protestant Christians in Germany but many people far beyond took an interest in his fate and that he was more than just the priest of Dahlem parish. But this bon mot is also an apt motto of his ecumenical work. His ecumenical activism only started in 1945 when Niemöller met representatives of the WCC after his liberation from the concentration camp. Initially, Niemöller's ecumenical commitment was rather ambivalent, which most clearly came to the fore during his long trip to the USA in 1946–7. Like other ecumenical contacts this journey aimed to pave the way for integrating the EKD into the international community of Protestant churches after the crimes of the 'Third Reich'. But in direct contact with American society and the depletion of the meaning of Christ's crucifixion to an exercise in moral pedagogy, which Niemöller considered typical of US Protestantism, his anti-American resentment and underlying national Protestantism erupted without restraint. Only the encounter with the young churches of the new nations in Asia and Africa that broke away from the clutches of colonialism changed this, starting with Niemöller's journey to India in 1952.

During the 1950s, Niemöller's understanding of the 'coloured world' in the global South and the 'races' who lived there was considerably shaped by semantic and intellectual inconsistencies, not only from the perspective of current postcolonial theory.[70] However, more importantly in the long-term was that the de-Westernization and globalization of ecumenical work, which he welcomed, enabled him to overcome the legacy of national Protestantism for good. Niemöller showed a habitual flexibility on his ecumenical journeys that was well received by his interlocutors. Finally, it is striking that Niemöller developed a strong affinity for Evangelical groups and adopted elements of the Evangelicals' melodramatic style of promulgating the Gospel. This is yet again indicative of an openness in matters of faith that Niemöller understood as crucial for ecumenism and which he himself practised.

18

Hopes and Disappointments in Old Age

The summer of 1961 was a hectic time for Niemöller. In February 1960, the steering committee of the German Protestant Church Congress (*Kirchentag*)—an event organized by a lay association—had confirmed Berlin as the venue of the 1961 *Kirchentag*, triggering controversial debates. According to Reinold von Thadden-Trieglaff, the president of the *Kirchentag*, the decision for Berlin was an attack on the GDR that would prohibit events in East Berlin. The West German government promised generous financial support, and thus the *Kirchentag*, given tensions over the divided city, became a site of Cold War conflicts. Niemöller exploited the decision for an 'all-out attack on the *Kirchentag*' and pronounced he would urge the EKHN to boycott the event. On 7 July 1961, the GDR imposed a ban on all events in East Berlin except those in church buildings.[1] When the Kirchentag opened on 19 July, Niemöller was on a preaching tour in the GDR which had extensive media coverage. From Dresden, Halle upon Saale, and Halberstadt he travelled to Nordhausen. On 30 July, back in Wiesbaden, his bottom line was: 'Tired!!!'. The next day he went to see a doctor who diagnosed him with laryngitis. Niemöller urgently needed a holiday.[2]

But first he had to give several interviews, riposting media reports on his appearances in the GDR, and assuring he had only 'expressed the unity of Christians'. On 6 August, Martin and Else Niemöller, their housekeeper Dora Schulz and the seven-year-old grandson Martin von Klewitz—from Hertha's marriage with the diplomat Wilhelm von Klewitz—headed off to Denmark in their Volkswagen Beetle. After an overnight stop, they continued in the morning of 7 August, taking the Autobahn to Hamburg, Flensburg, and the border. Shortly behind Apenrade the car drifted off the road and collided with a tree. Else Niemöller died at the scene of the accident, Dora Schulz passed away in hospital. Martin was unconscious for two days; his grandson remained almost unharmed.[3]

When Niemöller woke up, a considerable 'deployment at his bedside' awaited him. Three of his children—Hertha, Jan, and Martin jr—and his brother Wilhelm were there and tried their best to help him come to terms with the shock of his wife's death. Niemöller was heavily injured and had to stay in hospital for several weeks, first in Apenrade, then in Frankfurt, and could not attend Else's funeral. In autumn, his eldest son Heinz-Hermann, who lived in the USA, visited his father for a prolonged period of time.[4] After more than four decades together, it was very hard for Niemöller to cope with his wife's death.[5] In addition to his grief over the loss of the most important person in his life, he felt overwhelmingly lonely, a feeling that persisted despite the hustle and bustle that marked the eighth decade of his life. In autumn 1963 he confided to a close friend how he really felt:

> In the meantime I have become really lonely. When I came home on Sunday, nobody from my family was there, except for Tini [Martin Niemöller jr], who is working on his assessor thesis at the moment. What can you do with your life when you no longer live and work for someone who is very close and dear to you?![6]

Niemöller should have treated himself to a longer 'break', as Else had advised him to do in a letter to his sister Pauline in 1950. 'You Niemöller family', she wrote to Pauline, 'you are so intense, you need this more than others'.[7] Even after his wife's death Niemöller was not willing to simply give up his intensive life. He rather resumed his frequent travelling for peace and ecumenical work to flee the empty house in Wiesbaden, particularly once he had resigned as church president of the EKHN in 1964. In his 1967 diary Niemöller noted 'abroad: 182, within Germany: 139, Wiesbaden: 44'.[8] He only spent a bit more than one month in Wiesbaden during his 75th year.

And yet, travelling had its positives. In April 1968, Niemöller was in New York to give some talks. Sibylle Donaldson, the wife of an American television producer who had just separated from her husband, contacted him. Her father, Ulrich von Sell, a member of the Dahlem parish and trustee of the privy purse of Wilhelm II, had made a statement in favour of Niemöller in the trial before the special court in 1938. Sibylle von Sell, born in 1923, had always admired the father figure Niemöller, who had confirmed her in Dahlem. She became closer to him, despite the fact he was almost 30 years her senior. In 1971 they got married. As Niemöller wrote to an old friend, he was 'happy' his family was favourable towards him remarrying and that 'the loneliness was over'.[9] Shortly after the wedding, Sibylle Niemöller-von Sell and Marcus, her son from her first marriage, moved into the house in Brentanostraße, Wiesbaden.

In Favour of the Revolution

After the wedding with Sibylle von Sell, Niemöller started to calm down. In the ninth decade of his life, he finally had time for extensive holidays in Mallorca and Madeira, which became a 'second home' for him.[10] However, cutting down his political activities due to old age did not mean Niemöller had made his peace with the political situation in the Federal Republic—on the contrary. Even in old age, he still had new hopes to put the Christian message into practice. After his 80th birthday he was more radical than ever, now siding with the political left. This was to some extent the continuation of his robust criticism of the Federal Republic's party democracy from the 1950s. However, he now particularly criticized the 'allegedly "Christian"' Christian Democratic Union. When the CDU/CSU issued a constructive vote of no-confidence in the Bundestag against Chancellor Willy Brandt in April 1972, Niemöller started 'to think of where I can emigrate when Barzel and Strauß [two leading Christian democratic politicians] take over our state'.[11] Helmut Gollwitzer, who was an important dialogue partner for many left-wing protest movements in the 1970s, could always count on Niemöller's support. Following his friend's suggestion, Niemöller was more than happy to endorse causes such as the second Russell tribunal on the human rights situation in Latin America.[12]

Niemöller not only polemicized against the superficially Christian nature of the CDU. His radical critique of West German society was based on the fundamental rejection of acquisitiveness and greed for money. This view was not completely new. Returning to Germany after having been a Soviet POW in 1950, Gollwitzer thought about whether to accept a chair in Berlin or Bonn. Niemöller firmly recommended the Rhenish city. In the West, he reasoned, it was necessary to put up 'resistance', for if 'one falls prey to Western civilization', then the Church would be rendered pointless.[13] The perception of a lifestyle shaped by materialism also permeated his criticism of the USA, as we have seen in the previous chapter. Where the 'idol of mammon' ruled, he argued, man was 'no longer God's called child' but only 'masses, garbage that the consumer has to dispose of'.[14] In Niemöller's eyes, the Federal Republic was a 'republic of mammon' (Matt 6:24), to which the 'socialists'—referring to the SPD—had contributed. 'Everything', he concluded gloomily, 'was about money.'[15]

This critique led Niemöller to a radical conclusion: he championed a revolution, namely a 'radical revolution', which he defined as a 'Jesus revolution'.[16] The Protestant Church, he claimed, was nothing more than an organization for the distribution of church tax resources and had therefore lost all legitimacy. With this allegation, he took up the critique of Protestant regional churchdom since the Reformation which he had developed in 1939. In his eyes, the Church had been downgraded to a 'department of the state administration' and was only concerned with the self-preservation as an organization. In 1975 he was even more convinced that most of the church members were not 'believing' Christians than in 1939. Yet unlike in his notes written in Sachsenhausen, which had left the future path of the Church open-ended, Niemöller could now answer how Christians should practise their faith and where they would find the true Church: 'Like my Lord and Saviour Jesus I stand by those who have been abandoned by everyone—including the communists—the outcasts, the wretched, the famishing, and the starving of this world!'[17]

To adopt this standpoint, Niemöller did not need the 'theology of revolution' that was proposed by Protestant theologians like Jürgen Moltmann in the context of debates on Liberation Theology and in the wake of the 1968 rebellion.[18] At the end of his life, Niemöller was no longer interested in the insights of theology. He wrote that he had failed to find an answer to the question of what Christian belief really was in theology, which he had studied thoroughly; he rather had to 'find it myself'. No theologian could give him a satisfying answer.[19] Niemöller took up the cause of those living in the exclusion zones of modern society, those that even state welfare or charitable aid did not reach. He referred to the simple idea of the imitation of Christ and the adoption as children of God of every Christian.[20]

During the 1970s, debates on Niemöller's political statements continued unabated, for instance when he firmly declared that pastors could be members of the German Communist Party (DKP), which had been re-established in 1968 after the ban of the KPD in 1956.[21] In the politically active circles of left-wing Protestantism, which had gained substantial importance in the regional churches during the 1970s, Niemöller's views were met with broad approval. He thus became an iconic figure for all those who believed that the Protestant faith was predominantly a way to critique social conditions in the Federal Republic and the world. Reactions to his political statements in the GDR, which Niemöller visited frequently, were more sceptical. In December 1976, he was in Dresden, where he first met with friends of the theologian Walter Feurich. On 7 December, he gave a talk to an audience of superintendents and pastors from Dresden. The following debate revolved around the priest Oskar Brüsewitz. His public self-immolation in August 1976 had become a symbol of civil society opposition in the GDR. A young pastor criticized the deliberate misinformation of GDR media coverage on Brüsewitz's act of public protest. But Niemöller did not want to hear anything about this. He pointed out that the media in the Federal Republic depended on advertisement. Some audience members shouted 'you have no idea!' When Niemöller declared that for him socialism was the only possible social order and billionaires should be dispossessed, pastor Eberhard Pampel said: 'You can talk about pacifism in the West, but not here!'[22]

Until the end of his life, Niemöller found himself in the middle of political disputes, though he no longer participated in these discussions as a man of the Church but as an ordinary Christian (Fig. 15). In 1977 he declared:

> With reference to reports on Niemöller['s] alleged intention to leave the Church, he answered he had already stated years ago "if I were not relying on my pension, I would have become a Quaker ages ago". The reason for this was, he explained, that he had become "more and more repugnant" of a Church ruled and bound by laws.[23]

In 1974, Niemöller stressed that his social and political commitment had fully shifted towards secular groups and movements where he tried to practice 'faith as the imitation of Christ'. Time and again he asked himself whether 'an honest person' could still be a member of the organization Church. Politically

Fig. 15 The Committee for Peace, Disarmament, and Cooperation, controlled by the
DKP, the West German Communist Party, published this poster in 1984, shortly
after Niemöller's death. It marks the transition from Niemöller as a person, who held
many positions during his lifetime—including *völkisch*-nationalist and antisemitic
ones—to Niemöller as a site of memory, symbolizing the progressive values of the
peace movement. 'Whoever wants peace must want to live together with the enemy.
We must dare to trust. Therefore, stop rearmament.' With this quote, Niemöller
was enshrined in the pantheon of German pacifism, whose ideas and goals he did
not embrace until after his 60th birthday. Archiv der sozialen Demokratie Bonn,
6/PLKA014071.

speaking, he declared candidly, he was 'miles left of the communists' because as a Christian he had taken up the cause of those who had even been abandoned by communists.[24] Around his 90th birthday, Niemöller gave an interview to the widely read *Stern* magazine in 1982 under the slogan: 'Aged 90, I am now a revolutionary'.[25]

Even in old age, Niemöller championed views that deviated from the political mainstream of the Federal Republic. And yet, Niemöller also fell back into some of his old habits. One example is his relationship with Judaism. After 1945, Niemöller took first steps to detach himself from Christian anti-Judaism, which had also marked the half-hearted approach of the Confessing Church towards the racial policies of the Nazi regime. In a speech from 1957, Niemöller went one step further, stressing the intrinsic connection between nationalism and antisemitism, particularly in German history. The 'hatred of Jews', he stated, was different to the hatred of other nations, even though both were closely interwoven. While nationalism was based on the 'divinization of man', 'the Jew' was perceived as an 'allegation' because he had no nation, basically just his 'bare' existence as 'being man'. Niemöller explicitly recognized the Christian churches' historical responsibility for depriving 'the Jew' of his 'humanity'. This begged the question whether the Church had 'come to terms' with its past fraught with guilt.[26]

This was a question many other Protestant theologians debated at the time. Some of them—including the Berlin student pastor Friedrich-Wilhelm Marquardt and Niemöller's close friend Helmut Gollwitzer—answered with a theology of Israel. Gollwitzer, very well aware of the legacy of the Holocaust, visited Israel for the first time in 1958 with his wife Brigitte and her parents Adolf and Elsa Freudenberg. In Jerusalem, he was excited that Judaism was neither a theological abstraction nor an ancient relict, but a living practice. The journey was a 'milestone' for him and his efforts to incorporate the challenge of Judaism and the existence of the state of Israel into his theological thinking. These feelings were shared by Marquardt and the Berlin Provost, Heinrich Grüber, both of whom also travelled to Israel for the first time in 1958–9, recognizing the German guilt towards the Jews. The positions of these theologians of Israel varied in detail, but agreed on one point: in light of the Holocaust, Germans had a specific responsibility towards the state of Israel and were bound to support its right to exist. And they recognized that the people of Israel—which they prematurely equated with the same-named state—had significance for the prospect of salvation also from a Protestant perspective.[27]

Grüber in particular felt responsible for the state Israel and Jews who had found refuge here from the National Socialists. He had headed the 'Office Grüber' which helped more than 1,000 Christians of Jewish descent to leave Germany between 1938 and 1940. For his support of these victims of the racial policies of the Nazi state, he was brought to Sachsenhausen concentration camp in late 1940. For Grüber, travelling to Israel was a moral obligation, but more importantly a shared experience. In November 1962 he guided a group of 32 people, a quasi-official delegation of the EKD, to Israel. The destination was Yad Vashem, the official memorial to the Shoah, where the group took part in an event in remembrance of the pogrom on 9 November 1938.[28] Grüber invited his friend Niemöller to come to Israel, at least for the commemorative event, particularly in light of his contribution to the EKD's Declaration of Guilt in 1945. But Niemöller did not have the time—at least that was his answer: 9 November, he replied, was the beginning of the annual meeting of the DFG, which was in a 'rather dire situation', so he could not miss it.[29] Grüber planned another group trip for the following year, and Niemöller again declined. He had been planning a lecture tour to London for a long time. Grüber did not give up and answered that Niemöller could do this at any time. 'Israel', on the other hand, 'can only be experienced with others.' It would be good for Niemöller, 'as you always travel on your own and give talks', to experience something in the community of other people.[30]

There are good reasons to assume that Niemöller did not decline Grüber's invitations due to a lack of time. Rather, he was ill-disposed towards both the Christian-Jewish dialogue and West German rapprochement with the state of Israel. He firmly rejected theologically charged justifications for the existence of Israel as 'Christian Zionism'.[31] When a group of theologians turned to Niemöller in 1963, asking for his support in initiating diplomatic relations between the Federal Republic and Israel, they were met with a harsh rebuff. Niemöller answered it was 'incomprehensible' for him why the Church was so interested in the state of Israel. Moreover, he could not 'hold it against' the Arabs that they felt 'threatened and under attack' by the Jewish state.[32] The position of West German Protestants towards the state of Israel remained controversial, particularly during the Six-Day War in June 1967, which resulted in the annexation of the West Bank, Sinai Peninsula, and other territories.

During these debates, Niemöller engaged in doublespeak. At events where the discussion revolved around Israel in the context of the Middle East conflict he emphasized the need to achieve peace and the impossibility of holding only one side responsible.[33] In private conversations he revealed his resentment against the state of Israel—and implicitly against the Jews. Shortly after the Six-Day War in 1967 he had dinner with his old friends Elsa and Adolf Freudenberg. He expressed his 'conviction' that 'if I were an Arab I would certainly be an antisemite, because here on my soil, where my forefathers have lived for 1,200 years, an alien people have founded a state.' And he could not relate the state of Israel to the 'salvation history' of the Jewish people, because the majority of the Jews did not live in this state.[34] These remarks were not only insensitive towards Elsa Freudenberg, who was of Jewish descent. More importantly, Niemöller showed no understanding for the fact that the state of Israel was also a refuge for Jews who had been persecuted by Germany, and that its right to exist was based on this past. Elsa Freudenberg was stunned that her friend of 33 years could say something that she 'could not comprehend'. She also pointed out the blind spot in his line of argument and thus his own, implicit antisemitism: 'The Arabs' hatred' of the Jews, Freudenberg wrote, 'is as cruel and remorseless as Hitler's hatred against Jews, because it is just a play of words that it is directed against the state of Israel rather than against the individual Jew.'[35] In his addresses and speeches after 1945, Niemöller often talked about 'the Jew' and about the Germans who were in 'the Jew's' debt. But this 'Jew' remained a chimera, an abstract figment of his imagination. Even after the Shoah, Niemöller failed to grasp the reality of Judaism and of the people who practised it. His adamant refusal to travel to Israel with theologians like Grüber was one facet of this problem.

Life in the Crew 1910

The habits of a career officer are another element of continuity in Niemöller's life. After years of pacifist commitment, he had friends in the peace movement, and shortly before his 85th birthday he attended the Federal congress of the DFG.[36] But during the last 15 years of his life he really felt at home among his comrades in Crew 1910. For context, we must briefly look at the history of the Crew. The last gathering of the 1910 naval cadets Niemöller attended before his arrest was in 1935 on occasion of the 25th anniversary celebration of the Crew in Kiel. First, a speech of praise 'to the Führer' was held. Then Walter Lohmann—commander of the Naval School Mürwik from 1939 to 1942—interpreted the nature of the Crew. It was 'not only a shared youth experience, not only war comradeship [...] but also "Crew" as such', a form of manly-soldierly experience that went beyond 'the shared deployment for the Imperial Navy and the Navy of the Third Reich' and created a connection 'in the service for people and fatherland'. Then, Karl Diederichs talked about the comrades that were still active, who 'during the difficult years of the un-German intermediate Reich'—with this awkward term he referred to the Weimar Republic—had paved the way for the 'freedom to defend ourselves' (*Wehrfreiheit*) that the 'Führer' had declared with the re-introduction of conscription.[37] After the speeches, the sociable part began. Niemöller noted it lasted 'until 4am', 'but nice!'[38] Niemöller felt at home among his Crew comrades. The context of the Nazi dictatorship—which at any rate did not transform the radical nationalist coordinate system of the crew that had emerged after 1918, but only strengthened it—did not change this.

On 30 March 1939, Niemöller instructed his wife to inform comrade Lohmann of his 'resignation' from the membership of Crew 1910.[39] This decision was part of his reaction to a newspaper article by Joseph Goebbels. The propaganda minister had insulted Niemöller's sense of honour as a soldier, so he felt called upon to abandon the right to wear uniform. Therefore he also wanted to leave the Crew. Like many other instructions that her husband gave her during the conflict-ridden months in autumn 1939, Else seemed to have also ignored this one. Shortly after the end of the war, Otto Kranzbühler, who defended Karl Dönitz at the Nuremberg Military Tribunal, contacted the old crew comrade on behalf of his client. He asked whether Niemöller was willing to make an official statement that Dönitz knew nothing about the conditions in the concentration camps. As a matter of course, Niemöller was happy to do so.[40] In contrast, Niemöller's pacifist commitment, in particular his Kassel speech from January 1959, was a major challenge for the Crew to accept. Following his appearance in Kassel, Otto Backenköhler received letters in which Niemöller was called a 'traitor to his country' and 'communist priest gone mad'. Backenköhler, by the end of the Second World War an admiral in the High Command of the Navy, was Crew leader and responsible for organizing the annual meetings. Niemöller's participation in the 50th anniversary of the Crew in 1960 was highly controversial and met with broad refusal. One Crew member wrote to Backenköhler that he would not 'sit down at the same table with this chatty pastor, who calls us professional criminals'.[41] Niemöller defended his position as well as his Kassel speech, and started to air his own dirty laundry. In a conversation with Backenköhler he 'bitterly' complained that his Crew comrades had not made a case to Admiral Raeder for his release from the concentration camp and that Raeder had not done anything either.[42]

It was Dönitz who now sought for a heart-to-heart talk so Niemöller could attend the Crew anniversary, and to defuse the conflict. He achieved his first goal, although only temporarily. On 5 January 1960, Niemöller welcomed Dönitz into his house in Wiesbaden. The minutes of the conversation that Dönitz drafted were met with Niemöller's approval. Confusion about his Kassel speech could be set aside after both men talked at length about the distorted mass media coverage. What remained was the dissent over the legitimacy of future wars. For Dönitz, Niemöller's rejection of any war was not 'morally unworthy', but a personal political statement. There was 'nothing', concluded the former grand admiral of Hitler's navy, 'that separates me as a crew comrade from Niemöller'.[43] Dönitz's words resonated with Crew 1910 members—some of them still referred to him as Chancellor!—and thus nothing stood in Niemöller's way to attend the 50th crew anniversary in Kiel in June 1960.[44]

Niemöller's appearance at the 1960 Crew meeting did not fully resolve the conflict, and the gathering was only superficially harmonious. Three members had previously declared they were not attending because Niemöller was coming.[45] Thus, Niemöller's participation remained an exception. Two Crew members complained about a speech that Niemöller gave in 1961, declaring himself ashamed of his former enthusiasm for the Navy. The conflict flared up again immediately. At this point, Niemöller wanted to break away from the Crew. Again it was Backenköhler who mediated. Niemöller stayed away from further Crew gatherings in the following years, but occasionally met with two Crew comrades,

Helmut Brümmer-Patzig and Lothar Zechlin, who both lived in Wiesbaden.[46] Crew members continued to meet and socialize, but many were apparently 'in low spirits due to the unresolved question' of Niemöller's participation. His old friend from Elberfeld, Carl Pagenstecher, assured him that 'nobody has yet questioned your sense of comradeship'. In 1966, Pagenstecher was convinced that Niemöller always 'steers a course towards the leading lights', but that it must be hard for him 'always to see only the sea and the sky and never another ship'.[47] This was a sentimental and yet also fitting maritime metaphor for Niemöller's stubbornness and the resulting loneliness, which had shaped large parts of his life. However, the conflict with the Crew still remained unresolved.

Again it was Backenköhler who dealt with the problem. Shortly before his death in early 1967, he instructed Alexander Magnus, who alongside himself was responsible for the social activities of the Crew, to repair the group's relationship with Niemöller. Among the 49 surviving Crew members only very few were still irritated with the prospect of Niemöller attending their gatherings. Others, such as Pagenstecher and Karlhans Heye—who as fortress commander had defended Brunsbüttel against the Royal Navy in 1945—were in extensive discussions after Backenköhler's funeral. Considering nuclear weaponry, they were 'very close' to Niemöller's pacifism.[48] All remaining questions could be cleared up in a conversation between Niemöller and Pagenstecher. From the background, the latter's wife interrupted: 'Don't be so full of yourselves, you old geezers!'[49] This paved the way for Niemöller's participation in the meeting in Boppard upon Rhine from 23 to 25 September 1968. The event included a boat trip and several convivial meetings of the Crew members, somewhat advanced in years, and the Crew sisters, the wives and widows, who were in the majority by then. Patzig was the first to welcome Niemöller, but Pagenstecher and Dönitz joined him not long after. At the end, Niemöller extended a personal farewell to Dönitz and Heye. Once again, Niemöller was part of the Crew and felt at home in this community. He noted in his diary: 'Circle very nice! Good, conciliatory course of events.'[50]

In the following years, Niemöller did not miss a single gathering—Kiel in 1970, Überlingen in 1971, Kassel in 1972 and 1973. When Zechlin and Magnus died shortly one after another in 1971, it was a matter of course that 'the old crew comrade Niemöller' celebrated the memorial service. The Crew had shrunk considerably by that time—out of 30 surviving naval cadets who had commenced their service in 1910, only 13 attended the annual gathering in 1973.[51] At the meeting in 1976, again with Niemöller but without his second wife, Helmut Brümmer-Patzig stated it was wrong to lament the faults of fate in one's personal life that were caused by two world wars and the 'dismemberment of our fatherland'. From the 'position of eternity', these misfortunes had to be put into perspective. Those 'on the highest step of the ladder fall the deepest': these remarks were directed towards Dönitz, the 'grand admiral and chancellor', who had always felt the 'sympathy of your friends' in the Crew.[52] Dönitz was once again the topic at the 1979 meeting when the Crew sister Marlene Maertens, widow of Vice Admiral Erhard Maertens, gave a speech. She had met Dönitz in the Second World War as a young secretary in the Navy Command, but had been living in the USA for many years. There she met Niemöller in early 1979 and asked him about his relationship to Dönitz. 'You are such different people!' But Niemöller disagreed. 'Martin banged his fist on the table. "Rubbish!", he shouted out, "we are not different, we only took different paths!"'[53]

The Crew meeting in Kiel in 1980 was the last one Niemöller attended.[54] During the last 15 years of his life he received several honours. It seems that the Lenin Peace Prize, awarded in 1967—the highest award of the Soviet Union for non-nationals—was his favourite. During interviews he often wore the badge of the Lenin Prize on his lapel.[55] His Crew comrade and fellow pacifist Heinz Kraschutzki remarked ironically that Niemöller now could no longer hope to also get the Nobel Peace Prize. But this did not trouble Niemöller. On the contrary,

> Being awarded the Lenin Peace Prize gave me great joy. May the people finally realize that peace is something that can only be achieved and lived with the adversary or enemy. Thus, I prefer a prize from the other world over one from the Western world.[56]

In 1974, Niemöller wrote in a letter to his brother Wilhelm that his strength was waning 'slowly but steadily'. Two years later he came to the conclusion that 'the globe keeps on turning without us' and swore to retire on his 85th birthday.[57] During his final months, Niemöller was confined to bed. He passed away shortly after his 92nd birthday on 6 March 1984, which he had celebrated with family and close friends in his house in Wiesbaden. The official memorial service took place on 25 March 1984 in a church in Wiesbaden. A gravesite had actually been reserved for him at the cemetery of St Annen Church in Dahlem. But in 1980 he had left it to Rudi Dutschke, after Dutschke's widow Gretchen failed to find a gravesite in Berlin for the figurehead of the 1968 student rebellion.[58] At his own request, Niemöller was laid to rest at the family grave in Wersen in Tecklenburg Land, where his grandfather Gerhard Heinrich Niemöller had been a teacher and cantor.

Conclusion

Who was Martin Niemöller? His contemporaries were already asking this question, especially after he rose to international fame due to his leading role in the Confessing Church. It is worthwhile to note some of the answers. Paul Winckler voiced his opinion writing to Praeses Koch in December 1934. From 1925, he was the director of the Protestant Press Association for Westphalia, and in this role involved in the Inner Mission, where he must already have met Niemöller. In 1934, he urged the members of the Confessing Church to find a 'calm' way of dealing with the First VKL. Yet he was under the firm impression that Niemöller was not capable of doing so. 'Brother Niemöller's demeanour is absolutely toxic when he is not keeping himself in discipline. I have experienced a scene with him, during which I immediately thought he was weird. Immoderate, unjust, and sadly also arrogant.'[1] Winckler was by far not the only churchman who complained about Niemöller's brusque behaviour from 1933 to 1937.

From 1945, many observers arrived at a more favourable assessment, and not by chance. During his active role in building up the Confessing Church, Niemöller had demonstrated he could revise his thinking, move beyond his established Lutheran positions, and defend the principles laid down in Barmen and Dahlem without compromises, both against the Nazi state and their opponents within the Church. When the church political conflicts intensified in 1936–7, he did not shy away from taking risks for himself, not least by publicly criticizing the regime's church policies. Historian Friedrich Meinecke acknowledged this courage in his 1946 reflections on the *German Catastrophe*, characterizing Niemöller as a 'preacher of protest'.[2] Lutz Count Schwerin von Krosigk, who served as Reich Finance Minister from 1932 to 1945, used a metaphor. Krosigk was a conservative Protestant who initially sympathized with the Confessing Church, but whose sympathies cooled off as he observed the many rifts and conflicts within the Church. In his post-war memoirs, he wrote: 'Niemöller is the balance spring in the clock of the Protestant Church. The balance spring does not indicate the time, but without it the clock cannot work.'[3]

Bishop Theophil Wurm had a much more critical view of Niemöller's engagement in church politics during the post-war period. More than anybody else, Wurm could promise to unify the highly fractured Protestant churches. Writing in 1951, he expressed his disappointment about the compromise he had sought to build in Treysa in 1945:

In 1945, he [Niemöller] apparently expected I would relinquish the playing field to him, hence in his eyes he entered a *Burgfrieden* [temporary truce] with me; in my view it was an authentic alliance between two currents who came from different corners, but were moving towards the same goal. He is lacking any humour, and he is way too full of himself. I am afraid he will not find a happy ending, as he is entirely bound up in playing power games.[4]

On another occasion Wurm used a metaphor to describe how he experienced the first steps in rebuilding the Church after the war. He had travelled to Treysa in 1945 with high hopes, 'but between the volcano Martin Niemöller and the iceberg Hans Meiser there was no proper place left for him'.[5]

These opinions are only impressionistic snapshots. However, they demonstrate that many contemporaries were highly suspicious of Niemöller's motives and his modus operandi, even when they largely agreed with his aims. In the following, I will condense the key findings of this book. Rather than proceeding in chronological order, I develop four more general conclusions that situate Niemöller as a person against the wider backdrop of twentieth-century German history.

There is, first, the issue of biographical determination by character. Many of his contemporaries agreed that Niemöller had an impulsive and bossy personality, as we have just seen. But does this mean the course of his biography was shaped by certain character traits? This argument is sometimes invoked when Niemöller's character is condensed to his 'male fantasies', a toxic mixture of misogyny, hatred of Bolshevism, and soldierly nationalism that many Freikorps activists displayed in the early 1920s. Based on a superficial reading of *From U-Boat to Pulpit*, and without any further contextualization, literary scholar Klaus Theweleit counted Niemöller among those whose fascist mentality was based on these 'male fantasies'.[6] It is, however, flawed to reduce Niemöller's character to a fascist form of hegemonic masculinity. His personal testimony during the Great War demonstrates that Niemöller's masculinity did not conform to the hegemonic soldierly ideal, very much to his own dissatisfaction. It is also erroneous to interpret Niemöller's biography as the extension of a fascist masculinity because this means ignoring the importance of contingent decisions. Niemöller could have decided to join the Marine Brigade Loewenfeld in early 1919, henceforth participating in paramilitary combat against the Weimar Republic. Other protagonists in Theweleit's book, for instance Rudolf Höß, did exactly this. Yet Niemöller did not. He could have joined the NSDAP in 1923 in protest against the French occupation of the Ruhr, as his brother Wilhelm did, and then embark on a career in the Nazi Party. Yet he did not. Instead, he opted to build a family and to engage—via his work for the Inner Mission—the bureaucratic rules and democratic routines of the Weimar welfare state. When the German Christians appeared in his Dahlem parish in 1932, he could have sided with them, as he shared many of their core political ideas, from the aim of a unified German Protestant Church, resentment against Bolshevism and secularism to hopes for a *Volksgemeinschaft*. Yet he did not. All this demonstrates the need to account for the role of contingency of his biography. Niemöller certainly had core character traits, and the habits of the Navy officer that he retained into old age were an important part of them. But his character did not determine the contingent choices he made at various moments over the course of his life.

Niemöller's religious and political preferences, at any rate, did change considerably, especially in the post-war period. This is a second crucial point. The Niemöller legend—as epitomized by the Niemöller 'quotation' mentioned in the Introduction—is based on the notion that the man fundamentally changed his political preferences and his outlook on Christianity. But when did he do so? The claim of the Niemöller legend is that his political views, and especially his attitudes towards political and religious enemies, fundamentally changed during the seven long years of detention as Hitler's personal prisoner. Yet as Karl Barth has already noticed with his usual wit, it was the 'historical' Niemöller rather than the 'legend' that returned from captivity in 1945. Neither his Protestant nationalism, nor his antisemitism and anti-Catholic resentment had simply disappeared, and neither had his militarism. On all these accounts, Niemöller's positions only gradually changed, and did so in a protracted process that took the better part of a decade before it was mostly completed by the mid-1950s. Within this process, the adoption of new positions occurred in different timeframes, depending on the topic. The easiest thing for Niemöller was to part from his militarist values, which did not make much sense after German defeat anyway. But this was not the same as embracing pacifism. It took him another seven years to establish close rapport with pacifist circles, partly influenced by his wife Else, partly in the wake of contacts with US and German representatives of the Fellowship of Reconciliation. Yet he only fully embraced pacifism by 1954, after West German nuclear physicists had conveyed to him the capacity of nuclear weapons to destroy mankind altogether.

In spring 1945, Niemöller's Protestant nationalism was entirely intact. It provided him with a pretence for accusing the Western Allies of victimizing the Germans, and with a rationale to fight against Adenauer's policy of Western integration. Only years after that battle was lost and his investment in neutralist positions had not paid dividends did he mark his farewell to nationalism with a landmark speech in 1953. Niemöller's turn to ecumenism followed yet another chronology. It was not derived from the services that he celebrated with an interdenominational congregation during the final months at Dachau, as is often suggested. It was, in the first instance, an attempt to leverage international church relations to bring food and other relief to the Germans, who were, in Niemöller's national Protestant perception, worse off than concentration camp inmates during the 'Third Reich'. Starting in the mid-1950s, his ecumenical engagement acquired a new meaning, as Niemöller discovered the relevance of the 'young churches' in Africa and Asia for the future of Christianity. He now hoped the centre of gravity in Christianity would shift from the North to the global South. For Niemöller, ecumenism never had the meaning that is nowadays most often associated with it: a gradual reconciliation of the confessional rift between the Catholic Church and the various Protestant churches. Well into the 1950s, he displayed a virulent anti-Catholic attitude, a position he had criticized from 1935–6, when the Nazi crackdown against the churches had briefly turned Catholics into an unlikely ally. Even during the last three decades of his life, prejudice against the Catholics was simmering under the surface, traceable in his attacks on the Christian Democratic Union, at that point still a majority Catholic party, which he denounced of abusing the capital letter 'C' for secular political purposes.

Third, there is the issue of Niemöller's attitudes towards Judaism and the Jews. It is of such fundamental importance that it needs to be discussed separately, even though it is bound up with the notion of change. The discrepancy between the popular perception of this issue and the historical reality is stark, and indeed troubling. At first glance, a reassuring story can be told. Niemöller co-founded the Pastors' Emergency League (PEL) to defend the right of baptized Jews to serve as ministers in the Protestant Church. This was a bold act of resistance against the application of anti-Jewish legislation in the Church. But after this initial act, Niemöller's subsequent words and actions undermined the very premise of the PEL. By November 1933, he already distanced himself from the third point of the PEL pledge he had himself devised, as he placed limits on the solidarity with ministers of Jewish descent. Once the Confessing Church had been founded, the fight against the application of the 'Aryan paragraph' completely receded into the background. When the Steglitz synod of the Old Prussian Church discussed this topic again in September 1935, the debates revealed an astonishing terminological confusion, paired with deep reservations against the baptism of Jews by some members of the synod—but not by Niemöller. Yet he had nothing to say about the much more urgent question: what stance should the Church take in regard to members of the Jewish faith, who were persecuted and killed by the Nazi regime?

The key reason for his silence on this question was Niemöller's own persistent antisemitism. As misconceptions on this point abound, the key facts need to be restated. Niemöller had in fact been a *völkisch* antisemite and had embraced racial antisemitism, as evidenced by his membership in the first German fascist mass party, the DVSTB.[7] Only by 1932 did he start to reflect on Judaism and the Jews in theological categories. Yet even then, he denied the legitimacy of Judaism as a religion, and accepted that the critique of the Jewish faith by *völkisch* theologians could not be refuted. In regard to Judaism, Niemöller was much closer to the thinking of the German Christians than usually assumed.[8] More important, however, was the persistence of a cultural and social antisemitism after he finally abandoned his racial antisemitism. Through the lens of this cultural and social antisemitism, he perceived the Germans as victims of the Jews. In combination with his Lutheran conception of state and Church as two separate spheres, his antisemitism was reason enough to remain indifferent in the face of the Nazi persecution of the Jews. Contrary to what the Niemöller 'quotation' suggests, this was more than just silence.[9] Through his engagement with *völkisch* theology, Niemöller was actively involved in denigrating Judaism.[10] Members of his Dahlem parish repeatedly asked him to speak out on behalf of the Jews, which he actively refused on the grounds of his own antisemitism. Thus, he was rather complicit in the Nazi persecution of the Jews, which he implicitly acknowledged as legitimate.

After 1945, Niemöller gradually changed. On several occasions, he took part in—mostly haphazard—efforts by church bodies to confront the legacy of theological anti-Judaism. Yet his cultural and social antisemitism was undiminished, as he demonstrated on various occasions from 1945 to 1947, both in public and private. A crucial element of his post-war antisemitism was its fusion with anti-Americanism. In his view, the US occupation forces were controlled by Jews who were keen to victimize the Germans. During his lengthy US trip in 1946–7, his antisemitic resentment surfaced once he arrived in New York in early March 1947. In a press conference organized by Samuel Cavert, he argued that antisemitism in Germany 'had been overcome' and 'would be dead' as a result of Hitler's persecution of the Jews. The critical press coverage of these rather strange remarks convinced him this was the work of those 'who live off hate propaganda' and had an interest in portraying Germans as 'criminals'. With these barely coded remarks, he referred to American Jews as 'a group of people who are not only strongly represented in the East of the United States but also have significant influence on the newspapers.' Following this twisted antisemitic logic, he also found an explanation for his 'wonder' [*Verwunderung*] about the 'fact' that there was a 'strong antisemitism' in the USA.[11] For dyed-in-the-wool antisemites like Niemöller, the Jews only ever had themselves to blame for the resentment against them.

His persistent, deep-seated antisemitism also affected Niemöller's public statements on the issue of German guilt. In this context, he invoked the barbarity of the Holocaust in no uncertain terms. But his references to the Jewish victims of the genocide remained either clumsy or highly abstract, condensed in the collective singular expression 'the Jew', a hallmark of antisemitic discourse.[12] Unlike his fellow brethren of the Confessing Church, Helmut Gollwitzer and Heinrich Grüber, Niemöller never made a concerted effort to reflect on the relevance of Judaism for Christian tradition. When yet another scandal about one of his antisemitic statements severely damaged his public reputation in 1947, he stopped talking about German guilt altogether. Whether isolated statements from the 1960s on the legacy of Christian anti-Judaism reflect a genuine change of heart remains doubtful.[13] Niemöller's old friend Elsa Freudenberg, a Christian of Jewish descent, thought she had reason enough to accuse him of antisemitism when, in 1967, they talked about the state of Israel and its policies towards the Palestinians.[14]

All these issues relate—fourth—to the question of Martin Niemöller's historical legacy. Left-liberal Protestants in the Federal Republic consistently refer to him as a champion of progressive causes, from ecumenism to pacifism, and as a radical critic of authoritarian tendencies and anti-communism in Cold War West Germany. Yet his engagement for progressive causes must be balanced against the fact that, by assuming the role of prophetic guardian for himself and the remaining brethren of the Confessing Church, Niemöller refused to acknowledge the pluralism of opinions and compromise as core elements of parliamentary democracy. Even Gustav Heinemann, a close friend, was annoyed by the mis-guided righteousness and lack of respect for professional politicians that Niemöller displayed in these debates.

Overall, Niemöller's legacy should be assessed against the benchmark that he himself consistently used. Looking back on his life in old age, he repeatedly stated that from earliest childhood one question had been paramount on his mind: 'What would Jesus say to this?', and what would he ask him to do.[15] Seen from this angle, the tremendous malleability of the Protestant faith becomes apparent. Across five decades, Niemöller acted in the name of the Lord in hugely different and contradictory ways:

- in 1914, when he related the notion of Christian brotherly love only to the Germans and wished as many people as possible in the United Kingdom, France, the USA, and other 'rabble' dead
- in 1933, when he expressed his hopes regarding the realization of the National Socialist people's community and a re-Christianization of the German people
- in 1934, when he approved of the Barmen Theological Declaration
- in 1944, when he invoked God's help against the 'Bolshevik wave' which threatened to submerge his German 'fatherland'
- in 1945, when he accused the American occupation forces of wanting to eliminate the German people
- in 1952, when he declared to henceforth support pacifism
- in 1965, when he publicly called for a boycott of the Federal elections.

From 1924, Niemöller lived and acted in, for, and off the Protestant Church. In the book that he penned in Sachsenhausen in 1939, he was certain the notion of a 'Christendom without Church' was nothing but the 'product of modern individu-alistic thought', lacking 'any foundation in Scripture'.[16] Yet at the end of his long life, when the Protestant churches in the Federal Republic were marked by rapid membership decline and operated in a largely secular society, he was not any longer sure of this. It is one of the deep ironies of Niemöller's life that he battled about the right shape and course of the Protestant Church for half a century, but ultimately concluded that one would be better off living a Christian life outside the Church.

More than anything, the Niemöller 'quotation' cited at the beginning of this book nowadays seems to encapsulate the historical legacy of a Protestant Christian who tried to make up for his personal guilt during the 'Third Reich'. Yet when we consider the 'historical' Niemöller, this version of the quotation represents a myth. It is hence time, based on the facts presented in this book, to rephrase the Niemöller 'quotation' in a form that bears a closer resemblance to the life of the man:

> First they came for the Communists, and I did not speak out—because I resented the 'Godless' Communists for their attacks on Christianity.
>
> Then they came for the trade unionists, and I did not speak out—because I believed in the Nazi *Volksgemeinschaft*.
>
> Then they came for the Jews, and I did not speak out—because I 'disliked' the Jews and denied the legitimacy of their faith.
>
> Then they came for me and detained me for eight long years—yet when I was finally liberated, my views on Communists and Jews had not substantially changed.

Such a rewording of the 'quotation' should not be read as an attempt to downplay the historical significance of Niemöller's work in the Confessing Church during the 'Third Reich'. Yet Niemöller did not act as a man alone heroically facing a brutal dictatorship. He did so rather as part of a broader national Protestant milieu. It is time to question whether Martin Niemöller can still be seen—as he is often presented—as a beacon of Christian morality in dark times.

Notes

Notes to Introduction

1. The version on the USHMM website, which omits the communists, is problematic, as is the version on the website of the Niemöller Foundation in Germany, which omits the Jews. See https://encyclopedia.ushmm.org/content/en/article/martin-niemoeller-first-they-came-for-the-socialists, and http://martin-niemoeller-stiftung.de/martin-niemoeller/als-sie-die-kommunisten-holten (both accessed 3 Jan. 2023). For reasons and further context, see Harold Marcuse, 'The Origin and Reception of Martin Niemöller's Quotation "First They Came for the Communists..."', in Michael Berenbaum, Richard Libowitz, and Marcia Sachs Littell, (eds), *Remembering for the Future: Armenia, Auschwitz, and Beyond* (St. Paul, 2016), 173–99, esp. 192–4.
2. Friedrich Wilhelm Graf, *Die Wiederkehr der Götter. Religion in der modernen Kultur* (Munich, 2004), 102–32.
3. Ibid., 115.
4. See Manfred Gailus and Hartmut Lehmann (eds), *Nationalprotestantische Mentalitäten. Konturen, Entwicklungslinien und Umbrüche eines Weltbildes* (Göttingen, 2005).
5. See Todd Weir, 'The Christian Front against Godlessness: Anti-Secularism and the Demise of the Weimar Republic', *Past and Present* 229 (2015), 201–38.
6. Claudia Lepp, Klaus Fitschen, Siegfried Hermle et al. (eds), *Die Politisierung des Protestantismus. Entwicklungen in der Bundesrepublik während der 1960er und 70er Jahre* (Göttingen, 2011).
7. On these changes, see Benjamin Ziemann, 'Religion and the Search for Meaning, 1945–1990', in Helmut Walser Smith (ed.), *The Oxford Handbook of Modern German History* (Oxford, 2011), 693–714.
8. Benjamin Ziemann, 'Militarism', in Matthew Jefferies (ed.), *The Ashgate Research Companion to Imperial Germany* (Farnham, 2015), 367–82.
9. Walter Conrad, *Der Kampf um die Kanzeln. Erinnerungen und Dokumente aus der Hitlerzeit* (Berlin, 1957), 54.
10. Thomas Kühne (ed.), *Von der Kriegskultur zur Friedenskultur? Zum Mentalitätswandel in Deutschland seit 1945* (Hamburg, 2000).
11. Günther Gaus, *Zur Person. Portraits in Frage und Antwort* (Munich, 1965), 103–20, quotes 114–15.
12. Ibid., 114.
13. A substantial review article on recent research is missing, but see the reflections by Robert P. Ericksen, 'Church Historians, "Profane" Historians, and our Odyssey since Wilhelm Niemöller', *Kirchliche Zeitgeschichte* 27 (2014), 43–55.
14. James Bentley, *Martin Niemöller* (Oxford, 1984). The same hagiographic approach was taken more recently by Michael Heymel, *Martin Niemöller. Vom Marineoffizier zum Friedenskämpfer* (Darmstadt, 2017).

15. Matthew D. Hockenos, *Then They Came for Me: Martin Niemöller, the Pastor Who Defied the Nazis* (New York, 2018).

16. Lyndal Roper, *Martin Luther: Renegade and Prophet* (London, 2016).

17. See the documents in LkA EvKvW, 5.1, 1047; BArch, BDC, OPG NA, Film A 0041 Niemoeller, Wilhelm.

18. Wilhelm Niemöller, *Kirchenkampf im Dritten Reich* (Bielefeld, 1946), 10.

19. Robert P. Ericksen, 'Wilhelm Niemöller and the Historiography of the "Kirchenkampf"', in Manfred Gailus and Hartmut Lehmann (eds), *Nationalprotestantische Mentalitäten. Konturen, Entwicklungslinien und Umbrüche eines Weltbildes* (Göttingen, 2005), 433–51.

20. AK 4 June 1968. According to a stipulation by Sybille Niemöller-von Sell (1923–2022), his second wife, the *Amtskalender* for the years 1969 to 1983 are not accessible for research.

Notes to Chapter 1

1. Paraphrased by Günter Gaus, *Zur Person*, 114, after Niemöller's account in the 1938 trial: Hans Buchheim, 'Ein NS-Funktionär zum Niemöller-Prozeß', *Vierteljahrshefte für Zeitgeschichte* 4 (1956), 307–15, 313; letter to EN 5 Nov. 1937: MN, *Briefe aus der Gefangenschaft. Moabit*, ed. Wilhelm Niemöller (Frankfurt am Main, 1975), 86 ('Bauernnatur').

2. WN, *Vater Niemöller. Ein Lebensbild* (Bielefeld, 1946), 7–8; HN, *Aus goldener Jugendzeit* (Bielefeld, 1947), 9–15.

3. HN, *Aus goldener Jugendzeit*, 30–9.

4. WN, *Vater Niemöller*, 16–19; HN, *Aus goldener Jugendzeit*, 62–87.

5. WN 15 Jan. 1974 to Alfred Engelhardt: ZEKHN, 35/678.

6. Ibid., quote 215.

7. HN, *Aus goldener Jugendzeit*, 87–8; WN 15 Jan. 1974 to Alfred Engelhardt (quote): ZEKHN, 35/678; WN 1 Oct. 1958 to Clarissa Davidson: LkA EvKvW, 5.1, 456 F. 1, fo. 379.

8. Magdalene Niemöller, 'Mein Bruder Martin. Jugenderinnerungen', undated [*c.*1970], 5: ZEKHN, 35/1533.

9. School reports MN 1899 to 1900: ZEKHN, 62/6063.

10. MN, Was ich noch von meinem Vater weiß, undated [1939]: ZEKHN, 62/1873.

11. HN, *Ein Pastorenspiegel* (Elberfeld, 1929), quotes 123, 125, 127.

12. Magdalene Niemöller, 'Mein Bruder Martin. Jugenderinnerungen', undated [*c.*1970], 2: ZEKHN, 35/1533.

13. WN, *Vater Niemöller*, 45.

14. WN, *Vater Niemöller*, 45–6; MN, Was ich noch von meinem Vater weiß, undated [1939], id., Lippstadt, undated [1939]: ZEKHN, 62/1873.

15. MN 23 Nov. 1943 to EN: ZEKHN, 35/573.

16. WN 1 Oct. 1958 to Clarissa Davidson: LkA EvKvW, 5.1, 456 F. 1, fo. 379.

17. WN, Stürmische See-leuchtende Sonne. Ein Lebensbericht (typewritten ms., 1982), 6: ZEKHN, 35/578.

18. HN, *Aus 56 Amtsjahren* (Bielefeld, 1946), 37, 44–5, 58–67.

19. HN; *Aus 56 Amtsjahren*, 13–16.

20. HN, *Aus 56 Amtsjahren*, 23–36, quotes 31, 36.

21. MN, Was ich noch von meinem Vater weiß, undated [1939]: ZEKHN, 62/1873; HN, *Hinauf gen Jerusalem* (Berlin, 1899).

22. MN, Lippstadt, undated [1939] (quotes): ZEKHN, 62/1873.

23. MN, Lippstadt, undated [1939]: ZEKHN, 62/1873.

24. HN, *Aus 56 Amtsjahren*, 36–42.

25. MN, 'Was ich noch von meinem Vater weiß', undated [1939]: ZEKHN, 62/1873; HN, *Aus 56 Amtsjahren*, 41.

26. MN, 'Meine Großeltern', 7 Feb. 1939: LkA EvKvW, 5.1, 440 F. 1, fos 161–70, here fo. 169.

27. School reports 1900 to 1909, quotes 8 Apr. 1903, 30 Mar. 1904, 2 Apr. 1909: ZEKHN, 62/6063.

28. Gymnasium Elberfeld, school leavers report 4 Mar. 1910 (transcript): ZEKHN, 62/6063.

29. MN 3 Apr. 1911 to Hermann Bremer: ZEKHN, 62/6065.

30. MN 3 July 1910 to Hermann Bremer: ZEKHN, 62/6065.

31. MN diary London 2 Aug.–11 Sept. 1908, quotes 2 Aug. and 30 Aug. 1908: ZEKHN, 62/6063.

32. MN 11 Aug. 1909 to Hermann Bremer: ZEKHN, 62/6065.

33. MN, diary I, 1 Jan. 1909: ZEKHN, 62/6063.

34. MN, diary I, 1, 2, and 12 Jan. 1909: ZEKHN, 62/6063.

35. MN, diary 1912, entry 23–5 July 1912: ZEKHN, 62/6063.

36. Gaus, *Zur Person*, 104; WN, *Martin Niemöller. Ein Lebensbild* (Munich, 1952), 8 (quote).

37. Thomas Nipperdey, *Deutsche Geschichte 1866–1918*.Vol. 2: *Machtstaat vor der Demokratie* (Munich, 1992), 629–39; for details, see Michael Epkenhans, *Die wilhelminische Flottenrüstung 1908–1914: Weltmachtstreben, industrieller Fortschritt, soziale Integration* (Munich, 1991).

38. Jan Rüger, *The Great Naval Game: Britain and Germany in the Age of Empire* (Cambridge, 2009), 57–67.

39. MN 11 Aug. 1909 to Hermann Bremer: ZEKHN, 62/6065. Magdalene Niemöller, 'Mein Bruder Martin. Jugenderinnerungen', undated [*c*.1970], 3–4: ZEKHN, 35/1533.

40. 'Das Flottenkränzchen' (MN and three of his friends, among them Karl Gerstberger) 23 July 1908 to Hermann Bremer: ZEKHN, 62/6065; quote: Magdalene Niemöller, 'Mein Bruder Martin. Jugenderinnerungen', undated [*c*.1970], 4: ZEKHN, 35/1533.

41. Bruno Weyer (ed.), *Taschenbuch der Kriegsflotten*, 2nd edn (Munich, 1905), 304–7; see school reports 2 Apr. and 22 Dec. 1909: ZEKHN, 62/6063.

42. Holger H. Herwig, *The German Naval Officer Corps: A Social and Political History 1890–1918* (Oxford, 1973), 50.

43. Herwig, *Officer Corps*, 61.

44. Helmut Donat, 'Kapitänleutnant a.D. Heinz Kraschutzki (1891–1982). Ein Offizier im Kampf für ein "anderes" Deutschland', in Wolfram Wette and Helmut Donat (eds), *Pazifistische Offiziere in Deutschland 1871–1933* (Bremen, 1999), 338–62, 340–1.

45. Karl Gerstberger, *Seekadetten-Briefe* (Berlin, 1914).

46. MN, diary entries 1 Sept. 1912 and 28 Jan. 1913 (quote): ZEKHN, 62/6063.

Notes to Chapter 2

1. Karl Dönitz, *Mein wechselvolles Leben* (Göttingen, 1968), 24–5; Gerd Sandhofer, 'Dokumente zum militärischen Werdegang des Großadmirals Dönitz', *Militärgeschichtliche Mitteilungen* 1 (1967), 59–81, 66.

2. Cited in Thomas Kühne, *Kameradschaft. Die Soldaten des nationalsozialistischen Krieges und das 20. Jahrhundert* (Göttingen, 2006), 9.

3. Dieter Hartwig, *Großadmiral Karl Dönitz. Legende und Wirklichkeit* (Paderborn, 2010), 216.

4. Donat, 'Kraschutzki'.

5. Herwig, *Officer Corps*, 17–36, quote 33.

6. Ibid., 37–60, figure 47; see the breakdown for the years 1883 to 1907, 18 Feb. 1908: BArch, RM 2, 515, fo. 83.

7. Herwig, *Officer Corps*, 40.

8. Thomas Scheerer, *Die Marineoffiziere der Kaiserlichen Marine. Sozialisation und Konflikte*, PhD thesis, Hamburg, 1993, 42, 46; Weyer, *Taschenbuch*, 307–8.

9. Nipperdey, *Machtstaat*, 222.

10. Herwig, *Officer Corps*, 69–70, 102–53. On details of naval officer training, see Scheerer, *Marineoffiziere*, 83–123.

11. Herwig, *Officer Corps*, 63–4.

12. MN 1 Apr. 1910 to Hermann Bremer: ZEKHN, 62/6065; Sandhofer, 'Dokumente', 61; Dönitz, *Leben*, 26.

13. MN 5 May ('monkey jacket') and 10 May 1910 ('enjoy himself') to Hermann Bremer: ZEKHN, 62/6065.

14. MN 19 May 1910 to Hermann Bremer: ZEKHN, 62/6065; Dönitz, *Leben*, 28; Gerstberger, *Seekadetten-Briefe*, 5–6.

15. MN 9 Nov. (quotes), 12 and 26 Dec. 1910 to Hermann Bremer: ZEKHN, 62/6065; Gerstberger, *Seekadetten-Briefe*, 18, 38–9.

16. MN 26 Dec. 1910 to Hermann Bremer: ZEKHN, 62/6065.

17. MN 19 Nov. 1910 to Hermann Bremer: ZEKHN, 62/6065.

18. MN 1 Apr. and 24 Aug. 1910 to Hermann Bremer: ZEKHN, 62/6065.

19. MN 1 Apr. (quote), 1 Aug. and 18 Sept. 1910 to Hermann Bremer: ZEKHN, 62/6065.

20. Sandhofer, 'Dokumente', 66.

21. MN 19 Nov. 1910 to Hermann Bremer: ZEKHN, 62/6065; see Dönitz, *Leben*, 26–8.

22. Karl H. Peter, *Seeoffizieranwärter. Ihre Ausbildung von 1848 bis heute* (Mürwik, 1969), 93, online: http://www.pkgodzik.de/fileadmin/user_upload/Geschichte_und_ Politik/Karl_Peter__Seeoffizieranwaerter.pdf (accessed 24 Oct. 2018); Scheerer, *Marineoffiziere*, 90–2.

23. MN 30 Mar. 1911 to Hermann Bremer: ZEKHN, 62/6065; Dönitz, *Leben*, 34; see *Rangliste der Kaiserlich Deutschen Marine für das Jahr 1910–1914* (Berlin, 1910–14), *1911*, 165; *Rangliste 1914*, 171.

24. Scheerer, *Marineoffiziere*, 108–15; Peter, *Seeoffizieranwärter*, 86–92, 161.

25. MN 23 Jan. 1912 to Hermann Bremer: ZEKHN, 62/6065.

26. MN, Meine Großeltern, 7 Feb. 1939: LkA EvKvW, 5.1, 440, fasc. 1, fo. 170.

27. See Benjamin Ziemann, 'Ambivalente Männlichkeit. Geschlechterbilder und-praktiken in der kaiserlichen Marine am Beispiel von Martin Niemöller', *L'Homme. Europäische Zeitschrift für Feministische Geschichtswissenschaft* 29 (2018), 91–108.

28. MN 17 Apr. 1910 to Hermann Bremer: ZEKHN, 62/6065.

29. See, for instance, Oskar Pfennigsdorf, *Praktisches Christentum im Rahmen des kleinen Katechismus Luthers,* part 1, 3rd edn (Schwerin, 1910).

30. MN, diary entry 7 July 1912: ZEKHN, 62/6063.

31. MN 13 Sept. 1912 to Hermann Bremer: ZEKHN, 62/6065.

32. MN, diary entry 29 Apr. 1913: ZEKHN, 62/6063.

33. MN, diary entry 8 July 1912: ZEKHN, 62/6063.

34. MN 25 May 1913 to Hermann Bremer: ZEKHN, 62/6065.

35. HN, *Aus 56 Amtsjahren*, 19, 25.

36. WN, *Vater Niemöller*, 48.

37. MN 18 July 1912 to his sister Magdalene: ZEKHN, 62/6065.

38. Herwig, *Officer Corps*, 79.

39. Ibid., 79–82.

40. MN, diary entry 28 Jan. 1913: ZEKHN, 62/6063.

41. MN, diary entry 28 Jan. 1913: ZEKHN, 62/6063.

42. Martin Greschat, 'Krieg und Kriegsbereitschaft im deutschen Protestantismus', in Jost Dülffer and Karl Holl (eds), *Bereit zum Krieg. Kriegsmentalität im Wilhelminischen Deutschland* (Göttingen, 1986), 33–55, quote 46.

43. For details, see Ziemann, 'Ambivalente Männlichkeit'.

44. MN 18 July 1912 to his sister Magdalene: ZEKHN, 62/6065.

45. MN, diary entry 26 Nov. 1912: ZEKHN, 62/6063.

46. MN, diary entry 3 July 1915: ZEKHN, 62/6063.

47. Quoted in Herwig, *Officer Corps*, 89.

48. Ibid., 89.

49. Donat, 'Kraschutzki', 343–7.

50. Ziemann, 'Ambivalente Männlichkeit'.

51. Inspektion des Bildungswesens der Marine, Vorschlagsliste, 24 Oct. 1912: BArch, RM 2/525, fo. 12; see *Rangliste*, 1913: 168; Scheerer, *Marineoffiziere*, 92.

52. Scheerer, *Marineoffiziere*, 115, 375.

53. Ibid., 119–23; MN to Hermann Bremer 11 Dec. 1912: ZEKHN, 62/6065; MN, diary entry 3 Sept. 1912: ZEKHN, 62/6063.

54. MN 15 Jan. 1913 to Hermann Bremer: ZEKHN, 62/6065.

55. MN 16 Feb. and 20 Sept. 1913 to Hermann Bremer: ZEKHN, 62/6065.

56. Herwig, *Officer Corps*, 72, 93–4.

57. MN 15 Jan. 1912 to Hermann Bremer: ZEKHN, 62/6065. This letter was wrongly dated 15 Jan. 1911 by Niemöller.

58. MN 15 Jan. 1912 to Hermann Bremer: ZEKHN, 62/6065; see Epkenhans, *Flottenrüstung*, 93–137, 97.

59. Epkenhans, *Flottenrüstung*, 138–42.

60. Ibid., 108.

61. MN 30 July 1911 to Hermann Bremer: ZEKHN, 62/6065.

62. MN 5 Sept. 1911 to Hermann Bremer: ZEKHN, 62/6065.

63. Dirk Bönker, *Militarism in a Global Age: Naval Ambitions in Germany and the United States Before World War I* (Ithaca/London, 2012), 87; Epkenhans, *Flottenrüstung*, 96–105.

64. MN 23 Sept. 1911 to Hermann Bremer: ZEKHN, 62/6065; see Epkenhans, *Flottenrüstung*, 108.

65. WN 15 Jan. 1974 to Alfred Engelhardt: ZEKHN, 35/678.

66. WN, *Martin Niemöller. Ein Lebensbild*, 8–9.

67. MN, *U-Boat*, 216.

68. MN 18 July 1912 to his sister Magdalene: ZEKHN, 62/6065.

Notes to Chapter 3

1. MN to his parents, 28 June 1914, ZEKHN, 62/6065.

2. MN to his parents, 13 and 26 July 1914, ZEKHN, 62/6065.

3. MN to his parents, 31 July 1914, ZEKHN, 62/6065; Jeffrey Verhey, *The Spirit of 1914: Militarism, Myth and Mobilization in Germany* (Cambridge, 2000).

4. MN to his parents, 2 Aug. 1914, ZEKHN, 62/6065.

5. Sven Oliver Müller, *Die Nation als Waffe und Vorstellung. Nationalismus in Deutschland und Großbritannien im Ersten Weltkrieg* (Göttingen, 2002), 81.

6. Ibid., 84.

7. Ibid., 111–23, quote 111.

8. Dieter Langewiesche, *Nationalismus im 19. und 20. Jahrhundert. Zwischen Partizipation und Aggression* (Bonn, 1994).

9. Matthew Stibbe, *German Anglophobia and the Great War 1914–1918* (Cambridge, 2001),10–48.

10. MN to his parents, 2 Aug. 1914, ZEKHN, 62/6065.

11. MN to his parents, 9 Aug. 1914, ZEKHN, 62/6065.

12. MN to his parents, 22 Aug. 1914, ZEKHN, 62/6065.

13. MN to his parents, 30 Aug. 1914, ZEKHN, 62/6065.

14. MN, diary entry 17 Sept. 1914, ZEKHN, 62/6063.

15. Friedrich Wilhelm Graf, *Die Wiederkehr der Götter. Religion in der modernen Kultur* (Munich, 2004), 124.

16. MN to his parents, 2 Aug. 1914, ZEKHN, 62/6065.

17. MN to his parents, 18 Aug. 1914, ZEKHN, 62/6065.

18. Graf, *Wiederkehr*, 124.

19. MN to his parents, 10 Dec. 1914, ZEKHN, 62/6065; Müller, *Nation als Waffe*, 116.

20. MN to his parents, 4 Dec. 1914, ZEKHN, 62/6065.

21. MN to his parents, 22 Sept. 1914, ZEKHN, 62/6065.

22. MN to his parents, 8, 12, 22 Aug. and 27 Oct. 1914, ZEKHN, 62/6065.

23. Werner Rahn, 'Die Kaiserliche Marine und der Erste Weltkrieg', in Stephan Huck (ed.), *Ringelnatz als Mariner im Krieg 1914–1918* (Bochum, 2003), 39–89; Frank Nägler, 'Operative und strategische Vorstellungen der Kaiserlichen Marine vor dem Ersten Weltkrieg', in Michael Epkenhans (ed.), *Skagerrakschlacht. Vorgeschichte, Ereignis, Verarbeitung* (Munich, 2009), 19–56.

24. Rahn, 'Marine', 40.

25. Ibid., 40–3.

26. Michael Epkenhans, 'Die Kaiserliche Marine 1914/15. Der Versuch der Quadratur des Kreises', in Epkenhans (ed.), *Skagerrakschlacht*, 113–38, quote 119.

27. Nicolas Wolz, *Das lange Warten. Kriegserfahrungen deutscher und britischer Seeoffiziere 1914 bis 1918* (Paderborn, 2008), 386–400.

28. MN to his parents, 19 May 1915, MN to Magdalene, 1 July 1915, ZEKHN, 62/6066.

29. MN, diary entry 20 Mar. 1915, ZEKHN, 62/6063.

30. MN to his parents, 23 Aug. 1915, ZEKHN, 62/6066.

31. MN, diary entry 20 Mar, 1915, ZEKHN, 62/6063.

32. Wolz, *Warten*, 153–97.

33. MN to WN, 10 June 1916, ZEKHN, 35/265.

34. Ziemann, 'Ambivalente Männlichkeit'.

35. MN, diary entry 9 July 1915, ZEKHN, 62/6063.

36. MN to his parents, 28 Aug. 1915, ZEKHN, 62/6066.

37. MN, 6 Sept. and 11 Nov. 1915, ZEKHN, 62/6066.

38. Excerpts from the qualification reports of the lieutenants at sea as of 1 Dec. 1915; BArch, RM 2, 840, fo. 1.

39. MN to his parents, 28 Aug. 1915, ZEKHN, 62/6066.

40. MN, diary entry 22 Sept. 1914, ZEKHN, 62/6063.

41. Joachim Schröder, *Die U-Boote des Kaisers. Die Geschichte des deutschen U-Boot-Krieges gegen Großbritannien im Ersten Weltkrieg* (Bonn, 2003), 21–49, quote 41.

42. Ibid., 96–122, quote 111.

43. Ibid., 102.

44. Ibid., 126–35.

45. Ibid., 164–70; for figures, see 428, 430.

46. Ibid., 167–9.

47. MN to his parents, 16 Oct. 1915, ZEKHN, 62/6066; Rahn, 'Marine', 62.

48. Benjamin Ziemann, 'Schiffe versenken. Martin Niemöllers Bericht über die deutsche U-Bootflotte im Ersten Weltkrieg', *Krieg und Literatur/War and Literature* 28 (2017), 21–46.

49. Hockenos, *Then They Came for Me*, 34–48.

50. MN to his parents, 27 Feb. 1916, ZEKHN, 62/6066.

51. MN to his parents, 22 June, 8 July, 20 Aug. 1916, ZEKHN, 62/6066; MN to WN, 23 Aug. 1916, ZEKHN, 35/265.

52. Commission to First Lieutenant at Sea for the current Lieutenant at Sea Niemöller (Martin), issued by the Great Headquarters, 22 Mar. 1916, ZEKHN, 62/6063.

53. MN to his parents, 4 Dec. 1916, ZEKHN, 62/6066.

54. MN to his parents, 6 Mar. 1917, ZEKHN, 62/6066.

55. MN to his parents, 10 June 1917, ZEKHN, 62/6066.

56. SE 5 Dec. 1940; MN to Lene (quote), 18 July 1912, ZEKHN, 62/6065.

57. Hannes Karnick and Wolfgang Richter (eds), *Protestant. Das Jahrhundert des Pastors Niemöller* (Frankfurt am Main, 1992), 139–42; Edita Sterik (ed.), *Else Niemöller. Geborene Bremer 1890–1990. Die Frau eines bedeutenden Mannes* (Darmstadt, 1990).

58. Report of the Ardmore School, Tunbridge Wells, n.d. [July 1911], ZEKHN, 62/6077.

59. Leaving school exam certificate from 3 Oct. 1918: Universitätsarchiv der Humboldt Universität zu Berlin, Bestand Rektor und Senat, no. 2007.

60. EN, diary entries 10 to 16 Sept. 1916, ibid.

61. EN, diary entries 1 and 2 Nov. 1916, ibid.

62. MN to his mother, 29 May 1917 (quote), to his parents 13 and 17 June 1917, ZEKHN, 62/6066.

63. MN to WN, 14 Aug. 1917, ZEKHN, 35/265.

64. Else in retrospect, quoted from Karnick/Richter, *Protestant*, 143.

65. MN to HN, 16 Aug. 1918, ZEKHN, 62/6067; Scheerer, *Marineoffiziere*, 153–8.

66. MN to WN, 30 Mar. 1918, ZEKHN, 35/265.

67. Engagement announcement made by the Bremer parents, ZEKHN, 62/6063.

68. MN to his parents, 13 Aug. 1918, ZEKHN, 62/6067.

69. MN to WN, 10 June 1916, ZEKHN, 35/265.

70. MN to his mother, 9 May 1917, ZEKHN, 62/6066; MN, *From U-Boat to Pulpit* (London, 1936), 63–99, quote 99.

71. Schröder, *U-Boote*, 253–320.

72. MN to his parents, 20 Feb. 1917, ZEKHN, 62/6066.

73. MN to WN, 11 July 1917, ZEKHN, 35/265.

74. MN to his parents, 10 Feb. 1917, ZEKHN, 62/6066.

75. Benjamin Ziemann, 'Germany 1914–1918: Total War as a Catalyst of Change', in Helmut Walser Smith (ed.), *The Oxford Handbook of Modern German History* (Oxford, 2011), 378–99, 388–9.

76. MN to his parents, 4 Feb. 1915, ZEKHN, 62/6066. Text of the speech in Gerhard Granier (ed.), *Die deutsche Seekriegsleitung in Ersten Weltkrieg. Dokumentation*, vol. 2 (Coblenz, 2000), 52–3.

77. MN to WN, 14 Aug. 1917, ZEKHN, 35/265.

78. MN to his parents, 2 Oct. 1918, ZEKHN, 62/6066.

79. MN to his parents, 12 Oct. 1918, ZEKHN, 62/6066.

80. Excerpts from the qualification reports on the lieutenants at sea from 1 Dec. 1917, 26 Feb. 1918, BArch, RM 2, 839, fo. 71. Regarding Dönitz they read curtly: 'Suitable as submarine commander' (ibid).

81. MN to WN, 3 May 1918, ZEKHN, 35/265.

82. MN, *From U-Boat*, 104–16.

83. Ziemann, 'Schiffe versenken', 26–7.

84. List with number of ships sunk by 'Lieutenant at Sea Niemüller' [*sic!*], n.d., BArch, RM 27-XIII/357.

85. 'The most successful submarine commanders', 5 May 1922, BArch, RM 27-XIII/357.

86. Halpern, *Naval History*, 381–401; for figure, see 388.

87. MN to his parents, 19 Oct. 1918, ZEKHN, 62/6067.

88. Michael Geyer, 'Insurrectionary Warfare: The German Debate about a Levée en Masse in October 1918', *Journal of Modern History* 73 (2001), 459–527.

89. MN to his parents, 19 Oct. 1918, ZEKHN, 62/6067.

90. MN to his parents, 25 Oct. 1918, ZEKHN, 62/6067.

91. MN, *From U-Boat*, 139.

92. Wolz, *Warten*.

93. See references in Peter Ghosh, *Max Weber and 'The Protestant Ethic': Twin Histories* (Oxford, 2014), 126–7.

94. MN to his parents, 20 Feb. 1917, ZEKHN, 62/6066.
95. See examples in Dietmar Molthagen, Das *Ende der Bürgerlichkeit? Liverpooler und Hamburger Bürgerfamilien im Ersten Weltkrieg* (Göttingen, 2007), 373–86.

Notes to Chapter 4

1. Wolfram Wette, *Gustav Noske. Eine politische Biographie* (Düsseldorf, 1987), 218–25.
2. Niemöller, *From U-Boat*, 143.
3. MN to his parents, 3 Dec. 1918, ZEKHN, 62/6067.
4. See http://www.denkmalprojekt.org/u-boote/uboote_wk1/wk1_ub104.htm (accessed 12 May 2019).
5. MN to his parents, 3 Dec. 1918, ZEKHN, 62/6067.
6. Sandhofer, 'Dokumente', 66.
7. MN to his parents, 9 Dec. 1918, ZEKHN, 62/6067.
8. MN to his parents, 17 Dec. 1918, ZEKHN, 62/6067.
9. AK 10 Jan. 1919.
10. In what follows, racial antisemitism does not refer to hostility towards Jews under-pinned through pseudo-scientific 'Rasseforschung' as it was practised during the 'Third Reich'. In the *völkisch* student milieu of the early Weimar Republic, the concept of race served to substantiate the 'biologically determined value of peoples', which meant according to the concept of antisemitism: the biologically determined inferiority of the Jews. Ulrich Herbert, *Best. Biographische Studien über Radikalismus, Weltanschauung und Vernunft 1903–1989* (Bonn, 1996), 60–1.
11. Alice Salomon, 'Die Frauen vor der Nationalversammlung', *Berliner Tageblatt*, 5 Dec. 1918.
12. MN to his parents, 19 Dec. 1918, ZEKHN, 62/6067. 'German women' is most probably an allusion to 'German women, German faithfulness / German wine and German song', the beginning of the second verse of the 'Song of the Germans' ('Lied der Deutschen'). It was a popular and widespread patriotic song during the First World War and became the German national anthem in 1922.
13. AK 31 Jan. 1919.
14. For a different version of the story see Niemöller, *From U-Boat*, 148.
15. Wette, *Noske*, 243–55.
16. AK 28 Jan. 1919.
17. AK 26 Jan., 17 Feb., 28 Mar. 1919.
18. AK 10 Mar. and 15 Mar. 1919.
19. Bernward Vieten, *Medizinstudenten in Münster. Universität, Studentenschaft und Medizin 1905 bis 1945* (Cologne, 1982), 104–5.
20. MN to WN, 18 Mar. 1919, ZEKHN, 35/265.
21. AK 8 Mar, 1919; Niemöller, *From U-Boat*, 152.
22. MN to his parents, 17 Dec. 1918, ZEKHN, 62/6067.
23. MN to WN, 18 Mar. 1919, ZEKHN, 35/265.
24. MN to WN, 5 Apr. 1919, ZEKHN, 35/265; see Sandhofer, 'Dokumente', 66.
25. AK 20, 27, and 30 Apr. 1919; EN, diary entry, n.d., ZEKHN, 62/6077.
26. AK 8, 9, 12, 15, 22 May, 30 Aug., 16 and 17 Sept. 1919.
27. EN to Helene Bremer, 19 Nov. 1919, ZEKHN, 62/6079.

28. AK 29 June, 6, 13 July, 3, 10 Aug. 1919.

29. EN, diary entry, 15 June 1919, ZEKHN, 62/6077.

30. AK 19 Jan. 1919.

31. Niemöller, *From U-Boat*, 158, 163–4, quote 164. The German original of the book contains the original wording of the diary entry: 'Am I becoming a theologian?' (AK 17 Sept. 1919).

32. Niemöller, *From U-Boat*, 164–5.

33. Ibid., 165.

34. MN to WN, 5 Apr. 1919, ZEKHN, 35/265.

35. AK 29 June 1919; EN diary entry, 31 Aug., 6 Sept. 1919, ZEKHN, 62/6077; see MN to EN, 22 July 1919, ZEKHN, 35/372. In article 228 of the Versailles Treaty, the German government had agreed to extradite German war criminals so that they could be tried by courts in the Allied countries. The extent and details of this extradition request were widely discussed in the German media in the summer and autumn of 1919.

36. AK 17 (quote), 18, 21, and 24 Sept. 1919; EN diary entry, 31 Aug., 1, 6 Sept. 1919, ZEKHN, 62/6077.

37. Hockenos, *Then They Came for Me*, 55, reiterates this element of the Niemöller legend without evidence.

38. AK June–Sept. 1919, quotes 8 June and 24 Aug. 1919. Martin also slept in the chair in the morning of 14 September.

39. Lucian Hölscher, *Datenatlas zur religiösen Geographie im protestantischen Deutschland. Von der Mitte des 19. Jahrhunderts bis zum Zweiten Weltkrieg*, 4 vols (Berlin, 2001), vol. IV, 696; see EN diary entry, 1 and 22 June 1919, ZEKHN, 62/6077.

40. AK 29 Sept., 5, 12 (quote), 19, and 26 Oct. 1919.

41. Carl-Ludwig Holtfrerich, *Die deutsche Inflation 1914–1923. Ursachen und Folgen in internationaler Perspektive* (Berlin/New York, 1980), 15.

42. Martin H. Geyer, 'Korruptionsdebatten in der Zeit der Revolution 1918/19: Der "Fall Sklarz", das Pamphlet "Der Rattenkönig" und die (Ab)Wege des politischen Radikalismus nach dem Ersten Weltkrieg', in Heidrun Kämper, Peter Haslinger, and Thomas Raithel (eds), *Demokratiegeschichte als Zäsurgeschichte. Diskurse der frühen Weimarer Republik* (Berlin, 2014), 333–58, 343; see the election appeal of the DNVP from Jan. 1919 (quote) at http://www.dhm.de/datenbank/dhm.php?seite=5&fld_0=D2004137.

43. EN diary entry, 29 July 1919, ZEKHN, 62/6077; see Geyer, 'Korruptionsdebatten', 341–2; Holtfrerich, *Inflation*, quote 124.

44. Oliver Janz, *Bürger besonderer Art. Evangelische Pfarrer in Preußen 1850–1914* (Berlin, 1994), 151–4, quote 152.

45. CV of theology student Martin Niemöller, 14 Aug. 1922, ZEKHN, 62/6063.

46. Käthe Dilthey to MN, 26 Nov. 1919, ZEKHN, 62/6080.

47. AK Nov./Dec. 1919.

48. AK 3 Oct. 1919.

49. AK 18 and 21 Oct., 12 Dec. 1919. Personnel form Martin Niemöller, 22 July 1922, LkA EvKvW, 1 new no. 2032.

50. Ludger Grevelhörster, *Münster zu Anfang der Weimarer Republik. Gesellschaft, Wirtschaft und kommunalpolitisches Handeln in der westfälischen Provinzialhauptstadt 1918 bis 1924* (Schernfeld, 1993), 17–18, 146.

51. Benjamin Ziemann, 'Martin Niemöller als völkisch-nationaler Studentenpolitiker in Münster 1919 bis 1923', *Vierteljahrshefte für Zeitgeschichte* 67 (2019), 209–34, 212.

52. Hans-Erdmann von Lindeiner-Wildau (1929), quoted in ibid., 213.

53. Ibid., 212–14.

54. AK 27 Jan. 1921, 27 Feb. 1922.

55. Helene Bremer to Heinrich and Paula Niemöller, 7 Mar. 1920, ZEKHN, 62/6067.

56. Ziemann, 'Studentenpolitiker', 216.

57. Ibid., 217–18.

58. AK 13 Mar. 1920; WN diary entry, 13 Mar. 1920, ZEKHN, 35/703.

59. Ziemann, 'Studentenpolitiker', 218–22.

60. Ibid.

61. Niemöller, *From U-Boat*, 181.

62. AK 27 Apr. 1920.

63. Ziemann, 'Studentenpolitiker'.

64. Ibid.

65. Uwe Lohalm, *Völkischer Radikalismus. Die Geschichte des Deutschvölkischen Schutz- und Trutz-Bundes 1919–1923* (Hamburg, 1970), 214.

66. See the evidence in Ziemann, 'Studentenpolitiker'.

67. AK 2 Mar. 1921.

68. WN, 'Martin Niemöller' (MS, 1982) (quote),: ZEKHN, 62/1233; see the notebooks with lecture notes, ZEKHN, 62/6064.

69. Manfred Jacobs, 'Die evangelisch-theologische Fakultät der Universität Münster 1914–1933', in Wilhelm H. Neuser (ed.), *Die Evangelisch-Theologische Fakultät Münster 1914 bis 1989* (Bielefeld, 1991), 42–71, 49, 52, 54, 61; see AK 29 Apr. 1921 and 26 June 1922; Niemöller, *From U-Boat*, 191.

70. CV of the theology student Martin Niemöller, 14 Aug. 1922, ZEKHN, 62/6063.

71. Kollegheft Professor Smend, Liturgik, WS 1921/22, ZEKHN, 62/6064.

72. AK 8–15 Dec. 1921, quotes 10, 12, 14, and 15 Dec.; Niemöller, *From U-Boat*, 188–90.

73. AK 17 Apr, 1922.

74. Janz, *Bürger*, 225–7; WN, 'Stürmische See-leuchtende Sonne' (1982), 57, ZEKHN, 35/578.

75. Holtfrerich, *Inflation*, 207–10; Gerald D. Feldman, *The Great Disorder: Politics, Economics & Society in the German Inflation, 1914–1924* (Oxford, 1993), 211–54, 418–52.

76. Niemöller, *From U-Boat*, 193; WN, 'Stürmische See-leuchtende Sonne' (1982), 56, ZEKHN, 35/578.

77. Niemöller, *From U-Boat*, 194–6.

78. MN to Konsistorium Münster, 12 Nov. 1923 (quotes), LkA EvKvW, I new no. 2032. The original of his thesis is archived in Registratur der Kirchenverwaltung der EKHN, Darmstadt, Personalakten Martin Niemöller, vol. 1.

79. Frank-Michael Kuhlemann, 'Protestantische "Traumatisierungen". Zur Situationsanalyse nationaler Mentalitäten in Deutschland 1918/19 und 1945/46', in Manfred Gailus and Hartmut Lehmann (eds), *Nationalprotestantische Mentalitäten. Konturen, Entwicklungslinien und Umbrüche eines Weltbildes* (Göttingen, 2005), 45–78.

80. MN to Leni Niemöller, 8 Jan. 1921, ZEKHN, 62/6067.

81. Quoted in Kurt Nowak, *Evangelische Kirche und Weimarer Republik. Zum politischen Weg des deutschen Protestantismus zwischen 1918 und 1932*, 2nd edn (Göttingen, 1988), 38.

82. Ziemann, 'Studentenpolitiker', 229–30.

83. WN to MN, 13 Nov. 1940, LkA EvKvW, 5.1, no. 440 bundle 2, fos 148–50.

84. AK 8 June 1923; Stefan Zwicker, *"Nationale Märtyrer". Albert Leo Schlageter und Julius Fučík. Heldenkult, Propaganda und Erinnerungskultur* (Paderborn, 2006), 32–73.

Notes to Chapter 5

1. Benjamin Ziemann, 'Kampf gegen die "Gottlosen". Martin Niemöller als Geschäftsführer des westfälischen Provinzialverbandes der Inneren Mission 1924–1931', *Westfälische Forschungen* 68 (2018), 357–80, quote 360–1.

2. See Jochen Christoph Kaiser, *Evangelische Kirche und sozialer Staat. Diakonie im 19. und 20. Jahrhundert* (Stuttgart, 2008).

3. Kaiser, *Kirche*, 18–27.

4. Quoted in Kaiser, *Kirche*, 27.

5. Benjamin Ziemann, 'Zur Entwicklung christlicher Religiosität in Deutschland, 1900–1960', in Christof Wulf and Matthias Koenig (eds), *Religion und Gesellschaft* (Wiesbaden, 2013), 99–122, 109–10.

6. Jochen Christoph Kaiser, 'Die Diakonie als subsidiärer Träger des Sozialstaats der Weimarer Republik', in Traugott Jähnichen (ed.), *Protestantismus und Soziale Frage. Profile in der Zeit der Weimarer Republik* (Münster, 2000), 113–28, quotes 120, 125.

7. Jochen Christoph Kaiser, *Sozialer Protestantismus im 20. Jahrhundert. Beiträge zur Geschichte der Inneren Mission 1914–1945* (Munich, 1989), 89.

8. Ibid., 67–89.

9. Ziemann, 'Kampf', 358.

10. AK 5 Mar. 1924.

11. Niemöller, *U-Boat*, 213; Beglaubigung der Ordination, 29 June 1924: LkA, EvKvW, I neu Nr. 2032.

12. MN to EN, 31 Jan. 1924, ZEKHN, 62/6063.

13. Ziemann, 'Kampf', 364.

14. Ibid., 365.

15. Ibid., 365–7.

16. Ibid., 368–9.

17. Ibid., 368–9.

18. Ibid., 369–70.

19. EN to Leni, 18 Mar. 1926, ZEKHN, 62/1875.

20. EN to her father, 22 Mar. (quotes) and 28 Mar. 1926, ZEKHN, 62/1875.

21. Ziemann, 'Kampf', 370.

22. EN to her parents, 21 Aug. 1925, ZEKHN, 62/6079.

23. EN to her parents, 29 Sept. 1925, ZEKHN, 62/6079.

24. EN to Leni, 7 July ('unnahbar') and 23 Oct. 1926, ZEKHN, 62/1875.

25. EN to her father, 16 Aug. 1925, ZEKHN, 62/6079; EN to Leni (quotes), 2 Apr. and 21 Nov. 1926; EN to her father and Leni, 9 June 1926, 12 May 1928 ('recht unglücklich'), and 24 Jan. 1931, ZEKHN, 62/1875; see also AK 9–11 May 1928.

26. EN to Leni, 6 Mar. 1926, ZEKHN, 62/1875.

27. EN to her father, 10 Feb. 1927, ZEKHN, 62/1875. Emphasis in the original.

28. EN to her father and Leni, 10 Feb. 1928, ZEKHN, 62/1875; see also AK 10 Feb. 1928.

29. Barbara Beuys, 'Die Pfarrfrau: Kopie oder Original?', in Martin Greiffenhagen (ed.) *Das evangelische Pfarrhaus. Eine Kultur- und Sozialgeschichte* (Stuttgart, 1984), 47–61, quote 59.

30. EN to Leni, 6 May 1926, ZEKHN, 62/1875.

31. AK 28 Aug. 1921.

32. EN to her father, 4 Mar. 1927, ZEKHN, 62/1875.

33. EN to her father, 15 and 22 Jan. 1927 ('children making noise'), ZEKHN, 62/1875.

34. EN to her father, 15 Oct. 1927, ZEKHN, 62/1875; see Andreas Gestrich, 'Erziehung im Pfarrhaus', in Martin Greiffenhagen (ed.), *Das evangelische Pfarrhaus. Eine Kultur- und Sozialgeschichte* (Stuttgart, 1984), 63–82, 68, 81.

35. EN to Leni, 6 Mar. 1926, ZEKHN, 62/1875.

36. EN to Leni, 6 Mar. (quote) and 18 Mar. 1926, ZEKHN, 62/1875; see also Sterik (ed.), *Else Niemöller*, 24.

37. EN to Leni, 9 Apr. 1926, ZEKHN, 62/1875.

38. EN to Leni, 21 Nov. 1926, ZEKHN, 62/1875.

39. EN to Leni and her father, 29 Dec. 1930, ZEKHN, 62/1875.

40. MN, 'Gemeinschaft und Persönlichkeit des Wohlfahrtspflegers', *Ziele und Wege* 7 (1931), issue 1, quote 18.

41. EN to Leni and her father, 1 Feb. 1930; see also EN to Leni, 28 May 1926 and to her father, 30 May 1926, ZEKHN, 62/1875; Ziemann, 'Schiffe versenken', 27–8.

42. Annerose Sieck and Jörg-Rüdiger Sieck, *Die U-Bootfahrer und das Ehrenmal in Möltenort. Von der Kaiserzeit bis in die Gegenwart* (Heikendorf, 2006), 40–1.

43. AK 20 June 1930.

44. EN to her and her husband's parents, 25 June 1930, ZEKHN, 62/1875.

45. Text of the speech in ZEKHN, 62/1439; text of the speech from 31 May 1926 in ZEKHN, 62/6076.

46. EN to her and her husband's parents, 25 June 1930, ZEKHN, 62/1875.

47. Ibid.

48. Buchheim, 'NS-Funktionär', 312.

49. MN, undated sheet of paper loosely inserted in the diary with entries 1936–8, ZEKHN, 62/1873; see also AK 19 Jan. 1919, 6 June 1920, 20 Feb. 1921, 10 and 24 Apr. 1932, 5 Mar. 1933.

50. Buchheim, 'NS-Funktionär', 312.

51. Jürgen Kampmann, 'Bekenntnispfarrer, Archivar und Geschichtsschreiber: Wilhelm Niemöller zwischen Weltwirtschaftskrise und Wirtschaftswunder', in Reimund Haas (ed.), *Fiat voluntas tua. Theologe und Historiker, Priester und Professor. Festschrift zum 65. Geburtstag von Harm Klueting* (Münster, 2014), 467–85, 471–2.

52. Telegrams Dr Funccius/DNVP Elberfeld to MN and his same day response, 31 Aug. 1927, LkA, EvKvW, 5,1, 463, fo. 59; Stahlhelm, Bund der Frontsoldaten, Ortsgruppe Münster to MN, 5 June and 6 Aug. 1928, and MN response from 12 Sept. 1928 (quote), LkA, EvKvW, 5,1, 463, fos 35, 163, 168.

53. AK 9 Mar. 1929.

54. Major a.D. Boden from Papenburg to MN, 11 Sept. 1927 and MN response from 20 Sept. 1927, LkA EvKvW, 5,1, 463, fos 60, 66.

55. Hermann Jordan, *Von deutscher Not und deutscher Zukunft. Gedanken und Aufsätze* (Leipzig/Erlangen, 1922); Reinhold Seeberg, *Was sollen wir denn tun? Erwägungen und Hoffnungen* (Leipzig, 1915), 13–18, 22–8; Friedrich Wilhelm Graf, *Der heilige Zeitgeist. Studien zur Ideengeschichte der protestantischen Theologie in der Weimarer Republik* (Tübingen, 2011), 211–63.
56. Quoted in Ziemann, 'Kampf', 371.
57. Ibid., 372.
58. Thomas Mergel, 'Führer, Volksgemeinschaft und Maschine. Politische Erwartungsstrukturen in der Weimarer Republik und dem Nationalsozialismus 1918–1936', in Wolfgang Hardtwig (ed.), *Politische Kulturgeschichte der Zwischenkriegszeit 1918–1939* (Göttingen, 2005), 91–127, quote 91.
59. Quoted in Ziemann, 'Kampf', 372.
60. Ibid., 373.
61. Ibid., 373.
62. Ibid., 373.
63. Ibid., 373–4.
64. Quoted in ibid., 374.
65. Ibid., 374.
66. MN to Friedrich von Bodelschwingh, 28 Sept. 1929, HAB, 2/37–94; see Günter Opitz, *Der Christlich-soziale Volksdienst. Versuch einer protestantischen Partei in der Weimarer Republik* (Düsseldorf, 1969), 63–85, 108–27, 137–55.
67. 'Was will der Evangelische Volksdienst?', *Münstersche Zeitung* no. 80, 23 Mar. 1930; see Opitz, *Volksdienst*, 131; Joachim Kuropka, 'Auf dem Weg in die Diktatur. Politik und Gesellschaft in der Provinzialhauptstadt Münster 1929 bis 1934', *Westfälische Zeitschrift* 134 (1984), 154–99, 162–78.
68. MN, 'Lebenslauf', undated [May 1931], AKG Dahlem, 2034, Hefter 1.
69. Ziemann, 'Kampf', 375.
70. Quoted in Ziemann, 'Kampf', 375.
71. MN, Curriculum Vitae, undated [May 1931], AKG Dahlem, 2034, Hefter 1.
72. Ziemann, 'Kampf', 376.
73. MN and EN to father Bremer and Leni, 16 Jan. 1931, ZEKHN, 62/1875; AK 6 Jan. 1931.
74. Quoted in Ziemann, 'Kampf', 377.
75. See the concise analysis by Karl Rohe, *Wahlen und Wählertraditionen in Deutschland* (Frankfurt am Main, 1992), 140–63.

Notes to Chapter 6

1. Manfred Gailus, *Protestantismus und Nationalsozialismus. Studien zur nationalsozialistischen Durchdringung des protestantischen Sozialmilieus in Berlin* (Cologne, 2001), 311–15.
2. GKR Dahlem to consistory, 7 Mar. 1930, ELAB, 14/6367.
3. Gailus, *Protestantismus*, 314–15, 684.
4. Ibid., 316.
5. Consistory Berlin-Brandenburg to EOK, 28 Mar. 1931, GKR Dahlem to EOK, 16 Apr. 1931, EZA, 14/6367.

6. MN to father Bremer and Leni, 16 Jan. 1931, ZEKHN, 62/1875; see also AK 13 Jan. 1931.

7. Theodor Lang to MN, 14 Jan. 1931 (emphasis in original), ZEKHN, 62/6074.

8. Eberhard Röhricht to MN (draft), 22 Apr. 1931, AKG, 2034, Hefter 1.

9. Sterik (ed.), *Else Niemöller*, 30; MN to his parents, 10 Dec. 1931 and 5 Jan. 1932, ZEKHN, 62/6067.

10. 'Probeaufstellung des Pfarrers Nietmöller' [!], *Zehlendorfer Bezirksblatt* no. 60, 19 May 1931.

11. Graf, *Zeitgeist*, 179–80, 187.

12. Todd Weir, 'The Christian Front against Godlessness: Anti-Secularism and the Demise of the Weimar Republic', *Past and Present* 229 (2015), 201–38, 218–20.

13. AK 14 Dec. 1931; MN, *Dahlemer Predigten. Kritische Ausgabe*, ed. Michael Heymel (Gütersloh, 2011) 83–8, quotes 83–4.

14. AK 15 Aug. 1931.

15. Gailus, *Protestantismus*, 315–19.

16. Ibid., 317. See also AK 9 Aug. 1931.

17. EN and MN to father Bremer, 17 Aug. 1932, ZEKHN, 62/6079.

18. MN, 'Fritz Müller–Dahlem', in Wilhelm Niemöller (ed.), *Lebensbilder aus der Bekennenden Kirche* (Bielefeld, 1949), 74–80, quotes 74–5.

19. MN, *Dahlemer Predigten*, 80.

20. MN to his parents, 2 Sept. 1931, ZEKHN, 62/6067.

21. EN to Paula Niemöller, 9 May 1932, ZEKHN, 62/1875.

22. EN to her father, 21 Sept. 1931, ZEKHN, 62/6079.

23. EN to her father and Leni, 20 Nov. 1931, ZEKHN, 62/1875. See also EN to her father, 25 Sept. 1931 and 24 June 1932, ZEKHN, 62/6079.

24. MN to his parents, 3 June 1932, ZEKHN, 62/6067; see also MN, *Dahlemer Predigten*, 75–94.

25. MN to EN, 5 July 1932, ZEKHN, 62/6080.

26. Gailus, *Protestantismus*, 686.

27. MN to his parents, 2 Sept. and 10 Dec. 1931 (quote), ZEKHN, 62/6067, and AK 20, 21 Aug., 9, 12, 24 Sept. 1931, 13 Apr. and 16 May 1932.

28. MN to his parents, 2 Sept. 1931 (quotes) and 16 Jan. 1933, ZEKHN, 62/6067; see also EN to her father, 7 Aug. 1931, ZEKHN, 62/1875.

29. EN to her father and Leni, 16 Sept. 1931, ZEKHN, 62/6079.

30. EN to her father and Leni, 12 Mar. 1932, ZEKHN, 62/1875. Abbreviations in the original written out.

31. MN to his parents, 2 Sept. 1931, ZEKHN, 62/6067.

32. EN to her father and Leni, 4 Sept. 1931, ZEKHN, 62/6079.

33. EN to Paula Niemöller, 9 May 1932, ZEKHN, 62/1875; AK 11, 24 Sept., 1 Nov., 12 and 24 Dec. 1931.

34. MN to his parents, 10 Dec. 1931 (quote) and 5 Jan. 1932, ZEKHN, 62/6067.

35. AK 17 and 22 Dec. 1931, 29 Oct., 11 Nov., and 16 Dec. 1932, 2 and 3 Jan. 1933; Jürgen Schmidt, *Martin Niemöller im Kirchenkampf* (Hamburg, 1971), 30–2; Gerhard Schäberle-Koenigs, *Und sie waren täglich einmütig beieinander. Der Weg der Bekennenden Gemeinde Berlin/Dahlem in den Jahren 1937–1943 mit Helmut Gollwitzer* (Gütersloh, 1998), 98, 103.

36. Käthe Miethe, 'Kreuz und Schwert. Lebensgeschichte des früheren U-Boot-Kommandanten Martin Niemöller', *Beyers für Alle. Die Große Familien-Illustrierte*, issue 30 (1932), 9.

37. Gailus, *Protestantismus*, 91–5.

38. Ibid., 89–90.

39. Ibid., 416–20; Klaus Scholder, *Die Kirchen und das Dritte Reich*. Vol. I: *Vorgeschichte und Zeit der Illusion 1918–1934* (Munich, 2000), 284–96.

40. Guidelines of the list 'Deutsche Christen' from 26 May 1932, AKG, 171, 2.

41. Scholder, *Kirchen*, I, 298–303, quote 301. See Richard Steigmann-Gall, *The Holy Reich: Nazi Conceptions of Christianity, 1919*–1945 (Cambridge, 2003), 13–50.

42. Gailus, *Protestantismus*, 179–96, 449–80.

43. At least the DC's election proposal named him. See 'Ein Wort an die Wahlberechtigten zu den Kirchenwahlen in Dahlem', undated, AKG, 171, 2.

44. Helene Goldmann to the members of the Protestant Women's League in Dahlem, 25 Aug. 1932, AKG, 171, 2. For the number of offered seats, see Entwurf eines Aufrufs an die Wähler, undated, AKG, 171, 2. On single lists, see Gailus, *Protestantismus*, 95.

45. 'Ein Wort an die Wahlberechtigten zu den Kirchenwahlen in Dahlem', undated, AKG, 171, 2.

46. Eberhard Röhricht, Entwurf eines Flugblattes für die Kirchenwahlen, undated, AKG, 171, 2.

47. Appel, Erdmann et al., 'An die Wahlberechtigten', undated, AKG, 171, 2.

48. Niemöller, Zu den Dahlemer Kirchenwahlen (draft), undated, AKG, 171, 2.

49. Clipping from the *Dahlemer Kirchenblatt* no. 47, 20 Nov. 1932, AKG, 1311, 7; see also Gailus, *Protestantismus*, 96–9, 320.

50. AK 16 Sept. 1930; Verband Evangelischer Büchereien für Westfalen und Lippe to MN, 24 Dec. 1930, LkA EvKvW, 5.1, 464, fo. 278; statement by Ludwig Bartning on 22 Feb. 1938, GSA, P 3 Niemöller, Martin 2/1, 6.

51. Scholder, *Kirchen*, I, 194–212, quote 199.

52. Gerhard Jacobi to Helmuth Schweitzer, 7 Jan. 1931, and Walter Künneth's reply to Jacobi on 12 Jan. 1931 with Künneth insisting that only 'those men' were able to talk about national problems, 'whose names are known among the national movement', ADE, CA/AC, 151, fos 308–10. See also Dr Bornikoel, '3. Pastorenkursus der Apologetischen Centrale, 28. bis 31. Januar 1931', *Wort und Tat. Hefte der Apologetischen Centrale* 1931, issue 1, 18–20.

53. Clemens Vollnhals, 'Theologie des Nationalismus. Der christlich-völkische Publizist Wilhelm Stapel', in Manfred Gailus and Clemens Vollnhals (eds) *Für ein artgemäßes Christentum der Tat. Völkische Theologen im "Dritten Reich"* (Göttingen, 2016), 97–117, 107–8.

54. AK 30 Jan. 1931. The title of Stapel's lecture in ADE, CA/AC, 151, fos 38–9.

55. Ibid.

56. Scholder, *Kirchen*, I, 201–2.

57. Wilhelm Stapel, *Sechs Kapitel über Christentum und Nationalsozialismus*, 3rd edn (Hamburg/Berlin, 1931) (first 1931), quotes 6–7, 12, 28–9.

58. Scholder, *Kirchen*, I, 202.

59. MN, *Dahlemer Predigten*, 81–3; see Schmidt, *Niemöller*, 39–40.

60. EN to her father and Leni, 7 Aug. 1931, ZEKHN, 62/1875. See also AK 4 Aug. 1931; Hagen Schulze, *Otto Braun oder Preußens demokratische Sendung* (Frankfurt am Main/ Berlin/Vienna, 1977), 660–9.

61. Ursula Büttner, *Weimar. Die überforderte Republik 1918–1933. Leistung und Versagen in Staat, Gesellschaft, Wirtschaft und Kultur* (Stuttgart, 2008), 447–51; Opitz, *Christlich-soziale Volksdienst*, 226–30, 256–8.

62. EN to her father and Leni, 16 Oct. 1931, ZEKHN, 62/6079.

63. Reinhard Gaede, *Kirche, Christen, Krieg und Frieden. Die Diskussion im deutschen Protestantismus während der Weimarer Zeit* (Hamburg-Bergstedt, 1975), 39; Weir, 'Christian Front', 237.

64. Büttner, *Weimar*, 461–3.

65. Walter Conrad, a higher civil servant in the Ministry of the Interior in 1932–3, repeatedly stated after 1945 that Niemöller in 1932 had said: 'Hitler must come to power.' Niemöller vehemently repudiated this insinuation and, like any other non-contemporary statement, it must be treated with caution. See letter to Franz Beyer, 8 Aug. 1950 (quote), Walter Conrad to MN, 22 July 1950, and his reply from 18 Aug. 1950, ZEKHN, 62/130.

66. Statements of Max von Schätzell on 21 Feb. 1938 (quote) and Ludwig Bartning on 22 Feb. 1938, GSA, P 3 Niemöller, Martin 2/1, 5th day of the trial, fo. 81, 6th day of the trial, fo. 79.

67. Statement Ernst Brandenburg on 21 Feb. 1938, GSA, P 3 Niemöller, Martin 2/1, 5th day of the trial, fo. 109.

68. MN to his parents, 2 Sept. 1931, ZEKHN, 62/6067.

69. See the relevant undated references in AK 1932, 272, 282–3, 286, 298–300, 308–11. Niemöller referred to Barth's 'Zwischen den Zeiten 1923' (AK 1932, 273), that is the article 'Not und Verheißung der christlichen Verkündigung', published in 1923 in the first issue of the journal *Zwischen den Zeiten* and based on a speech given in 1922. Karl Barth, *Vorträge und Kleinere Arbeiten 1922–1925* (Zurich, 1990), 65–97.

70. AK 3 Oct. 1932, and AK 1932, 298–306. Friedrich Gogarten, 'Schöpfung und Volkstum', *Zwischen den Zeiten* 10 (1932), 481–505. Niemöller also cited Friedrich Gogarten, *Wider die Ächtung der Autorität* (Jena, 1930).

71. AK 1932, 278–80.

72. AK 1932, quotes 273–4.

73. AK 1932, quotes 282–3, 285, 290, 299.

74. Gogarten, 'Schöpfung und Volkstum', quotes 483, 494, 499, 501–2. See Graf, *Zeitgeist*, 265–328.

75. AK 1932, 298–306, quote 306.

76. Weir, 'Christian Front', 238.

Notes to Chapter 7

1. Peter Fritzsche, *Life and Death in the Third Reich* (Cambridge, MA, 2008), 19–75, quote 31.

2. Manfred Gailus, '1933 als protestantisches Erlebnis. Emphatische Selbsttransformation und Spaltung', *Geschichte und Gesellschaft* 29 (2003), 481–511, quotes 481, 483, 498.

Time of Illusion is the subtitle of Scholder, *Kirchen*, I; see Richard Steigmann-Gall, 'Apostasy or Religiosity? The Cultural Meanings of the Protestant Vote for Hitler', *Social History* 25 (2000), 267–85.

3. Quoted in Steigmann-Gall, 'Apostasy', 278.

4. Paula Niemöller to WN, 3 and 13 Feb. 1933, ZEKHN, 35/880.

5. Paula Niemöller to WN and his wife Ingeborg, 3 June 1933, ZEKHN, 35/880. Abbreviations in the original written out.

6. Paula Niemöller to WN and his wife Ingeborg, 16 Sept. 1933, ZEKHN, 35/880.

7. Quoted in Friedrich Baumgärtel, *Wider die Kirchenkampf-Legenden*, 2nd edn (Neuendettelsau, 1959), 25–6.

8. Kampmann, 'Bekenntnispfarrer', 472–3, quote 476.

9. 'Bielefelder Archiv des Kirchenkampfes im Dritten Reich. Pfarrer D. Wilhelm Niemöller', 1 July 1962, 17, ZEKHN, 62/674.

10. See, in hindsight, EN, 'Kleine Streiflichter aus der Kirchenkampfzeit der Jahre 1933–1937 [Nov. 1958], LkA EvKvW, 5.1, 456, F. 1, fos 189–95, here fo. 189.

11. MN, 'Was ich noch von meinem Vater weiß', undated [1939], ZEKHN, 62/6063.

12. AK 20 Apr. 1933.

13. AK 5 Mar. 1933. Abbreviations in the original written out.

14. MN, *Dahlemer Predigten*, 103–9, quotes 104.

15. Ibid., 105. For the NSDAP manifesto of 1920, see https://germanhistorydocs.ghi-dc.org/sub_document.cfm?document_id=4625 (last accessed 28 Mar. 2022).

16. MN, *Dahlemer Predigten*, 106.

17. Ibid. For the quote from a speech, see Scholder, *Kirchen*, I. 1, 319.

18. MN, *Dahlemer Predigten*, 106.

19. Ibid., 106–9.

20. Gailus, '1933 als protestantisches Erlebnis', 481.

21. MN, *Dahlemer Predigten*, 107; see also Gailus, '1933 als protestantisches Erlebnis', 484–94.

22. See D. Timothy Goering, *Friedrich Gogarten (1887–1967). Religionsrebell im Jahrhundert der Weltkriege* (Berlin/Boston, 2017), 249–78.

23. MN, *Dahlemer Predigten*, 124–8.

24. Ibid., 129–31, 130–1 (quotes), 133.

25. Hans-Günter Hockerts, 'Konfessionswechsel im Dritten Reich. Zahlenbilder und Fallbeispiele in typologischer Absicht', in Siegfried Hermle and Hans Maier (eds), *Konvertiten und Konversionen* (Annweiler, 2010), 149–65, 153; Gerhard Besier, *Die Kirchen und das Dritte Reich*. Vol. 3: *Spaltungen und Abwehrkämpfe 1934–1937* (Munich, 2001), 218–19.

26. MN, *Dahlemer Predigten*, 131.

27. Ibid., 137–41, quote 141.

28. Ibid., 152–3, 159, 163.

29. Ibid., 265–70, quote 266.

30. Jonathan R.C. Wright, *Über den Parteien. Die politische Haltung der evangelischen Kirchenführer 1918–1933* (Göttingen, 1977), 197–207; Kurt Meier, *Der evangelische Kirchenkampf*. Vol. I: *Der Kampf um die Reichskirche* (Halle an der Saale, 1976), 90–2; Thomas M. Schneider, *Reichsbischof Ludwig Müller. Eine Untersuchung zu Leben, Werk und Persönlichkeit* (Göttingen, 1993), 103–10.

31. AK 5 Apr. 1933

32. EN, Kleine Streiflichter aus der Kirchenkampfzeit der Jahre 1933–1937 [Nov. 1958], LkA EvKvW, 5.1, 456, F. 1, fos 189–95, here fo. 189; Schneider, *Ludwig Müller*, 93, 109. On the contact in Münster, see the minutes of Arbeitsausschuss of the Inner Mission in Westphalia of 15 Sept. 1930, ZEKHN, 62/6072.

33. EN, Kleine Streiflichter aus der Kirchenkampfzeit der Jahre 1933–1937 [Nov. 1958]: LkA EvKvW, 5.1, 456, F. 1, fo. 189; AK 13 and 17 May 1933; Peter Neumann, *Die Jungreformatorische Bewegung* (Göttingen, 1971), 21–37, 40–6; Walter Künneth, *Lebensführungen. Der Wahrheit verpflichtet* (Wuppertal, 1979), 108–9; Scholder, *Kirchen*, I, 458–9.

34. AK 12, 16, and 19 May 1933; Schmidt, *Niemöller*, 55–7.

35. Quoted in Meier, *Kirchenkampf*, I, 93; see also Neumann, *Jungreformatorische Bewegung*, 88–97.

36. Mitteilungen der Jungreformatorischen Bewegung No. 5, 19 June 1933, 2, LkA EvKvW, 5.1, 53, F. 1, fos 10–11.

37. Organisationsplan der Jungreformatorischen Bewegung, undated [June 1933]: LkA EvKvW, 5.1, 53, F. 1, fo. 16.

38. Holger Roggelin, *Franz Hildebrandt. Ein lutherischer Dissenter im Kirchenkampf und Exil* (Göttingen, 1999), 150–1; see also Heinrich Rusterholz, *"... als ob unseres Nachbarn Haus nicht in Flammen stünde". Paul Vogt, Karl Barth und das Schweizerische evangelische Hilfswerk für die Bekennende Kirche Deutschland 1937–1947* (Zurich, 2015).

39. *Martin Niemöller und sein Bekenntnis*, ed. Schweizerisches Evangelisches Hilfswerk für die Bekennende Kirche in Deutschland, 8th edn (Zollikon, 1939), 10.

40. Quotes: 'Was fordert das Kampfprogramm der Jungreformatorischen Bewegung?', undated [May 1933], EZA, 619/1 (emphasis in the original); see also Neumann, *Jungreformatorische Bewegung*, 108–18.

41. 'Was fordert das Kampfprogramm der Jungreformatorischen Bewegung?', undated [May 1933], EZA, 619/1; see also Schmidt, *Niemöller*, 61–2, 458.

42. Meier, *Kirchenkampf*, I, 95.

43. Friedrich von Bodelschwingh, Dreißig Tage an einer Wegwende deutscher Kirchengeschichte, 29 Oct. 1935, 14, HAB, 2/39–176; see also Schmidt, *Niemöller*, 63–5.

44. Meier, *Kirchenkampf*, I, 98–102; see also Schmidt, *Niemöller*, 80–2.

45. Speech of the leadership of the Young Reformation Movement at the Reich Bishop, 15 June 1933, HAB, 2/39–176; Neumann, *Jungreformatorische Bewegung*, 50–69; Schmidt, *Niemöller*, 65, 73–9.

46. AK 17 June 1933.

47. Schmidt, *Niemöller*, 85–6; cf. Wright, *Über den Parteien*, 220–30.

48. MN to Friedrich von Bodelschwingh, 21 June 1933, HAB, 2/39–176, fos 94–6; 'Demission': AK 21 June 1933.

49. Declaration of pastors from Mark Brandenburg, undated [July 1933], ZEKHN, 62/6022; Schmidt, *Niemöller*, 89–93.

50. Text in *JK* 1 (1933), no. 2, 16.

51. Scholder, *Kirchen*, I, 515, 527–8.

52. Ibid., 528; quotes MN, *Dahlemer Predigten*, 147–9.

53. Scholder, *Kirchen*, I, 528; see also Schmidt, *Niemöller im Kirchenkampf*, 98–9.

54. Scholder, *Kirchen*, I, 522–3.

55. Unsigned minutes of the meeting on 3 July 1933, LkA EvKvW, 5.1, 53 F. 1, fo. 18; see also Schmidt, *Niemöller*, 100–1.

56. Scholder, *Kirchen*, I, 529–40.

57. 'Kundgebung der Jungreformatorischen Bewegung', *JK* 1 (1933), No. 4, 44–7; AK 14 July 1933. The average number of souls in Berlin was 22,793 in 1933. See Gailus, *Protestantismus*, 684.

58. 'Volkskirche unter dem Evangelium', *JK* 1 (1933), No. 4, 50. This appeal was written by Fritz Söhlmann, the editor of the *Junge Kirche*; see also Scholder, *Kirchen*, I, 910.

59. Scholder, *Kirchen*, I, 524, 626–31; Schmidt, *Niemöller*, 103.

60. 'Richtlinien für die Kirchenwahlen', *JK* 1 (1933), No. 4, 43–4.

61. 'Zur Kirchenwahl. Ein Wort an alle Gemeindeglieder', *JK* 1 (1933), No. 4, 43.

62. AK 20 July 1933; Schmidt, *Niemöller*, 103–4.

63. 'Dahlemer Gemeindeabend', *Dahlemer Nachrichten*, 22 Mar. 1933; AK 19 Mar. 1933 ('Schlußwort'). On Klinge, who was active in the Christian-German Movement, which merged into the DC in 1933, see Christoph Weiling, *Die 'Christlich-deutsche Bewegung'. Eine Studie zum konservativen Protestantismus in der Weimarer Republik* (Göttingen, 1998), 227, 269–70, 272.

64. 'Worum es bei den Kirchenwahlen geht', *Dahlemer Nachrichten*, 19 July 1933 (excerpt in ZEKHN, 62/6021).

65. Quoted in Friedrich Müller, Anlage zum Schreiben an das Geheime Staatspolizeiamt, 24 Mar. 1934; see Evangelisches Konsistorium Berlin to the ApU regional bishop, 14 Apr. 1934, EZA, 7/11665.

66. 'Worum es bei den Kirchenwahlen geht', *Dahlemer Nachrichten*, 19 July 1933 (excerpt in ZEKHN, 62/6021).

67. Scholder, *Kirchen*, I, 630–4, quote 634; Meier, *Kirchenkampf*, I, 103–5.

68. Scholder, *Kirchen*, I, 634–5; Mitteilungen des Dahlemer Pfarramtes, undated [30 July 1933], ZEKHN, 62/6022; AK 23 July 1933.

69. Seminal on the theology and ideology of the German Christians: Doris Bergen, *Twisted Cross: The German Christian Movement in the Third Reich* (Chapel Hill, 1996).

70. Künneth/Lilje/Niemöller, Die neue Aufgabe der jungreformatorischen Bewegung, 24 July 1933, LkA EvKvW, 5.1, F. 568, fos 259–60; Schmidt, *Niemöller*, 109.

71. Sitzung der Reichsleitung 'Evangelium und Kirche', 27 July 1933 (minutes by Fritz Müller), ZEKHN, 62/6022; Neumann, *Jungreformatorische Bewegung*, 136–7.

72. Schmidt, *Niemöller*, 110; see also Gerhard Stratenwerth to MN, 18 Aug. 1933, ZEKHN, 62/6022.

73. MN, 'Die Jungreformatorische Bewegung und die Kirchenpolitik. 16 Thesen', *JK* 1 (1933), No. 9, 99–101.

74. Ibid.

75. Drafts of this text with the title *Die JB am Wendepunkt* can be found in LkA, EvKvW, 5.1., 53, F. 1, fos 22–9, quotes fos 23, 25.

76. Scholder, *Kirchen*, I, 644–5; Schmidt, *Niemöller*, 112–13.

77. Gailus, '1933 als protestantisches Erlebnis'.

Notes to Chapter 8

1. For the perception of the foreign press, see 'Der Kirchenstreit in Deutschland', *Neue Züricher Zeitung*, 8 Dec. 1933 (clipping in LkA EvKvW, 5.1., 435, F. 2, fo. 33).
2. Scholder, *Kirchen*, I, 663–6, quote 665.
3. Ibid., 667–71; Schmidt, *Niemöller*, 117–19.
4. Schmidt, *Niemöller*, 119–20.
5. MN to Friedrich von Bodelschwingh, 9 Sept. 1933, HAB, 2/39–50.
6. Schmidt, *Niemöller*, 120–6.
7. MN to Bodelschwingh, 19 Sept. 1933, HAB 2/39–69.
8. MN, circular from 21 Sept. 1933, LkA EvKvW, 5.1, 435 F. 1, fo. 81.
9. Cf. Scholder, *Kirchen*, I, 686.
10. WN (ed.), *Texte zur Geschichte des Pfarrernotbundes* (Berlin, 1958), 24–5 (quotes); see Schmidt, *Niemöller*, 127–8.
11. Scholder, *Kirchen*, I, 697–8.
12. *Martin Niemöller und sein Bekenntnis*, ed. Schweizerisches Evangelisches Hilfswerk für die Bekennende Kirche in Deutschland, 8th edn (Zollikon, 1939), 52–3; see Peter Noss, *Martin Albertz (1883–1956). Eigensinn und Konsequenz* (Neukirchen-Vluyn, 2001), 406.
13. Circular of the PEL no. 1, 2 Nov. 1933, LkA EvKvW, 5.1, 816 F. 1, fos 10–11; Schmidt, *Niemöller*, 129–31.
14. MN, 'Die Verpflichtung des Pfarrer-Notbundes', Oct. 1933, LkA, EvKvW, 5.1., 435 F. 1, fo. 99.
15. Hartmut Ludwig and Eberhard Röhm (eds), *Evangelisch getauft—als "Juden" verfolgt. Theologen jüdischer Herkunft in der Zeit des Nationalsozialismus* (Stuttgart, 2014), 394.
16. Marikje Smid, *Deutscher Protestantismus und Judentum 1932/1933* (Gütersloh, 1990), 362–97.
17. MN, 'Ehre und Vaterland. Die Verantwortung des Studenten vor seinem Volk', *Ziele und Wege* 4 (1928), issue 4/5, 14–24, quote 18.
18. Smid, *Protestantismus*, 221–41, 264–72, 301–10.
19. Alfred Rosenberg, *Der Mythus des 20. Jahrhunderts. Eine Wertung der seelisch-geistigen Gestaltenkämpfe unserer Zeit*, 33rd–34th edn (Munich, 1934), 218, 246–7, 603–7, 614; Carsten Nicolaisen, 'Die Stellung der "Deutschen Christen" zum Alten Testament', in Nicolaisen, *Zur Geschichte des Kirchenkampfes. Gesammelte Aufsätze II* (Göttingen, 1971), 197–220.
20. AK 1932, 278. Abbreviations in the original written out.
21. Johannes Hempel, *Fort mit dem Alten Testament?* (Gießen, 1932), 19, 26–7; see Cornelia Weber, *Altes Testament und völkische Frage. Der biblische Volksbegriff in der alttestamentlichen Wissenschaft der nationalsozialistischen Zeit, dargestellt am Beispiel von Johannes Hempel* (Tübingen, 2000), 100–36.
22. AK 1932, 278f. Abbreviations in the original written out. Emphasis in the original.
23. Friedrich Baumgärtel, *Ist die Kritik am Alten Testament berechtigt?* (Schwerin, 1927); Hempel, *Fort*; Hempel, *Altes Testament und völkische Frage* (Göttingen, 1931); Emanuel Hirsch, 'Etwas von der christlichen Stellung zum Alten Testament', *Glaube und Volk. Christliche-deutsche Monatsschrift*, issue 1, 1932, 7–10, 20–3.

24. AK 1932, 279.
25. Hempel, *Fort*, 26.
26. AK 1932, 279–80. Abbreviations in the original written out.
27. AK 1932, 279.
28. 'Nochmals: Was geht in der Kirche vor?', *Dahlemer Nachrichten*, 31 May 1933; see Kurt Meier, *Kirche und Judentum. Die Haltung der evangelischen Kirche zur Judenpolitik des Dritten Reiches* (Halle an der Saale, 1968), 49–50.
29. Quoted in Meier, *Kirche und Judentum*, 82; see Scholder, *Kirchen*, I, 298–302.
30. 'Nochmals: Was geht in der Kirche vor?', *Dahlemer Nachrichten*, 31 May 1933.
31. EN to her sister Käthe, 7 Sept. 1933, ZEKHN, 6079a; Schmidt, *Niemöller*, 120; AK 6 Sept. 1933.
32. Quoted in Wolfgang Gerlach, *Als die Zeugen schwiegen. Bekennende Kirche und die Juden* (Berlin, 1987), 64.
33. AK 21 and 22 Aug. 1933; see MN to Pastor Kampffmeyer, 15 Aug. 1933, ZEKHN, 62/6022.
34. Martina Voigt, '"Die Gemeinde hat die Pflicht, an den allgemeinen Menschenrechten interessiert zu sein". Elisabeth Schiemann', in Manfred Gailus (ed.), *Mit Herz und Verstand. Protestantische Frauen im Widerstand gegen die NS-Rassenpolitik* (Göttingen, 2013), 100–27, 108.
35. MN to Elisabeth Schiemann, 7 Sept. 1933, EZA, 50/258, fos 3–4. On attitudes within the Protestant Churches in regard to the Nazi persecution of the Jews in the spring of 1933 more generally, see now the painstaking analysis by Hermann Beck, *Before the Holocaust: Antisemitic Violence and the Reaction of German Elites and Institutions during the Nazi Takeover* (Oxford, 2022), 311–76.
36. Smid, *Protestantismus*, 205–7.
37. MN to Elisabeth Schiemann, 7 Sept. 1933, EZA, 50/258, fos 3–4.
38. MN to Pastor Holtz, 5 Oct. 1933, LkA EvKvW, 5.1, 435, Fasz. 1, fo. 86.
39. MN, 'Sätze zur Arierfrage in der Kirche', *Junge Kirche* 1 (1933), 269–71.
40. Ibid., 269–70.
41. Gerlach, *Zeugen*, 86–7.
42. Eberhard Busch (ed.), *Reformationstag 1933. Dokumente der Begegnung Karl Barths mit dem Pfarrernotbund in Berlin* (Zurich, 1998), 94. MN also talked about a 'minor matter' in 'Die Anschauungen des Pfarrernotbundes', *Der Ring. Konservative Wochenschrift*, no. 48, 1 Dec. 1933, 765.
43. Circular no. 1 of the PEL, 2 Nov. 1933, LkA EvKvW, 5.1, 816 F. 1, fos 10–11.
44. Reader's letter by Wilhelm Harnisch in *Protestantische Monatshefte* 18 (1957), 222; transcript in LkA EvKvW, 5.1, 435 F. 1, fo. 94.
45. MN, 'Die Anschauungen des Pfarrernotbundes', 765.
46. Franz Hildebrandt to MN, 24 Oct. 1933, LkA EvKvW, 5.1, 435 F. 1, fo. 97.
47. Roggelin, *Hildebrandt*, 61–7.
48. Busch, *Reformationstag*, 72–3; Schmidt, *Niemöller*, 139–40.
49. Busch, *Reformationstag*, 71–92, esp. 77.
50. Ibid., 72, 87.
51. Ibid., 93–113, quotes 103–4.
52. Scholder, *Kirchen*, I, 769.

53. Schmidt, *Niemöller*, 144, is incorrect on this point.

54. Rudolf Erbar for the DC parish group to EOK, 6 Nov. 1933, EZA 7/11661; figures: Gailus, *Protestantismus*, 686.

55. Protestant Consistory Berlin Brandenburg to EOK, 15 Nov. 1933, EZA, 7/1661; see Schmidt, *Niemöller*, 145-7.

56. Scholder, *Kirchen*, I, 783-5, quotes 785.

57. Scholder, *Kirchen*, I, 641-3.

58. Minutes of the meeting on 14 Nov. 1933, LkA, EvKvW, 5.1, 99 F. 1, fos 63-5.

59. Ibid.

60. Cf. the minutes of various meetings on 16 Nov. 1933 in ZEKHN, 62/6043; Scholder, *Kirchen*, I, 786.

61. Minutes in Busch, *Reformationstag*, 121-31, quotes 122-4.

62. Ibid., 128.

63. Karl Barth to Günther Jacob, 15 Dec. 1933, KBA, 9233.371; text of the petition in WN, *Der Pfarrernotbund. Geschichte einer kämpfenden Bruderschaft* (Hamburg, 1973), 41.

64. Arnold Wiebel (ed.), *Christa Müller. Theologin im Kirchenkampf. Vikarin bei Martin Niemöller. Ihre Briefe an Rudolf Hermann (1933-1935)*, https://theologie.uni-greifswald.de/fileadmin/uni-greifswald/fakultaet/theologie/ls-sys/Unpublizierte_ Quellen/Korr__Briefe_Christa_Mueller_1933-1935.pdf (accessed 14 Jan. 2019), 13, 19. Emphasis in the original.

65. Karl Barth, *Vorträge und kleinere Arbeiten 1930-1933* (Zurich, 1994), quote 584, the text 587-9.

66. Karl Barth to Richard Karwehl, 17 Nov. 1933, quoted in ibid., 586.

67. Karl Barth to Gerhard Jacobi, 23 Dec. 1933, KBA, 9233.378; Scholder, *Kirchen*, I, 789.

68. MN to the members of the PEL, 16 Nov. 1933, LkA EvKvW, 5.1, 100, Fasc. 1, fos 27-9.

69. Quote: note of MN on the 'Lage, Geschehen, Forderungen', 24 Nov. 1933, ZEKHN, 62/6043; figures: WN, *Pfarrernotbund*, 29; Schmidt, *Niemöller*, 153-4.

70. Scholder, *Kirchen*, I, 799f.

71. Ibid., 800-12.

72. Minutes of a meeting between MN, Erich Seeberg, and Gerhard Stratenwerth on 18 Nov. 1933, ZEKHN, 62/6043.

73. Susanna Niesel, Bericht über einen offenen Abend bei Niemöller, 6 Dec. 1933, EZA, 619/4.

74. Scholder, *Kirchen*, I, 813-23.

75. Schmidt, *Niemöller*, 163-7.

76. Quote: AK 11 Jan. 1934; see Klaus Scholder, *Die Kirchen und das Dritte Reich.* Vol. 2: *Das Jahr der Ernüchterung. 1934, Barmen und Rom* (Frankfurt am Main and Berlin, 1988), 37-50.

77. Scholder, *Kirchen* II, 50, 53.

78. Quoted in ibid., 54.

79. Bentley, *Niemöller*, 85-7.

80. EN, Kleine Streiflichter aus der Kirchenkampfzeit der Jahre 1933-1937 [Nov. 1958], LkA EvKvW, 5.1, 456 F. 1, fo. 192; quote AK 25 Jan. 1934.

81. Scholder, *Kirchen*, II, 59-61. On Eisenhardt, see WN, *Hitler und die evangelischen Kirchenführer* (Bielefeld, 1959), 38. Quote 'Adjutant': *Karl Barth—Charlotte von*

Kirschbaum. Briefwechsel. Vol. 1: *1925–1935*, ed. Rolf-Joachim Erler (Zurich, 2008), 355, footnote 8.

82. EN to Walther Künneth, 19 Oct. 1938, ZEKHN, 62/6091.
83. Theophil Wurm to Hammerschmidt, 5 Apr. 1939, EZA 50/81, fo. 18 ('deliberately overlooked'); Scholder, *Kirchen*, II, 61–2.
84. Scholder, *Kirchen*, II, quotes 61–2.
85. AK 26 Jan. 1934.
86. Scholder, *Kirchen*, II, 62–4.
87. AK 25 Jan. 1934.
88. MN to the pastors of the Emergency League, 16 Feb. 1934, LkA EvKvW, 5.1, 435 F. 2, fo. 153; see Susanna Niesel, Bericht über den offenen Abend on 27 Feb. 1934, EZA, 619/6.
89. MN to the pastors of the Emergency League, 15 Feb. 1934, LkA EvKvW, 5.1., 99 F. 1, fo. 109.
90. Georg Schulz to the Sydow brethren, 13 Nov. 1933, LkA EvKvW, 5.1, 99 F. 1, fos 51–3, quote fo. 51.

Notes to Chapter 9

1. AK 27, 28 and 30 Jan. 1934; see WN, *Hitler und die evangelischen Kirchenführer*, 41.
2. 'German Church Conflict. Collapse of Opposition', *The Times*, 29 Jan. 1934, 11; see 'German Pastors' Struggle', *Manchester Guardian*, 29 Jan. 1934; Tagesmeldung des Geheimen Staatspolizeiamts 30 Jan. 1934: BArch, R 58, 3144, fo. 217.
3. Hans-Rainer Sandvoß, *"Es wird gebeten, die Gottesdienste zu überwachen." Religionsgemeinschaften in Berlin zwischen Anpassung, Selbstbehauptung und Widerstand von 1933 bis 1945* (Berlin, 2014), 59 (quote); Tagesmeldung des Gestapa, 29 Jan. 1934, BArch, R 58, 3441, fo. 202.
4. Daily report by the Gestapa, 12 Feb. 1934, BArch, R 58, 3145; Reich Ministry of the Interior to Prussian Minister President, 12 Feb. 1934, GStA PK, I. HA Rep. 90, Annex P, Nr. 52/1, fo. 34.
5. Schmidt, *Niemöller*, 181.
6. MN, *Dahlemer Predigten*, 103, 183–7.
7. ApU regional bishop to Consistory Berlin-Brandenburg, 26 Jan. 1934, EZA, 7/11661.
8. Schmidt, *Niemöller*, 186–8.
9. Quotes: MN to Müller, 1 Mar. 1934, ZEKHN, 62/6069; see petition of the Council of Brethren of the PEL of ApU, 13 Feb. 1934, LkA EvKvW, 5.1, 435 F 2, fo. 157; Ludwig Bartning et al. to Müller, 14 Feb. 1934, EZA, 7/11661
10. Schmidt, *Niemöller*, 181.
11. Letter to Erwin Sutz, 28 Apr. 1934, Dietrich Bonhoeffer, *Werke*, Vol. 13: *London 1933–1935*, ed. Goedeker, Hans, Heimbucher, Martin and Schleicher, Hans-Walter (Gütersloh, 1994), 128. Abbreviations in the original written out. See AK, 17 Feb. 1934.
12. Aussprechabend (conversation evening), 27 Mar. 1934, LkA EvKvW, 5.1, 435, F. 2, fo. 160.
13. Pastor Schaerffenberg to Consistorium Berlin with memo Otto Gruhl, 3 Apr. 1934, 9 Apr. 1934; memo of DC Consistory Councillor Otto Eckert undated [April 1934] ('open rebellion'); protocol note from meeting Gruhl with Röhricht, 7 Apr. 1934, and further documents in ELAB, 14/6367. See 'German Church Conflict. Primate's New Measures', *The Times*, 5 Apr. 1934.

14. Oscar Berger to Consistorium Berlin-Brandenburg, 9 June 1934, and verdict of Landgericht Berlin from 5 July 1934, ELAB, 14/6367; Schmidt, *Niemöller*, 189–91.

15. Ernst Fraenkel, *Der Doppelstaat. Recht und Justiz im "Dritten Reich"* (Frankfurt am Main, 1984).

16. Gailus, *Protestantismus*, 322.

17. 'German Pastor Preaches Gospel, Unafraid', *Literary Digest*, 12 May 1934, 18; see 'Nazi Primate's Opponents', *Manchester Guardian*, 26 Feb. 1934.

18. 'Ein Deutscher spricht', *National-Zeitung* (Basel), 6 Mar. 1934 (excerpt in LkA EvKvW, 5.1, 435 F. 2, fo. 70).

19. 'Der Pfarrer von Dahlem', *Neue Freie Presse*, 8 Apr. 1934.

20. Ibid.

21. 'Eine Predigt Niemöllers', *Neue Züricher Zeitung*, 9 Apr. 1934 (excerpt in LkA, EvKvW, 5.1, 435, F. 2, fo. 106).

22. MN, *Dahlemer Predigten*, 200–4.

23. Steigmann-Gall, *Holy Reich*, 86–113, 218–60; Manfred Gailus, '"Ein Volk – ein Reich – ein Glaube"? Religiöse Pluralisierungen in der NS-Weltanschauungsdiktatur', in Friedrich Wilhelm Graf and Klaus Große Kracht (eds), *Europäische Religionsgeschichte im 20. Jahrhundert* (Cologne, 2007), 203–24.

24. Schmidt, *Niemöller*, 176–7.

25. MN, 'Kirche? – Kirche! Ein Wort zur Stunde ernster Entscheidung', *JK* 2 (1934), 139–43, here 141.

26. Ibid., 142.

27. For example in the speech from 6 Feb. 1935, MN, 'Dienst der Kirche', quote 4.

28. MN to Pastor Walter Treu, 19 Dec. 1934, ZEKHN, 62/6016.

29. MN, 'Kirche? – Kirche!', 142.

30. 'Gemeinde und Kirche', *Bergisch-Märkische Zeitung*, undated [March 1934], excerpt in LkA EvKvW, 5.1, 435, F. 2, fo. 82.

31. Scholder, *Kirchen*, II, 75–85, quote 78.

32. Ibid., 85.

33. MN to the PEL members, circular no. 11, 28 Feb. 1934, LkA EvKvW, 5.1, 435, F. 2, fo. 155; cf. Schmidt, *Niemöller*, 196–7.

34. Scholder, *Kirchen*, II, 87–94.

35. Schmidt, *Niemöller*, 195–200; Scholder, *Kirchen*, II, 98–101.

36. MN, circular no. 12 of the PEL, 28 Mar. 1934, LkA EvKvW, 5.1, 816 F. 1, fo. 56.

37. Scholder, *Kirchen*, II, 102, 112–13.

38. AK 29 May 1934; see Scholder, *Kirchen*, II, 181–2.

39. AK 29 May 1934. Abbreviation in the original written out.

40. Nicolaisen, *Weg*, 24, 27–46.

41. Scholder, *Kirchen*, II, 173f.; Nicolaisen, *Weg*, 48–9; quote: Schmidt, *Niemöller*, 206.

42. Gerhard Niemöller (ed.), *Die erste Bekenntnissynode der Deutschen Evangelischen Kirche zu Barmen. Vol. 2: Text, Dokumente, Berichte* (Göttingen, 1959), 43–72, quote 47; Nicolaisen, *Weg*, 50–6.

43. AK 30 May 1934.

44. Statement by D. Hermann Sasse, 31 May 1934 (transcript), LkA EvKvW, 5.1, 70 F. 1, fos 81–2; cf. Scholder, *Kirchen*, II, 186.

45. Niemöller, *Bekenntnissynode zu Barmen*, II, 100, 104, 128 (quotes), 132–3, 137, 186, 188–9.

46. AK 31 May 1934. Abbreviations in the original written out; see MN, 'Die Bekenntnissynode', *Deutsche Allgemeine Zeitung* 1 July 1934 ('peak'); Niemöller, *Bekenntnissynode zu Barmen*, II, 150–7.

47. MN, 'Die Bekenntnissynode', *Deutsche Allgemeine Zeitung*, 1 July 1934.

48. Quoted in Meier, *Kirchenkampf*, I, 189.

49. MN, *Ein Wort zur kirchlichen Lage* (Wuppertal, 1936), 2–3.

50. Quoted in Meier, *Kirchenkampf*, I, 190. See online version with preamble at https://www.ekd.de/Barmer-Theologische-Erklarung-11292.htm (accessed 25 July 2017).

51. Niemöller, *Bekenntnissynode zu Barmen*, II, 56.

52. The text titled 'Unser Wort an die Gemeinden', signed by Asmussen, Niemöller, and other pastors on 5 Apr. 1934, postulated that 'Christ's community' wanted 'to finally be liberated from all dead liberalism', LkA EvKvW, 5.1, 100 F. 2, fo. 9.

53. See the interpretation by Scholder, *Kirchen*, II, 192; Wolf-Dieter Hauschild, *Konfliktgemeinschaft Kirche. Aufsätze zur Geschichte der Evangelischen Kirche in Deutschland* (Göttingen, 2004), 164–8, 201–20.

54. Matthew D. Hockenos, 'Pastor Martin Niemöller, German Protestantism, and German National Identity, 1933–1937', in John Carter Wood (ed.), *Christianity and National Identity in Twentieth-Century Europe Conflict, Community, and the Social Order* (Göttingen, 2016), 113 30, 121 2; quote: MN, *Dahlemer Predigten*, 127. See ibid., 123, 141, 148–9, 164, 174.

55. MN to Karl Barth, 3 May 1966, KBA 9125.404.0.

56. Scholder, *Kirchen*, II, 187, 203.

57. Andreas Kersting, *Kirchenordnung und Widerstand. Der Kampf um den Aufbau der Bekennenden Kirche der altpreußischen Union aufgrund des Dahlemer Notrechts von 1934 bis 1937* (Munich, 1994), 94–103, quotes 96, 101.

58. Quote: AK 21 June 1934; cf. Schmidt, *Niemöller*, 212–17; see materials in LkA EvKvW, 5.1, 474 F. 2.

59. *Martin Niemöller und sein Bekenntnis*, 46–8, 51.

60. Ibid., 49; see Rangliste 1914, 143; AK 19 July and 22 Aug. 1933; Roggelin, *Hildebrandt*, 66.

61. AK 11 July and 25 Dec. 1934.

62. Ziemann, 'Schiffe versenken', 24–5.

63. Niemöller, *U-Boat*, 217. The German original of the book used the term *völkisch* instead of 'our people'.

64. Ziemann, 'Schiffe versenken', quote 43.

65. Hannelore Braun and Carsten Nicolaisen (eds), *Verantwortung für die Kirche. Stenographische Aufzeichnungen und Mitschriften von Landesbischof Hans Meiser. 1933–1955*. Vol. I: *Sommer 1933 bis Sommer 1935* (Göttingen, 1985), 303–4, footnote 2. Quote: AK 30 June 1934.

66. Minutes from the meeting of the Reich Brethren on 2 July 1934, ZEKHN, 35/372; see Braun and Nicolaisen, *Verantwortung*, I, 308–9.

67. Schmidt, *Niemöller*, 218–20, 255.

68. MN to Rudolf Buttmann (transcript), 14 Aug. 1934, LkA EvKvW, 5.1, 436 F. 1, fos 143–5; Scholder, *Kirchen*, II, 336.

69. Sermon from 28 Oct. 1934: MN, *Dahlemer Predigten*, 243.

70. Scholder, *Kirchen*, II, 309–35, quote 332.
71. Schmidt, *Niemöller*, 222–4.
72. Braun and Nicolaisen, *Verantwortung*, I, 313.
73. Ibid.
74. Scholder, *Kirchen*, II, 206–12.
75. Arno Spranger, Warum können wir nicht Notbündler sein? undated [autumn 1934], LkA EvKvW, 5.1, 100 F. 2, fos 22–3; Meier, *Kirchenkampf*, I, 478–9.
76. Scholder, *Kirchen*, II, 295–7.
77. WN (ed.), *Die Preußensynode zu Dahlem. Die zweite Bekenntnissynode der Evangelischen Kirche der altpreußischen Union. Geschichte—Dokumente—Berichte* (Göttingen, 1975), 96–7, 104–5, 118–19 (quotes), 129, 131, 137.
78. Ibid., 143–4, quote 149.
79. Ibid., quote 150.
80. Scholder, *Kirchen*, II, 345, 348.
81. Kersting, *Kirchenordnung*, 121–2.
82. Scholder, *Kirchen*, II, 297–306; Schmidt, *Niemöller*, 234–5.
83. Scholder, *Kirchen*, II, 348–52.
84. Schmidt, *Niemöller*, 236–9.
85. Minutes from the meeting of the Reich Brethren from 9 Nov. 1934 in Dahlem, LkA EvKvW, 5.1, 79 F. 1, fos 38–43, quotes fo. 39, 42. Abbreviations in the original written out. See Meier, *Kirchenkampf*, I, 512–16.
86. Minutes from the meeting of the Reich Brethren from 9 Nov. 1934 in Dahlem, LkA EvKvW, 5.1, 79 F. 1, fos 40–1.
87. WN, Von der Dahlemer Synode bis zur Gründung der ersten Vorläufigen Kirchenleitung (auch in: *Evangelische Theologie* 19 (1959)), LkA EvKvW, 5.1, 79 F. 2, fos 145–64, here fo. 149.
88. 'Große Kundgebungen der Bekenntniskirche in Berlin', *Basler Nachrichten*, 10 Nov. 1934, LkA EvKvW, 5.1, 436 F. 1, fo. 57.
89. Schmidt, *Niemöller im Kirchenkampf*, 239–40.
90. MN to Wilhelm Frick, 4 Dec. 1934, LkA EvKvW, 5.1, 436 F. 1, fos 153–4.
91. Meier, *Kirchenkampf*, I, 514, 518–23.
92. Ibid., 515–16, 520–1.
93. MN to Georg Wehrung, 7 Dec. 1934, LkA EvKvW, 5.1, 79 F. 2, fo. 100; Schmidt, *Niemöller*, 244; Braun and Nicolaisen, *Verantwortung*, I, S, 357–8, 376; Meier, *Kirchenkampf*, I, 519.
94. Schmidt, *Niemöller*, 244–5; see Paul Humburg to Praeses Koch, 31 Oct. 1934, ZEKHN, 62/6069. See also Scholder, *Kirchen*, II, 184.
95. Karl Barth to MN, 22 Nov. 1934, KBA 9234.333.
96. MN to Karl Barth, 26 Nov. 1934, KBA 9125.356.

Notes to Chapter 10

1. Schmidt, *Niemöller*, 246–50.
2. MN to Wilhelm Zoellner, 16 Jan. 1935, ZEKHN 35/373; on Marahrens' letter, see Schmidt, *Niemöller*, 245.

370 NOTES

3. Circular no. 18 of the PEL, 9 Feb. 1935, LkA EvKvW, 5.1, 436 F. 1, fo. 130.

4. Paul Winckler, member of the VKL, to MN, 29 Jan. 1935 and MN's reply from 30 Jan. 1935, LkA EvKvW, 5.1, 81 F. 1, fos 45–6; Schmidt, *Niemöller*, 280–7.

5. MN to Karl Immer, 31 Jan. 1935, WN, *Preußensynode zu Dahlem*, 6–7.

6. Brochure 'To the Parishes', draft from 28 Feb. 1935, adopted by the synod on 5 March without changes of this part: WN, *Preußensynode zu Dahlem*, 15–16.

7. Besier, *Kirchen*, 62.

8. MN to Pastor Schapper, 13 Mar. 1935, WN, *Preußensynode zu Dahlem*, 21–2; Schmidt, *Niemöller*, 272–4, quote 272.

9. Besier, *Kirchen*, 62–4.

10. Schmidt, *Niemöller*, 275.

11. MN to Lutz Graf Schwerin von Krosigk, 1 May 1935, ZEKHN, 35/403; see MN to Lutz Graf Schwerin von Krosigk, 16 June 1934, LkA EvKvW, 5.1, 436 F. 1, fo. 138; Besier, *Kirchen*, 31.

12. MN to Praeses Karl Koch, 3 May 1935, LkA EvKvW, 5.1, 436 F. 2, fos 1–3.

13. Schmidt, *Niemöller*, 285–7.

14. Ibid., 292.

15. WN (ed.), *Die dritte Bekenntnissynode der Deutschen Evangelischen Kirche zu Augsburg. Text, Dokumente, Berichte* (Göttingen, 1969), 85–7.

16. Schmidt, *Niemöller*, 291.

17. Braun and Nicolaisen, *Verantwortung*, I, 424.

18. Besier, *Kirchen*, 107–9; Hans-Jörg Reese, *Bekenntnis und Bekennen. Vom 19. Jahrhundert zum Kirchenkampf der nationalsozialistischen Zeit* (Göttingen, 1974), 333–55.

19. WN, *Augsburg*, 165.

20. Text of the circular in Dietrich Bonhoeffer, *Gesammelte Schriften*. Vol. 2: *Kirchenkampf und Finkenwalde. Resolutionen, Aufsätze, Rundbriefe, 1933 bis 1943* (Munich, 1965), 205–9, quotes 206–7; Schmidt, *Niemöller*, 294–6.

21. Bonhoeffer, *Gesammelte Schriften*, II, 205.

22. Bodelschwingh to Karl Immer, 8 Aug. 1935, quoted in Besier, *Kirchen*, 110–11; see WN, *Die zweite Bekenntnissynode*, 38.

23. Braun and Nicolaisen, *Verantwortung*, I, 420, 423–4; Besier, *Kirchen*, 110.

24. Kreutzer, *Reichskirchenministerium*, 75–130; Besier, *Kirchen*, 287–336.

25. Besier, *Kirchen*, 305.

26. Bodelschwingh, notes from a meeting with Church Minister Kerrl on 23 Aug. 1935 (quotes), as well as notes from this meeting by the office of the VKL, 4 Sept. 1935. HAB, 2/39–44; cf. Besier, *Kirchen*, 305–18. The quote 'solely ecclesiastic' in Niemöller's notes from this meeting, which diverge in some details from Bodelschwingh's notes written down in shorthand: MN, 23 Aug. 1935, LkA EvKvW, 5.1 19 F. 1, fos 7–11, here fo. 9.

27. Bodelschwingh, notes of a meeting with Church Minister Kerrl on 23 Aug. 1935, HAB, 2/39–44.

28. Notes MN, 23 Aug. 1935, LkA EvKvW, 5.1, 19 F. 1, fo. 10. Abbreviations in the original written out.

29. Bodelschwingh, notes from a meeting with Church Minister Kerrl on 23 Aug. 1935, HAB, 2/39–44; on anti-liberal tendencies of 1920s theology, cf. Graf, *Zeitgeist*, 425–46.

Niemöller's notes on this read: 'The Church is no slave to liberalism. [...] (not more liberal).' Notes MN, 23 Aug. 1935, LkA EvKvW, 5.1, 19 F 1., fo. 11.

30. Besier, *Kirchen*, 318.

31. MN, report about his meeting with Kerrl on 26 Aug. 1935 (quotes) and 29 Aug. 1935, HAB, 2/39–44; MN to Marahrens, 29 Aug. 1935, HAB, 2/39–44.

32. Schmidt, *Niemöller*, 302–5.

33. Besier, *Kirchen*, 322–3, quote 323.

34. MN to Julius Stahn, 2 and 4 Sept. 1935 (quotes), LkA EvKvW, 5.1, 19 F. 1, fo. 22, 36–7.

35. Besier, *Kirchen*, 326–7, 337–46.

36. WN (ed.), *Die Synode zu Steglitz. Die Dritte Bekenntnissynode der Evangelischen Kirche der Altpreußischen Union. Geschichte, Dokumente, Berichte* (Göttingen, 1970), 166–70, quote 168.

37. Kurt Meier, *Der evangelische Kirchenkampf.* Vol. II: *Gescheiterte Neuordnungsversuche im Zeichen staatlicher 'Rechtshilfe'*, 2nd edn (Göttingen, 1984), 159–62; WN, *Synode zu Steglitz*, 106–19.

38. MN to RBR/Karl Koch, 12 Aug. 1935, LkA EvKvW, 5.1, 99 F. 1, fo. 148.

39. Siegfried Knak, 'Ein Wort der Mission zur Rassenfrage', *Berliner Missionsberichte* 111 (1935), 157–9, quotes 158–9; see Bergen, *Twisted Cross*, 31; Meier, *Kirchenkampf*, II, 25.

40. WN, *Synode zu Steglitz*, 84, 120, 133.

41. Günter Jacob to MN, 13 Sept. 1935, LkA EvKvW, 5.1, 59 F. 1, fo. 25; see MN, *Das Bekenntnis der Väter und die bekennende Gemeinde. Zur Besinnung dargeboten von einem Kreise von evangelischen Theologen* (Munich, 1933), 24.

42. Schmidt, *Niemöller*, 315–16.

43. WN, *Synode zu Steglitz*, 20.

44. Ibid., 234.

45. Noss, *Albertz*, 326–7; Roggelin, *Hildebrandt*, 94–5.

46. WN, *Synode zu Steglitz*, 302.

47. Ibid., 304–9.

48. Stapo-Leitstelle Bielefeld to Gestapa Berlin (copy), 4 Sept. 1935, LkA EvKvW, 5.1, 19 F. 1, fo. 27.

49. WN, *Synode zu Steglitz*, 132.

50. Ibid., 302. With the formulation 'of the flesh', Niemöller might refer to passages such as Romans 8: 1–17, where St Paul talks about 'life through the spirit'. But it remains open whether Niemöller wanted to emphasize the inclusion of the baptized brethren in the spirit, or whether he emphasizes their origins as Jews 'of the flesh', for instance through circumcision. It might well be the case that Niemöller used this ambiguous formulation to obfuscate his own position on this thorny issue. I am indebted to Stefan Meili for pointing out this problem to me.

51. MN, *Dahlemer Predigten*, 355–9, quotes 357. Cf. MN, *Dahlemer Predigten*, 155–60, 258–64, 345–9, also the sermons from 20 Aug. 1933, 16 Jan. and 4 Aug. 1935.

52. MN, *Die Bedeutung des Alten Testaments für die christliche Kirche* (Berlin, undated [1936]), quotes 5, 12.

53. MN, 'Der Friede Gottes und die Kraft des wehrhaften Mannes', in: Eberhard Müller (ed.), *Wahrheit und Wirklichkeit der Kirche. Vorträge und geistliche Reden, gehalten auf*

der Eeutschen Evangelischen Woche, 26.–30. August 1935 in Hannover (Berlin, 1935). A slightly different manuscript of this talk in ZEKHN, 62/6076.

54. SE 24 June 1943. Else Niemöller shared this view. See her letter from 18 Sept. 1939 to MN, ZEKHN, 62/6081.

55. MN, 'Der Friede Gottes', quotes 244–6, 248, 251.

56. Quoted in Besier, *Kirchen*, 919; see also 57.

57. MN, *Dahlemer Predigten*, 265–270, quote 269.

58. Besier, *Kirchen*, 337–48, quote 348.

59. Quoted in ibid., 345.

60. Schmidt, *Niemöller*, 321, 338–47; see Kurt Dietrich Schmidt (ed.), *Dokumente des Kirchenkampfes*. Vol. 2: *Die Zeit des Reichskirchenausschusses 1935–1937. Zweiter Teil (29. Mai 1936 bis Ende Februar 1937)* (Göttingen, 1965), 83–94, quote 94.

61. MN to Landgerichtsrat Kramer in Allenstein (quote), 22 Oct. 1935; MN to Kueßner, 29 Oct. 1935, LkA EvKvW, 5.1, 201 F. 1, fo. 194, 202; see Meier, *Kirchenkampf*, II, 190–2.

62. Minutes from the meeting of the Reich Brethren Council on 3 Jan. 1936, LkA EvKvW, 5.1, 93 F. 2, fo. 107. Emphasis in the original, abbreviations in the original written out.

63. See WN (ed.), *Die Vierte Bekenntnissynode der Deutschen Evangelischen Kirche zu Bad Oeynhausen. Text, Dokumente, Berichte* (Göttingen, 1960), 33–6; Schmidt, *Niemöller*, 347–51. For the resolution of the Reich Brethren Council on 3 Jan. 1926, see Schmidt, *Dokumente*, II/1, 188–9.

64. See Schmidt, *Dokumente*, II/1, 189–91, 199–205, 226–45.

65. As Besier correctly argues, *Kirchen*, 429.

66. MN, Woher kommt die Spaltung in der Bekennenden Kirche, speech on 1 Feb. 1935, LkA EvKvW, 5.1, 436 F. 2, fos 179–89.

67. Pastor Theodor Moldaenke to MN, 28 Oct. 1935 and his reply 30 Oct. 1935 (quote), LkA EvKvW, 5.1, 19 F. 2, fos 65, 69.

68. Praeses Koch to Asmussen, 12 Jan. 1936, quoted in WN, *Bekenntnissynode Bad Oeynhausen*, 37.

69. Schmidt, *Niemöller*, 351–3.

70. WN, *Bekenntnissynode Bad Oeynhausen*, 157–75, quotes 170, 173–4.

71. MN, 'Missionierende Kirche', *Die Stimme der Gemeinde* 16 (1936), issue 9, 6–15, quotes 13–14.

72. WN, *Bekenntnissynode Bad Oeynhausen*, 112–15, 221–35, 318–19.

73. Besier, *Kirchen*, 426–8.

74. Gailus, *Protestantismus*, 333.

75. MN to Röhricht (the quote from an earlier letter by Röhricht to Niemöller), 10 Oct. 1936, ZEKHN, 62/6074.

76. MN to Bodelschwingh (quote), 11 Sept. 1936, HAB, 2/39–183, fo. 1094; see MN, Friedrich Müller, and Franz Hildebrandt to Röhricht, 20 Nov. 1936, ZEKHN, 62/6074.

77. Gertrud Freyss for the group helping with Sunday school to MN, 6 June 1937, and his reply 8 June 1937, LkA EvKvW, 5.1, 474 F. 1, fos 31–2; Gailus, *Protestantismus*, 334–5.

78. Besier, *Kirchen*, 399, 440–3, 461–7, quote 441.

79. Schmidt, *Niemöller*, 361–5, quote 362.

80. MN to Bodelschwingh, 6 Apr. 1936, ZEKHN 62/6002; see MN to Kurt Frör, 24 Apr. 1936, LkA EvKvW, 5.1, 77 F. 2, fos 57–8.

81. Meier, *Kirchenkampf*, II, 12–35.
82. MN to Zoellner, 30 Apr. 1936, LkA EvKvW, 5.1, 368a, fo. 5; Ley quoted in Schmidt, *Niemöller*, 402.
83. 'Brief von Martin Niemöller', n.d. [1936]: EZA 50/686.
84. See Martin Greschat (ed.), *Zwischen Widerspruch und Widerstand. Texte zur Denkschrift der Bekennenden Kirche an Hitler (1936)* (Munich, 1987), 25–9, quote 26.
85. Ibid., 34–78.
86. Greschat, *Widerspruch und Widerstand*, 97–103, quotes 97, 100.
87. Ibid.; for the final draft with appendix, see 104–43, quote 105–6.
88. Ibid., 7.
89. Quotes from the final draft, ibid., 104, 114, 117.
90. Manfred Gailus, *Friedrich Weißler. Ein Jurist und Bekennender Christ im Widerstand gegen Hitler* (Göttingen, 2017), 125–89; see also Besier, *Kirchen*, 488–96.
91. Gailus, *Friedrich Weißler*, 148, thinks that responsibility for the leak cannot be established. Greschat, *Widerspruch und Widerstand*, 148–52, rules out Weißler's responsibility.
92. Gailus, *Friedrich Weißler*, 231.
93. MN to Pastor Max Goosmann, 11 Sept. 1936, ZEKHN, 35/373.
94. Cf. MN quote in AK 28 Apr. 1936.
95. Quoted in Gailus, *Friedrich Weißler*, 160. Emphasis in the original.
96. See ibid., 187; Noss, *Albertz*, 279. In a letter from 6 Jan. 1937 to Pastor Georg Kühn in Solnhofen, Niemöller claimed that 'no-one' in the VKL believed Weißler 'capable of a morally condemnable attitude' (ZEKHN, 35/403). But this belated declaration of honour did not balance out his behaviour at the crucial meetings.
97. Text in Greschat, *Widerspruch und Widerstand*, 182–5, quote 185.
98. Text in ibid., 189–97, quotes 192, 195, 197.
99. Schmidt, *Niemöller*, 400–1; Besier, *Kirchen*, 502.
100. 'Nazis and the Church', *The Times*, 24 Aug. 1936; see MN, *Dahlemer Predigten*, 479–82.
101. AK 23 Aug. 1936.
102. MN, *Die Staatskirche ist da. Denkschrift aus der Bekennenden Kirche* (Wuppertal, 1936); see Schmidt, *Niemöller*, 327–8.
103. MN, *Staatskirche*, 4, 8.
104. Degree certificate, 3 June 1936: Eden Theological Seminary, archive, Niemöller files. I am grateful to Scott Holl, archivist at Eden Theological Seminary, for providing me copies of these documents. See AK 8 Jan. 1947.

Notes to Chapter 11

1. Schmidt, *Niemöller*, 401.
2. Gestapo report from 21 Sept. 1936, LkA EvKvW, 5.1, 467 F. 2, fos 17–20; see AK 18 Sept. 1936.
3. Gestapo report from 21 Sept. 1936, LkA EvKvW, 5.1, 467 F. 2, fos 17–20.
4. Statement MN on 18 Feb. 1938, GSA, P 3 Niemöller, Martin 2/1, fos 89–90.

5. Attorney General at the Regional Court Berlin, indictment from 13 July 1937, LkA EvKvW, 5.1, 466 F. 1, fos 6–23.

6. Gestapa II I B I 24 [November] 1936 to the Reich Minister for Church Affairs (copy), LkA EvKvW, 5.1, 467 F. 2, fos 30–5, fo. 30; see Besier, *Kirchen*, 324.

7. Report about the meeting of Westphalian theology students of the Confessing Church in Dortmund on 17–18 Oct. 1936, LkA EvKvW, 5.1, 467 F. 2, fos 24–9, quote fos 27–8.

8. Gestapa II I B I, 24 Nov. 1936 to the Reich Minister for Church Affairs, LkA EvKvW, 5.1, 467, F. 2, fo. 35.

9. Report about the theological course in Dahlem from 1 to 30 Sept. 1936, LkA EvKvW, 5.1, 467 F. 2, fos 21–3.

10. Report about the meeting of Westphalian theology students of the Confessing Church in Dortmund on 17–18 Oct. 1936, LkA EvKvW, 5.1, 467 F. 2, fos 24–9, fo. 27.

11. Statement August Kopff from 22 Feb. 1938, GSA, P 3 Niemöller, Martin 2/2, fo. 123; see SD II 1133 2 June 1937 to Heydrich, BArch, R 58, 5729.

12. EN to MN, 18 Sept. 1939, ZEKHN, 62/6081.

13. Benjamin Ziemann, 'Der Prozess gegen Martin Niemöller vor dem Berliner Sondergericht 1938', *Zeitschrift für Geschichtswissenschaft* 66 (2018), 299–317, 301.

14. Besier, *Kirchen*, 638–41; Schmidt, *Niemöller*, 411–16, quote 415.

15. Meier, *Kirchenkampf*, II, 148–54, quote 148.

16. Ibid., 149.

17. Schmidt, *Niemöller*, 418–21, quote 419.

18. MN to Pastor Dr Kühn in Leipzig, 17 Mar. 1937, ZEKHN, 35/403.

19. MN to Pastor Georg Kühn, 6 Jan. 1937, ZEKHN, 35/403.

20. Walter Adolph, *Geheime Aufzeichnungen aus dem nationalsozialistischen Kirchenkampf 1935–1943*, ed. Ulrich von Hehl (Mainz, 1979), 58.

21. Schmidt, *Niemöller*, 391.

22. Notes about the open evening on 7 June 1937, ZEKHN, 62/6020.

23. Schmidt, *Niemöller*, 421–2; quote: Benjamin Ziemann, 'Martin Niemöller und die Wartestandsaffäre 1939/40. Ein Kapitel aus der Geschichte des Kampfes gegen die Bekennende Kirche', *Schweizerische Zeitschrift für Religions- und Kulturgeschichte* 111 (2017), 317–38, 333.

24. Schmidt, *Niemöller*, 422–5.

25. Ziemann, 'Prozess', 302.

26. Quoted in ibid., 302–3.

27. Ibid., 303.

28. For the following, see Ziemann, 'Prozess'.

29. Ziemann, 'Prozess', 306.

30. Notes about the open evening on 7 June 1937, ZEKHN, 62/6020.

31. Notes about the open evening on 21 June 1937, ZEKHN, 62/6020; see Schmidt, *Niemöller*, 428–9.

32. Notes about the open evening on 28 June 1937, ZEKHN, 62/6020.

33. Schmidt, *Niemöller*, 432. Text of his last sermon in MN, *Dahlemer Predigten*, 649–56.

34. *Völkischer Beobachter*, No. 183, 2 July 1937, BArch, R 8034 II, 1864, fo. 68.

35. Letters from 6 July 1937 and 12 Feb. 1938, MN, *Briefe Moabit*, 22, 300–1.

36. WN, *Synode zu Steglitz*, 347, 351, 358–60.

37. MN to WN, 24 Nov. 1951, ZEKHN, 62/672; see the correspondence in ZEKHN, 62/1504 (here especially MN to Holstein, 9 Sept. 1945) and 62/6069.

38. Sebastian Sigler, 'Hans Koch – ein deutsches Schicksal im Widerstand', *Einst und Jetzt* 57 (2012), 339–50.

39. *Handbuch der dt. evangelischen Kirchen*, vol. 2, 105.

40. WN, *Macht*, 30; MN, *Briefe Moabit*, 186, 279.

41. MN, *Briefe Moabit*, quotes 76 (30 Oct. 1937), 86 (5 Nov. 1937).

42. Schäberle-Königs, *Und sie waren*, 38–45.

43. MN, *Briefe Moabit*, 227.

44. WN, *Macht geht vor Recht. Der Prozeß Martin Niemöllers* (Munich, 1952), 32–3; on further activities after Niemöller was sent to the concentration camp, see Günter Brakelmann (ed.), *Kirche im Krieg. Der deutsche Protestantismus am Beginn des Zweiten Weltkriegs* (Munich, 1979), 77–97.

45. Scholder, *Kirchen*, II, 102–3 (quote); see Ronald C.D. Jasper, *George Bell, Bishop of Chichester* (London, 1967).

46. Andrew Chandler, *Brethren in Adversity: Bishop George Bell, the Church of England and the crisis of German Protestantism, 1933–1939* (Woodbridge, 1997), 1–32, quotes 122–3.

47. George Bell to Rudolf Heß, 2 July 1937, BArch, NS 15/430, fo. 7.

48. Rudolf Heß to George Bell, 11 July 1937, BArch, NS 15/430, fos 2–5. The original in: LPL, Bell papers 10, fos 23–4.

49. George Chichester, 'Letter to the editor', *The Times*, 3 July 1937.

50. Chandler, *Brethren in Adversity*, 91.

51. Research in Times Digital Archive: http://find.galegroup.com.sheffield.idm.oclc.org (accessed 30 Jan. 2018).

52. Research in ProQuest Manchester Guardian Archive: https://search-proquest-com.sheffield.idm.oclc.org (accessed 22 Feb. 2018). On the coverage of German Protestant Church politics in the *Times* until 1939, see Markus Huttner, *Britische Presse und nationalsozialistischer Kirchenkampf. Eine Untersuchung der "Times" und des "Manchester Guardian" von 1930 bis 1939* (Paderborn, 1995), 205–39.

53. Alfred Wiener, 'Untersuchungen zum Widerhall des deutschen Kirchenkampfes in England (1933–1938)', in Max Beloff (ed.), *On the Track of Tyranny: Essays presented by the Wiener Library to Leonard G. Montefiore, O.B.E., on the occasion of his seventieth birthday* (London, 1960), 211–32, 221.

54. Keith Robbins, 'Martin Niemöller, the German Church Struggle and English Opinion', *Journal of Ecclesiastical History* 21 (1970), 149–70, 162–5.

55. Meier, *Kirchenkampf*, vol. 2, 152.

56. Gottfried Abrath, *Subjekt und Milieu im NS-Staat: Die Tagebücher des Pfarrers Hermann Klugkist Hesse 1936–1939. Analyse und Dokumentation* (Göttingen, 1994), quote 268.

57. Ibid., 175–6, quote 314 (abbreviation in the original written out).

58. Ibid., 319–20 (quotes), 370, 372.

59. MN, *Briefe Moabit*, 212, 207.

60. Indictment of 13 July 1937, LkA EvKvW, 5.1, 466 F. 1, quote fo. 8.

61. Ziemann, 'Prozess', 308–9.

62. MN, *Briefe Moabit*, 70, 150, 175, quote 197 (31 Dec. 1937).

63. Ibid., 104 and 199 (quotes), 251.

64. Ziemann, 'Prozess', 309.

65. File memo by the Reichskirchenministerium, 1 Feb. 1938, BArch, R 5101/23696.

66. Ralf Georg Reuth (ed.), *Joseph Goebbels Tagebücher 1924–1945*, 5 vols (Munich, 1992), vol. 3, 1198–9.

67. File memo for Hermann Muhs, 16 Dec. 1937, BArch, R 5101/23696.

68. Ziemann, 'Prozess', 310.

69. Report SDHA II 1133/Gahrmann, 8 Feb. 1938, BArch, R 58/5453, fos 159–60.

70. Buchheim, 'NS-Funktionär', 312–13.

71. Ibid., 313.

72. Ibid., 314–15.

73. Ziemann, 'Prozess', 313.

74. Reuth, *Goebbels Tagebücher*, vol. 3, 1206.

75. Ziemann, 'Prozess', 314.

76. Ibid.

77. Ibid.

78. MN, *Briefe Moabit*, 257.

79. Ziemann, 'Prozess', 315.

80. Ibid., 315.

81. Ibid., 316. Hockenos, *Then They Came for Me*, 135, repeats the legend that Hitler ordered Niemöller's transfer to Sachsenhausen only after hearing the verdict.

82. MN to Ehrenberg (copy), 26 Sept. 1945, LPL, CFR, LRC 43/1, fo. 3.

83. From the extensive literature, see only Gerhard Besier, 'Ansätze zum politischen Widerstand in der Bekennenden Kirche. Zur gegenwärtigen Forschungslage', in Jürgen Schmädeke and Peter Steinbach (eds), *Der Widerstand gegen den Nationalsozialismus: Die deutsche Gesellschaft und der Widerstand gegen Hitler* (Munich/Zurich, 1985), 265–80; Robert P. Ericksen, 'A Radical Minority: Resistance in the German Protestant Church', in Francis R. Nicosia and Lawrence D. Stokes (eds), *Germans Against Nazism. Nonconformity, Opposition and Resistance in the Third Reich: Essays in Honour of Peter Hoffmann* (New York/Oxford, 1990), 115–35; Klaus Scholder, 'Politischer Widerstand oder Selbstbehauptung als Problem der Kirchenleitungen', in Jürgen Schmädeke and Peter Steinbach (eds), *Der Widerstand gegen den Nationalsozialismus: Die deutsche Gesellschaft und der Widerstand gegen Hitler* (Munich/Zurich, 1985), 254–64; Günther van Norden, 'Widerstand im deutschen Protestantismus 1933–1945', in Christoph Kleßmann and Falk Pingel (eds), *Gegner des Nationalsozialismus. Wissenschaftler und Widerstandskämpfer auf der Suche nach historischer Wirklichkeit* (Frankfurt am Main, 1980), 103–25. On Bonhoeffer, see Charles Marsh, *Strange Glory: A Life of Dietrich Bonhoeffer* (New York, 2014), 318–19, 325–32, 340–5.

84. Scholder, 'Politischer Widerstand', 260.

85. Niemöller's speech on 10 Feb. 1937. Gestapa to the Minister for Church Affairs, 11 Mar. 1937, LkA EvKvW, 5.1, 467 F. 2, fo. 40.

86. Here I am following Richard Löwenthal, 'Widerstand im totalen Staat', in Richard Löwenthal and Patrik von zur Mühlen (eds), *Widerstand und Verweigerung in*

Deutschland 1933 bis 1945 (Berlin/Bonn, 1984), 11–24, and especially Peter Steinbach, 'Der Widerstand als Thema der politischen Zeitgeschichte', in Gerhard Besier and Gerhard Ringshausen (eds), *Bekenntnis, Widerstand, Martyrium. Von Barmen 1934 bis Plötzensee 1944* (Göttingen, 1986), 11–74, 37. Ian Kershaw, *The Nazi Dictatorship: Problems and Perspectives of Interpretation*, 4th edn (London, 2015), 240, suggests using the term 'opposition' for practices of this kind.

87. Dietrich Bonhoeffer, *Werke*, ed. Hans Goedeker, Martin Heimbucher, and Hans-Walter Schleicher, vol. 13: *London 1933–1935* (Gütersloh, 1994), 349–58, quote 353–4; see Norden, 'Widerstand', 107.

88. Michael Geyer, 'Resistance as Ongoing Project: Visions of Order, Obligations to Strangers, Struggles for Civil Society', *Journal of Modern History* 64 (1992), Supplement, 217–41, 225–6.

Notes to Chapter 12

1. 'Erinnerung Martin Niemöllers über die Verschleppung ins KZ Sachsenhausen', *c.*1946, ZEKHN, 35/1521.

2. Ibid.

3. SDHA/II 1133 to the Staff of the Führer's Deputy, 3 Mar. 1938, BArch, R 58, 5453, fo. 238. It was well-known in the Ministry for Church Affairs that Niemöller was 'under special protection of the camp commander at the Führer's command'. Note of Dr Albrecht in the Ministry for Church Affairs on 30 Aug. 1938, BArch, R 5101/23696.

4. Volker Koop, *In Hitlers Hand: Sonder- und Ehrenhäftlinge der SS* (Cologne/Weimar/Vienna, 2010), 79–110.

5. Parish church council Dahlem to the Führer and Chancellor, 31 Mar. 1938, and Lammer's reply, 26 Apr. 1938, Ludwig Bartning to Lammers, 11 May 1938, Lammers to Admiral Raeder, 30 May 1938, BArch, R 43/II, 155, fos 172–4, 183.

6. EN to 'Mein Führer!', 18 Apr. 1939, Lammers to EN, 25 Apr. 1939, BArch, R 43/II, 155, fos 206–7, 210.

7. File memo Dr Meerwald, 14 July 1939, BArch, R 43/II, 155, fos 241–2.

8. Lammers to the Fuehrer's adjutancy, 16 July 1939, note by Dr Meerwald, 19 July 1939, BArch, R 43/II, 155, fos 243–4.

9. Note by Marotzke in the office of the Prussian Minister President Göring, 4 Dec. 1939, GStA PK, I. HA Rep. 90, Annex P, No. 53/1, fo. 2; see Hermann Göring to Prof. Friedrich Bremer, 16 Dec. 1938, ZEKHN, 35/1511.

10. According to Berggrav's note on the meeting from 13 Feb. 1941, quoted in Alex Johnson, *Eivind Berggrav: Mann der Spannung* (Göttingen, 1960), 188.

11. MN, *Briefe Moabit*, 180, 189 (22 and 27 Dec. 1937).

12. 'Fate of Dr. Niemöller', *Manchester Guardian*, 4 Mar. 1938.

13. MN to the 'commander of the Sachsenhausen concentration camp' (his own written copy), 8 May 1938, ZEKHN 62/6063. Emphasis in the original.

14. In his notes written in Polish imprisonment in 1946–7, Rudolf Höß claimed Niemöller had rejected Lans's suggestion. It is, however, very likely that—contrary to his claim—Höß, who at that time was adjutant of the camp commander, did not have access to all

the correspondence relating to Niemöller. Rudolf Höß, *Kommandant in Auschwitz. Autobiographische Aufzeichnungen*, ed. Martin Broszat (Munich, 1992), 83–4.

15. See the evidence added by WN in MN, *Briefe aus der Gefangenschaft. Konzentrationslager Sachsenhausen (Oranienburg)*, ed. Wilhelm Niemöller (Bielefeld, 1979), 39, note 2.

16. [WN], note about the visitor's permit from 29 Aug. 1938, ZEKHN, 62/6179.

17. EN to Raeder, 16 June 1938, ZEKHN, 62/6090; cf. Schmidt, *Niemöller*, 345.

18. Erich Raeder to EN, 24 June 1938, ZEKHN, 35/1512. Publicly, Raeder denied his commitment to Niemöller. See his letter from 28 May 1938 to Fritz Klingler, leader of the Reichsbund der Deutsch-Evangelischen Pfarrervereine (Reich League of German Protestant Pastors' Associations), a copy of which the chief of staff of the commander-in-chief of the German navy sent, among others, to the Ministries for Propaganda and for Church Affairs on 31 May 1938. BArch, R 5101/23696.

19. According to a remark during a conversation with Else, Niemöller himself had also written to Raeder, namely on 16 Aug. 1939. The context, however, suggests this letter was about him being placed into temporary retirement *(Wartestand)*, rather than his release. SE 24 Aug. 1939.

20. Erich Raeder to HN, 16 Jan. 1939, LkA EvKvW, 5.1, 440 F. 1, fo. 16.

21. Hildegard von Kotze (ed.), *Heeresadjudant bei Hitler 1938–1943. Aufzeichnungen des Majors Engel* (Stuttgart, 1974), 44 (17 Jan. 1939).

22. 'The German Church. Politics and the Pulpit', *The Times*, 14 July 1938.

23. Hans Böhm to the Bishop of Gloucester, 18 July and 1 Aug. 1938 and his reply from 8 Aug. 1938, EZA, 50/550, fos 4–6.

24. Instructions for the press from 7 Jan. and 3 June 1939: Karen Peter (ed.), *NS-Presseanweisungen der Vorkriegszeit. Edition und Dokumentation*. Vol. 7/I: *1939, Quellentexte Januar bis April* (Munich, 2001), 24, and Karen Peter, *NS-Presseanweisungen der Vorkriegszeit. Edition und Dokumentation*. Vol. 7/II: *1939, Quellentexte Mai bis August* (Munich, 2001), 534; MN, *Briefe Sachsenhausen*, 29, note 1; WN, *Aus dem Leben eines Bekenntnispfarrers* (Bielefeld, 1961), 219–20.

25. SE 30 Mar. 1939.

26. Reuth, *Goebbels Tagebücher*, vol. 4, 1512.

27. Theophil Wurm to EN, 24 Aug. 1943, ZEKHN, 62/6090; see EN to Wurm, 7 Dec. 1944, Wurm to Kaltenbrunner (draft),18 Dec. 1944, LkA Stuttgart, A 126, 2156, fos 164–5.

28. See the erroneous remark by Richard J. Evans, *The Third Reich in Power 1933–1939* (London, 2006), 232, who relies, without source criticism, on the invented account of a fictitious Sachsenhausen inmate under the name of Leo Stein.

29. Interview with Harry Dubinski, 11, GSA, P 3, Dubinsky, Harry; Nachtrag zu den Erinnerungen des ehemaligen Schutzhäftlings 1245 G. Wackernagel, GSA, P 3 Wackernagel, Günter, fo. 41.

30. SE 20 Feb. and 6 Mar. 1941 (quote).

31. Hans Reichmann, *Deutscher Bürger und verfolgter Jude. Novemberpogrom und KZ Sachsenhausen 1937 bis 1939*, ed. Michael Wildt (Munich, 1998), 141.

32. MN to Rudolf Wunderlich, 11 Mar. 1961, GSA, Ordner ZB.

33. Kommandantur KL Sachsenhausen to SS-Oberführer von Alvensleben, 6 Mar. 1939, BArch, R 43/II, 155, fo. 236.

34. Nationale Mahn- und Gedenkstätte Sachsenhausen, Minutes of the visit of Bishop Dr Kurt Scharf on 21 Apr. 1985, GSA, Ordner ZB.
35. SE 25 Apr. 1939.
36. SE 26 May 1939.
37. EN to MN, 31 May 1939, ZEKHN, 62/6081.
38. SE 11 Aug. 1939.
39. SE 7 and 21 Sept., 19 Oct. 1939, 1 and 15 Feb. 1940; MN, *Briefe Sachsenhausen*, 45; Schäberle-Königs, *Und sie waren*, 46–57.
40. SE 6 June 1940.
41. As a typical case in point, see SE 4 Apr. 1940.
42. MN, *Briefe Sachsenhausen*, 25, 27, 29, 34, 46, 48; EN to Heinrich Himmler, 2 Mar. 1939, Baranowski to Ludolf von Alvensleben, 6 Mar. 1939, BArch, R 43/II, 155, fos 235–40.
43. The Gestapo explicitly reported Niemöller had a medical examination every week. Gestapa to Reich Minister for Church Affairs, 30 Jan. 1939, BArch, 5101/23696.
44. MN, *Briefe Sachsenhausen*, 28.
45. Ibid., 31. See also Chapter 1.
46. Ibid., 44.
47. EN to MN, 20 Feb. 1939, ZEKHN, 62/6081.
48. MN, *Briefe Sachsenhausen*, 47.
49. MN to EN, 19 Aug. 1939, ZEKHN, 62/6081. Abbreviations in the original written out.
50. EN to MN, 15 Apr. 1940 and 20 Jan. 1941, ZEKHN, 62/6081; see also SE 19 Sept. 1940; MN, *Briefe Sachsenhausen*, 36–7.
51. EN to MN, 19 Oct. 1938, ZEKHN, 62/6081.
52. EN to MN, 6 Jan., 4 Sept. 1939 and 15 Apr. 1940 (quote), ZEKHN, 62/6081.
53. EN to MN, 18 Sept. 1939 (quote) and 8 June 1940, ZEKHN, 62/6081.
54. MN, *Briefe Moabit*, 291 (10 Feb. 1938).
55. EN to MN, 27 Aug. 1939, ZEKHN, 62/6081.
56. SE 30 Mar. 1939; MN, *Briefe Sachsenhausen*, 40, 71–2.
57. Ziemann, 'Wartestandsaffäre', 317.
58. Ibid., quotes 324.
59. Quote ibid., 335.
60. MN to Johannes Heinrich, 12 Dec. 1939, ibid., 327.
61. SE 4 Jan. 1940; MN, *Briefe Sachsenhausen*, 85.
62. MN to the High Command of the Navy, 7 Sept. 1939, LkA EvKvW, 5.1, 440, F. 2, fo. 127. The handwritten original is not marked as a copy. As it does not contain any date stamp or processing comments, it can be assumed it is a copy of the original letter made by Niemöller himself.
63. Ibid.
64. WN, note about the visitor's permit from 29 Aug. 1938, ZEKHN, 62/6179.
65. SE 24 Aug. 1939.
66. EN to MN, 4 Sept. 1939, ZEKHN, 62/6081. This letter reached the concentration camp only on 9 September, that is, after the application for voluntary service.
67. SE 7 Sept. 1939.
68. WN, 'Geschichtliche Einführung', in MN, *Briefe Sachsenhausen*, 7–18, here 12–13. Here, against better knowledge, Wilhelm Niemöller claims his brother had reported to

the High Command of the Armed Forces (Oberkommando der Wehrmacht, OKW), presumably to create the impression that Martin Niemöller's application had nothing to do with returning to his previous profession as a navy officer.

69. Eberhard Bethge, *Dietrich Bonhoeffer. Theologe, Christ, Zeitgenosse* (Munich, 1967), 569, points out that Dietrich Bonhoeffer, when the war started, supported Niemöller's and other imprisoned Confessing Church pastors' decision to join the Wehrmacht, because this would protect them from the harassment and attacks by the SS. However, there is no evidence that Niemöller knew about Bonhoeffer's position.

70. MN to the Gestapa, 7 Sept. 1939, LkA EvKvW, 5.1, 440, F. 2, fo. 127.

71. SE 19 Oct. 1939; see Chief of the OKW to MN, 27 Sept. 1939, LkA EvKvW, 5.1, 440 F. 2, fo. 128.

72. SE 2 Nov. 1939.

73. Joseph Goebbels, 'Krieg in Sicht', *Völkischer Beobachter* 25 Feb. 1939, reprinted in Joseph Goebbels, *Die Zeit ohne Beispiel. Reden und Aufsätze aus den Jahren 1939/40/41* (Munich, 1941), 38–47, quote 41.

74. MN to the High Command of the Navy, 25 Feb. 1939 and (draft) to Erich Raeder (quote), 16 Aug. 1939, ZEKHN, 62/1873. Höß, *Kommandant*, 84, erroneously dates this waiver back to 1938 and concludes this was the reason for Hitler to refuse Niemöller's application for voluntary military service. The latter cannot be proven, but is not without a certain plausibility.

75. MN to EN, 15 Sept. 1939, ZEKHN, 62/6081.

76. EN to MN, 24 Oct. 1939, ZEKHN, 62/6081.

77. MN to EN, 26 Apr. 1943, ZEKHN, 35/573.

78. Otto Schiller, 'Auhagen, Otto', *Neue Deutsche Biographie* 1 (1953), 454–5.

79. MN to EN, 13 June 1943, ZEKHN, 35/573.

80. Helmut Gollwitzer, 'Meine lieben Freunde', n.d. [17 Dec. 1939], LkA EvKvW, 5.1, 440 F. 2, fos 132–3.

81. This is implied by Bernhard H. Forck, *Und folget ihrem Glauben nach. Gedenkbuch für die Blutzeugen der Bekennenden Kirche* (Stuttgart, 1949), 75. It is confirmed by Wilhelm Niemöller in a remark to MN, *Briefe Sachsenhausen*, 93, note 1.

82. Karl Barth, *Offene Briefe 1935-1942* (Zurich, 2001), 196–204, quote 197–8.

83. Excerpt from *Nieuwe Rotterdamsche Courant* No. 489, 17 Oct. 1939, EZA, 7/11667, fo. 121.

84. 'Dr. Niemöller's Offer to Join Up', *The Times*, 20 Oct. 1939.

85. 'War Items', in *The Observer*, 26 Nov. 1939.

86. Bentley, *Niemöller*, 148; see also Hockenos, *Then They Came for Me*, 146–7.

87. For further details, see Alf Christophersen and Benjamin Ziemann, 'Einleitung', in Martin Niemöller (ed.), *Gedanken über den Weg der christlichen Kirche* (Gütersloh, 2019), 7–59.

88. MN, *Briefe Sachsenhausen*, quotes 31, 52.

89. Ibid., 61.

90. Ibid., 155.

91. SE 22 Feb. 1941.

92. EN to MN, 25 Feb. 1941, ZEKHN, 62/6081.

93. SE 6 Mar. and 17 Apr. 1941.

94. Schäberle-Königs, *Und sie waren*, 259–60.

95. EN to MN, 22 Apr. 1941, ZEKHN, 62/6081.

96. MN, *Briefe Sachsenhausen*, 173–83, quote 173.

97. SE 18 July 1941.

98. MN to EN, 20 July 1939, MN, *Briefe Sachsenhausen*, 62.

99. Ziemann, 'Wartestandsaffäre', 332.

100. See Gailus, 'Ein Volk-ein Reich-ein Glaube?'; Benjamin Ziemann, 'Conversion as a Confessional Irritant: Examples from the Third Reich', in Mark Edward Ruff and Thomas Großbölting (eds), *Germany and the Confessional Divide, 1871-1989* (New York, 2021), 145–69, figure 152.

101. MN, *Gedanken über den Weg der christlichen Kirche*, ed. Alf Christophersen and Benjamin Ziemann (Gütersloh, 2019), 160.

102. Ibid., 160.

103. Ibid., 161. Emphasis in the original.

104. MN, *Gedanken*, 164.

105. Ibid., 164

106. Ibid, quotes 168, 178.

107. Ibid., 204–5.

108. See Christophersen and Ziemann, 'Einleitung', 40–52.

109. See also for the following, ibid., 26–39, quote 34.

110. Letter by Heinz Kloppenburg, 11 Mar. 1941, cited in Ziemann, 'Conversion as a Confessional Irritant', 158.

111. Quotes ibid.

112. WN to MN, 13 Nov. 1940, LkA EvKvW, 5.1 440 F. 2, fos 148–50.

113. Schäberle-Königs, *Und sie waren*, 261–9.

114. SE 5 Dec. 1940.

115. 'Pastor Niemöller. Reported Conversion to Rome', *The Times*, 6 Feb. 1941.

116. Pius XII to Bischof Preysing, 19 Mar. 1941: Burkhart Schneider (ed.), *Die Briefe Pius' XII. an die deutschen Bischöfe. 1939-1944* (Mainz, 1966), 132–5, here 134.

117. MN to EN, 28 Feb. 1940, ZEKHN, 62/6081.

118. SE 2 Nov. 1939. Abbreviations in the original written out.

119. Ibid.

120. SE 8 Aug. 1940.

121. SE 3 Oct. 1940; see EN to MN, 22 July 1940, ZEKHN, 62/6081.

122. EN to MN, 9 Oct. 1940, ZEKHN, 62/6081.

123. EN to MN, 26 Aug. 1940, ZEKHN, 62/6081.

124. EN to MN, 20 Dec. 1939, ZEKHN, 62/6081.

125. According to canon law, the sacrament of marriage ranks higher than that of celibacy, which is a precondition for the ordination of priests, from which the pope, however, can dispense. But it is fair to assume neither Else nor her husband knew about this.

126. MN to EN, 10 Nov. 1937, MN, *Briefe Moabit*, 97.

127. MN to EN, 23 Feb. 1941, ZEKHN, 62/6081. On Klapproth, see the fascinating study by Albrecht Beutel, *Erich Klapproth—Kämpfer an den Fronten. Das kurze Leben eines Hoffnungsträgers der Bekennenden Kirche* (Tübingen, 2019).

128. Christophersen/Ziemann, 'Einleitung', 24–5.

129. There is a lot of evidence for this tenderness and how important it was for both Else and Martin Niemöller. See SE 6 Feb. 1941. EN to MN, 2–5 Feb. 1940 (this letter was written over several days), MN to EN, 6 July 1941, ZEKHN, 62/6081.
130. SE 11 Aug. 1939.
131. SE 7 Dec. 1939, 7 Mar. and 3 May 1940 (quote).
132. SE 5 Sept. 1940.
133. MN to Hans Koch, 9 Nov. 1940, '3. Entwurf', ZEKHN, 62/1873.
134. MN to Koch, Oct. 1940, '1. Entwurf', ZEKHN, 62/1873.
135. Hans Koch to MN, 10 Sept. 1940, ZEKHN, 62/1873.
136. SE 19 Sept. 1940; cf. MN to EN, 22 Sept. 1940, ZEKHN, 62/6081.
137. EN to MN, 9 Oct. and 16 Nov. 1940, MN to EN (quote), 21 May 1941, ZEKHN, 62/6081.
138. On Neuhäusler's biography before and after 1945, see Mark Edward Ruff, *The Battle for the Catholic Past in Germany 1945–1980* (Cambridge, 2018), 23–9.
139. Angelika Pisarski, *Um nicht schweigend zu sterben. Gespräche mit Überlebenden aus Konzentrationslagern* (Munich, 1989) 146–58.
140. Bentley, *Niemöller*, 148.
141. Christophersen and Ziemann, 'Einleitung'.
142. Stanislav Zámečnik, *Das war Dachau* (Frankfurt am Main, 2007), 172–3; Höß, *Kommandant*, 84.
143. Dirk Riedel, *Kerker im KZ Dachau. Die Geschichte der drei Bunkerbauten* (Dachau, 2002), 35–48.
144. Statement MN, 9 Oct. 1951, StAM, Staatsanwaltschaften 34475/5; Riedel, *Kerker*, 49.
145. MN to EN, 20/21 July 1941, ZEKHN, 35/573.
146. MN to Hans Joachim Niemöller, 28 Dec. 1941, ZEKHN, 35/573.
147. MN to EN, 25 Aug. 1941, ZEKHN, 35/573; see Pisarski, *Gespräche*, 165.
148. MN to EN, 18 Jan. 1942, ZEKHN, 35/573.
149. Neuhäusler, Taschen Termin-Kalender 1942, AEM, NL Neuhäusler, No. 358/4; see Pisarski, *Gespräche*, 163.
150. Pisarski, *Gespräche*, 162.
151. MN to EN, 8 Feb. 1942, ZEKHN, 35/573.
152. MN to EN, 1 Apr. 1942, ZEKHN, 35/573.
153. MN to EN, 27 Sept. 1941, ZEKHN, 35/573.
154. MN to EN, 23 Oct. 1941, ZEKHN, 35/573.
155. MN to EN, 15 Nov. 1941, ZEKHN, 35/573.
156. MN to EN, 7 Dec. 1941, ZEKHN, 35/573.
157. MN to EN, 24 Mar. 1942, ZEKHN, 35/573.
158. MN to EN, 31 Jan. 1942, ZEKHN, 35/573. It is striking that, after 1945, Höck did not even mention Jansen; he only mentioned Corbinian Hofmeister, who came to the group in April 1944. Pisarski, *Gespräche*, 165; Michael Höck, 'Nec laudibus nec timore. Mit Abt Corbinian Hofmeister im KZ Dachau', *Beiträge zur Geschichte des Bistums Regensburg* 15 (1981), 363–6, 363.
159. MN to EN, 28 June 1942 ('Sanguiniker') and 14 Apr. 1943 ('Melancholische'), ZEKHN, 35/573.
160. MN to EN, 31 Jan. and 19 May 1942, ZEKHN, 35/573.

161. See documents in BArch, VBS 286/6400003146 and R 9361-II/13237. His own statement in the denazification trial contains different details on his period of service in Dachau: biography Wilhelm Beyer, 1 Aug. 1947, Staatsarchiv Ludwigsburg, EL 903/1, Bü. 598.

162. Ibid.

163. AK 28 Apr., 30 Apr., 4 June, 9 June, 24 June, 16 July, and 12 Aug. 1943 (quote).

164. Dirk Riedel, 'Der "Wildpark" im KZ Dachau und das Außenlager St. Gilgen. Zwangsarbeit auf den Baustellen des KZ-Kommandanten Loritz', *Dachauer Hefte* 16 (2000), 54–70, 55–6, 59–63.

165. MN to EN, 21/22 Mar. 1943, ZEKHN, 35/573; cf. AK 20 Mar. 1943.

166. AK 14, 17, 19 Apr., 6, 12, 17, 28 May, 14, 29 June, 27 July, 30 Aug., 19 Oct. 1943.

167. AK 7 July, 1 and 7 Sept. 1943; quote SE 8 July 1943.

168. AK 21 June 1943 and 3 April 1944; the latter is evidence that some of the privileges remained in place even after Untersturmführer Beyer had left.

169. AK 1 July 1943. Abbreviation in the original written out.

170. SE 8 July and 21 Oct. 1943.

171. SE 8 July 1943.

172. SE 8 Apr. and 22 Apr. 1942 (quote).

173. SE 26 Aug. 1943.

174. SE 10 Sept. and 17 Dec. 1942, 8 July 1943.

175. SE 12 Aug. 1943; Götz Bergander, 'Vom Gerücht zur Legende. Der Luftkrieg über Deutschland im Spiegel von Tatsachen, erlebter Geschichte, Erinnerung, Erinnerungsverzerrung', in Thomas Stamm-Kuhlmann, Jürgen Elvert, Birgit Aschmann, and Jens Hohensee (eds), *Geschichtsbilder. Festschrift für Michael Salewski zum 65. Geburtstag* (Wiesbaden, 2003), 591–616, 601.

176. SE 12 Aug. 1943; see Schmidt, *Niemöller*, 370–1.

177. SE 26 Aug., 9 Sept. ('Weisung'), 21 Oct. and 4 Nov. 1943, 20 Jan. 1944 ('Kontrollkommission').

178. Schäberle-Königs, *Und sie waren*, 183–242.

179. SE 2 Dec. 1943 and 6 Apr. 1944 (quote); cf. MN to EN, 13 July 1943, ZEKHN, 35/573; AK 5 July 1943.

180. MN to EN, 26 Jan. 1944, ZEKHN, 35/573.

181. MN to EN, 26 July 1943, ZEKHN, 35/573.

182. MN to EN, 26 Mar. 1944, ZEKHN, 35/573.

183. AK 25 Feb. 1944 and *passim* for 1944.

184. AK 8 Nov. 1944.

185. MN to EN, 9 Aug. 1944, ZEKHN, 35/573.

186. MN to EN, 6 Nov. 1944, ZEKHN, 35/573.

187. AK 3 Mar. 1945. Abbreviation in the original written out.

188. SE 22 Jan. 1945.

189. MN to EN, 3 Apr. 1945, ZEKHN, 35/573.

190. SE 1 Feb. 1945.

191. Nicholas Stargardt, *Der deutsche Krieg 1939–1945* (Frankfurt am Main, 2015), 619 (quote), 641–2.

192. Höck, 'Nec laudibus', 363.

193. Koop, *In Hitlers Hand*, 219; SE 15 Mar. 1945; Zámečnik, *Dachau*, 380.

194. AK 13 Jan. 1945; on Bossenigk, see 'Vernehmung des Paul Wauer am 16.7.1951', StAM, Staatsanwaltschaften 34475/2, fo. 11.

195. See AK 20, 23, 25, 27, and 30 Jan., 3 and 8 Feb., and 1 Mar. 1945; MN to EN, 2 Mar. 1945, ZEKHN, 35/573.

196. MN to EN, 17 Mar. 1945, ZEKHN, 35/573.

197. AK 3 Apr. 1945. The Bundesarchiv does not hold an SS personnel file for Lenzkowski. See, however, the brief information from a US military tribunal: Gedenkstätte Dachau Archiv, A 4913.

198. Höck, 'Nec laudibus', 365; SE 20 Apr. 1945.

199. Diary Johannes Neuhäusler (copy), 5 Apr. 1945, StAM, Staatsanwaltschaften 34475/2.

200. AK 16 Apr. 1945; see Zámečnik, *Dachau*, 344–5; 'Niederschrift der Vernehmung von Johannes Neuhäusler am 3.12.1951', StAM, Staatsanwaltschaften 34475/5; Karl Kunkel, '"Geheime Staatspolizei – Sie sind verhaftet!" Tagebuchaufzeichnungen des Sonderhäftlings Karl Kunkel', *Ermlandbuch* 116 (1983), 40–113, 63.

201. Kunkel, 'Tagebuchaufzeichnungen', 64; cf. diary Neuhäusler, 17 Apr. 1945, StAM, Staatsanwaltschaften 34475/2.

202. SE 20 Apr. 1945.

203. Quote: Kunkel, 'Tagebuchaufzeichnungen', 66; AK 23 and 24 Apr. 1945; diary Neuhäusler, 23 Apr. 1945, StAM, Staatsanwaltschaften 34475/2.

204. Hans-Günter Richardi, *SS-Geiseln in der Alpenfestung. Die Verschleppung prominenter KZ-Häftlinge aus Deutschland nach Südtirol* (Bolzano, 2005), 261.

205. John S. Conway, 'The Political Theology of Martin Niemöller', *German Studies Review* 9 (1986), 521–46, 539–40; Bentley, *Niemöller*, 164–5; Hockenos, *Then They Came for Me*, 156, mostly—and in my view wrongly—relates change during the years in Dachau to his post-war ecumenical work. See Chapter 17.

Notes to Chapter 13

1. AK 5 May 1945.

2. 'Niemoeller Holds Church Only Hope', *New York Times*, 8 May 1945; see 'Pastor Niemoeller's Views on Future of Germany', *Manchester Guardian*, 8 June 1945.

3. AK 11 May 1945.

4. AK 11, 19 and 30 May 1945; WN, *Neuanfang 1945. Zur Biographie Martin Niemöllers nach seinen Tagebuchaufzeichnungen aus dem Jahre 1945* (Frankfurt am Main, 1967), 27.

5. AK 5 June 1945.

6. 'Niemoeller Asks Iron Rule of Reich', *New York Times*, 6 June 1945.

7. Ibid.; Clemens Vollnhals (ed.), *Die evangelische Kirche nach dem Zusammenbruch. Berichte ausländischer Beobachter aus dem Jahre 1945* (Göttingen, 1988), XXV.

8. 'A Hero with Limitations', *New York Times*, 7 June 1945.

9. WN, *Neuanfang 1945*, 29–30.

10. AK 18 June 1945; see Vollnhals (ed.), *Die evangelische Kirche*, XIII.

11. AK 18 June 1945.

12. OSS report 18 June 1945: Vollnhals (ed.), *Die evangelische Kirche*, 21–4, quotes 24.

13. M. Knappen, report 18 June 1945, ibid., 19–21, quotes 20–1.

14. Vollnhals (ed.), *Die evangelische Kirche*, XXVI.

15. Thomas Wenner to Mr Heath in the US Embassy, 21 June 1945, IfZ, OMGUS, POLA/733/18.

16. Vollnhals (ed.), *Die evangelische Kirche*, X.

17. George Bell to MN, 6 July 1945 and MN's reply, 31 Oct. 1945 (quote), LPL, Bell papers 10, fos 322, 335.

18. On several other occasions, for instance during his trip to the USA in 1947, Niemöller explicitly said that he wanted to contribute to Hitler's downfall by signing up voluntaryrily. 'Niemoeller Tells Of Fight On Hitler', *New York Times*, 21 Jan. 1947.

19. AK 21–24 June 1945; see WN, *Neuanfang 1945*, 32–6.

20. M. Knappen, Report on the Niemöller Case to Date, 10 July 1945, IfZ, OMGUS, 5/342–1/32.

21. Memo M. Knappen 7 July 1945, IfZ, OMGUS, 5/342–1/32.

22. Note Adcock 7 July 1945 for General Frank W. Milburn, IfZ, OMGUS, 5/342–1/32.

23. M. Knappen to the Director of the Public Health and Welfare Division, 13 July 1945, IfZ, OMGUS, 5/342–1/32; see WN, *Neuanfang 1945*, 37.

24. Printed in WN, *Neuanfang 1945*, 37–45, quotes 38, 40, 42.

25. See Benjamin Ziemann, 'The Theory of Functional Differentiation and the History of Modern Society: Reflections on the Reception of Systems Theory in Recent Historiography', *Soziale Systeme* 13 (2007), 220–9.

26. Martin Greschat, 'Kirche und Öffentlichkeit in der deutschen Nachkriegszeit', in *Kirchen in der Nachkriegszeit. Vier zeitgeschichtliche Beiträge* (Göttingen, 1979), 100–24., 103; Schmidt, *Niemöller*, 404–5.

27. Percy Knauth, *Germany in Defeat* (New York, 1946), 144–5.

28. Ibid., 145.

29. Based on a search in https://search-proquest-com.sheffield.idm.oclc.org/hnpnewyorktimes/ (accessed 14 May 2018).

30. On the rise and fall of Niemöller's image in British public opinion, see Hannah Tetlow, 'The Making and Unmaking of a Protestant Hero: British Perceptions on Martin Niemöller in Context of the German Church Struggle, 1934–1945', *Schweizerische Zeitschrift für Religions- und Kulturgeschichte* 116 (2022), 283–300.

31. Henry Smith Leiper, 'Niemoeller Held Christian Symbol', *New York Times*, 25 June 1939; see Hockenos, *Then They Came for Me*, 142.

32. Hockenos, *Then They Came for Me*, 142.

33. 'Niemoeller Stand Praised By Rabbis', *New York Times*, 2 July 1939; Hockenos, *Then They Came for Me*, 143.

34. Leo Stein, *I was in Hell with Niemoeller* (London/New York/Melbourne, n.d. [1942]).

35. Heymel, 'Wer war Leo Stein? Spurensuche nach dem Verfasser des Buches "I was in Hell with Niemoeller, New York 1942"', *Mitteilungen zur kirchlichen Zeitgeschichte* 5 (2011), 53–87; see 'What Hitler Told Me about Christianity. Pastor Martin Niemoeller', *Liberty Magazine*, 20 Sept. 1941, 16; 'The Last Word: Pastor Niemoeller and Dr. Stein', *Liberty Magazine*, 7 Feb. 1942, 56.

36. 'Pickets Would Quit for Mrs. Roosevelt', *New York Times*, 10 Aug. 1940; see Ernst Toller, *Gesammelte Werke. Vol. 3: Politisches Theater und Dramen im Exil 1927/1939*

(Munich, 1978), 245–316; Nancy Copeland Halbgewachs, 'Censorship and Holocaust Film in the Hollywood Studio System', PhD thesis, The University of New Mexico, 2011, 17, 107–11. The film *The Hitler Gang* (1944), produced by Paramount, also presented Niemöller as the pinnacle of the 'good German'. Raimund Lammersdorf, 'Verantwortung und Schuld. Deutsche und amerikanische Antworten auf die Schuldfrage, 1945–1947', in Heinz Bude and Bernd Greiner (eds), *Westbindungen. Amerika in der Bundesrepublik* (Hamburg, 1999), 231–56, 245.

37. Karl Barth to MN, 9 July 1945, ZEKHN, 62/544. Emphasis in the original.

38. MN to WN, 9 Nov. 1945, ZEKHN, 62/671.

39. See his remarks in 'Presseempfang mit Pfarrer Niemöller', 30 June 1947, ELAB 55.1/672.

40. AK 13, 14 (quote) and 16 Aug. 1945; cf. MN to WN ('tiny'), 2 Sept. 1945, ZEKHN, 62/671; see MN to Franz Hildebrandt, 28 Sept. 1945, ZEKHN, 62/394; MN to the parish Dahlem, 9 Sept. 1945, AKG Dahlem, 2034, Hefter II.

41. AK 19, 20, 23, and 24 Sept. 1945 (quote).

42. AK 21 Oct. 1945; see Schäberle-Königs, *Und sie waren*, 119; WN, *Neuanfang 1945*, 62.

43. Jürgen J. Seidel, *'Neubeginn' in der Kirche? Die evangelischen Landes- und Provinzialkirchen in der SBZ/DDR im gesellschaftlichen Kontext der Nachkriegszeit (1945–1953)* (Göttingen, 1989), 201–2.

44. MN to Franz Hildebrandt, 28 Sept. 1945, ZEKHN, 62/394.

45. MN to Otto Dibelius, 18 July 1946, ZEKHN, 62/564.

46. Seidel, *Neubeginn*, 197–202; Noss, *Albertz*, 504–5.

47. Minutes of the GKR meeting on 29 Oct. 1945, AKG Dahlem, GKR-Protokolle 1934–1950.

48. MN to Wolf-Dieter Zimmermann, 13 July 1946, ELAB, 37/25.

49. MN to Martin Albertz, 18 Nov. 1946, EZA 600/102601.

50. Minutes of the GKR meetings on 28 June and 2 July 1947, AKG Dahlem, GKR-Protokolle 1934–1950.

51. MN to the GKR Dahlem, 3 Nov. 1947, AKG Dahlem, 2034, Hefter II.

52. MN to WN, 10 Dec. 1951, ZEKHN, 62/672.

53. See Alfred Reinelt, 'Pastor Martin Niemöller', *Der Standpunkt*, no. 6 (1946), 4–9.

54. Morrison C. Stayer to Lucius D. Clay, 19 Sept. 1945, IfZ, OMGUS, USG4/1/2.

55. 'Niemöller Sympathisierender der NSDAP', *Der Tagesspiegel*, 29 Mar. 1947; 'Schwankende Gestalt', *Neue Ruhr-Zeitung*, 9 Apr. 1947. A balanced account that highlights Niemöller's later merits in the Confessing Church: 'Fall Niemöller?', *Neues Abendland* 11 (1947), No. 3, in LkA EvKvW, 5.1, 443 F. 1, fos 15–16.

56. 'Zum Fall Niemöller', *Der Kurier*, 27 May 1947.

57. Letter to the editor by Böhm in ibid.

58. 'Martin Niemöller ohne Maske', *Aufbau*, 16 May 1947, 7.

59. On Forell, see Eberhard Röhm and Jörg Thierfelder, 'Ein langer Weg von Breslau nach New York. Der Flüchtlingspfarrer Friedrich Forell', in Joachim Mehlhausen (ed.),... *und über Barmen hinaus. Studien zur Kirchlichen Zeitgeschichte. Festschrift für Carsten Nicolaisen* (Göttingen, 1995), 376–85.

60. MN to Rev. Frederik J. Forell, 6 May 1947, LkA EvKvW, 5.1, 443 F. 1, fos 134–6.

61. Günter J. Trittel, *Hunger und Politik. Die Ernährungskrise in der Bizone, 1945–1949* (Frankfurt am Main, 1990), 216; Hans-Ulrich Wehler, *Deutsche Gesellschaftsgeschichte*,

vol. IV, *1914–1949* (Munich, 2003), 951; on calories as a symbol of victimization, see Atina Grossmann, 'Grams, Calories, and Food: Languages of Victimization, Entitlement, and Human Rights in Occupied Germany, 1945–1949', *Central European History* 44 (2011), 118–48.

62. MN to Rev. Frederik J. Forell, 6 May 1947, LkA EvKvW, 5.1, 443 F. 1, fos 134–6.

63. Edwin M. Sears, 'Wirklichkeitsfremd', *Der Tagesspiegel*, 17 Oct. 1947. Sears worked at the Office of Chief of Counsel for War Crimes, a department of the Office of Military Government, United States (OMGUS).

64. 'Weniger als KZ-Rationen', *Hannoversche Neueste Nachrichten*, 31 May 1947.

65. 'Die Angelegenheit Niemöller' (quote), authorless, n.d. [8 Sept. 1947], Archiv der Gedenkstätte Dachau, A 705; 'Nur Judenfreunde. Zusatzkarte für Martin Niemöller', *Der Spiegel*, 9 Aug. 1947, 4; Constantin Goschler, *Wiedergutmachung. Westdeutschland und die Verfolgten des Nationalsozialismus, 1945–1954* (Munich, 1992), 206.

66. AK 14 June 1947.

67. 'Nur Judenfreunde. Zusatzkarte für Martin Niemöller', *Der Spiegel*, 9 Aug. 1947, 4. According to 'Niemöller antwortet von der Kanzel', *Frankfurter Rundschau*, 16 Aug. 1947, Niemöller refused to comment on this remark, that is, he did not deny it.

68. Speech by Dr Hans Mayer 30 July 1947, Archiv der Gedenkstätte Dachau, A 705 (also in BArch, SAPMO, BY 6/V 280/152).

69. 'Pastor Niemoeller "Not a Nazi Victim"', *Manchester Guardian*, 28 July 1947; 'Niemöller is Ousted by Nazi Victims Unit. Termed Anti-Semite', *News of Germany*, 31 July 1947 (IfZ, OMGUS, 5/342-1/32); 'Nazi Victim Status Denied to Niemöller', *New York Times*, 28 July 1947.

70. 'Der nichtverfolgte Verfolgte', *Die Zeit*, 7 Aug. 1947.

71. Hans Mayer, Persönliche Information für die Interzonensekretäre, n.d. [*c.*10 Aug. 1947], BArch, SAPMO, BY 6/V 280/152; see 'L/La.-M.' to Hans Schwarz, VVN Hamburg, 12 Aug. 1947, Archiv der Gedenkstätte Dachau, A 705.

72. 'Ein neuer Fall Niemöller', *Hamburger Freie Presse*, 30 July 1947.

73. 'Nur Judenfreunde. Zusatzkarte für Martin Niemöller', *Der Spiegel*, 9 Aug. 1947, 4.

74. AK 10 Aug. 1947.

75. 'Niemöller und die VVN', *Badische Zeitung*, 19 Aug. 1947. On Niemöller's clumsiness in handling the media, see also 'Der Fall Niemöller', *Der Tagesspiegel*, 26 Aug. 1947.

76. AK 10 Aug. 1947.

77. 'Nochmals Niemöller', *Hamburger Volkszeitung*, 13 Aug. 1947.

78. AK 18 Aug. 1947; see Goschler, *Wiedergutmachung*, 78–81.

79. 'Eine Aussprache mit Niemöller', *Münchener Mittag*, 22 Aug. 1947; see 'Pastor Niemöller rechtfertigt sich', *Frankenpost*, 20 Aug. 1947.

80. 'Dr. Auerbach vermittelt', *Fränkischer Tag*, 20 Aug. 1947.

81. MN, speech in Neustädter Kirche in Erlangen on 22 Jan. 1946, LkA EvKvW, 5.1, 220 F. 1, fos 71–2. Number of participants in Barbara Wolbring, *Trümmerfeld der bürgerlichen Welt. Universität in den gesellschaftlichen Reformdiskursen der westlichen Besatzungszonen, 1945–1949* (Göttingen, 2014), 70.

82. MN, speech in Neustädter Kirche in Erlangen on 22 Jan. 1946, LkA EvKvW, 5.1, 220 F. 1, fos 71–2.

83. MN, *Der Weg ins Freie* (Stuttgart, 1946), 26–7.

84. Ibid., 26.

85. *Martin Niemöller über die deutsche Schuld, Not und Hoffnung* (Zollikon-Zurich, 1946), 5.

86. Quoted in Siegfried Hermle, *Evangelische Kirche und Judentum—Stationen nach 1945* (Göttingen, 1990), 216.

87. At the time Niemöller was by no means the only one saying this. On the persistence of antisemitism after 1945, see Hermle, *Evangelische Kirche*, 57–63.

88. 'Interview mit Niemöller', *Neue Zeitung*, 21 Feb. 1947 (ELAB, 55.1/672); see 'Antisemitism End in Germany Denied', *New York Times*, 25 Jan. 1947.

89. Kurt Kersten, 'Interview mit Niemöller', *Aufbau*, 31 Jan. 1947.

90. 'Presseempfang mit Pfarrer Niemöller', 30 June 1947, ELAB 55.1/672.

91. See Klaus Holz, *Nationaler Antisemitismus. Wissenssoziologie einer Weltanschauung* (Hamburg, 2001), 157–65.

92. Rusterholz, *Nachbars Haus nicht in Flammen*, 62–146, 521–5.

93. Minutes of the meeting on 7 Mar. 1946, KBA, 9107.302.

94. Ibid. See Rusterholz, *Nachbars Haus nicht in Flammen*, 266–80.

95. Minutes of the meeting on 7 Mar. 1946, KBA, 9107.302.

96. Ibid.

97. Langewiesche, *Nationalismus im 19. und 20. Jahrhundert*.

98. Hockenos, *Then They Came for Me*, 175.

99. MN to Ewart Turner, 5 Oct. 1947, ZEKHN, 62/533. I am grateful to Matthew Hockenos for bringing this source to my attention.

Notes to Chapter 14

1. Clemens Vollnhals, 'Die Evangelische Kirche zwischen Traditionswahrung und Neuorientierung', in Martin Broszat, Klaus-Dietmar Henke, and Hans Woller (eds), *Von Stalingrad zur Währungsreform. Zur Sozialgeschichte des Umbruchs in Deutschland*, 3rd edn (Munich, 1990), 113–67, 113–16, quote 113.

2. See ibid., 164–7; Greschat, *Die evangelische Christenheit*, 310–14.

3. See Chapter 13.

4. For example, the letters to Otto Fricke and Hans Böhm: Besier et al. (eds), *Kapitulation*, vol. 2, 141 (quote), 223–4.

5. MN to Otto Fricke, 18 July 1945: Besier et al. (eds), *Kapitulation*, vol. 2, 140.

6. MN, Lage und Aussichten der Evangelischen Kirche, 20 July 1945, ZEKHN, 62/1233.

7. Figure in Meier, *Kirchenkampf*, III, 152.

8. MN, Lage und Aussichten der Evangelischen Kirche, 20 July 1945, ZEKHN, 62/1233.

9. Ibid.

10. Greschat, *Christenheit*, 104–5; in detail, Jörg Thierfelder, *Das kirchliche Einigungswerk des württembergischen Landesbischofs Theophil Wurm* (Göttingen, 1975), here 267–9 the thirteen sentences.

11. Quoted in Besier et al. (eds), *Kapitulation*, vol. 1, 246.

12. Greschat, *Christenheit*, 107–11; quotes from the invitation letter from 25 July 1945: Besier et al. (eds), *Kapitulation*, vol. 2, 210–11.

13. Greschat, *Christenheit*, 116–17; Besier et al. (eds), *Kompromiß*, 179–99, quote 189.

14. Colonel R.L. Sedgwick, Report on the Conference of Evangelical Church Leaders at Treysa, 27 Aug.–1 Sept. 1945 (n.d.), LPL, George Bell Papers 9–11, 414–21, here 414–16 the list with names. The American observer counted 87 participants: Vollnhals (ed.), *Die evangelische Kirche*, 121; see Jörg Thierfelder, 'Die Kirchenkonferenz von Treysa 1945', in Besier et al. (eds), *Treysa*, 32–44, here 32.

15. Besier et al. (eds), *Treysa*, 215–79.

16. Sedgwick, Report on the Conference, LPL, George Bell Papers 9, fo. 414.

17. Ibid., fo. 420.

18. Ibid., fo. 420.

19. Ibid., fo. 419.

20. Hans Asmussen to Wurm, 6 Sept. 1945: Besier et al. (eds), *Treysa*, 372.

21. Ibid., 232f. (quotes), 256, 359; cf. Smith-von Osten, *Treysa*, 108–9, 120–3.

22. AK 29 Aug. 1945 (quote); see Sedgwick, Report on the Conference, LPL, George Bell Papers 9, fo. 420.

23. Karl Barth, Bericht, n.d.: Vollnhals (ed.), *Die evangelische Kirche*, 116.

24. Greschat, *Christenheit*, 119–23; Smith-von Osten, *Treysa*, 115–40.

25. Besier et al. (eds), *Treysa*, 324–5.

26. Matthew D. Hockenos, *A Church Divided: German Protestants Confront the Nazi Past* (Bloomington, 2004), 49.

27. Gniss, *Gerstenmaier*, 167.

28. Meiser 18 Sept. 1945: Besier et al. (eds), *Treysa*, 381–3; see Wolf-Dieter Hauschild, 'Vom "Lutherrat" zur VELKD 1945-1948', in Joachim Mehlhausen (ed.), *... und über Barmen hinaus. Studien zur Kirchlichen Zeitgeschichte. Festschrift für Carsten Nicolaisen* (Göttingen, 1995), 451–70.

29. MN to Wurm, 2 Sept. 1945: Besier et al. (eds), *Treysa*, 363; see Ralf Tyra, 'Treysa 1945. Neue Forschungsergebnisse zur ersten deutschen Kirchenversammlung nach dem Krieg', *Kirchliche Zeitgeschichte* 2 (1989), 239–76, 242–3.

30. MN to WN, 2 Sept. 1945, ZEKHN, 62/671.

31. MN to the regional brethren, 3 Sept. 1945: Besier et al. (eds), *Treysa*, 365–9, quotes 368.

32. WN, *Neuanfang 1945*, 56.

33. Besier et al. (eds), *Treysa*, 373.

34. Scholder, *Kirchen*, II, 104.

35. Besier et al. (eds), *Treysa*, 248.

36. MN to Emmi Kümpel, 13 Dec. 1947, ZEKHN, 62/057. On Niemöller as head of the *Außenamt*, see Benjamin Ziemann, 'Martin Niemöller als Leiter des Kirchlichen Außenamtes 1945-1956', in Andreas Gestrich, Siegfried Hermle, and Dagmar Pöpping (eds), *Evangelisch und deutsch? Auslandsgemeinden im 20. Jahrhundert. Zwischen Nationalprotestantismus, Volkstumspolitik und Ökumene* (Göttingen, 2020), 323–43.

37. Dietrich Bonhoeffer, *Ethik*, quoted in Martin Greschat (ed.), *Die Schuld der Kirche. Dokumente und Reflexionen zur Stuttgarter Schulderklärung vom 18./19. Oktober 1945* (Munich, 1982), 20–4, here 23; see Boyens, 'Schuldbekenntnis', 378.

38. Boyens, 'Schuldbekenntnis', 375–8.

39. See Chapter 12.

40. MN to Colonel Hugh O. Davis, Public Relations Division, US Military Government Frankfurt, 24 July 1945, ZEKHN, 62/1233. English in the original. See Dibelius to MN,

17 July 1945, ZEKHN, 62/564; Hartmut Ludwig, 'Tagung der Bekennenden Kirche in Frankfurt/M.', in Besier et al. (eds), *Treysa*, 10–20, here 12.

41. In a conversation with Marshall Knappen on 18 June 1945, Niemöller had rejected the idea of re-educating the youth. Rather, he claimed, the most important thing was that a young person could again proudly say 'I am a German youth'. Vollnhals (ed.), *Die evangelische Kirche*, 20. In his reply to the questionnaire of US Army Chaplain Ben L. Rose, in September 1945 Niemöller still wrote that 'the German people has been punished already by God', and 'the Christians in the world' should simply say 'we forgive you'. MN, [Antworten auf Fragen von Ben L. Rose], n.d., ZEKHN 62/43.

42. MN to Colonel Hugh O. Davis, 24 July 1945, ZEKHN, 62/1233.

43. Besier et al. (eds), *Treysa*, 142–3.

44. Hans Asmussen, 'An die Herren Amtsbrüder', in Besier et al. (eds), *Treysa*, 164–9, here 164–5.

45. Ibid., 108–9 (quote), 134.

46. MN, Ansprache in Treysa, 28 Aug. 1945, in ibid., 290–5, here 291.

47. Ibid., 292.

48. Ibid., 293–4.

49. MN to Karl Barth, 14 Sept. 1945, ZEKHN, 62/544.

50. Karl Barth to MN, 28 Sept. 1945, ZEKHN, 62/544; cf. Greschat, *Christenheit*, 141.

51. MN to Karl Barth, 5 Oct. 1945, ZEKHN, 62/544.

52. Boyens, 'Schuldbekenntnis', 374.

53. Hockenos, *A Church Divided*, 75–100. It is understandable that Niemöller soon firmly denied such a deal had been made. Cf. MN to WN, 3 Sept. 1947, LkA EvKvW, 5.1, 443 F. 1, fo. 170.

54. Greschat (ed.), *Schuld der Kirche*, 91–5; on the schedule of the Stuttgart conference, cf. 'Bericht und Dokumente' in Carsten Nicolaisen and Nora Andrea Schulze (eds), *Die Protokolle des Rates der Evangelischen Kirche in Deutschland*, vol. 1: *1945/46* (Göttingen, 1995), 23–111.

55. Nicolaisen and Schulze (eds), *Protokolle des Rates der EKD*, vol. 1: *1945/46*, 99–102.

56. Text versions and discussion in Greschat (ed.), *Schuld der Kirche*, 95–109, quotes 102; see also Greschat, *Christenheit*, 144–7.

57. Greschat, *Christenheit*, 146–9.

58. Ibid., 154–5; Clemens Vollnhals, 'Im Schatten der Stuttgarter Schulderklärung. Die Erblast des Nationalprotestantismus', in Manfred Gailus and Hartmut Lehmann (eds), *Nationalprotestantische Mentalitäten in Deutschland (1870-1970). Konturen, Entwicklungslinien und Umbrüche eines Weltbildes* (Göttingen, 2005), 379–431, 393–9; Greschat (ed.), *Schuld der Kirche*, 163–72.

59. Greschat (ed.), *Schuld der Kirche*, 132–43, quote 143.

60. Greschat, 'Kirche und Öffentlichkeit', 115.

61. 'Der Rat der EKD an die Christen in England', 14 Dec. 1945: Greschat (ed.), *Schuld der Kirche*, 129–31; Greschat, *Christenheit*, 152–3.

62. Greschat, *Christenheit*, 159–61.

63. MN to Asmussen, 17 Nov. 1946, ZEKHN, 62/539.

64. The figure given on the sign was higher than the total of around 200,000 inmates in Dachau. The number of deaths, which was only later officially confirmed, amounted to

42,000, of which 15,000 to 20,000 had been cremated in the crematory. Harold Marcuse, 'The Origin and Reception of Martin Niemöller's Quotation "First They Came for the Communists…"', in Michael Berenbaum, Richard Libowitz, and Marcia Sachs Littell (eds), *Remembering for the Future: Armenia, Auschwitz, and Beyond* (St. Paul, 2016), 173–99, 196.

65. MN, *Erneuerung unserer Kirche* (Munich, 1946), 9.

66. AK 8 Nov. 1945 (quote). Cf. MN, *Die Brücke über den Abgrund. Wort Martin Niemöllers am 6. Juni 1946 in der Johannis-Kirche zu Saarbrücken* (Saarbrücken, 1946), 8–10; MN, *Weg ins Freie*, 17–19; MN, *Zur gegenwärtigen Aufgabe der evangelischen Christenheit: Predigt über 1. Johannes 4, 9–14* (Frankfurt a.M., 1946), 11–12; MN, *Zur gegenwärtigen Lage der evangelischen Christenheit* (Tübingen, 1946), 12; MN, Ansprache am 27 March 1946 in Elberfeld, LkA EvKvW, 5.1, 435 F. 1, fos 237–9, here fo. 238.

67. MN, *Zur gegenwärtigen Aufgabe*, 10–11.

68. Hockenos, *Then They Came For Me*, 179–80; on the many versions used in 1946–7 and the later transformation of the quote, see Marcuse, 'Origin and Reception'.

69. Pfarrer Niemöller D.D. an die Göttinger Studenten, 17 Jan. 1946, LkA EvKvW, 5.1, 441 F. 2, fo. 67.

70. See Chapter 8.

71. MN, *Not und Aufgabe der Kirche in Deutschland*, Stuttgart 1947 (2nd edn), quotes 4, 6, 8–9; see MN, *Über die deutsche Schuld, Not und Hoffnung* (Zurich, 1946), 8–9.

72. MN, *Über die deutsche Schuld*, 8.

73. Pfarrer Niemöller D.D. an die Göttinger Studenten, 17 Jan. 1946, LkA EvKvW, 5.1, 441 F. 2, fo. 67.

74. Ibid. Explicitly also in the letter to WN, 9 Nov. 1945, ZEKHN, 62/671.

75. MN, *Erneuerung unserer Kirche*, 6–7.

76. Benjamin Ziemann, 'Martin Niemöller', in Norbert Frei (ed.), *Wie bürgerlich war der Nationalsozialismus?* (Göttingen, 2018), 334–50, here 346–7.

77. Bernd Weisbrod, '"Ein Vorsprung, der uns tief verpflichtet". Die Wiedereröffnung der Universität Göttingen im Wintersemester 1945/46', in *'Ein Vorsprung, der uns tief verpflichtet'. Die Wiedereröffnung der Universität Göttingen vor 70 Jahren* (Göttingen, 2016), 21–38, 25–8.

78. AK 22.1946 (quote); see Wolbring, *Trümmerfeld*, 43–74.

79. Diethild Pohl to Emil Dofivat, 6 Feb. 1946, GStA PK, VI. HA, NL Dovifat, No. 1236.

80. AK 4 Feb. 1946 (quote, abbreviations in the original written out); Andreas Lippmann, *Marburger Theologie im Nationalsozialismus* (Berlin, 2003), 458; Rudolf Bultmann, *Briefwechsel mit Götz Harbsmeier und Ernst Wolf: 1933–1976* (Tübingen, 2017), 137.

81. Bultmann, *Briefwechsel*, 137 (quote). MN, *Die politische Verantwortung des Christen im akademischen Stand. Vortrag, gehalten auf Einladung der evangelischen Studentengemeinde vor Studierenden der Philipps-Universität zu Marburg an der Lahn am 4. Mai 1946* (Gießen, 1946).

82. Harold Marcuse, *Legacies of Dachau: The Uses and Abuses of a Concentration Camp, 1933–2001* (Cambridge, 2001), 277–8.

83. Clemens Vollnhals, *Evangelische Kirche und Entnazifizierung 1945–1949. Die Last der nationalsozialistischen Vergangenheit* (Munich, 1989), 45–52, 156–70, figures 49–50.

84. Ibid., 52–77, quote 77. Text of the resolution in Vollnhals, *Selbstreinigung*, 126–7.
85. Barth to MN, 7 June 1946: Clemens Vollnhals (ed.), *Entnazifizierung und Selbstreinigung im Urteil der evangelischen Kirche. Dokumente und Reflexionen 1945–1949* (Munich, 1989), 133–4.
86. MN to Barth, 15 June 1946, ibid., 135–6.
87. Ibid., 202–3, further documents, 203–23; on the context, see Vollnhals, *Entnazifizierung*, 103–6.
88. Martin Greschat, 'Martin Niemöller. Repräsentant des deutschen Protestantismus im 20. Jahrhundert', *Pastoraltheologie* 81 (1992), 324–38, 334.
89. Vollnhals, *Entnazifizierung*, 106–15.
90. Diary entry 15 Feb. 1948: Bergsträsser, *Befreiung*, 284.
91. Clemens Vollnhals, 'Die Hypothek des Nationalprotestantismus. Entnazifizierung und Strafverfolgung von NS-Verbrechen nach 1945', *Geschichte und Gesellschaft* 18 (1992), 51–69, 58–65.
92. Tom Lawson, *The Church of England and the Holocaust: Christianity, Memory and Nazism* (Woodbridge, 2006), 153–55.
93. AK 30 Sept. (quote) and 1 Oct. 1947; see Karnick and Richter (eds), *Protestant*, 221–7.
94. MN to Ludwig Bartning, 7 Oct. 1947, ZEKHN, 62/1295a.
95. MN to E. Theodore Bachmann, 4 Oct. 1947, ZEKHN, 62/499; see MN to Ludwig Bartning, 7 Oct. 1947, ZEKHN, 62/1295a.
96. Karnick and Richter (eds), *Protestant*, 291.
97. Greschat, *Christenheit*, 164–74, quote 169.
98. Ibid., 359–69; see Smith-van Osten, *Treysa*, 364–81.
99. Greschat, *Christenheit*, 369–70; quote in Besier (ed.), *Intimately Associated*, 481.
100. For details, see Ziemann, 'Außenamt'.
101. MN to Haug, 18 Apr. 1952, LkA Stuttgart, A 126, No. 389, fo. 196; memorandum Weeber 30 Apr. 1952, also MN to Haug, 26 Apr. 1952, LkA Stuttgart, A 126, No. 2185, fo. 21.
102. Dibelius to Heinrich Held, 31 May 1955, EZA, 81/1009.
103. Dibelius to Constantin von Dietze, 22 July 1955, EZA, 81/1010.
104. Quoted in Greschat, *Protestantismus im Kalten Krieg*, 255. See Flemming, *Heinemann*, 93–127, 240–9.
105. MN to Hans Asmussen, 22 June 1946, ZEKHN, 62/539.
106. On this conflict, which deserves further analysis, see the letters in ZEKHN, 62/539 and 62/540.
107. Asmussen to MN, 2 July 1946, ZEKHN, 62/539.

Notes to Chapter 15

1. MN, [reply to questions by Ben L. Rose], n.d. [Sept. 1945], ZEKHN, 62/43.
2. MN, [replies to a questionnaire of the US military], n.d. [1945], ZEKHN, 62/43. Hockenos, *Then They Came For Me*, 169, assumes with good reason that Niemöller answered this questionnaire during the short period of internment in Wiesbaden.
3. Vollnhals (ed.), *Die evangelische Kirche*, 39 (6 July 1945).

4. 'Presseempfang mit Pfarrer Niemöller', 30 June 1947, ELAB 55.1/672.

5. Gerhard Besier, Hartmut Ludwig, and Jörg Thierfelder (eds), *Der Kompromiß von Treysa. Die Entstehung der Evangelischen Kirche in Deutschland (EKD) 1945. Eine Dokumentation* (Weinheim, 1995), 294.

6. Michael J. Inacker, *Zwischen Transzendenz, Totalitarismus und Demokratie. Die Entwicklung des kirchlichen Demokratieverständnisses von der Weimarer Republik bis zu den Anfängen der Bundesrepublik 1918–1959* (Neukirchen-Vluyn, 1994), 189–92; Dorothee Buchhaas-Birkholz, 'Einleitung', in Buchhaas-Birkholz (ed.), *"Zum politischen Weg unseres Volkes". Politische Leitbilder und Vorstellungen im deutschen Protestantismus 1945–1952. Eine Dokumentation* (Düsseldorf, 1989), 9–33, here 25–7.

7. Text of the declaration at https://www.ekd.de/Barmer-Theologische-Erklarung-11292. htm; Buchholz-Birkhaas, 'Einleitung', 20. On the theological premises of 'kingship', see Hyun-Beom Choi, *Die Politische Ethik der protestantischen Theologie im 20. Jahrhundert: Karl Barth, Barmen und die koreanische evangelische Kirche* (Münster, 2003), 109–11.

8. Besier et al. (eds), *Treysa*, 266.

9. Ibid., 249.

10. Friedrich Wilhelm Graf, 'Vom Munus Propheticum Christi zum prophetischen Wächteramt der Kirche? Erwägungen zum Verhältnis von Christologie und Ekklesiologie', *Zeitschrift für Evangelische Ethik* 32 (1988), 88–106.

11. Martin Greschat, *Die evangelische Christenheit und die deutsche Geschichte nach 1945. Weichenstellungen in der Nachkriegszeit* (Stuttgart, 2002), 322–30, quote 329.

12. Minutes of the meeting on 6–7 July 1947: Buchholz-Birkhaas (ed.), *"Zum politischen Weg"*, 77–104, quote 101.

13. Ibid., 101–2; see Greschat, *Christenheit*, 288–96.

14. Buchholz-Birkhaas (ed.), *"Zum politischen Weg"*, 104–6. Niemöller's draft in: Martin Greschat (ed.), *Im Zeichen der Schuld. 40 Jahre Stuttgarter Schuldbekenntnis. Eine Dokumentation* (Neukirchen-Vlyn, 1985), 81–2.

15. Inacker, *Transzendenz*, 206.

16. Greschat, *Christenheit*, 332–4, quote 334.

17. Minutes of the meeting on 15–16 Oct. 1947: Buchholz-Birkhaas (ed.), *"Zum politischen Weg"*, 116–32, quote 127.

18. Ibid., 128.

19. Ibid., 122.

20. Ibid., 121–2.

21. 'Kontrollbericht' des Volkspolizei Kreisamtes Halle, 21 Oct. 1952 and Volkspolizei Berlin to Ministerium des Innern der DDR, 12 Feb. 1954, BStU, HA XX AP 11907/92, fos 5–7, 27–8.

22. Buchholz-Birkhaas (ed.), *"Zum politischen Weg"*, 129.

23. Inacker, *Transzendenz*, 207.

24. Ibid.; Graf, 'Munus Propheticum', 98.

25. MN to Gisevius, 30 Dec. 1947, ZEKHN, 35/923.

26. MN from Auckland (New Zealand) to Heinemann, 22 Oct. 1949, AdsD, NL Heinemann, 0492.

27. 'Niemoeller For United Reich, Even if It's Red', *New York Herald Tribune*, 14 Dec. 1949, reprint in Karnick and Richter (eds.), *Protestant*, 247.

28. Hans-Joachim Oeffler, Hans Prolingheuer, Martin Schuck, et al. (eds), *Martin Niemöller. Ein Lesebuch* (Cologne, 1987), 154–5.

29. Martin Greschat, *Protestantismus im Kalten Krieg. Kirche, Politik und Gesellschaft im geteilten Deutschland 1945–1963* (Paderborn, 2010), 76–7.

30. MN to Hans Bernd Gisevius, n.d. [presumably June 1953], ZEKHN, 35/923.

31. 'Martin Niemöller zum Higgins Interview', first published in *Wiesbadener Tageblatt*, 16 Dec. 1949, LkA EvKvW, 5.1, 444 F. 2, fos 69–70. Here also some further press coverage.

32. MN to Heinemann, 22 Dec. 1949, AdsD, NL Heinemann, Allgemeine Korrespondenz; see Franz Beyer, *Menschen warten. Aus dem politischen Wirken Martin Niemöllers seit 1945* (Siegen, 1952), 169–70.

33. Benjamin Ziemann, 'Religion and the Search for Meaning, 1945–1990', in Helmut Walser Smith (ed.), *The Oxford Handbook of Modern German History* (Oxford, 2011), 693–714, 690.

34. Kristian Buchna, *Ein klerikales Jahrzehnt? Kirche, Konfession und Politik in der Bundesrepublik während der 1950er Jahre* (Baden-Baden, 2014), 348–68, quotes 349–50.

35. As he wrote in a letter to Hermann Kunst from 1953: ibid., 354.

36. Ulrich Herbert, *Geschichte Deutschlands im 20. Jahrhundert* (Munich, 2014), 629–36; in detail, Norbert Wiggershaus, 'Die Entscheidung für einen westdeutschen Verteidigungsbeitrag 1950', in *Anfänge westdeutscher Sicherheitspolitik: 1945–1956*, vol. 1: *Von der Kapitulation bis zum Pleven-Plan* (Munich, 1982), 325–402.

37. MN to Heinemann, 11 Feb. 1950, AdsD, NL Heinemann, Allgemeine Korrespondenz.

38. MN to Heinemann, 4 July 1950, AdsD, NL Heinemann, Allgemeine Korrespondenz.

39. Paul Mahlmann to Franz Beyer, 27 Sept. 1950, ZEKHN, 62/879; see Beyer to Mahlmann, 29 Sept. 1950, ZEKHN, 62/879.

40. MN, open letter of 4 Oct. 1950, LkA EvKvW, 5.1 446 F. 2, fo. 202.

41. Thomas Flemming, *Gustav W. Heinemann. Ein deutscher Citoyen. Biographie* (Essen, 2013), 218–24.

42. 'Paul Mahlmann', *Frankfurter Neue Presse*, 18 Oct. 1950; Mahlmann to Beyer, 16 Oct. 1950, ZEKHN, 62/879.

43. See dpa main editorial office to MN, 16 Nov. 1950, and 'betr. Thema Niemoeller/ Mahlmann', ibid.

44. Dibelius in the EKD Council, 5 Dec. 1950: Anke Silomon (ed.), *Die Protokolle des Rates der evangelischen Kirche in Deutschland*, vol. 4: *1950* (Göttingen, 2007), 367, footnote 1.

45. Dibelius to MN, 23 Oct. 1950, and his reply of 26 Oct. 1950, ZEKHN, 62/564; Greschat, *Protestantismus im Kalten Krieg*, 79; the flyer of the National Council of the National Front of the GDR in LkA EvKvW, 5.1, 447 F. 1, fo. 272.

46. Greschat, *Protestantismus im Kalten Krieg*, 86.

47. Adenauer im Bundeskabinett, 17 Oct. 1950, http://www.bundesarchiv.de/cocoon/ barch/0000/index.html (accessed 3 Sept. 2018).

48. IfD Allensbach, Die Stimmung im Bundesgebiet. Die Resonanz des Pfarrers Niemöller, Dezember 1950, 'Vertraulich', IfZ Archiv, MS 1003.006.

49. Johanna Vogel, *Kirche und Wiederbewaffnung. Die Haltung der Evangelischen Kirche in Deutschland in den Auseinandersetzungen um die Wiederbewaffnung der Bundesrepublik 1949–1956* (Göttingen, 1978), 83–153.

50. Hans Asmussen to the members of the EKD Council, 23 Oct. 1950, AdsD, NL Heinemann, Allgemeine Korrespondenz.
51. Dibelius to Hans Wellhausen, 10 Nov. 1950, AdsD, NL Heinemann, Allgemeine Korrespondenz.
52. Kirchlich-Theologischer Arbeitskreis der Gesellschaft für Innere und Äußere Mission, Einspruch gegen die Entschließung des Rates der EKD vom 17 Nov. 1950 zum Fall Niemöller, LkA EvKvW, 5.1, 446 F. 2, fos 303–4; Greschat, *Protestantismus im Kalten Krieg*, 110–11 (quote); see Chapter 14.
53. MN, *Kriegsschauplatz*. The first version of this text was published in October 1950 as MN, 'Die Not der Deutschen', *Die Stimme der Gemeinde* 2 (1950), No. 10 (LkA EvKvW, 5.1, 446 F. 2, fos 52–3.).
54. MN, *Kriegsschauplatz oder Brücke? Ein evangelisches Wort zu der Not der Deutschen* (Frankfurt am Main, n.d. [1951]) (no page numbers).
55. Michael Geyer, 'Der Kalte Krieg, die Deutschen und die Angst. Die westdeutsche Opposition gegen Wiederbewaffnung und Kernwaffen', in Klaus Naumann (ed.), *Nachkrieg in Deutschland* (Hamburg, 2001), 267–318, 281–2.
56. Lawrence S. Wittner, *One World or None: A History of the World Nuclear Disarmament Movement through 1953* (Stanford, 1994), 171–90, 238–9.
57. Martin Greschat, '"Er ist ein Feind dieses Staates!" Martin Niemöllers Aktivitäten in den Anfangsjahren der Bundesrepublik Deutschland', *Zeitschrift für Kirchengeschichte* 114 (2003), 333–56, 348–50.
58. Niemöller still made the same claim when Dibelius travelled to Moscow as part of an official delegation of the EKD Council in November 1952, accompanied by the bishops Hahn and Lilje. Dibelius to MN, 4 Nov. 1952 and his reply of 7 Nov. 1952, ZEKHN, 62/564.
59. Greschat, 'Feind', 350.
60. Quoted in Jan Niemöller, *Erkundung gegen den Strom 1952. Martin Niemöller reist nach Moskau. Eine Dokumentation* (Stuttgart, 1988), 18–20. Emphasis in the original.
61. Ibid., 35–80.
62. MN, 'Meine Reise nach Moskau', *Der Spiegel*, no. 3, 16 Jan. 1952.
63. Ibid.; see Greschat, 'Feind', 351–2.
64. Greschat, 'Feind', 352; Edgar Büttner, '"Ich bin ganz harmlos hingefahren und bin ganz harmlos zurückgekommen." Zur Moskaureise Martin Niemöllers im Jahr 1952', in Klaus Oldenhage, Hermann Schreyer, and Wolfram Werner (eds), *Archiv und Geschichte. Festschrift für Friedrich P. Kahlenberg* (Düsseldorf, 2000), 845–57, 850–4.
65. File memorandum about a visit of Pastor Martin Niemöller to Ambassador Appelt, 4 Jan. 1952, PA/AA, MfAA, A 15546, fos 2–4.
66. File memorandum about a visit of Ambassador Appelt to the head of the 3rd European Department of the Foreign Office, 4 Jan. 1952, PA/AA, MfAA, A 15546, fo. 5.
67. File memorandum about the reception for Pastor Niemöller on 7 Jan. 1952, PA/AA, MfAA, A 15546, fos 6–7.
68. 'Unruhe', *Göttinger Tageblatt*, 16 Jan. 1952, LkA EvKvW, 5.1, 448 F. 1, fo. 46; see press coverage in ELAB 55.1/675.
69. Claudia Lepp, *Tabu der Einheit? Die Ost-West Gemeinschaft der evangelischen Christen und die deutsche Teilung (1945–1969)* (Göttingen, 2005), 138–9; see *Der Spiegel*, no. 3, 16 Jan. 1952, 15.

70. Quoted in Greschat, 'Feind', 354.

71. Greschat, *Protestantismus im Kalten Krieg*, 107, 109.

72. MN, *Deutschland wohin? Krieg oder Frieden? Rede vom 17. Januar in Darmstadt* (Darmstadt, 1952), 3 (quote), 25; Hermine Hermes to WN, 5 Mar. 1952, LkA EvKvW, 5.1, 448 F. 1, fo. 178.

73. MN, *Deutschland wohin?*, 16–21, 26, 28.

74. MN to Heinemann, 1 Mar. 1951, AdsD, NL Heinemann, Allgemeine Korrespondenz.

75. MN to Ulrich Noack (copy), 26 Jan. 1951, AdsD, NL Heinemann, Allgemeine Korrespondenz; Flemming, *Heinemann*, 251–2.

76. MN to Heinemann, 26 Nov. 1951, AdsD, NL Heinemann, part 2, 0640; Flemming, *Heinemann*, 252–4, 275–82.

77. MN to Hans Bernd Gisevius, 17 Apr. 1953, ZEKHN, 62/923.

78. MN, 'Meine Reise nach Moskau', *Der Spiegel*, no. 3, 16 Jan. 1952.

79. Herbert, *Geschichte*, 638.

80. MN to Heinemann, 21 Nov. 1950, AdsD, NL Heinemann, part 2, 0639.

81. Flemming, *Heinemann*, 282–99, quote 289.

82. MN, *Reden 1945–1954* (Darmstadt, 1958), 266–7.

83. Greschat, *Protestantismus im Kalten Krieg*, 157–60, quote 160.

84. MN to Mochalski, 23 July 1953, ZEKHN, 62/661.

85. Greschat, *Protestantismus im Kalten Krieg*, 160.

86. Ibid., 162.

87. MN, 'Unser Volk unter den Völkern', in MN, *Reden 1945–1954*, 253–65, quotes 255, 259, 261–2; Lepp, *Tabu der Einheit*, 170–3.

88. Greschat, *Protestantismus im Kalten Krieg*, 161.

89. MN, 'Dreißig Jahre Bundesrepublik. Erlebnisse und Gedanken', *Blätter für deutsche und internationale Politik* 24 (1979), 13–26, quotes 14–16, 18–19, 23. Emphasis in the original.

90. Greschat, *Christenheit*, 377–87, quote 387; see Besier, *Die Rolle der Kirchen im Gründungsprozeß der Bundesrepublik Deutschland* (Lüneburg, 2000), 26–30, 35–6.

91. Graf, 'Munus Propheticum', 100.

Notes to Chapter 16

1. MN [answers to the questions by Ben L. Rose], undated [Sept. 1945], ZEKHN 62/43.

2. MN, *Reden 1945–1954*, 153–8, quotes 154, 157; Greschat, *Christenheit*, 385–6.

3. AK 18 Apr. 1949.

4. MN, *Reden 1945–1954*, 159–69, quote 160.

5. Michael Werner, 'Zur Relevanz der "Ohne mich"-Bewegung in der Auseinandersetzung um den Wehrbeitrag', in Detlef Bald and Wolfram Wette (eds), *Friedensinitiativen in der Frühzeit des Kalten Krieges 1945–1955* (Essen, 2010), 79–86.

6. Hans Karl Rupp, *Außerparlamentarische Opposition in der Ära Adenauer: Der Kampf gegen die Atombewaffnung in den fünfziger Jahren. Eine Studie zur innenpolitischen Entwicklung der BRD* (Cologne, 1970), 52.

7. Niemöller's speech in Potsdam on 13 Jan. 1951, BStU, HA XX AP 11907/92, fos 81–91, quote fo. 89.

8. Ibid.

9. MN, *Reden 1945–1954*, 226.

10. EN, 'Was kann die christliche Frau für den Frieden tun?', 29 Apr. 1950, ZEKHN, 62/6093.

11. EN, 'We Women and Peace', undated [1952], ZEKHN, 62/6093.

12. Eckart Dietzfelbinger, *Die westdeutsche Friedensbewegung 1948 bis 1955. Die Protestaktionen gegen die Remilitarisierung der Bundesrepublik Deutschland* (Cologne, 1984), 119; Klara Marie Faßbinder, 'Unserer Ehrenpräsidentin Else Niemöller zum Gedächtnis', *Frau und Frieden* 10 (1961), no. 9, 8–9; Helga Meyer, *Women's Campaign against West German Rearmament, 1949–1953* (Ann Arbor, 1989), 147–82.

13. Matthew D. Hockenos, 'Martin Niemöller, the Cold War, and his Embrace of Pacifism, 1945–1955', *Kirchliche Zeitgeschichte* 27 (2014), 87–101, 90–1; Helmut Donat and Karl Holl (eds), *Die Friedensbewegung. Organisierter Pazifismus in Deutschland, Österreich und in der Schweiz* (Düsseldorf, 1983), 200–1.

14. Hockenos, 'Embrace', 91.

15. A.J. Muste to MN, 23 Aug. 1950, EZA, 626/232.

16. Friedrich Siegmund-Schultze to MN, 7 Nov. 1950, EZA, 626/232.

17. 'Die Jahrestagung des Versöhnungsbundes in Heidelberg', *Die Versöhnung* 3 (1952), no. 2, 1–14, 7–8.

18. MN, 'Unser Glaubenskampf gegen die Angst', in MN et al., *Frieden. Der Christ im Kampf gegen die Angst und den Gewaltgeist der Zeit* (Zurich, 1954), 11–30.

19. International Fellowship of Reconciliation/Hans Maier to MN (quote), 29 May 1954 and his reply of 2 June 1954, ZEKHN, 62/781. Here also the correspondence between Niemöller and Siegmund-Schultze in previous years. On the Fellowship simultaneously reaching out to Heinemann and his circle, see Andreas Permien, *Protestantismus und Wiederbewaffnung 1950–1955. Die Kritik in der Evangelischen Kirche im Rheinland und der Evangelischen Kirche von Westfalen an Adenauers Wiederbewaffnungspolitik* (Cologne, 1994), 126–30.

20. Martin Greschat, 'Reaktionen der evangelischen Kirche auf den 17. Juni 1953', in Martin Greschat and Jochen-Christoph Kaiser (eds), *Die Kirchen im Umfeld des 17. Juni 1953* (Stuttgart, 2003), 85–108, 93–6, quote 96.

21. Text of the speech in Greschat and Kaiser (eds), Die Kirchen, 105–8; Greschat, 'Reaktionen', 97.

22. Hockenos, 'Embrace', 98.

23. MN, 'Christ und Krieg' (1960), in MN, *Reden 1958–1961* (Frankfurt am Main, 1961), 179–205, here 193–4; Hockenos, 'Embrace', 100–1, overreaches when suggesting that the process of revision happened during the years of Niemöller's concentration camp imprisonment.

24. Ilona Stölken-Fitschen, *Atombombe und Geistesgeschichte. Eine Studie der fünfziger Jahre aus deutscher Sicht* (Baden-Baden, 1995), 91–5; Lawrence Wittner, *Resisting the Bomb: A History of the World Nuclear Disarmament Movement, 1954–1970* (Stanford, 1997), 146–8, 153–4.

25. Appeal from 21 May 1954: Karl-Heinz Fix (ed.), *Die Protokolle des Rates der Evangelischen Kirche in Deutschland*, vol. 8: *1954/55* (Göttingen, 2012), 234–5.

26. AK 9 June 1954.

27. Copy of the transcript by Prof. Gollwitzer, sent to the members of the EKD council by MN on 5 July 1954, EZA, 87/1068.

28. MN to Gollwitzer, 22 June 1954, EZA, 87/1068.

29. MN, *Martin Niemöller zur atomaren Rüstung, Zwei Reden* (Darmstadt, 1959), 6, and in January 1960, MN, *Reden 1958-1961*, 194.

30. Fix (ed.), *Protokolle des Rates der EKD*, vol. 8, 234–5 (quote); Greschat, *Protestantismus im Kalten Krieg*, 268.

31. Bruno Thoß, *NATO-Strategie und nationale Verteidigungsplanung. Planung und Aufbau der Bundeswehr unter den Bedingungen einer massiven atomaren Vergeltungsstrategie 1952 bis 1960* (Munich, 2006), 446–50.

32. Quoted in Greschat, *Protestantismus im Kalten Krieg*, 269.

33. Benjamin Ziemann, 'German Angst? Debating Cold War Anxieties in West Germany, 1945-1990', in Matthew Grant and Benjamin Ziemann (eds), *Understanding the Imaginary War: Intellectual Reflections of the Nuclear Age, 1945-90* (Manchester, 2016), 116–39, 119–22.

34. Robert Lorenz, *Protest der Physiker. Die Göttinger Erklärung von 1957* (Bielefeld, 2011), 31–2 for the text of the Manifesto.

35. Ibid., 58–61.

36. Axel Schildt, '"Atomzeitalter" – Gründe und Hintergründe der Proteste gegen die atomare Bewaffnung der Bundeswehr Ende der fünfziger Jahre', in *"Kampf dem Atomtod!" Die Protestbewegung 1957/58 in zeithistorischer und gegenwärtiger Perspektive* (Munich/Hamburg, 2009), 39–56, 42–5.

37. Greschat, *Protestantismus im Kalten Krieg*, 273–6; Ulrich Möller, *Im Prozeß des Bekennens. Brennpunkte der kirchlichen Atomwaffendiskussion im deutschen Protestantismus 1957-1962* (Neukirchen-Vluyn, 1999).

38. Rupp, *Opposition*, 120–30.

39. Ibid., 130–2, 283–4.

40. Heinz Kloppenburg, Protokoll der Sitzung am 22.2.1958 im Schaumburger Hof, Bad Godesberg, EZA 613/84. Abbreviations in the original written out.

41. Eva Horn, 'The Apocalyptic Fiction: Shaping the Future in the Cold War', in Matthew Grant and Benjamin Ziemann (eds), *Understanding the Imaginary War: Culture, Thought and Nuclear Conflict, 1945-90* (Manchester, 2016), 30–50, 43–4, 46–7; see MN, *Reden 1958-1961*, 95.

42. Heinz Kloppenburg, Protokoll der Sitzung am 22.2.1958 im Schaumburger Hof, Bad Godesberg, EZA 613/84. Abbreviations in the original written out.

43. Ibid.; Rupp, *Opposition*, 133 (quote).

44. Rupp, *Opposition*, 162–93, figure 191; Schildt, 'Atomzeitalter', 47–8; Annegret Jürgens-Kirchhoff, '"Artists against Nuclear War" (1958–1962): A Touring Exhibition at the Time of the Cold War', in Benjamin Ziemann (ed.), *Peace Movements in Western Europe, Japan and the USA during the Cold War* (Essen, 2007), 211–36.

45. AK May/June 1958, esp. 27 May, 3, 12, and 19 June 1958.

46. Holger Nehring, *Politics of Security: British and West German Protest Movements and the Early Cold War, 1945-1970* (Oxford, 2013), 63–156.

47. AK 7 Apr. 1958. Shortly afterwards, Niemöller travelled to London again and participated in the Annual Meeting of the PPU, AK 20 Apr. 1958; Martin Ceadel, *Pacifism in Britain, 1914-1945: The Defining of a Faith* (Oxford, 1980), 242–92.

48. Nehring, *Politics of Security*, 156–89.

49. Rupp, *Opposition*, 194–202.

50. Ibid., 6–7.

51. *Martin Niemöller zur atomaren Rüstung*, 13–14.

52. Ibid., 18.

53. Jason Dawsey, 'After Hiroshima: Günther Anders and the History of Anti-Nuclear Critique', in Matthew Grant and Benjamin Ziemann (eds), *Understanding the Imaginary War: Culture, Thought and Nuclear Conflict, 1945–90* (Manchester, 2016), 140–64, 147–8; Günther Anders, 'Thesen zum Atomzeitalter' (1960), *Das Argument*, special issue 1/1 (1974), 226–34.

54. Benjamin Ziemann, 'Situating Peace Movements in the Political Culture of the Cold War: Introduction', in Benjamin Ziemann (ed.), *Peace Movements in Western Europe, Japan and the USA during the Cold War* (Essen, 2007), 11–38.

55. Karl Holl, *Pazifismus in Deutschland* (Frankfurt am Main, 1988), 138–58, 220–1.

56. Stefan Appelius, *Pazifismus in Westdeutschland. Die Deutsche Friedensgesellschaft 1945–1968*, vol. 1 (Aachen, 1999), 405; Michael Werner, 'August Bangel – Hermann L. Brill – Fritz Wenzel. Drei Sozialdemokraten in der Deutschen Friedensgesellschaft', in Detlef Bald and Wolfram Wette (eds), *Alternativen zur Wiederbewaffnung. Friedenskonzeptionen in Westdeutschland 1945–1955* (Essen, 2008), 71–85, 82–3.

57. Max Stierwaldt to the groups of the DFG Landesverband Nord, 30 Oct. 1957, LAV NRW R, RW 115, no. 256, fo. 125; August Bangel to Fritz Küster, 31 Oct. 1957, LAV NRW R, RW 115, no. 256, fo. 126.

58. Erica Küppers to Pauline Kredel, 28 Jan. 1960, LkA EvKvW, 5.1, 458 F. 2, fos 104–5.

59. Max Stierwaldt to Walter Auerbach, 9 Oct. 1950, quoted in Appelius, *Friedensgesellschaft*, vol. 1, 254.

60. Maria Häffner to August Bangel, 2 Sept. 1957, LAV NRW R, RW 115, no. 256, fo. 219; see Maria Häffner to Dr Müller, 5 Oct. 1957, LAV NRW R, RW 115, no. 256, fos 156–7.

61. Heinz Kraschutzki to August Bangel, 10 Nov. 1957, LAV NRW R, RW 115, no. 256, fo. 104; Appelius, *Friedensgesellschaft*, vol. 2, 561–3.

62. AK 25 Jan. 1959.

63. Einstellungsbescheid des Oberstaatsanwalts beim Landgericht Frankfurt/M., 20 May 1959, LAV NRW W, Q 211, no. 480.

64. MN, *Niemöllers Kasseler Rede vom 25. Januar 1959 im vollen Wortlaut. Was Niemöller sagt—wogegen Strauß klagt* (Darmstadt, 1959), quote 6.

65. 'Wehrdienst Hohe Schule des Berufsverbrechertums', *Kasseler Post*, 27 Jan. 1959; see Niemöller, 'Die Ausbildung zum Soldaten muß als eine Hohe Schule für Berufsverbrecher bezeichnet werden', *Frankfurter Abendpost*, 27 Jan. 1959. Both in BArch, BW 1, 9879.

66. MN, Erklärung, 27 Jan. 1959, BArch, BW 2, 20198.

67. Memo VR II 7, 27 Jan. 1959, and telex Wehrbereichskommando IV 26 Jan. 1959 to BMVtg-Pressereferat, BArch, BW 1, 9879.

68. BMVtg, VR II 7 27 Jan. 1959 to UAL VR II, BArch, BW 1, 9879.

69. BMVtg, VR II 7, signed Strauß, 27 Jan. 1959 to chief prosecutor Kassel, BArch, BW 1, 9879.

70. Telex Wehrbereichskommando I 27 Jan. 1959 to Bundeswehrverband Bonn via BMVtg, memo Major Bauer Fü B I 6, 28 Jan. 1959, and Bodo Zimmermann 27 Jan. 1959 to EKD (quotes), BArch, BW 1, 9879.

71. Greschat, *Protestantismus im Kalten Krieg*, 287; Gerstenmaier as president of the Bundestag to Strauß, 28 Jan. 1959, BArch, BW 1, 9879.

72. Erica Küppers, 'Zur Kampagne gegen Niemöller', *Stimme der Gemeinde* no. 4/1959, 105–18; Heinrich David, 'Niemöller und die "böse Presse"', *DIE ZEIT*, 27 Feb. 1959. These and further articles in, LkA EvKvW, 5.1, 456 F. 2; see LkA EvKvW, 5.1, 457 F. 1, fo. 32.

73. Letter to the editor Dr Lucie Jacobi, 'Immer im Recht', *FAZ*, 2 Feb. 1959.

74. BMVtg, VR II 7, 24 Apr. 1959 to the head of department VR II and Federal Minister of Defence 14 May 1959 to chief prosecutor at the Landgericht Frankfurt/Main, BArch, BW 1, 9879.

75. Nehring, *Politics of Security*, 67, 120–1, 203.

76. See *Pläne* Heft 4/5 (1961), no page numbers, LkA EvKvW, 5.1, 462 F. 1, fo. 138.

77. Adolf Freudenberg, speech on 22 Apr. 1962, EZA 686/575.

78. MN, 'Die Zündschnüre durchschneiden!' (1964), in MN, *Reden, Predigten, Denkanstöße 1964–1976*, ed. Hans Joachim Oeffler (Cologne, 1977), 16–18, quotes 17.

79. Andrew Oppenheimer, 'By Any Means Necessary? West German Pacifism and the Politics of Solidarity, 1945–1974', in Benjamin Ziemann (ed.), *Peace Movements in Western Europe, Japan and the USA during the Cold War* (Essen, 2007), 41–60.

80. MN, *Reden 1958–1961*, 26.

81. MN, 'Pazifistische Realpolitik', *Neue Wege. Beiträge zu Religion und Sozialismus* 53 (1959), no. 12, 329–36, quotes 334.

82. Oppenheimer, 'Politics of Solidarity', 51.

83. MN, 'Die Bedeutung des Widerstandes in der heutigen Zeit' (1967), in MN, *Reden, Predigten, Denkanstöße*, 110–13, quote 112.

84. Oppenheimer, 'Politics of Solidarity', 51–2; Daniel Gerster, *Friedensdialoge im Kalten Krieg. Eine Geschichte der Katholiken in der Bundesrepublik 1957–1983* (Frankfurt am Main/New York, 2012), 132–3.

85. AK 2–9 Jan. 1967, quotes 3, 5, and 8 Jan. 1967.

86. 'Lasst diesen Unsinn endlich aufhören!', *Der Spiegel*, no. 4, 16 Jan. 1967, 74.

87. MN, 'Bericht über die Reise nach Hanoi in Nord-Vietnam', 17 June 1967, BStU, HA XX AP 11890/92, quotes fos 60–1, 64.

88. See epd 24 Oct. 172, ELAB 55.1/679. This is one of the reasons why I think it is wrong to see Niemöller's pacifism motivated by Gandhi's notion of non-violent resistance. See Hockenos, *Then They Came for Me*, 232–3.

89. MN, 'Bericht über die Reise nach Hanoi in Nord-Vietnam', 17 June 1967, BStU, HA XX AP 11890/92, quote fo. 50.

90. MN, 'Erfahrungen im Einsatz für eine friedliche Welt' (1967), in MN, *Reden, Predigten, Denkanstöße*, 135–44, quote 139.

91. Thomas Wolf, 'Die Rede Martin Niemöllers im Siegener Lyzeum, 30. Juni 1959. Eine Episode in der Geschichte der Siegerländer Friedensbewegung. Textabdruck mit kurzer Einführung', *Siegener Beiträge* 11 (2006), 209–19, 209; 'Mann der Brandung', *Westdeutsche Allgemeine Zeitung*, 26 Mar. 1962, LAV NRW R, RW 115, no. 184, fo. 70.

92. Appelius, *Friedensgesellschaft*, vol. 2, 510.

93. Ibid., 511–12, 523–5.

94. Ibid., 507.

95. Quoted in ibid., 534.
96. Gustav Heinemann to Pastor Gottfried Wandersleb, 25 Jan. 1965, LAV NRW R, RW 115, no. 198, fo. 121. His public criticism in Gustav Heinemann, 'Antwort an Niemöller', *Sozialdemokratischer Pressedienst*, 6 Jan. 1965, 2–3.
97. Appelius, *Friedensgesellschaft*, vol. 2, 452–3, 560–1, 664–7.
98. Helge Heidemeyer, 'NATO-Doppelbeschluss, westdeutsche Friedensbewegung und der Einfluss der DDR', in Philipp Gassert, Tim Geiger, and Hermann Wentker (eds), *Zweiter Kalter Krieg und Friedensbewegung. Der NATO-Doppelbeschluss in deutsch-deutscher und internationaler Perspektive* (Munich, 2011), 247–67, 253–4.
99. Christoph Becker-Schaum et al. (eds), *'Entrüstet Euch!' Nuklearkrise, NATO-Doppelbeschluss und Friedensbewegung* (Paderborn, 2012); Gerster, *Friedensdialoge*, 220–314; Jan Hansen, *Abschied vom Kalten Krieg? Die Sozialdemokraten und der Nachrüstungsstreit, 1977–1987* (Munich, 2016); on the legend of the remote-controlled peace movement, see Holger Nehring and Benjamin Ziemann, 'Do all Paths Lead to Moscow? The NATO Dual-Track Decision and the Peace Movement – A Critique', *Cold War History* 12 (2012), 1–24.
100. MN, 'Für unser Handeln Verantwortung tragen', in Volkmar Deile (ed.), *Bonn 10.10.1981. Friedensdemonstration für Abrüstung und Entspannung in Europa. Reden, Fotos* (Bornheim, 1981), 111–12.
101. August Bangel to Ingeborg Küster, 10 June 1964, LAV NRW R, RW 115, no. 184, fo. 158.
102. Donat, 'Kraschutzki', 343.

Notes to Chapter 17

1. David Thompson, 'Ecumenism', in Hugh McLeod (ed.), *The Cambridge History of Christianity*, vol. 9: *World Christianities c.1914–c.2000* (Cambridge, 2006), 50–70, 50–3.
2. Ibid., 54–9.
3. Armin Boyens, *Kirchenkampf und Ökumene. 1939–1945. Darstellung und Dokumentation unter besonderer Berücksichtigung der Quellen des Ökumenischen Rates der Kirchen* (Munich, 1973), 96–101.
4. Otto Langmann, 'Aufzeichnung', 16 June 1937, PA/AA, R 61621.
5. Boyens, *Kirchenkampf*, 144–51.
6. MN, *Briefe Moabit*, 81.
7. MN, *Gedanken über den Weg der christlichen Kirche*, 208–9.
8. MN to EN, 31 Oct. 1942, ZEKHN, 35/573.
9. MN to EN, 30 May 1944, ZEKHN, 35/573.
10. Christophersen and Ziemann, 'Einleitung', 16, with footnote 35 at 216.
11. MN to EN, 26 Apr. 1943 and 30 May 1944, ZEKHN, 35/573.
12. MN, *Sechs Dachauer Predigten*, 4.
13. Ibid., 3, 5–12, quote 12.
14. Turner, 'Niemöllers in Amerika', 306.
15. MN to EN, 27 Dec. 1944, ZEKHN, 35/573.

16. Ibid.

17. MN, ...zu verkündigen ein gnädiges Jahr des Herrn! Sechs Dachauer Predigten (Munich, 1945), esp. 17.

18. Willem Adolph Visser 't Hooft, Die Welt war meine Gemeinde. Autobiographie (Munich, 1972), 228.

19. Visser 't Hooft to MN, 9 Nov. 1945, WCC Files, Box 42.0059, MF no. 1023.

20. Visser 't Hooft to MN, 21 Dec. 1945, WCC, GC Box 42.0059, MF no. 1024; Visser 't Hooft to MN, 27 Sept. 1945, WCC Files, Box 42.0059, MF no. 1023; Hockenos, Then They Came for Me, 192; Gerhard Besier, Armin Boyens, and Gerhard Lindemann, Nationaler Protestantismus und Ökumenische Bewegung: Kirchliches Handeln im Kalten Krieg (1945–1990). Mit einer Nachschrift von Horst-Klaus Hofmann (Berlin, 1999), 331–2.

21. Minutes of the meeting on 7 March 1946, KBA 9107.302; MN to Visser 't Hooft, 10 Oct. 1045, WCC Files, Box 42.0059, MF no. 1023 ('Erholungsfahrt'); AK 15–25 Feb. and 7–8 Mar. 1946; see Rusterholz, Nachbars Haus, 70–1.

22. His report in 'Pastor Niemöller: Amerikanische Predigt', VVN-Nachrichten. Mitteilungsblatt der Vereinigung der Verfolgten des Nazi-Regimes Württemberg-Baden no. 18, 21 June 1947.

23. MN, Reden 1945–1954, 39–40 (quote); see Visser 't Hooft, Welt, 235–7.

24. AK 3–9 Nov. 1946.

25. AK 15 May 1945; see MN, 'Bericht über meine Amerikafahrt im Winter 1946/47', 1 (undated), ZEKHN, 62/171.

26. AK 21 Nov. 1946; see Hockenos, Then They Came For Me, 187–209, quote 189. Hockenos provides an excellent account of Niemöller's journey across the USA in 1946–7. However, he only uses sources of American provenance and is hence limited in his analysis of Niemöller's ambivalent attitude towards the USA.

27. Hockenos, Then They Came For Me, 194; see Turner, 'Niemöllers in Amerika', 301–2.

28. AK 19 May 1947; Turner, 'Niemöllers in Amerika', 302–3; Hockenos, Then They Came For Me, 187–9.

29. Ewart E.Turner, 'Niemöllers in Amerika', Bekennende Kirche. Martin Niemöller zum 60. Geburtstag (Munich, 1952), 301–7, 302–4, quote 303; Hockenos, Then They Came For Me, 194–5, 211–12; MN, 'Bericht über meine Amerikafahrt im Winter 1946/47' (undated), ZEKHN, 62/171.

30. MN, 'Bericht über meine Reise nach den Vereinigten Staaten' (June 1947), EZA, 2/42, fos 48–54.

31. Ibid., fo. 48.

32. Balbier, 'Billy Graham's Cold War Crusades'.

33. 'Pastor Niemöller: Amerikanische Predigt', VVN-Nachrichten. Mitteilungsblatt der Vereinigung der Verfolgten des Nazi-Regimes Württemberg-Baden, no. 18, 21 June 1947.

34. MN, 'The faith that sustains me, Ansprache in Seattle', 4 Dec. 1946, LkA EvKvW, 5.1, 442 F. 2, fos 150–2; see Hockenos, Then They Came For Me, 197–200.

35. Address by Pastor Martin Niemöller, Dayton (Ohio), 4 Feb. 1947, WCC-Files, Box 42.0059, MF no. 1026.

36. EN to MN, 7 Feb. 1947, ZEKHN, 62/6080; Turner, 'Niemöllers in Amerika', 304–5.

37. AK 26 Dec. 1946, 1, 3, 4, 8 Jan. and 1 Feb. 1947 (quote). The same quote also in MN, 'Bericht über meine Reise nach den Vereinigten Staaten' (June 1947), EZA, 2/42, fo. 50; Hockenos, *Then They Came For Me*, 205–7.

38. Don E. Smucker to 'dear brother Lehmann', 20 Mar. 1947, IfZ, OMGUS, Shipment 5, Box 342–1, Folder 32.

39. Caitlin Carenen, *The Fervent Embrace: Liberal Protestants, Evangelicals, and Israel* (New York, 2012), 49–57. Niemöller met Niebuhr for two conversations in New York. AK 22 and 23 Jan. 1947.

40. 'Gegen Niemöller', *FAZ*, 6 Mar. 1952.

41. AK 15 Jan. 1947 ('bad press'); MN, 'Bericht über meine Reise nach den Vereinigten Staaten' (June 1947), EZA, 2/42, fo. 48.

42. MN to Ludwig Bartning, 19 Mar. 1947, ZEKHN, 62/1411.

43. [MN], 'Die "guten" Amerikaner' (undated) [summer 1947], ZEKHN, 62/171.

44. Ibid.

45. Ibid.

46. Robert N. Bellah, 'Civil Religion in America', *Journal of the American Academy of Arts and Sciences* 96 (1967), 1–21.

47. MN to Ludwig Bartning, 19 Mar. 1947, ZEKHN, 62/1411; see [MN], 'Die "guten" Amerikaner'.

48. MN, 'Bericht über meine Amerikafahrt im Winter 1946/47' (undated), ZEKHN, 62/171 ('Ethospredigt'); see Besier et al. (eds), *Treysa*, 109.

49. MN from New York to Hans Bernd Gisevius, 12 May 1947, ZEKHN, 35/923.

50. MN to Paula Niemöller, 2 May 1947, ZEHKN, 62/1287.

51. MN to Ludwig Bartning, 19 Mar. 1947, ZEKHN, 62/1411.

52. Jan C. Behrends, Árpád von Klimó, and Patrice G. Poutrus, 'Antiamerikanismus und die europäische Moderne. Zur Einleitung', in Behrends, von Klimó, and Poutrus (eds), *Anti-Amerikanismus im 20. Jahrhundert. Studien zu Ost- und Westeuropa* (Bonn, 2005), 10–33, 17.

53. AK 11 and 31 Jan., 24 Mar. (quote), and 5 Apr. 1947.

54. MN, 'Bericht über meine Reise nach den Vereinigten Staaten' (June 1947), EZA, 2/42, fo. 53.

55. MN to Elsa Freudenberg, 11 Feb. 1947, ZEKHN, 62/6089.

56. Wilhelm Stählin, *Via vitae. Lebenserinnerungen* (Kassel, 1968), 505; see Annemarie Smith-von Osten, *Von Treysa 1945 bis Eisenach 1948. Zur Geschichte der Grundordnung der Evangelischen Kirche in Deutschland* (Göttingen, 1980), 277–87.

57. On Amsterdam, see Greschat, *Christenheit*, 351–9; Greschat, *Protestantismus im Kalten Krieg*, 368–73.

58. AK 26 Aug. 1948.

59. Cited in Besier et al., *Nationaler Protestantismus*, 333.

60. MN from Sydney to Adolf Freudenberg, 24 Sept. 1949, EZA 686/7319.

61. Katharina Kunter and Annegreth Schilling, '"Der Christ fürchtet den Umbruch nicht". Der Ökumenische Rat der Kirchen im Spannungsfeld von Dekolonisierung, Entwestlichung und Politisierung', in Kunter and Schilling (eds), *Globalisierung der Kirchen. Der Ökumenische Rat der Kirchen und die Entdeckung der Dritten Welt in den 1960er und 1970er Jahren* (Göttingen, 2014), 19–74, here 23, 25.

62. Hans A. De Boer, *Unterwegs notiert. Bericht einer Weltreise. Mit einem Vorwort an den Herrn Kritiker* (Kassel, 1959), 178–9.

63. MN, *Reden 1945–1954*, 229–36, esp. 230.

64. MN, *Reden 1955–1957* (Darmstadt, 1957), 130–6, quotes 133–4.

65. Kunter and Schilling, '"Der Christ fürchtet den Umbruch nicht"', quote 29.

66. MN, *Reden 1958–1961*, 269–82; MN, *Eine Welt oder keine Welt. Reden 1961–1963* (Frankfurt am Main, 1964), 80–6.

67. Visser 't Hooft, *Welt*, 379–80; Besier et al., *Nationaler Protestantismus*, 64–6, 88–99, 105–10.

68. Hockenos, *Then They Came For Me*, 239–41.

69. MN, *Briefe Moabit*, 204.

70. As an example, see the talk he repeatedly gave in 1960: 'Wir und die farbige Welt', in MN, *Reden 1958–1961*, 62–70.

Notes to Chapter 18

1. Dirk Palm, *'Wir sind doch Brüder!' Der evangelische Kirchentag und die deutsche Frage 1949–1961* (Göttingen, 2002), 278–302, quote 294.

2. AK 20 July–1 Aug. 1961, quotes 30 July and 1 Aug. 1961.

3. 'Neuer Streit um Martin Niemöller entbrannt', *Die Welt,* 7 Aug. 1961, LkA EvKvW, 5.1, 460 F. 1, fos 77, 83, 96; AK 6 and 7 Aug. 1961.

4. AK 9 Aug.–22 Oct. 1961, quote 9 Aug. 1961; interview with Dr Heinz-Hermann Niemöller, 23 Mar. 2015.

5. MN to Franz Beyer, 20 Oct. 1961, quoted in Sterik (ed.), *Else Niemöller*, 147.

6. MN to Gerda Gisevius, 13 Nov. 1963, ZEKHN, 35/923.

7. EN to Pauline Kredel, 18 July 1950, LkA EvKvW, 5.1, 446 F. 1, fo. 99.

8. AK 1967, front page.

9. Quote: MN to Paul Herring, 22 Aug. 1971, LkA EvKvW, 5.1, 973; see AK 20 Apr. 1968, 25 and 16 Dec. 1968.

10. MN and Sibylle Niemöller-von Sell to the couple Gollwitzer, 6 Aug. 1972, EZA, 686/7337.

11. MN to Gollwitzer, 26 Apr. 1972, EZA, 686/7337.

12. MN to Gollwitzer, 22 June 1972, EZA, 686/7337. On the Russell tribunal, see MN to Gollwitzer, 30 Nov. 1974; Claudia Lepp, 'Helmut Gollwitzer als Dialogpartner der sozialen Bewegungen', in Siegfried Hermle, Claudia Lepp, and Harry Oelke (eds), *Umbrüche. Der deutsche Protestantismus und die sozialen Bewegungen in den 1960er und 70er Jahren* (Göttingen, 2007), 226–46.

13. MN to Gollwitzer, 13 Jan. 1950, EZA, 686/7337.

14. MN, 25 Jan. 1980: Hans-Joachim Oeffler, Hans Prolingheuer, Martin Schuck et al. (eds), *Martin Niemöller. Ein Lesebuch* (Cologne, 1987), 282–5, quotes 283–4.

15. Discussion on 10 Aug. 1975: MN, *Reden, Predigten, Denkanstöße*, 247–8.

16. Ibid., 247–8.

17. MN, 'Wozu heute noch Kirche?' (1975), in MN, *Reden, Predigten, Denkanstöße*, 222–30, quotes 223–4, 226.

18. See Thomas Kroll, 'Der Linksprotestantismus in der Bundesrepublik Deutschland der 1960er und 1970er Jahre; Helmut Gollwitzer, Dorothee Sölle und Jürgen Moltmann', in Thomas Kroll and Tilman Reitz (eds), *Intellektuelle in der Bundesrepublik Deutschland. Verschiebungen im politischen Feld in den 1960er und 1970er Jahren* (Göttingen, 2013), 103–22; for a critical perspective, see MN, 'Theologie der Revolution?' (1967), in MN, *Reden, Predigten, Denkanstöße*, 120–8.

19. MN, 'Christentum und Sozialismus', 1976, in MN, *Reden, Predigten, Denkanstöße*, 264–73, here 272.

20. MN, 'Wozu heute noch Kirche?' (1975), in MN, *Reden, Predigten, Denkanstöße*, 230.

21. See MN, *Reden, Predigten, Denkanstöße*, 249–50, and newspaper clippings in ELAB, 55.1/679.

22. Bezirksverwaltung für Staatssicherheit Dresden Abt. XX 22 to Oberst Bormann, Dec. 1976, BStU, HA XX AP 11891/92, fos 7–10, quotes fos 9–10.

23. 'Scharfe Kritik an Entwicklung der Evangelischen Kirche seit 1945', epd Landesdienst Hessen und Nassau, 7 Feb. 1977, ELAB, 55.1/679; 'Christentum bedeutet nur noch anständiges Benehmen', epd ZA No. 8, 13 Jan. 1982, ELAB, 55.1/679.

24. See epd ZA, 6 Dec. 1974, ELAB, 55.1/679.

25. 'Mit 90 bin ich jetzt ein Revolutionär', *Stern*, 7 Jan. 1982.

26. MN, 'Nationalismus—Antisemitismus als Schuld und Bedrohung der Kirche', in MN, *Reden 1955–1957*, 147–56, quotes 154–6.

27. Gronauer, *Staat Israel*, 126–39, 289–314, quote 129.

28. Ibid., 139–40.

29. Grüber to MN, 17 Aug. 1962 and Niemöller's reply of 20 Aug. 1962, GStA PK, VI. HA, NL Heinrich Grüber, No. 520.

30. MN to Grüber, 14 Aug. 1963 and Grüber's reply of 20 Aug. 1963 (quote), GStA PK, VI. HA, NL Heinrich Grüber, No. 520.

31. For instance in 1976, quoted in Leonore Siegele-Wenschkewitz, 'Auseinandersetzungen mit einem Stereotyp. Die Judenfrage im Leben Martin Niemöllers', in Ursula Büttner (ed.), *Die Deutschen und die Judenverfolgung im Dritten Reich* (Hamburg, 1992), 293–319, 312.

32. Gerhard Gronauer, *Der Staat Israel im westdeutschen Protestantismus. Wahrnehmungen in Kirche und Publizistik von 1948 bis 1972* (Göttingen, 2013), 182 (quote), 210.

33. Ibid., 220–1.

34. MN to Elsa Freudenberg, 22 July 1967, ZEKHN, 62/577.

35. Elsa Freudenberg to MN, 28 June 1967, ZEKHN, 62/577.

36. MN to WN, 28 Oct. 1976, ZEKHN, 62/1295.

37. Dr Diederichs, '25jähriges Crewfest', Aug. 1935, ZEKHN, 62/1439.

38. AK 9 June 1935.

39. SE 30 Mar. 1939.

40. Kranzbühler to MN, 30 Jan. 1946 and Niemöller's reply of 4 Apr. 1946, ZEKHN, 62/1439

41. Hartwig, *Karl Dönitz*, 32–3.

42. Backenköhler to MN (quote), 10 Mar. 1959 and Niemöller's reply of 12 Mar. 1959, ZEKHN, 62/1439.

43. Hartwig, *Karl Dönitz*, 33–4.

44. Minutes of the crew meeting on 12 June 1960, enclosure 5 of the circular of crew 1910 4/1960, Oct. 1960, ZEKHN, 62/1439.

45. Backenköhler to Stäcker, 2 June 1960, ZEKHN, 62/1439

46. Various letters, for example MN to Backenköhler, 9 and 23 Jan. 1962, MN to Egbert Begemann, 14 Jan. 1964, Backenköhler to MN, 31 Mar. 1964, all in ZEKHN, 62/1439.

47. Carl Pagenstecher to MN, 10 June 1965 ('Bedrückung') and 13 Dec. 1966, ZEKHN, 62/1439.

48. Carl Pagenstecher to MN, 25 Mar. 1967, ZEKHN, 62/1439.

49. Pagenstecher to MN (here a remark by Niemöller that the conversation took place on 16 May 1967), 30 Mar. 1967 and Pagenstecher to MN (quote), 23 Feb. 1968, ZEKHN, 62/1439.

50. AK 23–5 Sept. 1968, quote 24 Sept. 1968.

51. Circular of the crew and other documents in ZEKHN, 62/1439.

52. Helmut Brümmer-Patzig, speech 29 Sept. 1976 at the crew celebration, ZEKHN, 62/1439. See MN to Elsa Freudenberg, 20 Sept. 1976, ZEKHN, 62/577.

53. Marlene Maertens, 'Für die Crew 1910. Ansprache in Wilhelmshaven', 5 Sept. 1979, ZEKHN, 62/1439.

54. Crew meeting 18–20 Sept. 1980, list of participants, ZEKHN, 62/1439.

55. 'Ruhm und Rubel', Der Spiegel, No. 20, 8 May 1967.

56. MN to Kraschutzki, 13 July 1967, ZEKHN, 62/1439.

57. MN to WN, 3 Oct. 1974 and 20 Sept. 1976, ZEKHN, 62/1295.

58. This was arranged by Helmut Gollwitzer, who was good friends with Dutschke. See https://tagungshaus.ekhn.de/die-tagungshaeuser-der-ekhn/das-tagungshaus-martin-niemoeller/einzelansicht-mn/news/martin-niemoeller-und-die-suche-nach-einem-grab-fuer-rudi-dutschke-1.html (accessed 21 Nov. 2018).

Notes to Conclusion

1. Dr Paul Winckler to Praeses Koch, 29 Dec.1934, LkA EvKvW, 3.25/7. I am grateful to Jens Murken for pointing out this source to me.

2. Friedrich Meinecke, Die deutsche Katastrophe. Betrachtungen und Erinnerungen (Wiesbaden, 1947), 123.

3. Lutz von Schwerin-Krosigk, Es geschah in Deutschland. Menschenbilder unseres Jahrhunderts, 3rd edn (Tübingen 1952), 333.

4. Theophil Wurm to Gottfried Traub, 7 Apr. 1951, BArch, N 1059/38, fo. 84.

5. As referenced by Wilhelm Stählin, Via vitae. Lebenserinnerungen (Kassel, 1968), 502–3.

6. Klaus Theweleit, Male Fantasies, 2 vols, trans. Erica Carter, Stephen Conway, and Chris Turner (Minneapolis, 1987–9).

7. Hockenos, Then They Came For Me, 116–17, is imprecise and incorrect on this point.

8. As a perceptive introduction into different typologies, see Christian Wiese, 'An "Indelible Stigma": The Churches between Silence, Ideological Involvement, and Political Complicity', in Christian Wiese and Paul Betts (eds), Years of Persecution, Years of Extermination: Saul Friedländer and the Future of Holocaust Studies (London/ New York, 2010), 157–92, here 180–3.

9. See the important intervention by Wiese, 'An "Indelible Stigma"', 180, on this point.

10. The few, isolated anti-Judaist tropes in his Dahlem sermons from 1933 to 1937, for instance referenced by Hockenos, *Then They Came for Me*, 117, are in this regard less relevant than the personal reflections in his 1932 diary, as only they demonstrate the relevance of these issues for him.

11. MN, 'Bericht über meine Amerikafahrt im Winter 1946/47', n.d. [1947], EKHN, 62/171, quotes 27.

12. For further evidence and reflections, see Benjamin Ziemann, 'Martin Niemöllers Antisemitismus und die Frage der Schuld nach 1945', in Lukas Bormann and Michael Heymel (eds), *Martin Niemöller und seine internationale Rezeption* (Göttingen, 2023).

13. The statements mentioned by Hockenos, *Then They Came For Me*, 246–8 are isolated and not proof of a substantial engagement with these issues.

14. Hockenos, *Then They Came for Me*, 214, mentions that Adolf Freudenberg defended his close friend Niemöller in 1947 against allegations he was an antisemite, yet fails to mention the debate between Elsa Freudenberg and Niemöller in 1967.

15. As quoted in Karnick and Richter (eds), *Protestant*, 20–1.

16. MN, *Gedanken*, 134.

Bibliography

1. Primary Sources

Archiv der Gedenkstätte Dachau
Bestand A   Dokumente und Unterlagen zu Niemöller und anderen Häftlingen

Archiv der sozialen Demokratie, Bonn
Nachlass Gustav Heinemann

Archiv der Kirchengemeinde Dahlem, Berlin
Gemeinderatsprotokolle
Sachakten

Archiv des Erzbistums München und Freising, München
Nachlass Michael Höck
Nachlass Johannes Neuhäusler

Archiv für Demokratie und Entwicklung, Berlin
CA   Central-Ausschuss für Innere Mission
CA/AC   Apologetische Centrale des Central-Ausschusses

Bundesarchiv Berlin-Lichterfelde
DO 1   Ministerium des Innern der DDR
DO 4   Staatssekretär für Kirchenfragen der DDR
NS 6   Partei-Kanzlei der NSDAP
NS 8   Kanzlei Rosenberg
R 43-II   Reichskanzlei
R 3001   Reichsjustizministerium
R 5101   Reichsministerium für die kirchlichen Angelegenheiten
R 58   Reichssicherheitshauptamt
R 601   Präsidialkanzlei
R 8034 III   Reichslandbund Pressearchiv Personen
R 9361-II   NS Parteikorrespondenz
R 9361-III   SA und SS Mitglieder
R-9361-VIII   NS Mitgliederkartei
BDC, OPG   Oberstes Parteigericht der NSDAP
VBS   Vorläufige Bestandssignatur (previously BDC)

Bundesarchiv Koblenz
B 136   Bundeskanzleramt
N 1059   Nachlass Gottfried Traub

Bundesarchiv/Militärarchiv, Freiburg im Breisgau

BW 1	Bundesministerium der Verteidigung. Leitung, zentrale Stäbe und zivile Abteilungen
BW 2	Bundesministerium der Verteidigung. Generalinspekteur und Führungsstab der Streitkräfte
RM 2	Kaiserliches Marinekabinett
RM 3	Reichsmarineamt
RM 27-XIII	Inspektion des Unterseebootwesens der Kaiserlichen Marine
RM 86	Befehlshaber der Unterseeboote der Kaiserlichen Marine
RM 97	Unterseeboote der Kaiserlichen Marine

Bundesbeauftragter für die Stasi-Unterlagen, Berlin

Ministerium für Staatssicherheit

Handakten zu Martin Niemöller

Eden Theological Seminary, St. Louis, MO

Niemöller files

Evangelisches Landeskirchliches Archiv in Berlin

Bestand 14	Konsistorium der Kirchenprovinz Brandenburg
Bestand 15	Personalakten, Pfarrer
Bestand 37	Nachlass Wolf-Dieter Zimmermann
Bestand 55.1	Pressearchiv Personen

Evangelisches Zentralarchiv, Berlin

Bestand 2	Kirchenkanzlei der EKD
Bestand 6	Kirchliches Außenamt der EKD
Bestand 7	Evangelischer Oberkirchenrat der Evangelischen Kirche der ApU
Bestand 50	Archiv für die Geschichte des Kirchenkampfes
Bestand 81/1	Ratsvorsitzender Dibelius
Bestand 600	Nachlasssplitter und kleine Erwerbungen
Bestand 613	Nachlass Heinz Kloppenburg
Bestand 619	Nachlass Wilhelm Niesel
Bestand 626	Nachlass Friedrich Siegmund-Schultze
Bestand 686	Nachlass Helmut Gollwitzer

Gedenkstätte Sachsenhausen, Archiv

P 3 Dubinsky, Harry
P 3 Koch, Werner
P 3 Niemöller, Martin
P 3 Wackernagel, Günter
Ordner ZB (Zellenbau), N-R

Geheimes Staatsarchiv Preußischer Kulturbesitz, Berlin

I. HA Rep. 90 Staatsministerium, Annex P Geheime Staatspolizei
NL Emil Dovifat
NL Heinrich Grüber

Hauptarchiv der von Bodelschwinghschen Anstalten Bethel, Bielefeld

2/37   Dankort und Öffentlichkeitsarbeit
2/39   Teilbestand Kirchenkampf und Euthanasie
2/62   Innere Mission und Wohlfahrtspflege

Institut für Zeitgeschichte München, Archiv

ED
Fg
MA
MS
OMGUS
ZS

Karl Barth Archiv, Basel

Nachlass Karl Barth

Lambeth Palace Library, London

CFR LRC   Council of Foreign Relations, Lutheran and Reformed Churches
George Bell papers
Dorothy Buxton papers
Arthur Headlam papers

Landesarchiv Berlin

A Rep. 339   Landgericht Berlin
A Rep. 358-02   Generalstaatsanwaltschaft bei dem Landgericht

Landesarchiv Nordrhein-Westfalen, Abteilung Rheinland, Duisburg

RW 115, RW 477   Deutsche Friedensgesellschaft–VK, Bundesverband

Landesarchiv Nordrhein-Westfalen, Abteilung Westfalen, Münster

C 43   Soldatenverbände
Q 211   Generalstaatsanwaltschaft Hamm

Landeskirchliches Archiv der Evangelischen Kirche von Westfalen, Bielefeld

Bestand 0.0 alt   Sachakten des Konsistoriums
Bestand 13.110   Diakonisches Werk der EvKvW
Bestand 5.1   Sammlung Wilhelm Niemöller

Landeskirchliches Archiv Stuttgart

A 126   Allgemeine Akten des Oberkirchenrats
D 1   Nachlass Theophil Wurm

Politisches Archiv des Auswärtigen Amtes, Berlin

Ministerium für Auswärtige Angelegenheiten der DDR
Reichsaußenministerium

Staatsarchiv Ludwigsburg

Bestand EL 903/1   Spruchkammer der Interniertenlager

Staatsarchiv München
Staatsanwaltschaften

Stiftung Archiv der Parteien und Massenorganisationen der DDR im Bundesarchiv, Berlin
BY 6   Rat der Vereinigung der Verfolgten des Naziregimes

Universitätsarchiv der Humboldt Universität, Berlin
Bestand Rektor und Senat
Matrikelverzeichnis

Universitätsarchiv Münster
Bestand 4   Rektor, Sachakten
Bestand 31   Personalakten

World Council of Churches Files, Geneva
General Correspondence Archive [I have used the microfiche edition, Leiden 1997]

Zentralarchiv der Evangelischen Kirche in Hessen und Nassau, Darmstadt
Bestand 35   Nachlass Wilhelm Niemöller
Bestand 62   Nachlass Martin Niemöller
Bestand 368   Nachlass Gerhard Niemöller

2. Periodicals

Blätter für das Münsterland. Organ des Landesverbandes Münster der DNVP 1 (1921)–3 (1924).
Dahlemer Nachrichten. Nachrichtenblatt für Dahlem, Nikolassee, Wannsee und Zehlendorf 6 (1931)–8 (1933).
Der Westfale. Volkszeitung für deutschnationale Politik 1 (1920).
Hochschul-Stimmen. Zeitschrift für das akademische Leben der Westfälischen Wilhelms-Universität 1 (1919–20)–2 (1920–1).
Junge Kirche 1 (1933)–4 (1936).
Manchester Guardian 1934–47.
New York Times 1934–47.
Stimme der Gemeinde zum kirchlichen Leben, zur Politik, Wirtschaft und Kultur. Eine Halbmonatsschrift der Bekennenden Kirche 1 (1949)–11 (1959).
The Times 1934–47.
Ziele und Wege. Monatsschrift des Westfälischen Provinzialverbandes für Innere Mission 1 (1924)–7 (1931).

3. Printed Primary Sources and Literature

Abrath, Gottfried, *Subjekt und Milieu im NS-Staat: Die Tagebücher des Pfarrers Hermann Klugkist Hesse 1936–1939. Analyse und Dokumentation* (Göttingen, 1994).

Adolph, Walter, *Geheime Aufzeichnungen aus dem nationalsozialistischen Kirchenkampf 1935–1943*, ed. Ulrich von Hehl (Mainz, 1979).

Anders, Günther, 'Thesen zum Atomzeitalter' (1960), *Das Argument*, special issue 1/1 (1974), 226–34.

Appelius, Stefan, *Pazifismus in Westdeutschland. Die Deutsche Friedensgesellschaft 1945–1968*, 2 vols (Aachen, 1999).

Barth, Karl, *Offene Briefe 1935–1942* (Zurich, 2001).

Barth, Karl, *Vorträge und kleinere Arbeiten 1922–1925* (Zurich, 1990).

Barth, Karl, *Vorträge und kleinere Arbeiten 1930–1933* (Zurich, 1994).

Baumgärtel, Friedrich, *Ist die Kritik am Alten Testament berechtigt?* (Schwerin, 1927).

Baumgärtel, Friedrich, *Wider die Kirchenkampf-Legenden*, 2nd edn (Neuendettelsau, 1959).

Beck, Hermann, *Before the Holocaust: Antisemitic Violence and the Reaction of German Elites and Institutions during the Nazi Takeover* (Oxford, 2022).

Becker-Schaum, Christoph, Gassert, Philipp, Klimke, Martin, Mausbach Wilfried, and Zepp Marianne, eds, *'Entrüstet Euch!' Nuklearkrise, NATO-Doppelbeschluss und Friedensbewegung* (Paderborn, 2012).

Behrends, Jan C., Klimó, Árpád von, and Poutrus, Patrice G., 'Antiamerikanismus und die europäische Moderne. Zur Einleitung', in Behrends, Klimó, and Poutrus, eds, *Anti-Amerikanismus im 20. Jahrhundert. Studien zu Ost- und Westeuropa* (Bonn, 2005), 10–33.

Bellah, Robert N., 'Civil Religion in America', *Journal of the American Academy of Arts and Sciences* 96 (1967), 1–21.

Bentley, James, *Martin Niemöller* (Oxford, 1984).

Bergander, Götz, 'Vom Gerücht zur Legende. Der Luftkrieg über Deutschland im Spiegel von Tatsachen, erlebter Geschichte, Erinnerung, Erinnerungsverzerrung', in Stamm-Kuhlmann, Thomas, Elvert, Jürgen, Aschmann, Birgit, and Hohensee, Jens, eds, *Geschichtsbilder. Festschrift für Michael Salewski zum 65. Geburtstag* (Wiesbaden, 2003), 591–616.

Bergen, Doris, *Twisted Cross: The German Christian Movement in the Third Reich* (Chapel Hill, 1996).

Besier, Gerhard, 'Ansätze zum politischen Widerstand in der Bekennenden Kirche. Zur gegenwärtigen Forschungslage', in Schmädeke, Jürgen and Steinbach, Peter, eds, *Der Widerstand gegen den Nationalsozialismus: Die deutsche Gesellschaft und der Widerstand gegen Hitler* (Munich and Zurich, 1985), 265–80.

Besier, Gerhard, *Die Kirchen und das Dritte Reich. Vol. 3: Spaltungen und Abwehrkämpfe 1934–1937* (Munich, 2001).

Besier, Gerhard, *Die Rolle der Kirchen im Gründungsprozeß der Bundesrepublik Deutschland,* (Lüneburg, 2000).

Besier, Gerhard, Boyens, Armin, and Lindemann, Gerhard, *Nationaler Protestantismus und Ökumenische Bewegung: Kirchliches Handeln im Kalten Krieg (1945–1990). Mit einer Nachschrift von Horst-Klaus Hofmann* (Berlin, 1999).

Besier, Gerhard, Ludwig, Hartmut, and Thierfelder, Jörg, eds, *Der Kompromiß von Treysa. Die Entstehung der Evangelischen Kirche in Deutschland (EKD) 1945. Eine Dokumentation* (Weinheim, 1995).

Bethge, Eberhard, *Dietrich Bonhoeffer. Theologe, Christ, Zeitgenosse* (Munich, 1967).

Beutel, Albrecht, *Erich Klapproth—Kämpfer an den Fronten. Das kurze Leben eines Hoffnungsträgers der Bekennenden Kirche* (Tübingen, 2019).

Beuys, Barbara, 'Die Pfarrfrau: Kopie oder Original?', in Greiffenhagen, Martin, ed., *Das evangelische Pfarrhaus. Eine Kultur- und Sozialgeschichte* (Stuttgart, 1984), 47–61.

Beyer, Franz, *Menschen warten. Aus dem politischen Wirken Martin Niemöllers seit 1945* (Siegen, 1952).

Bönker, Dirk, *Militarism in a Global Age: Naval Ambitions in Germany and the United States Before World War I* (Ithaca and London, 2012).

Bonhoeffer, Dietrich, *Gesammelte Schriften*. Vol. 2: *Kirchenkampf und Finkenwalde. Resolutionen, Aufsätze, Rundbriefe, 1933 bis 1943* (Munich, 1965).

Bonhoeffer, Dietrich, *Werke*. Vol. 13: *London 1933–1935*, ed. Goedeker, Hans, Heimbucher, Martin, and Schleicher, Hans-Walter (Gütersloh, 1994).

Boyens, Armin, *Kirchenkampf und Ökumene. 1939–1945. Darstellung und Dokumentation unter besonderer Berücksichtigung der Quellen des Ökumenischen Rates der Kirchen* (Munich, 1973).

Brakelmann, Günter, ed., *Kirche im Krieg. Der deutsche Protestantismus am Beginn des Zweiten Weltkriegs* (Munich, 1979).

Braun, Hannelore and Nicolaisen, Carsten, eds, *Verantwortung für die Kirche. Stenographische Aufzeichnungen und Mitschriften von Landesbischof Hans Meiser. 1933–1955*. Vol. I: *Sommer 1933 bis Sommer 1935* (Göttingen, 1985).

Buchhaas-Birkholz, Dorothee, ed., *'Zum politischen Weg unseres Volkes'. Politische Leitbilder und Vorstellungen im deutschen Protestantismus 1945–1952. Eine Dokumentation* (Düsseldorf, 1989).

Buchheim, Hans, 'Ein NS-Funktionär zum Niemöller-Prozeß', *Vierteljahrshefte für Zeitgeschichte* 4 (1956), 307–15.

Buchna, Kristian, *Ein klerikales Jahrzehnt? Kirche, Konfession und Politik in der Bundesrepublik während der 1950er Jahre* (Baden-Baden, 2014).

Bultmann, Rudolf, *Briefwechsel mit Götz Harbsmeier und Ernst Wolf: 1933–1976* (Tübingen, 2017).

Busch, Eberhard, ed., *Reformationstag 1933. Dokumente der Begegnung Karl Barths mit dem Pfarrernotbund in Berlin* (Zurich, 1998).

Büttner, Edgar, '"Ich bin ganz harmlos hingefahren und bin ganz harmlos zurückgekommen". Zur Moskaureise Martin Niemöllers im Jahr 1952', in Oldenhage, Klaus, Schreyer, Hermann, and Werner, Wolfram, eds, *Archiv und Geschichte. Festschrift für Friedrich P. Kahlenberg* (Düsseldorf, 2000), 845–57.

Büttner, Ursula, *Weimar. Die überforderte Republik 1918–1933. Leistung und Versagen in Staat, Gesellschaft, Wirtschaft und Kultur* (Stuttgart, 2008).

Carenen, Caitlin, *The Fervent Embrace: Liberal Protestants, Evangelicals, and Israel* (New York, 2012).

Ceadel, Martin, *Pacifism in Britain, 1914–1945: The Defining of a Faith* (Oxford, 1980).

Chandler, Andrew, *Brethren in Adversity: Bishop George Bell, the Church of England and the Crisis of German Protestantism, 1933–1939* (Woodbridge, 1997).

Choi, Hyun-Beom, *Die Politische Ethik der protestantischen Theologie im 20. Jahrhundert: Karl Barth, Barmen und die koreanische evangelische Kirche* (Münster, 2003).

Christophersen, Alf and Ziemann, Benjamin, 'Einleitung', in Niemöller, Martin, *Gedanken über den Weg der christlichen Kirche* (Gütersloh, 2019), 7–59.

Conrad, Walter, *Der Kampf um die Kanzeln. Erinnerungen und Dokumente aus der Hitlerzeit* (Berlin, 1957).

Conway, John S., 'The Political Theology of Martin Niemöller', *German Studies Review* 9 (1986), 521–46.

Dawsey, Jason, 'After Hiroshima: Günther Anders and the History of Anti-Nuclear Critique', in Grant, Matthew and Ziemann, Benjamin, eds, *Understanding the Imaginary War: Culture, Thought and Nuclear Conflict, 1945–90* (Manchester, 2016), 140–64.

De Boer, Hans A., *Unterwegs notiert. Bericht einer Weltreise. Mit einem Vorwort an den Herrn Kritiker* (Kassel, 1959).

Deile, Volkmar, ed., *Bonn 10.10.1981. Friedensdemonstration für Abrüstung und Entspannung in Europa. Reden, Fotos* (Bornheim, 1981).

Dietzfelbinger, Eckart, *Die westdeutsche Friedensbewegung 1948 bis 1955. Die Protestaktionen gegen die Remilitarisierung der Bundesrepublik Deutschland* (Cologne, 1984).

Donat, Helmut and Holl, Karl, eds, *Die Friedensbewegung. Organisierter Pazifismus in Deutschland, Österreich und in der Schweiz* (Düsseldorf, 1983).

Donat, Helmut, 'Kapitänleutnant a.D. Heinz Kraschutzki (1891–1982). Ein Offizier im Kampf für ein "anderes" Deutschland', in Wette, Wolfram, assisted by Donat, Helmut, eds, *Pazifistische Offiziere in Deutschland 1871–1933* (Bremen, 1999), 338–62.

Dönitz, Karl, *Mein wechselvolles Leben* (Göttingen, 1968).

Epkenhans, Michael, 'Die Kaiserliche Marine 1914/15. Der Versuch der Quadratur des Kreises', in Epkenhans, ed., *Skagerrakschlacht. Vorgeschichte, Ereignis, Verarbeitung* (Munich, 2009), 113–38.

Epkenhans, Michael, *Die wilhelminische Flottenrüstung 1908–1914: Weltmachtstreben, industrieller Fortschritt, soziale Integration* (Munich, 1991).

Ericksen, Robert P., 'A Radical Minority: Resistance in the German Protestant Church', in Nicosia, Francis R. and Stokes, Lawrence D., eds, *Germans Against Nazism: Nonconformity, Opposition and Resistance in the Third Reich: Essays in Honour of Peter Hoffmann* (New York and Oxford, 1990), 115–35.

Ericksen, Robert P., 'Church Historians, "Profane" Historians, and our Odyssey since Wilhelm Niemöller', *Kirchliche Zeitgeschichte* 27 (2014), 43–55.

Ericksen, Robert P., 'Wilhelm Niemöller and the Historiography of the "Kirchenkampf"', in Gailus, Manfred and Lehmann, Hartmut, eds, *Nationalprotestantische Mentalitäten. Konturen, Entwicklungslinien und Umbrüche eines Weltbildes* (Göttingen, 2005), 433–51.

Evans, Richard J., *The Third Reich in Power 1933–1939* (London, 2006).

Feldman, Gerald D., *The Great Disorder: Politics, Economics & Society in the German Inflation, 1914–1924* (Oxford, 1993).

Fix, Karl-Heinz, ed., *Die Protokolle des Rates der Evangelischen Kirche in Deutschland.* Vol. 8: *1954/55* (Göttingen, 2012).

Flemming, Thomas, *Gustav W. Heinemann. Ein deutscher Citoyen. Biographie* (Essen, 2013).

Forck, Bernhard H., *Und folget ihrem Glauben nach. Gedenkbuch für die Blutzeugen der Bekennenden Kirche* (Stuttgart, 1949).

Fraenkel, Ernst, *Der Doppelstaat. Recht und Justiz im "Dritten Reich"* (Frankfurt am Main, 1984).

Fritzsche, Peter, *Life and Death in the Third Reich* (Cambridge, MA, 2008).

Gaede, Reinhard, *Kirche, Christen, Krieg und Frieden. Die Diskussion im deutschen Protestantismus während der Weimarer Zeit* (Hamburg-Bergstedt, 1975).

Gailus, Manfred, '1933 als protestantisches Erlebnis: Emphatische Selbsttransformation und Spaltung', *Geschichte und Gesellschaft* 29 (2003), 481–511.

Gailus, Manfred, '"Ein Volk – ein Reich – ein Glaube"? Religiöse Pluralisierungen in der NS-Weltanschauungsdiktatur', in Graf, Friedrich Wilhelm and Große Kracht, Klaus, eds, *Europäische Religionsgeschichte im 20. Jahrhundert* (Cologne, 2007), 203–24.

Gailus, Manfred, *Friedrich Weißler. Ein Jurist und Bekennender Christ im Widerstand gegen Hitler* (Göttingen, 2017).

Gailus, Manfred, *Protestantismus und Nationalsozialismus. Studien zur nationalsozialistischen Durchdringung des protestantischen Sozialmilieus in Berlin* (Cologne, 2001).

Gailus, Manfred and Lehmann, Hartmut, eds, *Nationalprotestantische Mentalitäten. Konturen, Entwicklungslinien und Umbrüche eines Weltbildes* (Göttingen, 2005).

Gaus, Günther, *Zur Person. Portraits in Frage und Antwort* (Munich, 1965).

Gerlach, Wolfgang, *Als die Zeugen schwiegen. Bekennende Kirche und die Juden* (Berlin, 1987).

Gerstberger, Karl, *Seekadetten-Briefe* (Berlin, 1914).

Gerster, Daniel, *Friedensdialoge im Kalten Krieg. Eine Geschichte der Katholiken in der Bundesrepublik 1957–1983* (Frankfurt am Main and New York, 2012).

Gestrich, Andreas, 'Erziehung im Pfarrhaus', in Greiffenhagen, Martin, ed., *Das evangelische Pfarrhaus. Eine Kultur- und Sozialgeschichte* (Stuttgart, 1984), 63–82.

Geyer, Martin H., 'Korruptionsdebatten in der Zeit der Revolution 1918/19: Der "Fall Sklarz", das Pamphlet "Der Rattenkönig" und die (Ab-)Wege des politischen Radikalismus nach dem Ersten Weltkrieg', in Kämper, Heidrun, Haslinger, Peter, and Raithel, Thomas, eds, *Demokratiegeschichte als Zäsurgeschichte. Diskurse der frühen Weimarer Republik* (Berlin, 2014), 333–58.

Geyer, Michael, 'Der Kalte Krieg, die Deutschen und die Angst. Die westdeutsche Opposition gegen Wiederbewaffnung und Kernwaffen', in Naumann, Klaus, ed., *Nachkrieg in Deutschland* (Hamburg, 2001), 267–318.

Geyer, Michael, 'Insurrectionary Warfare: The German Debate about a Levée en Masse in October 1918', *Journal of Modern History* 73 (2001), 459–527.

Geyer, Michael, 'Resistance as Ongoing Project: Visions of Order, Obligations to Strangers, Struggles for Civil Society', *Journal of Modern History* 64 (1992), Supplement, 217–41.

Ghosh, Peter, *Max Weber and "The Protestant Ethic": Twin Histories* (Oxford, 2014).

Goebbels, Joseph, *Die Zeit ohne Beispiel. Reden und Aufsätze aus den Jahren 1939/40/41* (Munich, 1941).

Goering, D. Timothy, *Friedrich Gogarten (1887–1967). Religionsrebell im Jahrhundert der Weltkriege* (Berlin and Boston, 2017).

Gogarten, Friedrich, 'Schöpfung und Volkstum', *Zwischen den Zeiten* 10 (1932), 481–505.

Gogarten, Friedrich, *Wider die Ächtung der Autorität* (Jena, 1930).

Goschler, Constantin, *Wiedergutmachung. Westdeutschland und die Verfolgten des Nationalsozialismus,1945–1954* (Munich, 1992).

Graf, Friedrich Wilhelm, *Der heilige Zeitgeist. Studien zur Ideengeschichte der protestantischen Theologie in der Weimarer Republik* (Tübingen, 2011).

Graf, Friedrich Wilhelm, *Die Wiederkehr der Götter. Religion in der modernen Kultur* (Munich, 2004).

Graf, Friedrich Wilhelm, 'Vom Munus Propheticum Christi zum prophetischen Wächteramt der Kirche? Erwägungen zum Verhältnis von Christologie und Ekklesiologie', *Zeitschrift für Evangelische Ethik* 32 (1988), 88–106.

Granier, Gerhard, ed., *Die deutsche Seekriegsleitung im Ersten Weltkrieg. Dokumentation*, vol. 2 (Coblenz, 2000).

Greschat, Martin, *Die evangelische Christenheit und die deutsche Geschichte nach 1945. Weichenstellungen in der Nachkriegszeit* (Stuttgart, 2002).

Greschat, Martin, ed., *Die Schuld der Kirche. Dokumente und Reflexionen zur Stuttgarter Schulderklärung vom 18./19. Oktober 1945* (Munich, 1982).

Greschat, Martin, '"Er ist ein Feind dieses Staates!" Martin Niemöllers Aktivitäten in den Anfangsjahren der Bundesrepublik Deutschland', *Zeitschrift für Kirchengeschichte* 114 (2003), 333–56.

Greschat, Martin, ed., *Im Zeichen der Schuld. 40 Jahre Stuttgarter Schuldbekenntnis. Eine Dokumentation* (Neukirchen-Vlyn, 1985).

Greschat, Martin, 'Kirche und Öffentlichkeit in der deutschen Nachkriegszeit', *Kirchen in der Nachkriegszeit. Vier zeitgeschichtliche Beiträge* (Göttingen, 1979), 100–24.

Greschat, Martin, 'Krieg und Kriegsbereitschaft im deutschen Protestantismus', in Dülffer, Jost and Holl, Karl, eds, *Bereit zum Krieg. Kriegsmentalität im Wilhelminischen Deutschland* (Göttingen, 1986), 33–55.

Greschat, Martin, 'Martin Niemöller. Repräsentant des deutschen Protestantismus im 20. Jahrhundert', *Pastoraltheologie* 81 (1992), 324–38.

Greschat, Martin, *Protestantismus im Kalten Krieg. Kirche, Politik und Gesellschaft im geteilten Deutschland 1945–1963* (Paderborn, 2010).

Greschat, Martin, 'Reaktionen der evangelischen Kirche auf den 17. Juni 1953', in Greschat, Martin and Kaiser, Jochen-Christoph, eds, *Die Kirchen im Umfeld des 17. Juni 1953* (Stuttgart, 2003), 85–108.

Greschat, Martin, ed., *Zwischen Widerspruch und Widerstand. Texte zur Denkschrift der Bekennenden Kirche an Hitler, 1936* (Munich, 1987).

Greschat, Martin and Kaiser, Jochen-Christoph, eds, *Die Kirchen im Umfeld des 17. Juni 1953* (Stuttgart, 2003).

Grevelhörster, Ludger, *Münster zu Anfang der Weimarer Republik. Gesellschaft, Wirtschaft und kommunalpolitisches Handeln in der westfälischen Provinzialhauptstadt 1918 bis 1924* (Schernfeld, 1993).

Gronauer, Gerhard, *Der Staat Israel im westdeutschen Protestantismus. Wahrnehmungen in Kirche und Publizistik von 1948 bis 1972* (Göttingen, 2013).

Grossmann, Atina, 'Grams, Calories, and Food: Languages of Victimization, Entitlement, and Human Rights in Occupied Germany, 1945–1949', *Central European History* 44 (2011), 118–48.

Halbgewachs, Nancy Copeland, 'Censorship and Holocaust Film in the Hollywood Studio System', PhD thesis, The University of New Mexico, 2011.

Halpern, Paul G., *A Naval History of World War I* (London, 1994).

Hansen, Jan, *Abschied vom Kalten Krieg? Die Sozialdemokraten und der Nachrüstungsstreit, 1977–1987* (Munich, 2016).

Hartwig, Dieter, *Großadmiral Karl Dönitz. Legende und Wirklichkeit* (Paderborn, 2010).

Hauschild, Wolf-Dieter, *Konfliktgemeinschaft Kirche. Aufsätze zur Geschichte der Evangelischen Kirche in Deutschland* (Göttingen, 2004).

Hauschild, Wolf-Dieter, 'Vom "Lutherrat" zur VELKD 1945–1948', in Mehlhausen, Joachim, ed., *... und über Barmen hinaus. Studien zur Kirchlichen Zeitgeschichte. Festschrift für Carsten Nicolaisen* (Göttingen, 1995), 451–70.

Heidemeyer, Helge, 'NATO-Doppelbeschluss, westdeutsche Friedensbewegung und der Einfluss der DDR', in Gassert, Philipp, Geiger, Tim, and Wentker, Hermann, eds, *Zweiter Kalter Krieg und Friedensbewegung. Der NATO-Doppelbeschluss in deutsch-deutscher und internationaler Perspektive* (Munich, 2011), 247–67.

Hempel, Johannes, *Altes Testament und völkische Frage* (Göttingen, 1931).

Hempel, Johannes, *Fort mit dem Alten Testament?* (Gießen, 1932).

Herbert, Ulrich, *Best. Biographische Studien über Radikalismus, Weltanschauung und Vernunft 1903–1989* (Bonn, 1996).

Herbert, Ulrich, *Geschichte Deutschlands im 20. Jahrhundert* (Munich, 2014).

Hermle, Siegfried, *Evangelische Kirche und Judentum—Stationen nach 1945* (Göttingen, 1990).

Herwig, Holger H., *Das Elitekorps des Kaisers. Marineoffiziere im Wilhelminischen Deutschland* (Hamburg, 1977).

Heymel, Michael, *Martin Niemöller. Vom Marineoffizier zum Friedenskämpfer* (Darmstadt, 2017).

Heymel, Michael, 'Wer war Leo Stein? Spurensuche nach dem Verfasser des Buches *I was in Hell with Niemoeller*, New York, 1942', *Mitteilungen zur kirchlichen Zeitgeschichte* 5 (2011), 53–87.

Hirsch, Emanuel, 'Etwas von der christlichen Stellung zum Alten Testament', *Glaube und Volk. Christliche-deutsche Monatsschrift*, issue 1 (1932), 7–10, 20–3.

Höck, Michael, 'Nec laudibus nec timore. Mit Abt Corbinian Hofmeister im KZ Dachau', *Beiträge zur Geschichte des Bistums Regensburg* 15 (1981), 363–6.

Hockenos, Matthew D., *A Church Divided: German Protestants Confront the Nazi Past* (Bloomington, 2004).

Hockenos, Matthew D., 'Martin Niemöller, the Cold War, and his Embrace of Pacifism, 1945–1955', *Kirchliche Zeitgeschichte* 27 (2014), 87–101.

Hockenos, Matthew D., 'Pastor Martin Niemöller, German Protestantism, and German National Identity, 1933–1937', in Wood, John Carter, ed., *Christianity and National Identity in Twentieth-Century Europe: Conflict, Community, and the Social Order* (Göttingen, 2016), 113–30.

Hockenos, Matthew D., *Then They Came for Me: Martin Niemöller, the Pastor Who Defied the Nazis* (New York, 2018).

Hockerts, Hans-Günter, 'Konfessionswechsel im Dritten Reich. Zahlenbilder und Fallbeispiele in typologischer Absicht', in Hermle, Siegfried and Maier, Hans, eds, *Konvertiten und Konversionen* (Annweiler, 2010), 149–65.

Holl, Karl, *Pazifismus in Deutschland* (Frankfurt am Main, 1988).

Hölscher, Lucian, ed., *Datenatlas zur religiösen Geographie im protestantischen Deutschland. Von der Mitte des 19. Jahrhunderts bis zum Zweiten Weltkrieg*, 4 vols (Berlin, 2001).

Holtfrerich, Carl-Ludwig, *Die deutsche Inflation 1914–1923. Ursachen und Folgen in internationaler Perspektive* (Berlin and New York, 1980).

Holz, Klaus, *Nationaler Antisemitismus. Wissenssoziologie einer Weltanschauung* (Hamburg, 2001).

Horn, Eva, 'The Apocalyptic Fiction: Shaping the Future in the Cold War', in Grant, Matthew and Ziemann, Benjamin, eds, *Understanding the Imaginary War: Culture, Thought and Nuclear Conflict, 1945–90* (Manchester, 2016), 30–50.

Höß, Rudolf, *Kommandant in Auschwitz. Autobiographische Aufzeichnungen*, ed. Martin Broszat (Munich, 1992).

Hull, Isabel, *A Scrap of Paper: Breaking and Making International Law during the Great War* (Ithaca and London, 2014).

Huttner, Markus, *Britische Presse und nationalsozialistischer Kirchenkampf. Eine Untersuchung der "Times" und des "Manchester Guardian" von 1930 bis 1939* (Paderborn, 1995).

Inacker, Michael J., *Zwischen Transzendenz, Totalitarismus und Demokratie. Die Entwicklung des kirchlichen Demokratieverständnisses von der Weimarer Republik bis zu den Anfängen der Bundesrepublik 1918–1959* (Neukirchen-Vluyn, 1994).

Janz, Oliver, *Bürger besonderer Art. Evangelische Pfarrer in Preußen 1850–1914* (Berlin, 1994).

Jasper, Ronald C.D., *George Bell, Bishop of Chichester* (London, 1967).

Johnson, Alex, *Eivind Berggrav. Mann der Spannung* (Göttingen, 1960).

Jordan, Hermann, *Von deutscher Not und deutscher Zukunft. Gedanken und Aufsätze* (Leipzig and Erlangen, 1922).

Jürgens-Kirchhoff, Annegret, '"Artists against Nuclear War" (1958–1962): A Touring Exhibition at the Time of the Cold War', in Ziemann, Benjamin, ed., *Peace Movements in Western Europe, Japan and the USA during the Cold War* (Essen, 2007), 211–36.

Kaiser, Jochen Christoph, 'Die Diakonie als subsidiärer Träger des Sozialstaats der Weimarer Republik', in Jähnichen, Traugott, ed., *Protestantismus und Soziale Frage. Profile in der Zeit der Weimarer Republik* (Münster, 2000), 113–28.

Kaiser, Jochen Christoph, *Evangelische Kirche und sozialer Staat. Diakonie im 19. und 20. Jahrhundert* (Stuttgart, 2008).

Kaiser, Jochen Christoph, *Sozialer Protestantismus im 20. Jahrhundert. Beiträge zur Geschichte der Inneren Mission 1914–1945* (Munich, 1989).

Kampmann, Jürgen, 'Bekenntnispfarrer, Archivar und Geschichtsschreiber: Wilhelm Niemöller zwischen Weltwirtschaftskrise und Wirtschaftswunder', in Haas, Reimund, ed., *Fiat voluntas tua. Theologe und Historiker, Priester und Professor. Festschrift zum 65. Geburtstag von Harm Klueting* (Münster, 2014), 467–85.

Karl Barth—Charlotte von Kirschbaum. Briefwechsel. Vol. 1: *1925–1935*, ed. Rolf-Joachim Erler (Zurich, 2008).

Karnick, Hannes and Richter, Wolfgang, eds, *Protestant. Das Jahrhundert des Pastors Niemöller* (Frankfurt am Main, 1992).

Kershaw, Ian, *The Nazi Dictatorship: Problems and Perspectives of Interpretation*, 4th edn (London, 2015).

Kersting, Andreas, *Kirchenordnung und Widerstand. Der Kampf um den Aufbau der Bekennenden Kirche der altpreußischen Union aufgrund des Dahlemer Notrechts von 1934 bis 1937* (Munich, 1994).

Knauth, Percy, *Germany in Defeat* (New York, 1946).

Koop, Volker, *In Hitlers Hand. Sonder- und Ehrenhäftlinge der SS* (Cologne, Weimar, and Vienna, 2010).

Kotze, Hildegard von, ed., *Heeresadjutant bei Hitler 1938–1943. Aufzeichnungen des Majors Engel* (Stuttgart, 1974).

Kroll, Thomas, 'Der Linksprotestantismus in der Bundesrepublik Deutschland der 1960er und 1970er Jahre. Helmut Gollwitzer, Dorothee Sölle und Jürgen Moltmann', in Kroll, Thomas and Reitz, Tilman, eds, *Intellektuelle in der Bundesrepublik Deutschland. Verschiebungen im politischen Feld in den 1960er und 1970er Jahren* (Göttingen, 2013), 103–22.

Kuhlemann, Frank-Michael, 'Protestantische "Traumatisierungen". Zur Situationsanalyse nationaler Mentalitäten in Deutschland 1918/19 und 1945/46', in Gailus, Manfred and Lehmann, Hartmut, eds, *Nationalprotestantische Mentalitäten. Konturen, Entwicklungslinien und Umbrüche eines Weltbildes* (Göttingen, 2005), 45–78.

Kühne, Thomas, *Kameradschaft. Die Soldaten des nationalsozialistischen Krieges und das 20. Jahrhundert* (Göttingen, 2006).

Kühne, Thomas, ed., *Von der Kriegskultur zur Friedenskultur? Zum Mentalitätswandel in Deutschland seit 1945* (Hamburg, 2000).

Kunkel, Karl, '"Geheime Staatspolizei – Sie sind verhaftet!" Tagebuchaufzeichnungen des Sonderhäftlings Karl Kunkel', *Ermlandbuch* 116 (1983), 40–113.

Künneth, Walter, *Lebensführungen. Der Wahrheit verpflichtet* (Wuppertal, 1979).

Kunter, Katharina and Schilling, Annegreth, '"Der Christ fürchtet den Umbruch nicht". Der Ökumenische Rat der Kirchen im Spannungsfeld von Dekolonisierung, Entwestlichung und Politisierung', in Kunter and Schilling, eds, *Globalisierung der Kirchen. Der Ökumenische Rat der Kirchen und die Entdeckung der Dritten Welt in den 1960er und 1970er Jahren* (Göttingen, 2014), 77–88.

Kunter, Katharina and Schilling, Annegreth, eds, *Globalisierung der Kirchen. Der Ökumenische Rat der Kirchen und die Entdeckung der Dritten Welt in den 1960er und 1970er Jahren* (Göttingen, 2014).

Kuropka, Joachim, 'Auf dem Weg in die Diktatur. Politik und Gesellschaft in der Provinzialhauptstadt Münster 1929 bis 1934', *Westfälische Zeitschrift* 134 (1984), 154–99.

Lammersdorf, Raimund, 'Verantwortung und Schuld. Deutsche und amerikanische Antworten auf die Schuldfrage, 1945-1947', in Bude, Heinz and Greiner, Bernd, eds, *Westbindungen. Amerika in der Bundesrepublik* (Hamburg, 1999), 231–56.

Langewiesche, Dieter, *Nationalismus im 19. und 20. Jahrhundert. Zwischen Partizipation und Aggression* (Bonn, 1994).

Lawson, Tom, *The Church of England and the Holocaust: Christianity, Memory and Nazism* (Woodbridge, 2006).

Lepp, Claudia, 'Helmut Gollwitzer als Dialogpartner der sozialen Bewegungen', in Hermle, Siegfried, Lepp, Claudia, and Oelke, Harry, eds, *Umbrüche. Der deutsche Protestantismus und die sozialen Bewegungen in den 1960er und 70er Jahren* (Göttingen, 2007), 226–46.

Lepp, Claudia, *Tabu der Einheit? Die Ost-West Gemeinschaft der evangelischen Christen und die deutsche Teilung (1945-1969)* (Göttingen, 2005).

Lepp, Claudia, Fitschen, Klaus, Hermle, Siegfried et al., eds, *Die Politisierung des Protestantismus. Entwicklungen in der Bundesrepublik während der 1960er und 70er Jahre* (Göttingen, 2011).

Lippmann, Andreas, *Marburger Theologie im Nationalsozialismus* (Berlin, 2003).

Lohalm, Uwe, *Völkischer Radikalismus. Die Geschichte des Deutschvölkischen Schutz- und Trutz-Bundes 1919-1923* (Hamburg, 1970).

Lorenz, Robert, *Protest der Physiker. Die Göttinger Erklärung von 1957* (Bielefeld, 2011).

Löwenthal, Richard, 'Widerstand im totalen Staat', in Löwenthal, Richard and von zur Mühlen, Patrik, eds, *Widerstand und Verweigerung in Deutschland 1933 bis 1945* (Berlin and Bonn, 1984), 11–24.

Ludwig, Hartmut and Eberhard Röhm, eds, *Evangelisch getauft—als "Juden" verfolgt. Theologen jüdischer Herkunft in der Zeit des Nationalsozialismus* (Stuttgart, 2014).

Marcuse, Harold, *Legacies of Dachau: The Uses and Abuses of a Concentration Camp, 1933-2001* (Cambridge, 2001).

Marcuse, Harold, 'The Origin and Reception of Martin Niemöller's Quotation "First They Came for the Communists..."', in Berenbaum, Michael, Libowitz, Richard, and Sachs Littell, Marcia, eds, *Remembering for the Future: Armenia, Auschwitz, and Beyond* (St. Paul, 2016), 173–99.

Marsh, Charles, *Strange Glory: A Life of Dietrich Bonhoeffer* (New York, 2014).

Martin Niemöller und sein Bekenntnis, ed. Schweizerisches Evangelisches Hilfswerk für die Bekennende Kirche in Deutschland, 8th edn (Zollikon, 1939).

Meier, Kurt, *Der evangelische Kirchenkampf*. Vol. I: *Der Kampf um die Reichskirche* (Halle an der Saale, 1976).

Meier, Kurt, *Der evangelische Kirchenkampf*. Vol. II: *Gescheiterte Neuordnungsversuche im Zeichen staatlicher "Rechtshilfe"*, 2nd edn (Göttingen, 1984).

Meier, Kurt, *Kirche und Judentum. Die Haltung der evangelischen Kirche zur Judenpolitik des Dritten Reiches* (Halle an der Saale, 1968).

Meinecke, Friedrich, *Die deutsche Katastrophe. Betrachtungen und Erinnerungen* (Wiesbaden, 1947).

Mergel, Thomas, 'Führer, Volksgemeinschaft und Maschine. Politische Erwartungsstrukturen in der Weimarer Republik und dem Nationalsozialismus 1918-1936', in Hardtwig, Wolfgang, ed., *Politische Kulturgeschichte der Zwischenkriegszeit 1918-1939* (Göttingen, 2005), 91–127.

Meyer, Helga, *Women's Campaign against West German Rearmament, 1949-1953* (Ann Arbor, 1989).

Möller, Ulrich, *Im Prozeß des Bekennens. Brennpunkte der kirchlichen Atomwaffendiskussion im deutschen Protestantismus 1957-1962* (Neukirchen-Vluyn, 1999).

Molthagen, Dietmar, *Das Ende der Bürgerlichkeit? Liverpooler und Hamburger Bürgerfamilien im Ersten Weltkrieg* (Göttingen, 2007).

Mommsen, Wolfgang J., 'Die nationalgeschichtliche Umdeutung der christlichen Botschaft im Ersten Weltkrieg', in Krumeich, Gerd and Lehmann, Hartmut, eds, *'Gott mit uns'. Nation, Religion und Gewalt im 19. und frühen 20. Jahrhundert* (Göttingen, 2000), 249-61.

Müller, Sven Oliver, *Die Nation als Waffe und Vorstellung. Nationalismus in Deutschland und Großbritannien im Ersten Weltkrieg* (Göttingen, 2002).

Nägler, Frank, 'Operative und strategische Vorstellungen der Kaiserlichen Marine vor dem Ersten Weltkrieg', in Epkenhans, Michael, ed., *Skagerrakschlacht. Vorgeschichte, Ereignis, Verarbeitung* (Munich, 2009), 19–56.

Nehring, Holger, *Politics of Security: British and West German Protest Movements and the Early Cold War, 1945-1970* (Oxford, 2013).

Nehring, Holger and Ziemann, Benjamin, 'Do all Paths Lead to Moscow? The NATO Dual-Track Decision and the Peace Movement – A Critique', *Cold War History* 12 (2012), 1–24.

Neumann, Peter, *Die Jungreformatorische Bewegung* (Göttingen, 1971).

Nicolaisen, Carsten, *Der Weg nach Barmen. Die Entstehungsgeschichte der Theologischen Erklärung von 1934* (Neukirchen-Vluyn, 1985).

Nicolaisen, Carsten, 'Die Stellung der "Deutschen Christen" zum Alten Testament', *Zur Geschichte des Kirchenkampfes. Gesammelte Aufsätze II* (Göttingen, 1971), 197–220.

Nicolaisen, Carsten and Schulze, Nora Andrea, eds, *Die Protokolle des Rates der Evangelischen Kirche in Deutschland. Vol. 1: 1945/46* (Göttingen, 1995).

Niemöller, Gerhard, ed., *Die erste Bekenntnissynode der Deutschen Evangelischen Kirche zu Barmen. Vol. 2: Text, Dokumente, Berichte* (Göttingen, 1959).

Niemöller, Heinrich, *Aus 56 Amtsjahren* (Bielefeld, 1946).

Niemöller, Heinrich, *Aus goldener Jugendzeit* (Bielefeld, 1947).

Niemöller, Heinrich, *Ein Pastorenspiegel* (Elberfeld, 1929).

Niemöller, Heinrich, *Hinauf gen Jerusalem* (Berlin, 1899).

Niemöller, Jan, *Erkundung gegen den Strom 1952. Martin Niemöller reist nach Moskau. Eine Dokumentation* (Stuttgart, 1988).

Niemöller, Martin, *Briefe aus der Gefangenschaft. Konzentrationslager Sachsenhausen (Oranienburg)*, ed. Wilhelm Niemöller (Bielefeld, 1979).

Niemöller, Martin, *Briefe aus der Gefangenschaft. Moabit*, ed. Wilhelm Niemöller (Frankfurt am Main, 1975).

Niemöller, Martin, *Dahlemer Predigten. Kritische Ausgabe*, ed. Michael Heymel (Gütersloh, 2011).

Niemöller, Martin, *Das Bekenntnis der Väter und die bekennende Gemeinde. Zur Besinnung dargeboten von einem Kreise von evangelischen Theologen* (Munich, 1933).

Niemöller, Martin, 'Der Friede Gottes und die Kraft des wehrhaften Mannes', in Müller, Eberhard, ed., *Wahrheit und Wirklichkeit der Kirche. Vorträge und geistliche Reden, gehalten auf der Deutschen Evangelischen Woche, 26.-30. August 1935 in Hannover* (Berlin, 1935), 243–52.

Niemöller, Martin, *Der Weg ins Freie* (Stuttgart, 1946).

Niemöller, Martin, *Deutschland wohin? Krieg oder Frieden? Rede vom 17. Januar in Darmstadt* (Darmstadt, 1952).

Niemöller, Martin, *Die Bedeutung des Alten Testaments für die christliche Kirche* (Berlin, undated [1936]).

Niemöller, Martin, *Die Brücke über den Abgrund. Wort Martin Niemöllers am 6. Juni 1946 in der Johannis-Kirche zu Saarbrücken* (Saarbrücken, 1946).

Niemöller, Martin, *Die Erneuerung unserer Kirche* (Munich, 1946).

Niemöller, Martin, *Die politische Verantwortung des Christen im akademischen Stand. Vortrag, gehalten auf Einladung der evangelischen Studentengemeinde vor Studierenden der Philipps-Universität zu Marburg an der Lahn am 4. Mai 1946* (Gießen, 1946).

Niemöller, Martin, *Die Staatskirche ist da. Denkschrift aus der Bekennenden Kirche* (Wuppertal, 1936).

Niemöller, Martin, 'Dreißig Jahre Bundesrepublik. Erlebnisse und Gedanken', *Blätter für deutsche und internationale Politik* 24 (1979), 13–26.

Niemöller, Martin, *Ein Wort zur kirchlichen Lage* (Wuppertal, 1936).

Niemöller, Martin, *Eine Welt oder keine Welt. Reden 1961-1963* (Frankfurt am Main, 1964).

Niemöller, Martin, 'Fritz Müller–Dahlem', in Niemöller, Wilhelm, ed., *Lebensbilder aus der Bekennenden Kirche*, Bielefeld 1949, 74–80.

Niemöller, Martin, *Gedanken über den Weg der christlichen Kirche*, ed. Christophersen, Alf and Ziemann, Benjamin (Gütersloh, 2019).

Niemöller, Martin, *Kriegsschauplatz oder Brücke? Ein evangelisches Wort zu der Not der Deutschen* (Frankfurt am Main, undated [1951]).

Niemöller, Martin, *Martin Niemöller über die deutsche Schuld, Not und Hoffnung* (Zollikon-Zurich, 1946).

Niemöller, Martin, *Martin Niemöller zur atomaren Rüstung. Zwei Reden* (Darmstadt, 1959).

Niemöller, Martin, *Not und Aufgabe der Kirche in Deutschland* (Geneva, 1947).

Niemöller, Martin, *Reden 1945–1954* (Darmstadt, 1958).

Niemöller, Martin, *Reden 1955–1957* (Darmstadt, 1957).

Niemöller, Martin, *Reden 1958–1961* (Frankfurt am Main, 1961).

Niemöller, Martin, *Reden, Predigten, Denkanstöße 1964–1976*, ed. Oeffler, Hans Joachim (Cologne, 1977).

Niemöller, Martin, *From U-Boat to Pulpit* (London, 1936).

Niemöller, Martin, *... zu verkündigen ein gnädiges Jahr des Herrn! Sechs Dachauer Predigten* (Munich, 1945).

Niemöller, Martin, *Zur gegenwärtigen Aufgabe der evangelischen Christenheit: Predigt über 1. Johannes 4, 9-14* (Frankfurt am Main, 1946).

Niemöller, Martin, *Zur gegenwärtigen Lage der evangelischen Christenheit* (Tübingen, 1946).

Niemöller, Martin, Lüthi, Walter, Casalis, Georges, and van der Meulen, Daniel, eds, *Frieden. Der Christ im Kampf gegen die Angst und den Gewaltgeist der Zeit* (Zurich, 1954).

Niemöllers Kasseler Rede vom 25. Januar 1959 im vollen Wortlaut. Was Niemöller sagt— wogegen Strauß klagt (Darmstadt ,1959).

Niemöller, Wilhelm, *Aus dem Leben eines Bekenntnispfarrers* (Bielefeld, 1961).

Niemöller, Wilhelm, *Der Pfarrernotbund. Geschichte einer kämpfenden Bruderschaft* (Hamburg, 1973).

Niemöller, Wilhelm, ed., *Die dritte Bekenntnissynode der Deutschen Evangelischen Kirche zu Augsburg. Text, Dokumente, Berichte* (Göttingen, 1969).

Niemöller, Wilhelm, ed., *Die Preußensynode zu Dahlem. Die zweite Bekenntnissynode der Evangelischen Kirche der altpreußischen Union. Geschichte—Dokumente—Berichte* (Göttingen, 1975).

Niemöller, Wilhelm, ed., *Die Synode zu Steglitz. Die Dritte Bekenntnissynode der Evangelischen Kirche der Altpreußischen Union. Geschichte, Dokumente, Berichte* (Göttingen, 1970).

Niemöller, Wilhelm, ed., *Die Vierte Bekenntnissynode der Deutschen Evangelischen Kirche zu Bad Oeynhausen. Text, Dokumente, Berichte* (Göttingen, 1960).

Niemöller, Wilhelm, *Hitler und die evangelischen Kirchenführer* (Bielefeld, 1959).

Niemöller, Wilhelm, *Kirchenkampf im Dritten Reich* (Bielefeld, 1946).

Niemöller, Wilhelm, *Macht geht vor Recht. Der Prozeß Martin Niemöllers* (Munich, 1952).

Niemöller, Wilhelm, *Martin Niemöller. Ein Lebensbild* (Munich, 1952).

Niemöller, Wilhelm, *Neuanfang 1945. Zur Biographie Martin Niemöllers nach seinen Tagebuchaufzeichnungen aus dem Jahre 1945* (Frankfurt am Main, 1967).

Niemöller, Wilhelm, ed., *Texte zur Geschichte des Pfarrernotbundes* (Berlin, 1958).

Niemöller, Wilhelm, *Vater Niemöller. Ein Lebensbild* (Bielefeld, 1946).

Nipperdey, Thomas, *Deutsche Geschichte 1866–1918*. Vol. 1: *Arbeitswelt und Bürgergeist* (Munich, 1990).

Nipperdey, Thomas, *Deutsche Geschichte 1866–1918*. Vol. 2: *Machtstaat vor der Demokratie* (Munich, 1992).

Norden, Günther van, 'Widerstand im deutschen Protestantismus 1933–1945', in Kleßmann, Christoph and Pingel, Falk, eds, *Gegner des Nationalsozialismus. Wissenschaftler und Widerstandskämpfer auf der Suche nach historischer Wirklichkeit* (Frankfurt am Main, 1980), 103–25.

Noss, Peter, *Martin Albertz (1883–1956). Eigensinn und Konsequenz* (Neukirchen-Vluyn, 2001).

Nowak, Kurt, *Evangelische Kirche und Weimarer Republik. Zum politischen Weg des deutschen Protestantismus zwischen 1918 und 1932*, 2nd edn (Göttingen, 1988).

Oeffler, Hans-Joachim, Prolingheuer, Hans, Schuck, Martin, et al., eds, *Martin Niemöller. Ein Lesebuch* (Cologne, 1987).

Opitz, Günter, *Der Christlich-soziale Volksdienst. Versuch einer protestantischen Partei in der Weimarer Republik* (Düsseldorf, 1969).

Oppenheimer, Andrew, 'By Any Means Necessary? West German Pacifism and the Politics of Solidarity, 1945–1974', in Ziemann, Benjamin, ed., *Peace Movements in Western Europe, Japan and the USA during the Cold War* (Essen, 2007), 41–60.

Palm, Dirk, *'Wir sind doch Brüder!' Der evangelische Kirchentag und die deutsche Frage 1949–1961* (Göttingen, 2002).

Permien, Andreas, *Protestantismus und Wiederbewaffnung 1950–1955. Die Kritik in der Evangelischen Kirche im Rheinland und der Evangelischen Kirche von Westfalen an Adenauers Wiederbewaffnungspolitik* (Cologne, 1994).

Peter, Karen, ed., *NS-Presseanweisungen der Vorkriegszeit. Edition und Dokumentation.* Vol. 7/I: *1939, Quellentexte Januar bis April* (Munich, 2001).

Peter, Karen ed., *NS-Presseanweisungen der Vorkriegszeit. Edition und Dokumentation.* Vol. 7/II: *1939, Quellentexte Mai bis August* (Munich, 2001).

Peter, Karl H., *Seeoffizieranwärter. Ihre Ausbildung von 1848 bis heute* (Mürwik, 1969). www.pkgodzik.de/fileadmin/user_upload/Geschichte_und_Politik/Karl_Peter__Seeoffizieranwaerter.pdf [accessed 24 Oct. 2018].

Pfennigsdorf, Oskar, *Praktisches Christentum im Rahmen des kleinen Katechismus Luthers.* Part 1, 3rd edn (Schwerin, 1910).

Pisarski, Angelika, *Um nicht schweigend zu sterben. Gespräche mit Überlebenden aus Konzentrationslagern* (Munich, 1989).

Rahn, Werner, 'Die Kaiserliche Marine und der Erste Weltkrieg', in Huck, Stephan, ed., *Ringelnatz als Mariner im Krieg 1914–1918* (Bochum, 2003), 39–89.

Rangliste der Kaiserlich Deutschen Marine für das Jahr 1910–1914 (Berlin, 1910–14).

Reese, Hans-Jörg, *Bekenntnis und Bekennen. Vom 19. Jahrhundert zum Kirchenkampf der nationalsozialistischen Zeit* (Göttingen, 1974).

Reichmann, Hans, *Deutscher Bürger und verfolgter Jude. Novemberpogrom und KZ Sachsenhausen 1937 bis 1939*, ed. Michael Wildt (Munich, 1998).

Reuth, Ralf Georg, ed., *Joseph Goebbels Tagebücher 1924–1945*, 5 vols (Munich, 1992).

Richardi, Hans-Günter, *SS-Geiseln in der Alpenfestung. Die Verschleppung prominenter KZ-Häftlinge aus Deutschland nach Südtirol* (Bozen, 2005).

Riedel, Dirk, 'Der "Wildpark" im KZ Dachau und das Außenlager St. Gilgen. Zwangsarbeit auf den Baustellen des KZ-Kommandanten Loritz', *Dachauer Hefte* 16 (2000), 54–70.

Riedel, Dirk, *Kerker im KZ Dachau. Die Geschichte der drei Bunkerbauten* (Dachau, 2002).

Robbins, Keith, 'Martin Niemöller, the German Church Struggle and English Opinion', *Journal of Ecclesiastical History* 21 (1970), 149–70.

Roggelin, Holger, *Franz Hildebrandt. Ein lutherischer Dissenter im Kirchenkampf und Exil* (Göttingen, 1999).

Rohe, Karl, *Wahlen und Wählertraditionen in Deutschland* (Frankfurt am Main, 1992).

Röhm, Eberhard and Thierfelder, Jörg, 'Ein langer Weg von Breslau nach New York. Der Flüchtlingspfarrer Friedrich Forell', in Mehlhausen, Joachim, ed., *… und über Barmen hinaus. Studien zur Kirchlichen Zeitgeschichte. Festschrift für Carsten Nicolaisen* (Göttingen, 1995), 376–85.

Roper, Lyndal, *Martin Luther: Renegade and Prophet* (London, 2016).

Rosenberg, Alfred, *Der Mythus des 20. Jahrhunderts. Eine Wertung der seelisch-geistigen Gestaltenkämpfe unserer Zeit*, 33rd–34th edn (Munich, 1934).

Ruff, Mark Edward, *The Battle for the Catholic Past in Germany 1945–1980* (Cambridge, 2018).

Rüger, Jan, *The Great Naval Game: Britain and Germany in the Age of Empire* (Cambridge, 2009).

Rupp, Hans Karl, *Außerparlamentarische Opposition in der Ära Adenauer: Der Kampf gegen die Atombewaffnung in den fünfziger Jahren. Eine Studie zur innenpolitischen Entwicklung der BRD* (Cologne, 1970).

Rusterholz, Heinrich, '… als ob unseres Nachbarn Haus nicht in Flammen stünde'. Paul Vogt, Karl Barth und das Schweizerische evangelische Hilfswerk für die Bekennende Kirche Deutschland 1937–1947* (Zurich, 2015).

Sandhofer, Gerd, 'Dokumente zum militärischen Werdegang des Großadmirals Dönitz', *Militärgeschichtliche Mitteilungen* 1 (1967), 59–81.

Sandvoß, Hans-Rainer, *'Es wird gebeten, die Gottesdienste zu überwachen.' Religionsgemeinschaften in Berlin zwischen Anpassung, Selbstbehauptung und Widerstand von 1933 bis 1945* (Berlin, 2014).

Schäberle-Koenigs, Gerhard, *Und sie waren täglich einmütig beieinander. Der Weg der Bekennenden Gemeinde Berlin/Dahlem in den Jahren 1937–1943 mit Helmut Gollwitzer* (Gütersloh, 1998).

Scheerer, Thomas, 'Die Marineoffiziere der Kaiserlichen Marine. Sozialisation und Konflikte', PhD thesis, University of Hamburg, 1993.

Schildt, Axel, '"Atomzeitalter"—Gründe und Hintergründe der Proteste gegen die atomare Bewaffnung der Bundeswehr Ende der fünfziger Jahre', in *'Kampf dem Atomtod!' Die Protestbewegung 1957/58 in zeithistorischer und gegenwärtiger Perspektive* (Munich and Hamburg, 2009), 39–56.

Schilling, René, *'Kriegshelden'. Deutungsmuster heroischer Männlichkeit in Deutschland 1813–1945* (Paderborn, 2002).

Schmidt, Jürgen, *Martin Niemöller im Kirchenkampf* (Hamburg, 1971).

Schmidt, Kurt Dietrich, ed., *Dokumente des Kirchenkampfes*. Vol. 2: *Die Zeit des Reichskirchenausschusses 1935–1937*. Second Part *(29. Mai 1936 bis Ende Februar 1937)* (Göttingen, 1965).

Schneider, Burkhart, ed., *Die Briefe Pius' XII. an die deutschen Bischöfe. 1939–1944* (Mainz, 1966).

Schneider, Thomas M., *Reichsbischof Ludwig Müller. Eine Untersuchung zu Leben, Werk und Persönlichkeit* (Göttingen, 1993).

Scholder, Klaus, *Die Kirchen und das Dritte Reich*. Vol. 1: *Vorgeschichte und Zeit der Illusion 1918–1934* (Munich, 2000).

Scholder, Klaus, *Die Kirchen und das Dritte Reich*. Vol. 2: *Das Jahr der Ernüchterung. 1934, Barmen und Rom* (Frankfurt am Main and Berlin, 1988).

Scholder, Klaus, 'Politischer Widerstand oder Selbstbehauptung als Problem der Kirchenleitungen', in Schmädeke, Jürgen and Steinbach, Peter, eds, *Der Widerstand gegen den Nationalsozialismus: Die deutsche Gesellschaft und der Widerstand gegen Hitler* (Munich and Zurich, 1985), 254–64.

Schröder, Joachim, *Die U-Boote des Kaisers. Die Geschichte des deutschen U-Boot-Krieges gegen Großbritannien im Ersten Weltkrieg* (Bonn, 2003).

Schulze, Hagen, *Otto Braun oder Preußens demokratische Sendung* (Frankfurt am Main, Berlin, and Vienna, 1977).

Schwerin-Krosigk, Lutz von, *Es geschah in Deutschland. Menschenbilder unseres Jahrhunderts*, 3rd edn (Tübingen, 1952).

Seeberg, Reinhold, *Was sollen wir denn tun? Erwägungen und Hoffnungen* (Leipzig, 1915).

Seidel, J. Jürgen, *'Neubeginn' in der Kirche? Die evangelischen Landes- und Provinzialkirchen in der SBZ/DDR im gesellschaftlichen Kontext der Nachkriegszeit, 1945–1953* (Göttingen, 1989).

Sieck, Annerose and Sieck, Jörg-Rüdiger, *Die U-Bootfahrer und das Ehrenmal in Möltenort. Von der Kaiserzeit bis in die Gegenwart* (Heikendorf, 2006).

Siegele-Wenschkewitz, Leonore, 'Auseinandersetzungen mit einem Stereotyp. Die Judenfrage im Leben Martin Niemöllers', in Büttner, Ursula, ed., *Die Deutschen und die Judenverfolgung im Dritten Reich* (Hamburg, 1992), 293–319.

Sigler, Sebastian, 'Hans Koch – ein deutsches Schicksal im Widerstand', *Einst und Jetzt* 57 (2012), 339–50.

Silomon, Anke, ed., *Die Protokolle des Rates der evangelischen Kirche in Deutschland*. Vol. 4: *1950* (Göttingen, 2007).

Smid, Marikje, *Deutscher Protestantismus und Judentum 1932/1933* (Gütersloh, 1990).

Smith-von Osten, Annemarie, *Von Treysa 1945 bis Eisenach 1948. Zur Geschichte der Grundordnung der Evangelischen Kirche in Deutschland* (Göttingen, 1980).

Stählin, Wilhelm, *Via vitae. Lebenserinnerungen* (Kassel, 1968).

Stapel, Wilhelm, *Sechs Kapitel über Christentum und Nationalsozialismus*, 3rd edn (Hamburg and Berlin, 1931 [first 1931]).

Stargardt, Nicholas, *Der deutsche Krieg 1939–1945* (Frankfurt am Main, 2015).

Steigmann-Gall, Richard, 'Apostasy or Religiosity? The Cultural Meanings of the Protestant Vote for Hitler', *Social History* 25 (2000), 267–85.

Steigmann-Gall, Richard, *The Holy Reich: Nazi Conceptions of Christianity, 1919–1945* (Cambridge, 2003).

Stein, Leo, *I was in Hell with Niemoeller* (London, New York, and Melbourne o. J. [1942]).

Steinbach, Peter, 'Der Widerstand als Thema der politischen Zeitgeschichte', in Besier, Gerhard and Ringshausen, Gerhard, eds, *Bekenntnis, Widerstand, Martyrium. Von Barmen 1934 bis Plötzensee 1944* (Göttingen, 1986), 11–74.

Sterik, Edita, ed., *Else Niemöller. Geborene Bremer 1890–1990. Die Frau eines bedeutenden Mannes* (Darmstadt, 1990).

Stibbe, Matthew, *German Anglophobia and the Great War 1914–1918* (Cambridge, 2001).

Stölken-Fitschen, Ilona, *Atombombe und Geistesgeschichte. Eine Studie der fünfziger Jahre aus deutscher Sicht* (Baden-Baden, 1995).

Tetlow, Hannah, 'The Making and Unmaking of a Protestant Hero: British Perceptions on Martin Niemöller in Context of the German Church Struggle, 1934–1945', *Schweizerische Zeitschrift für Religions- und Kulturgeschichte* 116 (2022), 283–300.

Theweleit, Klaus, *Male Fantasies*, 2 vols, trans. Erica Carter, Stephen Conway, and Chris Turner (Minneapolis, 1987–9).

Thierfelder, Jörg, *Das kirchliche Einigungswerk des württembergischen Landesbischofs Theophil Wurm* (Göttingen, 1975).

Thompson, David, 'Ecumenism', in McLeod, Hugh, ed., *The Cambridge History of Christianity. Vol. 9: World Christianities c.1914–c.2000* (Cambridge, 2006), 50–70.

Thoß, Bruno, *NATO-Strategie und nationale Verteidigungsplanung. Planung und Aufbau der Bundeswehr unter den Bedingungen einer massiven atomaren Vergeltungsstrategie 1952 bis 1960* (Munich, 2006).

Toller, Ernst, *Gesammelte Werke. Vol. 3: Politisches Theater und Dramen im Exil 1927/1939* (Munich, 1978).

Trittel, Günter J., *Hunger und Politik. Die Ernährungskrise in der Bizone, 1945–1949* (Frankfurt am Main, 1990).

Turner, Ewart E., 'Niemöllers in Amerika', *Bekennende Kirche. Martin Niemöller zum 60. Geburtstag* (Munich, 1952), 301–7.

Tyra, Ralf, 'Treysa 1945. Neue Forschungsergebnisse zur ersten deutschen Kirchenversammlung nach dem Krieg', *Kirchliche Zeitgeschichte* 2 (1989), 239–76.

Verhey, Jeffrey, *The Spirit of 1914: Militarism, Myth and Mobilization in Germany* (Cambridge, 2000).

Vieten, Bernward, *Medizinstudenten in Münster. Universität, Studentenschaft und Medizin 1905 bis 1945* (Cologne, 1982).

Visser 't Hooft, Willem Adolph, *Die Welt war meine Gemeinde. Autobiographie* (Munich, 1972).

Vogel, Johanna, *Kirche und Wiederbewaffnung. Die Haltung der Evangelischen Kirche in Deutschland in den Auseinandersetzungen um die Wiederbewaffnung der Bundesrepublik 1949–1956* (Göttingen, 1978).

Voigt, Martina, '"Die Gemeinde hat die Pflicht, an den allgemeinen Menschenrechten interessiert zu sein". Elisabeth Schiemann', in Gailus, Manfred, ed., *Mit Herz und Verstand. Protestantische Frauen im Widerstand gegen die NS-Rassenpolitik* (Göttingen, 2013), 100–27.

Vollnhals, Clemens, ed., *Die evangelische Kirche nach dem Zusammenbruch. Berichte ausländischer Beobachter aus dem Jahre 1945* (Göttingen, 1988).

Vollnhals, Clemens, 'Die Evangelische Kirche zwischen Traditionswahrung und Neuorientierung', in Broszat, Martin, Henke, Klaus-Dietmar, and Woller, Hans, eds, *Von Stalingrad zur Währungsreform. Zur Sozialgeschichte des Umbruchs in Deutschland*, 3rd edn (Munich, 1990), 113–67.

Vollnhals, Clemens, 'Die Hypothek des Nationalprotestantismus. Entnazifizierung und Strafverfolgung von NS-Verbrechen nach 1945', *Geschichte und Gesellschaft* 18 (1992), 51–69.

Vollnhals, Clemens, ed., *Entnazifizierung und Selbstreinigung im Urteil der evangelischen Kirche. Dokumente und Reflexionen 1945–1949* (Munich, 1989).

Vollnhals, Clemens, *Evangelische Kirche und Entnazifizierung 1945–1949. Die Last der nationalsozialistischen Vergangenheit* (Munich, 1989).

Vollnhals, Clemens, 'Im Schatten der Stuttgarter Schulderklärung. Die Erblast des Nationalprotestantismus', in Gailus, Manfred and Lehmann, Hartmut, eds,

Nationalprotestantische Mentalitäten in Deutschland (1870-1970). Konturen, Entwicklungslinien und Umbrüche eines Weltbildes (Göttingen, 2005), 379-431.

Vollnhals, Clemens, 'Theologie des Nationalismus. Der christlich-völkische Publizist Wilhelm Stapel', in Gailus, Manfred and Vollnhals, Clemens, eds, *Für ein artgemäßes Christentum der Tat. Völkische Theologen im 'Dritten Reich'* (Göttingen, 2016), 97-117.

Weber, Cornelia, *Altes Testament und völkische Frage. Der biblische Volksbegriff in der alttestamentlichen Wissenschaft der nationalsozialistischen Zeit, dargestellt am Beispiel von Johannes Hempel* (Tübingen, 2000).

Wehler, Hans-Ulrich, *Deutsche Gesellschaftsgeschichte.* Vol. 4: *1914-1949* (Munich, 2003).

Weiling, Christoph, *Die "Christlich-deutsche Bewegung". Eine Studie zum konservativen Protestantismus in der Weimarer Republik* (Göttingen, 1998).

Weir, Todd, 'The Christian Front against Godlessness: Anti-Secularism and the Demise of the Weimar Republic', *Past and Present* 229 (2015), 201-38.

Weisbrod, Bernd, '"Ein Vorsprung, der uns tief verpflichtet". Die Wiedereröffnung der Universität Göttingen im Wintersemester 1945/46', in *'Ein Vorsprung, der uns tief verpflichtet'. Die Wiedereröffnung der Universität Göttingen vor 70 Jahren* (Göttingen, 2016), 21-38.

Werner, Michael, 'August Bangel – Hermann L. Brill – Fritz Wenzel. Drei Sozialdemokraten in der Deutschen Friedensgesellschaft', in Bald, Detlef and Wette, Wolfram, eds, *Alternativen zur Wiederbewaffnung. Friedenskonzeptionen in Westdeutschland 1945-1955* (Essen, 2008), 71-85.

Werner, Michael, 'Zur Relevanz der "Ohne mich"-Bewegung in der Auseinandersetzung um den Wehrbeitrag', in Bald, Detlef and Wette, Wolfram, eds, *Friedensinitiativen in der Frühzeit des Kalten Krieges 1945-1955* (Essen, 2010), 79-86.

Wette, Wolfram, *Gustav Noske. Eine politische Biographie* (Düsseldorf, 1987).

Weyer, Bruno, ed., *Taschenbuch der Kriegsflotten*, 2nd edn (Munich, 1905).

Wiebel, Arnold, ed., *Christa Müller. Theologin im Kirchenkampf. Vikarin bei Martin Niemöller. Ihre Briefe an Rudolf Hermann (1933-1935).* https://theologie.uni-greifswald.de/fileadmin/uni-greifswald/fakultaet/theologie/ls-sys/Unpublizierte_Quellen/Korr__Briefe_Christa_Mueller_1933-1935.pdf [accessed 14 Jan. 2019].

Wiener, Alfred, 'Untersuchungen zum Widerhall des deutschen Kirchenkampfes in England (1933-1938)', in Beloff, Max, ed., *On the Track of Tyranny: Essays presented by the Wiener Library to Leonard G. Montefiore, O.B.E., on the occasion of his seventieth birthday* (London, 1960), 211-32.

Wiggershaus, Norbert, 'Die Entscheidung für einen westdeutschen Verteidigungsbeitrag 1950', in *Anfänge westdeutscher Sicherheitspolitik: 1945-1956.* Vol. 1: *Von der Kapitulation bis zum Pleven-Plan* (Munich, 1982), 325-402.

Wittner, Lawrence S., *One World or None: A History of the World Nuclear Disarmament Movement through 1953* (Stanford, 1994).

Wittner, Lawrence S., *Resisting the Bomb: A History of the World Nuclear Disarmament Movement, 1954-1970* (Stanford, 1997).

Wolbring, Barbara, *Trümmerfeld der bürgerlichen Welt. Universität in den gesellschaftlichen Reformdiskursen der westlichen Besatzungszonen, 1945-1949* (Göttingen, 2014).

Wolf, Thomas, 'Die Rede Martin Niemöllers im Siegener Lyzeum, 30. Juni 1959. Eine Episode in der Geschichte der Siegerländer Friedensbewegung. Textabdruck mit kurzer Einführung', *Siegener Beiträge* 11 (2006), 209-19.

Wolz, Nicolas, *Das lange Warten. Kriegserfahrungen deutscher und britischer Seeoffiziere 1914 bis 1918* (Paderborn, 2008).

Wright, Jonathan R.C., *Über den Parteien. Die politische Haltung der evangelischen Kirchenführer 1918-1933* (Göttingen, 1977).

Zámečnik, Stanislav, *Das war Dachau* (Frankfurt am Main, 2007).

Ziemann, Benjamin, 'Ambivalente Männlichkeit. Geschlechterbilder und -praktiken in der kaiserlichen Marine am Beispiel von Martin Niemöller', *L'Homme. Europäische Zeitschrift für Feministische Geschichtswissenschaft* 29 (2018), 91–108.

Ziemann, Benjamin, 'Conversion as a Confessional Irritant: Examples from the Third Reich', in Ruff, Mark Edward and Großbölting, Thomas, eds, *Germany and the Confessional Divide, 1871–1989* (New York, 2021), 145–69.

Ziemann, Benjamin, 'Der Prozess gegen Martin Niemöller vor dem Berliner Sondergericht 1938', *Zeitschrift für Geschichtswissenschaft* 66 (2018), 299–317.

Ziemann, Benjamin, 'German Angst? Debating Cold War Anxieties in West Germany, 1945–1990', in Grant, Matthew and Ziemann, Benjamin, eds, *Understanding the Imaginary War: Intellectual Reflections of the Nuclear Age, 1945–90* (Manchester, 2016), 116–39.

Ziemann, Benjamin, 'Germany 1914–1918: Total War as a Catalyst of Change', in Smith, Helmut Walser, ed., *The Oxford Handbook of Modern German History* (Oxford, 2011), 378–99.

Ziemann, Benjamin, 'Kampf gegen die "Gottlosen". Martin Niemöller als Geschäftsführer des westfälischen Provinzialverbandes der Inneren Mission 1924–1931', *Westfälische Forschungen* 68 (2018), 357–80.

Ziemann, Benjamin, 'Martin Niemöller', in Frei, Norbert, ed., *Wie bürgerlich war der Nationalsozialismus?* (Göttingen, 2018), 334–50.

Ziemann, Benjamin, 'Martin Niemöller als völkisch-nationaler Studentenpolitiker in Münster 1919 bis 1923', *Vierteljahrshefte für Zeitgeschichte* 67 (2019), 209–34.

Ziemann, Benjamin, 'Martin Niemöller und die Wartestandsaffäre 1939/40. Ein Kapitel aus der Geschichte des Kampfes gegen die Bekennende Kirche', *Schweizerische Zeitschrift für Religions- und Kulturgeschichte* 111 (2017), 317–38.

Ziemann, Benjamin 'Martin Niemöllers Antisemitismus und die Frage der Schuld nach 1945', in Bormann, Lukas and Heymel, Michael, eds, *Martin Niemöller und seine internationale Rezeption* (Göttingen, 2023).

Ziemann, Benjamin, 'Militarism', in Jefferies, Matthew, ed., *The Ashgate Research Companion to Imperial Germany* (Farnham, 2015), 367–82.

Ziemann, Benjamin, 'Religion and the Search for Meaning, 1945–1990', in Smith, Helmut Walser, ed., *The Oxford Handbook of Modern German History* (Oxford, 2011), 693–714.

Ziemann, Benjamin, 'Schiffe versenken. Martin Niemöllers Bericht über die deutsche U-Bootflotte im Ersten Weltkrieg', *Krieg und Literatur/War and Literature* 28 (2017), 21–46.

Ziemann, Benjamin, 'Situating Peace Movements in the Political Culture of the Cold War: Introduction', in Ziemann, Benjamin, ed., *Peace Movements in Western Europe, Japan and the USA during the Cold War* (Essen, 2007), 11–38.

Ziemann, Benjamin, 'The Theory of Functional Differentiation and the History of Modern Society: Reflections on the Reception of Systems Theory in Recent Historiography', *Soziale Systeme* 13 (2007), 220–9.

Ziemann, Benjamin, 'Zur Entwicklung christlicher Religiosität in Deutschland, 1900–1960', in Wulf, Christof and Koenig, Matthias, eds, *Religion und Gesellschaft* (Wiesbaden, 2013), 99–122.

Zwicker, Stefan, *'Nationale Märtyrer'. Albert Leo Schlageter und Julius Fučík. Heldenkult, Propaganda und Erinnerungskultur* (Paderborn, 2006).

Index

For the benefit of digital users, indexed terms that span two pages (e.g., 52–53) may, on occasion, appear on only one of those pages.